BAUDELAIRE
AND THE
SECOND REPUBLIC

BAUDELAIRE
AND THE
SECOND REPUBLIC

Writing and Revolution

RICHARD D. E. BURTON

CLARENDON PRESS · OXFORD

1991

Oxford University Press, Walton Street, Oxford OX2 6DP
Oxford New York Toronto
Delhi Bombay Calcutta Madras Karachi
Petaling Jaya Singapore Hong Kong Tokyo
Nairobi Dar es Salaam Cape Town
Melbourne Auckland
and associated companies in
Berlin Ibadan

Oxford is a trade mark of Oxford University Press

Published in the United States
by Oxford University Press, New York

British Library Cataloguing in Publication Data
(data available)

Library of Congress Cataloging in Publication Data
Burton, Richard D. E., 1946–
Baudelaire and the second republic : writing and revolution /
Richard D.E. Burton.
Includes bibliographical references and index.
1. Baudelaire, Charles, 1821–1867—Political and social views.
2. Revolutionary poetry, French—History and criticism.
3. Political poetry, French—History and criticism. 4. France—
Politics and government—1848–1852. 5. Radicalism in literature.
I. Title.
PQ2191.Z5B78 1991
841'.8—dc20 91-4774
ISBN 0-19-815469-0

Typeset by Downdell Ltd, Oxford
Printed and bound in
Great Britain by Bookcraft Ltd.
Midsomer Norton, Bath

Preface

Until the early 1970s, it was possible for readers, critics, and scholars of Baudelaire to treat the poet's political views and actions as, at most, a subject of peripheral importance to a life and work dominated by such 'non-political' considerations as sex, money, clothes, drugs, poetry, painting, and the passionate and unremitting pursuit of 'le beau' in life and art alike. It was generally conceded that, for one brief interlude in his life, during the early months of the Second Republic (1848–51), Baudelaire had indeed been not merely interested in, but actively involved in, the politics of his time, but the significance of that interest and involvement was regularly called in question. For most critical opinion, Baudelaire's undisputed participation in the street-fighting that brought down the Bourgeois Monarchy in February 1848 and again in the predominantly working-class uprising of June that year was to be attributed to 'personal' rather than to 'political' considerations. If he was on the streets in February and June, it was emphatically as a *révolté* rather than as a *révolutionnaire*: what he sought was not so much—or, in some views, not at all—a transformation of society by revolutionary political means as release from the *individual* constraints and obsessions that had held him captive in the last years of the Bourgeois Monarchy and, beyond that, revenge against that archetypal man of the Bourgeois Monarchy, his stepfather General Jacques Aupick, to whom he ascribed all the woes and humiliations he had had to endure since the enforced voyage to the South Seas in 1841–2 and the constitution of the *conseil judiciaire* in 1844. 'Il faut aller fusiller le général Aupick': these words, allegedly uttered by Baudelaire on the barricades at the Carrefour de Buci on the evening of 24 February 1848, have, since they were reported by Jules Buisson in 1886,[1] been used by critics of all political hues and none to devalue Baudelaire's participation in the *événements* of 1848 and his commitment to the Republic to which they gave birth and, by reducing both to no more than an outlet for personal frustrations and resentments, to deprive them of all properly *political* significance.

[1] Letter from Jules Buisson to Eugène Crépet, quoted from BPZ, 257.

Summarizing this widespread view, Claude Pichois has argued that 'Baudelaire s'est sans doute moins mis à la politique qu'il n'a témoigné de curiosité pour le socialisme et cherché dans les événements de 1848 un prétexte à libérer ses instincts de révolte.'[2] Not only this, but, according to the same scholar, 'la révolution de 1848 et ses prodromes entraînent Baudelaire dans des directions qui ne sont pas conformes à son génie'; his 'fièvre socialiste et révolutionnaire' in the early months of 1848 is seen in some way as 'un alibi', an escape from artistic sterility, perhaps even as a symptom of physical illness or as a consequence of incipient alcoholism.[3] Even those critics who admitted the 'genuineness' of Baudelaire's 'radicalism' usually undercut that genuineness by forthwith emphasizing its brevity. By April 1848, or May at the latest, Baudelaire had, it was commonly claimed, 'seen through' the naïve utopianism of the men of *quarante-huit* and, by the end of June, disgusted by the violence of both sides during that month's blood-bath on the streets of Paris, was already well embarked on the road towards apoliticism which the Bonapartist coup of December 1851 would complete but not, in this perspective, cause. The interlude opened up by the parricidal call to arms of February 1848 was thus closed, four years later, by the seemingly conclusive statement in the well-known and much-quoted letter to Ancelle of 5 March 1852: 'LE 2 DÉCEMBRE m'a *physiquement dépolitiqué*' (C, i. 188). To be sure, some critics conceded that Baudelaire's 'depoliticization' after December 1851 was not 'definitive' or 'total'. After all, the poet himself admitted to Nadar in May 1859, at the time of Napoleon III's Italian adventure, that, though he had convinced himself 'vingt fois' that 'je ne m'intéressais plus à la politique', none the less 'à chaque question grave, je suis repris de curiosité et de passion' (C, i. 578). As late as January 1862 he would confide to Sainte-Beuve that 'le vieux fonds d'esprit révolutionnaire' which 'il y a longtemps'—presumably during or around the time of the Second Republic—prompted him to 'faire des projets de constitution' (C, ii. 220) had still not entirely disappeared beneath the inspissated pessimism and cynicism of the ensuing years. None the less, such short-lived and in any case velleitary resurgences of his revolutionary past could, like that past itself, be safely fenced off within parentheses. There seemed, in short, no reason to query or add to the poet's devastating later

---

[2] 'Baudelaire en 1847, Petit essai de sociologie littéraire', BET, 96.
[3] 'La Maladie de Baudelaire', BET, 239.

verdict on the naïve idealism of 1848, his own, of course, included: '1848 ne fut amusant que parce que chacun y faisait des utopies comme des châteaux en Espagne. 1848 ne fut charmant que par l'excès même du Ridicule' (*Mon cœur mis à nu* (OC, i. 680)). Any remaining doubts as to the thoroughness of Baudelaire's post-1851 repudiation of 1848 and all it stood for were scotched by one of his very last texts, the prose poem 'Assommons les pauvres!' (1865) with its seemingly unanswerable 'put-down' of the socialist thinker held to be typical of 'tous ces entrepreneurs de bonheur public' of the time: 'Qu'en dis-tu, Citoyen Proudhon?'

Then, beginning in the early 1970s, there appeared a succession of works, mainly by German scholars strongly influenced by the work of Walter Benjamin, that radically called in question the received view of the place of politics, and particularly of the revolution of 1848, in Baudelaire's life and work.[4] Though these works differed in their emphases and conclusions, all insisted on the centrality of politics to an understanding of Baudelaire's work and, especially, on the centrality of the experience of 1848–51 to his development as writer, thinker, and human being. In one way or another, all of these studies reread Baudelaire's experience of *quarante-huit* and its aftermath through their authors' own recent experience of *soixante-huit* and its aftermath and, in general, drew from their rereading political meanings of an unabashedly revolutionary kind.[5] One scholar, Dolf Oehler, went even further in this reinstatement of Baudelaire's youthful radicalism. Not only was Baudelaire held to be a committed revolutionary, a 'frère spirituel

[4] The principal works in German are as follows: Oskar Sahlberg, *Baudelaire 1848: Gedichte der Revolution* (Wagenbachs Taschenbücherei, 1977) and *Baudelaire und seine Muse auf den Weg zur Revolution* (Suhrkamp, 1980); Wolfgang Fietkau, *Schwanengesang auf 1848: Ein Rendez-vous au Louvre: Baudelaire, Marx, Proudhon und Victor Hugo* (Das neue Buch, Rowohlt, 1978); Dolf Oehler, *Pariser Bilder, i (1830–1848): Antibourgeoise Ästhetik bei Baudelaire, Daumier und Heine* (Suhrkamp, Frankfurt-on-Main, 1979) (this is an elaboration of Oehler's thesis *Die antibourgeoise Ästhetik des jungen Baudelaire*, Frankfurt-on-Main, 1975); and Hartmut Stenzel, *Der historische Ort Baudelaires: Untersuchungen zur Entwicklung des französischen Literatur um die Mitte des 19. Jahrhunderts* (Wilhelm Fink Verlag, 1980). All of these works are reviewed by Claude Pichois in 'Baudelaire devant la socio-critique ouest-allemande', *Études baudelairiennes*, 9 (1981), 226–33; see also the review of Fietkau, Sahlberg, and Oehler by Jacques Le Ridier, 'Baudelaire agent secret . . .', *Le Monde Dimanche* (20 July 1980), p. xvi. For Fietkau, see the review of *Schwanengesang auf 1848* by Hartmut Stenzel: *Études baudelairiennes*, 9 (1981), 213–18.

[5] On the link between 1848 and 1968, see Pichois, 'Baudelaire devant la socio-critique', 227.

d'Auguste Blanqui', during the Second Republic, but both his pre-1848 and post-1851 writings were similarly informed by a radical socialist or, at the very least, aggressively anti-bourgeois ideology. In particular, Oehler challenged the widely held view that Baudelaire's writings of the Bourgeois Monarchy were essentially 'non-political' and that, by corollary, his appearance on the barricades in February 1848 constituted some fundamental break with his previously apolitical, or even anti-political, stance in society. Oehler's case turned on a particular reading, or way of reading, of the *Salon de 1846* which, he argued, was no 'disinterested' disquisition on art and aesthetics, but 'un plaidoyer tantôt engagé, tantôt ironique, voire satanique, en faveur d'un iconoclasme en même temps esthétique et politique: révolte contre le classicisme en art, révolte contre le juste-milieu en politique'.[6] Nothing in this text or, for that matter, in any other Baudelairean text, was quite what it seemed. In the *Salon*'s preface 'Aux Bourgeois', for example, Baudelaire's apparent eulogy of the bourgeoisie was in fact an ironic, elliptical deconstruction of bourgeois ideology in which, mimicking bourgeois ways of thinking and turning them on their head, Baudelaire adumbrated, for those readers who could see what he was doing, a radically *anti-bourgeois* stance in art, society, and politics which the rest of the *Salon*, again by ironic, roundabout, and disguised means, developed and exemplified. Moreover, far from being 'depoliticized' by December 1851, Baudelaire continued under the Second Èmpire to oppose the French bourgeoisie in its now politically unchallengeable form by, so to speak, infiltrating its thought-patterns and sabotaging them from within. The revolutionary option having comprehensively failed, Baudelaire transformed himself after *le 2 décembre* into a kind of secret agent[7] dedicated to undermining the bourgeois hegemony from within, a change of tactics necessitated by changed political circumstances which in no way diminished his fundamental commitment to revolution. Far from becoming less radical, as the 'traditional' view maintained, Baudelaire in fact became more so as his career as a writer approached its close, with his final political texts, *Pauvre Belgique!* and the prose poems 'Le Mauvais Vitrier', 'Le Gâteau', and, above all, 'Assommons les pauvres!' presenting that radical-

[6] Dolf Oehler, 'Le Caractère double de l'héroïsme et du beau modernes', *Études baudelairiennes*, 8 (1976), 190–1.
[7] See Le Ridier, 'Baudelaire agent secret . . .', p. xvi.

ism in an exacerbated, even satanic form. The secret agent becomes at the last a sadistic *agent provocateur*, committed to '(un)satanisme essentiellement émancipateur', who, by thrashing the hapless beggar who accosts him, 'veut provoquer une réaction violente du côté des opprimés'.[8] In the 'conservative' perspective, as articulated most persuasively by Claude Pichois, 'la seule caractéristique politique de Baudelaire est une pensée résolument anarchiste. Il a été anarchiste de gauche. Il va devenir anarchiste de droite.'[9] In the 'radical' counter-perspective, as advanced most forcefully by Dolf Oehler, Baudelaire underwent no such mid-career 'conversion' from left to right. 'Anarchist' he may have been, but an anarchist *à la Blanqui*, an *anarchiste de gauche*, not some *petit bourgeois révolté* looking to politics for release from personal frustrations, but a man and writer with a lifelong revolutionary project which assumed different forms in keeping with changing political conditions but which, beneath manifold surface discontinuities, is characterized by an impressive, if necessarily devious, *continuity*.

Faced with two such radically different readings of the significance of the Second Republic to Baudelaire's life and writing, I should say at the outset that it is no part of my intention in this book to arbitrate between them and still less to attempt to reconcile their many divergences in some transcendent overview of Baudelaire's political evolution. The present project has been many years in gestation and has its origins in an interpretation of 'Le Vin' cycle of *Les Fleurs du mal*, the main lineaments of which were defined before I encountered the works by German scholars that caused such a *remuement* in Baudelairean circles in the 1970s. As the present work grew out of its early nucleus, I obviously had to take into account the arguments and interpretations advanced in the works in question, but *Baudelaire and the Second Republic* is no more intended as a 'réponse' to the radical readings of 1970–80 than it is to the more conservative approach of traditional Baudelaire criticism. Furthermore, although any study of 1848 and its aftermath cannot but be influenced by *The Class Struggles in France* and *The Eighteenth Brumaire of Louis Napoleon*, it will soon become clear that the present work has its interpretative point of departure elsewhere, notably in the work of those modern historians—above all Maurice Agulhon—who have modified in

---

[8] Oehler, 'Le Caractère double', 199 and 211.
[9] BPZ, 285.

fundamental ways our understanding of the events of 1848–51, not least in their insistence that radical republicanism did not perish on the barricades of June 1848 but revived to fight on in 1849, 1850, and 1851 under the name of *démocratie sociale* or *la Montagne*, with its focus now more in provincial France than in the capital. Baudelaire, I shall argue, did indeed undergo a 'conversion' after June 1848, but it was not, as the traditional reading would have it, from 'left' to 'right' (or to an 'apolitical' stance of detachment) but from one kind of leftism to another: in shorthand terms, from Blanqui to Proudhon who, in this study, is shown to be the determining influence on Baudelaire's thought and actions from the aftermath of the *journées de juin* (and conceivably from as early as the end of 1846) until the early months of 1852. The Baudelaire of 1848 has received much attention from critics and scholars, that of 1849, 1850, and 1851 hardly any at all, in large part because of the dearth of both texts published and letters written during these crucial years in nineteenth-century French history which also coincided with and stimulated crucial changes in Baudelaire's life and development as a writer. Taking *Du vin et du haschisch* (March 1851) as my point of departure, I have tried to reconstruct the Baudelaire of 1849–51 from the fragmentary evidence that survives. The man and writer who emerges from my investigation is, I think, both considerably more radical than the Baudelaire of the 'traditional' interpretation and more moderate, more pragmatic, and more conscious of the constant need for cumulative political effort than the Baudelaire of the 'radical' counter-interpretation: in short, a seriously committed radical republican close not only to Proudhon but to the whole *démoc-soc* movement which, coming together in early 1849, provided the main focus of resistance to the Bonapartist advance during what remained of the Second Republic. Baudelaire, Claude Pichois has written, 'n'a rien d'un marxiste': true enough, no doubt, but, in the terms of 1849–51 (and perhaps beyond), he was—or so the present study seeks to show—without question a *rouge*, as red as the wine he celebrated in what are, I argue here, his most characteristic and politically significant writings of the Second Republic period.

This is a lengthy and at times difficult study, made so by the problematic nature of many of the Baudelaire texts it discusses— dating and variant readings are a constant and necessary consideration—and by the need to refer throughout to broader historical contexts, as well as to a mass of intertextual material, in order to grasp the significance of what Baudelaire is doing and writing. My first two chapters are concerned with the 'Baudelaire-Dufaÿs' of the last years of the Bourgeois Monarchy and confront the hotly disputed issue of the political beliefs and affiliations of the author of the *Salon de 1846* and *La Fanfarlo*. Chapters 3 and 4 give a detailed chronological account of Baudelaire's actions and writings between February 1848 and December 1852: no new facts are adduced (except, perhaps, with regard to the period the poet spent in Dijon during late 1849 and early 1850), but the contextualizing interpretation I give differs, I think, in certain fundamental ways from those current on both the 'Right' and the 'Left' of Baudelaire criticism, each of which, it seems to me, fails to grasp that June 1848 did not destroy radical republicanism as such but only one of its phases, expressions, or manifestations. Chapter 5 discusses at length the whole controversy surrounding wine in mid-nineteenth-century France and attempts to reconstruct what I have called 'le discours du vin', in other words the repertoire of images and themes in radical writings on the wine question which, I argue, Baudelaire drew on in writing *Du vin et du haschisch* and the wine poems themselves. Chapter 6 is perhaps the core of the book: here I analyse the numerous successive versions of 'Le Vin des chiffon-niers', the first of them dating from perhaps as early as 1841 up to the 'definitive' text of the second edition of *Les Fleurs du mal*, in an attempt to chart in detail, as refracted in the multiple variant readings of a single text, Baudelaire's political evolution from the high point of the Bourgeois Monarchy, through the conflicts of the Second Republic and the early years of the Second Empire to that regime's meridian in 1861. The gradual stabilization of an unstable text is seen as an analogue both of Baudelaire's own search for stability after the profoundly destabilizing experience of 1848–51 and of the progressive (but in many ways illusory) stabilization of French society after 1851, pending the further cataclysmic explo-sion, four years after Baudelaire's death, in 1871. Chapter 7 focuses on 'Châtiment de l'orgueil' (first published June 1850), possibly the worst poem from a purely literary standpoint in *Les Fleurs du mal* but, because it is the only poem which Baudelaire both wrote and published exclusively within the Second Republic period, takes on a quite crucial significance for a study of his political development during the years in question. Chapter 8 gives a political reading of a number of the poems that Baudelaire published, submitted for publication, wrote, or revised between 1850 and the end of 1852, most notably 'Voyage à Cythère' and 'Spleen' ('Pluviôse, irrité contre la ville entière . . .'), the first of the sequence of sonnets published under the title *Les Limbes* in *Le Messager de l'Assemblée* in April 1851. Chapter 9 engages, as any book on Baudelaire and the Second Republic must, with the text 'Assommons les pauvres!' in which, at the very end of his creative life, Baudelaire returned to the experience of 1848–51 to draw from it a message of, it is argued here, the uttermost ambiguity, one which is 'ni droite ni gauche' but an incendiary fusion of both and which, if it seems to herald certain forms of late nineteenth-century and twentieth-century ultra-leftism, also points disquietingly in the direction of fascism. A final section attempts, none too confidently, to draw some general conclusions from the mass of materials convoked in the previous chapters.

A word, finally, on the general critical approach I have adopted in this book. My first concern throughout has been to locate the texts I am studying with the maximum historical precision—no easy task, as will rapidly become clear—and, correspondingly, to situate them in relation to as broad a range of contextual and intertextual materials as I can muster. In the most general sense, each of the main poetical works analysed, and particularly 'Le Reniement de saint Pierre' and 'Le Vin des chiffonniers', is treated as a political allegory—allegory being, according to Baudelaire, 'l'une des formes primitives et les plus naturelles de la poésie' despite its misuse by countless 'peintres maladroits' of past and present (*Le Poème du haschisch* (OC, i. 430))—which, I believe, can only be deciphered through reference to the rich arsenal of political images that the revolution of 1848 inherited either from its predecessor of 1789–94 or from socialist-republican propaganda of the 1830s and 1840s. Such images include the figures of the republican Christ and revolutionary Satan, the colour red, the opposition of light and dark and of the seasons of the year, and a whole range of images associated with the production and consumption of wine. If Baudelaire had recourse to this widely diffused *dictionnaire d'images*, it was, I argue, partly in order to evade government censorship (increasingly coercive after June 1848), partly because he was consciously addressing his work to a *démoc-soc* public familiar with coded or allegorical political communication, and partly because the intensity and complexity of his political feelings forbade anything other than indirect expression by means of a series of 'objective correlatives' drawn originally from the radical republican tradition. But Baudelaire's political allegories are not fixed, closed, and monosemic like those of most of his radical republican contemporaries, but open and subject to all kinds of polyvalences and ambiguities.[10] Some, I argue, were not allegories of any kind when first written in the early 1840s but were retrospectively invested with an allegorical significance by the Revolution itself, often without Baudelaire's having to change a single word in the texts as they were first drafted. Changed historical contexts conferred political meanings where there was initially only description, evocation, or straightforward moralizing, and as further political changes occurred (and as Baudelaire's own ideological stance evolved), so too those new meanings changed or were made to change. All the main poetic texts discussed here are, therefore, in some way secret or esoteric, conveying political meanings through images and figures which, to the exoteric eye, are wholly 'apolitical'. Most of the texts studied are also fundamentally unstable: the society of the poem, to use Jonathan Raban's expression, is as turbulent as the society in which it was written or rewritten or which, by its very turbulence, conferred a succession of changing meanings on texts dating from the pre-revolutionary period. Allegorical readings such as those I am proposing here carry with them an inevitable risk of over-interpretation, and there will no doubt be occasions—perhaps many such—when the reader will feel that my contextualizing approach, and constant invocation of intertextual parallels, have caused me to see concealed political meanings where none were intended by Baudelaire. I have preferred, though, the error of over-politicizing the texts of this crucial period of Baudelaire's life to the more common error of emptying them of any political significance whatsoever: it is up to the reader to make the corrections or rejections that he or she thinks necessary.

To acknowledge fully all the intellectual debts I have incurred in writing *Baudelaire and the Second Republic* would still further

---

[10] On 'open' and 'closed' allegory, see Marie Maclean, *Narrative as Performance: The Baudelairean Experiment* (Routledge, 1988), 164. On the inexhaustibility of Baudelaire's allegories, see Nathaniel Wing, 'The Danaides Vessel: On Reading Baudelaire's Allegories', in Wing, *The Limits of Narrative: Essays on Baudelaire, Flaubert, Rimbaud and Mallarmé* (Cambridge Univ. Press, 1986), 8–18.

burden an already substantial text. Suffice it to say that, of the many scholars and critics who have written on this period of Baudelaire's life and on his politics generally, I have benefited particularly from the pioneering study *Baudelaire en 1848* by Jules Mouquet and the late W. T. Bandy and from the more recent work of Annie Becq, Hartmut Stenzel, Richard Terdiman, and Gretchen van Slyke. Like everyone who writes on Baudelaire, I would be nowhere without the editions, critical studies, and, most recently, the biographical work of Claude Pichois, and I owe a special debt to T. J. Clark's *The Absolute Bourgeois* and *Image of the People* which first alerted me as a graduate student to the engrossing question of the relationship between literature, painting, and politics in mid-nineteenth-century France and to which I have frequently returned in admiration in the course of writing this book. My personal debts are also many. I owe particular thanks to Professor Ralph Grillo, Dean of the School of African and Asian Studies at Sussex University, both for his constant encouragement of a research project which, to say the least, was peripheral to the intellectual focus of the school of studies of which he and I are members, and who also made available the research funds that permitted me the dubious pleasure of spending a week in a Dijon as torpid and rain-swept as when Baudelaire was there in the winter of 1849–50. I am also grateful to the British Academy for providing me with financial assistance in the preparation of my manuscript for publication. Dr J. A. Hiddleston of Exeter College, Oxford subjected an early version of Chapters 5 and 6 to a searching critical reading and also gave me invaluable practical assistance when I decided to use them as the basis of a full-length study of Baudelaire's politics. Once again Margaret Ralph produced for me a typescript of quite exemplary accuracy. My principal debt, however, is, as in my first book on Baudelaire, to Professor Ross Chambers of the University of Michigan who not only provided encouragement when spirits were low and made countless incisive comments on what I had written, but also gave me the use—in return only for looking after 'l'esprit familier du lieu'—of his house in Ann Arbor during the autumn of 1989 when the final version of the manuscript was laboriously Scotched and Gloyed together from the numerous fragments which, *chiffonnier*-like, I had been collecting over the years. Had he not written with typical insight on the ironies, ambiguities, and frequent sheer perversity of Baudelaire's own 'pratique de la dédicace', it is assuredly to Ross Chambers that the present work on Baudelaire would be dedicated.

R.D.E.B.
Lewes

Contents

Abbreviations — xviii

1 'Baudelaire-Dufaÿs' and the Politics of Consensus, 1842–1848 — 1

2 Proteus and his Texts: Opposition in Writing and Everyday Life, 1844–1848 — 54

3 Street-fighting Years (I): Baudelaire in 1848 — 94

4 Street-fighting Years (II): Baudelaire and the Second Republic, 1849–1852 — 142

5 Red Wine, Red Politics: The Wine Poems in Context — 185

6 Metamorphoses of the Ragpicker: Interpreting 'Le Vin des chiffoniers' — 220

7 Baudelaire and Proudhon (I): 'Châtiment de l'orgueil' in Context — 276

8 The Revenge of Pluviosus: Baudelaire and the Agony of the Second Republic — 291

9 Baudelaire and Proudhon (II): A Reading of 'Assommons les pauvres!' — 324

Conclusion: Ni Droite ni Gauche? Baudelaire and the Politics of Nineteenth-Century France — 353

Bibliography — 367

Index of Works by Baudelaire — 375

General Index — 377

Abbreviations

BET   Claude Pichois, *Baudelaire: Études et témoignages* (La Baconnière, Neuchâtel, 1967).

BPZ   Claude Pichois and Jean Ziegler, *Baudelaire* (Julliard, Paris, 1987).

C   Claude Pichois (ed.), *Correspondance de Baudelaire*, 2 vols. (Gallimard, Paris, 1973).

OC   Claude Pichois (ed.), *Œuvres complètes de Baudelaire*, 2 vols. (Gallimard, Paris, 1975).

1

'Baudelaire-Dufaÿs' and the Politics of Consensus, 1842–1848

When Baudelaire landed at Bordeaux in February 1842 at the end of his seven-month round trip to Mauritius and the Île Bourbon, he returned to a country which, not just on the surface but in fact, was enjoying a period of prosperity, security, and political stability such as it had not known since before the Great Revolution. Having withstood the numerous threats to its survival during what Baudelaire later called 'le temps des grandes fureurs politiques'— the years 1830–1834 when no fewer than three major insurrections in Paris and Lyon, together with the republican and socialist infrastructures that sustained them, were suppressed by a combination of 'massacres, emprisonnements, arrestations, perquisitions, procès, assommades de la police' (OC, ii. 550–1)—the Bourgeois Monarchy had, by 1842, succeeded in some large measure in creating that 'depoliticized consensus'[1] that had been its objective ever since it had been brought to power by the barricades of July 1830. Following the imposition of the infamous *lois de septembre* which, amongst other things, made it illegal even to call oneself a republican, the republican–socialist opposition had been driven underground, and the death of the great republican journalist Armand Carrel in a duel with Émile de Girardin, the editor of *La Presse*, in 1836 was widely interpreted as marking not only the demise of the republican cause but also the eclipse of traditional committed political journalism at the hands of the new-style depoliticized mass press of the Bourgeois Monarchy; 'le parti républicain est avec Carrel dans le cercueil', wrote Edgard Quinet in August 1836, 'il ressuscitera mais il lui faudra le temps'.[2]

---

[1] See Roger Magraw, *France 1815–1914: The Bourgeois Century* (Fontana, 1983), 69.

[2] Quoted A. Jardin and A. J. Tudesq, *La France des notables*, i. *L'Évolution générale 1815–1848* (Seuil, 1973), 141–2.

Its first attempted resurrection—the botched, almost self-parodying Blanquist uprising of 12–13 May 1839—seems to have disrupted the Aupick household, already thrown into disarray by Baudelaire's expulsion from Louis-le-Grand in April, considerably more than it did the Bourgeois Monarchy itself. As he had been in Lyon in 1831–2, Aupick was involved in the operation of repression, causing his wife, in Baudelaire's words, 'une horrible inquiétude' when he was obliged to spend the night of the uprising away from home at the *poste de garde* on the Place du Carrousel (C, i. 70).[3] Far more significant was the resurgence, in August–September 1840, of the social and economic unrest that had marked the early years of the regime. On 3 September, in what amounted to a general strike which brought the Parisian economy to a standstill, 10,000 building workers met on the plain of Bondy outside the city, while other groups of workers—*serruriers, fileurs, tanneurs, menuisiers, tailleurs d'habit, cordonniers*—likewise downed tools and foregathered in the traditional manner at the *barrières* of Pantin, Vaugirard, Saint-Mandé, and Ménilmontant.[4] But, although barricades were briefly raised in the Faubourg Saint-Antoine on 7 September, these social discontents did not, as they had in 1830–4, erupt into sustained political action; the 'social' and 'political' wings of opposition to the status quo which had, at the time of the Société des Droits de l'Homme, come close to converging were, in the absence of coherent political leadership and organization, as far apart as ever. 1840 saw the publication of numerous books, tracts, and newspapers—Blanc's *L'Organisation du travail*, Proudhon's *Qu'est-ce que la propriété?*, Cabet's *Voyage en Icarie*, as well as the first numbers of *L'Atelier*—which would decisively influence the growth of working-class radicalism in the coming decade;[5] at the same time, though, it marked an end to *open* labour unrest until the economic crisis of 1847 brought workers once more into direct confrontation with their employers and the forces of law and order. The disorder that had threatened to erupt in September 1840 had been largely contained and neutralized by the following December when, in one of the Bourgeois

[3] See BPZ, 114.

[4] Jean-Pierre Aguet, *Les Grèves sous la Monarchie de Juillet 1830–1847* (Droz, Geneva, 1954), 207–12. See also Martin Nadaud, *Mémories de Léonard*, ed. Maurice Agulhon (Hachette, 1976), 224–6.

[5] See David H. Pinkney, *Decisive Years in France 1840–1847* (Princeton Univ. Press, Princeton, NJ, 1986), 93.

Monarchy's most eloquent public occasions—eloquent for what it silenced or elided rather than for what it said—Napoleon's remains were returned to Paris from Saint-Helena. Baudelaire witnessed this event, or rather pseudo-event, in the company of Gustave Le Vavasseur.[6] He nowhere refers to it, but it is likely that, in common with Victor Hugo, he would have seen through the regime's attempt to co-opt and 'recuperate' the Bonapartist tradition to its own advantage and wrest it from the hands of Louis Napoleon Bonaparte who in August 1840 had launched the second of his ludicrous attempts to seize political power by force:

Il est certain que toute cette cérémonie a eu un singulier caractère d'escamotage. Le gouvernement semblait avoir peur du fantôme qu'il évoquait. On avait l'air tout á la fois de montrer et de cacher Napoléon. On a laissé dans l'ombre tout ce qui eût été trop grand ou trop touchant. On a dérobé le réel et le grandiose sous des enveloppes plus ou moins splendides, on a escamoté le cortège impérial dans le cortège militaire, on a escamoté l'armée dans la garde nationale, on a escamoté les chambres dans les Invalides, on a escamoté le cercueil dans le cénotaphe.[7]

Despite its mystificatory character, the *retour des cendres* undoubtedly consolidated support for Louis-Philippe who, as recently as 15 October 1840, had been subjected to yet another attempt on his life by a republican die-hard. On 29 October, after a prolonged ministerial crisis, a new cabinet was formed under the nominal presidency of Marshall Soult but led in fact by Guizot, a cabinet which, in marked contrast to the fifteen ministries that had succeeded each other between 1830 and 1840, would hold power uninterruptedly until September 1847 when Guizot assumed in person the presidency of the Conseil, retaining it until his dismissal by the king on 23 February 1848. Having reduced the radical republican or socialist opposition once more to a subterranean existence, defused by co-option any possible Bonapartist threat, and, in addition, largely healed its breach with the Legitimist-dominated Church, the Bourgeois Monarchy enjoyed a virtually complete political monopoly by the time of the general election of July 1842, which resulted in an overwhelming victory for supporters of the regime, though the Soult–Guizot ministry still failed to

---

[6] See BPZ, 133.
[7] Victor Hugo, *Œuvres complètes*, 35, *Choses vues*, i. (Éditions Rencontre, Lausanne, 1968), 144–5.

secure an overall majority. With personalities taking the place of issues, the elections of August 1846 were even more 'apolitical' in character. In February of that year, just a month before the opening of the exhibition that would inspire Baudelaire's first major publication, the *Salon de 1846*, Leon Faucher wrote that 'l'esprit politique est mort dans ce pays, pour plusieurs années; on ne pense qu'à s'enrichir et à faire des chemins de fer'; at the end of June the *Revue des Deux Mondes* announced that 'les élections générales se préparent et se feront dans un des moments les plus tranquilles dont la France ait joui depuis longtemps'.[8] Not surprisingly, the Soult–Guizot ministry gained an absolute majority for the first time with 291 supporters in parliament out of 459, though it is noteworthy in Paris itself that 9,000 out of 14,000 votes in the severely restricted franchise were cast for anti-government (but not necessarily anti-regime) candidates who were returned in 11 of the 12 *arrondissements*. Opposition in parliament to the regime itself— 12 republican deputies and 12 legitimists—was as good as non-existent.[9] To many observers, like the young radical republican Gustave Lefrançais, it seemed that the Bourgeois Monarchy would go on for ever.[10]

Having effectively depoliticized politics, the Bourgeois Monarchy was scarcely less successful in depoliticizing art, architecture, and, in the name of eclecticism, thought itself. It is well known that Delacroix's *Liberty Leading the People* was removed from public view as early as 1833 lest its celebration of insurrection legitimize the uprisings of Lyon and Paris in 1831–2 and justify further unrest;[11] in 1839 *all* paintings of the *Trois Glorieuses* were taken from public galleries and placed in storage as the regime endeavoured to obliterate its origins in popular revolutionary violence.[12] On the other hand, and as an adjunct to its deliberate recuperation of the Napoleonic legend, official artistic policy encouraged 'an alternate and highly specialized "official" history of the Revolution which was self-contained, politically inert, and systematically

[8] Quoted Jardin and Tudesq, *La France des notables*, i. 167.

[9] See H. A. C. Collingham, *The July Monarchy: A Political History of France 1830–1848* (Longman, 1988), 387.

[10] Gustave Lefrançois, *Souvenirs d'un révolutionnaire* (Bibliothèque des Temps Nouveaux, Brussels, 1902(?)), 20.

[11] See William Fortescue, *Revolution and Counter-Revolution in France 1815–1852* (Basil Blackwell, 1988), 40.

[12] Pinkney, *Decisive Years*, 3.

purged of the Terror' and, to that end, systematically 'incorporated imagery of the Great Revolution into its official iconography and ultimately redirected it to support the status quo'.[13] The Hugolian principle of *escamotage* applied to the very structure and texture of Parisian life. Just as Guizot congratulated himself on the reduction of the *retour des cendres* to the level of a 'pure spectacle',[14] devoid of meaningful political substance, so in its urban policy the Bourgeois Monarchy sought to obliterate or obfuscate the all-too-pertinent political significance of certain Parisian locations, most notably the former Place de la Révolution where Louis XVI had been guillotined and which the Restoration Monarchy had renamed in his memory. On its accession to power, the new regime not only gave the square a new name—the suitably 'apolitical' and 'consensualist' Place de la Concorde—but, in 1836, replaced the statue of Louis XV at its centre with a monument, the *obélisque de Louqsor*, which was chosen precisely for its meaninglessness, since, as Louis-Philippe informed his Préfet de Paris, 'il ne rappellera aucun événement politique et qu'il est sûr d'y rester tandis que vous pourriez y voir quelque jour un monument expiatoire ou une statue de la Liberté.'[15] For many contemporaries, the Place de la Concorde's hybrid confusion of styles and proliferation of architectural signs devoid of social or political referent came to epitomize the hollowness at the core of that living contradiction, a *bourgeois* monarchy; it was the equivalent, in stone, of the eclecticism that was the regime's official philosophy—a blurring and merging of oppositions in the name of some underlying unity of thought—and, increasingly, as the *Salon de 1846* makes clear, its ideal in painting and sculpture as well. In art, architecture, and philosophy, the Bourgeois Monarchy's goal was *hypo-significance* in the name of consensus; its systematic pursuit of *vacuousness* is unequalled in French political history.

The *escamotage* of substance that Hugo had seen in operation at the Invalides in 1840 was also at work in the realm of literature. In a celebrated article, 'Quelques vérités sur la situation en littérature',

---

[13] Michael Marrinan, *Painting Politics for Louis-Philippe: Art and Ideology in Orleanist France 1830–1848* (Yale Univ. Press, 1988), 140–77.
[14] Letter to Baron Mounier, 18 Dec. 1840, quoted ibid. 195.
[15] See Nerval's article 'Embellissements de Paris' published in *Le Messager* on 30/31 July 1838 and reproduced in *Œuvres complémentaires de Gérard de Nerval*, viii. *Variétés et fantaisies*, ed. Jean Richer (M. J. Minard, 1964), 99–100.

Baudelaire-Dufaÿs

that appeared in the *Revue des Deux Mondes* in July 1843,[16] Sainte-Beuve contrasted the 'stérile abondance' of French literary production in the late 1830s and early 1840s with its genuine vitality under the Restoration Monarchy and during the first few years of the new regime. 'Il y a treize ans', Sainte-Beuve wrote, 'une révolution s'accomplissait après une lutte prolongée, régulière, d'idées et de convictions, qui semblaient ardentes et profondes', giving rise to hopes for literature as grandiose as those for political and social progress. However, the 'solution mixte imposée à cette révolution' had the effect, by virtue of its very mixed-ness and lack of definition, of gradually neutralizing the passions and energies released by the *Trois Glorieuses*, so that 'dès 1837, le calme presque universel s'établissait et . . . voilà que, littérairement, ce calme social d'apparence propice n'enfantait rien et ne faisait que mettre à nu le peu de courant'. By 1843, 'dans toute l'étendue d'une certaine souche sociale'—that which produced the bulk of writers and painters as well as politicians—a single phenomenon was to be observed: 'en religion, politique, arts, modes et costumes, réaction sur toute la ligne'. But unlike the 'grandes et vraies réactions' of the 1800s or 1820s, the reaction of the 1840s, 'superficielle et sans grand fond', was, characteristically, not reactionary enough to provoke vigorous counter-movements in either literature or politics, whence the feeling that the former, in this a precise reflection of the latter, had for some years been stranded in an 'espèce de halte' which, for the moment, seemed unlikely to end.[17] The closing, on 22 April 1843, after just one month at the Théatre-Français,[18] of Hugo's drama *Les Burgraves* was widely seen as marking the end of the romantic revolution in the theatre, particularly as, on the same day, François Ponsard's *Lucrèce*—a pseudo-classical pseudo-tragedy, typical of the compromise eclecticism of the Bourgeois Monarchy—had opened at the Odéon to massive public and critical acclaim. By the time Baudelaire launched his impassioned defence of romanticism in the *Salon de 1846*—'Qui dit romantisme dit art moderne,—c'est-à-dire intimité, spiritualité, couleur, aspiration vers l'infini, exprimées par tous les moyens que contiennent les arts' (OC, ii. 421)—he was celebrating a movement which was widely believed to be moribund, whence, no doubt, the fervour of

---

[16] All quotations from *Revue des Deux Mondes*, 3 (1843), 7–10.
[17] Ibid. 20.
[18] See Max Milner, *Le Romantisme*, i. *1820–1843* (Arthaud, 1973), 70.

his advocacy. Just as the republican-socialist opposition seemed, by the mid-1840s, to have been defused, so romanticism, the romanticism of *grands* and *petits romantiques* alike, seemed to have been in large measure reabsorbed into the mainstream consensus. In 1846, Pétrus Borel, in whom Baudelaire would later see the epitome of 'cet esprit à la fois littéraire et républicain' of the early 1830s which was for him so different from 'la passion démocratique et bourgeoise qui nous a plus tard si cruellement opprimés' (OC, ii. 155) went to Algeria as a minor colonial official. In 1845 Hugo himself entered the Chambre des Pairs, whence, in part, Baudelaire's decidedly unenthusiastic response to the man and his writing in the *Salon de 1846*.[19] The rebel had been co-opted by the establishment: it was the literary equivalent of the *retour des cendres* on which Hugo had written so scathingly five years previously.

Despite its domination—scarcely challenged after 1840—of the institutions and discourses of the *pays légal*, the Bourgeois Monarchy remained sufficiently alert to possible threats to its existence from the *pays réel* to commit huge resources to the consolidation of the apparatus of surveillance and repression it had inherited from earlier regimes and which had been further extended to contain the manifold disturbances of the 1830s. In 1840, at the instigation of Thiers, and at a cost of 145 million francs, the government embarked upon the construction of a 24-mile-long fortified wall which, by its completion in 1844, encircled Paris in its entirety and which, though in theory designed to protect the city from external invaders, was widely seen by Parisians 'as the symbol and the proof of internal repression and containment', as an expression, in Lamennais's words, of 'la guerre chez nous' and of the government's determination to spare no effort or expense to contain the 'enemy within'.[20] Within the perimeter of the *mur de Thiers*, the enforcement of law and order took on an increasingly military character, as the army assumed many of the functions that had previously been assured by civilian bodies such as the *sergents de ville* and *officiers de la paix*. Writing in 1840, an English visitor stated that Paris 'may be said to be in the hands of the military . . . When, for instance, any quarrel takes place in a house, or disturbance occurs in the streets, the police, instead of themselves inter-

[19] See OC, ii. 431.
[20] Patricia O'Brien, *'L'Embastillement de Paris*: The Fortification of Paris during the July Monarchy', *French Historical Studies*, 9/1 (1975), 80–2.

posing to prevent any unpleasant consequences, call in one or more
soldiers.'[21] Not surprisingly, the number of troops stationed in and
around Paris rose from 12,000 in 1830 to 48,000 in 1848, while
paramilitary forces such as the *garde municipale*—one of whose
members makes an unscheduled and highly controversial appearance in the *Salon de 1846* (OC, ii. 490)—were not only strengthened
in numbers but became an increasingly visible presence in the day-
to-day policing of the city. Under the Soult–Guizot ministry,
government, police, army, and civil administration interlocked to
form an all-embracing system of containment and surveillance
whose 'panoptic' character—usually expressed through the related
mythological images of Argus, Briareus, and Proteus[22]—became
one of the commonplaces of Bourgeois Monarchy writing on Paris.
Having at its command both the 'géant aux mille bras, aux mille
oreilles' of the regular police force and a vast 'invisible réseau' of
spies, secret agents, and informers, the Préfecture de Police, wrote
Armand Durantin in 1840, constituted an 'œil d'Argus . . . qui se
promène du haut sur la cité et dont la mission est de toujours
châtier, jamais récompenser'.[23] But the powers of the ordinary
civilian *préfet* were scarcely less awesome than those of the *Préfet
de police*, making of him, according to *Le Charivari* in 1843,
'quelque chose d'obéliscal, de gigantesque, de formidable, un titan
en habit brodé'; if he was also, as was increasingly the case, a
conseiller d'État, 'alors il acquière des proportions tellement
colossales qu'il passe à l'état de demi-dieu'.[24]

Baudelaire, then, took his first steps as a writer in the capital city
of state which was, at the level of the *pays légal*, almost totally
depoliticized, whose security, prosperity, and stability were, up to
at least the beginning of 1847, not merely apparent but *real* and
which, thanks to the regulatory and repressive powers at its
disposal, had succeeded in crushing, neutralizing, or driving underground the counter-forces in the *pays réel* that, between 1830 and
1834, had undeniably threatened its existence. This *conjoncture* of

[21] James Grant, *Paris and its People* (1840), quoted Patricia O'Brien, 'Urban
Growth and Public Order: The Development of a Modern Police in Paris 1829–1854'
(D.Phil. thesis, Faculty of Political Science, Columbia Univ., NY, 1973), 71.
[22] See Richard D. E. Burton, 'The Unseen Seer, or Proteus in the City: Aspects of
a Nineteenth-Century Parisian Myth', *French Studies*, 42/1 (1988), 50–68.
[23] Armand Durantin, 'Le Sergent de ville', in *Les Français peints pas eux-mêmes*
(1840), quoted Burton, 'The Unseen Seer', 55.
[24] Quoted O'Brien, 'Urban Growth and Public Order', 141.

depoliticization and regulation obviously had important consequences both for the nature of Baudelaire's literary output up to
and including *La Fanfarlo* (January 1847) and, more generally, for
his whole stance and day-to-day comportment in a society which—
to repeat—gave scarcely a sign at the beginning of 1847 that within
barely more than a year its political order would be comprehensively transformed by revolution and its social and economic structure decisively challenged from below. In the first place, the
conditions of, say, 1844–6 could give a political significance to
statements and gestures which, to us, may seem wholly 'apolitical'.
If, for example, the regime was doing its utmost to promote an art
and literature that would be 'impartial', 'dispassionate', and
'apolitical', eclectic in viewpoint and devoted to the concealing
rather than the revealing of truth, then to insist, as Baudelaire does
in the *Salon de 1846* (OC, ii. 418), that 'la critique doit être partiale,
passionnée, politique, c'est-à-dire faite à un point de vue exclusif,
mais au point de vue qui ouvre le plus d'horizons' becomes a
potentially explosive *prise de position*. More specifically, if, as we
have seen, the regime sought to sanitize the Great Revolution by
eliminating any allusion to the Terror, an admiring reference—such
as that in Baudelaire's review of 'Le Musée classique du Bazar
Bonne-Nouvelle' (January 1846)—to David's painting of 'le *divin*
Marat' with his 'poitrine percée de la blessure *sacrilège*' (OC, ii. 409)
must once more be interpreted as a *political* gesture of some consequence. In the most general sense, then, the regime's determination
to empty art and literature of explicit political content gave writers
and artists ample scope for politicizing their works through hidden
reference, in-joke, irony, and paradox; texts and images that to the
exoteric eye—not least to that of the censor—might seem wholly
'apolitical' could, to an esoteric élite, be replete with concealed
political meaning. As we shall see, all of Baudelaire's published
works of the 1840s (and especially the *Salon de 1846* and *La
Fanfarlo*) are, in one way or another, *secret works*. If all they
required was careful decoding, such works would already be perplexing enough, but they seem determined to thwart through irony,
paradox, and contradiction the very possibility of univocal interpretation, playing one set of codes and meanings off against
another, retracting with one hand what is being advanced by the
other, until the reader begins to suspect that, like Flaubert's
Dictionnaire des idées reçues, the texts have been deliberately

written 'de telle manière [qu'il] ne sache pas si on se fout de lui, oui ou non'.[25] When the *doxa* is as all-powerful and all-embracing as it was in 1844–6, paradox is the dissident artist's and writer's one resource: how better to elude the Argus-eye of authority than to become a Proteus in the texts one is writing and in the text of one's life?

While the conditions of the mid-1840s opened up *certain* possibilities of expression to a writer like Baudelaire, they placed self-evident restrictions on what and how he could write and, as the examples of his early literary cronies Alphonse Esquiros (fined 600 francs and imprisoned for eight months for publishing *L'Évangile du peuple* in 1840) and the ex-Abbé Constant (brought to trial for his *Bible de la liberté* in 1841 and again for *La Voix de la famine* in 1846) showed,[26] made the unequivocal expression of radical ideas— if, that is, as is by no means proven, the Baudelaire of 1844–6 had radical ideas to express—virtually unthinkable. When the established order enjoys as great a monopoly of political and ideological power as the Bourgeois Monarchy did at the time Baudelaire wrote the *Salon de 1846* and *La Fanfarlo*, there is, Michel de Certeau has argued, no chance of any counter-force in society developing a coherent *strategy* of opposition, since the very possibility of constructing such a strategy depends on the existence of a locus outside the existing order—de Certeau calls it an 'elsewhere'—from which that order can be invested and attacked. Unable to develop such a strategy, dissident individuals and groups are compelled to fall back on *tactics*, an 'art of the weak' which tacitly acknowledges that the status quo is at present unchangeable but seeks via a series of disconnected 'oppositional practices' to introduce what de Certeau calls 'cracks, glints, slippages, brainstorms within the established grids of a given system'. Unlike strategy, tactics in de Certeau's sense 'has no place except in that of the other' and must consequently 'play with the terrain imposed upon it, organized by the law of a strange force'. It lacks 'the possibility of giving itself a global project [or] of totalizing the adversary in a distinct space, visible and objectifiable' and accordingly 'operates blow by blow': 'It poaches there. It creates surprises. It is possible for it to be where no one expects it. It is wile.' Many of these 'tricks of the

25 See Flaubert's letter to Louis Bouilhet, 4 Sept. 1850, in Flaubert, *Correspondance*, i. (Jan. 1830–June 1851), ed. Jean Bruneau (Gallimard, 1973), 679.
26 On Esquiros and Constant, see Pichois, 'Baudelaire en 1847', BET, 107–9.

"weak" within the order established by the "strong"' are apparently trivial in character—de Certeau instances 'dwelling, walking, spelling, shopping, cooking'—but individually and collectively they represent 'an art of scoring within the realm of the other', 'polymorphous maneuvers and mobilities' whose effect is to 'transfigure the normal language of a given space with an alien flash, thereby stupefying the recipient'.[27]

Using (in a much simplified form) de Certeau's distinction between 'strategy' and 'tactics', the present chapter argues that, up to the beginning of 1847 at the very earliest, Baudelaire's only option, in the absence of an 'elsewhere' constituted by an organized republican–socialist opposition to the Bourgeois Monarchy, was to confront the existing order *on its own ground*, deploying a diverse repertoire of oppositional devices not only in his style of life but also in his style of writing. I prefer to call such tactics pre-political rather than apolitical or anti-political; they were all that was possible in the circumstances of 1844–6 and took the form of an apparently compulsive urge to construct intellectual, textual, vestimentary, and related systems of meaning only to undercut them by no less carefully contrived counter-systems and, by dint of such ploys and subterfuge, throw the Other's interpretative processes into confusion and subvert the very possibility of detection or categorization. This does not mean, however, that I am falling back on the 'traditional' view of Baudelaire in the 1840s as an uncertain, half-formed, confused figure whose consuming passions—poetry, painting, money, sex, clothes—were essentially non-political (even anti-political) in character and whose stance in the society of the Bourgeois Monarchy was, at best, that of a petty bourgeois *révolté* of the type excoriated by Sartre: the rebel who positively *needs* what he is rebelling against in order to evade his freedom, in order, ultimately, to have any sense of identity—even counterfeit—at all. The case argued here is broadly that Baudelaire's stance, from the time that the imposition of the *conseil judiciaire* in the late summer of 1844 deprived him of his *financial* autonomy until, at the very earliest, the publication of *La Fanfarlo* in January 1847, consisted of a set of survival tactics designed to preserve an inner *existential* autonomy by extrapolating from within himself and juxtaposing in disorientating fashion a variety of identities, codes, and discourses,

[27] Michel de Certeau, 'On the Oppositional Practices of Everyday Life', *Social Text*, 3 (1980), 6–9.

each of which expressed a *part* of his complex and internally divided personality but which neither individually nor collectively expressed that personality in its totality. Tactics in de Certeau's sense are largely a question of style—style of dressing, walking, eating, drinking, and, not least, the way one 'styles' oneself, one's name or names: significantly, as we shall see, it was in the immediate aftermath of the imposition of the *conseil judiciaire* that Baudelaire added his mother's maiden name to his surname and so transformed himself into that bicephalous and curiously bisexual being Baudelaire-Dufaÿs (or, alternatively, Baudelaire De Fayis, Charles Dufaÿs, Defayis, or de Feyis and even, using his second given name, Pierre Dufaÿs or de Fayis) who would sign almost all his letters and all his published writings between September 1844 and January 1847,[28] before giving way to plain straightforward Baudelaire a month before the outbreak of revolution in 1848. *Larvatus prodeo*, indeed . . .

But such Protean tactics are not the whole story of Baudelaire in the years immediately before the revolution of 1848. Despite Claude Pichois's celebrated *petit essai de sociologie littéraire* 'Baudelaire en 1847', we actually know next to nothing about what he was doing, thinking, reading, and writing during that critical year when, for the first time since the early 1830s, political, economic, and social factors converged to create a real possibility that the Bourgeois Monarchy was not, as it surely seemed between 1842 and 1846, immune to all challenge from within and without. Following the appearance (under the name of Charles Defayis) of *La Fanfarlo* in January 1847, Baudelaire published nothing at all until 18 January 1848 when, using his proper surname, he reviewed some short stories by Champfleury for *Le Corsaire*. A twelve months' silence from a writer whose *Salon de 1846* had, according to Asselineau,[29] earned him an honoured place amongst the 'écrivains-artistes' of his generation surely suggests that some kind of inner revolution was at work, by the end of which, discarding his dichotomous,

---

[28] For the whole question of the names used by Baudelaire, see W. T. Bandy, 'What's in a Name? Variant Signatures in Baudelaire's Letters', *Rivista di letteratura moderne et comparate*, 12/4 (1959), 71–4. The only important occasion when Baudelaire used his proper surname between Sept. 1844 and Jan. 1847 was in signing the so-called 'suicide letter' of 30 June 1845 to Ancelle when, as Bandy says (p. 72), he was in effect signing his last will and testament.

[29] See Jacques Crépet and Claude Pichois (eds.), *Baudelaire et Asselineau* (Nizet, 1953), 79–80.

'hermaphroditic', and pseudo-aristocratic persona 'Baudelaire-Dufaÿs', the writer emerged in early 1848 in full possession of his true identity: Charles Baudelaire. Nothing can, of course, be proved beyond doubt, but it is my belief, which I hope to support with some evidence in the chapter that follows, that it was *in the course of 1847* (in all likelihood in the second rather than the first half of the year) that Baudelaire's previously 'pre-political' *tactics* of survival-through-opposition were transformed into at least the possibility of a *strategy* of political resistance to the Bourgeois Monarchy. This transformation was made possible by the re-emergence, after a lengthy subterranean sojourn in the depths of the *pays réel*, of a relatively coherent radical republican movement which, since 1840 (and arguably since 1834–5), had been so conspicuously absent not only at the level of the *pays légal* but also in those interstitial strata of society that Baudelaire inhabited; in 1847, thanks mainly, I shall argue, to his friendship with Pierre Dupont and Courbet and to his reading of Proudhon, Baudelaire at last encountered an 'elsewhere' from which an effective assault on the existing order might be launched. If I am right, it becomes possible to reconcile the widespread evidence, derived from both Baudelaire's writing and from the testimony of contemporaries, that no coherent political vision informed either his life or his work from his return to France in 1842 up to the beginning of 1847 with the incontrovertible fact that, from the moment revolution broke out, Baudelaire had a very clear perception indeed of where he stood politically and from which, I shall argue, he did not deviate significantly until after the Bonapartist coup of December 1851. In an attempt to impose some order on a vast mass of perplexing material, I have divided my treatment of Baudelaire under the Bourgeois Monarchy into two somewhat artificially separate sections. In the present chapter, I survey the different kinds of evidence that have been adduced in support of the numerous attempts by critics and biographers to affix this or that label— 'Fourierist', 'republican', 'socialist', 'reactionary', and the like— to Baudelaire's political position as expressed in his published writings of the 1840s. Finding none of these labels wholly appropriate (but none of them wholly inappropriate either), I turn in the chapter that follows to a discussion of the various 'oppositional tactics' Baudelaire displays in his writings, actions, and general demeanour or life-style up to and including January 1847, before speculating on some of the transformations he may have undergone in 1847 itself and which led him, logically and directly, to the barricades in February 1848.

Fourierist?

Thanks to the researches of, in particular, David Kelley,[30] the influence of Fourierism on Baudelaire's thought in the 1840s can no longer be doubted. That Baudelaire should have been so influenced is hardly surprising, for, as Peter Hambly has written, 'le milieu que fréquentait le futur auteur des *Fleurs du mal* est imprégné de Fouriérisme'. Of his early literary acquaintances, Privat d'Anglemont, Alphonse Esquiros, and the Abbé Constant were all sympathetic to Fourierism without being out-and-out Fourierists, and Baudelaire was clearly in contact with the Fourierist milieu in the years immediately following his return from the South Seas, submitting—without success—the manuscript of a story to the movement's daily newspaper *La Démocratie pacifique* towards the end of 1843 (C, i. 103). Indeed, such was the diffusion of Fourierist ideas in the 1840s that Baudelaire could have encountered them even in Mauritius where, remarkably, M. Autard de Bragard (to whose wife 'A une dame créole' was dedicated) is said to have had Fourierist sympathies by Désiré Laverdant,[31] the Mauritius-born art-critic of the Fourierist *La Phalange* whose writings (especially his *Salon de 1845*) were, as Kelley has shown, the likely source of many of the aesthetic categories and criteria used by Baudelaire himself in the *Salon de 1846*. Whether Baudelaire read the works of Fourier himself at this or any other stage of his career is open to doubt; his Fourierism, like his Swedenborgian-

[30] See above all his introduction to his edition of the *Salon de 1846* (Oxford Univ. Press, 1975) and also the article 'L'Art: l'Harmonie du beau et de l'utile', *Romantisme*, 5 (1973) 18–36. The question of Baudelaire's Fourierism has also been authoritatively discussed in Ivanna Bugliani, *Baudelaire: l'Armonia e la discordanza* (Bulzoni, 1980), 9–76, and in her earlier article 'Baudelaire tra Fourier e Proudhon', *Critica Storica*, 10/4 (1973), 591–679. A more cautious view of the extent of Fourier's influence on Baudelaire is taken in the pioneering article by Émile Lehouck, 'Baudelaire fut-il fouriériste?', *Revue de l'Université de Bruxelles* (Sept. 1966), 466–73.

[31] Peter S. Hambly, 'Idéologie et poésie: Notes sur Baudelaire et ses contemporains', *Australian Journal of French Studies*, 16/2 (1979), 202–3. The reference to Autard de Bragard and Désiré Laverdant is on p. 199.

ism, was in all likelihood second-hand, derived from regular reading of *La Démocratie pacifique* and *La Phalange*, especially the contributions of the movement's leader, Victor Considerant, and its most outrageously fantastical writer, Alphonse Toussenel. The title, *Les Limbes*, which Baudelaire gave to his forthcoming collection of poetry between 1848 and 1851 (and under which a sequence of twelve poems was published in April of the latter year) has commonly, if restrictively, been interpreted as referring to the 'périodes lymbiques' which, in the Fourierist system,[32] characterize the transition from the organic social order of the past to the 'harmonian' social organization of the future to be created by the implementation of the Fourierist programme; the years of the Bourgeois Monarchy would, it goes without saying, constitute just such a period, a 'chaos civilisé barbare et sauvage', in Fourier's scathing expression.[33] The penultimate section of the *Salon de 1846*, 'Des écoles et des ouvriers', is shot through with Fourierist concepts and terminology and the whole work—a treatise on modern painting rather than the standard *salon* review—is based, in Kelley's words, on the key insight of Fourierist art-critics such as Laverdant and Pelletan that 'les rapports internes de l'œuvre d'art sont analogues à ceux de la société' and that if a painting lacks harmony, order, and vitality, it is because the personality of its maker and, still more, the society that makes that personality, are similarly deficient.[34] Baudelaire's thought in the mid-1840s clearly overlapped at many points with that of the Fourierists: is it, therefore, legitimate to call him a Fourierist and the *Salon de 1846* a Fourierist treatise on art? And, even if his Fourierism was only partial, or assumed heterodox forms, does that make him a revolutionary in the terms current in the 1840s? It is to these and related questions that the present section is devoted.

[32] The starting-point of most 'Fourierist' interpretations of the meaning of the title *Les Limbes* is the well-known reaction of Jean Wallon in 1849 to the collection's announcement in *L'Écho des marchands de vin*: 'Ce sont sans doute des vers socialistes et par conséquent de mauvais vers. Encore un devenu disciple de Proudhon par *trop* ou trop peu d'ignorance' (OC, i. 794–5). Wallon presumably mistook 'les limbes' for a Proudhonian rather than a Fourierist term, or interpreted the title in the light of Baudelaire's enthusiasm—of which he, as an acquaintance, would probably have been aware—for Proudhon in the second half of 1848 and early 1849. For a full discussion of the range of meanings suggested by *Les Limbes*, see Léon Cellier, 'Baudelaire et les Limbes', *Studi Francesi*, 24 (1964), 432–41.

[33] Quoted J. L. Talmon, *Political Messianism: The Romantic Phase* (Secker and Warburg, 1960), 144.

[34] Kelley, 'L'Art', 32.

As indicated above, 'Des écoles et des ouvriers' is the most obviously Fourierist section of the *Salon de 1846* and, on the face of it, is no more than a restatement, with regard to contemporary painting, of the Fourierists' horror of the disintegrative effects of modern individualism and of the need to counter the latter with a new form of associative community of which the *phalanstère* is the ultimate ideal. But, as the painstaking readings of Hartmut Stenzel,[35] Annie Becq,[36] and Ivanna Bugliani[37] have revealed, Baudelaire has given a number of highly personal twists to the Fourierist commonplace and ends with a view of society and art which stands at some considerable distance from that expounded in the pages of *La Phalange* and *La Démocratie pacifique*. Not only does Baudelaire's ideal artistic association lie in the past where the *phalanstère* remains to be realized in the future, but that association is not so much anti-individualist, as it is in the orthodox Fourierist conception, as hyper-individualist in that the association's *raison d'être* is not the collective good of its members but the triumph of 'la force et la souveraineté du génie' of the individual master-artist who is its founder and lodestar. What appals Baudelaire is not so much the chaotic individualism of modern painting (the 'tohu-bohu de styles et de couleurs' that results in an 'absence complète d'unité, dont le résultat est une fatigue effroyable pour l'esprit et pour les yeux') but rather that the 'individual' visions, styles, and personalities it expresses are so mediocre, so derivative, so lacking in, precisely, authentic individuality. In contrast to past conditions which allegedly fostered the growth of true originality of style and vision, modern painting is dominated by 'une vaste population de médiocrités, singes de races diverses et croisées, nation flottante de métis qui passent chaque jour d'un pays dans un autre, emportent de chacun les usages qui leur conviennent, et cherchent à se faire un caractère par un système d'emprunts contradictoires'. Fourierist critics such as Laverdant or Pelletan would not have disagreed with this assessment, but *their* concern was with the need to bring about, in Pelletan's words, cited by Bugliani, 'le passage de la peinture individuelle à la peinture collective', to create conditions in which

[35] Stenzel, *Der historische Ort*, 106–16.
[36] Annie Becq, 'Energie, nostalgie et création artistique selon Baudelaire: A propos du *Salon de 1846*', in *Approches des lumières: Mélanges offerts à Jean Fabre* (Klincksieck, 1974), 31–7.
[37] Bugliani, *Baudelaire*, 46–8. The quotation from Pelletan is on p. 47.

all painters would collaborate and associate with each other on an egalitarian basis for the greater good of all. Baudelaire, though, is concerned only with 'les forts', the true geniuses of painting of whom, for him, the archetype is Delacroix and to whom lesser figures—the simple *ouvriers*, 'les tièdes'—should, he believes, submit themselves and their talents as to 'la férule d'une foi vigoureuse'. Far from being a democratic or egalitarian association, the ideal artistic school for Baudelaire is nothing other than 'la force d'invention organisée' in which 'les individus vraiment dignes de ce nom absorbent les faibles' (all quotations from *Salon de 1846* (OC, ii. 490–2)). Many readers will agree with Bernard Howells that 'there is a whiff of cultural fascism in "Des écoles et des ouvriers"'—which, as he says, is expressive of 'the undercurrents of Baudelaire's sensibility in 1846: eclecticism must be put down; the purpose of life is to produce culture, a coherent, unified culture in which self is sustained and nourished and irresolution pacified'.[38]

Authoritarianism, to be sure, is by no means absent from Fourierist thought itself—from *Phalange* to *Falange* is no distance at all—but that authoritarianism is of a corporate, anti-individualist kind rather than, as in Baudelaire, a glorification of the supremely gifted individual before whom no ordinary artist or lesser person appears to have any rights whatsoever. Consciously or unconsciously, Baudelaire has used Fourierist categories of thought to produce a thoroughly anti-Fourierist conclusion. For all its ostensibly associationist terminology, 'Des écoles et des ouvriers' points forward not so much to Baudelaire's socialism of the Second Republic as to the unabashed artistic élitism of the post-1852 period of which 'Bénédiction' and 'Les Phares', both perhaps drafted between 1845 and 1847, are the supreme poetic expressions.

It is sometimes implied that Baudelaire's evident interest in Fourierist ideas placed him in some way at the vanguard of 'advanced' social (or even socialist) thinking in the mid-1840s and brought him into contact with the working-class radicalism that gained momentum throughout the decade; it is also suggested that Fourierism was a revolutionary ideology at the time when Baudelaire became interested in it. None of these claims can be sustained. A well-informed article in the *Revue des Deux Mondes* in 1845 by the Milan-born philosopher Giuseppe Ferrari argued that, despite

[38] Bernard Howells, 'Baudelaire: Portrait of the Artist in 1846', *French Studies*, 37 (1983), 436.

its superficial vitality and the wide diffusion of its ideas, 'au fond, le fouriérisme se dissout' and survived only as 'une fraction excentrique du parti radical, dont il a usurpé les tendances et revendiqué les succès'; 'l'école tout entière,' he concludes, 'flotte entre la banalité et l'absurde'.[39] Moreover, although there is evidence of working-class support for Fourierist ideas in Lyon in the 1830s,[40] by the 1840s even this strictly localized popular constituency had vanished, as workers were attracted increasingly to the ideas and organizations of more radical (and often themselves working-class) theorists such as Louis Blanc and Étienne Cabet, the founder of the Icarian communist movement and author of the *Voyage en Icarie* (1840) to which Baudelaire refers in a celebrated line of 'Le Voyage' (1859): 'Notre âme est un trois-mâts cherchant son Icarie.' Even when given a more radical and democratic slant by Victor Considerant after 1843, Fourierism, in the words of a modern historian, 'seems to have attracted mostly well-educated professionals'.[41] For some radical workers, such as those associated with *L'Atelier*, Fourierism was not merely irrelevant to their demands but actively opposed to them in that its model community, the *phalanstère*, was to embrace all classes in society arranged still in a fundamentally hierarchical fashion.[42] Not only, according to *L'Atelier*, did Fourierists maintain that 'les droits appartiennent aux classes supérieures' but the fact that the *phalanstère* would continue, like existing units of production, to be financed by private capital made it merely 'un moyen nouveau de perpétuer l'infériorité des ouvriers', 'une forme nouvelle de l'exploitation du travailleur par le capitalisme'.[43] Even after Considerant's attempted radicalization and democratization of the movement, *La Démocratie pacifique* remained, according to Ferrari, basically 'conservatrice au point de vue politique': 'elle ne

[39] Ferrari, 'Des idées et de l'école de Fourier depuis 1830', *Revue des Deux Mondes*, 11 (1845), 389–90 and 484.

[40] See Christopher H. Johnson, *Utopian Communism in France: Cabet and the Icarians 1839–51* (Cornell Univ. Press, 1974), 188.

[41] Ibid. 156 (n.). See also the entry on Considerant in Jean Maitron, *Dictionnaire biographique du mouvement ouvrier français*. On working-class indifference to Fourierism in Paris, Lyon, and Reims, see Johnson, *Utopian Communism*, 192. See also Félix Arnand, *Les Fouriéristes et les luttes révolutionnaires de 1848 à 1851* (Presses Universitaires de France, 1948), 11.

[42] See Considerant's definition of his ideal form of social organization in his *Principes du socialisme* (1843) cited in Arnand, *Les Fouriéristes*, 26.

[43] Quotations from Armand Cuvillier, *Hommes et idéologies de 1840* (Marcel Rivière, 1956), 103–5.

cesse pas d'attaquer la féodalité industrielle, et pourtant ne cesse pas de faire l'apologie de la politique qui la maintient.'[44] Lacking, as we shall see shortly, a commitment to Republicanism or to any other form of organized political action, the Fourierist school was, in Ferrari's words, unable to escape 'cette contradiction du socialisme sans politique' and was reduced to promising not 'une révolution' but 'une transfiguration' which Considerant and his fellows believed would come about as it were magically through the diffusion of their Master's ideas. By 1846 the Fourierist movement was seriously compromised in the eyes of other radicals by its impenetrable jargon, its resolutely anti-political stance, and above all by its authoritarian élitism which has led one modern writer to speak of its incipiently Nietzschean and even fascist character.[45] If it is true, as Bugliani and others have argued, that 'Des écoles et des ouvriers' represents a 'deformation' of Fourierist orthodoxy, the fact remains that the deformation in question goes along with, rather than against, the movement's increasingly authoritarian tendency. This is not to say that, after February 1848, someone with Fourierist convictions or interests might not move, as Considerant himself did,[46] in a more radical and democratic direction. It simply means that to be a Fourierist in the last years of the Bourgeois Monarchy, or to advance Fourierist ideas (even, like Baudelaire, in a modified version) was not to be in the forefront of the radical movement and could well indicate the existence of—to use Howells's expression—personal and ideological 'undercurrents' which, in changed circumstances (say after the Bonapartist coup of 1851) were as likely to propel one to the authoritarian right as to the left (authoritarian or otherwise), as the post-1851 career of Leconte de Lisle[47]—by 1845 virtually the official poet laureate of the Fourierist school—abundantly illustrates.

Republican?

The view that, by the time he wrote the *Salon de 1846*, Baudelaire had become an active supporter of the Republican cause rests

---

[44] Ferrari, 'Des idées', 423, 425, 391.

[45] See Arnand, *Les Fouriéristes*, 32–3.

[46] Ibid. 58–9.

[47] See Hambly, 'Idéologie et poésie', 203. On p. 205 Hambly argues that 'Baudelaire et Leconte de Lisle ont tous les deux la même religion dans les années 1840'.

almost entirely on a particular reading of the opening paragraph
of, once again, 'Des écoles et des ouvriers':

Avez-vous éprouvé, vous tous que la curiosité du flâneur a souvent fourrés
dans une émeute, la même joie que moi à voir un gardien du sommeil
public,—sergent de ville ou municipal, la véritable armée,—crosser un
républicain? Et comme moi, vous avez dit dans votre cœur: 'Crosse, crosse
un peu plus fort, crosse encore, municipal de mon cœur; car en ce crosse-
ment suprême, je t'adore, et te juge semblable à Jupiter, le grand justicier.
L'homme que tu crosses est un ennemi des roses et des parfums, un
fanatique des ustensiles; c'est un ennemi de Watteau, un ennemi de
Raphaël, un ennemi acharné du luxe, des beaux-arts et des belles-lettres,
iconoclaste juré, bourreau de Vénus et d'Apollon! Il ne veut plus travailler,
humble et anonyme ouvrier, aux roses et aux parfums publics; il veut être
libre, l'ignorant, et il est incapable de fonder un atelier de fleurs et de
parfumeries nouvelles. Crosse religieusement les omoplates de l'anarchiste!'
(OC, ii. 490)

The problem presented by this paragraph has been well formulated
by Gretchen van Slyke. 'Decoded on a strictly literal level', she
writes, it 'sums up the reactionary esthetic and political attitudes of
the bourgeoisie of the July Monarchy: "vive l'art académique et
Louis-Philippe, roi des bourgeois"'; if, on the other hand (and here
she tersely summarizes the argument of Dolf Oehler),[48] it is read
ironically, 'we then run to the conclusion that this passage means
the opposite of what it ostensibly signifies—that Baudelaire, acting
like an *agent provocateur* for the republican opposition, hopes to
exacerbate existing conflicts and to trigger, *à la Blanqui*, the revolt
of the proletariat'.[49] Following and adding to the cases argued by
Stenzel[50] and Becq,[51] van Slyke sees the resolution to the conflict of
interpretations in the widely attested hostility of Fourierists to
Republicanism which, for them, was no more than the 'anarchic'
political expression of the chaotic individualism characteristic of
the 'période lymbique' in which they were living. By Republicans,
Fourierists meant essentially the moderate middle-class 'con-

[48] See Oehler, *Parisen Bilder I*, 119–22.

[49] Gretchen van Slyke, 'Riot and Revolution in the *Salon de 1846*', *French
Forum*, 10/3 (1985), 295.

[50] Hartmut Stenzel, 'Les écrivains et l'évolution idéologique de la petite bourgeoisie dans les années 1840: Le cas de Baudelaire', *Romantisme*, 17–18 (1977),
85–6.

[51] Becq, 'Énergie', 32–4.

stitutional' Republicans centred on *Le National*, a group whose 'decorous programme of electoral and educational reform'[52] envisaged only a change of *political* regime that would leave the underlying structure of society and the economy unaltered and whose view of society as an aggregate of free individuals ran directly counter to the Fourierist ideal of the organic, hierarchical association. If Baudelaire shared this Fourierist definition of what Republicanism was at the time that he wrote the *Salon de 1846*, the virulent anti-Republicanism of the opening paragraph of 'Des écoles et des ouvriers' is wholly consistent with the critique of pseudo-individualism and pseudo-freedom in painting developed in what follows. Discerning, in van Slyke's phrase, an 'analogy between mimetic art and republican politics',[53] Baudelaire condemns both as expressions of the same atomistic individualism that, in the Fourierist perspective, is the cause and curse of the 'sociétés subversives' of the present;[54] the fact that, unlike their Fourierist counterparts, Republican artists and art-critics commonly held to a narrowly didactic and utilitarian view of painting was a further reason for dismissing Republicans *en bloc* as 'fanatiques des ustensiles' and sworn enemies of everything that is merely beautiful. If 'les singes'—pseudo-individualistic and derivative painters—are, as Baudelaire says, 'les républicains de l'art' (OC, ii. 492), it follows that Republicans are 'les singes de la politique': from the heterodox Fourierist standpoint of the *Salon de 1846*, both stand accused as enemies not only of cultural, social, and artistic unity but of the expression of authentic individuality in art and life as well.

If one accepts, as (with some misgivings) I do, the validity of this interpretation, there is no need to look, as Oehler does, beneath the ostensible meaning of 'Des écoles et des ouvriers' for a pro-Republican subversion by imitation and exaggeration of the anti-Republican discourse of these sections of the middle and upper-middle classes who still, in 1846, gave their support to Louis-Philippe and his regime: the anti-Republicanism of the *Salon de 1846* is sincerely held and consistent with Baudelaire's other beliefs

[52] See Magraw, *France 1815–1914*, 88.
[53] Van Slyke, 'Riot', 299.
[54] On the Fourierist concept of 'société subversives', see Victor Considerant, *Exposition abrégée du système phalanstérien de Fourier* (Libraire phalanstérienne, 1848), 70–4.

at the time and with the Fourierist outlook as a whole. At the same time, however, the sheer violence of the imagery, tone, and language of the opening paragraph of 'Des écoles et des ouvriers' is so wildly disproportionate to the case Baudelaire goes on to make that it is difficult to take it as a straightforward, 'sincere' attack on Republicans and their cause. Readers of *L'Éducation sentimentale* will not need reminding of the routine nature of police violence against Republicans in the 1840s, and one would need to be a fanatical anti-Republican indeed not only to take sides with 'la violence du Pouvoir' (Flaubert's phrase[55]) against the likes of a Dussardier but to hail the *sergent de ville* responsible for the drubbing as an Olympian bringer of justice and urge him on to still greater violence. The exorbitance of situation and language is clearly ironic, and van Slyke argues convincingly that Baudelaire's objective is to 'stage' a 'confrontation between the gendarme and the republican' that will 'throw into the face of the bourgeoisie a dilemma of their own making—a dilemma to which they can offer no response save that of violence, which can only exacerbate tensions and risk precipitating civil war'.[56] In this reading, then, Baudelaire is attacking both Republicans—particularly the 'constitutional' Republicans of *Le National*—and those sections of the middle and upper-middle classes opposed to them, the two antagonists being, from the Fourierist viewpoint, enemies only on the surface but, deep down, proponents of the same detested utilitarian and atomistic concept of society. The merit of this reading is that it offers not merely a coherent account of Baudelaire's position in 1846 but also makes his political choices in and after February 1848 intelligible and consistent. In equating Republicanism *in 1846* with the legalistic 'bourgeois' Republicanism of *Le National*, Baudelaire was doing no more than echoing the views of *La Démocratie pacifique* and *La Phalange*;[57] he can hardly be blamed for failing to appreciate that there were other submerged and repressed forms of Republicanism in France at this time—radical, socialist, working-class Republicanism—when even his close friend, the popular *chansonnier* and poet Pierre Dupont, in whose work Baudelaire would, in 1851,

[55] Gustave Flaubert, *L'Éducation sentimentale*, ed. Édouard Maynial (Garnier, 1964), 30.
[56] Van Slyke, 'Riot', 296.
[57] On the hostility of working-class radicals to *Le National* and its programme, see Georges Weill, *Historie du Parti Républicain en France 1814–1870* (Félix Alcan, 1928), 143.

find an expression of 'le goût infini de la République' (OC, ii. 33), was, in 1845–6, still, in the words of Jean Maitron, 'l'adepte d'un utopisme confus' and whose 'conversion' to the Republican cause does not seem to have occurred until 1847–8.[58] When in February 1848 (if not before) a popular and radical Republicanism revealed itself, Baudelaire, as we shall see, rallied immediately and unreservedly to its cause; his evident contempt for the merely constitutional Republicanism of the Provisional Government is a logical continuation of his earlier hostility to bourgeois Republicanism, especially as the Provisional Government was dominated by members of the editorial committee of *Le National*.

Whether Baudelaire was, in the distinction current in 1848, a *républicain de la veille* or *du lendemain* is unlikely ever to be established. If, swallowing all my doubts, I was asked to 'label' the *Salon de 1846*, I would describe it as a non-Republican, even anti-Republican treatise, shot through with a typically Fourierist mistrust of politics and erroneously—though in the circumstances of 1846, understandably—identifying Republicanism as a whole with its bourgeois, constitutional expression. If Baudelaire did become a Republican before February 1848 (and there were plenty of barricade conversions), it seems more likely that he did so after the publication of the *Salon de 1846*, perhaps as late as January 1848 when he for the first time published a work under his 'citizen's' name of Baudelaire. *Sero te amavi*: lateness or suddenness of conversion never meant lukewarmness.

Socialist?

The word 'socialiste' appears to have been used only once by Baudelaire in works published before 1848, and that in the highly ironic context of the concluding paragraph of *La Fanfarlo*: 'Pauvre chantre des *Orfraies*! Pauvre Manuela de Monteverde!—Il est tombé bien bas.—J'ai appris récemment qu'il fondait un journal socialiste et voulait se mettre à la politique.—Intelligence malhonnête!—comme dit cet honnête M. Nisard' (OC, i. 580). As we

---

[58] On Dupont's radicalization in 1846 (when 'Le Chant des Ouvriers' was published) and subsequent years, see D. Higgins, 'Pierre Dupont: A *Chansonnier* of the 1848 Revolution', *French Studies*, 3 (1949), 122–36. On Baudelaire's reaction to 'Le Chant des Ouvriers', see OC, ii. 31.

shall see, the relationship between the narrator of *La Fanfarlo* and the story's central character is ambiguous in the extreme, and great caution should be exercised before identifying either with Baudelaire himself. As noted above, *La Fanfarlo* was published in January 1847 but may have been completed as much as a year earlier;[59] the narrator's contempt—itself, like everything else in the story, expressed equivocally—for Cramer's 'conversion' to left-wing journalism and political activism cannot be taken as evidence that, in early 1847 or at any other time, Baudelaire himself viewed either activity in the same dismissive manner. Moreover, any discussion of Baudelaire's 'socialism' at this stage of his career must begin by recognizing that what was meant by the words 'socialism' and 'socialist' in the 1840s was, to say the least, extremely unspecific. In his study of Proudhon, K. Steven Vincent has written that 'to be a socialist in France before 1848 was to take a stance that was critical of the existing political and social order, especially of the conditions of the working class, and that advocated a new order, opposed to "individualism" and consistent with the religious-moral values of social justice'.[60] This is general stuff indeed, and though the definition of 'socialist' was tightened somewhat in 1848 itself, it was again relaxed in the years that followed as the Left strove to assemble the broadest possible coalition of groups and interests to check the advance of its enemies; in November 1849 the highly influential *La Feuille de village* declared typically that 'le socialisme, c'est l'esprit d'association, de solidarité. C'est tout ce qui tend à rendre la société meilleure, les hommes moins egoïstes, la vie moins dure.'[61] Given this broadness of definition, it may be thought that, short of being an out-and-out defender of the existing social, political, and economic order, it was difficult not to be a 'socialist' in some sense in the 1840s.

What is interesting about the final paragraph of *La Fanfarlo* is the way it equates two concepts—'socialism' and 'politics'—which, in the mid-1840s, were kept rigorously separate by most thinkers

---

[59] Pichois (OC, i. 1414) is of the opinion that '*La Fanfarlo* a pu être écrit entre 1843 et la fin de 1846'. In a letter of 10 June 1844 to his mother (C, i. 107), Baudelaire states that he is 'toujours sur mon interminable nouvelle': this could well be *La Fanfarlo*.

[60] K. Steven Vincent, *Pierre-Joseph Proudhon and the Rise of French Republican Socialism* (Oxford Univ. Press, 1984), 77.

[61] Quoted Philippe Vigier, *La Seconde République* (Presses Universitaires de France, 1967), 79.

who called themselves 'socialists'. According to Daniel Halévy, 'le mot *socialiste*, de recent usage, désignait alors [*he is referring precisely to 1846, the year Proudhon published his* Système des contradictions économiques] tous ceux qui mettaient l'ordre social, distinct de l'ordre politique, au premier rang de leurs préoccupations'.[62] An uncertainty concerning the relationship between 'le social' and 'le politique' is, as we shall see, typical of the French Left throughout the period covered by this book, and contempt for the 'merely political' would remain a leitmotiv of socialist thought and practice in France amongst certain sections of the Paris Commune, the Allemanistes of the 1880s and 1890s, the Anarcho-Syndicalists of the 1900s and even of the Parti Communiste Français in the years before the Popular Front. It is characteristic of the anti-political bent of much French socialism that in July 1847, shortly after the beginning of the banquet campaign for electoral reform, Proudhon could write in his notebooks not only that 'la réforme politique sera l'effet, non le moyen de la réforme sociale' but that 'la réforme politique est un moyen sûr d'enterrer la réforme sociale';[63] Proudhon, it need hardly be added, was, like so many on the French Left, in no real sense a Republican before February 1848, and his subsequent support for the Republic as a political regime would remain muted and conditional upon its commitment to social and economic change.[64] It would be too much to suggest that, as early as 1847, Baudelaire was pointing a way beyond the opposition of 'society' and 'politics' that would signally weaken the French Left for the next half-century or more, but his explicit linking of two spheres that much socialist thinking would long keep apart is none the less most striking.

How much did Baudelaire know, prior to the outbreak of revolution, of the socialist thought and movements of his time? There is ample evidence[65] that he was familiar with the heady mixture of prophecy, this-worldly mysticism, cosmological speculation, esotericism, and social romanticism to be found in the works of Alphonse Esquiros (one of his 'secondes liaisons littéraires' (OC, i. 785) and the author of a typically 1840s 'synthesis' of Christianity

[62] Daniel Halévy, *Le Mariage de Proudhon* (Stock, 1955), 22.

[63] Quoted in Pierre Haubtmann, *Pierre-Joseph Proudhon: Sa vie et sa pensée (1809–1849)* (Beauchesne, 1982), 807.

[64] See ibid. 821.

[65] Summarized Pichois, 'Baudelaire en 1847', BET, 106–17, from which most of the following is taken.

and socialism in *L'Évangile du peuple*), the ex-Abbé Constant (whose scandalous 'œuvre de folie', *La Bible de la liberté* (1841) is discussed at length, if hardly sympathetically, in a section of *Les Mystères galants des théâtres de Paris* (1844) that may be by Baudelaire (OC, ii. 1007–11)), Edgar Quinet, the author of *Ahasvérus* (1833) and held to be 'un homme d'un vrai mérite' by Baudelaire in 1846 (OC, ii. 9) and 'le paisible Pierre Leroux, dont les nombreux ouvrages sont comme un dictionnaire des croyances humaines' (OC, ii. 40) and who, as Gretchen van Slyke has shown, exercised an important influence on the thinking of the *Salon de 1846*.[66] To argue that Baudelaire was probably drawn as much or more to the cosmological speculations of such writers—and particularly to the theory of *correspondances* that he would have found expounded by, for instance, Constant—as to their social thinking is to establish a false distinction for, as Claude Pichois has memorably demonstrated, in the heated intellectual ambience of the 1840s,

théories sociales, idées esthétiques, attitudes politiques se commandent alors les unes les autres; n'est-il pas révélateur que le même Pierre Leroux ait été . . . le créateur des mots *symbolisme* et *socialisme*? Croire à la symbolique des fleurs, cela engage fortement alors dans le socialisme, et l'innocent fleuriste se retrouve un jour sur les barricades. Écrire que les parfums, les couleurs et les sons se répondent, ce pourrait être aussi grave que de signer sa propre condamnation aux pontons inhospitaliers de la Deuxième République. Et lire Swedenborg, c'est se promettre de serrer un jour la main de Proudhon.[67]

There was no clear cut-off point between writers such as Esquiros and Constant who, by modern standards, were, at most, humanitarian or 'socialistic' in outlook and the Fourierists who, 'Utopian' though they may have been, none the less come much closer to a modern understanding of what is meant by 'socialist'.[68] Again no clear distinction can be drawn between a sympathy for Fourierist aesthetic theories—which, on the evidence of the *Salon de 1846*, Baudelaire certainly possessed—and a sympathy for some aspects, at least, of their social thinking. At the very least, Baudelaire may

---

[66] See van Slyke, 'Riot', 297–305, and also her 'Les Lois du calorique: Le Discours de la nature chez Baudelaire et Leroux' (forthcoming).

[67] Pichois, 'Baudelaire en 1847', BET, 115. For a full, if highly partisan, discussion of the links between socialism, spiritualism, occultism, and esoterism in the 1840s, see Philippe Muray, *Le 19e siècle à travers les âges* (Denoël, 1984).

[68] Pichois, 'Baudelaire en 1847', 99–100.

be said to have shared their critique of the atomistic individualism in contemporary art and society though, as we have seen, the conclusions he drew from this were very different from those of the orthodox Fourierists. The conflict, apparent in 'Des écoles et des ouvriers', between the anti-individualism of a major contemporary school of socialist thought and Baudelaire's visceral need to protect and affirm the individuality of the authentic artist (i.e. himself) is but one of a number of tensions, to be brought out in the pages that follow, between his undoubtedly sincere espousal of certain socialist ideals and concepts before, during, and after 1848 and the deeper 'undercurrents' of his personality and ideology.

Turning now to other 'schools' of French socialism in the 1840s which commanded rather more popular support than either social romanticism or Fourierism (not that either of these was without important influence on the working classes), there is no evidence that Baudelaire had read either Louis Blanc or Étienne Cabet—between them overwhelmingly the best-known socialist thinkers amongst 'le peuple' before 1848—but, equally, it is difficult to imagine that he had not acquired, well before the outbreak of revolution, some second-hand knowledge, at least, of the state-centred theory of socialism expounded in *L'Organisation du travail* which, published in 1840, had gone into its tenth edition by 1848. Raspail he seems not to have known until the first number of *L'Ami du Peuple* appeared on 27 February 1848,[69] and it is most improbable that he read at any time the work of such important working-class socialist thinkers as Constantin Pecqueur, Philippe Buchez, and Théodore Dézamy. If Baudelaire's *reading* of the socialist literature of the 1840s seems to have been confined almost entirely to the work of middle-class theorists, he had a vital link with the dynamic world of workers' socialism through his friendship with Pierre Dupont who, the Lyon-born son of a blacksmith, was the only one of Baudelaire's acquaintances who can be described as of working-class origin, even though he had moved some considerable distance from his roots by the time Baudelaire met him in 1842. Until 1846, as we have seen, Dupont's poems and songs were of a bucolic, sentimental character and touched only peripherally on political and social questions. In 1846, though, Dupont published and performed 'Le Chant des Ouvriers' which, along with

[69] See the testimony of Charles Toubin, reproduced BPZ, 259, where Baudelaire's 'tendresse et admiration sans bonnes' for Raspail are recorded.

other such compositions, was to earn him a place amongst the front
rank of socialist *chansonniers* in the immediate pre-revolutionary
period. In each of his articles on Dupont (1851 and 1861), Baudelaire
memorably recalls the occasion when, in the course of one of their
'longues flâneries' together in 1846, Dupont first sang to him 'le
magnifique *Chant des Ouvriers*' in 'cette voix si charmante qu'il
possédait alors' (1861 article, OC, ii. 171):

Cependant Dupont, s'avançant dans sa voie naturelle, avait composé un
chant d'une allure plus décidée et bien mieux fait pour émouvoir le cœur
des habitants d'une grande ville. Je me rappelle encore la première confidence qu'il m'en fit, avec une naïveté charmante et comme encore indécis
dans sa résolution. Quand j'entendis cet admirable cri de douleur et de
mélancolie (*Le Chant des ouvriers, 1846*), je fus ébloui et attendri. Il y avait
tant d'années que nous attendions un peu de poésie forte et vraie! Il est
impossible, à quelque parti qu'on appartienne, de quelques préjugés qu'on
ait été nourri, de ne pas être touché du spectacle de cette multitude
maladive respirant la poussière des ateliers, avalant du coton, s'imprégnant
de céruse, de mercure et de tous les poisons nécessaires à la création des
chefs-d'œuvres, dormant dans la vermine, au fond des quartiers où les
vertus les plus humbles et les plus grandes nichent à côté des vices les plus
endurcis et des vomissements du bagne; de cette multitude soupirante et
languissante à qui *la terre doit ses merveilles*; qui sent *un sang vermeil et
impétueux couler dans ses veines*, qui jette un long regard chargé de
tristesse sur le soleil et l'ombre des grands parcs, et qui, pour suffisante
consolation et réconfort, répète à tue-tête son refrain sauveur: *Aimons-
nous!...* (1851 art., OC, ii. 30)

If there was any one experience that 'converted' Baudelaire to the
socialist cause, it was surely this, though of course he could well be
projecting back on to 1846 his populist enthusiasms of 1851.
Chapter 5 of this book will show how much of Baudelaire's writing
of the Second Republic period draws on the same matrix of theme
and image as Dupont's songs. But Dupont is important, too, as we
shall see, for the areas of working-class experience and culture to
which, but for his friendship, Baudelaire would probably not have
gained access, most notably the *goguettes* which, as again Chapter 5
will show, were one of the principal media through which socialist
ideas were disseminated before 1848 and which functioned, in
particular, as a point of contact between middle-class and working-
class concepts of socialism. If Baudelaire was, as Jacques Rancière

has argued, 'étroitement lié à la culture mixte des années 40–48',[70] it was, one suspects, in large part thanks to those aspects of working-class life opened up to him by friendship with Dupont.

Two other leading socialist thinkers and activists need to be mentioned at this point, pending a more detailed examination in later chapters of Baudelaire's attitude to them in and after 1848. The name of Blanqui must have been known to Baudelaire, as it was to all his contemporaries, before 1848, and the fact that Aupick had been actively engaged in the repression of the Blanquist coup of May 1839 may have made his stepson particularly sympathetic to *l'Enfermé* and the version of ultra-leftist Republicanism he embodied.[71] I shall discuss in the next chapter Baudelaire's probably brief membership of Blanqui's *Société Républicaine Centrale* in February–March 1848 together with the likelihood that he remained in contact with the Blanquist milieu until the very end of the June uprising; his pre-1848 view of the man and his methods remains yet another imponderable. Dolf Oehler's view that parts of the *Salon de 1846* are, as it were, literary equivalents of the Blanquist *coup de main* staged in order to precipitate ideological class conflict is fascinating but unverifiable,[72] though Walter Benjamin[73] may well have been right when he discerned 'the dark head of Blanqui' behind lines 16–17 of 'Les Litanies de Satan' ('une pièce assez ancienne', according to Pichois (OC, i. 1083)):

> Toi qui fais au proscrit ce regard calme et haut
> Qui damne tout un peuple autour d'un échafaud . . .

The likelihood is that, like so many of his contemporaries, Baudelaire had long possessed a mental image of Blanqui as the archetypal political conspirator which, in and after 1848, he would attempt to reconcile with his experience of the man himself, his strategy, and his followers.

The case of Proudhon is still more obscure. Given the notoriety of *Qu'est-ce que la propriété?* (1840), Baudelaire would presumably have heard of him despite the fact that he had somewhat slipped from public view in the mid-1840s, only fully to re-emerge after the

---

[70] Jacques Rancière, 'Ronds de fumée: Les Poètes ouvriers dans la France de Louis-Philippe', *Revue des sciences humaines*, 190 (1983), 40.

[71] See Baudelaire's letter to Alphonse around 18 May 1839 (C, i. 70 and BPZ, 114).

[72] See Oehler, 'Le Caractère double', 190–1.

[73] Benjamin, *Charles Baudelaire*, 23.

repression of the *journées de juin*. Through Jules Viard, an associate on the *Corsaire-Satan* in 1846 who would reappear at intervals in his life after 1848, Baudelaire had a distant contact with the milieu frequented by Proudhon before the revolution. It was Viard who, in October 1847, founded *Le Représentant du peuple* that would provide him with his principal journalistic platform in the months to come. Although it is almost certainly wrong to suggest, as Ivanna Bugliani does in her otherwise excellent study, that Baudelaire had read Proudhon when he wrote the *Salon de 1846* and that that work expresses a conflict between Fourierist and Proudhonian conceptions of art and society, it is true that some time between the autumn of 1846 and the beginning of the Second Empire he copied out—presumably with approval—a section from Proudhon's *Système des contradictions économiques* concerning the relationship between ethics, aesthetics, and economics (OC, ii. 979). Better known under its subtitle *Philosophie de la misère* (and savaged by Marx in *Misère de la philosophie*), the *Système* was published in October 1846 and could not, therefore, have influenced the writing of the *Salon*, published in May.[74] Though the book was reviewed only in *La Presse* (of which Baudelaire was, however, a reader) and found only a tiny readership, Baudelaire's range of intellectual interests was such that he could well have been drawn towards a work by a notorious author the title of which foregrounded two notions—'system' and 'contradiction'[75]—that were at the core of his preoccupations in the mid-1840s. It is entirely possible that, at the instigation, perhaps, of his new Franc-Comtois friends, Gustave Courbet and Charles Toubin, Baudelaire read the *Système* in late 1846 or during the 'missing year' of 1847 and that the 'théodicée envahissante et énigmatique'[76] that Proudhon elaborates in chapter 8, volume 1, 'De la responsabilité de l'homme et de Dieu, sous la loi de contradiction, ou solution du problème de la Providence' with its scandalous conclusion that 'Dieu, c'est le mal' influenced the thinking behind not only, as Lois B. Hyslop has argued,[77] 'Le Reniement de saint Pierre' (1851–2) but also other somewhat earlier poems such as 'L'Âme du vin' and 'Le Vin des

[74] See Halévy, *Le Mariage de Proudhon*, 22–4.

[75] On 'system', see OC, ii. 577–8, and on 'contradiction', OC, ii. 456.

[76] The expression is Edouard Droz's (1909) and is quoted in Haubtmann, *Pierre-Joseph Proudhon*, 667.

[77] See Lois B. Hyslop, 'Baudelaire, Proudhon and "Le Reniement de saint Pierre"', *French Studies*, 30/3 (1976), 281–4.

chiffonniers'. Baudelaire's passionate enthusiasm for Proudhon the man probably dates from the immediate aftermath of the *journées de juin* but had its roots, in all likelihood, in a fervent reading of one of his key works in the last fifteen months or so of the Bourgeois Monarchy.

Given the ecumenical definition of socialism and socialist in the 1840s to which we referred above, the evidence assembled in this chapter probably justifies our stating that Baudelaire had been a socialist in some very general sense for some indeterminable period before the outbreak of Revolution in February 1848 and that his actions between the *journées de février* and *journées de juin* and beyond were a logical extension of developments that had taken place in the last months or years of the Bourgeois Monarchy. The problem is, however, that that 'general sense' in which Baudelaire was a socialist before 1848 is very general indeed. There is no firm evidence to link him beyond doubt to any one of the schools of socialist theory and practice that abounded in the 1840s, except to the Fourierists whose influence on the *Salon de 1846* is not in question but with whom, as we have seen, Baudelaire had important points of difference when it came to the kind of community that, ideally, was to be opposed to the centreless individualism of modern life. It would certainly be legitimate to describe the *Salon de 1846* as a socialist treatise on art in the minimum sense that the deficiencies of modern painting are constantly traced back to the defects of modern society, that contemporary (pseudo-) individualism is roundly condemned (even if Baudelaire's solution to the threat it poses to art and society owes more to the Romantic cult of individualism than to any form, present or future, of socialism), and that—though here there is considerable room for disagreement— no 'merely political' solution seems to be envisaged for what are seen as a set of interlinked social, spiritual, and psychological problems. Since contemporary definitions of socialism were already so loose, it may be thought ultra-cautious if I still prefer to call the *Salon* pre- or proto-socialist. It is my view that, if Baudelaire became a socialist in some more specific, concrete sense before 1848, he did so, as suggested earlier, in the months after the *Salon*'s publication, in 1847 when the combined influences of the worsening social, economic, and political situation, Dupont's growing prowess as a socialist *chansonnier*, and the reading of the *Système des contradictions économiques* gave greater clarity, direction, and, above all, *positive content* to what had previously been essentially a disposition or stance founded on a set of ambivalences and negativities. One may readily agree, in short, that—to anticipate on the subject of the following section—the *Salon de 1846* and related texts are, again in some very unspecific sense, 'anti-bourgeois'; this, however, does not necessarily make them socialist but could, in another set of circumstances, cause their author to veer vertiginously to the Right in a desperate attempt to cling on to his own individual identity. There is already more than a hint of this in 'Des écoles et des ouvriers' with its proto-Nietzschean response to the scourge of modern pseudo-individualism. Sensing a conflict between his own need for individual freedom as man and artist and the anti-individualism of most existing forms of socialism—Proudhon who, as early as 1846 (in *Le Système*), condemned Cabet's communism as entailing 'la mort du moi, l'affirmation du néant'[78] was, as ever, an exception to the rule—Baudelaire does not hesitate to move in a direction which, to say the least, is not one that is normally associated with socialism: when one's own individuality is threatened, rather than that of sundry semi-talented 'ouvriers emancipés' about one, it is not, it appears, such a 'petite propriété' after all (OC, ii. 491–2). 'Baudelaire-Dufaÿs' may well have believed in the need for a 'harmonian' solution to the discordant individualism of the modern world, but, as he memorably puts it in the *Salon* itself, 'les poètes, les artistes et toute la race humaine seraient bien malheureux, si l'idéal, cette absurdité, cette impossibilité, était trouvé. Qu'est-ce que chacun ferait désormais de son pauvre *moi*,—de sa ligne brisée?' (OC, ii. 455). The whole of Baudelaire's post-1851 polemic against socialism is contained *in nuce* in these words.

'Anti-bourgeois'?

Following the lead given by Dolf Oehler,[79] most recent readings of the dedication 'Aux Bourgeois' of the *Salon de 1846* have insisted

---

[78] Quoted Haubtmann, *Pierre-Joseph Proudhon*, 663.

[79] See Oehler, *Pariser Bilder I*, 56–71. The present section was written before I read Gretchen van Slyke's typically searching article 'Les Épiciers au musée: Baudelaire et l'artiste bourgeois' (*Romantisme*, 55 (1987), 55–66) which, though broadly, I think, confirming my interpretation introduces many important and subtle distinctions into the social category 'bourgeois', and to which the reader is referred.

on the text's apparently systematic use of irony, ambivalence, exaggeration, and mimicry as a means, on Baudelaire's part, of turning bourgeois ideology against itself, of exposing its inner contradictions and absurdities and thus of defining himself and his work in oppositional terms over and against *juste-milieu* values in art, ethics, and politics.[80] Paradoxically, however, readings that dwell exclusively on the dedication's subversive ambiguity may make it considerably more straightforward than it actually is for, as Annie Becq has written, the main problem with 'Aux Bourgeois' is that, though the text may be ironic *in parts*, 'l'ironie mystificatrice ne le constitue pas totalement',[81] leading to the further problems of determining where the ironies start and finish and whether their object is the same throughout the text and raising, finally, the possibility that the ultimate irony of 'Aux Bourgeois' is that it is not an ironic text at all in the generally understood sense of saying the opposite of what it seems to mean but one which, much more perversely, tricks the reader into thinking it must contain some hidden subversive intent while all along it is the obvious surface level of the piece that carries its author's real meaning.

The dedication of the *Salon de 1846* was not the first time Baudelaire had addressed himself to the relationship of art and the middle classes, and recent interpretations of the text have not always made sufficiently clear how closely its argument parallels that already advanced in the 'Quelques mots d'introduction' that open the *Salon de 1845* and in the concluding paragraph of 'Le Musée Classique du Bazar Bonne-Nouvelle' (January 1846).[82] Although both these texts present, *en plus petit*, problems of tone and intentionality similar to those posed by 'Aux Bourgeois', taken together the three advance a case that is intelligible, consistent with the Fourierist perspective that informs so much of Baudelaire's writings of 1845–6, and not so utterly fatuous, above all in the particular conditions that obtained during those years, that there simply has

---

[80] For an important discussion of Baudelaire's use of dedications for 'oppositional' purposes, see Ross Chambers, 'Baudelaire et la pratique de la dédicace', *Saggi e ricerche di letteratura francese*, 24 (1985) 120–40. The *Salon de 1846* is discussed on p. 134.

[81] Annie Becq, 'Baudelaire et "l'Amour de l'Art": La Dédicace "aux bourgeois" du *Salon de 1846*', *Romantisme*, 17–18 (1977), 71.

[82] An important exception is Eliane Jasenas, 'Stendhal et Baudelaire: La Dédicace "Aux bourgeois", la problématique d'un texte', *Nineteenth-century French Studies*, 9/3–4 (1981), esp. 193–5.

to be some subversive anti-bourgeois intent lurking beneath the complimentary and respectful attitudes evident on the texts' surface level. The starting-point of Baudelaire's argument throughout is the reality of bourgeois power in politics, society, economy, thought, and culture, a power which he clearly believes to be, to all intents and purposes, unchallengeable; in the circumstances of 1845–6 this was not, as we have seen, an unreasonable assessment. The question posed by the three texts we are considering is a stark one—how are authentic art and authentic artists to survive in a society that is so wholly dominated by bourgeois tastes and bourgeois values and, above all, by bourgeois power and bourgeois money?—and the answers Baudelaire gives are notable for their pragmatism and their candour. First of all, he says, there must be an end to the routine attacks launched by 'nos grands confrères *artistiques*' (i.e. Baudelaire's fellow *salonniers* and art critics) as well as by many 'jeunes artistes' of his acquaintance on 'le bourgeois' as though 'le bourgeois' was intrinsically and by definition 'l'ennemi de toute chose grande et belle'. The practice—virtually automatic in the 'artistic' milieu Baudelaire frequented—of defining 'artist' and 'bourgeois' in tautological antithesis to each other (the artist is the non- or anti-bourgeois, the bourgeois is the non- or anti-artist) is not only dishonest—since the attackers are themselves just as much bourgeois by social class as those they attack—but devoid of meaning since the term bourgeois is in itself no more than a value-free description of a particular class of society; when used by artists, art-critics, and their journalistic hangers-on as an all-purpose, unthinking term of abuse, the word 'bourgeois', says Baudelaire, 'sent l'argot d'atelier d'une lieue' and should be quite simply 'supprimé du dictionnaire de la critique' (OC, ii. 352).

Having dealt with the professional bourgeois-haters and -baiters who dominate 'la critique des journaux, tantôt niaise, tantôt furieuse, jamais indépendante' and whose one achievement has been to drive the bourgeois public away in disgust from the kind of serious art criticism Baudelaire wants to write, he then goes on to attack 'une chose mille fois plus dangereuse que le bourgeois', namely 'l'artiste-bourgeois, qui a été créé pour s'interposer entre le public et le génie; il les cache l'un à l'autre'. In the present state of his intellectual and artistic awareness, the bourgeois certainly represents a danger to authentic art; the 'artiste-bourgeois'—an Ary Scheffer or a Horace Vermet—is, however, a thousand times more threatening since he panders to the bourgeois as he is and so prevents him from appreciating—and buying!—authentic works of art: 'Le bourgeois qui a peu de notions scientifiques va où le pousse le grande voix de l'artiste-bourgeois.—Si on supprimait celui-ci, l'épicier porterait E. Delacroix en triomphe' (OC, ii. 414). The irony of the expression should not deceive us as to the seriousness of Baudelaire's intention. In the *Salons* of both 1845 and 1846 he undoubtedly welcomes the democratization of the art public that has taken place since the revolution of 1830, particularly as expressed in the creation, thanks to 'l'esprit éclairé et librement paternel' of the new king (OC, ii. 352), of new galleries and museums such as the *Musée espagnol*. At the same time, he has nothing but contempt for those whom 'Aux Bourgeois' calls 'les accapareurs des choses spirituelles', namely all those would-be sophisticates in the art world who, bourgeois themselves, would none the less deny the new bourgeois public the right and the capacity to appreciate genuine art, and particularly the critics, those 'aristocrates de la pensée' whose self-ascribed monopoly of the power to praise and blame is dismissed by Baudelaire as simply 'leur comptoir et leur boutique' (OC, ii. 415–16). While approving in principle of the recent *embourgeoisement* of the art public, Baudelaire recognizes that the archetypal *épicier* of the new regime is incapable, in his present state of intellectual and artistic awareness, of appreciating the art of a Delacroix. So too, still more seriously, are members of the wealthier strata of the bourgeoisie— the *négociants* and *propriétaires*—who might actually buy a Delacroix painting in preference to a Scheffer or a Vernet had they but the necessary artistic awareness and were not their lives so dominated by work and the work ethic that, by 7 or 8 in the evening, their heads are already nodding 'vers les braises du foyer et les oreillards du fauteuil' (OC, ii. 416). Again it is important to look past the irony of expression to the wholly serious and sincere point Baudelaire is making. He is not, like 'les accapareurs', saying that the bourgeois can never and will never appreciate and purchase authentic art. He is saying rather that the bourgeois needs to be educated in artistic appreciation and brought to a position where it will be natural for him to prefer a Delacroix to a Vernet. It need hardly be added that the key role in this formation of an artistically aware bourgeois public will be played by serious art critics like himself.

Baudelaire believes—or feigns to believe—that nothing but good will come from the democratization of genuine art appreciation and enjoyment. It will, in the first place, be good for the bourgeoisie since 'l'art est un bien infiniment précieux, un breuvage rafraîchissant et réchauffant, qui rétablit l'estomac et l'esprit dans l'équilibre naturel de l'idéal' and, if 'taken' in the proper proportions and spirit, will restore the spiritual, intellectual, psychological, and physical equilibrium that the overemphasis on work in bourgeois culture has disrupted; like so much else in the *Salon de 1846*, this belief in the healing process of art is wholly in line with orthodox Fourierist teaching. Secondly, the existence of a sophisticated bourgeois public will be of obvious benefit to the authentic artist since he will at last be able to make a living without compromising his artistic and other standards; the status and income of the serious art critic will also be enormously enhanced. Still more, however, Baudelaire appears—or, again, feigns—to believe that the restoration, through art, of spiritual, psychological, and physical health to the bourgeoisie is linked in some way to the restoration of health to society as a whole: just as he claims that members of the bourgeoisie will be 'heureux, repus et bienveillants' once the elixir of authentic art has restored to them 'l'équilibre de toutes les parties de [leur] être', so, he says, 'la société sera repue, heureuse et bienveillante, quand elle aura trouvé son équilibre général et absolu' (OC, ii. 417). Is Baudelaire really saying that a healthy bourgeoisie will lead to a healthy society as many Fourierists would not hesitate to claim? Or is this not the point at which the essentially non-ironic reading of the content of 'Aux Bourgeois' and its companion-texts that we have so far proposed[83] needs to be

---

[83] Support for a non-ironic reading may be found in Asselineau's view—possibly influenced by discussions with Baudelaire himself—of the intention that lay behind the dedication of the *Salon* to 'la partie la plus publique du public', namely the bourgeoisie. This was done, according to Asselineau, 'non pas, comme on pourrait le croire, par amour du paradoxe, mais en haine et à exclusion du demi-bourgeois et du faux-artiste que l'auteur appelle les "accapareurs", les "pharisiens" '. 'Ce qui me paraît le plus clair là-dedans', Asselineau continues, 'c'est qu'en traitant directement avec le bourgeois, Baudelaire trouvait le moyen de passer par-dessus la tête à ses confrères et s'établissait de plein droit dans le ton affirmatif et dogmatique qui lui plaisait, en s'épargnant des discussions oiseuses'. (*Baudelaire et Asselineau*, 76–7, see also BPZ, 227–8.) Mention might also be made of the statement regarding the *Salon de 1846* attributed to Baudelaire by *La Silhouette* on 24 May 1846: 'Je me mets sous la protection des bourgeois et des artistes'. (See Auguste Vitu (?), *Le Corsaire-Satan en Silhouette*, ed. Graham Robb (Centre W. T. Bandy d'Études baudelairiennes, Nashville, 1985), 65.)

complemented by a reading that takes into account the many ironies and ambiguities to be found in the form and style in which the argument is advanced? The key, I believe, lies in the fact that Baudelaire is fully aware that he is arguing from a position of very real weakness. He may well have genuinely believed that the bourgeois needs the pleasure- and health-bringing 'breuvage' of art if he is to live fully; the problem is, of course, as the *Salon de 1845* starkly acknowledges ('il faut plaire à ceux aux frais de qui l'on veut vivre' (OC, ii. 352)), the artist needs the bourgeois if he is to be able to live and survive at all. In the unpromising circumstances of 1845–6, Baudelaire can see no possible alternative to this dependence on bourgeois purchasing power, which is why he is so anxious that the bourgeoisie should be educated, principally by art critics like himself, into appreciating and buying the genuine art of a Delacroix rather than the pseudo-art of a Vernet or a Scheffer; the fact remains, however, that even an educated and appreciative bourgeoisie would still be the dominant partner in the artist–public relationship. Baudelaire, in other words, despises the bourgeois as he is but considers his power in politics, the economy, society, thought, and culture to be an unchallengeable fact of mid-nineteenth-century life. His only hope—and it is a slender one—is that the bourgeois' sensitivity to authentic art might be enhanced through education, whence the genuine attempt to gain his sympathy and interest—or, at the very least, not to antagonize him by the knee-jerk bourgeois-ophobia of 'les accapareurs' and their like in the art world—in the three texts we have been discussing. Baudelaire's 'pro-bourgeois' stance in these texts is, if one may so put it, simultaneously genuine and bogus: genuine to the extent that he can see no alternative to seeking bourgeois sympathy if authentic art and artists are to survive at all, bogus in that his bourgeoisophilia is a matter of pragmatic necessity rather than of inner conviction and that it rests precariously upon a substratum of contempt for the bourgeoisie which, for urgent practical reasons, it is necessary for him to repress or, failing that, disguise. The ironies and ambiguities that pervade 'Aux Bourgeois' and other parts of the *Salon de 1846* are a suppressed, disguised form of the 'rire amer de l'homme vaincu' that erupts in the poem 'Obsession' and represent the one *tactical* resource open to a man who believes he has no *strategic* alternative to trying to enlist, without much hope of success, the support of a despised enemy whose power, in the uniquely unfavourable conditions of the mid-1840s, seemed wholly impervious to challenge: they are Baudelaire's way of trying to preserve an inner integrity as he goes about a wholly invidious supplicatory task.

Given the tension in 'Aux Bourgeois' between its pro-bourgeois programme and rhetoric and the substratum of anti-bourgeois sentiment on which they rest, it is hardly surprising if, in the course of the *Salon de 1846*, the full force of that sentiment sometimes breaks through the constraints and disguises that, in the preface, Baudelaire seeks to impose upon it. Unable to attack head-on either the bourgeoisie as a class or the Bourgeois Monarchy as a regime, Baudelaire assails certain specific individuals, groups, intellectual and artistic movements, or institutions, that it some way or other epitomize them and through which he can direct his fury at much broader targets. In the first place, one cannot fail to notice Baudelaire's loathing of the army which he is able to attack through and in conjunction with the military painter *par excellence*, Horace Vernet:

M. Horace Vernet est un militaire qui fait de la peinture.—Je hais cet art improvisé au roulement du tambour, ces toiles badigeonnées au galop, cette peinture fabriquée à coups de pistolet, comme je hais l'armée, la force armée, et tout ce qui traîne des armes bruyantes dans un lieu pacifique. Cette immense popularité, qui ne durera d'ailleurs pas plus longtemps que la guerre, et qui diminuera à mesure que les peuples se feront d'autres joies,—cette popularité, dis-je, cette *vox populi, vox Dei,* est pour moi une oppression. (OC, ii. 469)

There is much more involved here than a roundabout assault on General Aupick, though that, to be sure, is present as well! As we have seen, the militarization of the Bourgeois Monarchy had, by 1846, reached such a point that to attack the army, particularly at the height of its testing Algerian campaign against Abd-el-Kader (the 'guerre' to which Baudelaire refers), was tantamount to attacking the regime itself. But Baudelaire's loathing goes beyond Vernet, the army and the regime to embrace all those people—by implication the best part of the population of France—whom the sight of the nation's army, in the flesh or on a Vernet canvas, sends into swoons of orgiastic patriotic fervour.[84] Abandoning 'la ligne

---

[84] On Baudelaire's hatred of the army at this time, see the extract from Champfleury's *Souvenirs et portraits de jeunesse* (1872) quoted Stenzel, *Der historische Ort*, 84.

courbe en matière d'éreintage' to which tactical considerations have hitherto caused him to conform, Baudelaire, his fury mounting, now espouses 'la ligne droite' of an out-and-out frontal attack on everything Vernet and the army stand for and does so with a strength and conviction derived from the knowledge that 'à chaque phrase le *je* couvre un *nous, nous* immense, *nous* silencieux et invisible,—*nous*, toute une génération nouvelle, ennemie de la guerre et des sottises nationales; une génération pleine de santé, parce qu'elle est jeune, et qui pousse déjà à la queue, coudoie et fait ses trous,—sérieuse, railleuse et menaçante' (OC, ii. 471). It is a remarkable sentence, one of the most powerfully felt and expressed Baudelaire ever wrote, and one which, for the first time, opens up the possibility of an 'elsewhere' from which the Bourgeois Monarchy, its values, and supporters might be subjected to a systematic strategy of attack by and in the name of a '*nous* immense' acting in unison. It is a '*nous*' which, significantly, is conceived of in generational rather than class terms, as though for Baudelaire at this time the key conflict in French society was not that of class against class but of youth against age or—to put it only slightly differently—of sons against fathers.[85] The thrust of both his life and writings in the 1840s is not so much anti-bourgeois as anti-patriarchal. The titles and descriptions of his works of the period sometimes dwell insistently on the youthfulness of their author, subject-matter, or intended public: *Conseils aux jeunes littérateurs*,[86] *Le Jeune Enchanteur*, or *Les Limbes* intended, according to announcements of 1850–1, to depict 'les agitations et les mélancolies' or the 'agitations spirituelles' of 'la jeunesse moderne' (OC, i. 793). Baudelaire saw fit to publish only three poems before 1848: it is surely significant that one of them should have been 'L'Impénitent' (September 1846), the first version of 'Don Juan aux Enfers'. A 'fils audacieux', Don Juan is contemptuous of the 'front blanc' of his father Don Luis, of the mercantile grovelling of Sganarelle (in whom a later text, *La Fin de Don Juan* (1852–3?) will see a representative of 'la future bourgeoisie qui va remplacer la noblesse

---

[85] On the importance of the concept of generation in nineteenth-century France, see Anthony Esler, 'Youth in Revolt: The French Generation of 1830', in *Modern European Social History*, ed. Robert Bezucha (D. C. Heath, 1972), 300–34.

[86] In *Conseils aux jeunes littérateurs*, Baudelaire speaks significantly of the 'tendresse toute fraternelle' that he has brought to the composition of 'ces préceptes dédiés aux jeunes littérateurs' (OC, ii. 13).

tombante' (OC, i. 627)) and above all of the God-centred patriarchal order embodied in the 'grand homme de pierre' standing at
the helm of the boat that propels him, totally unrepentant, towards
Hell. Defiant of fathers, the family, the middle classes, and God,
Baudelaire's Don Juan points forward to the great rebel heroes—
Cain, Satan—who will rise up against a tyrannical father-God and
his oppressive world-order in 'La Révolte', that short sequence of
poems which, as we shall see, can be fully understood only in the
context of Baudelaire's radicalism of 1847–52. If Baudelaire did
indeed declare, gun in hand, on the evening of 24 February 1848
that 'il fallait aller fusiller le général Aupick', it was no more than
the logical climax of his whole development as man and writer since
1842. Nor were such patricidal promptings just a question of
individual psychology: what was involved was nothing less than
a whole generation's rejection of the Father.[87]

Populist?

Some time in 1846, as we have seen, Baudelaire was left 'ébloui et
attendri' by Pierre Dupont's rendering of 'Le Chant des Ouvriers',
that '*Marseillaise* du travail', as Baudelaire would call it in 1851
(OC, ii. 30), in which a searing indictment of working-class misery
is set off against the refrain's repeated call to a future of plenty,
peace, and communion:

> Aimons-nous, et quand nous pouvons
> Nous unir pour boire à la ronde,
> Que le canon se taise ou gronde,
>   Buvons, (Ter.)
> A l'indépendance du monde!

Precisely when in 1846 Baudelaire first heard Dupont's song
remains unclear. If it was before or during the composition of that
year's *Salon*, one might expect to find clear evidence in that text of
the populist sympathies which, if Baudelaire's account of 1851 is to

---

[87] On the 'parricidal' dimension of the Great Revolution, see Lynn Hunt,
Politics, Culture and Class in the French Revolution (Univ. of California Press,
Berkeley, Calif., 1984), 31–2: 'From the beginning radicals found themselves over-
turning the traditional familial analogues to power. They seemed to be rhetorically
killing the King, their father, long before the Convention actually voted the death
sentence.'

be trusted, the song aroused in him; the fact is, though, that such evidence is singularly elusive. The dedication 'Aux Bourgeois' refers, somewhat puzzlingly, to the working class as 'la minorité protestante et souffrante' (OC, ii. 416) only to dismiss it forthwith as 'l'ennemie naturelle de l'art', an observation which, like everything else in the dedication, is susceptible of both ironic and non-ironic interpretation. Amongst the examples of 'l'heroïsme de la vie moderne' given at the end of the *Salon* is that of a convicted murderer—referred to by Baudelaire as 'le sublime B.....' and identified by Dolf Oehler[88] as Pierre-Joseph Poulmann, executed in January 1844 for killing an old man—who, on his way to the guillotine, refuses priestly consolation and absolution with the words 'Laissez-moi tout mon courage!' Baudelaire's evident admiration for this 'funèbre fanfaronnade d'un criminel, d'un grand protestant, bien portant, bien organisé, et dont la féroce vaillance n'a pas baissé la tête devant la suprême machine' (OC, ii. 495) leads Oehler to the conclusion that, here as, in his view, elsewhere in the *Salon*, Baudelaire is expressing in a disguised, elliptical manner his sympathy for 'le peuple' in its (allegedly) most dangerous, 'anti-bourgeois' incarnation—the *classes dangereuses* or *Lumpenproletariat*—and that the celebration of Poulmann's Lacenaire-like defiance of God and society may be taken as evidence of Baudelaire's espousal, as early as 1846, of what he variously refers to as satanic socialism or revolutionary satanism.[89] A proletarian version of the unrepentant Don Juan, 'le sublime B.....' certainly points forward to the murderous and blasphemous drunkard of 'Le Vin de l'assassin' and to the antitheistic cosmic and social revolutionaries of 'La Révolte', whose political significance cannot be doubted. Oehler's case—which, as so often, could well be right—would be strengthened if there were other evidence in Baudelaire's writings of September 1844–January 1847 of those 'secret sympathies for the proletariat' which, he claims, inform the whole vision of the *Salon de 1846*. Such evidence, though, is extremely thin and, where it appears (as, for example, in 'A une mendiante rousse' (1845–6?)), is often better explained by poetic convention than by any political sympathy. It is also to be noted that when members of the Parisian lower classes appear in texts published before 1848, they invariably belong to marginal sub-categories of 'le peuple'—

---

[88] Oehler, 'Le Caractère double', 203.   [89] Ibid. 199, 210, and 212.

prostitutes, beggars, *saltimbanques*, street musicians, *chiffonniers* —rather than to its core of skilled and semi-skilled workers— *tailleurs d'habits, cordonniers, menuisiers, bijoutiers, serruriers*, and the like—who formed the backbone of every insurrectionary or revolutionary movement in Paris from 1789 up to and including the Commune of 1871. Significantly, when Baudelaire refers in the conclusion of the *Salon de 1846* to the 'milliers d'existences flottantes qui circulent dans les souterrains d'une grande ville', he immediately singles out 'criminels' as being, presumably, their most typical component (OC, ii. 495); it is as though, for him as for most other middle-class readers of *La Gazette des tribunaux* and *Les Mystères de Paris*, the threatening allure of the city's 'floating' population of thieves, prostitutes, scavengers, or vagrants was still blinding him, in May 1846, to the existence of the more settled and stable *classes laborieuses* who, in February and June 1848, as in July 1830, would constitute the core of the revolutionary crowd and who posed a far more concrete threat to bourgeois society than the so-called *classes dangereuses*, the latter being, in *political* terms, not 'dangerous' at all since they accounted, in Maurice Agulhon's estimate, for a mere 2.55 per cent of the more than 11,000 persons arrested during the *journées de juin*.[90] If Oehler is right, and Baudelaire really did see the murderer of a seventy-year-old *aubergiste* as an emblematic proletarian revolutionary, then he was merely demonstrating his remoteness from the nerve-centre of Parisian radicalism, his bondage—hardly to be wondered at in the circumstances of 1846—to a romantic-nihilist view of revolution that the actual experience of 'la foule' would cause him decisively to revise in 1848. On the other hand, it could be argued from the context in which the passage appears that Poulmann's 'heroism' is being commended to the reader not as an admirable political gesture but as one amongst many of the 'sujets poétiques et merveilleux' which, unbeknown to modern man, make up the daily atmosphere of his existence.[91] Once again, the whole character of the *Salon* as text precludes unequivocal judgement.

Fortunately there is one text that gives us the keenest possible insight into the paradoxes of Baudelaire-Dufaÿs's attitude towards 'le peuple'. This is to be found in an unexpected aside in 'Le Musée classique du Bazar Bonne-Nouvelle' (January 1846) where, before

[90] Maurice Agulhon, *Les Quarante-huitards* (Gallimard/Julliard, 1975), 32.
[91] This is the case argued by Pichois (OC, ii. 1325).

reviewing the paintings exhibited, Baudelaire sees fit to confide in his readers 'un fait assez curieux qui pourra leur fournir matière à de tristes réflexions'. The exhibition had been organized, Baudelaire continues, 'au profit de la caisse de secours de la société des artistes, c'est-à-dire en faveur d'une certaine classe de pauvres, les plus nobles et les plus méritants, puisqu'ils travaillent au plaisir le plus noble de la société'. It appears that when the exhibition opened a number of poor people—Baudelaire calls them 'les pauvres—les autres'—had 'raided' the gallery demanding that they be given a share of the money raised for the indigent artists and art-workers. Baudelaire's account of what followed is obscure—it seems that the interlopers, offered a fixed sum by the exhibition organizers, continued to insist on their right to a given proportion of the whole sum raised—but his language clearly conveys his outrage at what has taken place:

Ne serait-il pas temps de se garder un peu de cette rage d'humanité maladroite, qui nous fait tous les jours, pauvres aussi que nous sommes, les victimes des pauvres? Sans doute la charité est une belle chose; mais ne pourrait-elle pas opérer ses bienfaits, sans autoriser ces *razzias* redoutables dans la bourse des travailleurs?

To clinch his point, he reports a similar episode that has come to his attention:

Un jour, un musicien qui crevait de faim organise un modeste concert; les pauvres de s'abattre sur le concert; l'affaire étant douteuse, traite à forfait, deux cents francs; les pauvres s'envolent, les ailes chargées de butin; le concert fait cinquante francs, et le violoniste affamé implore une place de *sabouleux* surnuméraire à la cour des Miracles!—Nous rapportons des faits; lecteur, à vous les réflexions. (OC, ii. 408–9)

It would be difficult to imagine a sharper illustration of the ambiguities of the relationship between professional artist and the mass of 'le peuple'. Baudelaire clearly identifies with the lot of impoverished artists reduced to public charity ('pauvres aussi que nous sommes') and with the desperate fund-raising activities of the famished musician who appears as a double of the 'saltimbanque à jeun' of the early poem 'La Muse vénale'. He was acutely aware, as well he might be as his financial situation steadily worsened, of his own status as a producer of goods for the market—'Moi qui vends ma pensée, et qui veux être auteur', as 'Je n'ai pas pour maîtresse . . .'

so tellingly puts it—and it is interesting to note that, in April 1846, he applied for membership of the writers' equivalent of the *Société des artistes*, the *Société des gens de lettres* (see C, i. 136–7), in whose bulletin he would actually publish *La Fanfarlo* in January 1847. As well as identifying with fellow-workers in the art business, Baudelaire also sympathizes in a limited, begrudging way with the lot of 'les pauvres-les autres', knowing that they too are dependent on the money of others for their survival. When, however, they cease to be passive supplicants for charity and actively insist on what they claim as their rights, Baudelaire's partial identification is transformed into a characteristic *mélange* of horror, anger, and fear; his outrage, in 1846, at the '*razzia*' of the Musée classique by a bunch of uppity ne'er-do-wells points forward to his later (post-1852) outrage at the mob's violation of the Louvre and the Château de Neuilly in 1848.[92] This early encounter in Baudelaire's work of impoverished and oppressed artist and impoverished and oppressed members of 'le peuple' points forward, too, to a whole series of similar confrontations in his writings of the last decade of his life: 'Le Mauvais Vitrier', 'Le Vieux Saltimbanque', 'Le Gâteau', 'Mademoiselle Bistouri', and, above all, of course, 'Assommons les pauvres!' From early in his career it is clear that the spectacle of lower-class poverty provoked in Baudelaire reactions of the utmost ambivalence, and that the giving and receiving of charity—what he would later call 'le Paradoxe de l'aumône' (OC, ii. 607)[93]—presented itself to him as a hugely problematic area of experience, especially when giver and receiver share a common condition of misery and rejection and the giver is all too likely to become a victim of the receiver and of the act of giving itself.

Though susceptible, of course, to an 'ironic' reading (what in Baudelaire's writing of 1844–6 is not?), *Le Musée classique* seems to me to offer compelling evidence, at least as far as early 1846 is concerned, that, far from having any 'secret sympathies' with 'le peuple', 'Baudelaire-Dufaÿs' had an undisguised antipathy for it as soon as it stepped beyond the clearly defined limits to which he

[92] It is likely that the invasion of the Louvre is alluded to in ll. 9–10 of 'Causerie': 'Mon cœur est un palais flétri par la cohue; | On s'y soûle on s'y tue, on s'y prend aux cheveux'. See Ivanna Bugliani, 'I selvaggi di Baudelaire', in Bugliani, *Baudelaire*, 160. For the invasion of the Château de Neuilly, see OC, ii. 55.

[93] This is clearly the title of a projected short story or prose poem, in all likelihood 'La Fausse Monnaie' (see OC, ii. 1382).

believed it should keep. Had a *sergent de ville* or *garde municipal* been called to 'assommer les pauvres' at the Bazar Bonne-Nouvelle in January 1846, there was one critic present who would not, one imagines, have restrained him from his task! It may even be that it is the January incident that lies behind the dismissal, in the May *Salon*, of 'la minorité protestante et souffrante' as 'l'ennemie naturelle de l'art' (OC, ii. 416), conceivable, too, that the drubbing vicariously administered to the republican, that other 'ennemi acharné du luxe, des beaux-arts et des belles-lettres' (OC, ii. 490) in 'Des écoles et des ouvriers' owes something to the outrage he clearly felt on the earlier occasion. An entry in *Mon cœur mis à nu* (OC, i. 691) refers to 'La haine du peuple contre la beauté'; there is no reason to suppose that 'Baudelaire-Dufaÿs' thought any differently in 1846 from Baudelaire in the late 1850s and 1860s. Just how unaware Baudelaire was in 1846 of what was really happening in 'les souterrains' of his native city emerges from an entry Victor Hugo made in his diary just a month after the publication of *Le Musée classique*. It is worth quoting in full since, better than any argument I can advance, it throws into unmistakable relief the limitations to which in early 1846, Baudelaire's social and political perceptions were still subject:

Hier, 22 fevrier, j'allais à la Chambre des pairs. . . . Je vis venir rue de Tournon un homme que deux soldats emmenaient. . . . Il avait sous le bras un pain. Le peuple disait autour de lui qu'il avait volé ce pain et que c'était à cause de cela qu'on l'emmenait. En passant devant la caserne de gendarmerie, un des soldats y entra, et l'homme resta à la porte, gardé par l'autre soldat.

Une voiture était arrêtée devant la porte de la caserne. C'était une berline armoriée portant aux lanternes une couronne ducale, attelée de deux chevaux gris, deux laquais en guêtres derrière. Les glaces étaient levées, mais on distinguait l'intérieur tapissé de damas bouton-d'or. Le regard de l'homme fixé sur cette voiture attira le mien. Il y avait dans la voiture une femme en chapeau rose, en robe de velours noire, fraîche, blanche, belle, éblouissante, qui riait et jouait avec un charmant petit enfant de seize mois enfoui sous les rubans, les dentelles et les fourrures.

Cette femme ne voyait pas l'homme terrible qui la regardait. Je demeurai pensif. Cet homme n'était plus pour moi un homme, c'était le spectre de la misère, c'était l'apparition, difforme, lugubre, en plein jour, en plein soleil, d'une révolution encore plongée dans les ténèbres, mais qui vient. Autrefois le pauvre coudoyait le riche, ce spectre recontrait cette gloire; mais on ne se regardait pas. On passait. Cela pouvait durer ainsi longtemps.

Du moment où cet homme s'aperçoit que cette femme existe, tandis que cette femme ne s'aperçoit pas que cet homme est là, la catastrophe est inévitable.[94]

For Baudelaire, who would later respond so profoundly to 'les yeux des pauvres', 'les pauvres-les autres' were, in 1846, not subject-seers in their own right, as they were for Hugo, but objects—alluring, repulsive, frightening, as the case may be—seen from afar through a prism of preconceptions which are no less bourgeois for being placed in the service of a supposedly 'anti-bourgeois' ideology. On 22 February 1846, Hugo was able to predict the revolution which, with exquisite timing, would explode on 22 February 1848. In contrast to the woman in the carriage, 'Baudelaire-Dufaÿs' at the Bonne-Nouvelle—one can imagine him, *calepin* in hand, superb in that 'paletot droit en bure, dont il avait *le secret*'[95]—can at least see the poor—but not as potential makers of political and social revolution, only as defilers of an artistic sanctuary which, for him, means far more than their misery or resentment. The discovery of 'le peuple' as a positive and active social and political force clearly lies before him.

Reactionary?

All the labels we have so far tested for their 'fit' to Baudelaire's ideas and actions of the 1840s have been of a broadly 'left-wing', 'progressive', or—in the very unspecific sense of the time—'socialist' in character. We have finally to consider the view—perhaps the consensus opinion of critics until the early 1970s—that Baudelaire's radicalism of 1848–51 constitutes no more than a hiatus of two or three years (or, in some interpretations, of no more than two or three months) in what is in other respects a continuously and consistently anti-liberal, anti-republican, anti-humanist, anti-naturalist, anti-socialist—in a word, reactionary—vision of humanity and all its works. In this view, *le 2 décembre* (or, even more restrictively, the *journées de juin* or the *présidentielles* of December 1848) merely restored Baudelaire to what he had always been before the February revolution, namely an artist first and foremost, unconcerned by politics or, when he was, fundamentally opposed to the romantic-

---

[94] Hugo, *Choses vues*, i. 391–2.   [95] *Baudelaire et Asselineau*, 168.

socialist naïveties of his contemporaries in the 1840s. The publications of Clark, Oehler, Bugliani, and others may have made this an unfashionable view, as more and more critics have looked back to Baudelaire's writings of the Bourgeois Monarchy for premonitions of his radicalism of the Second Republic, but it is a serious view and deserves serious attention, not least because it has recently been revived, in a far more extreme form than its earlier versions, by Philippe Muray in his remarkable work *Le 19ᵉ siècle à travers les âges* (1984). Muray strenuously denies that Baudelaire ever subscribed to any of the complex of mystico-political beliefs which make up what he calls 'l'occulto-socialisme' of the 1830s and 1840s as evidenced in the works of, in particular, Hugo, Michelet, Comte, Lamartine, Sand, Fourier, Leroux, and Quinet. Where the 'occulto-socialistes' (or 'oc-socs') believed in the inherent goodness of both man and nature, Baudelaire always believed, Muray argues, that both were contaminated by the primordial calamity of Original Sin. Where they believed in indefinite progress towards perfection, he believed—in the 1840s as in the 1850s and 1860s—in an indefinite falling away from perfection. They believed in 'le Peuple', he in élites; they in democracy, he in an aristocracy of the spirit; they in Man divinized, he in the God-man Christ; they in Satan as the apotheosis of Humanity, he in God as a necessary check to the hubristic overreachings of sinful man. According to Muray, 'merveilleux Baudelaire phare-laser'[96] was—with Flaubert —alone capable of seeing through the 'oc-soc' miasmata of the 1840s. Though 'entouré, convoité' by 'les néo-païens, les pagano-socialistes, les archéo-plotiniens, les christiano-martinistes, les occulto-paganistes',[97] Baudelaire systematically resisted and rejected all their mystico-political flimflam—naturalism, populism, progressism, occultism, symbolism, harmonianism, feminism, and the rest—and, if he participated in the events of 1848 and seemed to share the *quarante-huitard* spirit, it was not, Muray insists, as a 'believer' but as 'le démon furtif, le mauvais génie parodique de la nouvelle piété qui s'installe'.[98] Baudelaire, for Muray, never varied and, as Baudelaire himself later wrote of Poe's horror of 'la démocratie, le progrès et le civilisation', 'il ne fut jamais dupe' (OC, ii. 321): in 1846, as in 1856 or 1866, he was ever the essentially

---

[96] Muray, *Le 19ᵉ siècle à travers les âges*, 423.
[97] Ibid. 205.   [98] Ibid. 483.

Christian moralist, ever the enemy of the humanist-naturalist delusions of his contemporaries, a rare beacon of lucidity amidst the
otherwise all-encompassing darkness of that truly Satantic amalgam
of socialism and occultism, *la dix-neuviémité.*

It is the nature of polemical writing to overstate its case, but
Muray's argument cannot be dismissed simply on the grounds of its
magnificent extravagance of expression. On the other hand, its
rhetorical force cannot conceal its limitations with regard to
Baudelaire *in the 1840s.* While it is true that, as we have seen,
Baudelaire shows little enthusiasm for some typical 'oc-soc' writers
such as Esquiros, Constant, and Louis Ménard, he had clearly
responded to others no less typical—Quinet, Leroux, Lamennais—
with genuine sympathy; there is, moreover, no evidence in the
writings of the 1840s of the later marked hostility towards Michelet
and George Sand.[99] It is also to be noted that when Baudelaire
attacks an orthodox 'oc-soc' 'prophet' like Ménard, he does not do
so from an anti-humanist, anti-naturalist standpoint, but, precisely,
from one that is itself shot through with 'occulto-socialist' pre-
suppositions: significantly, Ménard's *Prométhée délivré* is
condemned not—as it should be if Muray's interpretation is right—
praised for having 'esquivé le culte de la Nature, cette grande
religion de Diderot et d'Holbach, cet unique ornement de l'athéïsme'
and its author would, according to Baudelaire, have 'obtenu de
beaux effets' if he had developed further 'le côté panthéistique et
naturaliste' of his typically 'oc-soc' theme of republican-humanist
Prometheanism (OC, ii. 11). Nor is it possible to argue, as Muray
does, that *Les Lesbiennes*—the volume of poems whose imminent
appearance was announced several times between 1845 and 1847—
represented 'la première vision de Baudelaire pour décrocher de son
autel la Femme-Messie qu'on est en train de célébrer',[100] his anti-
humanist, anti-feminist retort, as it were, to the 'oc-soc' excesses of

[99] Michelet's view of the Revolution of 1789 having been made 'par le peuple' is
referred to approvingly in the first number of *Le Salut public* (OC, ii. 1032); the first
disparaging allusion to Michelet is in a letter to Madame Aupick of 11 Dec. 1858,
where Baudelaire condemns *L'Amour*—without having read it—as 'un livre
répugnant' (C, i. 532). As for Sand, as late as 1852 (in *Edgar Allen Poe: Sa vie et ses
ouvrages*), Baudelaire refers to her as 'un très grand et très justement illustre
écrivain' (OC, ii. 283). Baudelaire's almost hysterical hatred for her appears to date
from 1855 (see Léon Cellier, 'Baudelaire et George Sand', *Revue d'histoire littéraire
de la France*, 67/2 (1967), 239–59).
[100] Muray, *Le 19e siècle*, 207.

Constant's *L'Assomption de la Femme* (1841) or *La Mère de Dieu* (1844). Although Baudelaire's attitude towards lesbianism is as ambiguous as his attitude towards wine, there is no evidence that, until the catastrophe of December 1851 compelled a thoroughgoing revaluation of all his beliefs, he regarded lesbians as *femmes damnées* beyond the possibility of equivocation or appeal. It is well known that the final condemnatory stanzas of 'Delphine et Hippolyte' were added at the last moment in 1857 in a vain attempt to avoid prosecution (see OC, i. 1127). Otherwise, the three poems on explicit lesbian themes tend to praise the *chercheuses d'infini* and their quest for full human and sexual liberation. In setting, regardless of the consequences, the demands of Love above the Law of God and society, lesbians are, just as much as Don Juan, Cain, and Satan, rebelling against domination by the patriarchs ('Laisse du *vieux* Platon se froncer l'œil austère' ('Lesbos', l. 21)) in the name no longer of the sons but of the daughters with whom, there can be no doubt, 'Baudelaire-Dufaÿs' identifies with passion: 'Car Lesbos entre tous m'a choisi sur la terre' ('Lesbos', l. 41). The thematic links between the lesbian poems, 'Le Vin' and 'La Révolte' will be further explored in later chapters, together with their common links with Baudelaire's radicalism of the Second Republic. All, it will be argued, are poems of human liberation, based on the systematic rejection of what Muray memorably calls 'tout Dehors qui paternellement et surmoïquement nous précédait'.[101] Baudelaire may well have changed his attitude towards lesbianism after 1851 as he certainly (or so it will be argued) changed his attitude towards wine. To claim, though, that, as originally drafted in the 1840s, the lesbian poems were written in accordance with rather than against the 'father-values' of the Superego is to subject them to a fundamental misreading.

The main evidence in favour of Muray's case is, oddly, evidence that he himself does not adduce, namely, the essay on laughter, *De l'essence du rire*, which, though not published until 1855, has been shown by Claude Pichois to date, not merely in its conception but in something close to its final form, from the years 1844–7,[102]

---

[101] Ibid. 455.

[102] See Claude Pichois, 'La Date de l'essai de Baudelaire sur le rire et les caricatures' (BET, 80–94, esp. 92): 'A notre avis, la première version de l'*Essence du rire* n'est pas postérieure à 1846, et la deuxième version, publiée en 1855 . . . ne diffère que peu de la première.'

in that first burst of creativity that culminated in the *Salon de 1846*.
It would be difficult to imagine two more or less contemporaneous
texts more opposed to each other in their underlying world-views
than the two works in question. That of the *Salon* is essentially
humanist in that it rests on a postulate of natural human goodness
and, correspondingly, cf a primordial unity between man and
world which has been radically impaired by a distorted and distorting civilization but which is none the less recoverable by concerted
human effort; the *Salon's* world-view may derive immediately
from Baudelaire's reading of the Fourierists, but its ultimate source
lies in Rousseauistic naturalism, at the heart of which, as Baudelaire
would later write in *Le Peintre de la vie moderne* (OC, ii. 715),
resides 'la négation du péché originel'. But it is precisely the reality
of Original Sin, understood in a strictly Augustinian or Pascalian
sense, that *De l'essence du rire* asserts with such peremptory force.
Where the *Salon* postulates a primordial unity that has since been
fragmented (but not irremediably destroyed) by a defective civilization, the essay on laughter posits a radical dualism that is inscribed
naturally and (without divine grace) irredeemably at the very heart
of human existence. Laughter is the appropriately distorting expression of an aboriginally distorted human nature:

Maintenant, résumons un peu, et établissons plus visiblement les propositions principales, qui sont comme une espèce de théorie du rire. Le rire est
satanique, il est donc profondément humain. Il est dans l'homme la
conséquence de l'idée de sa propre supériorité; et, en effet, comme le rire
est essentiellement humain, il est essentiellement contradictoire, c'est-à-dire
qu'il est à la fois signe d'une grandeur infinie et d'une misère infinie, misère
infinie relativement à l'Être absolu dont il possède la conception, grandeur
infinie relativement aux animaux. C'est du choc perpétuel de ces deux
infinis que se dégage le rire. (C, ii. 532)

The contradiction between the two views of human nature is so
blatant that critics have commonly seen *De l'essence du rire* as a
product of Baudelaire's post-1852 anti-humanism and, specifically,
of his reading of Joseph de Maistre. But, as J. A. Hiddleston has
written, Baudelaire did not need to read de Maistre or Poe in order
to discover a conception of human nature that was embedded at the
core of the culture that produced him. Without the organizing concept of Original Sin, Hiddleston continues, it is difficult to see how
Baudelaire's theory of laughter, even in its pre-1848 formulation,

would have amounted to much more than 'un vague assortiment d'observations et d'anecdotes';[103] the 'Augustinian' dimension of the essay may have been accentuated after 1852 in accordance with Baudelaire's general ideological shift but it must have been insistently present in the original version for that version to have had any intellectual coherence at all.

The likely contemporaneity of the *Salon de 1846* and the first version of the essay on laughter complicates the reading of the two texts to an almost impossible degree and renders the classification of Baudelaire's political and other views in the mid-1840s still more problematic. If Pichois is right in his dating, there was a de Maistre in Baudelaire long before he read *Les Soirées de Saint-Pétersbourg*, and the Fourierist superstructure of the *Salon de 1846* was being undermined from within even as it was being elaborated from without. In his review of the *Exposition universelle* of 1855, his first substantial publication on the visual arts since the coup of December 1851 (indeed since the 1846 *Salon* itself),[104] Baudelaire speaks of how 'une fois'—clearly he is referring to the mid-1840s— he sought to 'm'enfermer dans un système pour y prêcher à mon aise', a system which, he says, seemed to him to be 'beau, vaste, spacieux, commode, propre et lisse surtout' but which was no sooner constructed than it was confounded by some 'produit spontané, inattendu, de la vitalité universelle' that revealed his will to systematize as the 'fille deplorable de l'utopie' it was. Baudelaire is speaking here of the inevitable tension between a 'Utopian' aesthetic system such as the one he elaborated in the *Salon de 1846* and the reality of 'le beau multiforme et versicolore, qui se meut dans les spirales infinies de la vie' (OC, ii. 577–8), but there is a no less obvious tension between the 'Utopian' ethical theory that underpins the *Salon*—essentially a Rousseauistic belief in the intrinsic goodness of man and nature—and the reality of death, corruption, pain, and suffering that is also part of 'la grande Nature' ('Une charogne', l. 11) but which the various forms of 'occulto-socialism' (notably Fourierism) to which Baudelaire was undoubtedly drawn were incapable of explaining satisfactorily and,

---

[103] J. A. Hiddleston, 'Baudelaire et le rire', *Études baudelairiennes*, 12 (1987), 92.

[104] On this question, see F. W. Leakey, 'Les Esthétiques de Baudelaire: Le "Système" des années 1844–1847', *Revue des sciences humaines*, 32/127 (1967), 481–5.

still less, of remedying or redeeming. Throughout the 1840s, as
F. W. Leakey has shown,[105] Baudelaire's thinking was dominated
by a 'Utopian' view of nature as beneficent and of man as intrinsically good. Such a view could not, however, permanently suppress
and conceal—and still less could it explain—the underside of
nature which, with truly explosive force, intermittently imposes
itself on Baudelaire's consciousness, in the form, for example, of
the pullulating carcass of 'Une charogne' (1842–3?) or of the
mutilated corpse of 'Un voyage à Cythère' (1844–6?). To account
for such radical evil, Baudelaire would, after 1851, turn to another
system that, in the 1840s themselves, he had already used to explain
the explosive, violent force of laughter: an anti-Utopian, anti-
naturalist counter-system with, at its core, the conviction that the
whole of nature—human and non-human, animate and inanimate
—is tainted by some aboriginal catastrophe the consequences of
which no degree of 'civilization' can ever entirely conceal, let alone
rectify or remove. During the 1840s, the Utopian system was able,
by and large, to screen out the negative underside of existence that
only the anti-Utopian counter-system could explain, but the counter-
system was, on the evidence of *De l'essence du rire*, already there in
place awaiting only changed circumstances—like the traumatic
disappointments of the Second Republic—to force its way through
and shatter the 'aveuglante forteresse' (OC, ii. 577) of theories and
concepts which, as Baudelaire himself admitted in 1855, he had
built around himself in the last years of the Bourgeois Monarchy.
Once the reality of Original Sin—as lived experience and hermen-
eutic principle—imposed itself on Baudelaire, it would of necessity
utterly transform his view not only of human nature but of society,
politics, and art as well. By 1855 the basically optimistic and
'progressive' Baudelaire of the 1840s had been supplanted by a
pessimistic figure who, as far as conscious ideology was concerned,
was an out-and-out reactionary in everything but his artistic theory
and practice. The roots of that reactionary ideology, however, are
to be found in the 1840s. Baudelaire was not a dandy-who-became-
a-radical-who-became-a-reactionary: at any stage of his career he
was simultaneously dandy, radical, *and* reactionary, with now one
now another 'tendency' apparently in the ascendant, but always
divided, always in conflict, so that when the repressed Catholic

[105] See Leakey, *Baudelaire and Nature* (Manchester Univ. Press, 1969),
chaps. 2–4.

counter-system of the 1840s became the repressive system of the 1850s and 1860s, the old utopianism remained present beneath the thoroughly de Maistrianized superstructure of Baudelaire's thinking, itself now a hidden counter-system secretly undermining the new kind of 'aveuglante forteresse' Baudelaire had built for himself in the wake of the December coup. The periodic but always explosive return of the 'Utopian repressed' after 1851 will be an important theme in later chapters.

2

Proteus and his Texts: Opposition in Writing and Everyday Life, 1844–1848

Mixing the Codes: Names

To the extent that our names are given names, given to us without our knowledge and consent, and impose a single social definition on the multiplicity of inner selves, actual and potential, we contain, they constitute a privileged terrain for the kinds of oppositional practice—opposition by subterfuge, irony, and paradox rather than by direct resistance—which, following Michel de Certeau, we outlined in the previous chapter. It was no accident that the installation of the Bourgeois Monarchy unleashed an unprecedented rage for pseudonyms in the Parisian literary world as writers sought by every anagrammatic, orthographic, or other means to differentiate their names as sharply as possible from those current in the *juste-milieu*, either—like Gérard Labrunie *alias* Gérard *de* Nerval— by adopting the aristocratic *particule* at a time when, supposedly, the power of the old aristocracy had been ended for ever or—like civil servant's son Théophile Dennoy transformed by inspired anagram into that wonderful combination of Hellene and hooligan known to literary history as Philothée O'Neddy—'identifying' in grotesque self-mocking manner with the 1830s' equivalents of the Viet Cong and Tupamaros of a later age, the Greeks and the Irish. In one sense, then, Baudelaire was merely conforming to an all too well-worn literary convention when in September 1844 he followed Jules Husson (Champfleury), Louis Ménard (L. de Senneville), Félix Tournachon (Nadar), and the rest and adopted what was at least a partial pseudonym, Baudelaire-Dufays (or, preferably, Dufaÿs), which, with certain variations, he would use for most of

his correspondence and all of his published work up to, as we have
seen, January 1848. What is interesting is not that Baudelaire
should have adopted a quasi-pseudonym, but that he should have
taken on (and then abandoned) the name(s) that he did at the time
that he did. An exploration of these questions will take us close to
the core of Baudelaire's apparently systematic use of the tactics of
polysemy and paradox in the struggle for survival in the uniquely
discouraging circumstances of the mid-1840s.

It is worth noting in the first instance that Baudelaire's pseudonyms have none of the extravagance, inventiveness, or, above
all, the totally conccaling (and hence liberating) quality of, say,
Stendhal's.[1] Indeed, compared to the latter's plethoric onomastic
progeny, Baudelaire's alternative identities are not true pseudonyms
at all, since they for the most part merely add to, complicate, and,
at best, blur his given identity. They do not so much signify a tran-
scendence or negation of his family origins as a whole as mark a
shift of allegiance from the paternal term Baudelaire to its maternal
counterpart Dufaÿs (or Defayis, de Fayis, etc.), his mother's
maiden name before her marriage to François Baudelaire in 1819,
pending her adoption of the surname Aupick on her remarriage to
the general in 1828. Until the autumn of 1844—until, in other
words, the creation of the *conseil judiciaire* to oversee and regulate
his finances—almost all of Baudelaire's letters were signed simply
'Charles' or 'C. Baudelaire'. The latter style is commonly used even
in his letters to his mother, as though he wished, none too subtly, to
confront her with the fact that he was not her second husband's
son, to underline, as it were, her betrayal of him in favour of a
stranger. It is significant in this respect that, having throughout the
1830s referred to Aupick as 'mon père' or 'papa', Baudelaire seems
first to have called him 'le général' in the letter he wrote his mother
from the *Paquebot-des-Mers-du-Sud* as it sailed out of Bordeaux
on 9 June 1841 bound for Calcutta (C, i. 88); thereafter 'ton mari'
was the best that Mme Aupick could hope for.

Baudelaire's adoption of the surname 'Baudelaire-Dufaÿs'
(usually abbreviated in letters to 'B.D.') almost immediately after
his financial freedom—indeed his freedom *tout court*—had been
taken from him by the setting up of the *conseil judiciaire* can, and

---

[1] On Stendhal, see the classic essay by Jean Starobinski, 'Stendhal pseudonyme',
in *L'Œil vivant* (Gallimard, 1961).

has, been interpreted both psychologically and sociologically. If, following Michel Butor[2] or Pierre Emmanuel,[3] we see the imposition of the *conseil* as some kind of symbolic castration or re-infantilization of the briefly independent adult male, the coupling of mother's maiden name to patronymic suggests a *regressio ad uterum*, a merging of the son's identity with that of the woman who, by virtually immaculate conception, gave birth to him. Through their Christian names, Caroline and Charles already shared the same name-day, 4 November, to which Charles refers instinctively as 'notre fête' in a letter of February 1842 (C, i. 91). For the son to take over the mother's maiden name as well was to make of her a kind of twin sister or, at least, to reincorporate into himself the person from whom he had been separated first by birth and then, more traumatically, by his mother's remarriage; it was as though, in the crisis occasioned by the constitution of the *conseil*, Baudelaire sought by that almost umbilical *trait d'union* to re-attach himself to his mother and so restore the 'vert paradis des amours enfantines' which they had inhabited together between François Baudelaire's death and the arrival of Aupick, that 'époque d'amour passionné' when, as Baudelaire wrote in May 1861, 'j'étais toujours vivant en toi; tu étais uniquement à moi' (C, ii. 153). But it is not just Aupick who is repudiated by Baudelaire's assumption of his mother's maiden name but also François Baudelaire with whose memory he would later, in the 1850s and 1860s, come to identify so powerfully.[4] In the 1840s, however, he seems to have sought to deny those paternal links even as he depended on them for such regular income as he had. The squandering of a large part of his inheritance between April 1842 (when Baudelaire came of age) and September 1844 (when the *conseil* was established) may be seen as a sustained gesture of, as it were, posthumous parricide,[5] while the double-barrelled appellation Baudelaire-Dufaÿs aptly suggests both a diminution of paternal *potestas* and, at the same time, a reluctant acknowledgement of dependence on it even beyond the grave.

There is, however, still another person from whom 'Baudelaire-Dufaÿs' was seeking to mark himself off: his elder half-brother

[2] Michel Butor, *Histoire extraordinaire* (Gallimard, 1961), 40–2.
[3] Pierre Emanuel, *Baudelaire, la femme et Dieu* (Seuil, 1982), 38.
[4] See Richard D. E. Burton, *Baudelaire in 1859: A Study in the Sources of Poetic Creativity* (Cambridge Univ. Press, 1988), 46–8.
[5] See BPZ, 195.

Alphonse ('Baudelaire-Janin'?)[6] who, having sided with Aupick over the South Seas journey and, now, over the *conseil judiciaire*, was, in the eyes of the younger man, a substitute for the father-substitute and, as someone more or less of his own generation, doubly a traitor. Even more than Aupick, it was Alphonse who epitomized for Baudelaire the time-serving bourgeoisie of the 1840s and 1850s, and his loathing of him was so great that, as he told his mother in January 1856, 'je n'aime pas m'entendre demander si j'ai un frère'; adding his mother's maiden name to his was at least as much fratricidal as parricidal. A 'nullité politique', totally lacking in '*esprit poétique*' or '*chevalerie dans les sentiments*', Alphonse was, despite his 'opinions cyniques sur les femmes' (C, i. 335), married to a woman—interestingly Baudelaire often refers to her as 'ma sœur' in letters to his half-brother—to whom Baudelaire was, or feigned to be, strongly attracted and to whom, on two occasions, he made highly indiscreet advances by letter. On 31 December 1840 he sent *to Alphonse* a somewhat *risqué* poem—he calls it 'des étrennes poétiques'—in the disingenuous hope that '[il] divertira peut-être ma sœur' (C, i. 84); 'eût-il ecrit: qui pervertira, qu'on eût mieux compris', is Claude Pichois' entirely appropriate comment.[7] It is to the same tactic of cuckolding-by-sonnet that Baudelaire resorted a few months later when he dispatched from Île Bourbon 'A une Créole' to the husband of its inspiration in Mauritius for, supposedly, his 'approval' (see letter to M. Autard de Bragard, 20 October 1841 (C, i. 89–90)). In March 1846, when his antipathy towards his half-brother was at its height, the tiro writer—by now, of course, 'Baudelaire-Dufaÿs'—went even further and sent Félicité Baudelaire a copy of the recently published (and pointedly amoral) *Choix de maximes consolantes sur l'amour*, accompanied by a remarkably indiscreet letter which combines all manner of scarcely disguised sexual provocation with a final leering reference to 'le *canal de l'amour*' and, as if his (mock?) purpose were not obvious enough already, he sent his highly compromising offering not to the family home in Fontainebleau but to the address of Félicité's mother in Paris (C, i. 134–5 and 773). 'Gardez-vous du paradoxe en amour', adjures the *Choix de maximes* with typical self-deconstructing irony, 'gardez-vous bien de singer l'illustre don

---

[6] On Alphonse Baudelaire, see Claude Pichois, 'Le Demi-frère du poète des *Fleurs du mal*: Alphonse Baudelaire ou le magistrat imprudent', BET, 44–58.
[7] BPZ, 134.

Juan' (OC, i. 550–2): 'Baudelaire-Dufaÿs' is the *burlador* of the bourgeois age, the crosser of boundaries, the mixer of roles, the flouter—armed, like his double Samuel Cramer, with a handful of sonnets—of the institution on which, before all else, the culture of that age is founded: the husband and father-centred nuclear family. But 'Baudelaire-Dufaÿs' threatens the patriarchal order not, like a commonplace adventurer, from without but, much more insidiously, from within. Flouting fathers and husbands, his desire arouses the prospect not merely of adultery but of incest, and of homosexual incest at that, for 'Baudelaire-Dufaÿs', like his *alter ego* Samuel Cramer (*alias* 'Manuela de Monteverde' (OC, i. 553)) is a man-woman drawn to women not as like to unlike but, much more subversively, as like to like. Bearing a name in which 'male' and 'female' meet hermaphroditically, 'Baudelaire-Dufaÿs' refuses to play the binary game and, in so doing, threatens to reduce the whole differentiated structure of social relationships to a magma of non-distinction where opposites meet and merge and the very possibility of relationship, communication, and exchange is swallowed up, as in the concluding stanza of 'Les Sept Vieillards', in 'une mer monstrueuse et sans bords'.

It was under the 'hermaphroditic' name of Baudelaire-Dufaÿs that Baudelaire published all his writings from the *Salon de 1845* (May 1845) up to and including 'L'Impénitent' ('Don Juan aux Enfers') in September 1846. According to Asselineau,[8] Baudelaire had, by the end of 1846, established himself as a writer of substance in the eyes of his peers, and it is, therefore, doubly appropriate that his one published work of 1847, *La Fanfarlo*, should have appeared under a signature, Charles Defayis, that suppressed the paternal filiation completely; it is as though, at 25 rising 26 and a fully fledged member of the *Société des gens de lettres* (in whose *Bulletin La Fanfarlo* was published), Baudelaire has at last truly come of age as a writer and has no further need of the father to whom he owes merely his physical existence. The shift in early 1847 from a 'hermaphroditic' identification to one that stresses the maternal connection (when first announced in October 1845, *Les Lesbiennes* was attributed to Baudelaire-Dufaÿs; in early 1847 its author is Charles Dufays) could suggest that Baudelaire felt that he had

---

[8] Jacques Crépet and Claude Pichois (eds.), *Baudelaire et Asselineau* (Nizet, 1953), 79.

crossed a critical threshold in his creative development.[9] Having at
last 'given birth'[10] to a work which may have been in gestation since
1843–4 (and which, in its conclusion, makes the analogy between
publishing and giving birth wholly explicit), Baudelaire may have
adopted an unambiguously maternal name in the confident hope of
being shortly 'delivered' of the litter of almost complete poems he
contained within him.[11] If such was indeed his hope, he was to be
sorely disabused, since, as far as literature was concerned, Charles
Defayis or Dufays would give birth to precisely nothing in the
twelve months following the publication of *La Fanfarlo*. In another
sense, though, this mysterious interlude could not have been more
fertile, since, at its term, 'Baudelaire-Dufaÿs', having first repudiated his father and then over-identified with his mother, was reborn
as, at last, the person he truly was: Charles Baudelaire.

In the first instance, therefore, the quasi-pseudonym 'Baudelaire-
Dufaÿs' suggests a condition of sexual indeterminacy, liminality,
or ambivalence of which the bearer is both victim and—since he
can exploit it in his code- and role-mixing game—beneficiary.
More generally, it indicates a state of social and political in-
betweenness or neither-nor-ness which, once again, 'Baudelaire-
Dufaÿs' half succeeds in transforming from a minus to a plus. By
adding 'Dufaÿs' to his legal surname and, still more, by juggling
with this or that combination of 'De' ('de') and 'Fayis' ('Feyis'),
Baudelaire was evidently seeking to blur his bourgeois origins and
upbringing and endow himself with a pseudo-aristocratic identity,
in the same way that, through their dandy's dress and demeanour,
he and kindred 'hommes déclassés, dégoûtés, désœuvrés, mais tous
riches de force native' were simultaneously engaged in creating 'une
espèce nouvelle d'aristocratie, d'autant plus difficile à rompre
qu'elle sera basée sur les facultés les plus précieuses, les plus
indestructibles, et sur les dons célestes que le travail et l'argent ne
peuvent conférer' (*Le Peintre de la vie moderne* (1863) (OC, ii.

---

[9] It is significant in this respect that in *La Fanfarlo* hermaphroditism is twice
explicitly associated with sterility or impotence ('le dieu de l'impuissance,—dieu
moderne et hermaphrodite' (OC, i. 553) and 'les anges sont hermaphrodites et
stériles' (OC, i. 577)).

[10] At the end of *La Fanfarlo* (OC, i. 580), Samuel Cramer is said to have 'mis bas
quatre livres de science'.

[11] On this whole question, see Burton, *Baudelaire in 1859*, esp. pp. 25–35 and
57–63, and Marie Maclean, 'Baudelaire and the Paradox of Procreation', *Studi
Francesi*, 76 (1982), 87–98.

711)). In this context, the name is a privileged item in the dandy's wardrobe of signs: Baudelaire-Dufaÿs is as obsessed by a missing *tréma* on his *y grec* as he would be by a missing button on the *gilet très long* or *habit en queue de sifflet* he affected.[12] Dandyism for Baudelaire was an ambivalent cult symptomatic of those 'époques transitoires' like the Bourgeois Monarchy 'où la démocratie n'est pas encore toute-puissante, où l'aristocratie n'est que partiellement chancelante et avilie' (OC, ii. 711). It is—to use a term made current by Fourier and his disciples and which Baudelaire would echo in another of the titles (*Les Limbes*) he gave to his forever forthcoming book of poetry—a characteristic product of a limbo-age, -society, or -regime, neither aristocratic nor bourgeois, monarchical nor democratic, and, to the extent that it looks both forward and back and yet is neither one thing nor the other, 'Baudelaire-Dufaÿs' takes on the air of a limbo-name custom-built for the Janus-faced, oxymoronic Bourgeois Monarchy in which its bearer remained, until its very end, stranded in a kind of perpetual adolescence, no longer a child but not yet an adult, neither wholly male nor wholly female, pregnant with works to which he cannot give birth, marooned, in common with a whole generation, in a condition of death-in-life and life-in-death: 'Nous célébrons tous quelque enterrement' (*Salon de 1846* (OC, ii, 494)). What's in a hyphen? A whole condition of doubleness, ambivalence, and latency which, by advertising it in his name, 'Baudelaire-Dufaÿs' assumes and turns against itself and in his favour, finding in the very source of his oppression the tactical resources with which to combat it.

Mixing the Codes: Homes

If Baudelaire multiplied identities in the 1840s, he also multiplied

[12] See letters of May 1846 to Julien Lemer: 'prenez bien garde, je vous en supplie, à l'orthographe de mon nom: du Faÿs, en deux mots, avec un *y*, un tréma et une *s*' (C, i. 139). Ironically, as this letter goes on to show, 'Baudelaire-Dufaÿs' ran the risk of being confused with the theatre critic, Gabriel Alexandre Dufaï (or Dufaÿ) (1807–57). It is presumably—though some might wish it were not!—to this Dufaÿ, and not to Baudelaire-Dufaÿs, that Delacroix was referring when he made the following entry in his diary on 2 Mar. 1847: 'Dufaÿs venu; Colin. Le premier des deux est frappé de la nécessité d'une révolution. L'immoralité générale le frappe. Il croit à l'avènement d'un état de choses où les coquins seront tenus en bride par les honnêtes gens' (*Journal d'Eugène Delacroix*, ed. André Joubin (Plon, 1960), i. 187). See also the entry for 4 Apr. 1847: 'A M. Dufaÿs, 150 francs, qu'il me demande pour deux mois' (ibid. i. 214).

addresses, though this, of course, was not always something he did voluntarily nor, unlike his experiments with pseudonyms, was it something that ceased after 1848. None the less, when one follows Baudelaire's tracks as he moves from address to address in the 1840s like 'le Bédouin de la civilisation' moving camp across 'le Sahara des grandes villes' evoked in *Un mangeur d'opium* (OC, i. 458), the picture that emerges is, in part, that of a man stricken with some sense of radical displacement even in his native city, but also of one who, turning that very displacement to his tactical advantage, is consciously avoiding social definition by playing one address off against another and by refusing, as a matter of policy, to stay over-long in this or that residence or *quartier*. The net result of these repeated switches of address, like the switches of identity we have already discussed, is a paradoxical kind of freedom within the interstices of an increasingly constraining urban society in which class and *quartier* were becoming more and more closely associated with each other.[13] Crosser of boundaries and scrambler of codes, 'Baudelaire-Dufaÿs' contrived to slip through the nets of social and political definition.

From his return to France in 1842 until the outbreak of revolution, Baudelaire 'tacked' at irregular intervals between left and right banks, rarely staying for more than a few months at any one address and largely avoiding those localities—above all the Quartier Latin itself—favoured by the 'artistic' milieu to which he both did and did not belong.[14] The only exception to this erratic pattern is the two and a half years or so that he spent at the celebrated Hôtel Pimodan on the Île Saint-Louis (the present Hôtel Lauzun, 17 Quai d'Anjou) from May? 1843 to November 1845, following a slightly earlier period of residence on the island, at 22 Quai de Béthune, from May to December 1842. There is a particular eloquence about this one period of residential stability enjoyed by Baudelaire in the 1840s, for, as Claude Pichois has written, 'on est de la rive gauche ou de la rive droite, on est à la rigueur de la Cité, on n'est pas de

[13] The literature on social change in mid-19th-century Paris is vast, and the reader will find a summary of the principal transformations in Richard D. Burton, *The Context of Baudelaire's 'Le Cygne'* (Durham Modern Language Series FM 1, Univ. of Durham, 1980), 35–47 (and nn.), 97–8.

[14] For a detailed discussion of Baudelaire's residences in the 1840s, see Claude Pichois, *Baudelaire à Paris* (Hachette, 1967), 14–20. Only one of his addresses during this time—7 Rue de Tournon—is in the Quartier Latin proper, and he seems not to have remained there for long (see the *billet à ordre* of 1 Dec. 1846 (C, i. 139)).

l'île Saint-Louis'.[15] It is as though, unable to reconcile the tensions in his life symbolized by left and right banks—the left bank of art, sex, youthful freedom, and, of course, the house on the Rue Saint-André-des-Arts which, as well as the 'blanche maison' at Neuilly, widow and only son occupied together in 1827, contrasted with the right bank and 'cette grande maison froide et vide' (letter of 3 March 1844, C, i. 105) on the Place Vendôme where Mme Aupick and the General had lived since November 1842—Baudelaire chose to take up residence in, precisely, a limbo-*quartier*, linking the two, partaking of both yet belonging to neither, the topographical equivalent, as it were, of the hyphen in 'Baudelaire-Dufays'.

In the early 1840s, the Île Saint-Louis had not changed greatly, at least on the surface, from what, according to one observer, it had been in 1830: a 'parfaite image d'une ville de province, qui serait tombé par hasard, avec son pavé verdoyant, au milieu de la bruyante métropole'.[16] As far as Baudelaire's peers in the literary milieu were concerned, the island was, in Ernest Prarond's words, 'un pays bien plus perdu que l'île Maurice',[17] inhabited by precisely the kind of 'vieux Paris' mix of skilled workers and *petits rentiers* that was beginning to disappear elsewhere in the city as the processes of class segregation gathered pace.[18] This mixed population was joined, from the mid-1830s onwards, by an influx of much poorer people driven there by demolition work and high rents from the neighbouring Île de la Cité and the slums on the right bank opposite. This presence, in a previously tranquil *quartier*, of a newly displaced population on the hazy borderline between *classes laborieuses* and *classes dangereuses* may have played as crucial a part in Baudelaire's discovery of *le peuple* in all its complexity as, according to T. J. Clark, it did in Daumier's. When Baudelaire arrived on the Île Saint-Louis, the only artist or writer of note to live there was, it seems, Meissonnier. Later, Roger de Beauvoir, Baudelaire's close friend Alexandre Privat d'Anglemont (under whose name—another surrogate identity—a number of his poems

---

[15] Pichois, *Baudelaire à Paris*, 15.

[16] Auguste Luchet, *Paris: Esquisse du peuple parisien* (J. Bart, 1830), 12.

[17] 'Sur la jeunesse de Baudelaire', BET, 35.

[18] For a detailed discussion of the social composition of the Île Saint-Louis, see T. J. Clark, *The Absolute Bourgeois: Artists and Politics in France 1848–1851* (Thames and Hudson, 1973), 101–3. Clark's comments on the importance of the island to Daumier as 'a place to hide as well as to see from, in close-up: detachment as much as contact' (p. 102) could well apply to Baudelaire as well.

were published in the 1840s), the painter Émile Boissard, and Gautier would move there, followed, in 1846, by the island's most famous resident, Honoré Daumier: this influx of other artists may have been one of the factors that prompted Baudelaire to leave in late 1845. While living on the Quai d'Anjou, Baudelaire, unlike the humbly born (and humbly housed and dressed) Daumier, appears to have made no attempt to 'merge' with the lower- and lower-middle-class population that inhabited the island. Not only did he occupy comparatively luxurious quarters—probably the most comfortable he would ever know—at the Hôtel Pimodan but, as Asselineau informs us,[19] habitually paraded 'un luxe de toilette inusité'—'bottes vernies' and 'gants clairs', not to mention 'des manchettes de mousseline plissée' which must have gone down well with the *teinturiers* who, in a manner typical of the social heterogeneity of 'le vieux Paris', occupied the ground floor and *entresol* of the Hôtel Pimodan[20]—as he sauntered about the 'quartiers déserts et pauvres' of what he liked to refer to as his 'terrier' or even as 'mon Île' (letter to Prarond of 19 April 1843, C, i. 98). Such behavior epitomizes Baudelaire's whole tactical stance in the 'limbic' society of the Bourgeois Monarchy. If the later Baudelaire, beginning in February 1848, longed to *épouser la foule* and lose himself in the masses teeming and swirling about him, 'Baudelaire-Dufaÿs' sought above all to assert his dissonance with his human and material surroundings. Not so much 'un *moi* insatiable du *non-moi*' like his successor, *l'homme des foules* (*Le Peintre de la vie moderne* (OC, ii. 690)), the dandy's first priority is to distinguish *moi* and *non-moi* to the evident advantage of the former, and this he does by playing one set of meanings (in the case that concerns us, a pseudo-aristocratic dress and demeanour) against another (residence in an unfavoured popular or petit-bourgeois *quartier*) in order to undercut both and confront the observer—that indispensable adversarial partner in the dandy's game—with an unfathomable and deeply unsettling semiotic enigma. And, as we shall see, a similar subversion of one code by another is the recurrent tactical device pursued in Baudelaire's most characteristic writings of the Bourgeois Monarchy, tactics designed to confuse, disturb, and undermine the reader's habitual modes and methods of interpretation, while protecting the writer's 'true self' beneath the innumerable and self-contradictory disguises and devices of his text.

[19] *Baudelaire et Asselineau*, 70.   [20] See BPZ, 179.

Mixing the Codes: Dress

If one reads attentively contemporaries' descriptions of Baudelaire's appearance, dress, and demeanour as they perceived them at different points in the 1840s, it is clear that all three underwent subtle but significant changes during the years 1844–6 when the *conseil judiciaire* was set up and Baudelaire began to establish his reputation as a writer. Before the journey to the South Seas and from his return until the fatal summer and autumn of 1844, Baudelaire's dress, though in no way ostentatious, was manifestly expensive and conformed largely to that associated with the now standard image of the dandy. Its principal constituent elements—'costume noir, toujours le même, à toute heure, en toute saison', 'chemise si fine, aux manchettes plissées', 'pantalon tirebouchonnant sur des souliers d'un lustre irréprochable' (Charles Cousin (1872), recalling how Baudelaire dressed in 1840)[21]—were all of a piece and combined together to form a coherent and immediately comprehensible vestimentary message, a message reinforced rather than undercut by the more extravagant accessories—'une légère canne à petite pomme d'or' (Prarond: Baudelaire in 1841–2), pale pink gloves (Nadar: 1843–4)—that he affected after his return to France. During these early years, Baudelaire clearly sought to impress, even to surprise, the perceiver with the meticulous elegance of his dress, but the surviving accounts suggest no concerted intention to disorientate or confound. At a time when close-fitting clothes tended to connote lower-class or, at best, petit-bourgeois status,[22] Baudelaire's clothes in the early 1840s appear to have been of generous cut and unconstricting. When Nadar first knew him in 1843–4, the black *habit* he invariably wore was 'démesurément évasé du torse en un cornet d'où émergeait comme bouquet la tête'; his 'gilet très long' that so impressed his contemporaries was buttoned high but does not seem to have impeded movement (Prarond), and Nadar also speaks of his 'col de chemise largement rabattu' and 'manchettes non moins amples en linge très blanc de fine toile'; only 'l'étroit pantalon

---

[21] All the descriptions of Baudelaire's appearance and dress that follow are taken from W. T. Bandy and Claude Pichois, *Baudelaire devant ses contemporains* (Éditions du Rocher, Monaco, n.d.), 15–26.

[22] See the passage from *La Mode* (Oct.–Dec. 1829) quoted Henriette Vanier, *La Mode et ses métiers: Frivolités et luttes des classes 1830–1870* (Armand Colin, 1960), 16–17.

sanglé par le sous-pied sur la botte irréprochable' and the *habit*'s 'basques infinitésimales, en sifflet' (Nadar again) suggest an element of constriction that would become more marked as the decade advanced. Still more eloquent was, in Banville's words, the 'longue, épaisse et soyeuse chevelure noire' that Baudelaire possessed in 1842. Referring to 1843–4, Nadar speaks of his 'chevelure bouclée et très noire qui retombait sur les épaules'; in the celebrated portrait by Émile Deroy (painted 1843–4 and described here by Asselineau), 'la chevelure, très épaisse, fait touffe sur les tempes', while in *La Fanfarlo* Samuel Cramer (in whom we might see a distillation of the pre-*conseil* Baudelaire) is described by the narrator (a figure, perhaps, of the acerbic and ironic post-*conseil* Baudelaire-Dufaÿs) as having 'la chevelure prétentieusement raphaélesque' (OC, i. 553). Moreover, while eschewing (or unable to grow) a full-flowing 'proletarian' beard, the young Baudelaire wore, according to Prarond, a 'barbe légère qu'il laissait libre et qui n'envahissait pas le visage'; Banville speaks of 'le noir duvet d'une barbe naissante' in 1842, and in the Deroy portrait 'une barbe vierge, drue et fine, frisotte à l'entour du menton et des joues' (Asselineau). All in all, the descriptions we have of Baudelaire up to and including 1844 give the impression of a young man at ease in his body and in his clothes, extroverted but not ostentatious, relaxed in bearing—Prarond speaks of his 'pas souple, presque rythmique'—and facial expression, with body, mind, emotions, and dress all broadly in accord: Banville writes convincingly of the 'profond rassemblement de son être' in 1842. Asselineau, it is true, finds the 'physionomie' in the Deroy portrait 'inquiète ou plutôt inquiétante', but this will not be everyone's impression; perhaps, as has been suggested,[23] Asselineau (who did not meet Baudelaire until March 1845), was projecting back on to the Baudelaire of 1843–4 memories of the more troubled figure of the later 1840s.

When one turns to descriptions of how Baudelaire looked and dressed after 1844, certain changes are immediately evident. In the first place, the thick, long, curly locks of the earlier period had, according to every surviving account, been replaced by close-cropped hair—descriptions vary from 'cheveux coupés très ras' (Gautier, referring to 1844–5) to 'la tête complètement rasée' (Asselineau on his first meeting with Baudelaire at the 1845 Salon)—and

[23] By Bandy and Pichois, *Baudelaire devant ses contemporains*, 19.

the beard too disappeared; 'une légère et soyeuse moustache' was, it seems, cultivated for a time, but then it too was removed on the grounds, according to Gautier, that 'c'était un reste de vieux chic pittoresque qu'il était puéril et bourgeois de conserver'. But it was not primarily, as had earlier been the case, from the bourgeoisie that Baudelaire appears to have sought to distinguish himself by dress and appearance from the mid-1840s onwards; indeed, the adoption of short hair, removal of beard and moustache, and abandonment of the more extravagant accessories he had previously affected could be interpreted as, precisely, *concessions* to bourgeois norms and tastes. A number of observers are at pains to stress Baudelaire's growing concern, in Gautier's words, to 'se séparer du genre artiste, à chapeau de feutre mou, à vestes de velours, à vareuses rouges, à barbe prolixe et à crinière échevelée'. Baudelaire's dress, never ostentatious, appears to have become still more re-strained (though no less meticulous) in the mid-1840s when Gautier described him as belonging to 'ce dandysme sobre qui râpe ses habits avec du papier de verre pour leur ôter l'éclat endimanché et tout battant neuf si cher au philistin et si désagréable pour le vrai gentleman'. A whole reorientation of Baudelaire's being-in-the-world is suggested by a comparison of the Deroy portrait of 1843–4 and that painted by Courbet sometime in the late 1840s.[24] In the first, Baudelaire confronts artist and viewer directly and confid-ently, with a quizzical half-smile playing about his eyes and lips. In the second, he is turned inwards, his attention monopolized by the book he is reading, the quill, ink-well, and paper on the table before him suggesting that here is a man who will shortly begin to write; the intentness with which he draws on his pipe only adds to his air of concentrated inwardness. His undemonstrative dress forms a kind of rampart about him and his close-cropped hair has some-thing of the 'espèce de casque sarrasin' of which Gautier speaks; together, dress and hair underline the impression of ascetic, almost monachal self-enclosure created by the whole image. The Deroy portrait depicts a dandy in all his extroverted glory, its successor a

---

[24] The exact date of the portrait is unknown. In 1855, Courbet himself ascribed the painting to 1850, but, according to Clark (*Image of the People: Gustave Courbet and the 1848 Revolution* (Thames and Hudson, 1973), 51), 'at that time he had reasons to confuse his audience on the issue of dating in general'; Clark himself prefers the first half of 1849. Pichois (BPZ, 241) states that Courbet 'peint en 1847 le portrait de Baudelaire conservé au musée Fabre de Montpellier', but admits in his notes (p. 636) that the dating is hypothetical.

reader, thinker, and writer whose external appearance is fundamentally *neutral*. It is significant that when Charles Bataille met Baudelaire 'vers 1848'—Bandy and Pichois do not indicate whether it was before or after February—he was struck, as everyone else was, by his 'chevelure presque rasée', his 'linge soigné' and 'paletot large et sans taille, rigidement brossé', but otherwise could distinguish 'rien qui indiquât les préoccupations de costume que la légende de sa jeunesse lui prête'.[25] The point is, one suspects, that those youthful preoccupations had, at least in their obvious form, disappeared by the eve of the revolution; the dandy had become a writer, and now that he was producing significant literary texts attached no undue importance to what Balzac memorably calls 'le texte de son existence' as constituted by dress.[26]

Courbet's portrait, together with descriptions of Baudelaire's appearance in the later 1840s, suggest that his dress moved progressively closer to the bourgeois norm as epitomized by the *habit* famously celebrated in the conclusion to the *Salon de 1846*:

Et cependant, n'a-t-il pas sa beauté et son charme indigène, cet habit tant victimé? N'est-il pas l'habit nécessaire de notre époque, souffrante et portant jusque sur ses épaules noires et maigres le symbole d'un deuil perpétuel? Remarquez bien que l'habit noir et la redingote ont nonseulement leur beauté politique, qui est l'expression de l'égalité universelle, mais encore leur beauté poétique, qui est l'expression de l'âme publique;— une immense défilade de croque-morts, croque-morts politiques, croquemorts amoureux, croque-morts bourgeois. Nous célébrons tous quelque enterrement.

Having evoked this 'livrée uniforme de désolation', Baudelaire goes on to contrast the 'excentriques' of old 'que les couleurs tranchées et violentes dénonçaient facilement aux yeux' with their contemporary counterparts (amongst whom he implicitly ranges himself) who concentrate on 'des nuances dans le dessin, dans la coupe, plus encore que dans la couleur': 'Ces plis grimaçants, et jouant comme des serpents autour d'une chair mortifiée, n'ont-ils pas leur grâce mystérieuse?' (OC, ii. 494). In other words, the modern equivalent of the dandy is so self-effacing that the term dandy is hardly applicable. Indistinguishable to the exoteric eye from the bourgeois generality, he adopts the outward rhetoric of

[25] *Baudelaire devant ses contemporains*, 26.
[26] Honoré de Balzac, 'Traité de la vie élégante' (1830), in Balzac, *Œuvres diverses*, ii. *(1830–1835)* (Conard, 1938), 180.

bourgeois dress only to undermine it through the 'plis grimaçants' of a profoundly ambiguous semiological game which only a tiny élite of kindred spirits—if that—will be able to penetrate. The new-style 'dandy' does not set out, in the manner of his predecessor, to *épater le bourgeois* but subtly, indeed imperceptibly, to subvert bourgeois codes even as he appears to subscribe to them most slavishly; the game he plays with 'le texte de son existence' is the exact equivalent of the literary-textual game that Baudelaire plays in his 'Aux Bourgeois' preface to the *Salon de 1846*. The funereal *habit* is the quintessential expression of the limbo-epoch, neither living nor dead, that is the Bourgeois Monarchy, and Baudelaire's adoption of something close to the 'livrée uniforme de désolation' of that epoch is both an acknowledgement of its hold on him and a way of challenging that hold from within; his dress is oppositional through mimesis rather than antithesis. With his close-cropped hair and mineralized, impenetrable exterior, the Baudelaire of the late 1840s resembles nothing so much as a living corpse, but the fact that he, unlike his contemporaries, has consciously chosen and created that condition has the effect of liberating him within it. To the uninitiated eye, he, like every other citizen of limbo, is just so much 'chair mortifiée'; thanks to the 'plis grimaçants' of his oppositional game, he remains alive when all around him are, effectively, dead.

In the chapter that follows, we shall frequently have cause to comment on the explicitly political meaning attached to certain items or styles of dress under the Second Republic, most notably the significance of the *blouse* and, more generally, of the colour red. Such symbolism already existed under the Bourgeois Monarchy, with, for example, pointed hats designating *juste-milieu* loyalists, while *bousingots* (glazed leather hats originally worn by sailors) signified republican sympathies; the colour red, too, had clear republican connotations.[27] Baudelaire seems to have incorporated such politically loaded signifiers into the text of his costume but in a manner, characteristically, that appeared to contemporaries to run counter to his political beliefs—or non-beliefs—as they understood them. Thus Charles Toubin, who knew Baudelaire well in the years immediately before 1848 and who is a precious source for his beliefs and actions in 1848 itself, states that, when he first met him in 1846, 'il portait, quoique non républicain, une cravate rouge à

---

[27] Vanier, *La Mode*, 20 and 53.

noeud quelque peu lâche'.[28] Whether Toubin was right in thinking
that Baudelaire was not a republican is, in the present context, of
no great importance. The point is rather that Toubin believed his
friend to be a non- or anti-republican and that Baudelaire had said
or done nothing to suggest otherwise but still persisted in wearing
an item of dress which, in the context of the times, could not but
connote republican sympathies. Still more intriguing is the testimony of Champfleury who knew Baudelaire as well as anyone in
the last years of the Bourgeois Monarchy:

Sur la blouse bleue, indice du socialisme, de 1845 à 1847 environ, il faut
prendre garde d'errer. C'était une forme nouvelle du 'dandysme' de
Baudelaire. Notez que sous la blouse passait un pantalon noir à pieds
(mode des écrivains à cette époque: Balzac, etc.) et que les pieds de ce
pantalon de chambre étaient insérés dans d'élégants souliers à la Moliére
que Baudelaire tenait à voir très reluisants toujours. Pas de socialisme
alors, du tout, du tout. Haine vigoureuse pour la démocratie, chez
Baudelaire particulièrement. Caractéristique de Baudelaire à cette époque:
cheveux rasés au rasoir, foulards de couleurs voyantes passé les ponts . . .
vin rouge et pipes neuves de terre dans les cafés du boulevard ou du Palais-
Royal; toilette du matin dans le faubourg Saint-Germain, blouse.
Discussions littéraires, jamais socialistes.[29]

Again the point is not (for the moment) the accuracy or otherwise
of Champfleury's categorical 'pas de socialisme alors, du tout, du
tout', but rather the way in which, once again, 'Baudelaire-Dufaÿs'
appears to be playing one set of signifiers or codes off against
another in order to render himself wholly 'illegible' to others,
setting up, on the one hand, a tension between the 'text' of his
political ideas (in so far as these were known to others or as he
chose to reveal them) and the 'text' of his actions and appearance
and, on the other, so combining contradictory signifiers in this
latter text as to thwart any attempt at decoding. Thus 'Baudelaire-
Dufaÿs' 'identifies' with *le peuple* by drinking red wine and
smoking a clay pipe, but he does so not in a *marchand de vin* in the
Faubourg Saint-Antoine where his game would be exposed forthwith but in the select cafés of the Palais-Royal where he can *épater
le bourgeois* without serious consequence. Not content with flaunting a *blouse* in the aristocratic Faubourg Saint-Germain, he creates
further confusion by offsetting it with the silk scarf, tight-fitting

[28] *Baudelaire devant ses contemporains*, 25.
[29] Letter of 1887 from Champfleury to Eugène Crépet, cited in OC, ii. 1553.

trousers and gleaming pump shoes of the dandy: it is as though he seeks at once to exhibit himself and, by systematically jumbling different vestimentary codes, to escape social definition and with it the need for any decisive political stance or statement. Pseudo-proletarian and pseudo-aristocrat, sometimes openly anti-bourgeois but at others mimicking and manipulating bourgeois codes so subtly that his oppositional stance is barely detectable, 'Baudelaire-Dufaÿs' plays out his elaborate game along the interfaces of class society, at once victim and beneficiary of what *De l'essence du rire* calls 'une dualité permanente, la puissance d'être à la fois soi et un autre' (OC, ii. 543).

Baudelaire's various oppositional practices suggest that there were two ways of reacting to and expressing the limbo-world of the Bourgeois Monarchy. The first, exemplified by Delacroix and 'cette mélancolie singulière et opiniâtre qui s'exhale de toutes ses œuvres', was tragic; even 'ce petit poème d'intérieur, plein de repos et de silence', *Femmes d'Alger dans leur appartement*, 'exhale je ne sais quel haut parfum de mauvais lieu qui nous guide assez vite vers les limbes insondées de la tristesse' (*Salon de 1846*, OC, ii. 440). It was these depths that Baudelaire was exploring and expressing in tragic mode in the poems—most of them completed or close to completion by 1846—that were scheduled to appear under the title of *Les Limbes* with the explicit object of depicting 'les agitations et les mélancolies de la jeunesse moderne' (OC, i. 793). For whatever reason, these explorations of modernity in the tragic mode were not published even as single texts, let alone in collected form, before 1848. Instead, what we find exemplified in 'Baudelaire-Dufaÿs''s *published* writings—almost all of them, significantly, in prose— and in his *public* behaviour of the 1840s is the other mode of response—the comic mode—to the experience of limbo. If, as *De l'essence du rire* claims, laughter is inconceivable 'dans le paradis terrestre (qu'on le suppose passé ou à venir, souvenir ou prophétie, comme les théologiens ou comme les socialistes)', the comic is, by corollary, the mode *par excellence* of the fallen, in-between world of the Bourgeois Monarchy, both as contradiction-ridden consequence of some 'chute ancienne' and as counter to 'les agitations et les mélancolies' that that Fall has brought about. In all of Baudelaire's oppositional practices of 1844–6—whether in his published literary texts or in the public text of his life—laughter erupts, as he self-consciously assumes the contradictions of the present (as expressed in names, in choice of residence, in clothes, even, as we shall see, in food and drink) and turns them into a source of savage, even satanic private pleasure; thus, as he says in *De l'essence du rire*, 'les phénomènes engendrés par la chute deviendront les moyens du rachat' (OC, ii. 528). It may be that the laughter of 'Baudelaire-Dufaÿs' was, like Melmoth's, that other 'contradiction vivante', 'l'explosion perpétuelle de sa colère et de sa souffrance' (OC, ii. 531) and it may be, too, that his 'faculté comédienne' (OC, i. 555) condemned him, like Samuel Cramer, to a life of sterile, narcissistic self-repetition. But, in 1844–6, the tactics of laughter were 'Baudelaire-Dufaÿs''s one resource, and they did enable him to survive until a more fertile strategy of resistance became available.

Mixing the Codes: La Fanfarlo

Almost from its first appearance in January 1847, readers of *La Fanfarlo* have made the mistake of reading it as though its title were *Samuel Cramer* and as though Baudelaire's purpose in it were to provide an ironic but essentially 'life-like' self-portrait after the manner of *René* or *Joseph Delorme*. More recent critical writing,[30] especially that of Ross Chambers, Nathaniel Wing, and Barbara Wright, has broken away from such 'confessional' readings to explore rather the extraordinary complexity and ambiguity of the story as a whole and in particular to probe the disconcerting and continually shifting relationship between narrator and 'hero', neither of whom is to be identified fully with the author himself. What is now perceived to be crucial is not so much the figure of Cramer himself, nor even what is represented by the contrasting (but at the same time troublingly similar) figures of Mme de Cosmelly and La Fanfarlo, but the way in which the novella is a nexus of distinct and often competing styles and voices, in which one narrative mode is continually undercut by another only to be undercut in its turn, leaving the reader reaching out in vain for

[30] See Ross Chambers, 'Le Fade et le pimenté: Modes de séduction dans *La Fanfarlo*', in *Littérature et gastronomie*, ed. Ronald W. Tobin, *Biblio*, 17 (1985), 175–201; Nathaniel Wing, 'The Poetics of Irony in Baudelaire's *La Fanfarlo*', *Neophilologus*, 59/2 (1985), 165–89; Barbara Wright, '*La Fanfarlo*', in Wright and David H. T. Scott, *'La Fanfarlo' and 'Le Spleen de Paris'* (Grant and Cutler, 1984), 9–35. The following pages are strongly influenced by all three articles.

some fixed point that would enable him to grasp in its entirety a text which, in Chambers' words, is 'capricieux, fantasque, impossible à récupérer parce que tout en mouvement et constamment oublieux de lui-même'.[31] In this reading, La Fanfarlo is a figure of the text to which she gives her name: a bewildering succession of signifiers without anchorage in the real, artifice without nature, metamorphosis without substance, in short nothing less than the archetypally polysemic 'open work' of modernism itself, for ever beyond the reader-spectator's efforts to tie her down to one or another fixed significance. *La Fanfarlo*, then, is 'about' both La Fanfarlo and *La Fanfarlo*. A dancer, she—like Fancioulle in 'Une mort héroïque' (1863) whom even her name seems to prefigure—is both the producer of the 'text' of her dance and that text itself; until her 'fall' in the final pages of the novella, it seems that, like Fancioulle later on, she can transcend the duality of artist and art-work just as the initial 'la' and final 'lo' of her name seem to make of her a wholly self-contained androgynous being unlike Cramer whose 'femininity' is just one more assumed role amongst many.[32] For a full discussion of these and related issues the reader is referred to the critical works in question; the purpose of the present section is first to situate the themes of *La Fanfarlo* and its particular use of dissonant narrative voices in the context of the mid-1840s and then to locate what is at first sight a wholly non-political work in the overall trajectory of Baudelaire's political development in the last years of the Bourgeois Monarchy.

Although the word 'limbes' is nowhere used in *La Fanfarlo*, everything in the novella—characters, setting, situation, style—is invested with a 'limbic' character that makes it a comic counterpart in prose of the poems in which Baudelaire was simultaneously exploring 'les agitations et les mélancolies de la jeunesse moderne'. The events narrated in the story take place in an unspecified limbo-epoch (the late 1830s or early 1840s?) which, while inferior to 'le bon temps du romantisme' (the early 1830s?), is none the less viewed as superior to the present (the mid-1840s) in which the narration itself occurs. If with his 'chevelure prétentieusement raphaélesque' (OC, i. 553), Cramer appears as both a belated

---

31 Chambers, 'Le Fade', 191.
32 See Wright, '*La Fanfarlo*', 10. It is interesting that the same combination of syllables is found in the first name of the actress, Lola Montès, who could well have inspired the figure of La Fanfarlo (see BPZ, 222–6).

parodic soul-brother of *Les Jeune-France*[33] and as a figure of the 'orthodox' dandy Baudelaire had been before the imposition of the *conseil judiciaire*, the narrator, in contrast, seems more to embody the ironic, deflatory stance of the post-*conseil* 'Baudelaire-Dufaÿs'; in this perspective, the first narrative sequence that treats Cramer's attempted seduction of Mme de Cosmelly might be read as a comic dismantling of *le premier Baudelaire*'s pseudo-romantic poses and pretensions conducted from his successor's proto-modernist ironic standpoint of 1845–6. But, as the narrator underlines, Samuel Cramer is much more than just an individual case. 'Dans le monde actuel,' he says, 'les rues, les promenades publiques, les estaminets, et tous les asiles de la flânerie fourmillent d'êtres de cette espèce' (OC, i. 554), a judgement Cramer himself endorses when, as we have already seen Baudelaire doing in his most characteristic works of the mid-1840s, he identifies his own sufferings and frustrations with those of a whole generation:

Madame, plaignez-moi, ou plutôt plaignez-nous, car j'ai beaucoup de frères de ma sorte; c'est la haine de tous et de nous-mêmes qui nous a conduits vers ces mensonges. C'est par désespoir de ne pouvoir être nobles et beaux suivant les moyens naturels que nous nous sommes si bizarrement fardé le visage. Nous nous sommes tellement appliqués à sophistiquer notre cœur, nous avons tant abusé du microscope pour étudier les hideuses excroissances et les honteuses verrues dont il est couvert, et que nous grossissons à plaisir, qu'il est impossible que nous parlions le langage des autres hommes. Ils vivent pour vivre, et nous, hélas! nous vivons pour savoir . . . Malheur, trois fois malheur aux pères infirmes qui nous ont faits rachitiques et mal venus, prédestinés que nous sommes à n'enfanter que des morts-nés! (OC, i. 559–60)

This outburst is greeted with an appropriately deflatory comment ('Encore des *Orfraies*!') by Mme de Cosmelly who, whatever she may owe to Balzac's *femmes de trente ans*, is close to the narrator in her ability to see through Cramer's 'marivaudage sentimental' (OC, i. 563) and to manipulate him to her own advantage. The point, though, is that, even in his hypocrisy and self-important posturing, Cramer is typical of the limbo-epoch and limbo-society that has produced him. The 'complications bizarres' of his personality are to be attributed not merely to his 'double origine' as

---

[33] On the relationship between Cramer and *Les Jeune-France*, see Ivanna Bugliani, 'Samuel Cramer: ritratto epico dell'artista moderne', in Bugliani, *Baudelaire*, 77–128 *passim*.

the 'produit contradictoire d'un blême Allemand et d'une brune Chilienne' but also to the 'éducation française' and 'civilisation littéraire' that have formed him, and if he possesses a 'nature ténébreuse, bariolée de vifs éclairs,—paresseuse et entreprenante à la fois,—féconde en desseins difficiles et en risibles avortements', that too needs to be seen in a broader social and historical context. 'L'homme des belles œuvres ratées', Cramer is only too characteristic of 'tous ces demi-grands hommes' that the narrator has known 'dans cette terrible vie parisienne'. His inner divisions and dissonances are, in typically Fourierist fashion, viewed as a refraction of the divisions and dissonances of the age; to the narrator he is the modern 'dieu de l'impuissance' incarnate, an 'impuissance si colossale et si énorme qu'elle en est épique' (OC, i. 553), reducing everything and everyone—save, it seems, the narrator and La Fanfarlo herself (and even they will eventually 'fall')—to a state of living death from which there appears to be no escape.

In the first narrative sequence, the narrator's attitude towards Cramer, though not without ambiguity, is essentially a critical one: it is as though he has left the stock language and stratagems of the old-style romantics and their Bohemian-dandy successors far behind him and can only view with contempt the hero's efforts to use them to seduce a woman who herself appears to epitomize the styles and values of a bygone age. There is a marked shift, however, in the narrator's stance when he comes to recount Cramer's relationship with La Fanfarlo whom, following recent readings of the story,[34] we may identify with the modern conception of romanticism as elaborated in the *Salon de 1846*—'Qui dit romantisme dit art moderne,—c'est-à-dire intimité, spiritualité, couleur, aspiration vers l'infini, exprimées par tous les moyens que contiennent les arts' (OC, ii. 421)—in contrast to the superannuated romanticism of Mme de Cosmelly and 'Manuela de Monteverde'. The 'entente profonde' (OC, i. 576) that rapidly develops between Cramer and La Fanfarlo is paralleled by the growing sympathy of narrator for hero and, correlatively, of reader for hero. As Cramer and La Fanfarlo draw closer together, so the outside world (Paris and specifically the 'natural' setting of the Jardin de Luxembourg in which the would-be seduction of Mme de Cosmelly was conducted) is supplanted first by the actress's *loge*, then by the 'calèche basse et

---

[34] See esp. Wing, 'The Poetics', 170.

bien fermée' in which actress and poet proceed to her home and finally by her *maisonnette* itself. But it is not in the intimacy of La Fanfarlo's bedroom, that 'ravissant taudis, qui tenait à la fois du mauvais lieu et du sanctuaire', that Cramer achieves his most intimate union with the living incarnation of modern beauty—it is precisely in the bedroom that their 'similitude de goûts' breaks down—but rather at her dinner-table from which 'les viandes niaises' and 'les poissons fades' are rigorously banished, along with champagne and 'les bordeaux les plus célèbres et les plus parfumés', in favour of dishes and drinks in which, as Chambers has shown,[35] sensation predominates over substance and whose common characteristic is their pungency (OC, i. 575–6). The modern beauty which La Fanfarlo both creates and embodies and which Cramer longs both to possess and create in his turn is neither 'natural' nor 'artificial', 'physical' nor 'spiritual', but a powerful amalgam of the two. Its salient characteristic is 'la bizarrerie' which, as Baudelaire would later put it, 'constitue et définit l'individualité' and which 'joue dans l'art . . . le rôle du goût ou de l'assaisonnement dans les mets, les mets ne différant les uns des autres, abstraction faite de leur utilité ou de la quantité de substance nutritive qu'ils contiennent, que par l'*idée* qu'ils révèlent à la langue' (*Exposition universelle* (1855) (OC, ii. 579)). Cramer's insistence that La Fanfarlo offer herself to him not naked but clad in her 'corsage de saltimbanque' and wearing the make-up of her role is not, therefore, an expression, as Sartre and others would have it,[36] of Baudelaire's alleged horror of the female body and of his desire to escape, come what may, from the clutches of the merely natural. What Cramer desires is not an escape from physicality into the spirituality of 'pure' art but an intensification of physical sensation through an art that is itself profoundly physical; and, as the narrator comments, 'ce matérialisme n'était pas loin de l'idéalisme le plus pur' (OC, i. 577).

But finally, of course, though Cramer 'possesses' La Fanfarlo physically and is able to enjoy the spectacle of her in any number of her dancer's roles and costumes, he cannot penetrate the inner sanctum of her being and appropriate for himself the creative secret she possesses. The Dancer may be the Muse of modernity, a projection, as Wright suggests,[37] of the consummate artist the Poet vainly

[35] Chambers, 'Le Fade', 185–8.
[36] Jean-Paul Sartre, *Baudelaire* (Gallimard, 1966), 143–5.
[37] See Wright, '*La Fanfarlo*', 31.

hopes to become, but his attitude towards her remains from first to last that of the uncreative spectator who sees 'l'infini derrière les yeux clairs' of his beloved and yet remains 'souvent seul dans sons paradis, nul ne pouvant l'habiter avec lui; et si, de hasard, il l'y ravissait et l'y traînait presque de force, elle restait toujours en arrière: aussi, dans le ciel où il régnait, son amour commençait d'être triste et malade de la mélancolie du bleu, comme un royal solitaire'. Significantly, in the paragraph that follows, Cramer is described as 'piétinant lestement sur un trottoir' as he leaves his 'réduit amoureux' first thing each morning (OC, i. 578). It is a striking early instance of the motif of stumbling which recurs throughout Baudelaire's work and which we shall encounter later in this study in 'Le Soleil' ('Trébuchant sur les mots comme sur les pavés', l. 7) and 'Le Vin des chiffonniers' ('Butant, et se cognant aux murs comme un poète', l. 6). The fact that Cramer stumbles 'lestement' should not disguise the parallels between his situation— he the poet of *Les Orfraies*!—and that of Baudelaire's two arche- typal 'bird-poets', the albatross and the swan, with their halting, impeded gait, and obsession with the absolute. Just as the swan is haunted by 'le ciel ironique et cruellement bleu' while its 'pieds palmés [frottent] le pavé sec', so Cramer is both 'triste et malade de la mélancolie du bleu' and tripped up each morning by reality in, literally, its most down-to-earth form. Because he is unable to synthesize the real and the ideal in the creation of an authentically modern art-work, Cramer is condemned to sterility and when at last he does 'give birth'—Baudelaire actually says 'mis bas'—it is to a series of books which the narrator holds to be plainly inferior to the works he might have produced had he been able to draw cre- atively on the example of La Fanfarlo. But the Dancer ultimately fares no better than the Poet. She in whose very person, as in the thyrsus Baudelaire would celebrate in his later work, the real and the ideal, the masculine and the feminine, the straight line and the arabesque, seemed fused in an 'amalgame tout-puissant et indivis- ible' ('Le Thyrse' (OC, i. 336)) is revealed, at the last, to be human, all too human as she is reclaimed by precisely that which she had sought to banish from her dining-table: the insipid substantiality of the merely natural and the socially acceptable. By the end of the novella, La Fanfarlo 'engraisse tous les jours' and has become 'une beauté grasse, propre, lustrée et rusée, une espèce de lorette minis- terielle'. The narrator predicts her imminent return to the Church and marriage to 'un jeune héritier'; 'En attendant, elle apprend à faire des enfants; elle vient d'accoucher heureusement de deux jumeaux' (OC, i. 580). *La Fanfarlo* ends with both Dancer and Poet, those would-be 'créatures d'élite' with their preternatural 'accord d'opinions pour le bien-vivre' (OC, i. 575), having been recuperated by the natural order and the social norm, fertile certainly, but giving birth to a progeny that is worthless indeed beside the authentic art-works that La Fanfarlo had—and Cramer might have—produced during their prime. Both are severally swallowed up by the limbo-world from which they seemed about to escape together.

Having come together at La Fanfarlo's dinner-table to partake in unison of the eucharist of modernity, hero and heroine, narrator, author, and reader are, by the end of the novella, once more held apart by a series of ironies so dense and complex that, as Wright says, 'the reader is left to pirouette in a state of uncertainty and ambiguity'.[38] If La Fanfarlo has definitely forfeited the sympathy of both narrator and author (and, consequently, of the reader as well), the situation regarding Cramer is considerably more complex. True, he has 'given birth' to four 'livres de science'—one on the four evangelists, another on the symbolism of colours, 'un mémoire sur un nouveau système d'annonces', and 'un quatrième dont je ne veux pas me rappeler le titre'—which, in the narrator's estimation, clearly represent a betrayal of the authentic artist Cramer might have become, a betrayal that is all the more 'épouvantable' in that the fourth unnamed book is 'plein de verve, d'énergie et de curiosités' and shows what its author might have achieved had he not 'sold out' to the values of society. But Cramer himself is conscious of the extent of his betrayal and has the effrontery ('a eu le front') to draw attention to it in the epigraph he appends to the fourth book, *Auri sacra fames*, a Virgilian tag (*Aeneid*, III. 57) which is worth quoting in its entirety: 'quid non mortalia pectora cogis | auri sacra fames' ('To what dost thou not drive the hearts of man, O accursed hunger for gold!'). Cramer is prostituting himself and his talent but is aware that he is doing so, and this ironic self-awareness preserves him from a total capitulation to the values of the establishment: it is worth noting that it is La Fanfarlo, and not Cramer himself, who wants him to enter the Institut, that 'sanctuaire

[38] Wright, '*La Fanfarlo*', 19.

courroucé' of establishment art and thinking (*Salon de 1846* (OC, ii. 431)), and who, 'lorette ministérielle' that she is, 'brigue au ministère pour qu'il ait la croix'.

If Cramer is conscious of having sinned against his talent, he is, at least in the terms of a later Baudelairean formulation according to which 'le mal se connaissant' is 'moins affreux et plus près de la guérison que le mal s'ignorant' ('Sur *Les Liaisons dangereuses*' (OC, ii. 68)), potentially redeemable, and it is the possibility of such redemption that seems to me to lie behind the involuted ironies of the novella's final disconcerting paragraph, already quoted, which we must now analyse in greater detail: 'Pauvre chantre des *Orfraies*! Pauvre Manuela de Monteverde!—Il est tombé bien bas.—J'ai appris récemment qu'il fondait un journal socialiste et voulait se mettre à la politique.—Intelligence malhonnête!—comme dit cet honnête M. Nisard!' (OC, i. 580). On the face of it, this is a straightforward condemnation of Cramer delivered by the narrator, endorsed by the author, and, presumably, to be accepted by the reader; for the 'chantre des *Orfraies*' to found 'un journal social- iste' and to want to 'se mettre à la politique' is just one more stage in Cramer's 'fall' from poetic grace and recuperation by the social order that has been described in the previous paragraph. At the same time, though, the whole passage can be read against itself to produce a diametrically opposed meaning or at least, as Wing argues,[39] one that 'does not totally abolish positive elements' in the reader's final view of the novella's central character. The 'pauvre chantre des *Orfraies*' was, on the evidence of the rest of the story, never much of a poet anyway and the fact that he has 'fallen' away from the posturing pseudo-romanticism of his youth could be to the long-term benefit of his talent. Likewise, if 'Manuela de Monte- verde' has had her/his day, perhaps at last the 'real' Samuel Cramer can emerge from his multiple disguises of the past and, renouncing that 'faculté comédienne' that made of him 'à la fois tous les artistes qu'il avait étudiés et tous les livres qu'il avait lus', give expression to his own personality which, we have been assured, 'restait profondément original' (OC, i. 555). As for the 'journal socialiste' and 'la politique', it is, as we have seen, impossible to determine whether, at the time he wrote the final paragraph of *La Fanfarlo* (perhaps as late as the second half of 1846, but

---

[39] Wing, 'The Poetics', 186.

conceivably as early as 1844–5), Baudelaire was himself a 'socialist' in even the broadest pre-1848 sense of the term. On the other hand, as a reader of and would-be contributor to, for instance, *La Démocratie pacifique*, it is unlikely that he would share the narrator's apparent view of political journalism as intrinsically risible and, even if he did, he would certainly know that no founder of a radical journal could hope—as La Fanfarlo hopes for Cranmer—to be accepted as a member of the Institut or the Légion d'honneur; at the very least, and irrespective of its actual content, Cramer's gesture will necessarily put him outside 'respectable' society and, in so doing, will give him the possibility of realizing himself as man and artist that will forever be denied to insiders like the archetypal establishment thinker, 'cet honnête M. Nisard'.

Such has been the narrator's dominance of story, characters, and reader that, up to this final paragraph, the reader has had little option but to take his ironic, all-knowing, totalizing voice for that of the author himself.[40] Throughout the preceding pages (except, significantly, in the discussion of food where author, narrator, characters, and reader were at one), the narrator has assumed an attitude of sardonic superiority towards both hero and reader which, the latter begins to suspect, may not have been—or may not always have been—the author's own. Early in the novella, the narrator describes *Les Orfraies* as a 'recueil de sonnets, comme nous en avons tous fait et tous lu, dans le temps où avions le jugement si court et les cheveux si longs' (OC, i. 558), typically implying that he, for his part, has come through the phase of naïve romanticism to which 'le romantique Samuel, l'un des derniers romantiques que possède la France' (OC, i. 571) remains, from his point of view, comically in thrall. Come through, though, to what? —to a worldly wise cynicism, to an integration into society far more complete than that of which he accuses Cramer, and also, apparently, to friendship with La Fanfarlo in her plump latter-day incarnation as 'ministerial tart'.[41] Indeed, there is more than a hint of ministerial authority in the narrator's voice throughout— sarcastic, sententious, always with more 'intelligence' (in every sense of the word) at his disposal than characters or reader yet

---

[40] The argument in this paragraph depends heavily on Chambers, 'Le Fade', 197.
[41] See OC, i. 577, where La Fanfarlo is said to have been questioned by 'ses camarades' on 'le commencement de sa liaison avec Samuel'. What follows suggests that the narrator is either one of these 'camarades' or one of their circle.

jealously protective of his 'sources'—and there is a particular appropriateness, rich in ironies not all of which the narrator can, for once, control, in his parting invocation of that *chien de garde* of Bourgeois Monarchy orthodoxy, Désiré Nisard.

Nisard (1806–88) embodied the regime's thinking on literature: he was to criticism what Victor Cousin was to philosophy or Horace Vernet to painting.[42] As the author of a *Manifeste contre la littérature facile* (1833) and an *Étude de mœurs et de critique sur les poètes latins de la décadence* (1834), he had led the classicists' assault on the 'excesses' of romantic writing and had been rewarded for his obdurate advocacy of literary tradition by a succession of promotions in the academic world which took him at an early age to the Chair of French Eloquence at the Sorbonne previously occupied by that other object of Baudelaire's loathing, Abel Villemain. His academic successes led on to a political career of note: *chef du secrétariat* at the Ministère de l'Instruction Publique (1836), *maître des requêtes* at the Conseil d'État (1837), followed by election to the Chambre des Députés in 1842 as ministerial candidate for Chatillon-sur-Seine, a seat he continued to occupy until February 1848. After a brief set-back in the early days of the Second Republic, Nisard's career continued its inexorable advance as the Republic moved to the right, and in 1850 he was elected to the Académie in preference to Musset; the Second Empire would bring him further honours, power, and prestige. In his *Histoire de la littérature française* which began to appear in 1844, Nisard formulated his characteristically dogmatic view of literary criticism. It is, he wrote,

une science exacte, plus jalouse de conduire l'esprit que de lui plaire. Elle s'est fait un idéal de l'esprit humain dans les livres; elle s'en est fait un du génie particulier de la France, un autre de sa langue; elle met chaque auteur et chaque livre en regard de ce triple idéal. Elle note ce qui s'en approche: voilà le bon; ce qui s'en éloigne, voilà le mauvais.[43]

Claude Pichois suggests that the ironic invocation of Nisard could be a side-swipe at Ancelle amongst whose clients was the critic's younger brother Charles (OC, i. 1429). More to the point, perhaps, are Nisard's similarities with Aupick: honest Professor Nisard and

---

[42] For Nisard, see Milner, *Le Romantisme*, i. 237 and 354 and OC, i. 1429.

[43] Quoted in Antoine Adam, *et al.*, *Littérature Française*, ii. (Larousse, 1968), 116.

honest General Aupick are typical of the 'honnêtes gens' of mid-nineteenth-century France who would serve Bourgeois Monarchy, Second Republic (in its reactionary phase) and Second Empire with equal enthusiasm, their combination of dogmatism and opportunism enabling them to switch their allegiance from regime to regime with scarcely any sense of compromise or inconsistency.

To give the 'last word' in *La Fanfarlo* to a critic accustomed to having the 'last word' on everything is, therefore, replete with multiple ironies some of which are willed and controlled by the narrator but of which others rebound on him and undermine the posture of moral superiority from which he has issued Nisard-like judgements on Cramer throughout the text. The ironic antiphrasis *malhonnête-honnête* is typical of the narrator's stylistic cleverness, an in-joke which those from the same anti-academic intellectual tradition as himself can be expected to savour and applaud. But far from 'closing the case' on Cramer as the narrator evidently intends it to, its actual effect is dramatically to reopen it and, as Wing suggests,[44] to imply that any attempt to 'fix' a proteiform figure like Samuel cannot be other than flawed. The narrator's apparently anti-authoritarian discourse is revealed to be authoritarian and judgemental through and through. His scoffing reference to 'cet honnête M. Nisard' inadvertently reveals the moral and intellectual *dis*honesty of the attitude he has assumed towards hero and reader. For what the 'conclusion' of *La Fanfarlo* reveals is that, for someone like Samuel, at least until he is definitively *'cloué sous la lame'* (OC, i. 580), there can be no conclusion. His is an open consciousness that the narrator has the illusion of having defined and tied down, but as the story ends for the narrator, so life begins again for Samuel as he moves forward into a future of new possibilities and commitments: 'Fonder un journal socialiste', 'se mettre à la politique'. Whether, when he wrote these last lines of *La Fanfarlo*, Baudelaire had already been 'converted' to the radical cause is, to repeat, impossible to determine; that, some time in 1845–6, he should have predicted so accurately what he would do scarcely more than a year after the novella's publication is less important than the fact that, by its end, Samuel has broken free not only of 'Manuela de Monteverde' and her/his dated 'jargon romantique' (OC, i. 569) but also of the facile anti-romantic ironies of the narrator. Throughout the novella, except at La Fanfarlo's dinner-table,

[44] Wing, 'The Poetics', 186.

author and hero (and reader) have been kept apart by the narrator's stance of ironic superiority; by the final paragraph, that stance has been undermined, and the gap between author, hero, and reader reduced to a minimum. Author and hero are not yet the authentic modern romantic artist both have glimpsed in La Fanfarlo, and neither has yet given birth to the authentic modern romantic poems he contains within him, but both are beginning to break free of the alienating pseudo-identities that have held them and their creativity in check. The hermaphroditic—and poetically sterile—'Baudelaire-Dufaÿs' has gone, to be replaced, over-optimistically as far as the production of poems was concerned, by 'Charles Defayis' out of whom, after a further twelve months' painful maturation, 'Charles Baudelaire' would be born on the very eve of revolution. *La Fanfarlo* is the last of Baudelaire's 'tactical' writings of the 1840s, the last in which he assumes a bewildering range of protean discourses and disguises in order to confound those who, after the manner of the narrator, seek to imprison him in a single psychological and social definition. In the twelve months that followed *La Fanfarlo*'s publication, political circumstances in France changed so much that at last a consistent *strategy* of opposition became a possibility, and, as it did so, so it became possible for Baudelaire, after four years of opposition by subterfuge and sleight of language, to speak at last with his own voice and in his own name.

Towards 1848

'Quelle année que 1847! Comme 1847 a amené 1848!' (Pasquier, President of the Chambre des Pairs under the Bourgeois Monarchy, speaking in 1849, as reported by Victor Hugo).[45] The elections of August 1846 had, as we have seen, given Louis-Philippe and the Soult–Guizot ministry its first overall majority in parliament and seemed to open the way for a further period of depoliticized social peace and economic prosperity. But at the very moment that the hegemony of the Bourgeois Monarchy seemed most assured it began to be undermined from both within and below and within eighteen months of Guizot's triumph would succumb to a combination of economic, social, and political crises whose effects began to be felt from early 1847 onwards. Looking back from the

[45] Quoted Claude Pichois, *Le Romantisme*, ii. *1843–69* (Arthaud, 1979), 24.

vantage-point of 1850, Tocqueville described France at that time as a country

divisé en deux parts ou plutôt en deux zones inégales: dans celle d'en haut, qui seule devait contenir toute la vie politique de la nation, il ne régnait que langueur, impuissance, immobilité, ennui; dans celle d'en bas, la vie politique, au contraire, commençait à se manifester par des symptômes fébriles et irréguliers que l'observateur attentif pouvait aisément sentir.[46]

The source of those 'symptoms' lay in the economic crisis which, beginning with the poor grain harvest of 1845, had gathered momentum in 1846 and, by mid-1847, had plunged the whole country into its worst recession since the late 1820s.[47] Disastrous grain harvests led to a doubling of bread prices in some parts of France between May 1846 and May 1847, provoking a wave of bread-riots, attacks on grain-convoys, and assaults on alleged hoarders (*accapareurs*) throughout northern and eastern France. With the potato harvest also failing in every year between 1845 and 1848, rural France was, from the spring of 1847, in the grip of a mounting panic which some historians have compared to the *grande peur* of 1789; an expanding popular and middle-class press ensured that stories of roaming bands of beggars and unemployed workers, attacks by peasants on rich landowners, and of food riots being quelled by troops and *gardes nationaux* reached large urban centres like Lille and Paris itself where raids on bakeries became a common occurrence in the spring of 1847. Soon industry as well as agriculture was sucked into the gathering crisis. A nation-wide slump in the building industry in 1846–7 had repercussions throughout the whole economy, especially in Paris where unemployment amongst building workers had already greatly increased since the completion of the *mur de Thiers*. The railway bubble burst abruptly and the Bordeaux–Sète line was abandoned uncompleted; it is estimated that as many of 700,000 construction and metal workers had been laid off by the end of 1847. In Roubaix 4,800 out of 13,000 workers were unemployed in February 1847; by May the figure had risen to 8,000. Salaries in Rouen were cut by 30 per cent while in Lille 29,000 out of 76,000 inhabitants were receiving some kind of public assistance by the end of 1847; in France as a whole

[46] Alexis de Tocqueville, *Œuvres complètes*, xii. *Souvenirs*, ed. Luc Monnier (Gallimard, 1964), 35.
[47] The account that follows is based on Jardin and Tudesq, *La France des notables*, i. 233–46 and Magraw, *France 1815–1914*, 76.

the death rate rose from 220 per 10,000 inhabitants in 1844 to 239 in 1847, close to a 10 per cent increase in the space of three years. Nor was it just the lower classes who were enveloped by the now systemic crisis. Railway shares dropped dramatically in value, and the number of bankruptcies doubled between 1846 and 1847; the resources of the Banque de France dropped by 65 million francs in October 1846 alone, and a major bank in Le Havre collapsed completely. To lower-class misery and anger were joined the fears and resentments of the *petite* and *moyenne bourgeoisie*; by the end of 1847 the regime had forfeited the support of even the *grande bourgeoisie* and *notables*.

All through 1847 the signs of impending catastrophe were there for those, like Tocqueville or Victor Hugo, who could see them. In *Choses vues* Hugo describes a ball given in early July at the Parc des Minimes in the Bois de Vincennes and attended by the *fine fleur* of the Bourgeois Monarchy including Guizot, Thiers, Rothschild, the Prefect of Police, Lord Normandy, Dumas *père* and *fils*, Gautier, Vigny, and Hugo himself. In order to reach the ball, guests had to drive eastwards from their fastnesses in the west of Paris through the working-class heartland of the Faubourg Saint-Antoine, with predictably calamitous results:

Depuis quinze jours on . . . parlait [de la fête], et le peuple de Paris s'en occupait beaucoup. Hier, depuis les Tuileries jusqu'à la barrière du Trône, une triple haie de spectateurs garnissait les quais, la rue et le faubourg Saint-Antoine, pour voir défiler les voitures des invités. A chaque instant, cette foule jetait à ces passants brodés et chamarrés dans leurs carrosses des paroles hargneuses et sombres. C'était comme un nuage de haine autour de cet éblouissement d'un moment. . . . Quand on montre le luxe au peuple dans des jours de disette et de détresse, son esprit . . . franchit tout de suite une foule de degrés; il ne se dit pas que ce luxe le fait vivre, que ce luxe qui est utile, que ce luxe lui est nécessaire. Il se dit qu'il souffre et que voilà des gens qui jouissent; il se demande pourquoi tout n'est pas à lui. . . . Ceci est plein de périls. Quand la foule regarde les riches avec ces yeux-là, ce ne sont pas des pensées qu'il y a dans les cerveaux, ce sont des événements.[48]

Slowly the crisis in the *pays réel* began to make itself felt in the *pays légal* of official politics. In July 1847 the *banquet* campaign for electoral reform was launched in Paris and by the end of the year had become a nation-wide movement; a series of financial and sexual scandals (notably the murder of the Duchesse de Choiseul-

---

[48] Hugo, *Choses vues*, i. 104–6.

Praslin by her husband and his subsequent suicide) further undermined the credibility not only of the government but also of the
regime in the eyes of its erstwhile supporters. 1847 also saw the
publication of three widely read histories of the Great Revolution
by Louis Blanc, Michelet, and, above all, Lamartine whose *Histoire
des Girondins* was one of the best-selling works of the nineteenth
century. 'C'est surtout le peuple qui m'aime et m'achète', ex-
claimed the future chief minister of the Provisional Government of
1848;[49] according to another observer, it was the popularity of the
Histoire des Girondins that was behind the frequency with which
street musicians played *Ça Ira* and *La Carmagnole* on their *orgues
de barbarie* during the summer and autumn of 1847.[50]

For all this, the widespread social and economic crisis was
remarkably slow in translating itself into an out-and-out political
crisis. As late as 29 January 1848, in a celebrated speech before
the Chambre des députés, Tocqueville conceded that the working
classes were not 'tourmentées par les passions politiques propre-
ment dites' in the manner that they had once been but went on to
argue that, since 'leurs passions, de politiques, sont devenues
sociales', it was no longer this or that ministry, or even this or that
political regime, that was under threat, but the very structure of
society and the economy.[51] None the less, even Tocqueville was
staggered when the crisis finally erupted on 22 February following
the banning of the last of the reform banquets. For almost all
French men and women, irrespective of class and political affilia-
tion, the Revolution of 1848 was born more or less *ex nihilo*, with
nothing to suggest that the anti-ministerial riots with which it began
would lead in less than forty-eight hours to the collapse of the
regime itself. Right up to the massacre on the Boulevard des
Capucines on the evening of 23 February it was possible to miss the
properly revolutionary character of what was happening on the
streets of Paris, and even then Frederic Moreau's off-hand reaction
—'Ah! on casse quelques bourgeois'[52]—must have been echoed by
not a few Parisians. We shall see how Baudelaire reacted in the
chapter that follows. Our first task, though, is the almost impossible one of tracing the possible trajectory of his political and other

---

[49] Cited Milner, *Le Romantisme*, v. 36.
[50] Poumiès de la Siboutie, *Souvenirs d'un médecin de Paris* (Plon, 1910), 312.
[51] Tocqueville, *Souvenirs*, 38.
[52] Flaubert, *L'Éducation sentimentale*, 285.

views in the twelve months that separated the publication of
La Fanfarlo from the appearance of the review of Champfleury's
stories in *Le Corsaire* on 18 January 1848.

The absence of published writings of any kind after January 1847
in itself suggests that Baudelaire was in the throes of a major crisis
affecting both his personal life and creative output, and this impression is amply confirmed by the one substantial piece of written
evidence that we have for his state of mind in 1847, the letter that
he addressed to his mother at the year's end on 4 December. In the
letter Baudelaire tells his mother that 'depuis quelques mois je vis
dans un état surnaturel', that the fraught tone of his letter stems
from 'des *souffrances inconnues à vous* que je subis' and, finally,
that 'l'oisiveté absolue de ma vie apparente, contrastant avec
l'activité perpétuelle de mes idées, me jette dans des colères
inouïes'. The letter of 4 December shows beyond doubt that Baudelaire was afflicted right up to the end of the Bourgeois Monarchy
with the two maladies most characteristic of limbo-epochs: idleness
and infertility: 'l'oisiveté me tue, me dévore, me mange,' he writes,
'supposez une oisiveté perpétuelle commandée par un malaise
perpétuel, avec une haine profonde de cette oisiveté, et l'impossibilité absolue d'en sortir, à cause du manque perpétuel d'argent'.
Clearly, too, Baudelaire feels that he is at a crucial turning-point in
his whole existence. He feels he is wasting his talent and he is half-
tempted by the offer of a private teaching post in Mauritius he has
received from contacts there and which he has until February 1848
to accept or refuse. On the other hand, he feels strongly that 'la
postérité me concerne' and he is determined, once the New Year
begins, to embark on what he calls 'un nouveau métier', namely 'la
création d'œuvres d'imagination pure—le Roman' by means of
which he hopes to be able to earn some sort of living in the future:
'*bon ou mauvais tout se vend*; il ne s'agit que d'assiduité'.

In all of this there is no mention of politics whatsoever, and no
suggestion that the 'situation d'esprit exceptionnelle' in which he
has spent the previous months is in any way linked to the broader
crisis of French society. What is interesting, though, is the way in
which Baudelaire's personal condition in 1847—exhaustion, desperation, sterility, combined with the feeling that, if he can just
bring himself to make 'un dernier grand effort' (C, i. 142–7), all
can yet be redeemed and the embryonic works he bears within him
brought to fruition—coincides almost point for point with the

broader condition of France itself, and especially of 'le peuple', as expressed in the work of popular poets and *chansonniers* in the months preceding the outbreak of revolution. In a song of 1847 entitled 'Le Fumier', Eugène Pottier (the future composer of 'L'Internationale') conveys a powerful sense of present sterility combined with the hope that sustained courage and effort will in time bring forth the growth that is at present held in check by a repressive political and economic system:

> Bon laboureur, peuple aux bras nus,
>   Le grain des idées
> Dans tes sillons, les temps venus,
>   Aura vingt coudées.
> Un engrais fétide et grossier
> Couvre encore le sol nourricier . . .
>   O plèbe
>   A la glèbe
>   Il faut du fumier! . . .
>
> Courage, ô laboureur trapu,
> Attends de pied ferme,
> Et sous ce fumier corrompu,
> Voyant ce qui germe,
> Pour la moisson du monde entier,
> Tiens ta faulx prête et ton grenier . . .
>   O plèbe
>   A la glèbe
>   Il faut du fumier.[53]

Closer to home, and on the very eve of revolution, Pierre Dupont expressed a similar sense of imminent resurrection and future fecundity in the refrain of 'La Chanson du Banquet' written for the banned banquet of 21 February 1848:

> La France dort, mais n'est pas morte;
> Elle a des sursauts en dormant.
> Le fruit divin que son flanc porte
> Va mûrir pour l'enfantement.[54]

Lamartine's celebrated 'la France s'ennuie' describes only part of the France of 1847–8, the 'official France' of the political classes, the *pays légal*; of the 'other France', the vast bulk of the nation, the

---

[53] Eugène Pottier, *Œuvres complètes*, ed. Pierre Brochon (Maspéro, 1966), 43–4.
[54] Pierre Dupont, *Chants et poésies* (Garnier, 1862), 92–4.

pays réel, it might better have been said 'La France attend'. In the limbo-months of 1847–8, Baudelaire too waited, without much hope, for deliverance from the internal and external constraints that held not just his artistic creativity but his whole life in thrall. When at last the February Revolution came, it was experienced throughout France as a miraculous *re*birth: for Baudelaire, after the sterile agitation of 1847, it may have seemed less like a new beginning than as the beginning *tout court*.

Baudelaire, Courbet, Proudhon

Although Baudelaire published nothing between January 1847 and January 1848 and probably wrote very little either in the twelve months preceding the outbreak of revolution, the letter of 4 December 1847 suggests that the year had been one of intense intellectual activity as well as of bitter personal suffering. If hearing Dupont's 'Chant des Ouvriers' in 1846 had had the impact on him that he later claimed, he cannot have remained indifferent to the signs of mounting social and economic distress amongst 'le peuple' in the course of 1847; he must have been aware, too, particularly if he was visiting *goguettes* and *marchands de vin* alone or in Dupont's company, of the spread of radical socialist ideas amongst the lower classes that Tocqueville referred to in his speech of January 1848. He seems to have read the first volume of Michelet's history of the Great Revolution and to have grasped and endorsed the historian's key thesis—quoted in the first number of *Le Salut public* in February 1848 (OC, ii. 1032)—that 'la Revolution de 89 a été faite par le peuple' and not, as the revolution's enemies might claim, by the nefarious ideas of a Voltaire, a Rousseau, or a Beaumarchais. The review of Champfleury's stories published in January 1848 suggests a reversion to precisely the kind of naturalist metaphysics, ethics, and aesthetics that *La Fanfarlo* had so pointedly called in question. Not only is Champfleury praised for having shown 'une confiance illimitée' in nature in his stories and for writing in a style that is 'large, soudain, brusque, poétique, comme la nature', but another story-teller of Baudelaire's acquaintance, Philippe de Chennevières, is also commended as 'un brave esprit tout voué au travail et à la religion de la nature' (OC, ii. 21–3). This unexpected endorsement of naturalism on the very eve of revolution when *La*

Fanfarlo had seemed to point in the direction of the anti-naturalism of the middle and later 1850s is of considerable significance, since, as we shall see, a positive view of 'Nature' and 'the natural' will be one of the organizing principles of Baudelaire's thought and literary practice throughout the Second Republic period. The tension between naturalism and anti-naturalism is all the greater if we recall Baudelaire's determination, announced in the letter of December 1847, to embark on 'la création d'œuvres d'imagination pure—le Roman', fictions which, one imagines, would have been very different from Champfleury's *contes* and closer to those of the writer—Edgar Allan Poe—the discovery of whose works (in a translation of *Le Chat noir* by Isabelle Meunier published in the Fourierist *Démocratie pacifique* on 27 January 1847) caused him, as he would later put it,[55] 'une commotion singulière' that would outlast not merely the Bourgeois Monarchy but the Second Republic as well. Paradoxically, the Revolution of 1848, erupting at a time when Baudelaire seems to have been moving in a radically new direction artistically, may actually have retarded rather than advanced his creative development. As we shall see, it is not the least of the many ironies of Baudelaire's revolutionary 'interlude' that his actual writings of the period are in form, tone, and style—in everything, in fact, except their political content—perceptibly more conservative than the writings of 1844–7 and of the post-1851 period.[56]

The broadly 'naturalist' view of life and art indicated in the review of Champfleury's stories is almost certainly linked to the discussions Baudelaire had been having in 1847 not only with Champfleury himself but also with Courbet.[57] Exactly when Baudelaire and Courbet met is not known—sometime in 1847, according to most scholarly opinion, and definitely not earlier than

---

[55] The expression 'commotion singulière' comes from a letter to Armand Fraisse of 18 Feb. 1860 (C, i. 676).

[56] See F. W. Leakey, 'Baudelaire: The Poet as Moralist', in L. J. Austin, Garnet Rees, and Eugène Vinaver (eds.), *Studies in Modern French Literature Presented to P. Mansell Jones* (Manchester Univ. Press, Manchester, 1961), 196–219, esp. the comment (p. 197): 'It would seem that, in the Revolution of 1848, Baudelaire's rebelliousness found a provisional outlet or safety-valve, and that by a familiar paradox, his new-found enthusiasm for social and political revolution was accompanied by a certain modified return to moral and aesthetic conformity.'

[57] For a full discussion of the relationship between Baudelaire and Courbet, see Alan Bowness, 'Courbet and Baudelaire', *Gazette des Beaux-Arts*, 90 (Dec. 1977), 189–99.

the latter part of 1846—and it needs to be stressed that, prior to
the winter of 1848 (when he began work on his first masterpiece,
Une après-dînée à Ornans), Courbet was, though two years older
than Baudelaire, considerably less well-known than the younger
man and far less sure than he of the artistic path he was pursuing.
According to Alan Bowness, when Baudelaire and Courbet met,
the painter was still 'searching for a style and for a subject'. The
wide range of subjects he attempted in the 1840s indicates, in
Bowness's view, 'an absence of commitment to what he was doing',
and, above all, his 'preoccupation with self portraiture when a
young artist suggests a certain search for identity: like an actor
[*and, we need hardly add, like 'Baudelaire-Dufaÿs' and Samuel
Cramer*], he appears before the public in a bewildering variety of
roles, surprising us at each appearance, and making it impossible
for us to decide which is the real self-portrait'.[58] It was not,
therefore, an established artist with a concerted artistic programme
and practice that Baudelaire encountered in Courbet in 1847, but a
fellow prisoner in limbo, one who, even more desperately than he,
was in quest of an authentic self and style, and this shared uncertainty of purpose must have added to the intensity of their exchange
of views on art, in which Champfleury also participated. A letter
from Courbet to his parents in January 1848, plainly referring to
Baudelaire and Champfleury, indicates that the discussions had
yielded some kind of consensus and that the three were about to
embark on a collaborative artistic venture:

My picture is progressing rapidly. I hope to finish it for the exhibition, and
if it is accepted it will be most helpful and will secure me a great reputation.
In any event I am on the threshold of success, for I am surrounded by
people, very influential in the press and the arts, who are enthusiastic about
my work. At last we are about to found a new school, of which I shall be
the representative in painting.[59]

Despite Bowness's caution against concluding that the 'school' in
question had the idea of realism as its lodestar, Baudelaire's article
on Champfleury which, appearing at the very time Courbet was
writing to his parents, may be seen as some kind of manifesto,
clearly endorses 'la peinture au naturel' of contemporary, everyday

[58] See Alan Bowness's introd. to *Gustave Courbet 1819–1877* (Arts Council of
Great Britain, 1978), 12.
[59] Quoted Bowness, 'Courbet and Baudelaire', 191. I have been unable to locate
the French original of this quotation.

life and, very significantly, commends Balzac as 'un naturaliste' and 'un observateur' no less than as 'un savant' and 'un inventeur' (OC, ii. 22), in marked contrast to Baudelaire's later view that Balzac was *not* primarily—or even at all—'un observateur' but a 'visionnaire, et visionnaire passioné' (*Théophile Gautier* (I) (1859) (OC, ii. 120)). What this suggests is that, under the influence of Champfleury, Baudelaire and Courbet were together moving towards the idea that both painting and literature—and it is worth recalling that, in the late 1840s, Baudelaire considered himself as much a writer of stories as of poetry and criticism—should concern themselves primarily, as the *Salons* of 1845 and 1846 had so memorably asserted, with 'l'héroïsme de la vie moderne'. Though, as Bowness points out,[60] the actual painting on which Courbet was working when he wrote to his parents (a *Nuit classique de Walpurgis* described by the painter himself as a 'tableau allégorique résumant le Faust de Goethe') can in no way be described as a 'realist' work, the evidence suggests that the 'school' of which Courbet wrote was, in theory if not yet in practice, committed to a view of art which may legitimately be described as 'realist' in the broad sense of the term. At the same time, however, Baudelaire's endorsement of 'naturalistic' representation in the article on Champfleury would appear to run counter to his desire, expressed in the letter of December 1847 to his mother and obviously linked to his recent discovery of Poe, to commit himself to 'la création d'œuvres d'imagination pure—le Roman'. It is a wholly characteristic tension. Baudelaire entered 1848 apparently espousing two theories of art—one broadly 'realist' or 'representative', directed towards the outside world, the other 'imaginary', concerned essentially with the world within—which could not, ultimately, be reconciled. The conditions and exigences of 1848–51 would incline him, broadly, towards an essentially 'realist' conception of art close to that championed with such ardour by Courbet, and many critics, beginning with Champfleury in 1850,[61] have seen *L'Enterrement à Ornans* as a sustained realization of the programme of the *Salon de 1846* as

[60] Ibid. 194.

[61] See the article by Champfleury in *L'Ordre* of 21 Sept. 1850 in which he draws the connection between Courbet's depiction of modern dress in *L'Enterrement à Ornans* and the eulogy of the *habit* in 'un livre rare et curieux (le *Salon de 1846*, par M. *Baudelaire*)' (quoted Bowness, 'Courbet and Baudelaire', 196). This whole question is discussed by Yoshio Abé, 'Un Enterrement à Ornans et l'habit noir baudelairien', *Études de langue et littérature françaises*, 1 (1962), 29–41.

regards both subject-matter and style: the 'heroic' representation of contemporaneity. At the same time, the non- or even anti-realist in Baudelaire remained strong and, having been suppressed or held in check throughout the Second Republic, would resurface with a vengeance after 1851, as is revealed not least by his repudiation, in 1855, of Courbet as one of those 'anti-surnaturalistes' whose systematic 'guerre à l'imagination' has been conducted 'au profit de la nature extérieure, positive, immédiate' (*Exposition universelle (1855)* (OC, ii. 586)). As so often, the source of Baudelaire's post-1851 position is to be found in the years before 1848 and the very virulence with which he later repudiated friends and causes of the Second Republic years ('Réalisme,—villageois, grossier, et même rustre, malhonnête', 'Courbet sauvant le monde', *Puisque réalisme il y a* (1855?) (OC, ii. 58–9)) may be seen as evidence of the intensity with which he had committed himself to them at the time.

Courbet's political position before February 1848 (and, for that matter, afterwards) is scarcely less obscure than Baudelaire's. In a letter of 1866 he described himself as a 'republican by birth' and as a follower of Fourier when he first arrived in Paris in 1839 or 1840.[62] In the 1840s he was, like so many others, drawn to the ideas of Étienne Cabet and Pierre Leroux and must, in the broad definition of the term, be considered to have been a 'socialist' when he and Baudelaire met in 1847, though scarcely yet in the radical sense of the famous letter to *Le Messager de l'Assemblée* in November 1851 when he declared himself to be 'non seulement socialiste, mais bien encore démocrate et républicain, en un mot partisan de toute la Révolution, et, par-dessus tout, réaliste, c'est-à-dire ami sincère de la vraie vérité'.[63] Perhaps Courbet's greatest contribution to Baudelaire's radicalization was to have introduced him, some time in 1847, to the work of his fellow Franc-Comtois, Pierre-Joseph Proudhon, whom he does not appear to have actually met until April 1851 but whose *Système des contradictions économiques* he may have known—and must have known of—before 1848.[64] As we

---

[62] Letter to Victor Frond, quoted (in trans.) *Gustave Courbet 1819–1877*, 12.

[63] Quoted Timothy J. Clark, 'A Bourgeois Dance of Death: Max Buchon on Courbet', in Petra Ten-Doesschate Chu (ed.), *Courbet in Perspective* (Prentice-Hall, Englewood Cliffs, NJ, 1977), 93.

[64] On Courbet and Proudhon, see Alan Bowness, 'Courbet's Proudhon', *Burlington Magazine*, 120/900 (1978), 123–30. For the importance of the *Système des contradictions économiques* to an understanding of Courbet's work (esp. of *L'Atelier du peintre*), see James Henry Rubin, *Realism and Social Vision in Courbet and Proudhon* (Princeton Univ. Press, Princeton, NJ, 1980), esp. pp. 55 and 74.

have seen, some time between the autumn of 1846 and the beginning of the Second Empire, Baudelaire copied out a passage from the *Système* which it is appropriate to cite at this stage of our argument:

L'art, c'est-à-dire la recherche du beau, la perfection du vrai, dans sa personne, dans sa femme et ses enfants, dans ses idées, ses discours, ses actions, ses produits: telle est la dernière évolution du travailleur, la phase destinée à fermer glorieusement le cercle de la nature. L'*Esthétique*, et au-dessus de l'esthétique, la *morale*, voilà la clef de voûte de l'édifice économique. (OC, ii. 979)

The importance of this passage—whenever Baudelaire read and transcribed it—to his thought and writing during the Second Republic will become evident in the chapters that follow. That Baudelaire should have seized upon it reveals his preoccupation, already manifest in his interest in Fourierism, with a 'totalizing' view of human activity which sees economics, aesthetics, and ethics as interrelated expressions of a single complex whole. For the moment, though, the massive influence of Proudhon's ideas and personality on Baudelaire in 1848–52 and again in the 1860s need not detain us: both the man and his thought will receive attention enough in the chapters that follow. Did Baudelaire read Proudhon before 1848? Let us, in the absence of compelling evidence either way, assume that he did and, with a quotation from the *Système* to which no young reader of the Bourgeois Monarchy's final months could have remained indifferent, leave the wintry limbo of 1847 behind and move into the early springtime of the year that followed.

Socialistes! éclaireurs perdus de l'avenir, pionniers dévoués à l'exploration d'une contrée ténébreuse, nous dont l'œuvre méconnue éveille des sympathies si rares et semble à la multitude un présage sinistre: notre mission est de redonner au monde des croyances, des lois, des dieux, mais sans que nous-mêmes, pendant l'accomplissement de notre œuvre, nous conservions, ni foi, ni espérance, ni amour. Notre plus grand ennemi, socialistes, est l'utopie! Marchant d'un pas résolu, au flambeau de l'expérience, nous ne devons connaître que notre consigne, EN AVANT! Combien parmi nous ont péri, et nul n'a pleuré leur sort! les générations auxquelles nous frayons la route passent joyeuses sur nos tombes effacées; le présent nous excommunie, l'avenir est sans souvenir pour nous, et notre existence s'abîme dans un double néant. . .[65]

---

[65] Pierre-Joseph Proudhon, *Système des contradictions économiques, ou Philosophie de la misère* (Marcel Rivière, 1923), ii. 85.

3

Street-fighting Years (I):
Baudelaire in 1848

February to June 1848

Paris Spring

To those on the left in France, wrote Gustave Lefrançais in 1886, the years 1845, 1846, and 1847 were worse even than the long 'cauchemar' of the Second Empire to which, by the middle 1860s, an end, sooner or later, could be foreseen. As it approached the end of its second decade, the Bourgeois Monarchy seemed, in contrast, destined to linger on *ad infinitum*, sclerosed and anaemic, but, for that very reason, apparently capable of withstanding indefinitely all challenges to its being from both within and without: to be young and radical at such a time was, said Lefrançais, quite simply 'la mort'. It is hardly surprising, then, that to Lefrançais and his generation—he was five years younger than Baudelaire—the proclamation of the Second Republic on 24 February 1848 should have appeared as nothing less than 'une résurrection' which, but four or five days previously, nothing seemed remotely to fore-shadow, a miraculous and totally unexpected 'retour à la vie' after the limbo years of the 1840s in which, swirling together in ecstatic collective effervescence, 'riches et pauvres, bourgeois et ouvriers oublièrent pour un moment ce qui les séparait'.[1] In three days, as replete with tension, horror, and ultimate joy as the Easter triduum, the streets and boulevards of Paris and, with them, the hearts, minds, and even, it seemed, the bodies of the city's inhabitants, were utterly transformed. Gone was the wintry darkness of the old regime, dispelled by a wondrous and all-encompassing radiance which, to all save the Orleanist rump and a few clear-headed

---

[1] Gustave Lefrançois, *Souvenirs d'un révolutionnaire* (Bibliothèque des Temps Nouveaux, Brussels, 1902(?)), 20.

observers like Proudhon and de Tocqueville, seemed to herald an everlasting springtime of health, prosperity, and social harmony:

L'aspect des boulevards etait féerique. Une longue guirlande de lumière diversement colorée, suspendue à tous les étages, unissait les maisons, joyeux emblème de l'union des cœurs. . . . L'allégresse était dans l'air, la satisfaction sur tous les visages. . . . Dans l'effusion de cette fête commune, bourgeois et prolétaires se donnaient les bras, habits et blouses se rapprochaient familièrement. Le sentiment d'une fraternité joyeuse débordait de tous les cœurs.[2]

In February 1848, Alain Faure has recently argued, 'Fête et Révolution étaient l'une dans l'autre'; 'l'insurgé fut tour à tour charivariseur, barricardier et bouffon', and the revolution that he made was at one and the same time a 'théâtre révolutionnaire' and a 'révolution théâtrale'.[3] Nor is this assimilation of Carnival and Revolution simply a fashionable product of modern historical-anthropological speculation shot through with *gauchiste* nostalgia for May '68; it is a recurring theme, even a cliché, of the literature of the period, irrespective of the class or political beliefs of the writers concerned. Thus—to take a working-class participant in the riots—Norbert Truquin states that on the 24th 'la ville était en fête, les rangs étaient confondus; les ouvriers causaient fraternellement avec les bourgeois'[4] while, turning to a middle-class and still essentially conservative observer of events, Hugo notes that on the 25th—the day afer the Republic was proclaimed at the Hotel de Ville—'les rues étaient toutes frémissantes d'une foule en rumeur et en joie . . .; les cafés regorgeaient, mais nombre de magasins etaient fermés, comme les jours de fête; et tout avait l'aspect d'une fête, en effet';[5] even Flaubert, writing some twenty years later, could speak almost wistfully of the 'gaieté de carnaval'[6] that reigned in Paris in the days following the fall of the monarchy. After the long Lenten years of the Bourgeois Monarchy, it seemed

[2] Daniel Stern, *Histoire de la Révolution de 1848* (Charpentier, 1862), ii. 196–7.
[3] Alain Faure, *Paris Carême-prenant: Du carnaval à Paris au xixe siècle, 1800–1914* (Hachette, 1978), 120.
[4] Norbert Truquin, *Mémoires et aventures d'un prolétaire à travers la révolution* (Maspéro, 1977), 63.
[5] Victor Hugo, *Choses vues 1847–1848* (Gallimard, Folio, 1972), 291.
[6] Gustave Flaubert, *L'Éducation sentimentale*, ed. Édouard Maynial (Garnier, 1964), 295.

that the *chansonnier* Eugène Pottier's prophecy, in 1847, of a
people's Easter had been miraculously fulfilled:

> La nation que Dieu bénit,
> La France rieuse et profonde,
> Comme l'oiseau tient dans son nid
> De beaux œufs blancs qu'elle féconde.
> Ces œufs de Pâques, mes amis,
> A ceux qui jeûnent sont promis.
> Quand Pâques viendra,
> Plus de carême au pauvre monde;
> Quand Pâques viendra,
> Comme on se décarêmera![7]

The characteristic figures and scenes of February–March 1848—
the *gamin*'s playful subversion of the rigid hierarchies of the
adults' social world, the *homme du peuple* flaunting beard, *blouse*,
casquette, and cutlass like so many insignia of historical election,
the popular feasts of wine and *saucisson* at the foot of *tricolore*-
bedecked *arbres de la liberté*, the ubiquitous presence of the Republican Christ—all these will receive extensive treatment in this and
the chapters that follow, for they constitute a common lexicon of
themes and images on which Baudelaire's writings of the Second
Republic draw repeatedly and without which their underlying
political meaning is indecipherable. For the moment, our concern is
to trace in as much detail as possible, and in essentially chronological mode, what Baudelaire did and thought between the revolutionary carnival of 22–24 February 1848 and the Bonapartist
legislative elections of 29 February 1852—a Lenten ritual if ever
there was one—in the wake of which he wrote to Ancelle of his
total and, he claimed, definitive disillusion with politics as such:
'LE 2 DÉCEMBRE m'a *physiquement dépolitiqué*' (C, i. 188). These
four years took Baudelaire, as they took an entire generation, from
rapturous rebirth, after the limbo-years of the declining Bourgeois
Monarchy, via what Charles de Rémusat was to call 'la plus violente
révolte des gouvernés contre les gouvernants, des pauvres contre les
riches, des ouvriers contre les patrons, du salaire contre le capital,
du prolétariat contre la bourgeoisie, une guerre enfin véritablement
civile ou plutôt une guerre sociale',[8] to an encounter with political

---

[7] Eugène Pottier, *Œuvres complètes*, ed. Pierre Brochon (Maspéro, 1966), 44.
[8] Charles de Rémusat, *Mémoires de ma vie*, ed. Charles-Henri Pouthas (Plon, 1962), iv. 326.

despair infinitely deeper than anything he or it had previously known. The beginning and the end of Baudelaire's journey from one experience of political death to another are well known, and the present account adds little by way of facts to what has already been uncovered concerning the period from February to June 1848 and his response to the Bonapartist coup of December 1851. But Baudelaire's radical Republicanism, no more than French radical Republicanism itself, did not perish on the barricades of June 1848; it is on what little we know of his thoughts, deeds, and associations in the second half of 1848, in 1849 and 1850, and during the build-up to the December coup that attention will principally be focused, as a new picture of strengthened rather than diminished radical republican conviction in the aftermath of June is gradually pieced together from the fragments of evidence at our disposal.

Revolutionary Parricide

As we have seen, Baudelaire had not waited for the events of late February to shed symbolically his false identity of the limbo-years. In publishing the *Corsaire-Satan* article on Champfleury under his real name on 18 January 1848, Baudelaire symbolically discarded the indeterminacy, dualism, and pseudo-aristocratic effeminacy of 'Baudelaire-Dufaÿs', 'Pierre de Fayis', *et al.* and for the first time confronted his public not only as an autonomous, adult individual but as an equal. In December 1847 Michelet had told his students at the Collège de France that 'non seulement dans la littérature, mais dans la vie, dans l'action, il y aura un mouvement immense de tous vers tous, une croisade des hommes à la recontre des hommes':[9] by becoming, at long last, 'Charles Baudelaire', it was as though the young writer was responding, consciously or unconsciously, to the same prophetic call.

How Baudelaire reacted to the accelerating banquet campaign against the Guizot ministry in January and February is not known, but, thanks to the unpublished memoirs of Charles Toubin, his actions from 22 February onwards can be charted in some detail and leave no doubt that, whether or not a 'républicain de la veille', no sooner did the crisis break than he committed himself passionately and unreservedly not merely to a change of ministry but to a

[9] Jules Michelet, *L'Étudiant* (Seuil, 1970), 63.

change of regime and, through and beyond that, to a thorough-going transformation of society. Around 3 p.m. on 22 February Baudelaire was with Toubin, Courbet, and Courbet's *franc-comtois* musician friend Promayet at the Place de la Concorde where, appalled, they witnessed the bayoneting of anti-regime demonstrators by two *gardes municipaux*. It is as though events conspired with wicked irony to confront the poet with the reality of what his real or mock incitement to anti-republican police violence in the *Salon de 1846* involved, but now Baudelaire's reaction admitted no complicity, ambivalence, or hesitation: sickened, he went, according to Toubin, with Courbet to the offices of *La Presse* to 'dénoncer à Émile de Girardin cet acte d'épouvantable ferocité'.[10] Around 1 p.m. on the following day, accompanied by Champfleury, Promayet, and Toubin, Baudelaire left the Café de la Rotonde on the corner of the Rue Hautefeuille and the Rue de l'École-de-médecine in the Latin Quarter, crossed the river and set out for the *quartier* Saint-Denis where they had been told there was fighting. Proceeding via the Place du Châtelet, they attempted with some difficulty to find a way through the numerous barricades that had already appeared—Proudhon would speak conservatively of Paris in February 1848 as 'un labyrinthe de 500 Thermopyles'[11]—to join the *boulevards intérieurs* between the Porte Saint-Denis and the Place de la Bastille. After witnessing, though not, it seems, participating in, sustained street-fighting between demonstrators and government forces, they had no sooner reached the Boulevard du Temple than they learned of the resignation of Guizot and his ministry. All along the boulevards, flags appeared at windows, lights lit up, *La Marseillaise* and *Les Girondins* rang out, while a massed phalanx of 'gardes nationaux en uniforme, ouvriers en blouse, polytechniciens, tous bras dessus bras dessous' (Toubin) approached from the direction of the Porte Saint-Martin. It was Baudelaire's first experience of such cross-class fraternity and euphoria, and his enthusiasm, attested to by Toubin, is no more than one would expect of a young bourgeois Bohemian *en rupture de ban*:

Il était enchanté de ce qu'il avait vu depuis deux jours. Le commencement

---

[10] Quoted from BPZ, 251.
[11] Quoted Édouard Dolléans and J.-L. Puech, *Proudhon et la Révolution de 1848* (Presses Universitaires de France, 1948), 24.

du drame l'avait fort intéressé; seulement, le dénouement lui plaisait peu, et il trouvait que le rideau était tombé trop tôt. Je ne l'avais jamais vu si gai, si leste, si infatigable, lui qui n'avait pas l'habitude de marcher. Ses yeux étincelaient.

Baudelaire's disappointment that the curtain had fallen 'too soon' on the scenes of revolutionary street-theatre that had so entranced him could indicate that, as early as the 23rd, his sights were set on the proclamation of a new Republic. Returning after dinner to the Café de la Rotonde, Baudelaire and Toubin found Courbet 'absolument seul en présence d'un bock et en compagnie de sa pipe'. On the streets once more, they witnessed further fighting in the Latin Quarter between demonstrators and the detested *gardes municipaux*, and eventually made their way to the Pont-Neuf where, prevented by troops loyal to Louis-Philippe from crossing, they learned of the massacre of demonstrators on the Boulevard des Capucines earlier that evening. Around 3 a.m. on the morning of the 24th, Toubin left Baudelaire to go home to sleep.[12]

If Baudelaire slept at all that night, he was in action first thing the following morning when he was seen by Toubin around 9 a.m. at the Carrefour de Buci in the company of Armand Barthet (1820–74), a minor poet and dramatist with whom Baudelaire had almost fought a duel a month before[13] and who, later in 1848, would earn some small renown in his native Franche-Comté for his national anthem 'La Républicaine'. Both Baudelaire and Barthet were, according to Toubin, 'armés de fusils de chasse et prêts à faire feu derrière une barricade qui ne les couvre encore que jusqu'à la ceinture', their improvised weaponry and general demeanour giving rise, in the eyes of some scholars, to severe doubts concerning the seriousness of their republican commitment.[14] But, according to a modern study, the Carrefour de Buci witnessed the heaviest fighting on the Left Bank on the 24th, with massive barricades, each manned by more than 400 insurgents, being constructed at each of the streets that fed into it: Buci, Mazarine, Dauphine, Saint-André-des-Arts, and l'Ancienne Comédie. For Baudelaire even to have been present there constituted a considerable risk, and

---

[12] Account based on, and quotations drawn from, BPZ, 251–3.
[13] See BPZ, 246.
[14] BPZ, 256–7. Pichois's comment on this episode is characteristic of this view: 'Ce n'était pas pour la République qu'il se battait; pas même pour la révolution. C'était pour satisfaire son instinct profond de révolte' (BPZ, 257).

it is to be noted that on the 24th the insurgents to be found in the *quartier* in question were overwhelmingly of working-class origin; only a handful of students, it seems, took part, and Baudelaire would certainly have stood out amongst the mass of working men who thronged the *carrefour*. It is also worth noting that on the morning of the 24th, before the king abdicated and before the Republic was officially proclaimed from the Hôtel de ville, the insurgents at the Carrefour de Buci had already taken it upon themselves to declare for a Republic.[15] No mere spectator, Baudelaire was, it is clear, at the heart of republican activity on the Left Bank as the *journées de février* approached their climax.

If Jules Buisson's account can be trusted, he was still at the Carrefour de Buci in the evening, brandishing 'un beau fusil à deux coups luisant et vierge' which he had just looted (or which had just been looted) from a nearby gunsmith's and resplendent in 'une superbe cartouchière de cuir jaune tout aussi immaculée'. The alleged exchange between Buisson and the agitated dandy-insurgent has passed into the *legenda aurea* of nineteenth-century literature:

Je le hélai, il vint à moi simulant une grande animation: 'Je viens de faire le coup de fusil!' me dit-il. Et comme je souriais, regardant son artillerie tout brillant neuve—'Pas pour la République, par example!'—Il ne me répondait pas, criait beaucoup et toujours son refrain: il fallait aller fusiller le général Aupick![16]

Buisson, whose one brush with fame this appears to have been, told his story to Eugène Crépet in 1886 and had, no doubt, been dining out on it for close to forty years. Damning in its implications, impossible to verify, Buisson's account has been widely used to discredit Baudelaire's radicalism in February 1848, providing the main evidence for the view that for him, as for Flaubert's Frédéric Moreau, the February revolution represented above all an outlet for frustrated personal emotions, an entrancing theatrical spectacle in which he was free to act out fantasy roles with relative impunity; 'Baudelaire aimait la Révolution', Asselineau would later write, confirming this view, 'plutôt, il est vrai, d'un amour d'artiste que d'un amour de citoyen'.[17] None the less, it is by no means im-

[15] See John G. Gallaher, *The Students of Paris and the Revolution of 1848* (Southern Illinois Univ. Press, Carbondale and Edwardsville, 1980), 60.

[16] Quoted from BPZ, 256–7.

[17] Jacques Crépet and Claude Pichois (eds.), *Baudelaire et Asselineau* (Nizet, 1953), 85. Asselineau, it might be noted, did not become a close friend of Baudelaire until 1850–1.

possible that Baudelaire did actually utter the quasi-patricidal wish attributed to him, and it is to be noted that, scarcely a mile away from the Carrefour de Buci, Aupick, head of the Polytechnique since November 1847, had been actively engaged in trying to dissuade his students from joining the insurgents on the streets on the evening of the 23rd and throughout the 24th. Failing in his aim, he had won credit for not finally standing in his students' way, but his name would none the less have been associated throughout the Latin Quarter with a despised regime that was about to yield up its dying gasp.[18] The archetypal man of the Bourgeois Monarchy (as he had been of the First Empire, the Restoration monarchy, and shortly after the *journées de février,* would be of the new Republic, pending his nomination to the Senate by Napoleon III in 1853), Aupick not only epitomized the political fudges and moral compromise inseparable from the Orleanist regime, but, in his ability to survive and prosper, embodied the continuity of conservative power which, it would soon become clear, underlay the transition from constitutional monarchy to republic. For Baudelaire to repudiate him and all he stood for was to assert his authentic manhood over and against the infantilizing constraints of the *conseil judiciaire,* to align himself unreservedly with his real father François Baudelaire who, in abandoning the priesthood, had himself espoused the revolutionary cause more than fifty years before, and symbolically to reject the bogus patriarchal or pseudo-patriarchal powers against which, as we have seen, much of his published writing of the 1840s had been explicitly directed. At the very outset of the Second Republic, Baudelaire emphatically declared himself to be his own man. The 'victime' of the Bourgeois Monarchy had become the would-be 'bourreau' of the revolution.

Even if, following an established critical and biographical tradition, we admit an undercurrent of dilettantism, histrionism, perhaps even of hysteria, in Baudelaire's behaviour on the streets of Paris in February 1848, the sections that follow will show his commitment to the revolution to have been serious, long-lasting, and profound. In addition to the properly political significance that events had for him and which we shall discuss shortly, February 1848 marked his first real encounter with 'la foule' whose ambiguous appeal he was to explore so profoundly in his later writing. It was on the February barricades that he first experienced what he

[18] See BPZ, 254–6.

calls 'l'ivresse des foules' (*Mon cœur mis à nu* (OC, i. 693)), here that he first knew the rapturous deliverance from self that fusion with the crowd affords: 'Ivresse religieuse des grandes villes.—Panthéisme. Moi, c'est tous; tous, c'est moi' (*Fusées* (OC, i. 651)). Merging with the delirious throng in the streets, Baudelaire derived, as he says in 'Les Foules', 'une singulière ivresse de cette universelle communion' (OC, i. 291). Quite simply, he was *intoxicated* by the sudden political and social convulsion and the carnival-like euphoria that succeeded it, and it is highly significant in the context of the wine poems whose properly revolutionary significance will be discussed in the chapters that follow that, in *Mon cœur mis à nu*, Baudelaire should speak without hesitation of 'mon ivresse en 1848' (OC, i. 679).

Le Salut public

After the declaration of the Republic and the formation of the Provisional Government, Baudelaire's position continued to be that of a convinced, even of a radical, republican, though the extent to which it may be termed 'socialist' must remain conjectural, particularly in view of the wide variety of 'socialisms' that coexisted and competed with each other in the weeks and months that followed the Revolution. Together with Toubin and Champfleury he founded an ephemeral republican journal *Le Salut public*—the Jacobin-sounding title was suggested by Baudelaire himself—which, clad in 'une de ses blouses blanches' (whether worn with 'pantalon de chambre' and 'élégants souliers à la Molière' is not, alas, recorded), he is said by Toubin to have sold on the streets and in the cafés of the Latin Quarter; Toubin adds that, in a twin gesture which well accords with the general mood of republican-socialist religiosity that reigned in Paris in February and early March, Baudelaire, 'dans la tête de qui rien n'était inconciliable', took copies of *Le Salut public* both to the Archbishop of Paris and to the radical socialist Raspail for whom, says Toubin, 'il professait tendresse et admiration sans bornes qu'il avait 'lu *L'Ami du Peuple*'.[19] *Le Salut public* had only two numbers (27 February and 1 or 2 March) and, although no one article can be decisively attributed to Baudelaire, he may, as co-founder of the journal, be

[19] See BPZ, 257–60.

assumed to share the sense of miraculous rebirth, of mystic populism, that finds expression in an article in the first number entitled 'LA BEAUTÉ DU PEUPLE':

Depuis trois jours la population Paris est admirable de beauté physique. Les veilles et la fatigue affaissent les corps; mais le sentiment des droits reconquis les redresse et fait porter haut toutes les têtes. Les physionomies sont illuminées d'enthousiasme et de fierté républicaine. . . . Qui veut voir des hommes beaux, des hommes de six pieds, qu'il vienne en France! (OC, ii. 1032)

Although *Le Salut public* contains no political philosophy or programme that can realistically be described as 'socialist', its commitment to the Republic clearly goes beyond the limited constitutional republicanism of the Provisional Government and its supporters. The tone of the journal is radical, populist, mystic, even rapturous, and, in a spirit wholly and typically *quarante-huitard*, it marries politics and religion, the Republic and Christ:

[Jésus-Christ] était avec nous aux barricades, et c'est par lui, par lui seul que nous avons vaincu. Jésus-Christ est le fondateur de toutes les républiques modernes; quiconque en doute n'a pas lu l'Évangile. (OC, ii. 1035)

The second number of *Le Salut public* carried on its masthead a vignette by Courbet depicting a man on the barricades wearing a *blouse* and top hat and holding in one hand a gun and in the other a flag proclaiming 'Voix du peuple, voix de Dieu'. Given the explicit political significance of dress in 1848—one of the most popular songs of the early weeks of the Republic began with the words 'Chapeau bas devant ma casquette | À genoux devant l'ouvrier!'— it is possible, as Claude Pichois has suggested, that Courbet, in typically *quarante-huitard* fashion, sought in this association of top hat and *blouse* to symbolize the union of bourgeoisie and *peuple* in the name of the Republic; it could, of course, be 'read' more personally (and less kindly) as a sharp comment by Courbet on the tensions and contradictions which Baudelaire, like all middle-class radicals of his generation, was attempting to reconcile not only in his thought and action but in his entire person as well.[20] Yet Baudelaire's stake in the unfolding pattern of events is not to be

---

[20] See BPZ, 258. For a discussion of Courbet's illustration, see T. J. Clark, *Image of the People: Gustave Courbet and the 1848 Revolution* (Thames and Hudson, 1973), 48–9.

doubted. If, as Toubin said, Baudelaire was more committed than Champfleury and himself to the success of the second number of *Le Salut public*, it seems reasonable to assume that it was because this time he was the author of most of what appeared in it. In highly Baudelairean manner, and using images of intoxication that are, to say the least, revealing, *Le Salut public* proclaimed that 'la République circule dans l'air, et *enivre* les poumons, comme un parfum'; not only are Paris and France seized by intoxicating republican fervour, but revolution is seething throughout Europe: 'au-delà de la mer, le peuple *bouillone*, la République *fermente* sourdement' (OC, ii. 1034, all italics added). There are attacks on the *gardes municipaux* and on the 'mendiants de place' who, recognizable by 'la bassesse de leurs figures empreintes de servilisme', are besieging the new government in search of power and position. Bandy and Mouquet have plausibly suggested that the journal's denunciation of 'ces insatiables dévoreurs de la République' constitutes a barely disguised attack on General Aupick who had indeed publicly rallied to the new regime on 1 March and would be duly confirmed as head of the Polytechnique two days later.[21] There is an attack, too, on the old regime's detested salt-tax (shortly to be abolished by the new government, pending its re-imposition after Louis Napoleon's electoral triumph in December) which, says *Le Salut public*, 'empêchait la fertilisation des terres, qui enrayait les socs des charrues' (OC, ii. 1038): the contrast between the sterility of the old regime and the hoped-for fecundity of the new is again, as we shall see, an integral part of Baudelaire's *magasin* of images and themes throughout the Second Republic. Stridently anti-monarchist, the second number of *Le Salut public* is, however, conciliatory towards both 'républicans de la veille' of whatever hue and 'républicains du lendemain', condemning Raspail and *L'Ami du Peuple* for their reservations *vis-à-vis* the Provisional Government and, despite its Jacobin title, actually criticizing Marat (Baudelaire's admiration for whom is, as we have seen, evident in his comments on David's painting in 1846) and other 'infatigables flaireurs de mauvaises intentions' bent on revolutionary purity at all costs: 'Des hommes de 93,' *Le Salut public* cautions, 'ne prenons que leur foi ardente à la République et leur admirable dévouement à la patrie' (OC, ii. 1036). A week after the proclamation of the

---

[21] Jules Mouquet and W. T. Bandy, *Baudelaire en 1848* (Éditions Émile-Paul Frères, 1946), 70–7.

Republic, when tensions within society and the polity were already apparent, the tone of *Le Salut public* remained radical, populist, mystic, rapturous, in a word Utopian. By the middle of March, and still more by the middle of April, intoxicated republican fervour would be on the wane, giving way to feelings of disillusion, rancour, even of anxiety concerning the Republic's very survival.

Blanqui and the Blanquistes

Baudelaire's name—shorn, needless to say, of the pseudo-aristocratic Dufaÿs—appears on the list of members of Blanqui's Société Républicaine Centrale published by *Le Courrier français* on 28 February. It is, however, unclear whether this formal adhesion indicates support for Blanqui's brand of radical activism: the Society's prospectus of 26 February to which Baudelaire responded merely invited 'tous les hommes d'intelligence et de dévouement consacrés par dix-sept années de luttes contre la tyrannie, les condamnés politiques, les penseurs, les savants, les écrivains de la presse démocratique, sans distinction de nuances' to meet at the Salle de la Redoute on the Rue de Grenelle-Saint-Honoré 'pour se constituer en association'. Not surprisingly, the initial membership of the Société Républicaine Centrale was extremely diverse in its opinions and included many more middle-class intellectuals than would be found amongst the hard core of Blanqui's supporters in the weeks to come: Saint-Beuve (whom Baudelaire had known since the early 1840s) was an early adherent, as was Leconte de Lisle, a Fourierist sympathizer like Baudelaire and, like him, a future reactionary, while other existing or future associates of Baudelaire to become founder-members included Théophile Thoré (an early vice-president of the Society), Alphonse Esquiros, the ex-Abbé Constant, Jean Wallon (who would shortly move sharply to the right), the Fourierist Alphonse Toussenel, Pierre Dupont, and, intriguingly, Richard Wagner; other adherents were, from the middle-class intelligentsia, Paul de Flotte, the Fourierist architect and sculptor César Daly and the future philosopher of Republicanism Charles Renouvier, and, from the secret societies and political prisons of the Bourgeois Monarchy, working-class revolutionaries such as Vilcoq, Crevat,

Espirat, and Joseph Mathie, known as 'La-Jambe-du-bois'.[22] Baudelaire's name (like that of Thoré and Dupont) does not appear on the second (or any subsequent) list of members published on 10 March, and it is commonly assumed that he abandoned the Society completely, repelled, it is often claimed, by its alleged rhetoric, sloganeering, and servile personality cult of Blanqui, as well as by its supposedly ultra-leftist, confrontational politics. But the fact that Baudelaire apparently ceased to be a *sociétaire* after the inaugural meeting would not have prevented him from attending subsequent meetings at the Salle Valentino or Salle des Menus-Plaisirs at the Conservatoire de Musique on a 'one-off' basis as an *auditeur*; and the 'public singulièrement mélangé et tapageur' that flocked to see and hear Blanqui—Daniel Stern says that 'les femmes du monde, sous des vêtements plus que modestes, s'y glissaient furtivement, protégées par la lumière crépusculaire des quinquets où l'huile était parcimonieusement mesurée'[23]—would have rendered his presence there wholly unexceptional, indeed imperceptible. Moreover, tenacious myths to the contrary, the Société Républicaine Centrale was, in the words of another member known to Baudelaire, Louis Ménard, 'un foyer de discussions sérieuses et d'éducation politique'.[24] The researches of, in particular, Peter Amann have shown that the Society's debates, though vigorous and unstructured, were neither chaotic nor, above all, monopolized by Blanqui; modern research also indicates that, again contrary to widespread belief both at the time and since, Blanqui exercised, or attempted to exercise, a consistently moderating influence on the events of 1848, conspicuously declining to give his backing to the invasion of the Constituent Assembly on 15 May (which Baudelaire may have witnessed).[25] In short, neither Baudelaire's adhesion to the Société Républicaine Centrale in February nor his apparent absence from its meetings subsequently tells us very much about his political opinions and options in 1848. Other evidence, to be considered now and in later sections, suggests, however, that, up to and including the *journées de juin*, Baudelaire's beliefs and actions are broadly consistent with a

[22] All information and quotations taken from Maurice Dommanget, *Auguste Blanqui et la Révolution de 1848* (Mouton, 1972), 19–20 and 38–44.

[23] Quoted ibid. 30.

[24] Quoted ibid. 35.

[25] See Peter H. Amann, *Revolution and Mass Democracy: The Paris Club Movement in 1848* (Princeton Univ. Press, Princeton, NJ, 1975), 61–2 and 218–30.

Blanquist perspective on the social and political crisis that gathered momentum from the middle of March onwards.

Whatever the character and duration of Baudelaire's association with the Société Républicaine Centrale, he, like all his contemporaries, retained a vivid memory of Blanqui's appearance, as his sketches of 'le plus terrible des révolutionnaires' (Daniel Stern[26]) on the manuscript of 'Le Guignon' (dated 1849–50 by Poulet-Malassis; perhaps Baudelaire was reminded of him by his widely reported trial at Bourges in March–April 1849[27]) clearly indicates. Moreover, such were the ramifications of the Blanquist network, and so diverse the social and intellectual background of his supporters, that Baudelaire could well have remained in indirect contact with *l'Enfermé* and his conspiratorial brand of club-based ultra-leftism. Although Baudelaire's scathing review in 1846 of Louis Ménard's *Promethée délivré* had caused them to sever relations, their common hostility to 'les républicains du lendemain' could have brought them together after February; without being an out-and-out Blanquist, Ménard was close to the Société Républicaine Centrale and its successors and would, like Baudelaire himself, fight on the barricades in June. Still more tantalizing is Baudelaire's reference, when met by Gustave Le Vavasseur at the close of the June insurrection, to Paul de Flotte, one of the most appealing minor figures of *quarante-huit*, a *Blanquiste à outrance*, and, as a close friend of Ménard and Leconte de Lisle, very much part of Baudelaire's own intellectual and social milieu. A noted naval officer, engineer, and chemist, and a *républicain de la veille*, de Flotte was from February onwards on the far left of the radical republican movement and was involved with Blanqui in all the major confrontations of the early months of the Republic. He marched with his mentor at the head of the huge demonstration of 17 March, supported, albeit reluctantly, the invasion of the Assembly on 15 May and, after Blanqui's arrest, was instrumental with Esquiros (another link between Baudelaire and the ultra-revolutionary clubs) in setting up new radical organizations to replace the disbanded Société Républicaine Centrale. In June, de Flotte was, according to the Blanqui scholar Maurice

---

[26] Quoted Dommanget, *Auguste Blanqui*, 27.

[27] Baudelaire's drawing is reproduced in *Album Baudelaire*, ed. Claude Pichois (Gallimard, Bibliothèque de la Pléiade, 1974), 83 (illus. 113). For a discussion of the possible link between Blanqui and 'Le Guignon', see Graham Chesters, 'A Political Reading of Baudelaire's "L'Artiste inconnu" ("Le Guignon")', *Modern Language Review*, 79/1 (1984), 64–76.

Dommanget, 'assurément le plus qualifié des chefs blanquistes libres pour donner des directions aux insurgés'.[28] De Flotte was actively engaged on 23 and 24 June in liaising between different insurgent groups but appears to have remained in hiding during the fighting itself. On 26 June he was arrested at the Divan Lepeletier, a café close to the Opéra of which Baudelaire would be a *habitué* after December 1851 but which he may have known already, and it was to this that Baudelaire referred when accosted by Gustave Le Vavasseur and Philippe de Chennevières at the Palais-Royal later that day. In Lefrançais's view, De Flotte was lucky to escape with his life, 'tant son nom soulevait alors de colères contre lui dans la bourgeoisie'.[29] As it was, he was sentenced to transportation to Algeria but, reprieved in December 1849, he returned to France and, following his election to the Assembly in March 1850, was one of the pillars of the Montagnard opposition to Louis Napoleon in the last eighteen months or so of the Republic's existence. Briefly exiled once more after December 1851, he returned to France and, a radical idealist to the end, finally died fighting for Italian unity at the battle of Reggio in 1860. That Baudelaire could well have known so dedicated a revolutionary republican and sympathized with his aims and strategy puts his known revolutionary commitment in June 1848 in a new and more significant context. It does not make a Blanquist of him, but it does suggest that there could be more to his radicalism than the immature anti-authoritarianism to which a leading body of scholarship still seeks to reduce it.

The April Elections

Baudelaire's experience of the Société Républicaine Centrale, combined, in all likelihood, with forays into other revolutionary-republican clubs and gatherings, may have inspired in him that loathing of demagoguery and empty political rhetoric that would never leave him. The projected epilogue to the 1861 edition of *Les Fleurs du mal* speaks pointedly of Paris's 'petits orateurs, aux enflures baroques | Prêchant l'amour' (OC, i. 192), and it is wholly in character that we should next encounter him heckling Arsène Houssaye and Alphonse Esquiros during the April election cam-

---

28 Dommanget, *Auguste Blanqui*, 195.
29 Lefrançois, *Souvenirs*, 109.

paign for the Constituent Assembly, exposing their ignorance on a variety of issues of the day and, according to Toubin, reducing each to a state of mammering confusion. It is unclear whether Baudelaire shared the widespread radical republican scepticism concerning the validity of any election held so early in the Republic's life when conservative pressures could so easily be brought to bear on wholly inexperienced new voters. In *Mon cœur mis à nu* (OC, i. 684), he evidently proposed to expound on 'ce que je pense du vote et des droits d'élection' as on the 'droits de l'homme' in general; his tone suggests a less than wholehearted endorsement of the principle of electoral democracy, though once again there is insufficient evidence to affirm—or deny—that such was his attitude in 1848 itself. On the other hand, the celebrated letter of March 1852 to Ancelle implies that his refusal to vote—'un parti pris chez moi' (C, i. 188)—in the previous month's election may not have been the first time he had deliberately abstained from formal processes of electoral democracy, and it could well be, therefore, that Baudelaire's republicanism, like that of so many of his radical contemporaries (not least Blanqui and Proudhon), was not, contradictory though it may seem to us, incompatible with a pronounced anti-electoralism. In his notice on Pétrus Borel dating from the late 1850s or early 1860s, he speaks witheringly of 'la passion démocratique et bourgeoise' which, beginning in 1848, 'nous a si cruellement opprimés' (OC, ii. 155). The reference, it can hardly be doubted, is to the succession of elections conducted under universal suffrage which, in April and December 1848, in May 1849, and again in the plebiscites of December 1851 and November 1852, returned parliamentary majorities or political decisions fundamentally opposed to the Republican cause. Republicans of Baudelaire's generation and beyond had every reason to fear and mistrust the Republican institution *par excellence*, universal manhood suffrage.

Whatever his views on the elections as such, the content of Baudelaire's exchanges with Esquiros and Houssaye (assuming, that is, that he was sincere and not simply intent upon humiliating the speakers with whatever arguments came to hand) suggests that, in economic matters at least, his 'socialism' stopped well short of the state socialism of Louis Blanc, the 'communism' of Étienne Cabet and his followers, as well as of other 'collectivist' strategies current at the time. Certainly his comments imply a concern for 'libre-échange' (which Baudelaire, according to Toubin, described as 'la clef de voûte de l'édifice social') and for 'les intérêts du petit commerce' (adjudged, reportedly, by Baudelaire to be 'aussi sacrés que ceux de la classe ouvrière') which would assort ill with a fully fledged socialist position, though not, it should be said, with the kind of co-operativism or mutualism advocated by Proudhon with whose ideas he could have been familiar even in April 1848 and of whom, as we shall see, he was to become a virtual disciple in the aftermath of the *journées de juin*.[30] When Baudelaire first encountered Proudhon and Proudhon's ideas and when, in particular, he first read the *Système des contradictions économiques* remains, as we have seen, one of the many unknowables of his intellectual and political development. What is certain, however, is that Baudelaire's visceral anti-statism and his no less deep-rooted individualism would, when the moment of encounter came, make him singularly receptive to the forthright defence of personal freedom against the encroachments of the state—monarchist, Jacobin, Bonapartist, 'moderate' or 'radical' Republican alike—in which we may discern the essence of Proudhon's otherwise bewilderingly contradictory social, economic, and political philosophy. Baudelaire would later claim to have been drawn by some preternatural force of spiritual and intellectual kinship towards the work of Poe and de Maistre. It would seem that his encounter with Proudhon, the man as well as the work, was—to use a term common to both the author of *Qu'est-ce que la propriété?* and of *Les Soirées de Saint-Pétersbourg* —no less 'providential' in character.

La Tribune nationale

In April 1848 Baudelaire was appointed *secrétaire de rédaction* of *La Tribune nationale* and his name appears with that attribution on the surviving numbers of the journal published daily between 26 May and 6 June. Two points should be made at the outset concerning the evidentiary value of *La Tribune nationale*: first, that, to my mind at least, the attempts by Jules Mouquet and W. T. Bandy in their pioneering study *Baudelaire en 1848* to ascribe specific articles in it to Baudelaire on largely stylistic grounds fail to carry conviction and, second, that as *secrétaire de rédaction*, Baudelaire

[30] Account based on, and quotations taken from, BPZ, 261–2.

would not necessarily share the political views the journal expressed. On the other hand, Baudelaire's clash with the owners and backers of *Le Représentant de l'Indre* in Châteauroux in October 1848 suggests that, if there were not some broad congruence of views and objectives between *secrétaire* and ownership—particularly if the *secrétaire* was as thoroughly difficult as Baudelaire—the relationship would rapidly become unworkable. The following discussion is accordingly based on the assumption that, while *La Tribune nationale* may not express Baudelaire's view on each and every subject, it is most unlikely that he could have disagreed fundamentally with its political line and have yet remained—or, indeed, have wanted to remain—in its employ.

What that political line was has been much debated. Drawing on biographical and bibliographical guides published at the time, Mouquet and Bandy argued that *La Tribune*, well to the left when its first numbers appeared in February–March, was taken over at some point (probably in May) by a wealthy and conservative member of the Constituent Assembly, the Comte Combarel de Leyval, and became steadily more right-wing as time went on; *Le Croque-mort de la Presse* of January 1849, which they quote, even speaks of the journal's 'tendances monarchiques' in its later manifestation.[31] Even a cursory reading of the journal's twelve surviving numbers makes it clear, however, that, as Marcel Ruff has argued,[32] *La Tribune* remained essentially true throughout its existence to the description *Le Croque-mort* gives of its original version in February–March: 'Républicain ardent, démocratique et socialiste'. Its principal backer, as well as its principal contributor, from beginning to end, was clearly Jules Schmeltz, the personal assistant of Émile de Girardin (we have already noted Baudelaire's apparent familiarity with the owner of *La Presse*) and, according to Proudhon's associate Darimon, an 'esprit essentiellement pratique . . . très versé dans la pratique des affaires'.[33] As such, he had been enlisted by Girardin to set up the latter's projected *Société universelle d'échange*. Failing to make anything of it, he was approached by Proudhon himself to drawn up the statutes for Proudhon's own

---

[31] See Mouquet and Bandy, *Baudelaire en 1848*, 311–12.
[32] See Marcel Ruff, 'La Pensée politique et sociale de Baudelaire', in *Littérature et société: Recueil d'études en l'honneur de Bernard Guyon* (Desclée de Brouwer, Bruges, 1973), 65–75, esp. 69–70.
[33] Quoted Pierre Haubtmann, *Pierre-Joseph Proudhon*, 868.

ambitious credit scheme, the *Banque national d'échange*, which were published in Proudhon's organ *Le Représentant du Peuple* on 10 May 1848. On 18 May *Le Représentant* listed Schmeltz and Charles Fauvéty as *secrétaires* of the *Banque national d'échange*, with Proudhon as president and Girardin and Jules Lechevallier (like Fauvéty, a close associate of Proudhon) as vice-presidents. Although Schmeltz can in no sense be described as a Proudhonist (an article in *La Tribune nationale* of 6 June acknowledges the credit scheme to be an 'institution désirable', but is critical of 'l'imagination trop vive de l'auteur' and, in particular, of his view of 'la propriété comme un vol'[34]), it may well have been him who introduced Baudelaire, if not to Proudhon himself, to Proudhon's ideas, and above all to the project of the *Banque nationale d'échange*. As late as 1865 Baudelaire could tell Ancelle that, 'en matière d'économie', Proudhon still struck him as 'singulièrement respectable' (C, ii. 453); my final chapter will discuss the possible relevance of Proudhon's economic theory in general, and of the *Banque* in particular, to an understanding of 'Assommons les pauvres!' If Schmeltz did initiate Baudelaire into Proudhon's ideas, he represents a crucial link between the poet's radicalism of February–June 1848 and the rather different kind of radicalism that would emerge in the aftermath of the insurrection.

The politics of *La Tribune nationale* are clear and consistent. Despite repeated attacks on the proposed nationalization of the railways (almost certainly, as Ruff argues, because Schmeltz was himself a private shareholder in the companies) which give it an anti-socialist colouring, *La Tribune* is unswerving in its view that 'la République n'aurait rien fait pour nous, qui ne répondrait que par une révolution politique à la rénovation sociale qui est notre droit et notre légitime exigence'.[35] As such, it regularly and scathingly attacked the constitutional republicans of *Le National*, together with their equivalents in the Provisional Government and Constituent Assembly for whom 'les questions politiques sont tout, les questions sociales ne sont rien',[36] this opposition of the political and the social being, as we have seen, wholly characteristic of

[34] *La Tribune Nationale* (6 June 1848), quoted Mouquet and Bandy, *Baudelaire en 1848*, 289–91.
[35] *Numéro spécimen* (10(?) Apr. 1848), quoted Mouquet and Bandy, *Baudelaire en 1848*, 93.
[36] 2/3 June 1848, quoted Mouquet and Bandy, *Baudelaire en 1848*, 238.

the radical French left at the time. While heaping contempt on bourgeois republicans (principally in the person of Lamartine), *La Tribune* was no less dismissive of 'le petit citoyen Louis Blanc' and his plans for the state organization of labour, and it is notably insulting about 'les vapeurs hermaphrodites répandues par la plume de George Sand'[37] in the pages of *La Vraie République*. Lamartine, Blanc, and Sand[38] figure prominently, of course, amongst the 'mature' Baudelaire's hatreds (Proudhon loathed them too); it is unlikely that, with the possible exception of Sand, he would have dissented from *La Tribune*'s scourging of them in 1848 itself.

The radicalism of *La Tribune nationale* is most evident in the candidates it supported in the by-elections of early June 1848. As well as backing Proudhon, Caussidière, and Pierre Leroux, radical republicans all of them, it urged its readers to give their votes to 'des hommes du peuple . . . des hommes qui ne font qu'un avec le peuple, des hommes prêts et à combattre et à mourir pour lui'.[39] Amongst the working-class candidates so commended are Jules Malarmé, a *monteur en bronze* who is described in Jean Maitron's authoritative *Dictionnaire biographique du mouvement ouvrier français* as a 'Babouviste', 'communiste matérialiste', and 'partisan d'associations réglées par la loi révolutionnaire et subordonnée à une dictature politique de la classe ouvrière'; Savary, described in *La Tribune* as an *ex-ouvrier cordonnier* and by Maitron as a 'propagandiste communiste de tendance néo-Babouviste' considered by the police to be 'un dangereux révolutionnaire'; and the *ouvrier cambreur* Adam whose candidature was also announced in *L'Aimable Faubourien: Journal de la Canaille* (the journal founded in February by Poulet-Malassis—whom Baudelaire had still to meet—Antonio Watripon, and Alfred Delvau) in its list of candidates 'adoptée par les clubs réunis'. That Baudelaire should have worked for six weeks or more for a journal prepared unambiguously to

---

[37] Mouquet and Bandy, *Baudelaire en 1848*, 247.
[38] For Baudelaire and Louis Blanc, see OC, i. 708. For Baudelaire and George Sand, see *Mon cœur mis à nu*, esp. OC, i. 686–7, but with the proviso (see Cellier, 'Baudelaire et George Sand', 246–7) that Baudelaire's attitude towards her may have been much more positive prior to 1855. For Baudelaire and Lamartine, see the letter to Jean Wallon of 29 July 1850 (C, i. 166).
[39] Mouquet and Bandy, *Baudelaire en 1848*, 239–40. It is also true that *La Tribune* supported the candidacy of Bureaud-Rioffrey as well—the *rédacteur en chef* of *Le Progrès* whom T. J. Clark (*The Absolute Bourgeois: Artists and Politics in France 1848–1851* (Thames and Hudson, 1973), 172) rightly includes amongst the 'stalwarts of property' in 1848.

endorse such ultra-left working-class candidates does not, of course, prove that he would have shared their views. All the evidence, though, points in the same direction: connected indirectly (and perhaps, through Ménard and De Flotte, directly) to the world of the revolutionary clubs, and with links, too, with the world of Proudhonian anarchism, Baudelaire was placed firmly on the left of Parisian politics as the confrontation between bourgeois republicans and their radical, largely working-class, adversaries approached its climax.

The Journées de Juin

The evidence concerning Baudelaire's actions between the April elections and the outbreak of the June insurrection is fragmentary in the extreme. The mounting political crisis did nothing to ease his strained relationship with his mother who, Aupick having been named 'envoyé extraordinaire et ministre plénipotentiaire' to the Ottoman Empire on 8 April, was clearly bent on having her say on all matters relating to her son's life prior to her departure for Constantinople. The fact that Aupick owed his appointment directly to the intervention of Lamartine (a friend of the family of at least ten years' standing) doubtless heightened Baudelaire's contempt both for his stepfather and for the leading light of the Provisional Government, and it comes as no surprise to find Baudelaire, writing to his mother in late April or early May, refusing to meet 'ton Mari' and requesting a time to see her 'où je ne le rencontrerai pas chez Toi' (C, i. 149). When they did meet, a violent argument—to which Baudelaire refers in a letter of 8 December 1848—evidently ensued concerning his relationship with Jeanne: 'Avec cet entête-ment nerveux, cette violence qui vous est particulière,' Baudelaire complained (in Baudelaire's letters to his mother, the shifts from *tutoiement* to *vouvoiement* and back are as highly charged as in any Racinian lovers' dialogue), 'vous m'avez maltraité, uniquement à cause d'une pauvre femme que *je n'aime depuis longtemps que par devoir*, voilà tout'. Claiming (in December) that it was only 'l'expiation et le désir de rémunerer un dévouement' that kept him from breaking with Jeanne, Baudelaire none the less refused point-blank to end the 'singulière liaison' that so scandalized his mother (C, i. 153–4). By 12 May, his mother and stepfather were already at

Marseille, about to embark for Constantinople, and Baudelaire seems to have had no contact with them until the letter of 8 December. At the same time that he was breaking decisively with bourgeois politics, so he was placing a greater distance than ever before between himself and his bourgeois family origins.

The demonstrations of 16–17 March and 16 April having already exploded February's fragile illusion of inter-class harmony, the first bloody confrontation between contending social and political forces took place in Rouen at the end of April. Breaking 'sur une ligne de lutte de classes l'euphorie de la fraternité nouvelle', the events of 26–8 April in Rouen put an end to what Maurice Agulhon has called the 'période heureuse et conciliante' of the Second Republic,[40] and their impact on public opinion was accordingly immense, particularly amongst the Blanquists who, according to a modern historian, were 'incensed by the massacre of workers in Rouen'[41] and determined to retaliate as soon as the opportunity arose. Where Baudelaire stood is clear from his reaction, recorded in *Quelques caricaturistes français* (first published in *Le Présent* on 1 October 1857, but probably written in 1852–3, before his lurch to the right in the mid-1850s), to a caricature by an unknown artist that he saw 'peu après les malheureux massacres de Rouen':

Sur le premier plan, un cadavre, troué de balles, couché sur une civière; derrière lui tous les gros bonnets de la ville, en uniforme, bien frisés, bien sanglés, bien attifés, les moustaches en croc et gonflés d'orgueil; il doit y avoir là-dedans des dandys bourgeois qui vont monter leur garde ou réprimer l'émeute avec un bouquet de violettes à la boutonnière de leur tunique; enfin, un idéal de *garde bourgeoise*, comme disait le plus célèbre de nos démagogues. A genoux devant la civière, enveloppé dans sa robe de juge, la bouche ouverte et montrant comme un requin la double rangée de ses dents tailées en scie, F.C. promène lentement sa griffe sur la chair du cadavre qu'il égratigne avec délices.—Ah! le Normand! dit-il, il fait le mort pour ne pas répondre à la Justice! (OC, ii. 551–2)[42]

To Baudelaire it must have seemed that the 'premiers temps du gouvernement de 1830' had returned with a vengeance, the time

[40] Maurice Agulhon, *1848 ou l'apprentissage de la république 1848–1852* (Seuil, 1973), 57.

[41] Anthony Denholm, 'Louis Auguste Blanqui: The Hamlet of Revolutionary Socialism?', in Eugene Kamenka and F. B. Smith (eds.), *Intellectuals and Revolution: Socialism and the Experience of 1848* (Edward Arnold, 1979), 25.

[42] 'F.C.' refers to Frank-Carré, the president of the court at Rouen before which the insurgents of Apr. 1848 were tried (see OC, ii. 1355).

of the 'lamentable massacre de la rue Transnonian' with its 'emprisonnements, arrestations, perquisitions, procès, assommades de la police', but with one crucial difference: in April 1848 as in April 1834, the sacrificial 'victime' was still a defenceless French worker, but the 'bourreau' was no longer a soldier or policeman of the monarchy but a bourgeois republican acting, moreover, in the name of republican legality (OC, ii. 550–2).

Feeling as he evidently did, and with, apparently, contacts in the world of the ultra-left clubs, it is just possible that Baudelaire was present at the invasion of the Constituent Assembly on 15 May: 'Le 15 mai.—Toujours le goût de la destruction. Goût légitime si tout ce qui est naturel est légitime.' (*Mon cœur mis à nu* (OC, i. 679)). As for the *journées de juin* themselves, we have two main pieces of evidence: a two-line entry in *Mon cœur mis à nu* ('Les horreurs de Juin. Folie du peuple et folie de la bourgeoisie. Amour naturel du crime' (OC, i. 679)) which suggests, if anything, a stance of appalled de Maistrian neutrality before the spectacle of generalized cross-class human violence, and a lengthy statement by Gustave Le Vavasseur—all the more valuable given the author's known conservatism—which shows that, his later disclaimers notwithstanding, Baudelaire's commitment to the radical cause in June 1848 was sufficiently strong for him, quite simply, to have risked his life fighting on its behalf:

Baudelaire prit part, comme insurgé, aux journées de Juin 1848. Nous étions restés, Chennevières et moi, à la garde du Louvre, pendant les journées de Juin. Aussitôt après la reddition du faubourg Saint-Antoine, nous sortîmes, allant à la découverte et aux informations. Nous recontrâmes, dans le jardin du Palais-Royal, un garde national de notre pays, et nous l'emmenâmes boire un coup. Dans la diagonale que nous suivions pour gagner le café de Foy, nous vîmes venir à nous deux personnages de différent aspect: l'un nerveux, excité, fébrile, agité; l'autre calme, presque insouciant. C'étaient Baudelaire et Pierre Dupont. Nous entrâmes au café. Je n'avais jamais vu Baudelaire en cet état. Il pérorait, déclamait, se vantait, se démenait pour courir au martyre: 'On vient d'arrêter de Flotte, disait-il, est-ce parce que ses mains sentaient la poudre? Sentez les miennes!' Puis des fusées socialistes, l'apothéose de la banqueroute sociale *et cætera*. Dupont n'y pouvait rien. Comment nos prudences normandes tirèrent-elles notre ami de ce mauvais pas? Je ne m'en souviens guère. Mais je pense que la cocarde de mon ami de garde national joua un rôle muet, apparent et salutaire dans la petite comédie du sauvetage.

Quoi qu'on ait pensé du courage de Baudelaire, ce jour-là, il était brave et se serait fait tuer.[43]

Two points only need to be stressed here. The first is that Baudelaire's presence on the insurgent side in June is wholly consistent with—it is indeed the logical culmination of—the entire process of radicalization that we have followed since the *journées de février*: typically 'Utopian' in February in his belief in universal regeneration and inter-class fraternity, Baudelaire had, by the end of April at the latest, come to accept the inevitability of social and political conflict and had already opted unambiguously for the radical cause. Secondly, it cannot be stressed too much how exceptional it was for someone of Baudelaire's class and intellectual background to commit himself so unreservedly to the radical cause *in June*. The young middle-class radicals—especially students—who had participated so widely and readily in the overthrow of the monarchy were conspicuously absent from the insurgent ranks in June.[44] Most of the leading radical republican politicians—Louis Blanc, Caussidière, Ledru-Rollin—lent their admittedly reluctant support to the Provisional Government, and though Proudhon was present at the fighting on the streets of Paris, and spent much time questioning insurgents as to their motives ('Je suis parti seul, j'ai interrogé des insurgés. C'etait l'idée sociale, vague, générale'[45]), his stance was decidedly that of a pained if critically sympathetic observer, not of a participant. Finally, of Baudelaire's present, former, or future associates, only Ménard, Dupont, Poulet-Malassis, and possibly Antonio Watripon seem actually to have fought on the insurgent side, though Alphonse Esquiros, Theophile Thoré, and Pierre Leroux were strongly sympathetic to their cause. The composition of the insurgent force in June 1848—as, indeed, of that of their adversaries—is one of the liveliest controversies of nineteenth-century French history,[46] but one conclusion may be asserted with confidence: the cross-class alliances that had existed in February

---

[43] Quoted from BPZ, 264–5.

[44] See Gallaher, *The Students of Paris*, 95–6.

[45] Quoted in Dolléans and Puech, *Proudhon*, 54.

[46] For the insurgents, see, amidst a voluminous literature, Charles Tilly and Lynn H. Lees, 'The People of June 1848', in Roger Price (ed.), *Revolution and Reaction: 1848 and the Second French Republic* (Croom Helm, 1975), 170–209. For the *gardes mobiles* who fought on the government side, see Mark Traugott, *Armies of the Poor: Determinants of Working-class Participation in the Parisian Insurrection of June 1848* (Princeton Univ. Press, Princeton, NJ, 1985).

had disintegrated by June, and the men and women who confronted the forces of law and order on the streets of Paris from the 23rd to the 26th of that month were overwhelmingly of working-class origin. What is still more remarkable is that Baudelaire should still —or so Le Vavasseur's account suggests—have been actively engaged in fighting at the end of the insurrection on the 26th. Middle-class sympathizers may well have joined the insurgents on the 23rd or 24th when the fighting was closer to the centre of Paris and, as the insurgents were beaten back to the east, slipped away and returned relatively unscathed to their homes in the western *quartiers*. Records do show that some middle-class radicals fought on to the bitter end. Resistance in the Faubourg Saint-Antoine was organized by a *lycée* professor named Louis Lacollange, the editor of a newspaper called *L'Organisation du Travail* and president of a club of the same name; sympathetic pharmacists are known to have made gunpowder for the insurgents, and a foundry in the Faubourg Saint-Antoine was captured by a force from the Club Républicain Démocratique des Quinze-Vingts headed by a mathematics teacher named Brutinel-Nadal.[47] No doubt there were more such, but not, one suspects, that many. Baudelaire had every right, in Le Vavasseur's words, to be 'nerveux, excité, fébrile, agité'. A displaced member of the cultivated middle classes, he had just participated, on the insurgent side, in the first head-on clash in French—indeed European—history between a radicalized working-class population (whether 'traditional' or 'modern', 'artisanal' or 'proletarian', matters no more here than the precise degree or nature of its radicalism) and the newly ascendant bourgeoisie. The stepson of a career soldier who had shown 'la plus grande énergie' and 'un zèle et . . . un dévouement à toute épreuve'[48] in helping to suppress the *canut* uprising of 1834 had risked his life fighting beside their desperate brothers and sisters on the streets of Paris fourteen years later. Ten years or so further on, the horror had still not abated, though the stance adopted towards the events, ideas, and persons that produced it had undergone a decisive transformation: '(Pour la guerre civile.) Le canon tonne, les membres volent . . . des gémissements de victimes et des hurlements de sacrificateurs se font entendre . . . C'est l'Humanité qui cherche le bonheur' (OC, i. 371). The 'fusées socialistes' with which, according to Le Vavasseur,

---

[47] See Amann, *Revolution and Mass Democracy*, 311.
[48] These were the terms of Aupick's citation in 1834. See BPZ, 91.

Baudelaire had exploded in June 1848 had, by the late 1850s, been succeeded by 'fusées' of a different order: de Maistre-inspired squibs and firecrackers, sardonic, despairing, aimed at subsuming and suppressing the political in the name of an all-encompassing moral pessimism, as though, having sided unambiguously with the 'victimes' against the 'sacrificateurs' in June 1848, Baudelaire now sought to distance himself from *both* participants in the political and social blood-letting that had taken place. The transition from the 'socialism' of 1848 to the 'de Maistrianism' of the middle-to-late 1850s and beyond will receive close attention in the pages and chapters that follow, but it did not take place overnight. On the contrary, the *journées de juin* were followed by a phase of heightened rather than diminished radicalism on Baudelaire's part, though it was a radicalism of a rather different order—more pragmatic, more populist, more social, in a word, more *Proudhonian*— than the Blanquist-inspired ultra-leftism that, once the 'illusion lyrique' of February had dissipated, appears to have propelled him inexorably towards the June barricades.

June to December 1848

Citizen Proudhon

Although, he claimed, a 'républicain de la veille et de l'avant-veille, républicain de collège, d'atelier, de cabinet',[49] Proudhon had been a belated and, at best, unenthusiastic participant in the events that led to the overthrow of the July Monarchy, and stood resolutely apart from the spasm of euphoria that seized all but the most out-and-out reactionary when the Republic was proclaimed on 24 February: 'C'est une cohue d'avocats et d'écrivains, tous plus ignorants les uns que les autres, et qui vont se disputer le pouvoir. Je n'ai rien à faire là-dedans.' Lacking, in his view, substantial intellectual or ideological content ('ON A FAIT UNE RÉVOLUTION SANS IDÉE'), the new Republic constituted merely a change of political superstructure and seemed to him incapable of bringing about that revolution in the social and economic infrastructure that was his obsessive life-long concern. As 'la blagologie' burst out around him and the affairs of the political Republic generated into

[49] *Le Peuple* (19 Feb. 1849), quoted Dolléans and Puech, *Proudhon*, 15.

a 'comédie réchauffée de 93',[50] Proudhon made his decision: 'On
n'avait que faire de moi; je rentrai dans ma mansarde, et me mis à
réfléchir sur la Révolution'.[51] In late March and early April, he
published the fruit of these reflections in *Solution du problème
social* in which he gave the clearest possible formulation of his view
of the primacy of social and economic revolution over mere political
change: 'il devient évident que la réforme sociale ne sortira jamais
de la réforme politique; que c'est la réforme politique, au contraire,
qui doit sortir de la réforme sociale'.[52] This scepticism concerning
the narrowly political did not, however, prevent him from standing
unsuccessfully for election to the Constituent Assembly in April
and again, this time successfully, in the complementary elections of
early June when he enjoyed the backing of a wide range of left-wing
opinion, including, as we have seen, that of *La Tribune nationale.*
Cut off on what he strikingly called 'le Sinaï parlementaire', 'cet
isoloir qu'on appelle une Assemblée nationale', Proudhon failed
utterly, by his own admission, to foresee the tragedy shortly to be
unleashed on the streets of Paris: 'Pour moi, le souvenir des
journées de juin pèsera éternellement comme un remords sur mon
cœur. Je l'avoue avec douleur: jusqu'au 25, je n'ai rien prévu, rien
connu, rien deviné.'[53] Having, again by his own admission, been
'un imbécile' in June, Proudhon sought to make amends by refusing to succumb to the despair that gripped the Parisian left in
the aftermath of the débâcle and by placing himself at the head of
the chastened radical movement: 'Orgueil ou vertige, je crus que
mon tour était venu.'[54] Convinced that, in the present calamity, he
alone could provide the focus for 'une deutérose de l'idée révolutionnaire, une nouvelle manifestation du socialisme', he set out, in
the Assembly and above all in the pages of *Le Représentant du
Peuple*, to 'relever le moral des travailleurs, venger l'insurrection
de juin des calomnies de la réaction' and to 'poser, avec un re-
doublement d'énergie, avec une sorte de terrorisme, la question
sociale'.[55] 'Le courant réactionnaire nous portait en arrière: il
fallait déterminer un contre-courant d'idées radicales qui nous

---

[50] All quotations from Haubtmann, *Pierre-Joseph Proudhon*, 827–8.
[51] Quoted ibid. 835.
[52] Quoted ibid. 847–8.
[53] Pierre-Joseph Proudhon, *Les Confessions d'un révolutionnaire pour servir à
l'histoire de la Révolution de Février* (Marcel Rivière, 1929), 168–9.
[54] Ibid. 171.
[55] Ibid. 192.

portât en avant', but, if the radical movement was to be revived, it was essential first to create 'un parti nombreux, énergique, défini' out of the 'pluralité de sectes' which had emerged since February and, second, to 'détourner (le peuple) de l'émeute, en le faisant entrer comme acteur dans les luttes parlementaires'. Recognizing that 'en prêchant, à travers une polémique ardente, le calme et la patience, nous nous exposions à passer pour des endormeurs et des traîtres',[56] Proudhon embarked upon a series of dramatic interventions in the Constituent Assembly which brought him to the forefront of Parisian political life and, in doing so, to the attention of Baudelaire whom, in the wake of the June disaster, we may imagine crying out for precisely the kind of leadership, political realism, and, above all, inspiration that Proudhon had to offer.

He was not, of course, alone in this. Proudhon's almost superhuman stature in the aftermath of June, his virtually single-handed resuscitation of the French radical movement, was acknowledged even by his arch-rival on the left, Louis Blanc:

Après juin, Proudhon fut admirable. Les esprits honnêtes étaient atterrés; la calomnie marchait la tête haute et les pieds dans le sang; la vérité se taisait et se cachait; la République semblait n'avoir plus que la force de porter son propre deuil. Lui, avec un talent qui n'eut d'égal que son courage, il ralluma la flamme des généreux sentiments, il tint la victoire en échec, il rappela l'imposture à la pudeur, il mit son journal en travers de la réaction, à laquelle il défendit fièrement de passer outre; il fut, je le répète, admirable. Les feuilles intrépides qu'il lançait chaque matin, le Peuple se les arrachait avec une ardeur mêlée de reconnaissance, et je retrouve vivante au fond de mes souvenirs l'impression que me fit cette conduite pleine de force et d'éclat.[57]

Proudhon's campaign began in early July with a series of articles in *Le Représentant du Peuple* urging that the June insurgents (those 'consciences assombries, dont l'égarement a été déplorable mais qui après tout ne sont point criminelles'[58]) be treated with justice and compassion: 'Il n'y a point de coupables, il n'y a que des victimes'.[59] At the same time, hoping to build bridges with those radicals who, however reluctantly, had sided with the Provisional

---

[56] Ibid. 207–8.
[57] *Le Nouveau Monde* (15 Dec. 1849), quoted Haubtman, *Pierre-Joseph Proudhon*, 1051.
[58] Quoted Halévy, *Le Mariage de Proudhon*, 164.
[59] Quoted Haubtmann, *Pierre-Joseph Proudhon*, 906.

Government, Proudhon notably refused to condemn the suppression of the uprising out of hand ('Si le droit était de ce côté-ci des barricades, il était aussi de ce côté-là'[60]), but in the supercharged Manichean atmosphere of July 1848, even so cautious a relativizing of the ascription of right and wrong was too much for those in power: on 8 July *Le Représentant* was suppressed and would remain so until 7 August. In mid-July, before the Constituent Assembly's Comité des Finances, Proudhon outlined his proposals for funding his long-cherished *Banque d'échange* project by a levy on rents, interest, and other unearned income which, rightly or wrongly, was interpreted by conservative members of the committee —especially by Thiers—as amounting to an income tax. A violent confrontation ensued which was carried on to the floor of the Constituent Assembly itself on 31 July when Proudhon made the speech that, in the words of a journalist of the time which he was happy to make his own, transformed him into 'l'*homme-terreur*' of the possessing classes. Formulating his proposals in terms of what 'nous' were demanding of 'vous', Proudhon was summoned by an increasingly agitated chamber to explain exactly whom or what these pronouns designated. His reply caused a sensation: 'Lorsque j'ai employé les deux pronoms *vous* et *nous*, il est évident que, dans ce moment-là, je m'identifiais, *moi*, avec le *prolétariat*, et que je vous identifiais, *vous*, avec la *classe bourgeoise*.' Against a background of scandalized protest ('C'est la guerre sociale', 'C'est le 23 juin à la tribune'), Proudhon launched a further provocative attack on his opponents ('Le capital a peur et son instinct ne le trompe pas: le socialisme a les yeux sur lui') and was promptly condemned by 691 votes to 2, himself and a Lyonnais weaver called Greppo, for 'une atteinte odieuse aux principes de la morale publique'.[61] 'Cet interminable discours m'a donné la pépie,' he said to his associate Darimon as he and Greppo left the Palais Bourbon in disgrace, 'allons boire un bock'.[62]

After 31 July, Proudhon was, as he put it, 'prêché, joué, chansonné, placardé, biographié, caricaturé, blâmé, outragé, maudit',[63] and there is every reason to believe him when he told his friend Maguet on 16 August that 'je vis comme la salamandre, je vis dans

[60] Quoted Haubtmann, *Pierre-Joseph Proudhon*, 907.
[61] Account based on, and quotations drawn from, ibid. 909–23.
[62] Quoted in Daniel Halévy's introduction to Proudhon, *Les Confessions*, 36.
[63] Ibid. 202.

le feu. Abandonné, proscrit, exécré par tout le monde, je tiens tête à tout le monde, je mets en échec la réaction et tous les ennemis de la République'.[64] On 7 August *Le Représentant* was allowed to reappear, but a succession of fiery articles by Proudhon and others (notably the radical sculptor Antoine Étex whose work Baudelaire had reviewed—hardly enthusiastically—in the *Salon de 1845* (OC, ii. 376 and 404–5)) led it to be seized on 16, 18, and 20 August 'pour excitation à la haine d'une classe de la société'—needless to say, the property-owning class. Along with other radical newspapers, *Le Représentant* was definitely suppressed on 21 August, but not before Proudhon had delivered a dire parting warning on the direction in which France was heading as the reaction strengthened its grip on the whole of society:

Nous ne sommes pas en République: tout ceci n'est qu'un interim. LA FRANCE VEUT UN ROI: ce sera Henri V, Bonaparte ou Joinville, peu importe, pouvu que le nouvel élu jure, sur les saints Évangiles, d'exterminer les socialistes, les derniers des chrétiens.[65]

At the height of its popularity, *Le Représentant* had a circulation of between 20,000 and 25,000 and a readership of perhaps ten times that number. Not surprisingly, Baudelaire was one such reader, and on 21 August 1848, the very day *Le Représentant* was suppressed, he was sufficiently alarmed by a rumoured threat to Proudhon's security he had overhead to go to the Palais Bourbon itself to warn the representative in person. Prevented by police from entering the building, Baudelaire tried unsuccessfully to get a message to Proudhon 'par d'autres représentants que je connais un peu', whereupon he retired to a café on the corner of the Rue de Bourgogne opposite the Palais to alert Proudhon by letter. The letter begins, famously, with the words 'Un ami passionné et inconnu *veut absolument vous voir*' and shortly afterwards Baudelaire describes himself to Proudhon as 'un misérable inconnu' (C, i. 150). There are grounds for thinking, however, that Baudelaire and Proudhon may have met and even dined together before 21 August. Many years later, in February 1865, in an article entitled 'Proudhon en Belgique' published in *La Petite Revue*, Poulet-Malassis described how an unnamed 'citoyen' encountered Proudhon eating 'son déjeûner énorme et frugal' at the offices of *Le Peuple*, the

---

64 Quoted Haubtmann, *Pierre-Joseph Proudhon*, 936.
65 Quoted ibid. 947.

newspaper Proudhon would found in September 1848 to take the place of the definitely banned *Représentant du Peuple*. The point of the anecdote is Proudhon's response to the anonymous citizen's amazement at his prodigious appetite: 'Vous vous étonnez de me voir tant manger, citoyen . . .; mon appetit est en raison des grandes choses que j'ai à faire' (quoted C, ii. 902). The 'citoyen' was, of course, Baudelaire, from whom Poulet-Malassis had evidently heard the story, but, in recounting it, he made a number of errors which Baudelaire corrected in a letter to him at the beginning of March 1865. Baudelaire is categorical that the offices in question were those of *Le Représentant du Peuple* and not *Le Peuple* and that he went there one evening in search of Jules Viard, the founder and owner of *Le Représentant*, whom he knew from his days on the *Corsaire-Satan*; it is worth noting, in confirmation of Baudelaire's identification of the paper concerned, that Viard had no connection with the later *Peuple*.[66] Viard having left, Proudhon invited Baudelaire to dine with him, which they did 'chez un petit traiteur récemment installé rue Neuve-Vivienne'. Baudelaire's account continues as follows:

Proudhon jasa beaucoup, violemment, amplement, m'initiant, moi, inconnu pour lui, à ses plans et à ses projects, et lâchant involontairement, pour ainsi dire, une foule de bons mots.

J'observai que ce polémiste mangeait énormément et qu'il ne buvait presque pas, tandis que ma sobriété et ma soif contrastaient avec son appétit. 'Pour un homme de lettres, lui dis-je, vous mangez étonnamment.'

'C'est que j'ai de grandes choses à faire', me répondit-il; avec une telle simplicité que je ne pus deviner s'il parlait sérieusement ou s'il voulait bouffonner.

Je dois ajouter,—puisque vous attachez aux plus petits détails une importance souvent légitime—, que, le repas fini, quand je sonnais le garçon pour payer notre dépense commune, Proudhon s'opposa si vivement à mon intention que je le laissai tirer sa bourse, mais qu'il m'étonna un peu en ne payant que strictement son dîner.—Peut-être en inférerez-vous un goût décidé de l'égalité et un amour exagéré du droit? (C, ii. 470)

The fact that Baudelaire recalled this occasion at the very time he was writing 'Assommons les pauvres!' with its provocative final reference (in the manuscript) to Proudhon ('Qu'en dis-tu, citoyen Proudhon?') will form part of our later discussion of that text. For the moment, it is worth mentioning that when Baudelaire contacted

---

[66] See Haubtmann, *Pierre-Joseph Proudhon*, 949.

Proudhon on 21 August 1848, he cannot have been the total stranger he claimed to be; it is, needless to say, most unlikely that the visit to *Le Représentant*'s offices recorded in the 1865 letter took place on the very day of the paper's suppression. Claude Pichois dates the dinner with Proudhon 'à la fin de 1848 ou dans les premières semaines de 1849'.[67] It is much more likely, given Baudelaire's punctiliousness about the name of the paper involved, that it took place before the meeting—if meeting there was—on 21 August: a minor point, no doubt, but one which suggests that the 'admiration', 'sympathie', and 'dévouement' for Proudhon of which Baudelaire writes in his letter of that day were founded not only on a reading of *Le Représentant* and of reports of Proudhon's speeches in *Le Moniteur* but also on a brief, but memorable encounter.

Having warned Proudhon of the alleged threat to his person, Baudelaire stated that he would wait '*indéfiniment*' in the café for a reply, adding, in a telling aside on the mood current in Paris at the time, that 'le trouble qui règne dans tous les esprits appelle les explications les plus promptes entre tous les gens de cœur' (C, i. 150). It seems that Proudhon did not at first respond, prompting Baudelaire, presumably on the same day, to address a further, and still more excited and explicit, letter to him. This time he spells out the threat directly:

On nous promet des troubles. Qui les fera? nous ne le savons pas. Mais à la prochaine manifestation, même anti-populaire, c'est-à-dire au prochain prétexte,—vous pouvez être *assassiné.* . . . Vous êtes le grand bouc.— Soyez sur qu'il n'y a là-dedans aucune exagération; je ne puis pas vous donner de preuves. Si j'en avais, sans vous consulter, je les aurais envoyées à la préfecture. Mais ma conscience et mon intelligence font de moi un excellent mouchard relativement à mes convictions. Ce qui veut dire que je suis sûr de ce que j'affirme, à savoir que l'homme qui NOUS est spécialement cher court des dangers. C'est à tel point que, me rappelant différentes conversations surprises, s'il y avait une tentative, *je pourrais vous donner des noms*, tant la férocité est imprudente.

Baudelaire's use of 'NOUS'—emphatic but unspecific, as though neither he nor Proudhon had any doubts as to whom it designated —could conceivably be a reference to the 'nous' that Proudhon had used to such sensational effect on 31 August. Certainly, it is as a

---

[67] BPZ, 268. The date of the meeting between Baudelaire and Proudhon is discussed, with somewhat different conclusions from those reached here, in Haubtmann, *Pierre-Joseph Proudhon*, 949–50.

co-believer and co-actor in a shared political cause that Baudelaire goes on to address Proudhon and what he says shows that he has thoroughly absorbed Proudhon's insistence on the need, in the present critical conjuncture, to avoid needlessly provocative conflicts with the forces of law and order:

J'ai cru aujourd'hui que vous daigneriez m'honorer d'une réponse. Je n'avais d'ailleurs à vous parler que d'améliorations que je crois importantes dans votre journal, par example pour l'édition hebdomadaire, de la réimpression de la collection totale, et en second lieu, de l'opportunité qu'il y aurait à faire une immense affiche, signée de vous, d'autres représentants, et des rédacteurs de votre journal, tirée à un nombre immense d'exemplaires et COMMANDANT au peuple de ne pas bouger. Votre nom est actuellement plus connu et plus influent que vous ne le croyez. Une insurrection peut commencer par être légitimiste, elle finit par être socialiste; mais aussi la réciproque peut avoir lieu.

Celui qui vous écrit ces lignes a une absolue confiance en vous, ainsi que beaucoup de ses amis, qui marcheraient les yeux fermés derrière vous pour les garanties de savoir que vous leur avez données.

Ainsi, à la prochaine émotion, la plus insignifiante, *ne soyez pas chez vous*. Ayez, si vous le pouvez, une garde occulte ou sommez la police de vous protéger. D'ailleurs le *gouvernement accepterait volontiers peut-être un pareil cadeau* de la part des bêtes féroces de la propriété: ainsi il vaut mieux peut-être vous protéger vous-même. (C, i. 151–2)

A note attached to Baudelaire's second letter ('Salle de la rotonde/ r.p.s.v.p.') suggests that Proudhon did eventually grant Baudelaire the interview he so urgently requested. It would appear too that Proudhon took Baudelaire's warning seriously, writing to his friend Pauthier on 24 August, 'Puis-je au besoin me réfugier chez vous?' It is symptomatic of the increasingly terroristic atmosphere of the summer of 1848 that Proudhon should have requested that Pauthier should address his reply pseudonymously to 'M. Gauthier, rue Mazarine, 70'.[68]

L'Ère du Soupçon

By the end of August when Baudelaire contacted Proudhon, to speak or to write in a manner even remotely critical of the Provisional Government, its supporters, and their values or ideology was

---

[68] See Haubtmann, *Pierre-Joseph Proudhon*, 947.

most emphatically dangerous. Having suppressed the June uprising and murdered, imprisoned, or banished thousands of the participants, the Government, headed now by General Cavaignac, proceeded to arm itself with hugely increased legal powers designed to quell that freedom of the word to which February had so egregiously given birth. A law of 28 July severely curbed freedom of expression in the clubs while stopping short of banning clubs as such. All meetings, public and private, became subject to police authorization and control; amongst other measures, it is interesting to note that women were henceforth prohibited from attending political meetings. The Draconian press laws of 9–11 August which we have already seen in operation against *Le Représentant du Peuple* effectively restored the publishing controls that had existed under the July Monarchy. Parisian daily papers had in future to pay caution money of 24,000 francs, a measure which caused numerous publications to close, most famously Lamennais' *Le Peuple constituant* which bade farewell to its readers with the all too pertinent headline *Silence au pauvre*. Finally, a revised seditious libel act of 13 August made it an offence to criticize the Republic, Provisional Government and Assembly or in any way to question the principles of private property and what were termed 'the rights of the family'.[69] For those on the left in France, the word was under threat and had to be used and protected accordingly.

In the circumstances, therefore, the sense of persecution and danger, and of the corresponding need for secrecy and conspiratorial solidarity with fellow believers that emerges from Baudelaire's letters to Proudhon is entirely justified and would recur as themes in his subsequent writing during and about the Second Republic. Born in part of Baudelaire's experience of the Second Republic in its counter-revolutionary phase, the theme of the conspiracy[70] surfaces in at least two projected short stories of the late 1850s or early 1860s and, most notably, in 'Une mort héroïque' where, it will be recalled, Fancioulle joins 'une conspiration formée par quelques gentilshommes mécontents' (OC, i. 319), the discovery of which ultimately brings about the Fool's death at the behest of his

---

[69] Account based on Thomas R. Forstenzer, *French Provincial Police and the Fall of the Second Republic: Social Fear and Counterrevolution* (Princeton Univ. Press, Princeton, NJ, 1981), 51–3.

[70] On the theme of conspiracy in Baudelaire's writing, see Pierre Pachet, *Le Premier Venu: Essai sur la politique baudelairienne* (Denoël, 1976), 47–55.

curiously sympathetic Prince-patron: one might envisage an interpretation of this text as, in part, an ironic (because partially
reversed) re-enactment in courtly dress of the relationship between
People and Prince between Louis Napoleon's return to France in
the summer of 1848 and his eventual apotheosis, after, precisely,
the *conspiracy* of December 1851, as Emperor Napoleon III in
December 1852. The theme of conspiracy is inseparable from that
of betrayal which, most unexpectedly, we find mentioned, apparently referring to the events of 1848, in 'Mademoiselle Bistouri'
in which the eponymous madwoman's gallery of famous doctors
includes a portrait of one who, during 'le temps des émeutes',
'denonçait au gouvernement les insurgés qu'il soignait à son
hôpital' (OC, i. 354). Betrayal in its turn leads to *self*-betrayal and
self-denunciation. The murderous anti-hero of the projected play
L'Ivrogne (1854) which, as we shall see, is replete with Baudelaire's
preoccupations of the Second Republic, denounces himself 'avec
une volubilité, une ardeur, une emphase extraordinaire, avec une
minutie extrême,—très vite, très vite, comme s'il craignait de
n'avoir pas le temps d'achever' (OC, i. 634), even as Baudelaire
would himself gratuitously reveal through disingenuous footnotes
the true significance of two of his most heavily encoded poems
'Le Reniement de saint Pierre' and 'A celle qui est trop gaie'. More
generally, the repressive and suspicious climate of the post-June
Republic—prolonged, in exacerbated form, into the early years of
the Second Empire—would impose severe constraints on what and
how Baudelaire could write and where he could publish what he
had written. Thus we find him resorting to obscure or improbable
trade or special-interest publications such as *L'Écho des marchands
de vin*, *Le Magasin des familles*, and *Jean Raisin, Revue joyeuse et
vinicole* as outlets for his writings: an author who, in December
1849, was reduced to publishing—or saying he would publish since,
almost invariably, the text announced never appeared—'Les Derniers
Buveurs' in *La Veillée pittoresque, Musée encyclopedique illustré*
was in desperate straits indeed.[71] More to the point, Baudelaire
was, as ensuing chapters will try to demonstrate, constrained to
write in what amounts to code in order to convey radical political
meanings in a repressively reactionary context. As we shall see, the
salient characteristic of each of the principal poems we shall discuss
—'L'Âme du vin', 'Le Vin des chiffonniers', 'Châtiment de

[71] On 'Les Derniers Buveurs', see BPZ, 272.

l'orgueil', 'Spleen' ('Pluviôse . . .'), and 'Le Reniement de saint Pierre'—is that it does not immediately or easily yield its meaning, depending rather on the reader's capacity to perceive, interpret, and respond to images whose true significance was hidden not from the *profanum vulgus*—they, one would like to think, would have understood Baudelaire only too clearly, *had they but read him*— but from those who detested and feared 'le peuple' and all it stood for. To the 'bêtes féroces de la propriété', a glass of wine was a glass of wine; to those in the know, as we shall see later, it was nothing less than *la République démocratique et sociale* itself.

The Manifeste du Peuple

For the moment, though, some measure of freedom still existed and on 2 September Proudhon launched a new paper, *Le Peuple: Journal de la République démocratique et sociale*, bearing the provocatively unambiguous masthead: 'Qu'est-ce que le producteur? Rien. Que doit-il être? Tout. Qu'est-ce que le capitaliste? Tout. Que doit-il être? Rien.'[72] The specimen number of 2 September consisted of an unsigned manifesto addressed to 'Patriotes' of all political hues; we may be sure that, having just entered into relations with Proudhon, Baudelaire would not have failed to read it and that, when the paper proper began publication on 1 November (it became a daily after 23 November), he would have followed it whenever possible right up to its final suppression on 13 June 1849. The manifesto began with a grim survey of the political situation in France now that the repressions of June, July, and August had all but destroyed the radical hopes awakened in February and March, leaving, according to Proudhon, only one course open to radicals:

Le succès de la contre-révolution nous a rejetés sur la défensive: c'est la défense qu'il s'agit en ce moment d'organiser, en attendant que nous puissions organiser la victoire. Et c'est comme gage de bataille que nous venons demander à votre patriotisme un dernier effort, l'acte de vertu suprême du chrétien et du citoyen, la PATIENCE!

The political orientation of the new journal is then spelt out unequivocally:

72 Quoted Haubtmann, *Pierre-Joseph Proudhon*, 950.

Nous ne sommes d'aucune secte, d'aucune école: nous ne jurons par l'autorité de personne. Nous sommes du peuple. . . .
Le peuple a nommé la *République démocratique et sociale*: Nous sommes de la République démocratique et sociale.
Nous avons, comme le peuple, pour principe la *liberté*, pour moyen l'*égalité*, pour but la *fraternité*.
La liberté, c'est-à-dire l'âme, la vie, le mouvement, la spontanéité, progressive dans son développement, infinie, absolue dans son essence et son idéal;
L'égalité, progressive et absolue;
La fraternité, progressive et absolue.

Toute notre science', the manifesto continues, 'consiste à épier les manifestations du peuple, à solliciter sa parole, à interpréter ses actes. Interroger le peuple, c'est pour nous toute la philosophie, toute la politique.' In order to counter reactionary opponents for whom socialism is by definition antagonistic to the principles of marriage, property, and religion, Proudhon goes on to give a resolute defence of each from a socialist standpoint and, having vindicated work 'comme droit et comme devoir', then defends the socialist legitimacy of ownership in the sense of 'la libre disposition pour chacun des fruits de son travail, de son industrie et de son intelligence'. If usury and other forms of unearned income are condemned, it is precisely because they constitute an 'obstacle au développement de la production, à l'accroissement et à l'universalisation de la propriété'. Let no radical, then, says Proudhon, preach 'la confiscation et le vol': 'Nul n'est plus ennemi du vol que celui qui travaille'. There follows a defence of the right to inheritance of goods (though not of privileges and titles), whereafter Proudhon—whose other notorious statement, to be discussed later, was, of course, 'Dieu, c'est le mal'—resonantly affirms the validity of religion which, he declares, is 'dans notre incomparable pays le ferment de tout ce qui a vie, autorité et durée'. Atheism and materialism are vigorously condemned, and Proudhon, in a manner wholly characteristic, as we shall see, of the humanist, naturalist, and republican interpretation of Christianity current on the French left in the 1830s and 1840s, explains that, for him, true religion means 'le surnaturalisme dans la nature, le ciel dans la société, Dieu dans l'homme': 'C'est quand la civilisation nous apparaîtra comme une perpétuelle apocalypse, et l'histoire comme un miracle sans fin; quand, par la réforme de la société, le christianisme aura été élevé à sa deuxième puissance, que nous connaîtrons la religion'. There follows a telling opposition of two models of government and society, the hierarchical-aristocratic-monarchical and the republican-democratic-egalitarian:

Nous voulons comme forme de gouvernement et de société la République. Nous sommes les irréconciliables ennemis de la royauté, de tout ce qui y touche, de tout ce qui y ressemble. . . . La République est l'égalité coordonnée des fonctions et des personnes: la royauté n'en est que la hiérarchie et la subalternisation. . . .

La République est, comme la religion, essentiellement expansive et universelle, embrassant le monde et l'éternité.—La royauté, toujours personnelle, locale, stationnaire, vivant chez soi et pour soi, la royauté est l'ennemie du genre humain et du progrès.

The manifesto concludes with a renewed exhortation to patience and self-discipline on the part of radicals:

Gardez-vous de céder aux perfides instigations de ceux qui vous poussent à la révolte et à la guerre civile: la guerre civile est le seul moyen de succès qu'ait en ce moment la royauté. Les choses, par la combinaison providentielle des événements, sont arrivées à ce point, que si le peuple reste quelque temps immobile, la royauté, avec son infernal cortège, est perdue à jamais.

Patience donc, citoyens; aucune vérité sur les hommes et sur les choses ne vous sera par nous dissimulée, aucune résolution timide suggérée. Mais, encore une fois, patience! c'est tout l'avenir du peuple, et le salut de la République.[73]

It would, of course, be excessive to claim that Proudhon's manifesto provided Baudelaire with a political and social programme for the months and years that followed. None the less, as we shall see in detail as we proceed, each of the 'planks' in Proudhon's platform finds significant expression and endorsement in his writings of the Second Republic period. The conviction that 'l'homme de labeur est aussi, et par excellence, l'homme d'amour' is fundamental to such texts as 'Du vin et du haschisch' (1851) and 'Pierre Dupont' (1851); at no other time in Baudelaire's career, one might add, is the family or marriage (the 'marriage of true minds' —his and Jeanne's—rather than the formal bourgeois marriage) viewed as positively as between 1848 and 1852. Future chapters will show the centrality of work to Baudelaire's republican world-view,

---

[73] All quotations are from Proudhon, *Les Confessions*, 392–8.

and there is no evidence that at any time before, during, or after the Second Republic he challenged the principle of individual property *as such*; his later condemnations of usury and commerce ('Le commerce est *naturel, donc* il est *infâme*', 'Le commerce est, par son essence, *satanique*', *Mon cœur mis à nu* (OC, i. 703)), commonly ascribed to his reading of de Maistre, have their roots in his Proudhonian (and indeed Fourierist) convictions of the 1840s. The view of Christianity outlined in the manifesto is Proudhon's version of the republican-socialist Christianity so widespread in 1848 and, as such, consistent with the conception of Christianity that underpins and gives meaning to such important texts as 'L'Âme du vin' and 'Le Reniement de saint Pierre'. Finally, although the later Baudelaire would hold that 'il n'y a de gouvernement raisonnable et assuré que l'aristocratique' (*Mon cœur mis à nu* (OC, i. 684)), what animates all his writing between February 1848 and the end of 1851 is, to use an expression he himself uses of Pierre Dupont, 'le goût infini de la République' (OC, ii. 33). To the extent that it makes significant concessions to the principle of private property, Proudhon's manifesto might be described as embodying a 'socialisme mitigé', the term by which Baudelaire would himself qualify one of his most characteristic Second Republic texts, 'La Rançon' (1851?), quoted here complete with the final stanza that was omitted, presumably for reasons of political prudence, on its first publication in *Le Présent* in November 1857:

L'homme a, pour payer sa rançon,
Deux champs au tuf profond et riche,
Qu'il faut qu'il remue et défriche
Avec le fer de la raison;

Pour obtenir la moindre rose,
Pour extorquer quelques épis,
Des pleurs salés de son front gris
Sans cesse il faut qu'il les arrose.

L'un est l'Art, et l'autre l'Amour.
—Pour rendre le juge propice,
Lorsque de la stricte justice
Paraîtra le terrible jour,

Il faudra lui montrer des granges
Pleines de moissons, et des fleurs
Dont les formes et les couleurs
Gagnent le suffrage des Anges.

Mais pour que rien ne soit jeté,
Qui serve à payer l'esclavage,
Elles grossiront l'apanage
De la commune liberté.

It was with convictions close to these and to those elaborated in
Proudhon's manifesto that we may imagine Baudelaire embarking
on the next bizarre stage of his republican Odyssey which would
take him out of Paris to, improbably, Châteauroux in the department of the Indre, in the first of two excursions into provincial
France which are essential to an understanding of his evolving
political position under the Second Republic.

Provincial Interlude (I): Châteauroux

Some time in late September or early October 1848, Baudelaire was
offered the post of *rédacteur en chef* of a newspaper that was about
to appear in Châteauroux: *Le Représentant de l'Indre,* bearing the
(for Baudelaire) discouraging subtitle *Journal des principes d'ordre
et de conservation.* The prefect of the Indre was informed of the
intention to publish on 19 October; caution money of 1,800 francs
was duly paid, and the first number of the newspaper appeared on
the following day carrying an article entitled 'Actuellement' which
Mouquet and Bandy claim is 'incontestablement de Baudelaire'.[74]
Baudelaire appears to have owed his post to the initiative of Arthur
Ponroy, like Viard a contact from his *Corsaire-Satan* days.
Ponroy's father, Jean-Sylvain Ponroy, was a lawyer from Issoudun
who presumably belonged to the consortium of conservatives—'les
réactionnaires de Chateauroux', according to Maxime Rude, one
of two sources we have for Baudelaire's brief stay in the town—
who provided the paper with its financial backing and were to determine its political orientation; presumably again it was financial
need, combined with the difficulty of finding journalistic employment in the straitened Parisian situation, that prompted Baudelaire
to accept a post which could, at best, be uncongenial to him.
Exactly when Baudelaire left for Châteauroux cannot be determined. If 'Actuellement' is indeed by him, he must have been there

---

[74] Mouquet and Bandy, *Baudelaire en 1848,* 51. The present account of
Baudelaire's stay at Châteauroux is based on this work (esp. pp. 48–50) and on
BPZ, 268–71. All quotations are from these two sources.

by 15 October at the latest, since another article in the first number of *Le Représentant de l'Indre*, 'Le Nouveau Ministère', is dated 'Châteauroux, 15 octobre 1848' and is without doubt by the writer responsible for 'Actuellement'. On 19 October Baudelaire wrote to another acquaintance of the early 1840s, Philippe de Chennevières (whom we have already encountered at the Palais-Royal on 26 June) asking him to send *'immédiatement* à Mlle Jeanne Lemer la totalité de vos œuvres. J'ai besoin de trois feuilletons; je vous reproduirai tout entier' (C, i. 152). The letter gives no indication of Baudelaire's whereabouts at the time, but the instruction to de Chennevières to send his work—the first number of *Le Représentant* announced that the paper would soon publish regularly 'un feuilleton pris dans les échantillons de la meilleure littérature'—to Jeanne's address in Paris suggests that he was already in Châteauroux where his mistress was to join him shortly.

According to Firmin Boissin, relaying (in *Le Figaro* in January 1887) the account given him many years earlier by Arthur Ponroy, on his arrival in Châteauroux Baudelaire was entertained to dinner by the principal shareholders of *Le Représentant*—'de riches et bons bourgeois, un peu prudhommesques', says Boissin—in the course of which Baudelaire reputedly 'ne desserra pas les dents'. An alternative account—that given in Maxime Rude's *Confessions d'un journaliste* (1876)—claims that Baudelaire arrived in Châteauroux sporting 'longs cheveux' and a 'cravate de foulard rouge', both indubitable signs, in the political semiology of the Second Republic to which we shall shortly return, of radical republican-socialist convictions. In the course of the dinner of welcome, Baudelaire was regaled by his employers with 'les considérations les plus anti-révolutionnaires' to which, invited to give a speech in reply, he responded, 'les lèvres serrées et sifflantes', as follows: 'Messieurs, dans cette Révolution dont on vient de parler, il y a un grand homme,—le plus grand de cette époque,—un des plus grands hommes de tous les temps: cet homme, c'est Robespierre.' In Boissin's version of events, two days after his arrival in Châteauroux, Baudelaire published an article in *Le Représentant* commending 'Marat, cet homme doux, et Robespierre, cet homme propre' for seeking to institute the Terror and the guillotine 'en permanence'. No such article has been discovered, but it is clear that at some point during his stay in Châteauroux, Baudelaire spoke or wrote in real or mock praise of Robespierre, Jacobinism, and the Terror. To do so in the context of the post-June repression was, to say the least, dangerous, for, as John M. Merriman has written, the new law on seditious libel meant that 'references to 1793 or to Robespierre could either fall under the legal statutes forbidding "inciting hatred" or be considered a public "apology for acts previously declared to be criminal" '.[75] The scandalized and incensed reaction of his employers is hardly to be wondered at.

How seriously should we take Baudelaire's apparent enthusiasm for Robespierre?[76] He had clearly read Robespierre extensively as an adolescent and young man and more than once commends his literary or oratorical style ('son style de glace ardente, recuit et congelé comme l'abstraction' (OC, i. 455), 'ce style sentencieux dont ma jeunesse s'est enivrée' (OC, i. 592)). On a number of occasions he quotes—with varying degrees of accuracy—from his speeches (particularly the terrifying speech of 11 Germinal An II in which Robespierre declared that 'quiconque tremble en ce moment est coupable, car jamais l'innocence ne redoute la surveillance publique'; Baudelaire relays this in edulcorated form as 'ceux qui tremblent se sentent coupables' (OC, ii. 223)); he appears, moreover, to have possessed a medallion depicting the great revolutionary (see C, ii. 431). But at no time in his life does Baudelaire's admiration for 'ce fou de Robespierre' (OC, ii. 223) seem to have gone beyond admiration for his style as man and, above all, as speaker and writer: 'Robespierre n'est estimable que parce qu'il a fait quelques belles phrases' (*Mon cœur mis à nu* (OC, i. 680)). He may not have had Proudhon's contempt for Robespierre and for the whole Jacobin-inspired tradition of revolutionary centralism, but it would seem that his Jacobinism of October 1848 is best put down as a classic case of bourgeois-baiting. To provoke M. Prudhomme —in person rather than in writing—in Châteauroux in October 1848 was a different matter, though, from addressing cleverly ambivalent prefaces to him in Paris in 1846. Baudelaire's 'Robespierrism', like his long hair and red necktie, may, in the context of place and period, be interpreted as a significant—because highly risky—political gesture.

[75] John M. Merriman, *The Agony of the Republic: The Repression of the Left in Revolutionary France 1848–1851* (Yale Univ. Press, New Haven, Conn., and London, 1978), 32.

[76] On Baudelaire and Robespierre, see Nicole Ward Jouve, *Baudelaire: A Fire to Conquer Darkness* (Macmillan, 1980), 28.

The content of 'Actuellement' will be discussed in our chapter on 'Châtiment de l'orgueil', the idea for which, it will be argued, came to Baudelaire shortly before, during, or shortly after his stay in Châteauroux. Mouquet's and Bandy's attribution of the article in question to Baudelaire (which, with some misgivings, I share) raises problems concerning the companion-article 'Le Nouveau Ministère' which is definitely by the same author. 'Actuellement', as we shall see, is broadly concordant with the Proudhonian position of July–December 1848 as elaborated in the manifesto of *Le Peuple*. To the extent, however, that it approves of the ministerial reshuffle of 15 October that for the first time admitted known anti-Republicans like Dufaure and Vivien into the Provisional Government, 'Le Nouveau Ministère' implies a political viewpoint considerably to the right of what I believe to have been Baudelaire's at the time.[77] On the other hand, the hostility manifested in the article towards the Montagnards can readily be squared with Proudhon's hearty contempt at the time—he would change his tune in 1849—for those he would drawlingly refer to as 'mêssieûrs les jâcôbîns':[78] Ledru-Rollin, Blanc, Délescluze, and their *démoc-soc* associates. Perhaps Baudelaire was simply mistaken as to the significance of the reshuffle; perhaps, again, 'Le Nouveau Ministère' is an exercise in journalistic chameleonism designed to satirize through mimicry his employers' political opinions; perhaps, of course, neither 'Actuellement' nor 'Le Nouveau Ministère' is by Baudelaire. The problem remains.

The Présidentielles

Baudelaire returned to Paris sometime between 20 and 31 October, his departure precipitated, according to Boissin, by the discovery made by the chairman of *Le Représentant*'s board of directors, 'un notaire qui avait lu Casimir Delavigne', that the woman with whom his *rédacteur en chef* was openly living was not his lawfully wedded wife, as Baudelaire had made out, but rather his 'favorite'; Baudelaire allegedly retorted that 'la "favorite" d'un poète peut quelquefois valoir la femme d'un notaire' and, according to Boissin, left

---

[77] 'Le Nouveau Ministère' is reproduced in Mouquet and Bandy, *Baudelaire en 1848*, 66–9.
[78] Quoted Haubtmann, *Pierre-Joseph Proudhon*, 951.

for Paris 'le soir même'.[79] It had, as Baudelaire told his mother in early December, been a thoroughly pointless excursion ('une expédition qui ne m'a rien rapporté' (C, i. 153)), though what happened there would have shown him how, with the presidential elections looming, conservative opinion was becoming increasingly mobilized and aggressive and how, as the counter-revolution gathered momentum, any infraction of the bourgeois consensus— be it speaking out in praise of Robespierre, living openly with a woman to whom one was not married, or even flaunting long hair and a red necktie—could bring dire penalties. The conservative reaction was taking on an increasingly monolithic character: opposition to any part of its ideology or practice more and more meant opposition to the whole.

It is all the more significant, therefore, that, on returning to Paris, Baudelaire should have aligned himself publicly with a radical—or at least anti-government—association and its short-lived journal. The association in question is the *Comité central des boissons* and the journal *L'Écho des marchands de vin, des vignerons et des ouvriers*.[80] It was almost certainly through Pierre Dupont (whose song 'Ma vigne' appeared in the specimen number of the journal on 18 October) that Baudelaire came into contact with *L'Écho*, whose principal objective was the repeal of the taxes on wine that, in the Republic's radical springtime, the Provisional Government had removed on 31 March 1848 only to reimpose them on the eve of the *journées de juin* (22 June 1848). A discussion of the political significance of wine as reality and symbol under the Second Republic must await a later chapter; the dates of the repeal and reimposition of the hated taxes will already have indicated the centrality of the issue to the conflicts of the time. The *Comité des boissons* organized a banquet at the Barrière du Roule on 24 November which was attended by Ledru-Rollin, a sure sign of the association's political orientation and of the radical implications of the proposed abolition of the wine tax; it is, of course, tempting to think that Baudelaire was also present. On 30 November, the second number of *L'Écho* announced the forthcoming publication by Michel Lévy of 'LES LIMBES. Poésies, par Charles Baudelaire.

---

[79] Quoted BPZ, 269.
[80] The following account is based on Jean Ziegler, '"Le Vin de l'assassin": 1848?' in *Du romantisme au surnaturalisme: Hommage à Claude Pichois* (La Baconnière, Neuchâtel, 1985), 189–97.

Ce livre paraîtra, à Paris et à Leipzig, le 24 février 1849'.[81] It was the belief of some nineteenth-century bibliographers that *L'Écho* had, in the same or a later number, published 'Le Vin de l'assassin', one of Baudelaire's most important 'Second Republic' texts to which we shall return later; the researches of Jean Ziegler, however, have shown that any such publication in 1848, at least in *L'Écho*, did not occur. None the less, Baudelaire had announced his intention to publish a collection of poems bearing a title which, as we have seen, seems to have had an unmistakably 'socialist' (*tendance Fourier*) ring to it in a journal that was publicly identified with the radical cause. In the climate of late 1848, with elections approaching and the party of order increasingly mobilized and vigilant, it was inevitable that a book so entitled and advertised would attract attention and so, in the December number of the *Bulletin de censure* (forbiddingly subtitled 'Revue indispensable comme avertissement aux familles contre les erreurs de l'époque'), it duly did.

The *Bulletin*'s notice, by Jean Wallon, was terse, sarcastic, and politically loaded, with even the book's proposed date of publication (the anniversary of the Republic's proclamation) marking the author out as a dangerous radical:

Charles Baudelaire ou Baudelaire du Fays, ou Pierre Defays, a fait deux volumes de critique sur les salons de 1845 et 1846, une nouvelle, *la Fanfarlo*, beaucoup de vers et quelquefois de beaux vers; aujourd'hui nous voyons annonce, dans *l'Écho des Marchands de vins: les Limbes*, pour paraître le 24 février à Paris et à Leipsick. Encore un devenu disciple de Proudhon par *trop ou trop peu* d'ignorance.

Wallon, whom Baudelaire had known well since his Île Saint-Louis days and with whom he would remain on surprisingly good terms, was, according to Gustave Lefrançais, actively associated with the so-called 'groupe de la rue de Poitiers', in Lefrançais's words 'un vrai bouquet de réactionnaires de toutes nuances' including Thiers, Barrot, Falloux, Faucher, Changarnier, and Montalambert, which, in the aftermath of June, was the principal focus of anti-socialist (and, increasingly, anti-republican) opinion and propaganda in France; Wallon, according to Lefrançais, was responsible for organizing the publication of 'des brochures à l'usage des *bons* ouvriers des villes et des campagnes, pour combattre les pernicieux effets de la propagande socialiste et les maintenir dans le pieux respect d'une saine morale et de la propriété . . . surtout'. Preceded by attacks on Nadar ('le voilà socialiste, démocrate rouge'), Pierre Dupont ('le chanteur officiel des banquets révolutionnaires') and another acquaintance of Baudelaire, Jules de la Madelène ('il s'est jeté à tête perdue dans le socialisme'),[82] the denunciation of Baudelaire was entirely predictable but no less invidious for that: to be labelled a 'disciple de Proudhon' by a right-wing hatchet-man in December 1848 was to be marked out publicly not only as an object of vilification but, if the political climate heated up still further, as a potential candidate for repression.

We do not know how, or even if, Baudelaire voted in the presidential elections of 10 December 1848 which swept Louis Napoleon to such a crushing victory over his various opponents; if Baudelaire voted at all (and there is evidence, noted above, that he was a long-term abstainer), he may have followed Proudhon in favouring Raspail (37,000 votes in all) whom he is known to have admired. The only indication of Baudelaire's attitude to the election comes from a comment in *Quelques caricaturistes français* on the poor quality of 'tous les plaidoyers politiques étalés aux carreaux lors de la grande élection présidentielle' which, he says, 'n'offraient que des choses pâles' in comparison to 'le temps des grandes fureurs politiques', namely the heyday of Daumier and *Le Charivari* between 1830 and 1834 (C, ii. 551). In the long letter he wrote to his mother in Constantinople of 8 December, he does not even mention the election to be held two days later, a sign, perhaps, of the small importance which, as a 'disciple de Proudhon', he attached to the processes of mere 'politics'. He does, however, mention his fear of an imminent 'mouvement insurrectionnel' (a fear consistent, as we have seen, with a broadly Proudhonian position), not least because 'rien n'est plus déplorable que d'être absolument privé d'argent dans ces moments-là'.

Financial matters were, inevitably, much on Baudelaire's mind as 1848 drew to a close, especially since the disruption of publishing and the restrictions on journalism limited his chances of supplementing his income from the *conseil judiciaire*; literature, he comments in his letter to his mother, was 'moins en faveur que

---

[82] All quotations from Ziegler, ' "Le Vin de l'assassin": 1848?', 193–4.

jamais'. None the less, it is clear from the letter that, at the year's end, Baudelaire's thoughts were moving back to—if they had ever abandoned—his career, or rather his 'destinée', *as a writer*. If he needs money so urgently, it is, he tells his mother, in order to 'accomplir plusieurs projets que j'ai à cœur depuis longtemps, entre autres de retirer mes pauvres chers manuscrits qui sont éternellement engagés; pourvu qu'ils existent encore!' There can be little doubt, as we shall see shortly, that the manuscripts concerned included some at least of the poems destined for *Les Limbes* which would ultimately form the core of the first edition of *Les Fleurs du mal*. As well as reaffirming his literary ambitions, Baudelaire makes his general moral and ideological position abundantly clear to his mother when, referring to his 'duty' to remain with Jeanne whom Mme Aupick wishes him to drop, he writes:

Mais pourtant j'en reviens à ceci, et je me crois obligé de vous donner ces explications: actuellement à vingt-huit ans moins quatre mois, avec une immense ambition poétique moi séparé à tout jamais du *monde honorable* par mes goûts et par mes principes, qu'importe si bâtissant mes rêves littéraires, j'accomplis de plus *un devoir*, ou ce que je crois un devoir au grand détriment des idées vulgaires d'honneur, d'argent, de fortune?

As at Châteauroux, Baudelaire is clearly placing his relationship with Jeanne—whether it be based on 'duty' or whatever—above all considerations of money, respectability, and social or religious legitimacy. At the end of 1848, Baudelaire strikes us as never before as a man whose mind is made up, whose sense of vocation is clear, and who, in terms of moral, social, and political values, knows precisely where he stands. In January 1848 he for the first time appeared publicly as 'Charles Baudelaire'. By the year's end he had completed the process of self-definition over and against his mother and stepfather, and it is, indeed, with a scarcely disguised attack on the latter's supposed opportunism and readiness to trim to the prevailing political wind that the letter concludes: 'Des gouvernements nouveaux ne vous déplaceront sans doute pas'. Yet, as this barbed sentence reveals, Baudelaire was, on the eve of Louis Napoleon's election, anticipating major political changes—changes, from his point of view, decidedly for the worse—and he signed off by telling his mother that 'peut-être dans un an, si je suis plus riche, irai-je à Constantinople, car ma rage de voyages me reprend perpétuellement' (C, i. 153–5). The seeds of the later 'depoliticized'

Baudelaire are dimly present in the subtext of the letter of December 1848. Money permitting, it might well have been Baudelaire, as well as Flaubert and Du Camp, who embarked on a *voyage en orient* in the wake of the collapse of the republican cause in 1849–50.

4

Street-fighting Years (II): Baudelaire and the Second Republic, 1849–1852

The 'Missing Years', 1849–1850

Delacroix's Visitor

Whatever advance signs we may discern in the letter of December 1848 of Baudelaire's eventual 'depoliticization', there can be no doubt, Louis Napoleon's massive victory notwithstanding, as to the continuing intensity of his radical beliefs in early 1849. We know this thanks to an entry which, thus earning the everlasting gratitude of Baudelaire scholars, Delacroix made in his diary on 5 February that year:

> M. Baudelaire venu comme je me mettais à reprendre une petite figure de femme à l'orientale, couchée sur un sofa, entreprise pour Thomas, de la rue du Bac. Il m'a parlé des difficultés qu'éprouve Daumier à finir. Il a sauté à Proudhon qu'il admire et qu'il dit l'idole du peuple. Ses vues me paraissent des plus modernes et tout à fait dans le progrès.[1]

To admire Proudhon in early 1849 was to align oneself with the remarkable series of attacks on Louis Napoleon launched in the pages of *Le Peuple* in January; to recognize further that he was 'l'idole du peuple' as 1849 began—as indeed he was—showed no little insight into the continuing strength, despite the débâcle of June and subsequent setbacks, of radical republicanism amongst the Parisian working classes. In an article entitled 'La Guerre' published in *Le Peuple* on 26 January 1849, Proudhon spelt out his view of the political situation with the utmost clarity. With the newly elected President already taking steps to limit the powers

---

[1] Eugène Delacroix, *Journal*, ed. André Joubin (Plon, 1960), i. 258.

of the Constituent Assembly, a critical turning-point had been reached with, as Maurice Agulhon has written, the anti-*socialist* reaction of June–December 1848 being transformed inexorably if at first imperceptibly into the anti-*republican* reaction that would dominate the political history of the next three years. 'La lutte est donc entre l'Assemblée et L. Bonaparte', Proudhon proclaimed,

entre l'Assemblée qui a salué la Révolution, qui a fondé la République démocratique, et posé dans l'article 13 de la Constitution, la pierre d'attente du socialisme, l'Assemblée qui veut le maintien de son ouvrage, et refuse de faire un seul pas rétrograde; et L. Bonaparte, incapacité de naissance, ambition de bas étage, personnification de toutes les idées réactionnaircs, qui, coupable envers la France du plus grand des attentats, amnistié par le vote qui l'a fait représentant, élu sans titre à la présidence de la République, conspire aujourd'hui avec toutes les coteries monarchiques, avec les jésuites, les absolutistes, l'esclavage du Peuple et le retour de tous les abus!

The following day, in a further article entitled 'Le Président de la République est responsable', Proudhon, after explaining that 'toutes les forces, toutes les idées, toutes les espérances de la Révolution sont aujourd'hui concentrées dans l'Assemblée nationale' just as surely as 'toutes les forces, toutes les idées, toutes les espérances de la Contre-Révolution sont réunies sur la tête de L. Bonaparte', drew the following dramatic conclusion:

Bonaparte, élu de la réaction, instrument de la réaction, personnification de la réaction, Bonaparte est en ce moment toute la réaction; à tel point que quiconque fait de l'opposition à Bonaparte est indubitablement révolutionnaire; et que, Bonaparte tombé, toute la conspiration doctrinaire, légitimiste, orléaniste, impérialiste, capitaliste et jésuite s'écroule avec lui.

Fears of arrest and prosecution did not deter Proudhon from launching a further attack on 31 January on 'le Picrochole de Strasbourg, le César de Boulogne, le socialiste de Ham, *le bâtard du suffrage universel*'[2] following the President's deployment of troops in Paris two days earlier, ostensibly in order to quell a threatened insurrection, in fact—or so Proudhon argued—to place further pressure on the Assembly to agree to the constitutional changes he sought. For the articles of 26 and 27 January, Proudhon would, in March 1849, be sentenced to three years' imprisonment.

---

[2] All quotations taken from Pierre Haubtmann, *Pierre-Joseph Proudhon: Sa vie et sa pensée (1809–1849)* (Desclée de Brouwer, Bruges, 1988), 1026–32.

Given these circumstances, the significance of Baudelaire's continuing enthusiasm for Proudhon can hardly be doubted: 'tout à fait dans le progrès' in Delacroix's terms, he remained, if we accept Proudhon's assessment of the situation, 'indubitablement révolutionnaire'.

1849

It is at this point that things become decidedly obscure. From 5 February 1849 to the middle of December that year, Baudelaire effectively disappears from view and the evidence at our disposal becomes fragmentary in the extreme. It is known that on 12 May Baudelaire copied out a letter for Courbet (imitating his signature) to the Duc de Luynes, president of a committee about to select paintings for a lottery intended to help artists impoverished by the Revolution and the consequent disruption of the Parisian art-world (see C, i. 787–8). The letter is addressed 30 rue Hautefeuille (the street on which, at No. 13, Baudelaire had been born), but this is evidently Courbet's home, not his; it is not, unfortunately, known where Baudelaire lived in Paris between August 1848 (when he was at 18 avenue de Neuilly, the present avenue Charles de Gaulle) and May 1850 (when he returned to the Avenue to live at No. 95). At the end of June, we have what is probably further evidence of Baudelaire's difficulty in finding outlets for his writings under the Second Republic when, on four successive days (27–30 June), *La Constitution, Journal du département du Loiret*, of which Baudelaire's friend Charles Barbara was *rédacteur en second*, announced that it would (re)publish *La Fanfarlo*; needless to say, the publication never occurred (see OC, i. 1416–17). On 13 July there is a tantalizing letter to an unknown addressee recommending to him a 'M. *Schoman*, musicien de grand talent, qui dut quitter Dresde, à la suite des journées révolutionnaires'. The mysterious 'Schoman' is said to want to publish a study on *Tannhäuser*, and the letter goes on to speak of 'notre commune admiration pour *Wagner*', suggesting that Baudelaire may have read Liszt's article on the composer that had appeared in the *Journal des Débats* on 18 May 1849 (C, i. 157 and 787). It is also worth mentioning that Alfred Rethel's woodcuts 'La Danse des morts en 1848' were reproduced in *L'Illustration* on 28 July and that Champfleury, possibly

Baudelaire's closest friend at this time, devoted an article to them and their successors 'La Danse des morts de l'année 1849' in *L'Artiste* on 15 September; Baudelaire would not discuss Rethel's work until 1859 (in *l'Art philosophique*), but the likelihood is that he first encountered it in the summer of 1849. Wagner, 'Schoman', Rethel: could it be that Baudelaire had contacts (possibly through Proudhon) with the German revolutionary milieu and with German political exiles in Paris? No one has ever explained, it might be added, why the publication of *Les Limbes* by Michel Lévy was scheduled for Paris and *Leipzig*. Like everything else concerning Baudelaire in 1849, even conjecture on this point would be out of place.

Provincial Interlude (II): Dijon

Some time in December 1849—possibly as early as the 3rd, and certainly by the 17th—Baudelaire left Paris for Dijon with the clear intention of remaining there for some time. Jeanne joined him soon after his arrival, and the two of them took up what they thought was temporary residence in a hotel pending, Baudelaire wrote to Ancelle on 10 January 1850, their installation in more permanent furnished accommodation where they could live far more cheaply than in Paris; it seems likely that this hope, like so many others, was to remain unfulfilled. It is not known how long Baudelaire remained in Dijon (it could well have been into February or even March 1850), nor is there conclusive evidence for his reasons for going there in the first place. The three letters, or fragments of letters, that survive from his stay in the city strongly suggest that he had been promised employment there which would enable him to pay off some of his Parisian debts (C, i. 161); that employment could only have been of a journalistic character,[3] and there is every reason to accept Claude Pichois's view (C, i. 788–9) that what took Baudelaire to Dijon was the offer of a position on the local *démoc-soc* newspaper *Le Travail* which, first published on 26 September 1849 (in succession to the banned *Citoyen de la Côte-d'Or*), appeared regularly three times a week until it too was forced to close on 20 March 1850. During its brief and precarious existence,

[3] Contrary to the case argued by Albert Ronsin in 'Le Problème du séjour de Charles Baudelaire à Dijon en 1849–1850', *Mémoires de l'Académie des Sciences, Arts et Belles-Lettres de Dijon*, 112 (1954–6), 57–74. See esp. pp. 70–1.

Le Travail went through a succession of editors, amongst them a Parisian journalist of Proudhonian persuasion whom Baudelaire knew well and whom we have already encountered: Jules Viard, the founder and editor of the now defunct *Représentant du Peuple*, who was brought down from the capital to edit *Le Travail* with effect from 21 December 1849 and who, after the journal's demise, remained in Dijon to edit its successor *Le Peuple* (first number 3 April 1850), returning to Paris in early 1851 after that journal had, in its turn, been forced to suspend publication on 22 December 1850. It seems reasonable to conclude, as Pichois does, that Baudelaire's arrival in Dijon was directly linked to Viard's imminent assumption of the editorship of *Le Travail* and that he worked on the newspaper, as he had done on *La Tribune nationale*, in some undefined sub-editorial or administrative capacity, without contributing any articles to it personally. The political orientation of *Le Travail* will be discussed shortly. Our first task is to indicate the political climate in Dijon and in the Côte-d'Or as a whole around the time of Baudelaire's stay in the city, a stay which may, indeed, be regarded as 'providential' in that it took him from Paris where, after the elections of 13 May 1849 and the botched uprising of 13 June, radical republicanism was decidedly on the retreat to one of the provincial centres where, henceforth, the *démoc-socs* would exert their greatest influence and where, correspondingly, social and political conflicts were at their most intense.[4] In leaving Paris when he did and heading for the centre-east of the country, Baudelaire, contrary to what a truncated 'Parisocentric' reading of the Second Republic might suggest, was actually moving *towards* the new epicentre of radical republicanism in France. Although by no means a hotbed of 'red republicanism' in the manner of the Var or the Jura, Dijon and the Côte-d'Or can legitimately be viewed as representing in microcosm the multiple political, social, and ideological conflicts that rent provincial France in the 'declining' phase of the Second Republic.[5] The following reconstruction of the

---

[4] On the shift of focus of radical republicanism from Paris to the provinces after Dec. 1848, see, amongst other sources, Roger Magraw, *France 1815–1914: The Bourgeois Century* (Fontana, 1983), 140–55.

[5] Pichois' comments on the political 'torpeur' of Dijon in 1849–50 are not entirely borne out by the facts, nor is it true to say that the city was 'réputée conservatrice' (BPZ, 271). On the contrary, Gustave Lefrançois told Viard in late 1850, 'la côte d'Or et Dijon surtout passent à Paris pour un vrai nid de *rouges*' (Lefrançois, *Souvenirs d'un révolutionnaire* (Bibliothèque des Temps Nouveaux, Brussels (1902)), 145).

various contexts of Baudelaire's stay in Dijon in 1849–50 will, it is hoped, set the tantalizingly brief comments he makes about it in a new and more revealing perspective than has hitherto been the case.

Before 1848, Paul Gonnet has written, 'Dijon, qui n'est pas une ville de fabriques, offre un mauvais terrain à la croisade socialiste'.[6] In the surrounding towns, villages, and countryside, however, and above all in areas associated with the production of wine, that terrain had, by the time Baudelaire arrived in Dijon, been amply prepared, and the city itself had, somewhat belatedly, witnessed a significant, if far from overwhelming, growth in support for the radical republican cause.[7] In wine-producing areas, traditional hostility to the *impôt sur les boissons*, a catastrophic drop in wine prices following the glut of 1847, 1848, and 1849 and widespread indebtedness had made *vignerons* both large and small receptive to the ideas disseminated by *démoc-soc* propagandists and particularly to the brand of peasant radicalism relayed by the widely read journal *La Feuille de village*, founded, edited, and largely written by the local Montagnard deputy Pierre Joigneaux whose possible influence on Baudelaire's political thinking is considered in the chapter that follows. With Dijon itself soon succumbing to the combined effects of high bread and potato prices and of slumps in the building and metal-working industries, a community of interests was forged between wine-producers, urban workers, and petty-bourgeois radicals throughout the Côte-d'Or that presented the various right-wing groups—Orleanists, Legitimists, Bonapartists, and 'moderate' Republicans—with a major challenge to their hold on the department and its *chef-lieu*. The close association between wine production and radical republicanism is, as the following chapter will show, of particular significance to our argument. Analysing the election results of April 1848, December 1848, and May 1849, Robert Laurent has shown how, in the Côte-d'Or as in many other wine-producing areas, 'à trois reprises, en l'espèce de deux ans et dans des conditions politiques bien différentes, le

[6] Paul Gonnet, 'La Conquête républicaine, 1830–1871', in Pierre Gras (ed.), *Histoire de Dijon* (Privat, Toulouse, 1981), 277–8.
[7] The following account is based on Pierre Lévêque, *La Bourgogne de la Monarchie de Juillet au Second Empire*, 5 vols. (Université de Lille III, 1980); id., 'Les Elections de 1849 en Côte-d'Or', *Bulletin de la Faculté des Lettres de Strasbourg* (1965), 293–326; and Paul Gonnet, 'La Société dijonnaise au 19e siècle, 1815–1890' (unpub. doctoral thesis, 7 fasc., n.d.).

vignoble a témoigné de la profondeur de ses sentiments républicains'; moreover, 'ce républicanisme est plus montagnard que bourgeois'. Dijon, too, moved steadily to the left, and in the election of May 1849 cast 48.1 per cent of its votes for Montagnard candidates (the same percentage as for wine-producing areas), in contrast to the 37.2 per cent cast for the left in the department as a whole; a subsequent by-election in the city in August 1849 produced a clear majority (57.9 per cent) for the Montagnard candidate.[8] By the time Baudelaire arrived in Dijon, 'moderate' Republicanism had effectively ceased to exist, and a majority of the city's shopkeepers, petit-bourgeois professionals, and skilled and unskilled workers, like the bulk of *vignerons* in the department as a whole, stood solidly behind the Montagne in its confrontation with the many-faceted 'party of order'. 'La lutte est plus nettement celle des riches et des pauvres,' Paul Gonnet comments, 'c'est encore le vieux combat démocratique'.[9]

The strength of Montagnard feeling in Dijon during and around Baudelaire's stay in the city is attested in successive reports by the local *procureur-général*, Duval. On 27 December 1849 he informed his superiors in Paris that 'dans les bas-fonds de l'organisation sociale, il s'établit une force irritée et brutale destinée à lutter violemment contre celle qui domine sur les sommets; ceux qui la préparent pour la mettre plus tard en œuvre disposent d'auxiliaires nombreux et actifs sur lesquels le gouvernement n'a pas de prise, ceux qui, par leur obscurité même, échappent trop facilement à sa surveillance'.[10] On 9 April 1850 Duval reported that 'les idées socialistes continuent d'agiter beaucoup les esprits' and, still more alarmingly, on 11 May 1850 that 'le respect de loi et de l'autorité . . . disparaît graduellement des mœurs publiques sous l'influence d'exaltations incessantes qui . . . font place presque toujours à la résistance par paroles et bien souvent incitent à des rébellions individuelles mal caractérisées.'[11] But it was not only, or not even mainly, in the city that public order was under threat. On 6 February 1850, it was reported that 'sur plusieurs points, à Saint-Dizier, à Charolles, à Gevrey-Chambertin [the last-named, the wine-

---

[8] Robert Laurent, *Les Vignerons de la Côte-d'Or au XIXe siècle* (Les Belles Lettres, 1958), i. 491–3.
[9] Gonnet, 'La Société dijonnaise', v. 968.
[10] Ibid. 960.
[11] Ibid. 966–7.

producing village *par excellence,* lying some 10 kms. south of Dijon], les délits forestiers commis avec voitures, et par bandes de cinquante à soixante personnes, ont pris le caractère d'une véritable dévastation. En maints endroits, les délinquants agissant à ciel découvert et sans se cacher disent hautement "que les propriétaires ont assez longtemps exploité, que leur tour est venu, à eux pauvres gens"'; the *procureur-général* had no doubt that these 'déprédations'—wholly typical, it should be stressed, of the rural discontents of 1849–51—'s'accomplissent sous l'influence, sous le patronage et au nom des idées socialistes'.[12] The articulation of these widespread urban and rural resentments was essentially the work of radical republican journals like *Le Citoyen* and its successors *Le Travail* and *Le Peuple* which not only linked Dijon to the outlying towns, villages, and hamlets of the Côte-d'Or but also ensured communication between the department as a whole and the central *démoc-soc* organizations in Paris. In February 1850, *Le Travail* had 1,500 *abonnés* and a readership of perhaps ten times that figure, with—to anticipate on the theme of the chapter that follows—*cabarets* and *marchands de vin* providing the vital nodes in a department-wide network of communication; it is highly significant that, of the 524 subscribers to *Le Peuple* whose professions are known, no fewer than 143 (36.6 per cent) were *aubergistes, débitants, cabaretiers,* or *limonadiers.*[13] Clearly, if Baudelaire did work with Viard on *Le Travail,* he was at the very hub of radical republican activity in the department.

The political line pursued by *Le Travail* throughout its troubled six months' existence was wholly consistent with that being advanced by *démoc-socs* the length and breadth of France in 1849–50. The definition of socialism that it gave in its first number of 26 September 1849 was one that could be accepted by a wide swathe of popular and lower middle-class opinion and is notable for its defence—again wholly in line with *démoc-soc* thinking at the time —of the principles of family and individual property that, according to reactionaries of every hue, socialism threatened before all else:

A nos yeux, le socialisme n'est point un minotaure altéré de sang humain, comme le publient les pharisiens des temps modernes . . .; il a pour but de vivifier toutes les branches de l'activité humaine par l'équilibre de tous les

[12] Lévêque, *La Bourgogne,* iii. 1171.   [13] Ibid. iv. 1324.

intérêts, par la satisfaction accordée à tous les besoins; il a pour but de soustraire le faible à l'empire du fort; il est le mot qui résume toutes les idées de justice et d'amour éparses dans le monde des intelligences; il est la formule synthétique de toutes les vues économiques qui tendent à améliorer la condition de l'homme, la destinée des peuples. Loin d'être l'ennemi de la famille et de la propriété, il aspire à les garantir l'une et l'autre contre les attentats du capital, de l'usure, du libertinage, de tous les mauvais instincts.

Le Travail goes on to describe socialism as 'la réforme de tous les abus, la mort de tous les privilèges, l'émancipation de tous les opprimés; c'est la justice, c'est le progrès, c'est la raison, c'est l'ordre dans la liberté, c'est le bonheur dans la fraternité, c'est la pensée de Dieu réalisée autant que possible sur la terre': an unspecific, question-begging 'definition', to be sure, but one which is broadly congruent with the 'socialisme mitigé' that Baudelaire was defending at much the same time in 'La Rançon'. But *Le Travail* was undeniably radical—'Nous provoquerons l'abaissement de cette puissance si oppressive qu'on nomme le capital, et la glorification de cette vertu si féconde qu'on nomme le travail'—and become more so after Viard assumed the editorship. On 4 January 1850 he went as far as to defend Marat, Saint-Just, and Robespierre—by now a very dangerous thing indeed—and two days later gave the following heavily Proudhonian definition of the Republic which one may imagine Baudelaire reading with approval:

La République, c'est l'absence d'AUTORITÉ *extérieure à la* SOCIÉTÉ, et dominant, exploitant, écrasant, affamant, rongeant une nation avec l'impunité du droit divin ou du droit de la force . . . C'est la LIBERTÉ ABSOLUE,—l'absence de *monarque*, d'*oligarque*, d'*omniarque* et de tous les *arques* du monde, c'est-à-dire de tous les bourreaux et de tous les dominateurs et maîtres du monde! . . . C'est l'*an-archie* (mot si calomnié, si incompris!), c'est la *liberté*, c'est le suffrage universel, c'est la souveraineté du peuple.[14]

Of all the journals with which Baudelaire was (or is likely to have been) associated during the Second Republic, it is *Le Travail*—populist, radical, anti-capitalist, and socialist in an unspecific but broadly Proudhonian manner—that was probably closest to his political viewpoint at the time. Having retreated, like so many radical republicans, from the ultra-leftism of June 1848, Baudelaire, heavily influenced by Proudhon, was probably prepared to back

[14] *Le Travail* (6 Jan. 1850).

the *démoc-soc* programme as it was formulated in the spring and summer of 1849. Whether, however, support for the *démoc-soc* programme implied approval of the *démoc-socs* themselves is another question entirely to which, in concluding this section, we now turn.

Baudelaire's one specifically political statement during his 'Dijon interlude' is to be found in an undated fragment that survives from a letter to Ancelle:

Madier de Montjau, qui revenait de je ne sais quel triomphe d'avocat, je ne sais quel triomphe de procès politique a passé par ici, il est venu nous voir. —Vous savez que ce jeune homme passe pour avoir un talent merveilleux. C'est un aigle démocratique. Il m'a fait pitié! Il faisait l'enthousiaste et le révolutionnaire. Je lui ai parlé alors du socialisme des paysans,—socialisme inévitable, féroce, stupide, bestial comme un socialisme de la torche ou de la faulx. Il a eu peur, cela l'a refroidi.—Il a reculé devant la logique. C'est un imbécile ou plutôt un très vulgaire ambitieux. (C, i. 157–8)

This fragment has sometimes been used as evidence that, by the end of 1849, Baudelaire had already thoroughly repudiated his radicalism of the previous year; Enid Starkie, for example, for whom Baudelaire 'had become conservative' by this time, sees it as an expression of his 'disgust with the socialism of the rabble' and, as such, as a pointer to the out-and-out reactionary political positions he allegedly adopted after the coup of 1851.[15] Noël Madier de Montjau (1814–92)—assuming, perhaps wrongly, that it is him and not the Madier de Montjau *jeune* also featured in Maitron's *Dictionnaire biographique*[16]—was a pivotal figure in the nationwide *démoc-soc* organization that had been created in the wake of the left's set-backs in June and December 1848 and, as Baudelaire's letter indicates, was renowned as a defender of republican publications; as Claude Pichois has shown (BPZ, 272), it is likely that his visit to the *démoc-socs* of Dijon—Baudelaire's 'nous' almost certainly refers to the editorial team of *Le Travail* (C, i. 789)—

---

[15] Enid Starkie, *Baudelaire* (Penguin, Harmondsworth, 1971), 222.

[16] The fact that Baudelaire, aged 28, refers to Madier as 'ce jeune homme' makes it more than likely that the younger man, rather than his 35-year-old namesake, is concerned. The younger Madier (whose date of birth is not given by Maitron) was also a lawyer, a noted left-wing militant in Montargis and Gien and a failed *démoc-soc* candidate for the Loiret in the elections of May 1849 and again in a by-election of July that year. The present analysis of the incident is not substantially altered if it was indeed the younger Madier whom Baudelaire encountered.

followed immediately upon his stirring defence of the Toulouse-based radical newspaper *L'Émancipation* towards the end of December 1849. In the Saône-et-Loire by-election of 10 March 1850, Madier came top of the list with over 60,000 of the 105,000 votes cast; his victory, like that of the other successful *démoc-soc* candidates, was contested by the authorities, but was confirmed in the re-run of 28 April by an even higher margin, after which, according to Maitron, Madier became 'une des têtes visibles de ce "péril rouge" insidieux que le pouvoir allait dénoncer, et l'un des chefs de la Montagne à la Législative'. A leading figure in the republican resistance to the 1851 coup, Madier was exiled to Belgium, returning towards the end of the Second Empire and, as deputy for the Drôme, playing a significant part in far-left parliamentary politics from 1874 to 1879 when, again according to Maitron, he 'étonnait les jeunes républicains ambitieux par sa fidélité intransigeante au souvenir de la Montagne, celle de la Première et celle de la Seconde République'.

If it was indeed this paragon of Montagnard virtue (and even if it was his possibly even more radical younger namesake) whom Baudelaire treated in Dijon as an 'imbécile' and 'très vulgaire ambitieux', the letter is, on the surface of things, evidence of a decisive shift to the right. But only on the surface: Claude Pichois is surely right when he argues (BPZ, 272) that 'le radicalisme de Baudelaire ne pouvait se satisfaire des naïvetés de la social-démocratie', even when that cause was championed by someone as committed as Madier. Thanks to the privileged vantage-point from which, it is argued here, Baudelaire was able to view the unfolding pattern of events in the Côte-d'Or (and, by inference, in France as a whole), it would have been clear to him, as it may not have been to someone like Madier, that there was a growing tension between the constitutionalism and electoralism of the predominantly middle-class *démoc-soc* politicians and the far more turbid political and social passions which, as we have seen, were erupting simultaneously in direct, illegal activity in the countryside around Dijon: what, in his letter, Baudelaire memorably calls 'un socialisme de la torche ou de la faulx'. The fragment suggests that, far from having moved to the right, Baudelaire was increasingly convinced that the constitutional legalism of the *démoc-soc* leadership would not ultimately be able to save the Republic from its enemies, and that, in entrusting its fate to men like Madier, the left was, in effect, condemning it to death. If this is so, then Baudelaire had reached the same conclusion that the ultra-leftist Gustave Lefrançois would come to when he stayed in Dijon under *résidence surveillée* in 1850–1. Lefrançois cannot find words harsh enough for the 'gros bonnets de la démocratie dijonnaise' and their 'tempêtes dans un vase de nuit', 'politicailleries', 'insipides bavardages', and the 'allures de pontife' of their 'cacique', Jules Carion.[17] When the crunch came in December 1851, resistance in Dijon itself was virtually non-existent; the Republic, Lefrançois lamented, had been 'égorgée par les républicains plus encore que par l'homme qui vient seulement de l'achever'.[18] Only in the wine-producing village of Nuits-Saint-Georges, where a policeman was killed, was there anything like concerted opposition to the coup: 'Ce fut le seul acte énergique qui se produisit dans tout le département,' wrote Lefrançois, 'Dans tout le reste de la Côte-d'Or, les rouges demeurèrent inactifs'.[19] In the Côte-d'Or, as in so much of France, the Second Republic ended not with a bang and scarcely with a whimper. Elsewhere, though, in the centre, south, and east of the country, in the Jura, the Allier, the Hérault, the Vaucluse, the Drôme, and, above all, the Var, the 'socialisme de la torche et de la faulx' would, for more than a week, hold the Bonapartists and their supporters at bay. Even in the Côte-d'Or the link between wine-production and resistance was apparent: in the departments to the south and east it was inescapable.

1850

After the sudden rush of information for December 1849–January 1850, we are once more reduced to virtually unsupported speculation for the remainder of the year which, like 1849, is marked by only a handful of surviving letters and the publication of a mere three poems: 'Châtiment de l'orgueil' and 'Le Vin des honnêtes gens' (i.e. 'L'Âme du vin'), both of them crucial texts for our argument, in *Le Magasin des familles* in June 1850 and, in July, 'Lesbos' in Julien Lemer's anthology *Les Poètes de l'amour*. 'Mere', though, is perhaps the wrong word since the three pieces effectively doubled the number of poems by Baudelaire that had so

[17] Lefrançois, *Souvenirs*, 145, 153, 158, 162, 175.
[18] Ibid. 174.
[19] Ibid. 181.

far appeared in public ('Don Juan aux enfers', 'A une Malabaraise', 'Les Chats'), and the fact that the June number of *Le Magasin des familles* said that the 'deux morceaux inédits' it was publishing formed part of *Les Limbes* scheduled to appear 'très prochainement' and 'destiné à representer les agitations et les mélancolies de la jeunesse moderne' (C, i. 792–3) suggests, especially when combined with other evidence shortly to be considered, that Baudelaire was at last making substantial progress on his long-delayed collection. There is evidence of other work conceived or actually in progress. In December 1849 *La Presse* announced the forthcoming publication in *La Veillée pittoresque* of '*Les Derniers Buveurs*, par M. Charles Baudelaire'—a tantalizing title if ever there was one, given the centrality of the wine theme to Baudelaire's Second Republic output—and in June 1850 *La Presse* further announced that Baudelaire would shortly contribute to *Le Magasin des familles* an article entitled 'L'influence des images sur les esprits'. Another notice in the same journal concerning yet another republication of *La Fanfarlo* by 'Chasles Beaudelaire' (in *La Semaine*—yet again it failed to materialize) suggests, however, that Baudelaire was still short of publishable copy and that finding outlets for what he did have was still a considerable problem.

As to Baudelaire's political opinions in 1850, there is only one piece of evidence which, though of a most general kind, suggests that he remained firmly on the left as the Bonapartist challenge to the Republic gathered momentum. In his biography of Baudelaire, Charles Asselineau (who had met Baudelaire in 1845 but had lost contact with him since the Revolution) wrote that during the period of 'cette grève littéraire de 1848 et des années suivantes' when, he said (perhaps over-hastily), Baudelaire 'produisait peu', the poet-critic lived 'retiré à l'extrémité de Paris'—in other words at Neuilly—where 'on le rencontrait, m'a-t-on-dit, sur les boulevards extérieurs, vêtu tantôt d'une vareuse et tantôt d'une blouse; mais aussi irréprochable, aussi correct dans cette tenue démocratique que sous l'habit noir des jours prospères'.[20] As we have seen already, and as Asselineau's adjective 'démocratique' underlines, dress was never more semiotically charged than under the Second Republic, and for Baudelaire, either for economic or political reasons (or, most likely, for a combination of both), to wear

---

[20] Jacques Crépet and Claude Pichois (eds.), *Baudelaire et Asselineau* (Nizet, 1953), 91.

clothes that signalled 'democratic' (i.e. *démoc-soc*) convictions in an ultra-bourgeois district like Neuilly in 1850–51 was, even more than at Châteauroux in 1848, to expose himself to the possibility, if not of physical violence, then at least of mockery and verbal abuse. No mention, unfortunately, is made of the colour of Baudelaire's dress and accessories or of the length of his hair. If he was still flaunting the shaggy locks, beard, and red necktie of Châteauroux, then he was taking a very real risk indeed for, by 1850, the wearing of red caps, red waistcoats, red ties, red braces, red buttonholes was, like the carrying of red flags and the ringing of red-painted handbells, forbidden by law; cafés with red marquees could be closed by the police, and at Amboise the presence of a red weather-cock on a local churchtower was thought serious enough for a detachment of fifty soldiers to be sent to remove it![21] Flaubert records in *l'Éducation sentimentale* that 'les barbes longues' were a target of reactionary hatred just as much as primary school teachers, *marchands de vin*, philosophy and history classes, novels, and indeed 'toute indépendance, toute manifestation individuelle';[22] after the 1851 coup, schoolteachers would be prohibited from having any kind of beard at all, that 'symbole d'anarchie' as a ministerial directive described it.[23] As the liberty trees came down throughout the length and breadth of France—most had been felled by the authorities by the end of 1850, sometimes provoking popular protest as at the Arts-et-Métiers in Paris in February 1850[24]—the cries that had accompanied the events of 1848 and could still be heard in 1849—'Vive Raspail', 'Vive Robespierre', 'Vive Barbès', 'A bas les blancs', 'Vivent les barricades', 'Vive la sociale'[25]—were banned by law, and, as we shall see, the full force of state repression would be turned against the focal institution of French (male) working-class culture, the café, cabaret, and *marchand de vin*. In such a context, to wear a 'democratic' *blouse* or *vareuse* must be seen as a serious political gesture.

[21] John M. Merriman, *The Agony of the Republic: The Repression of the Left in Revolutionary France 1848–1851* (Yale Univ. Press, New Haven, Conn., and London, 1978), 96–7.

[22] Flaubert, *L'Éducation sentimentale*, ed. Édouard Maynial (Garnier, 1964), 390.

[23] Maurice Agulhon, *1848 ou l'apprentissage de la république 1848–1852* (Seuil, 1973), 211.

[24] Merriman, *The Agony of the Republic*, 92 and 97. See also Lefrançois, *Souvenirs*, 113.

[25] Merriman, *The Agony of the Republic*, 94–5.

1851: The Collapse of the Republic

Les Limbes *and 'Douze poèmes'*

Even setting aside the shattering political developments it contained, 1851 was a crucial year in Baudelaire's life. It was, in the first instance, the year in which he reached the age of thirty—the age when, according to Gautier, 'le jeune homme' is transformed into 'l'homme jeune'—and, by coincidence or design, it was indeed precisely on his thirtieth birthday—9 April 1851—that *Le Messager de l'Assemblée* published a sequence of eleven of his poems under the title of *Les Limbes* together with the by now almost ritualistic announcement that the poems formed part of a larger collection of the same name destined to 'retracer l'histoire des agitations spirituelles de la jeunesse moderne' (OC, i. 793). This was almost the same description as had been announced in *Le Magasin des familles* in 1850, though the earlier reference to 'mélancolies' has disappeared and the emphasis is now less on representing than on retracing the history of the spiritual turmoil of modern youth. Not too much should be made of this slight variation; perhaps, though, by publishing a selection of his works on contemporary youth on the very day he entered *l'an trentiesme de son aage*, Baudelaire was seeking to divest himself of its miseries, consign it to history and advance at last into authentic manhood.

1851 also witnessed the publication of other works vital to an understanding of Baudelaire's personal, poetic, and political development under the Second Republic: *Du vin et du haschisch* (March 1851), the tribute to Pierre Dupont (late August), and, less than a week before the Bonapartist coup, *Les Drames et les romans honnêtes* (27 November). More important still, there is firm evidence that by late 1851, or early 1852 at the latest, Baudelaire really did have a substantial body of poetry ready for publication in book form. In his biography, Asselineau stated that some time in 1850 Baudelaire 'me montra chez lui, dans un logement proche du boulevard Poissonière, le manuscrit de ses poésies magnifiquement copié par un calligraphe, et qui formait deux volumes in-4° cartonnés et dorés. C'est ce manuscrit qui a servi pour l'impression des *Fleurs du Mal*'.[26] In his preparatory notes for his book, Asselineau said

[26] *Baudelaire et Asselineau*, 92.

that the 'viewing' in question took place 'un soir Boulevard Bonne-Nouvelle, c'est-à-dire vers le coup d'état';[27] the researches of F. W. Leakey have proved conclusively that it is the later date given in the notes that is to be preferred, and that Asselineau was probably shown the manuscript some time in October–November 1851, when Baudelaire was living (as he did from mid-July 1851 to April 1852) at 25 Rue des Marais-du-Temple (the present rue Albert Thomas), fairly close to both the boulevard Poissonnière and the boulevard Bonne-Nouvelle.[28] Some time between, it would seem, September 1851 and the beginning of 1852, Baudelaire also sent the manuscripts of twelve poems to Gautier for publication in *La Revue de Paris*; amongst them were four 'Second Republic texts' of fundamental importance, 'Les Deux Crépuscules' (i.e. 'Le Crépuscule du soir' and 'Le Crépuscule du matin'), 'Le Vin des chiffonniers' and 'Le Reniement de saint Pierre'. As the Second Republic approached its bathetic collapse in December 1851, so, clearly, Baudelaire's poetic career was moving towards the possibility of some kind of interim climax.

Towards the coup

Baudelaire's general political position in 1851 can be inferred with some confidence from what he did and what he wrote in the course of the year. Qualifications will be introduced as we proceed, but he remained, at root, a man of the left, his commitment to the Republic growing even as his confidence in the willingness and capacity of Republicans to resist the Bonapartist threat to its survival collapsed. In February—presumably on the 24th—he attended 'un banquet commémoratif de la révolution de Février to which he refers in some detail in *L'École païenne* (January 1852). Baudelaire's scathing comments on the pseudo-classical drivel uttered there on the subject of revolution by 'un de ces jeunes gens qu'on peut qualifier d'instruits et d'intelligents' (OC, ii. 44) should not lead us to conclude that he was by now antagonistic to the revolutionary cause and principle as such. On the contrary, Baudelaire was highly conscious of the symbolic significance of 24 February—we have

---

[27] Ibid. 188.
[28] F. W. Leakey, 'Baudelaire et Asselineau en 1851: Asselineau critique de Corot', *Bulletin baudelairien*, 8/2 (1973), 9–12.

already seen that *Les Limbes* was originally scheduled for publication on the day of the Republic's first anniversary—and, as late as
1859, writing to Poulet-Malassis on 24 February, he would speak of
it as a 'date à jamais mémorable et qui doit être chère à un vieux
faubourien comme vous' (C, i.

557), neatly side-stepping the fact
that he had been just as much a *faubourien* in 1848 as his publisher,
though not, it is true, to the extent of having edited and published,
as Poulet-Malassis had done, a popular newspaper entitled
L'Aimable Faubourien: Journal de la Canaille (see C, i. 1015).
Baudelaire would hardly have attended the banquet had he not
remained committed to the Republic, and his presence there calls
for two comments. In his *1848 ou l'Apprentissage de la République*,
Maurice Agulhon makes the valuable point that the Second Republic
had not one but two foundation dates: first, 24 February when the
Republic was hastily proclaimed amid the turmoil of the Hôtel de
Ville and, secondly, on 4 May when the duly elected Constituent
Assembly assembled for the first time at the Palais-Bourbon. Significantly, the official anniversary of the Republic was celebrated
on 4 May in 1849, 1850, and 1851, and Agulhon rightly points out
that 'toute une philosophie politique est incluse dans cette substitution: le régime veut être né dans une assemblée régulièrement élue,
et non pas sur des barricades'; 'à distance,' he further comments,
'on peut y voir une indication sur l'esprit du nouveau pouvoir'.[29]
The conclusion is obvious: for Baudelaire, especially in 1851, to
attend the celebrations of 24 February suggests a continued commitment to the revolutionary Republic of February 1848, the
popular, radical Republic, rather than to the formal, conservative,
and essentially bourgeois Republic that had succeeded it. Furthermore, John M. Merriman has shown how, beginning in 1849, the
commemorative banquets of the Republic—24 February and 4 May
alike—took on a decidedly popular character and, charging low
admission fees to attract workers and providing popular fare such
as pâté and wine (*toujours!*), became 'as a form of political organization and popular fraternal festivity . . . almost exclusively
characteristic of the extreme left'.[30] Once again a knowledge of
Second Republic imagery and practice allows us to decode the likely
political significance of Baudelaire's behaviour.

Any doubts concerning Baudelaire's commitment to the Republic,

[29] Agulhon, *1848*, 58.
[30] Merriman, *The Agony of the Republic*, 84.

right up to the military coup itself (and indeed beyond), should be dispelled by a reading of 'Du vin et du haschisch' and 'Pierre Dupont', both of which will be discussed in detail in the chapter that follows. Although, as we shall see shortly, there is a marked disparity between the public optimism of these texts and Baudelaire's private pessimism at the time (mainly, but not exclusively, brought about by his fears concerning the Republic's survival), 'Du vin et du haschisch' and 'Pierre Dupont', exhaling as they do what 'Pierre Dupont' calls 'le goût infini de la République' (OC, ii. 33), must count amongst the purest and most passionate defences of Republicanism made by any major French writer between 1848 and 1852, and the Republicanism they defend—indeed exalt—is popular, democratic, radical, the Republicanism of the barricades rather than of the Assembly. Once again, it is necessary to stress how risky it was, in the climate of 1850–1, to write, for example, in praise of a poet-*chansonnier* as closely associated with the popular revolutionary cause as Pierre Dupont. In June 1850, in an article in *Revue des Deux Mondes* entitled 'La Poésie et les poètes populaires', Émile Montégut launched an attack of quite exceptional violence on Dupont's 'chants de propagande socialiste' which, he says, were '(composés) pour certaines factions et (chantés) par des factieux'. 'Ces chants sont du reste son crime,' Montégut continues, 'et un jour ou l'autre seront son châtiment'. As if this were not enough, Montégut's conclusion, in the paranoid atmosphere of mid-1850, is scarcely less than a direct incitement to violence:

Fasse le ciel qu'il ne reçoive pas un jour la punition qui est due à tout homme qui, étourdiment ou après y avoir longtemps réfléchi, sincèrement ou avec hypocrisie, peu importe, met entre les mains de ses concitoyens un brandon de guerre civile![31]

Comment is hardly necessary: quite simply, it took courage, in August 1851, publicly and passionately to praise Pierre Dupont and his songs, as it did, in the teeth of generalized vituperation, to state without equivocation (as Baudelaire did in 'Les Drames et les romans honnêtes') that 'Proudhon est un écrivain que l'Europe nous enviera toujours' (OC, ii. 40–1). As the counter-revolution strengthened its grip on every aspect of French life, any sign or suspicion of sympathy for radicals or the radical cause could bring

---

[31] Émile Montégut, 'La Poésie et les poètes populaires', *Revue des Deux Mondes* (June 1850), 1147.

untold retribution on the suspect's head, as even Baudelaire's half-brother Alphonse discovered in 1851 when, as Juge d'Instruction at Fontainebleau, he was found guilty of entertaining what were described as 'relations inconvenantes' with prisoners in his charge—amongst other offences, he was alleged to have given a plumb-line, square, and compass to a detainee named Granger, a 'socialiste exalté, poursuivi et détenu pour avoir cherché à troubler la paix publique, en excitant la haine des citoyens les uns contre les autres' —and in November 1851 was demoted from the post of Juge d'Instruction to that of simple judge, a punishment that seems effectively to have ruined his career. If even someone as inoffensive and fundamentally conservative as Alphonse Baudelaire could, in the words of the Procureur-Général investigating his case, be suspected of nourishing 'mauvaises opinions politiques', what would the 'authorities' make of his fiery *blouse*-clad half-brother Charles? [32]

In the circumstances, Baudelaire's last published work before the coup, 'Les Drames et les romans honnêtes' (*La Semaine théâtrale*, 27 November 1851), reads as a calculated assault on counter-revolutionary ideology as epitomized by the so-called 'école du *bon sens*' and its 'grande fureur d'honnêteté' which, according to Baudelaire, was unleashed on stage and in the novel in the last years of the Bourgeois Monarchy and which, briefly interrupted by the February revolution, had rapidly established itself as the literary orthodoxy of the bourgeois Republic as well. Baudelaire's polemic is directed at three targets: first 'les débordements puérils de l'école dite romantique' (OC, ii. 38), then 'l'école du bon sens, l'école exclusivement morale' with 'ses types de bourgeois corrects et vaniteux', and finally 'l'école socialiste' and 'le sophisme social-istique', by which he means that socialist art that is written with an exclusively moralistic or propagandistic goal in mind and which, as he says, is curiously similar to the bourgeois literature it purports to challenge:

Il est douloureux de noter que nous trouvons des erreurs semblables dans deux écoles opposées: l'école bourgeoise et l'école socialiste. Moralisons! moralisons! s'écrient toutes les deux avec une fièvre de missionnaires. Naturellement l'une prêche la morale bourgeoise et l'autre la morale

[32] Details and quotations taken from Claude Pichois, 'Le Demi-frère du poète des *Fleurs du mal*', BET, 44–58.

socialiste. Dès lors l'art n'est plus qu'une question de propagande. (OC, ii. 41)

But Baudelaire's principal scorn is reserved for 'l'école du bon sens' and 'l'honnêteté bourgeoise' of which it is the literary or theatrical vehicle. Baudelaire does not hesitate to designate 'l'école du bon sens' as *'l'école de la vengeance'* (OC, ii. 40), of vengeance, above all, on Romanticism and its anti-bourgeois values, and it is not difficult to see that, under the transparent cover of an attack on literary counter-revolution, it is counter-revolutionary ideology—and, by implication, practice—as a whole that Baudelaire is taking on.

Mais la réaction l'emporte, la réaction bête et furieuse. L'éclatante préface de *Mademoiselle de Maupin* insultait la sotte hypocrisie bourgeoise, et l'impertinente béatitude de l'école du *bon sens* se venge des violences romantiques. Hélas, oui! il y a là une vengeance.

There follows a withering attack on the major theatrical exemplar of *l'école du bon sens*, Émile Augier's *Gabrielle* (1849) which received the Academy's Prix Montyon largely on the strength of its impassioned defence of the bourgeois family encapsulated in its heroine's celebrated 'declaration' to her lawyer-husband: 'Ô père de famille, ô poète, je t'aime!' This is simply too much for Baudelaire to stomach:

Un notaire! La voyez-vous, cette *honnête* bourgeoise, roucoulant amoureusement sur l'épaule de son homme et lui faisant des yeux alanguis comme dans les romans qu'elle a lus! Voyez-vous tous les notaires de la salle acclamant l'auteur qui traite avec eux de pair à compagnon, et qui les venge de tous ces gredins qui ont des dettes et qui croient que le métier de poète consiste à exprimer les mouvements lyriques de l'âme dans un rhythme réglé par la tradition! Telle est la clef de beaucoup de succès. (OC, ii. 39)

Claude Pichois (OC, ii. 1097) sees in this an attack on Ancelle who had in 1851 achieved a lifetime's ambition and become mayor of Neuilly. No doubt Ancelle is a target but, through him, Baudelaire's anger and contempt are directed at all the Ancelles throughout the length and breadth of France who, in the name of law, order, property, and, perhaps most stridently, 'the family', had, almost since the foundation of the Republic, been consciously or unconsciously preparing the way for the assault on its very existence which, like everyone else, Baudelaire must now have known to be imminent. Not content merely to attack one of the major social bases of the Bonapartist reaction, Baudelaire, with remarkable heedlessness in the circumstances, goes on to attack a leading Bonapartist minister by name: Léon Faucher who, he says, 'vient de blesser à mort la littérature avec son décret satanique en faveur des pièces honnêtes' (OC, ii. 43), the reference being to the decree of 12 October 1851 which, following the Riancey amendment of 16 July 1850 that placed severe restrictions on the publication of *roman-feuilletons* (believed, following the success of Eugène Suë, to promote 'socialism' and 'immorality' amongst working-class readers), proposed similarly to regulate and control the French stage. In the week before the military coup, fully aware that, sooner or later, some assault on the Republic must come, Baudelaire had described a ministerial decree—one that, with his growing ambition to write for the stage, would effect him directly—as nothing less than satanic. He could hardly have found a stronger term with which to denounce in advance the nexus of military, political, and ideological forces which, within days, would hold the whole of Paris, if not yet the whole of France, in its grip.

Le 2 décembre

For Baudelaire's reaction to the Bonapartist coup of 2 December 1851, we have one entry in *Mon cœur mis à nu* (OC, i. 679), as abrupt, summary, and conclusive as the event itself: 'Ma fureur au coup d'État. Combien j'ai essuyé de coups de fusil. Encore un Bonaparte! quelle honte!' Given Baudelaire's political trajectory as it had evolved since the February Revolution, his presence on the streets on 2 December (and, in all likelihood, on succeeding days) was no more than the logical culmination of the political options he had been making since the very beginning of the Second Republic. Having in all probability fought for no more than a change of political regime in February 1848, he had clearly been converted to the radical vision of the social Republic—'la sociale'—in the weeks and months that followed and had accordingly fought on the insurgent side during the *journées de juin*, unlike most Republicans of his class and generation who, with varying degrees of enthusiasm, had sided with the Provisional Government. Moreover, the defeat of the June uprising did not lead in Baudelaire's case, as it might so easily have done (and indeed as it is said so often by biographers and critics to have done), to a jettisoning of his radical political beliefs. On the contrary, under the influence of Proudhon, Baudelaire, as we have seen, became a more committed, coherent, and above all more pragmatic radical after June 1848 than he had been before. He had, as our discussion of the 'Dijon interlude' revealed, become thoroughly disillusioned with the Montagnard politicians who were attempting to organize *démoc-soc* opposition to the counter-revolution, but his writings of 1850–1, together with the other biographical and anecdotal data we have assembled, leave little doubt that Baudelaire remained committed to the Republic in its popular, radical, and social form even as his pessimism mounted as to its short-term, let alone long-term viability. Baudelaire's 'fureur' at the *coup d'état* is likely to have had two immediate targets: first, of course, fury at the Bonapartists themselves, and the diverse interest groups that backed them, but fury no less at the Republicans of various hues—moderate-constitutional, radical, even radical-socialist—whose vacillations and inner conflicts had so signally weakened the Republican cause ever since 1848 and who, when the crunch came, were incapable of effective action in its defence. An entry in *Mon cœur mis à nu* (OC, i. 692) suggests, however, that Baudelaire's fury went far beyond the Bonapartists and their ineffectual Republican opponents to embrace 'le peuple français' as a whole which, despite widespread resistance to the coup in the centre and south-west of the country (about which Baudelaire, in Paris, was probably ill-informed), not only failed determinedly to oppose the coup itself, but, in the plebiscite of 21 December 1851, endorsed and thus legitimated it by an overwhelming majority:

En somme, devant l'histoire et devant le peuple français, la grande gloire de Napoléon III aura été de prouver que le premier venu peut, en s'emparant du télégraphe et de l'Imprimerie nationale, gouverner une grande nation.

Imbéciles sont ceux qui croient que de pareilles choses peuvent s'accomplir sans la permission du peuple,—et ceux qui croient que la gloire ne peut être appuyée que sur la vertu.

But if 'le peuple français' in the broad, cross-class, sense of the term was responsible in Baudelaire's estimation for accepting and legitimating the coup, it may be that a still heavier responsibility weighed in his mind on 'le peuple' in the narrower, class-specific, sense of the term, and particularly on 'le peuple de Paris', the Parisian working classes who, having fought so valiantly in

February and June 1848, conspicuously failed to intervene in the Republic's defence in December 1851.[33] Paralysed in reality by their defeat of June 1848 and the subsequent repression, consumed with resentment at their abandonment and betrayal at the hands of the bourgeois Republicans, and undermined, furthermore, by sustained Bonapartist-inspired anti-Republican propaganda, the Parisian working classes would, in Baudelaire's embittered interpretation of events, stand condemned of having willed their own subjection under the Second Empire by their failure to act in December 1851. In *Mon cœur mis à nu* (OC, i. 685), Baudelaire would speak of the 'immense goût de tout le peuple français pour la pionnerie, et pour la dictature', and in 'Le Voyage' (February 1859) would evoke a nightmare vision of dictator and people bound together, like executioner and victim, in an embrace of sado-masochistic complicity:

> Le bourreau qui jouit, le martyr qui sanglote;
> La fête qu'assaisonne et parfume le sang;
> Le poison du pouvoir énervant le despote,
> Et le peuple amoureux du fouet abrutissant . . .

If, as *Mon cœur mis à nu* further suggests (OC, i. 692), 'les dictateurs sont les domestiques du peuple', it is only because 'le peuple', and particularly its working-class majority, wants at some unacknowledged level of itself to be domesticated and dominated. As we shall see, 'Assommons les pauvres!' may be read as a perverse attempt by a middle-class political sadist to jolt a lower-class masochist out of his passivity and into aggressive action on his own behalf and that of his fellow oppressed.

There is no need to doubt Baudelaire's word when he speaks of having risked his life in defence of the Republic in December 1851. He was, as already mentioned, living at the time on the rue du Marais-du-Temple at the entrance to the Faubourg du Temple, from which it would have been but a short walk to the Porte Saint-Martin which, as Victor Hugo wrote in *Histoire d'un crime*, was the focus of the essentially bourgeois opposition to the Bonapartist coup:

Paris, pour sa vaste tâche historique, se compose de deux personnages

---

[33] On the failure of working-class Parisians to resist the coup, see Agulhon, *1848*, 171, and, above all, chap. 12 ('2 décembre') of Jules Vallès, *Le Bachelier*.

révolutionnaires, la bourgeoisie et le peuple. Et à ces deux combattants correspondent deux lieux de combat: la Porte Saint-Martin, quand c'est la bourgeoisie qui se révolte; la Bastille, quand c'est le peuple.[34]

From the Porte Saint-Martin, Baudelaire would have been drawn naturally into the warren of streets south of the *boulevards intérieurs* between the rue Saint-Denis and the rue Montorgueil where the resistance to the coup was fiercest, and his description in *Mon cœur mis à nu* of undergoing heavy gunfire suggests that he could have been on the receiving end of the so-called 'fusillade des Boulevards' towards evening on 4 December when, in Agulhon's words,

Au signal de quelques coups de feu isolés partis du boulevard Bonne-Nouvelle, la troupe réplique par une fusillade intense, générale, propagée de proche en proche sur toute la ligne des boulevards, et visant comme autant d'ennemis les badauds, hostiles mais desarmés, des balcons et des fenêtres. Après plusieurs minutes de ce feu meurtrier, le Paris bourgeois est ensanglanté et terrorisé, et du coup la situation politique retournée.[35]

'Et cependant tout s'est pacifié' (*Mon cœur mis à nu* (OC, i. 679)). By nightfall on the 4th, with no signs of popular support from the Faubourg Saint-Antoine or the Faubourg du Temple, resistance in Paris, though not yet in the provinces, came to an end. Baudelaire's 'fureur' gave way, in his own words, to 'honte' at the realization that 'another Bonaparte' had, with the minimum of effort, and with the at least passive consent of the vast bulk of the people, first, of Paris and, then, of France as a whole, been able to sweep away the whole political superstructure of the Republic and supplant it with a system of personal, authoritarian rule sustained and justified by pseudo-democratic consensus; it was, as Gretchen van Slyke has suggested, more the plebiscite of 21 December than the coup of the 2nd that finally 'depoliticized' Baudelaire.[36] The Bonapartist triumph seemed so inevitable and so complete that Baudelaire believed—it was a view shared, if only briefly, by Proudhon—that Louis Napoleon's accession to power was in some sense necessary, predetermined, even providential:[37] 'Ce qu'est

---

[34] Victor Hugo, *Histoire d'un crime, Œuvres complètes*, xxx. 246.

[35] Agulhon, *1848*, 173.

[36] Gretchen van Slyke, 'Dans l'intertexte de Baudelaire et de Proudhon: Pourquoi faut-il assommer les pauvres?', *Romantisme*, 45 (1984), 76.

[37] On Proudhon's view of Louis Napoleon's 'rôle providentiel' in the development of socialism in France, see his *La Révolution sociale démontrée par le coup d'état du deux décembre* (Marcel Rivière, 1936), esp. pp. 174–7. For the link

l'empereur Napoléon III. Ce qu'il vaut. Trouver l'explication de sa nature, et sa providentialité' (*Mon cœur mis à nu* (OC, i. 679)).

Mysterious, inscrutable, fearful but weirdly attractive, the figure of Louis Napoleon began to haunt Baudelaire in the wake of the December coup and would never thereafter relinquish its grip on his imagination: 'Le Prince est l'être actuel qui, par ses actes et son visage, ressemble le plus à un *sphinx*' (letter to Poulet-Malassis, 8 January 1860 (C, i. 655)).

'Democratically' legitimized by the huge majority it obtained in the plebiscite of 21 December, the new regime moved rapidly to instal what has without exaggeration been described as a police state. Between December 1851 and December 1852 there was unleashed what Howard C. Payne has called 'a vast purge of real and fancied enemies of public order'.[38] 26,885 persons were tried before the so-called *commissions mixtes* established by a law of 3 February 1852, with over 4,500 being sentenced to penal detention in Algeria (the infamous 'Algerie + ') and a further 5,000 to simple residence there ('Algerie − '). In addition, close to a thousand of those arrested were forced into exile, among them many Republicans with whom Baudelaire was directly or indirectly associated: Paul de Flotte, Pierre Leroux, Edgar Quinet, Louis Ménard, Madier de Montjau, Alphonse Esquiros, and above all the man who for Baudelaire would become the poet-exile *par excellence*, Victor Hugo himself. More generally, primary and secondary schoolteachers were dismissed by the hundred, known Republicans were removed from national and local administration, political pressures forced many doctors, lawyers, and journalists to abandon their careers. Press laws still more Draconian than that of the post-June repression were promulgated on 17 February 1852, as a result of which, said Prévost-Paradol, the French press became 'entre les mains de l'autorité centrale à peu près comme Gulliver entre les mains du géant qui l'avait ramassé dans les blés'.[39] After the coup, one old

between Baudelaire and Proudhon on this point, see van Slyke, 'Dans l'intertexte', 68–71, and Stenzel, *Der historische Ort Baudelaires: Untersuchungen zur Entwicklung des französischen Literatur um die Mitte des 19. Jahrhunderts* (Wilhelm Fink, Munich, 1980), 170–4.

[38] Howard C. Payne, *The Police State of Louis Napoleon Bonaparte 1851–1860* (Univ. of Washington Press, Seattle, 1966), 34.

[39] Quoted in Roger Bellet, *Presse et journalisme sous le Second Empire* (Armand Colin, 1967), 13.

radical recalled in 1905, a red cravat had much the same effect on gendarmes and *mouchards* as the *muleta* on a Spanish bull;[40] we have already noted the fate of schoolteachers' beards. Finally, the link between public drinking, working-class sociability, and radical Republicanism was such that the police were given still greater powers than they had enjoyed under the Second Republic in its reactionary phase to coerce cafés, cabarets, *marchands de vin*, and *débits de boisson* into conformity with the new decrees on public order and freedom of speech; Tonnet, the prefect of Calvados, would close no fewer than 600 cafés and cabarets in the *département* in the next six years.[41] This was the context of repression in which elections to the new and essentially powerless Legislative Assembly took place on 29 February 1852, shortly after which (on 5 March) Baudelaire wrote to Ancelle saying that 'LE 2 DÉCEMBRE m'a *physiquement dépolitiqué*' (C, i. 188). What exactly he meant by this will be a principal theme of the section that follows.

1852: The Retreat from Politics

Public Persona and Private Self

Although Baudelaire's political position throughout the Second Republic was—or so I have argued—one of sustained radicalism, we have at intervals witnessed the existence of other interests, urges, and preoccupations which, running parallel, tangent, but not, so long as Baudelaire's republican enthusiasm survived, directly counter to the main radical current, might, in changed circumstances, become the dominant inflection of his thought. A constant theme of Baudelaire's Second Republic output was, as following chapters will reveal, a belief in the primacy of action and, above all, of work over what are seen, especially in *Du vin et du haschisch*, as sterile meditation and reverie; escapism and idleness are vigorously condemned, and the life of solitary reflection is seen as a culpable and inhuman retreat from the need for collective social action for the good of humanity as a whole. This is all very well, but Baudelaire's commitment to collective activism in 'Pierre Dupont' and

---

[40] Jean Fontane, quoted Payne, *The Police State*, 42.
[41] See Vincent Wright, 'The *coup d'état* of December 1851: Repression and the Limits to Repression', in *Revolution and Reaction*, 309.

Du vin et du haschisch often comes over as something he has had deliberately to will, and the suspicion remains that, by taste, temperament, and talent, he is drawn all too strongly towards the very inward-looking reflectiveness that his activist ideology requires him to condemn. Traces of that anti-activist and escapist predilection surface intermittently between 1848 and the December coup. We have already noted the 'rage de voyager' which, on the eve of the presidential elections of December 1848, Baudelaire told his mother seized him 'perpétuellement' (C, i. 155), and many of the intellectual and literary interests expressed at intervals during the Second Republic indicate a desire to withdraw inwards and away from the public sphere which his republican commitment demands that he inhabit. Thus the interest in Poe, whom Baudelaire had 'discovered' in early 1847, did not—far from it—disappear after the February revolution but continued in, as it were, counterpoint to the outer-directed activities and writings that were his principal preoccupation under the Second Republic. It is symptomatic of this tension that Baudelaire's first translation from Poe, *Révélation magnétique*, though probably completed before the February revolution, should have been published in *La Liberté de pensée* on 15 July 1848, some three weeks, that is, after Baudelaire's radical activism had led him to risk his life on the June barricades. The intellectual interests that prompted Baudelaire to translate this of all of Poe's works are not, to be sure, absolutely incompatible with the activism he was displaying on the streets and in other writings of the time, but there is an evident tension which, in the new political situation that the Bonapartist coup would bring about, could readily evolve into an out-and-out contradiction of his earlier activist posture. In August 1850, Baudelaire wrote to Wallon —Wallon the arch-reactionary who had commented so scathingly on the still-to-be published *Les Limbes* in 1848 (in another letter of 1850, Baudelaire would address him as 'mon cher ami')—concerning the work of Joseph Bouzeran (1799–1868) whom he had evidently met and on whom, he told Wallon, he intended to write an article 'quand j'aurai lu son livre, qu'il doit m'adresser dans trois jours' (C, i. 166). The book in question is probably Bouzeran's *Essai d'unité linguistique raisonnée ou de la philosophe du Verbe dans la Trinité catholique* (Agen, 1847) (see C, i. 794). Baudelaire's interest, in 1850, in a work so entitled does not, again, necessarily contradict his radical political stance of the time, but it does point to the continued (if largely submerged) presence, originating during the last years of the Bourgeois Monarchy, of those mystical, philosophical, and now more and more explicitly theological preoccupations which, shortly after the December coup (and perhaps even before) would take him in the direction of Joseph de Maistre and, in 1853, of the work of Hoëné Wronski (see letter of 24 September 1853 to Ancelle, C, i. 231 and 836–7).

More generally, the reader of Baudelaire's fragmentary correspondence between 1848 and 1852 cannot but be struck by how frequently his personal situation of loneliness and melancholy—principally, but not entirely, caused by his mounting political despair—runs counter to the essentially optimistic vision his Republican commitment required him to proclaim in public. As Baudelaire was publicly celebrating the joys of collective action in *Du vin et du haschisch* and 'Pierre Dupont', so, privately, he was slipping more and more into much the same limbo-world of non-creative subjectivism from which the 'ivresse' of February 1848 had briefly delivered him. In print he was commending the health- and hope-giving qualities of wine and condemning hashish as the drug of the desperate and the idle rich; in private, in that 'sombre solitude que j'ai faite autour de moi', as a letter from Dijon of 10 January 1850 tells us, he had 'l'estomac passablement détraqué par le laudanum' (C, i. 158). The contradiction between public optimism and private woe became still more blatant as time went on. In January 1851, at the very time, in all likelihood, that he was working on *Du vin et du haschisch*, that manifesto of hope, sociability, and positive action, to be published in March 1851, he was complaining to his mother of his 'douleurs incessantes' and 'la solitude de ma pensée' (C, i. 168–9). On 26 August 1851, again at the very time that a further 'official' declaration of Republican utopianism was about to be made public in 'Pierre Dupont', Baudelaire inscribed in an album belonging to a certain Mme Francine Ledoux thoughts whose autumnal tone and tenor could not have been more different from the springtime optimism that the soon-to-be-published notice would so rhetorically display:

A mesure que l'homme avance dans la vie, et qu'il voit les choses de plus haut, ce que le monde est convenu d'appeler la beauté perd bien de son importance, et aussi la volupté, et bien d'autres balivernes. Aux yeux désabusés et désormais clairvoyants toutes les saisons ont leur valeur, et l'hiver n'est pas la plus mauvaise ni la moins féerique. (OC, ii. 37)

On 30 August, in the very letter in which he enclosed the Dupont article with its extravagant eulogy of the 'divin caractère utopique' of poetry ('Non seulement elle constate, mais elle répare. Partout elle se fait négation de l'iniquité.' (OC, ii. 35)), Baudelaire was telling his mother of his sadness, anxiety, and, above all, of his fears lest, aged scarcely 30, he may already have exhausted such poetic creativity as he possessed, fears, too, that, in the present circumstances, the writing of poetry was no longer the activity it had been when he embarked upon it in the early 1840s:

> Mon livre de poésie? Je sais qu'il y a quelques années, il aurait suffi à la réputation d'un homme. Il eût fait un tapage de tous les diables. Mais aujourd'hui, les conditions, les circonstances, tout est changé. Et si mon livre *fait long feu*, après? quoi? Le drame, le roman, l'histoire même peut-être. Mais tu ne sais pas ce que c'est que les jours de doute. Il me semble quelquefois que je suis devenu trop raisonneur et que j'ai trop lu pour concevoir quelque chose de franc et de naïf. Je suis trop savant et pas assez laborieux. (C, i. 178)

Finally, of Baudelaire's misery in June–July 1851, we have the direct testimony of Mme Aupick herself, recorded in a letter of 1868 to Asselineau: 'Quel dénuement! Et moi, sa mère, avec tant d'amour dans le cœur, tant de bonne volonté pour lui, je n'ai pu le tirer de là!' (C, i. 798). Yet in 'Pierre Dupont', which Baudelaire began in July 1851 (C, i. 173), Republican ideology led him to declare that 'la nature est si belle, et l'homme est si grand, qu'il est difficile, en se mettant à un point de vue supérieur, de concevoir le sens du mot: irréparable' (OC, ii. 34). So sharp a dualism of public persona and private self could surely not be sustained for long.

'Depoliticization'?

By the late summer of 1851, then, the evidence suggests that Baudelaire's Republican faith was held together largely by will, making it only too likely that a collapse of the Republic would bring about a collapse of the faith and allow the emotions and interests that the needs of the faith had obliged Baudelaire to suppress or subordinate to explode through the increasingly fragile crust of Republican orthodoxy beneath which he sought to contain them. The effect of the December coup was not so much traumatic as seismic. On 27 March 1852, he wrote to his mother of 'l'influence *foudroyante'* that recent political events had had on him (C, i. 196, italics added). Still more elemental is the image he had used earlier that month in the celebrated letter to Ancelle: 'Ma tête devient littéralement un volcan malade. De grands orages et de grandes aurores' (C, i. 188). It was as though the earth-shattering events of the previous December had caused one stratum of preoccupations to subside—'LE 2 DÉCEMBRE m'a *physiquement dépolitiqué'*—and another, composed of the private melancolies and the various philosophical, theological, and moral concerns that the Republican commitment had caused him to underplay or suppress, to rise up in its stead: it was like the violent death of one self ('de grands orages') and the no less dramatic birth of another ('de grandes aurores'). The word that Baudelaire uses to describe the turbulent experience he has undergone—'dépolitiquer'—is not to be found in any of the major French dictionaries (there is no recorded mention even of the cognate 'dépolitiser' until the 1950s) and there is reason to believe that it is a Baudelairean *hapax legomenon.* Baudelaire's Fourierist and Proudhonian formation—both schools of thought, as we have seen, disparage the merely political, in the sense of the formal, the constitutional, the electoral, the parliamentary, in favour of the social—make it unlikely that he meant he was abjuring all concern with *la chose sociale,* as he is often interpreted as doing, but only with *la chose politique* in the narrower sense of the political regime superimposed (in the Proudhonian perception) on it and of the political measures and machinations associated with it. If that is what he did mean, then his renunciation of politics, even in the restricted sense, was premature, for as he himself admitted to Nadar in May 1859, on the occasion of Napoleon III's Italian adventure, 'je me suis vingt fois persuadé que je ne m' intéressais plus à la politique, et à chaque question grave, je suis repris de curiosité et de passion' (C, i. 578). Nor, needless to say, did Baudelaire become an out-and-out reactionary overnight, or even at all. Indeed, in the sense that he would never forgive or forget what the same letter to Nadar calls 'les horreurs commises en Décembre' (C, i. 579), Baudelaire would never abandon his hostility to the Bonapartist regime and, to that extent at least, may be said to have remained true to his Republican convictions of 1848–51. Moreover, as late as 1862, he confessed to Sainte-Beuve that the 'vieux fonds d'esprit révolutionnaire' which 'il y a longtemps' (presumably during the Second Republic) incited him 'à faire des projets de constitution' had still not completely disappeared (C, ii. 220), and a famous entry in *Pauvre Belgique!*, perhaps his most stridently anti-democratic work, indicates that, in spite of de Maistre and in spite, perhaps, of himself, Baudelaire retained a highly paradoxical attachment to the revolutionary beliefs of 1848:

MOI, quand je consens à être républicain, *je fais le mal, le sachant.* Oui! *Vive la Révolution!* Toujours! Quand même! Mais moi je ne suis pas dupe, je n'ai jamais été dupe! je dis *Vive la Révolution!* comme je dirais: *Vive la Destruction! Vive l'Expiation! Vive le Châtiment! Vive la Mort!* Non seulement je serais heureux d'être victime, mais je ne haïrais pas d'être bourreau, pour sentir la Révolution des deux manières! Nous avons tous l'esprit républicain dans les veines, comme la vérole dans les os, nous sommes Démocratisés et Syphilisés. (OC, ii. 961)

In a variation of the volcano image of 1852, what we witness here is the 'vieux fonds révolutionnaire' briefly but violently thrusting its way up through the thick crust of de Maistrian pessimism that had hardened over it since the coup or, to use *Pauvre Belgique!*'s appalling metaphor, a renewed outbreak of the republicanism with which, as with syphilis, he was infected as a young man and which, despite every would-be antidote, remained within him, corroding body and mind, always subject to sudden, unpredictable recrudescence. In this context, 'Assomons les pauvres!' represents, as it were, a terminal dose of revolutionary clap with which Baudelaire is determined to infect the old beggar who accosts him.

In the years immediately following the coup, however, Baudelaire retreated inwards away from the public, political sphere, though even this retreat was not without its paradoxes and intermittences. A letter to Poulet-Malassis of 20 March 1852 concerning 'le social-isme napoléonien' suggests that Baudelaire may briefly have held the view that his mentor Proudhon himself briefly entertained in the wake of the coup (notably in *La Révolution sociale démontrée par le coup d'état de deux décembre* of July 1852), namely that the new regime and its prince-president would actually, if not necessarily intentionally, advance the cause of socialism even as they dismantled the Republican political apparatus. The same letter emphasizes the need to 'se mettre au point de vue *providentiel*' in order to understand recent political events and concludes with an injunction to Poulet-Malassis to persuade himself 'comme moi, de plus en plus, que la Philosophie est *Tout*' (C, i. 189–90). Baudelaire may not have lost interest in politics but more and more he is situating himself, he the street-fighter of but three months previously, *au-dessus de la mêlée*, no longer a participant in society's conflicts but an observer from a 'providential' viewpoint, *sub specie aeternitatis*.

Baudelaire's use of the term 'providential' in the letter to Poulet-Malassis is probably Proudhonian rather than de Maistrian, but the fact that there are doubts as to his frame of reference indicates the speed and relative ease with which he was able to move from a world-view shaped by Proudhon to one moulded by de Maistre: Proudhon, it should be noted, was himself an avid and by no means disapproving reader of *Les Soirées de Saint-Pétersbourg*.[42] Asselineau suggests that Baudelaire was studying de Maistre *before* the coup, and there is no reason to question his view. The first actual reference to de Maistre appears to be in the notes Baudelaire drew up in February 1852 for *Le Hibou philosophe* (both noun and adjective are highly significant), the periodical he planned to publish with Champfleury and others: de Maistre's '*Lettres et mélanges*' (actually his *Lettres et opuscules inédits* (1851)) are included amongst the works *Le Hibou* should review (OC, ii. 50). Admiring references to de Maistre are to be found in the first article on Poe, 'Edgar Allan Poe: Sa vie et ses ouvrages', published in *La Revue de Paris* in March and April 1852 (OC, ii. 251 and 267), and a letter of 9 May 1852 to Maxime Du Camp cites with approval de Maistre's view, expressed in *Les Soirées*, of Islam as no more than '*une des phases du protestantisme*,—ou quelque chose comme cela' (C, i. 199). At the same time, translations of Poe began to appear at regular intervals—*Bérénice* (April 1852), *Philosophie de l'ameublement* (September), *Souvenirs de M. Auguste Bedloe* (December)—and the December number of *L'Illustration* in which the last-named text appeared announced that it formed part of a book of translations entitled *Histoires extraordinaires* to be published—some hopes!—by Victor Lecou the following month. 'De Maistre et Edgar Poe m'ont appris à raisonner,' Baudelaire would later write (OC, i. 669); by the end of 1852 at the latest they had replaced Proudhon (of whom, a single reference of 1858 apart (C, i. 505), neither published work nor correspondence would

---

[42] See K. Vincent, *Pierre-Joseph Proudhon and the Rise of French Republican Socialism* (Oxford Univ. Press, 1984), 24–5.

speak again before July 1864 (C, ii. 391)) as the focal points of his intellectual and moral universe.

Further evidence of withdrawal from the public world of politics into one of private reflection can be found in the range of titles Baudelaire proposed for the periodical he planned to edit with Champfleury. Some are directly suggestive of a quasi-monastic flight from the world (*La Chartreuse*, *L'Hermitage*, *La Thébaïde*, *Les Hermites volontaires*), others of a desperate fight for survival amidst an encircling desert of reactionary philistinism (*L'Oasis*, *La Citerne du désert*, *Le Dernier Asyle des Muses*). One proclaims its unabashed élitism (*Paucis*), while another implies that the only Republic that remains is *La République des Lettres*; two others, *Les Ouvriers de la dernière heure* and *La Réaction* suggest a confused hesitation between a vestigial populism and its diametrical opposite (OC, ii. 53).[43] Baudelaire's preferred title *Le Hibou philosophe* inevitably suggests 'Les Hiboux', published as the concluding—and conclusive—poem of the *Limbes* sequence of April 1851, in which Hartmut Stenzel[44] has seen evidence of a turning away from the political sphere and of a repudiation, even before the coup, of revolutionary activism in favour of an essentially spectatorial and 'philosophical' stance:

> Sous les ifs noirs qui les abritent
> Les hiboux se tiennent rangés
> Comme des idoles de jais,
> Dardant leur œil rouge; ils méditent.
>
> Sans remuer ils se tiendront
> Jusqu'à l'heure mélancolique
> Où, poussant le soleil oblique,
> Les ténèbres s'établiront.
>
> Cette attitude au sage enseigne
> Qu'il faut en ce monde qu'il craigne
> Le tumulte et le mouvement.
>
> L'homme, ivre d'une ombre qui passe
> Porte toujours le châtiment
> D'avoir voulu changer de place.
>
> (Text of 1851)

[43] The projected titles are discussed, unfortunately without reference to their possible political meanings, by Jacqueline Wachs, 'A propos des "Titres pour un recueil mensuel"', *Bulletin baudelairien*, 10/2 (1975), 2–10.

[44] Stenzel, *Der historische Ort*, 159–60. Stenzel does not comment on the possible political significance of the owls' 'œil *rouge*'.

Although, as with all the 1851 *Limbes* poems, nothing proves conclusively that 'Les Hiboux' was not written before the February revolution, the appearance of the key-word 'ivre' in the first line of the final tercet locates the poem at the heart of Baudelaire's pre-occupations of 1848–51 and beyond. If 'Les Hiboux' is indeed a text of, say, 1849–50 (and, as we shall see, 'l'heure mélancolique', 'le soleil oblique', and 'les ténèbres' could also have special meanings in a Second Republic context), then the poem could be read as an expression of that melancholic private self which we have seen to be increasingly at odds with the optimistic public persona of the later stages of the Republic. Once more Baudelaire's social, moral, and political conservatism of the later 1850s could be seen to have its roots in the 1848–51 period itself when his over-riding commitment to the Republic allowed it, at most, incidental expression.

A similar movement inwards is to be found in 'Paysage', a poem which I have argued elsewhere[45] was originally inspired not by any Parisian event (despite its title when first published of 'Paysage parisien') but by the memory of the insurrectionary turmoil which Baudelaire witnessed as a schoolboy in Lyon in April 1834. It is likely that disillusion in the wake of the events of 1848–51 prompted Baudelaire, some time in the second half of 1852 or early 1853, to return to this abandoned text of the late 1830s or early 1840s, and perhaps inspired by Gautier's preface to *Émaux et Camées* (July 1852), to 'recycle' it with slight modification as an expression of his post-December recoil from political activism into a private world of poetic creativity. The first published version of the poem (in *Le Présent* in November 1857) concluded as follows:

> Et l'émeute aura beau tempêter à ma vitre,
> Je ne lèverai pas le front de mon pupitre,
> Et ne bougerai plus de l'antique fauteuil,
> Où je veux composer pour un jeune cercueil
> (Il faut charmer nos morts dans leurs noires retraites)
> De doux vers tout fumants comme des cassolettes.

The version used as the liminary poem of the *Tableaux parisiens* section of the 1861 *Fleurs du mal* is even more explicit in its apolitical (even anti-political) aestheticism:

---

[45] Richard D. E. Burton, 'Baudelaire and Lyon: A Reading of "Paysage" ', *Nottingham French Studies*, 28/1 (1979), 26–38.

L'Émeute, tempêtant vainement à ma vitre,
Ne fera pas lever mon front de mon pupitre
Car je serai plongé dans cette volupté
D'évoquer le Printemps avec ma volonté,
De tirer un soleil de mon cœur, et de faire
De mes pensers brûlants une tiède atmosphère.

The capitalization of 'Émeute' implies a negative judgement of all forms of political violence, and a review of a history of Neuilly of 1855 in which Baudelaire speaks of the 'terribles journées de Février où le Château fut le théâtre et la proie des plus ignobles passions, l'orgie et la destruction' (OC, ii. 56) appears to mark a further step towards his 'mature' view of revolution—even the amiable revolution of February 1848—as a manifestation of man's innate depravity. In 1853, in *Morale du joujou*, Baudelaire had already likened the child's determination to break its toys to 'le peuple qui assiège les Tuileries' (OC, i. 587), pointing forward to his later view that 'l'enfant, en général, est relativement à l'homme, en général, beaucoup plus rapproché du péché originel' (*L'Œuvre et la vie de Delacroix* (1863), OC, ii. 767). Before long the influence of de Maistre will be obsessive, but, as we have already indicated, just as Baudelaire's republicanism was never wholly free of other, potentially discordant, elements, so the anti-republicanism and anti-socialism of his later years are always subject to sudden and apparently unmotivated reversals. There is no better evidence of this instability than 'Le Vin des chiffonniers', the pivotal text of the chapters that follow, a poem on which Baudelaire worked for a period of ten years or more and which shows a bewildering number of changes from version to version—changes that seem to run against the current of what we know or can surmise of the poet's general ideological development, so that the 'definitive' version of 1857 is, or appears to be, more 'revolutionary' or 'socialist' than those that preceded it.

'Le Reniement de saint Pierre'

Two final poems—'Le Reniement de saint Pierre', written before the coup, probably in September–October 1851, and published in *La Revue de Paris* in October 1852, and 'A une femme trop gaie' (i.e. 'A celle qui est trop gaie'), sent anonymously to Mme Sabatier on 9 December 1852, but not published until the 1857 edition—will complete this review of the shift in Baudelaire's political stance between the last months of the Second Republic and the proclamation, following the plebiscite of 21 November 1852, of the Second Empire on the first anniversary of the coup. Sent to Gautier in late 1851 or early 1852 (it is one of the so-called 'douze poèmes' and Baudelaire classes it amongst the pieces he prefers (C, i. 180)), 'Le Reniement' was understandably withheld from publication during the months of repression that followed the coup. Even when it was eventually published in October 1852, by which time the situation had eased somewhat, the piece was still sufficiently provocative (Baudelaire described it as 'fort dangereuse' in a letter to his mother of 26 March 1853) for its author almost to be prosecuted on its account (C, i. 217). It was for this reason that, when republishing the poem in the 'Révolte' section of the 1857 *Fleurs du mal*, Baudelaire added, apparently at the last moment, the following note which, intended to protect him from the threat of prosecution, inadvertently or by design drew attention to the political significance of a poem that might otherwise have been read as a variation (which, of course, is what it is in part) on the stock romantic theme of God's abandonment of Christ at Gethsemane and Calvary as expressed most memorably in Vigny's 'Le Mont des Oliviers' (1843) and Nerval's 'Le Christ aux Oliviers' (1844), neither of which seems to have provoked undue scandal when first published:

Parmi les morceaux suivants, le plus caractérisé a déjà paru dans un des principaux recueils littéraires de Paris, où il n'a été considéré, du moins par les gens d'esprit, que pour ce qu'il est véritablement: le pastiche des raisonnements de l'ignorance et de la fureur. Fidèle à son douloureux programme, l'auteur des *Fleurs du Mal* a dû, en parfait comédien, façonner son esprit à tous les sophismes comme à toutes les corruptions. Cette déclaration candide n'empêchera pas sans doute les critiques honnêtes de la ranger parmi les théologiens de la populace et de l'accuser d'avoir regretté pour notre Sauveur Jésus-Christ, pour la Victime éternelle et volontaire, le rôle d'un conquérant, d'un Attila égalitaire et dévastateur. Plus d'un adressera sans doute un ciel les actions de grâces habituelles du Pharisien: 'Merci, mon Dieu, qui n'avez pas permis que je fusse semblable à ce poète infâme!' (OC, i. 1075–6)

It was, of course, a commonplace of the *quarante-huitard* imagination to represent the Republic as Christ and to see in the Christian virtues of Faith, Hope, and Charity the prototypes and inspiration of the *Liberté, Égalité, Fraternité* of the Republic. The assimilation of Christ and Republic permeates the whole of the Second Republic experience, from the philosophical Republicanism of works such as Alphonse Esquiros's *L'Évangile du Peuple* (1849), cited by Hartmut Stenzel in his valuable discussion of 'Le Reniement',[46] to the humanitarian, egalitarian, and anti-clerical reinterpretation of Christianity, partly inspired by Lamennais, that gained such a hold on the French popular imagination during the Restoration and Bourgeois Monarchies and which gave the Republicanism of February–March 1848 its would-be sacred, ritualistic character. The theme is present, parodically, in Pellerin's painting in *L'Éducation sentimentale* of 'la République, ou le Progrès, ou la Civilisation, sous la figure de Jésus-Christ conduisant une locomotive'[47] and, tragically, in Daumier's awe-inspiring 'We want Barabbas!' which may be read as an allegory of the betrayal of the Republic by its Bonapartist and Orleanist enemies and its abandonment by the French people. The following, quoted from Edward Berenson's superbly documented *Populist Religion and Left-wing Politics in France, 1830–1852* (1984), are wholly typical expressions of the popular Christian Republicanism of the Second Republic which Montagnard propaganda systematically drew on and disseminated between 1849 and the coup and with which, self-evidently, Baudelaire was familiar:

Jesus Christ was not, therefore, merely the redeemer of humanity from the divine point of view. He was the emancipator of humanity in the here-and-now. *La Voix du Peuple* (Marseille, 5 Nov. 1848)

God is no longer separated from humanity . . . for the action of God is revealed as well through the liberation of all peoples, by universal association, by the application of the divine principle of fraternity proclaimed by Jesus . . . It is revealed through the abolition of all monopolistic privileges, and through the destruction of all obstacles which stand in opposition to the regime of liberty, equality, and human fraternity that we so ardently desire. *La République* (3 May 1849)

If Christ came down to earth . . . (the conservatives) would call him a utopian, an anarchist, a revolutionary. They would charge him with vagrancy and put him in chains . . . Christ would not be with the *Honnêtes Modérés*. He would be with the poor and the oppressed . . . He would

---

46 Stenzel, *Der historische Ort*, 162–9.
47 Flaubert, *L'Éducation sentimentale*, 300.

preach the abolition of the proletariat . . . He would be a socialist. *La République* (22 Feb. 1849)[48]

In 1848, unlike 1830, Maurice Agulhon has written, summarizing the whole tradition of popular egalitarian Christianity, 'l'arbre (de la liberté) n'est plus une anticroix, il en serait plutôt, si l'on ose dire, une esquisse, une approche'.[49] In March 1848 *Le Salut public* (probably Baudelaire himself) had declared Christ to be 'le fondateur de toutes les républiques modernes' (OC, ii. 1035). There is no more need to seek a 'source' for this declaration than there is for 'Le Reniement' itself: quite simply, Christ the Republican was a ubiquitous presence throughout the Second Republic period.

Given this abundance of contextual and intertextual material, the meaning of 'Le Reniement' is only too clear; the only mystery is why the prosecution threatened in 1852 did not take place and why, at the 1857 trial, the charge of 'atteinte à la morale religieuse' was not followed up (see OC, i. 1180). After two stanzas whose meaning will be discussed in the next chapter, the poem continues as follows:

> —Ah! Jesus, souviens-toi du Jardin des Olives!   9
> Dans ta simplicité tu priais à genoux
> Celui qui dans son ciel riait au bruit des clous
> Que d'ignobles bourreaux plantaient dans tes chairs vives,   12
>
> Lorsque tu vis cracher sur ta divinité
> La crapule du corps de garde et des cuisines,
> Et lorsque tu sentis s'enfoncer les épines
> Dans ton crâne où vivait l'immense Humanité;   16
>
> Quand de ton corps brisé la pesanteur horrible
> Allongeait tes deux bras distendus, que ton sang
> Et ta sueur coulaient de ton front pâlissant,
> Quand tu fus devant tous posé comme une cible,   20
>
> Rêvais-tu de ces jours si brillants et si beaux
> Où tu vins pour remplir l'éternelle promesse,
> Où tu foulais, monté sur une douce ânesse,
> Des chemins tout jonchés de fleurs et de rameaux,   24
>
> Où, le cœur tout gonflé d'espoir et de vaillance,
> Tu fouettais tous ces vils marchands à tour de bras,
> Où tu fus maître enfin? Le remords n'a-t-il pas
> Pénétré dans ton flanc plus avant que la lance?   28

[48] Edward Berenson, *Populist Religion and Left-wing Politics in France, 1830–1852* (Princeton Univ. Press, Princeton, NJ, 1984), 99–102.
[49] Agulhon, *1848*, 53.

—Certes, je sortirai, quant à moi, satisfait
D'un monde où l'action n'est pas la soeur du rêve;
Puissé-je user du glaive et périr par le glaive!
Saint Pierre a renié Jésus . . . il a bien fait!   32

Using the Gospel narratives, Baudelaire has provided nothing less
than a history and interpretation in code of the evolution and fate
of the Second Republic as he perceives them. After 'l'éternelle
promesse' of the spring of 1848 when the Christ-Republic briefly
rode 'monté sur une douce ânesse' along 'des chemins tout jonchés
de fleurs et de rameaux' (ll. 22–4), there followed a phase of
messianic radicalism as, 'le cœur tout gonflé d'espoir et de
vaillance', the Republic—or rather its ultra-leftist wing—attempted
to drive 'tous ces vils marchands' (the conservatives and their
bourgeois allies and backers) from the Republican Holy of Holies
(ll. 25–6). If Baudelaire's Christ is transfixed by a remorse more
piercing than the Roman soldier's lance, it is not because he used
excessive violence on that occasion when, for a short while, he
might at last have been the 'maître' of his people and the situation
(l. 27), but rather because he had lashed the merchants only 'à tour
de bras' (l. 26) rather than availing himself of a more powerful and
destructive weapon, whence Baudelaire's apocalyptic call to arms
in the poem's penultimate line: 'Puissé-je user du glaive et périr par
le glaive!' Having failed in April, May, and finally June to will the
violent means necessary to achieve its ends, the doomed Republic
moved month by month and year by year from one Station of the
Cross to the next: first vilification and mockery at the hands of 'la
crapule du corps de garde et des cuisines' (l. 14) (the *gardes mobiles*
of June 1848?), then the parodic coronation of its 'crâne où vivait
l'immense Humanité' (l. 16) and now, the ultimate humiliation,
crucifixion by 'd'ignobles bourreaux' (l. 12) on the Liberty Tree
itself, the 'pesanteur horrible' of its broken body wrenching its
'bras distendus' out of joint as, the target of universal hatred and
abuse ('Quand tu fus devant tous posé comme une cible'), blood
and sweat pours from its 'front pâlissant' in the final agony
(ll. 17–20).
    What of the final stanza of 'Le Reniement de saint Pierre'? In it,
Baudelaire certainly denies the Christ-Republic or, rather, he
denies it as it existed in 1848–51, but it is essential to grasp the
substance and significance of that denial. Far from making an anti-

Republican, or even out-and-out reactionary of him, 'Le Reniement' reveals Baudelaire to be a *jusqu'auboutiste* in his commitment to the Republic. In repudiating the Christ-Republic in its present humbled, non-violent, and essentially powerless incarnation, Baudelaire is lamenting, as his note of 1857 disingenuously indicates, that it was or had no 'Attila égalitaire et dévastateur' prepared to will the violent means necessary to protect it from its enemies and establish the Republic of Liberty, Equality, and Fraternity on earth; he is lamenting, quite simply, that the 'victime' was not a 'bourreau'. Had he been Simon Peter, Baudelaire is saying, he would not have let Christ be taken without a fight; he would not merely have cut off the high priest's servant's ear, but cut his throat as well, and that of Judas, Caiaphas, Annas, Pontius Pilate, and the rest . . . But since this Christ-Republic has failed to fight for its survival, he, Baudelaire,[50] can repudiate it, if not the Republican principle itself, without remorse. While the Republican Christ has gone like a lamb to the slaughter and all His disciples have fled or fallen by the wayside, he alone has remained saintly in his uncompromising revolutionary purity. His cause may have failed but he has not failed it, whence his perverse, embittered pride and satisfaction as, untainted to the end, he withdraws 'd'un monde où l'action n'est pas la sœur du rêve'. If Peter denies the doomed Christ-Republic, he is doing no more than the doomed Christ-Republic deserves: 'Saint Pierre a renié Jésus . . . il a bien fait!' The Republic is dead or dying: long live *Saint* Peter! With the death of his Messiah, the disciple becomes a Messiah—or a Satan—unto himself: 'Être un grand homme et un saint *pour soi-même*, voilà l'unique chose importante' (*Mon cœur mis à nu* (OC, i. 695), 'Si j'avais voté, je n'aurais pu voter que pour moi' (letter to Ancelle, 5 March 1852 (C, i. 188)). The ultra-revolutionary Satanism of 'Le Reniement''s conclusion leads on logically, if indirectly, to the virtually unqualifiable—anarcho-sadist, Faustian-fascist, Satano-Bolshevik, authoritarian-egalitarian, or whatever—extremism of 'Assommons les pauvres!' The collapse of republican humanism in 1851–2 deprived the anti-bourgeois oppositionist that Baudelaire remained of the framework of political and moral values that, since 1848, had given shape to his disaffections and displacements.

---

[50] One might note, without attaching undue importance to the fact, that Baudelaire's second given name was Pierre and that 'Pierre de Feyis' was one of his pseudonyms of the 1840s.

Alienated henceforth from both the bourgeoisie that had destroyed the Republic and from the people that, through its failure to resist, had collaborated in that destruction, Baudelaire now felt himself wholly isolated in his oppositional stance, whence the exclamation, at once proud and despairing, of the letter to Ancelle: 'Peut-être l'avenir appartient-il aux hommes *déclassés?* (C, i. 188). As he left behind the republican-humanist certainties of 1848–51, Baudelaire moved into the new decade carrying within him both the debris of an egalitarian anti-bourgeois populism and the seeds of an authoritarianism that was both anti-bourgeois and anti-populist. Morally and politically *jenseits von Gut und Böse*, he would be drawn as by 'deux postulations simultanées' (*Mon cœur mis à nu* (OC, i. 682)) towards the extremes of Right and Left, at once 'Jésuite et Révolutionnaire' as, in May 1859, Baudelaire told Nadar 'tout vrai politique doit l'être' (C, i. 579). Democrat and autocrat, Proudhonist and de Maistrian, proto-Bolshevik and proto-fascist: Baudelaire was all of these simultaneously, and 'Assommons les pauvres!' is the textual battleground in which these contradictory impulses will, quite literally, fight it out amongst themselves.

'A une femme trop gaie'

'Le Reniement' havers between a repudiation of the Second Republic as it stood in 1851 and a repudiation of the Republican principle itself. Baudelaire's last poem of 1852, 'A une femme trop gaie', has no explicit political meaning, nor does it contain a coded political message like 'Le Reniement', but there is a sense in which it goes much further than the earlier poem in repudiating the underlying world-view of Republicanism. As we have seen, a faith in the intrinsic goodness both of nature and of humanity is fundamental to the republican humanism to which, with some reservations, Baudelaire unquestionably subscribed and which, as the following chapters will argue, found its principal expression in 'Le Vin' cycle of *Les Fleurs du mal*. By the end of 1852, though, just as the woman to whom the poem is addressed is felt to be 'trop gaie', so nature as a whole is experienced as over-lush, over-fertile, replete with a surfeit of vitality:

> Quelquefois dans un beau jardin
> Où je traînais mon agonie,

J'ai senti comme une ironie
Le soleil déchirer mon sein.

Et le printemps et la verdure
Ont tant humilié mon coeur
Que j'ai puni sur une fleur
L'insolence de la Nature.

(Text of 1852, quoted from
C, i. 206)

Having celebrated the fecundity of 'great creating Nature' in the wine poems and other characteristic Second Republic texts, Baudelaire now turns against it to infect it, like the woman's body, with own physical and psychological malady (embodied in 'sang' rather than 'venin' in the 1852 text). But it is not simply an over-luxuriant garden or a woman's over-ripe body that Baudelaire violates, debases, and reneges in 'A une femme trop gaie': it is, by conscious or unconscious implication, all the hopes and dreams of a Republican heaven on earth, all the faith in 'Nature' and 'Humanity', that were Baudelaire's and his generation's in the great revolutionary springtime of February 1848. For the first time since the mid-1840s, Baudelaire gives voice to a strident anti-humanism, anti-naturalism, and, not least, anti-feminism. His reading of de Maistre, on which he seems to have embarked some months before the December coup, had, by the end of 1852, helped release and give shape to that loathing of self, nature, and sex which, erupting in early poems like 'Une charogne' (1842–4?) and 'Un voyage à Cythère' (1845–6?), had been overlaid and largely subdued by one or another form of naturalistic humanism since the time, approximately, of the *Salon de 1846*.

Baudelaire sent 'A une femme trop gaie' to Madame Sabatier on 9 December 1852, a week after the proclamation of the Second Empire on the first anniversary of the December coup. It was the anniversary-obsessed poet's first *explicit* repudiation of Nature since the mid-1840s and it was made (Baudelaire's anonymous accompanying note suggests the poem was a recent creation (C, i. 205)) in the first week of a regime which, universal male suffrage and the tricolore apart, repudiated everything the Second Republic had stood for: whether consciously intended by Baudelaire or brought about by the unconscious logic of the imagination, the fit between public context and private text is too close to be coincidental. Whether Baudelaire knew it or not, December 1852 marked a decisive, though still not definitive, break with the whole world-view of Republicanism. If thereafter he gave voice to Republican hopes and dreams, or wrote on Republican themes using Republican imagery, it would be in the teeth of an increasingly reactionary official ideology.

Red Wine, Red Politics:
The Wine Poems in Context

In both the 1857 and 1861 editions of *Les Fleurs du mal*, Baudelaire gave a place apart in the overall 'architecture' of his work to five poems on the theme of wine which, it will be argued here, are the fullest—because most complex and contradictory—poetic expression of his interrelated political, aesthetic, and ethical concerns during the period covered by the first four chapters of this book. The unique importance of the wine poems—and particularly of the two most substantial texts in the section, 'L'Âme du vin' and 'Le Vin des chiffonniers'—to an understanding of Baudelaire's politics before, during, and after the Second Republic stems from the fact that, though they undoubtedly existed in some form before 1848 (as early as 1843, according to the usually reliable testimony of Ernest Prarond), they underwent radical changes not only of expression but of underlying meaning as the political crisis unfolded and Baudelaire's political position shifted under the combined pressure of public events and private preoccupations. To follow the successive and often highly discrepant versions of, in particular, 'Le Vin des chiffonniers' from its earliest manuscript form (probably dating from 1848 itself but based on a text drafted as early as 1841–3), through its first publication in 1854 to its 'definitive' form in the 1857 *Fleurs du mal* is to follow the whole trajectory of Baudelaire's thinking over a fifteen-year period of unparalleled inner and outer turbulence as he struggles to reconcile all the contending political, ethical, and metaphysical 'pulls' to which he is exposed until finally, by a supreme paradox, he produces a text for the 1857 edition which, running against the grain of his whole political evolution since 1851, is—or seems to be—actually more 'revolutionary' in its implications than the versions that preceded it. Our understanding of the wine poems is both aided and complicated by the fact that prose 'doublets' of 'L'Âme du vin' and 'Le

Vin des chiffonniers' figure prominently in Baudelaire's most 'committed' work of the Second Republic period, *Du vin et du haschisch* (March 1851), and that 'Le Vin de l'assassin', a poem which Prarond claimed to have heard Baudelaire recite in 1843, would later (in 1854) provide the basic theme and plot for a play entitled *L'Ivrogne* which, though it never got beyond draft stage, would clearly have embodied a very different moral and political viewpoint from that contained in the original poem. As we shall see, Baudelaire's wine poems cannot be understood outside the whole question of wine production and consumption in nineteenth-century France—a question well to the fore in the debates, controversies, and conflicts of 1848–51—and our discussion will take us into areas far removed from the main currents of Baudelaire criticism before leading us back armed, it is hoped, with the contextual and intertextual insights necessary for the correct interpretation of the texts before us. Wine is a theme of the utmost ambiguity in Baudelaire's work, and we can best begin our exploration of it with a text in which, for reasons that will become clear, Baudelaire was at pains to deny, suppress, or disguise that ambiguity: *Du vin et du haschisch*, first published in *Le Messager de l'Assemblée* in March 1851, a work of insistently *démoc-soc* inspiration which, together with the slightly later *Pierre Dupont* (August 1851), represents Baudelaire's fullest and most orthodox radical republican statement throughout the entire Second Republic 'interlude'.

Du vin et du haschisch *and* Pierre Dupont (I)

The world-view of *Du vin et du haschisch* is, like that of the tribute to Pierre Dupont, essentially optimistic, naturalistic, and populist. As in the later *Paradis artificiels* (1860), the use of drugs is condemned on the grounds that they undermine the user's will-power, isolate him from his fellow men and encourage inaction and lethargic reverie. The recourse to drugs is seen as an attempt by the individual to 'déranger les conditions primordiales de son existence, et de rompre l'équilibre de ses facultés avec les milieux', an illegitimate bid, in other words, to transcend the limitations of the Real and attain to a god-like condition. Furthermore—and this is perhaps the crucial point in the present context—the use of hashish is, in Baudelaire's view, confined to the leisured classes, whereas the drinking of wine is for him essentially a working-class pursuit: 'Enfin le vin est pour le peuple qui travaille et qui mérite d'en boire. Le haschisch appartient à la classe des joies solitaires; il est fait pour les misérables oisifs. Le vin est utile, il produit des résultats fructifiants. Le haschisch est inutile et dangereux.' Hashish, in short, is dehumanizing and antisocial; it encloses the user within a solipsistic dream-world instead of binding him to his fellows; it is opposed to action and work which, for the Baudelaire of 1851, was tantamount to being opposed to life itself: 'Il faut avant tout vivre et travailler' (OC, i. 397).

In contrast to this negative view of the effects of hashish, Baudelaire's celebration of wine is entirely—even lyrically—positive. The essential argument in its favour is that 'le vin est profondément humain, et j'oserais presque dire homme d'action' (OC, i. 388), pointing forward to the injunction to the poet in *Pierre Dupont* to celebrate 'le génie de l'action' (OC, ii. 34) to the exclusion of other inner-directed preoccupations. Baudelaire summarizes his distinction between wine and hashish thus:

Le vin exalte la volonté, le haschisch l'annihile. Le vin est un support physique, le haschisch est une arme pour le suicide. Le vin rend bon et sociable. Le haschisch est isolant. L'un est laborieux pour ainsi dire, l'autre essentiellement paresseux. A quoi bon, en effet, travailler, labourer, fabriquer quoi que ce soit, quand on peut emporter le paradis d'un seul coup? (OC, i. 397)

The stress here on socially useful production gives the lie to Baudelaire's later assertion that 'être un homme utile m'a paru *toujours* quelque chose de bien hideux' (*Mon cœur mis à nu* (OC, i. 679), italics added). Such may well have been the case before 1848 and again after 1851. For the *démoc-soc* Baudelaire, however, not only are work and social usefulness the paramount values but the poet is himself defined in *Pierre Dupont* as first and foremost a worker who, like any other, must earn his living by his productive labour—'Il faut que son outil le nourrisse' (OC, ii. 30)—and so contribute to the common human enterprise evoked in 'La Rançon' (1851–2). *L'Art pour l'art*, and along with it any 'ivory tower' concept of the artist's place (or non-place) in society, is stigmatized almost as the artistic equivalent of hashish-smoking. The republican Baudelaire's preference is for 'le poète qui se met en communication permanente avec les hommes de son temps', who 'placé sur un des points de la circonférence de l'humanité, renvoie sur la même ligne en vibrations plus mélodieuses la pensée qui lui fut transmise' (OC, ii. 27) and the whole of whose gifts as man and writer are to be devoted to the task of inspiring his fellow workers by articulating the ideas and feelings that they themselves are unable to formulate. Work—artistic work like any other—is the social bond *par excellence*, and wine the supreme social lubricant, the instrument and sacrament of active community. Wine–hashish, work–idleness, production–consumption, 'socialism'–individualism: all these antitheses are explicitly present in *Du Vin et du haschisch* and are congruent with the basic opposition between 'travailleurs' and 'oisifs' on which so much of the socialist thought of the 1830s and 1840s was founded.[1]

Not surprisingly, Baudelaire has nothing but contempt for those 'pseudo-moralistes pharisiens' (OC, i. 381) who condemn wine and would deprive 'le peuple' of the joys, solace, and inspiration it affords. Against their insistence that drink provokes crime, he argues that it does no more than bring out the natural propensities of the drinker: 'Il y a des ivrognes méchants; ce sont des gens naturellement méchants. L'homme mauvais devient exécrable, comme le bon devient excellent' (OC, i. 387). In defending drink in this way, it goes without saying that Baudelaire was directly challenging the dominant middle-class view which saw in *le gros rouge* and other *tord-boyaux* too nefarious to mention proof of the underlying depravity of the working classes and a major cause— perhaps *the* major cause—of their poverty, desperation, and alarming proclivity towards violence. In answer to the charge that 'vous innocentez l'ivrognerie, vous idéalisez la crapule', Baudelaire admits that 'devant les bienfaits je n'ai pas le courage de compter les griefs' (OC, i. 382). Yet by 1851, Baudelaire already had ample evidence, both in his own life and from his observation of others, of the negative effects of the drunkenness he is so determined to celebrate in *Du vin et du haschisch*. In December 1847, he had told his mother, pointedly failing to distinguish, as he does in 1851, between drink and drugs, that 'le laudanum et le vin sont des mauvaises ressources contre le chagrin. Ils font passer le temps mais ne refont pas la vie' (C, i. 143). At the *Salon* of 1846 he had

---

[1] For an authoritative discussion of this opposition, see William H. Sewell, *Work and Revolution in France: The Language of Labour from the Old Regime to 1848* (Cambridge Univ. Press, 1980), esp. p. 214.

obviously been deeply struck by the 'ferocité' and 'brutalité' of a painting by Ignazio Manzoni entitled *La Rixe des mendiants* which, in addition to 'les faces les plus patibulaires qui se puissent voir', depicted 'un mélange singulier de chapeaux défoncés, de jambes de bois, de verres cassés, de buveurs vaincus; la luxure, la ferocité et l'ivrognerie agitant leurs haillons' (OC, ii. 452). This painting may well have suggested to Baudelaire the image of the drunkard in the tercets of 'Le Tonneau de la Haine' which, first published as one of *Les Limbes* in April 1851 but probably written before 1848, strikingly dramatizes the negative side of alcohol that *Du vin et du haschisch* is at such pains to deny:

> La Haine est un ivrogne au fond d'une taverne,
> Qui sent toujours la soif naître de la liqueur
> Et se multiplier comme l'hydre de Lerne.
>
> —Mais les buveurs heureux connaissent leur vainqueur,
> Et la Haine est vouée à ce sort lamentable
> De ne pouvoir jamais s'endormir sous la table.

(Text of 1851)

If we further recall that, by 1851, Baudelaire had certainly written (but not, as was long believed, published) at least a version of 'Le Vin de l'assassin', the exclusion of the negative from *Du vin et du haschisch* becomes all the more remarkable, to be explained only, as will become clear later in this chapter, by the highly positive significance of wine in *démoc-soc* political discourse in 1848–51 and by Baudelaire's consequent determination to protect wine and popular drinking habits from any possible counter-attack from those 'fanfarons de sobriété, buvant en cachette et ayant quelque vin occulte' (OC, i. 382), the French bourgeoisie.

Pierre Dupont is also characterized by a deliberate suppression of the negative that takes the form of a celebration—at a time (July–August 1851) when, as we have seen, Baudelaire's mood was anything but celebratory—of 'l'optimisme de Dupont, sa confiance illimitée dans la bonté native de l'homme, son amour fanatique de la nature'. It was political considerations similar to those which required that wine be presented in solely positive terms that led Baudelaire, in the teeth of his despair at the time, to assert that 'la nature est si belle, et l'homme est si grand, qu'il est difficile, en se mettant à un point de vue supérieur, de concevoir le sens du mot: irréparable.' *Pierre Dupont* concludes with a celebration of poetry that is uncannily similar to the eulogy of wine in *Du vin et du haschisch*:

Dans le cachot, elle se fait révolte; à la fenêtre de l'hôpital, elle est ardente espérance; dans la mansarde déchirée et malpropre, elle se pare comme une fée du luxe et de l'élégance; non seulement elle constate, mais elle répare. Partout elle se fait négation de l'iniquité.

Like wine, poetry always contains 'le divin caractère utopique' (OC, ii. 34–5). It restores health and encourages hope ('Tu lui verses l'espoir, la jeunesse et la vie', Baudelaire writes of wine in 'Le Vin du solitaire') and transfigures the most squalid surroundings exactly as wine does in 'Le Poison':

> Le vin sait revêtir le plus sordide bouge
> D'un luxe miraculeux,
> Et fait surgir plus d'un portique fabuleux
> Dans l'or de sa vapeur rouge,
> Comme un soleil couchant dans un ciel nébuleux.

Poetry and wine—no less than revolution—are 'Utopian' expressions of human desire; they are all forms of revolt against the limitations and miseries of the Real, challenges issued by the human imagination to 'un monde où l'action n'est pas la sœur du rêve'. Wine, poetry, and the collective action of the crowd all generate a particular form of 'ivresse' that negates things as they are and awakens the vision of a Promised Land in which all human longings would at last be satisfied.

Du vin et du haschisch and *Pierre Dupont* may be completed by a text, *Morale du joujou*, which, though published in April 1853, is very close in inspiration to Baudelaire's writings of the Second Republic and may, of course, have been conceived and drafted some considerable time before it appeared in print. What is most striking about *Morale du joujou* in the present context is Baudelaire's comparison of parents who deprive their children of toys to those members of the middle classes who would deny the right of the poor to seek in drink comfort and sustenance for the miseries which middle-class dominance has itself brought into being:

Ce sont les mêmes gens qui donneraient volontiers un franc à un pauvre, à condition qu'il s'etouffât avec du pain, et lui refuseront toujours deux sous pour se désaltérer au cabaret. Quand je pense à une certaine classe de personnes ultra-raisonnables et anti-poétiques par qui j'ai tant souffert, je sens toujours la haine pincer et agiter mes nerfs. (OC, i. 586)

Baudelaire's highly emotional identification with both deprived child and deprived worker is extremely significant. The child, as we know from this and other texts, is for Baudelaire an embryonic poet who lives in a state of inspirational rapture and whose love of toys is the expression of a deep-rooted spiritual and artistic impulse, a longing for the ideal. Still more significantly, the child is permanently intoxicated by the world in which he lives: 'L'enfant voit tout en *nouveauté*; il est toujours *ivre*' (OC, ii. 690). (Cf. 'L'Enfant désherité s'enivre de soleil' in 'Bénédiction'.) Those members of the bourgeoisie who would deprive the child of his toys and the worker of his drink are, in Baudelaire's view, the hardened enemies of poetry. The link between wine, poetry, and popular revolution is becoming steadily clearer.

'L'Âme du vin' ('Le Vin des honnêtes gens')

Ernest Prarond claimed that a version of 'L'Âme du vin' existed as early as 1843, and there is no reason to doubt him, particularly as the first line of the 1857 text (not, interestingly, that of the first published version of 1850) appeared as the epigraph, with the attribution 'Baudelaire-Dufaÿs', to Théodore de Banville's 'Chanson du vin', a poem dated September 1844 and published for the first time in *Les Stalactites* (1846). By the time it appeared in print under the title 'Le Vin des honnêtes gens' in *Le Magasin des familles* in June 1850, the original text must have undergone considerable rewriting for, together with its still more obviously *démoc-soc* prose 'doublet' in *Du vin et du haschisch*, the poem remains the fullest and most positive statement of Baudelaire's radical-socialist world-view of 1848–51. What prompted Baudelaire to publish so radical a text in so conspicuously unradical a journal remains obscure. His contact was probably Julien Lemer in whose anthology *Les Poètes de l'Amour* 'Lesbos' would appear in July 1850 and who, in *Le Magasin*'s April number, had begun a series of articles entitled 'Études historiques sur le vin' in which, mainly through the mouthpiece of a real or imaginary oenophile named 'Père Latreille', he dispensed advice on the purchase and keeping of wine to the journal's middle-class and probably mainly feminine readership. Lemer may have felt that some poems on wine would nicely offset his articles and Baudelaire, pressed for money and, in the circumstances of 1850, with few outlets for his writings, may be imagined to have accepted in spite—or even, conceivably, because —of *Le Magasin*'s conservative character. 'Le Vin de l'assassin' and 'Le Vin des chiffonniers' (both already available in publishable or near-publishable form) being far too controversial for such a journal, 'Le Vin des honnêtes gens' duly appeared in the June 1850 number as one of *Le Magasin*'s regular series 'Poésies de la famille', preceded by 'Châtiment de l'orgueil' and followed by the announcement that 'ces deux morceaux inédits sont tirés d'un livre intitulé LES LIMBES, qui paraîtra très prochainement, et qui est destiné à représenter les agitations et les mélancolies de la jeunesse moderne'. The incongruity of two such highly political poems—the political significance of 'Châtiment de l'orgueil' is discussed in a later chapter of this book—appearing in such a context is under-lined by the titles of the articles surrounding Baudelaire's poems: 'Histoire de la dentelle' by Charles Robin (pp. 323–9), 'Les Femmes de l'Empire: Madame Tallien' by Émile Marco de Saint-Hilaire (pp. 330–5), then Baudelaire's poems (pp. 335–7) and then, delightfully, 'Contes des veillées de famille: Le Soldat de plomb, tendre et constant' by Andre de Goy, beginning: 'Il y avait une fois vingt-cinq soldats de plomb; ils étaient tous frères, car ils étaient nés du même moule . . .'. It may be the character of *Le Magasin des familles* that explains 'L'Âme du vin' 's puzzling original title, 'Le Vin des honnêtes gens'. The term 'honnêtes gens' had a very precise meaning in *démoc-soc* discourse in 1848–51, that of 'moderates' who mouthed their loyalty to the Republic but were in reality ready to support anyone—Cavaignac, Changarnier, Louis Napoleon—who seemed able to deliver France from the spectre of *les rouges*. In 1848, Eugène Pottier, of whom we shall hear much in the pages that follow, had written a song entitled 'La Republique honnête' which featured Robert Macaire as the emblematic 'moderate' and began as follows:

> Robert Macaire a cinquante ans.
> Il fit sa pelote au bon temps.
> A la Bourse, gras et vermeil,
> Il fait la pluie et le soleil.
> Modéré féroce, il répète:

Vive la République honnête!
Et Bertrand dit de son côté:
Vive la Famille et la Propriété![2]

Similarly, in Dijon in late 1849, *Le Travail* repeatedly warned its readers against those who sought to 'amener une révolution dans le sens *honnête et modéré*', urging them to fight off 'cet état d'atonie, de honte, de misère, dans lequel nous a plongés, pieds et poings liés, la ligue des *honnêtes gens*' and always to remember that 'parmi les *honnêtes gens*, il est bon nombre de citoyens qui se sont laissés entraîner au courant de la réaction, sans trop se rendre compte de l'abus que le parti royaliste faisait de leur simplicité' (*Le Travail*, 14 Oct. and 5 Nov. 1849, italics in original). At the same time, there is some evidence that radicals used the term 'gens honnêtes' to designate their own working-class supporters.[3] If this is so, one may legitimately suspect some subversive intention in Baudelaire's publishing in a journal obviously intended for *honnêtes gens* a poem which, despite its title, expresses the ideology and world-view of *gens honnêtes* and could, presumably, only be correctly understood by them. It could be, therefore, that in the constraining circumstances of 1850, Baudelaire is reverting to the 'oppositional' tactics of disguise, subterfuge, and simulation that he appears to have used so frequently in his writings of the Bourgeois Monarchy. Significantly, when he republished the poem in *La République du Peuple, almanach démocratique* in September 1851 he gave it the title—'L'Âme du vin'—that it would have in the 1857 *Fleurs du mal*:[4] in a *démoc-soc* publication there was no need

[2] Pottier, *Œuvres complètes*, ed. Pierre Brochon (Maspéro, 1966), 54.
[3] The radical journal *L'Aimable Faubourien*, founded by Poulet-Malassis, changed it subtitle from *Journal de la canaille* to *Journal des gens honnêtes* in May 1849. An article by Antonio Watripon entitled 'Aux gens honnêtes' contained the exhortation 'Enfin, frères, nous sommes du parti des gens honnêtes' and another, also by Watripon, made a series of distinctions between 'les Républicains honnêtes et les honnêtes Républicains', which confusingly, uses the term 'honnêtes républicains' as designating true, radical republicans while denouncing 'les républicains honnêtes' as 'très-malhonnêtes gens qui conspirent, au nom de l'ordre, contre la République' (*L'Aimable Faubourien*, 2ᵉ année, 1 (May 1849), 1–2). In his first article on Poe, Baudelaire uses the term '*les honnêtes gens*' in its standard pejorative sense in radical-Bohemian discourse (OC, ii. 270).
[4] At least, I assume that this is the case, since none of the major editions of *Les Fleurs du mal* gives an alternative title for the *République du Peuple* text. There is another manuscript, written in a hand other than Baudelaire's, that has the title 'Le Vin des honnêtes gens' and which is presumably taken directly from *Le Magasin des familles*; Pichois dates it 'avant 1853' (see OC, i. 1045).

to conceal his meaning and no incentive to hoodwink his readers into thinking they were reading something 'honnête et modéré' when the poem was, as will become clearer as we proceed, a classic statement of the *démoc-soc* faith using the classic *démoc-soc* coupling of workers and their wine.

The essential theme of 'L'Âme du vin'[5] and its prose equivalent is the co-operative relationship between man, nature, and wine. Significantly, in view of the value that the republican Baudelaire attaches elsewhere to work, 'L'Âme du vin' celebrates the production as well as the consumption of wine. Born of the union of natural processes and human labour, wine owes its existence to the worker and, in gratitude, bestows its blessings upon him:

> Je sais combien il faut, sur la colline en flamme,
> De peine, de sueur et de soleil cuisant
> Pour engendrer ma vie et pour me donner l'âme;
> Mais je ne serai point ingrat ni malfaisant . . .

There is a creative exchange between man and nature in the making of wine, and an economic exchange between producers and consumers; the state induced by wine—itself the result of a biochemical 'exchange' with the drinker's organism—provokes a further exchange of sociability and friendship amongst the community of drinkers. At each of its 'stages', therefore, wine is suggestive of reciprocity, collaboration between man and nature and with each other, cosmic balance and community; it is entirely appropriate that it should sing 'un chant plein de lumière et de fraternité' for it embodies the kind of co-operativism to which Baudelaire, as an admirer of Proudhon, would have been deeply sympathetic. Furthermore, wine implies a natural continuum, an unending cycle of birth, growth, decay, death, and rebirth—the kind of cycle by which Baudelaire was nauseated in the earlier 'Une charogne' (1841–3?)—but which here suggests the underlying equilibrium and goodness of nature. Thus wine in its bottle ('Sous ma prison de verre et mes cires vermeilles') is in a state of death-like incarceration until it descends into the belly of the weary worker which is both tomb ('une douce tombe') and womb from which, after a further process of exchange, it is reborn as life-giving energy: 'Je fais dans

---

[5] For the sake of convenience, I am using this title to refer to all the published versions of the poem and, except where there are important variant readings, am using the text of the 1861 edition of *Les Fleurs du mal*.

l'estomac du travailleur un grand remue-ménage, et de là par des escaliers invisibles je monte dans son cerveau où j'exécute ma danse suprême.' Just as in February revolution is said in *Le Salut public* to have physically revitalized the people of Paris, so wine rejuvenates the worker's ailing wife, restoring her to her former tenderness and, perhaps, reawakening her sexual appetite. It also reinvigorates his son:

J'allumerai les yeux de ta vieille femme, la vieille compagne de tes chagrins journaliers et de tes plus vieilles espérances. J'attendrirai son regard et je mettrai au fond de sa prunelle l'éclair de sa jeunesse. Et ton cher petit, tout pâlot, ce pauvre petit ânon attelé à la même fatigue que le limonier, je lui rendrai les belles couleurs de son berceau, et je serai pour ce nouvel athlète de la vie l'huile qui raffermissait les muscles des anciens lutteurs. (OC, i. 380)

The theme of the natural cycle is still more pronounced in the first published version of the poem where the final stanza incorporates two archetypal symbols of cosmic continuity and transformation— the seed that must die before it can yield new life and the butterfly that is born of the tomb-like chrysalis:

En toi je tomberai, végétale ambroisie,
Comme le grain fécond tombe dans le sillon,
Et de notre union naîtra la poésie
Qui montera vers Dieu comme un grand papillon.

(Text of *Le Magasin des familles*)

These words suggest a sacramental relationship between man and wine, and indeed it would be virtually impossible for anyone of Catholic formation to write of wine without some reference, conscious or unconscious, to the Mass; the themes of union, communion, and fraternity in 'L'Âme du vin' gain added resonance from the association that many, if not most, readers will spontaneously make with the Christian mystery *par excellence*. But Baudelaire's sacrament celebrates not God or His Incarnation in Christ, but Man. In *Du Vin et du haschisch* he envisages an explicitly Trinitarian relationship between man, wine, and the Superman that is born of their union, writing of 'une sorte de psychologie double dont le vin et l'homme composent les deux termes' and going on, in terms that deliberately echo those of the Creed, to explain how certaines boissons contiennent la faculté d'augmenter outre mesure la personnalité de l'être pensant, et de créer, pour ainsi dire, une troisième personne, opération mystique, où l'homme naturel et le vin, le dieu animal et le dieu végétal, jouent le rôle du Père et du Fils dans la Trinité; ils engendrent un Saint-Esprit, qui est l'homme supérieur, lequel procède également des deux. (OC, i. 387)

This Trinity is, needless to say, profoundly blasphemous. The Third Person,[6] which Baudelaire assimilates in 'L'Âme du vin' to poetry, rises up 'vers Dieu', but, one surmises, in a spirit of revolt rather than of reverence; the poet-superman, born of the union of man and wine, represents the revolt of humanity against a divinely instituted and repressive order. Primitive communism has supplanted the communion of believers; the drinkers of the wine of revolutionary humanism have established the kingdom of love and justice on earth without God's aid or intervention. Much later, and in another context, Baudelaire was to write: 'La Révolution n'est pas une religion, puisqu'elle n'a ni prophètes, ni saints, ni miracles, et qu'elle a but de nier tout cela'. And he added, critically now of course: 'Pan doint tuer Dieu. Pan, c'est le peuple' ('Notes diverses sur *L'Art philosophique*' (1860–1?) (OC, ii. 606)). The close kinship of Pan and Dionysos, god of wine, and of both with the violent upheaval of the *status quo*, needs hardly to be stressed: 'c'est le dieu Pan qui a fait la révolution,' a young radical hothead told Baudelaire in February 1851, 'il est la révolution' (*L'École païenne* (1852) (OC, ii. 44)).

Republicanism, Socialism, and Antitheism

One of the most striking features of the wine poems is that each of them ends, as 'L'Âme du vin' does, on a note of auto-deification and of challenge to the divine order. Of the 'hubristic' conclusion to the 1857 version of 'Le Vin des chiffonniers' in which man creates wine almost as a retort to God's indifference, we shall say much later. In 'Le Vin du solitaire' wine endows the drinker with 'l'orgueil, ce trésor de toute gueuserie | Qui nous rend triomphants et semblables aux Dieux' and in 'Le Vin des amants', the weakest

---

[6] See Philippe Muray (*Le 19ᵉ siècle à travers les âges* (Denoël, 1984), 501) on 'le culte dixneuviémiste du Saint-Esprit' and the 'espèce de paraclétophilie progressiste' in the 'oc-soc' literature of the 1840s which Baudelaire seems to echo in *Du vin et du haschisch*.

poem of the cycle, it permits the lovers, united in 'un délire parallèle', to soar 'vers le paradis de [leurs] rêves'. In none of these poems is the urge towards self-divinization even implicitly criticized by Baudelaire, and even in 'Le Vin de l'assassin' he shows an undoubted complicity with the murderer and his final outright defiance of the divine order:

> Et je dormirai comme un chien!
> Le chariot aux lourdes roues
> Chargé de pierres et de boues,
> Le wagon enragé peut bien
>
> Écraser ma tête coupable
> Ou me couper par le milieu,
> Je m'en moque comme de Dieu
> Du Diable ou de la Sainte Table!

For the first edition of *Les Fleurs du mal*, Baudelaire having renounced his youthful radicalism or anxious to conceal it, attempted to reduce the blasphemous (and potentially revolutionary) implications of 'L'Âme du Vin'. In the final stanza the line 'Comme le grain fécond tombé dans le sillon' is replaced by 'Grain précieux jeté par l'éternel Semeur' so that wine, which in the first version of the poem was the product solely of the collaboration of man and 'great creating Nature', is now given a divine origin. But this subterfuge cannot disguise the anti-Christian or 'hubristic' implications of the poem which continues to postulate the irrelevance of God to the community of drinkers.

All this underlines the close relationship between the wine poems and the *Révolte* section of *Les Fleurs du mal*. 'Le Reniement de saint Pierre' (which, significantly, stresses Christ's '*H*umanité' rather than His '*d*ivinité') was, as we have seen, written in the immediate aftermath of the *coup d'état*, and it is virtually certain that 'Abel et Caïn' and 'Les Litaries de Satan' date from the very end of the Bourgeois Monarchy, if not from 1848 itself. The political significance of Satan and Satanism in the middle years of the nineteenth century has been brought out powerfully by Eugen Weber:

Satan n'est pas nécessairement le Mal, bien qu'en ce rôle il ait aussi sa place. Très souvent, il n'est que *l'Autre*, l'opposition à l'ordre établi, aux principes régnants, aux intérêts bien pensants qui se recommandent de Dieu. Et cette opposition devait suggérer une autre incarnation de Satan, celle de héros révolutionnaire toujours, mais cette fois-ci dans un sens non seulement littéraire mais politique. Si, pour les maîtres de la Restauration, la liberté était diabolique, pourquoi les libéraux ne prendraient-ils pas parti pour le diable? . . . Si, pour ses ennemis, la Révolution était le fait de Satan, les partisans de la Révolution devaient lui en savoir gré. Si les ennemis de la Révolution avaient cause liée avec Dieu, si les oppresseurs des peuples (comme, plus tard, du *peuple*) régnaient par sa grâce, le libéral et le romantique (souvent une et même personne) pouvaient bien suivre Satan en son exil et rejeter un ciel trop réactionnaire ou trop bourgeois, selon les régimes, pour les attirer.[7]

Thus there would be no contradiction for radical republicans and socialists to see Christ (particularly, as in 'Le Reniement de saint Pierre', when apparently abandoned by God in Gethsemane and on the cross) and Satan as embodiments of the revolt of Humanity (the poor) against divine oppression (the tyranny of the rich and powerful); social and political conflicts would be translated into Manichean terms with Satan now as revolutionary Lucifer aided in his struggle against God and the existing order by archetypal rebels such as Cain. The importance of Cain as a figure of metaphysical and artistic revolt in romantic writing is well known.[8] By 1848 that revolt had, predictably, been recast in political terms, so that when in April that year, Antoine Étex, the Saint-Simonian sculptor of *Cain and his Race Accursed of God* that had been the sensation of the 1833 Salon, stood for election in Seine-et-Oise, his placard read: 'Let us elect the great sculptor Étex, who, in his depiction of Cain, wished to embody the miseries of the proletariat'.[9] Later in the century, the prominent *communarde* Paule Minck would go even deeper into the culture of revolutionary satanism and call her youngest son Lucifer-Blanqui-Vercingétorix-Révolution Minck![10]

[7] Eugen Weber, *Satan Franc-maçon* (Julliard, 1964), 10–11.

[8] See above all the passage in *Splendeurs et misères des courtisanes*, quoted OC, i. 1081. Following Jacques Crépet, Pichois also quotes an article by Louis Goudall that appeared in *Le Figaro* in February 1856 in which Abel is seen as both 'le premier représentant de l'École du Bon Sens' and as 'le premier bourgeois' while 'Caïn le revolte, Caïn le fratricide' is said to stand for 'l'école . . . de l'insurrection morale, de la fantaisie déchevelée, de la rébellion à outrance et du romantisme à tous crins'.

[9] See Albert Boime, *Hollow Icons: The Politics of Sculpture in Nineteenth-Century France* (Kent State Univ. Press, Kent, Ohio, and London, 1987), 45. Baudelaire discussed Étex without enthusiasm in the *Salons* of 1845 and 1846 (OC, ii. 376 and 404–5).

[10] See Susanna Barrows, *Distorting Mirrors: Visions of the Crowd in Late Ninteenth-Century France* (Yale Univ. Press, New Haven, Conn., and London, 1981), 52.

In the circumstances, therefore, the political implications of Baudelaire's 'Abel et Caïn' can hardly be mistaken:

> Race de Caïn, au ciel monte,
> Et sur la terre jette Dieu!

Whether Baudelaire was inspired to write the *Révolte* poems by reading the notorious 'Dieu, c'est le mal' excursus in *Philosophie de la misère*[11] is perhaps less important than the fact that both he and Proudhon were drawing on the same tradition of radical republican antitheism. None the less, one can readily imagine the impact that the relevant passage must have had on Baudelaire:

Dieu, c'est sottise et lâcheté; Dieu, c'est hypocrisie et mensonge; Dieu, c'est tyrannie et misère; Dieu, c'est le mal . . . Esprit menteur, Dieu imbécile, ton règne est fini . . . Dieu, retire-toi! car des aujourd'hui, guéri de ta crainte et devenu sage, je jure, la main étendue vers le ciel, que tu n'es que le bourreau de ma raison, le spectre de ma conscience.[12]

Once again, it is impossible, once one knows the political-metaphysical contexts of the 1840s, to miss the revolutionary meaning of 'Les Litanies de Satan' where Lucifer is not only the sworn enemy of the 'Dieu jaloux' and the 'Crésus impitoyable et vil' who, between them, have denied mankind at large enjoyment of the earth's riches but also a source of consolation, hope, and inspiration to the poor, the suffering and the oppressed:

> Toi qui, même aux lépreux, aux parias maudits,
> Enseignes par l'amour le goût du Paradis . . .

Satan takes under his protection all those 'exilés', 'pendus', and 'conspirateurs' who have challenged the existing order and, in his compassion for the victims of God's wrath, shows a peculiar and, in the present context, highly significant concern for the welfare of the impoverished drunkard:

> Toi qui, magiquement, assouplis les vieux os
> De l'ivrogne attardé foulé par les chevaux . . .

More and more, a clear pattern is emerging. A family bond unites the poet, the worker, the drunkard, the revolutionary, and Satan and sets them against the tyrannical world-order of God and the bourgeoisie.

---

[11] As is argued by Lois B. Hyslop in 'Baudelaire and Proudhon'.
[12] Proudhon, *Système des contradictions économiques*, i. 384.

The Politics of Wine and Nineteenth-Century France

> Aimons-nous, et quand nous pouvons
> Nous unir pour boire à la ronde,
> Que le canon se taise ou gronde,
> Buvons, buvons, buvons
> A l'Indépendance du monde!
>
> Pierre Dupont, 'Le Chant des
> Ouvriers' (1846)

Many of the symbolic values that appear to attach to wine in the poems with which we are concerned—fraternity, exchange, productive labour, renewal, the goodness of nature and of man himself, self-divinization coupled with defiance of an oppressive God-ordained social and political order—find significant echoes in the poetry, songs, and other propaganda of the Left in France between, say, 1830 and 1880. Baudelaire may have given a personal inflexion to the theme of wine but the theme itself was a republican and socialist commonplace, so widespread that Maurice Agulhon has written of 'la liaison, longtemps tenue pour évidente, entre le vin, la vigne et les idées de progrès et d'émancipation'.[13] That wine should have attained such importance for the Left, both in itself and as a symbol of wider social and political issues, should cause no surprise if we recall that its production, distribution, and consumption were all equally surrounded with political controversy in the mid-nineteenth century, and that though we may now regard wine as the popular drink *par excellence* in France, it was not in fact until the 1880s that working-class wages had risen sufficiently to permit its generalized consumption.[14] What propelled wine to the forefront of political controversy in the first half of the nineteenth century was the bitter hostility of both producers and consumers to the wide range of national and local taxes levied on wine which, it has been estimated, not only increased the cost of wine to consumers by as much as 120 per cent[15] but also fell

[13] Maurice Agulhon, 'Attitudes politiques' and 'La Société paysanne et la vie à la campagne', in Étienne Juillard (ed.), *Histoire de la France rurale*, iii, *Apogée et crise de la civilisation paysanne 1789–1914* (Seuil, 1976), 173.

[14] For the whole of this question, see the excellent article by Michael R. Marrus, 'Social drinking in the *belle époque*', *Journal of Social History*, 7/2 (1974), 115–41.

[15] See the useful discussion in Leo A. Loubère, *The Red and the White: A History of Wine in France and Italy in the Nineteenth Century* (State Univ. of New York Press, Albany, NY, 1978), 322–4.

unequally on the poorer sections of society since it was the volume, not the quality, of the wine that determined the amount of tax due. The struggle over the wine tax from the end of the eighteenth century until the early years of the Third Republic replicates with almost uncanny precision the broader social and political struggles in France during the same period. One of the most detested legacies of the *ancien régime*—it was in order to facilitate its collection that the *mur d'octroi* had been built to encircle Paris in the 1780s, inspiring the celebrated pasquinade 'le mur murant Paris rend Paris murmurant'—the wine tax had been abolished in the early years of the revolution only to be reimposed in a modified form by Napoleon in 1808. According to Marx, Napoleon later came to believe that 'the reintroduction of the wine tax had contributed more to his overthrow than anything else, as it had alienated the peasants of southern France from him',[16] and both he, after his escape from Elba in 1815, and Louis-Philippe, in 1830, made promises to abolish the tax in an effort to build up lower-class support. In December 1830 Louis-Philippe did indeed lower all wine and alcohol taxes by a third, but it was a compromise measure that failed to allay the hostility of producers and consumers alike. By the mid-1840s there was probably no single issue that, uniting both large- and small-scale producers and lower-class consumers in towns and country alike, was more capable of focusing opposition to the government and the economic and social interests it represented. One of the earliest fiscal measures taken by the Provisional Government in 1848 was, accordingly, to abolish the wine tax (along with similarly detested taxes on salt and meat) on the grounds that, in the words of Garnier-Pagès who introduced the relevant bill on 31 March, 'de toutes les inventions du vieil esprit fiscal', the wine tax was 'celle qui blesse le plus profondément la justice et la dignité humaine, celle qui fomente le plus d'irritations, qui charge de plus d'entraves le travail industriel' and was, as such, 'incompatible avec les nouvelles institutions que la France veut fonder et maintenir'.[17] Predictably, however, as the philanthropic fervour of February and March gave way to the exacerbated class tensions of May and June,

[16] Karl Marx, *The Class Struggles in France*, in *Surveys from Exile* (Penguin, Harmondsworth, 1973), 113–15, gives a telling account of the significance of the wine tax in nineteenth-century France.
[17] See Alfred Antony, *La Politique financière du Gouvernement Provisoire, février–mai 1848* (Arthur Rousseau, 1910), 190–5.

the Right manœuvred to reimpose the tax the abolition of which, it was argued, had not only sharply reduced government revenue but, by encouraging working-class alcohol consumption, had created a potent source of social and political disorder; it is significant that the tax was eventually restored on the very same day—21 June 1848—that the Ateliers Nationaux were dissolved, the two measures combining to fuel the outbreak of the insurrection two days later. On his election to the presidency in December, Louis Napoleon not only retained the wine tax but induced the assembly to restore the salt tax as well (27 December 1848). Political expediency, however, led the Prince-President, on the eve of the legislative elections of May 1849, to promise the abolition of drink taxes as of the beginning of 1850; on 16 May, as its final act prior to dissolution, the Constituent Assembly went one better and voted for their immediate suppression, suspecting, quite rightly, that Louis Napoleon's promise was simply an electoral ploy to gain support amongst urban workers and peasants. If the President's words did prompt some voters to back him, they would have been rudely disillusioned when on 20 December 1849—pointedly the first anniversary of Louis Napoleon's proclamation as President—the wine tax was reimposed yet again, thereby sealing the alliance of small wine producer and lower-class consumer on which *démoc-soc* propaganda would work so effectively during what remained of the Second Republic's existence, thanks, in particular, to Claude Durand's 'Chant des vignerons' which was perhaps the song most frequently heard and read in France in 1850 and 1851:

> Bons villageois, votez pour la Montagne,
> C'est là l'espoir des pauvres vignerons,
> Car avec elle, bonnes gens des campagnes,
> Disparaîtront les impôts des boissons.
> > Bons, bons vignerons,
> > Aux prochaines élections
> > Il faudra, campagnards,
> > Voter pour les Montagnards.
> Ouvre les yeux, peuple, l'on t'escamote
> Les plus beaux fruits de la riche moisson.
> Tu sèmes, hélas, c'est l'oisif qui récolte.
> A eux la fleur, et à toi le gros son.[18]

[18] Quoted Agulhon, 'Attitudes politiques', 173.

Not only would Baudelaire, like any adult Parisian, have been aware of the wine tax and its political ramifications, but his network of contacts and the circumstances of his life almost certainly enabled him to witness at close quarters the grievances of small wine producers, *marchands de vin*, and lower-class drinkers during the Second Republic. Although it is now established that Baudelaire did not, contrary to a durable myth, first publish 'Le Vin de l'assassin' in *L'Écho des marchands de vins* in November 1848, he undoubtedly had in Pierre Dupont a personal link with the Comité Central des Boissons whose organ it was and on his return from Châteauroux could well have read the committee's statement of intent published in *L'Écho*'s *numéro spécimen* on 18 October. Although in no way a 'source' for 'L'Âme du vin', the editorial recognizably inhabits the same socio-political and imaginary universe as Baudelaire's poem, not least in its emphasis on the mutual interdependence of producer, retailer, and consumer:

> Vous tous, vignerons, débitants de boissons et ouvriers, vivez les uns par les autres, en voisins, amis ou clients; la prosperité vous arrive ou l'adversité vous atteint en même temps. . . . Vous êtes donc unis par le lien que la nature a établi forcément entre la bonne culture et l'usage facile de la plus savoureuse, de la plus exquise de ses productions. C'est aux vignerons de faire mûrir le sang écumeux de la vigne, frère de celui qui coule dans les veines de l'homme; c'est aux marchands de vin de distribuer à la table des ouvriers une bienfaisante liqueur, qui apporte la gaîté dans leurs maigres repas, et y verse au moins la consolation, quand toute autre nourriture y manque.[19]

The editorial concludes with a paean to wine that deploys many of the characteristic tropes and figures of 'le discours du vin' in nineteenth-century France on which, it should already be clear, 'L'Âme du vin' draws just as much as the numerous songs about wine to be discussed shortly. As well as reading *L'Écho*, Baudelaire could well have attended—and would almost certainly have heard about from Dupont—the Comité's *banquet* held at the Barrière du Roule on 24 November 1848 when no less a personage than Ledru-Rollin addressed an audience made up of 700 members of the wine trade and their sympathizers. 'Le dru' vigorously took to task those present who accused him of 'making politics' out of the wine tax issue, reminding them in no uncertain terms that 'il est certain que

---

[19] *L'Écho des marchands de vins, des vignerons et des ouvriers, numéro spécimen* (18 Oct. 1848), 1.

le gouvernement provisoire avait senti que votre cause était liée à celle de la classe ouvrière en France . . . Et vous voudriez qu'on ne vous parlât pas politique en vous parlant d'impôt: c'est un nonsens, c'est de la folie!' The number of *L'Écho* that reported the *banquet* was the same that announced the forthcoming publication of *Les Limbes*. It also contained as its *feuilleton* a further eulogy of wine which, as well as showing many *recoupements* with the language and imagery of 'L'Âme du vin' and *Du vin et du haschisch*, concludes with a fervent if over-optimistic invocation of *'le vin des Rois* que le peuple a bu au 24 février, qu'il ne boit plus, qu'il reboira' that clearly places wine at the heart of *démoc-soc* discourse:[20] the conviction that only a socialist republic would ensure the unfettered production, distribution, and consumption of wine led naturally to the transformation of wine into the symbol *par excellence* of Revolution, the radical Republic, and the coming socialist Kingdom of Heaven on Earth.

On 10 December 1849 *La Presse* announced the forthcoming publication in *La Veillée pittoresque* of ' "Les Derniers Buveurs", par M. Charles Baudelaire'; one would do much to know what this never-published, indeed probably never completed, text contained or was planned to contain and whether it was, as its title and timing suggest, in any way related to the wine tax controversy. With ironic appropriateness 'Les Derniers Buveurs' was readvertised in *L'Événement* on 20 December 1849,[21] the day the wine tax was reinstated for the second time, by which time Baudelaire was in Dijon and ideally positioned to pick up the reverberations of the wine question in provincial France. On 28 December the Dijon police closed the *Salle de concerts de la Fraternité* and the *Estaminet lyrique du passage Jouffroy* to prevent the singing of Gustave Mathieu's 'La Chanson de Jean Raisin', the words of which were reprinted in *Le Travail* on 30 December. Again it is reasonable to assume that Baudelaire (who certainly knew Mathieu in the mid-1850s and may already have met him at the Brasserie des Martyrs[22]) would have seen the song in question with its telling summary of the whole controversy surrounding wine:

> Inspiré par Dieu notre père
> De Février le parlement

[20] *L'Écho des marchands de vin*, 2 (Nov. 1848), 1–2.
[21] BPZ, 272.
[22] See BPZ, 299–300.

Un jour décréta sagement
Qu'on lâcherait le gai compère.
Ce jour-là, sur des airs nouveaux,
Le peuple chanta les bouteilles,
Le vin vieux, la vigne et les treilles,
La République et les tonneaux.
Au nom de la machine ronde,
De l'eau coulant par tout le monde,
Place, place pour Jean Raisin,
De Jean Raisin devenu vin;
Laissez donc passez Jean Raisin
Avec son vieil ami le pain . . .

Mais voici bien une autre affaire:
Survient un autre parlement,
Qui, raisonnant différement,
Vient d'empoigner le pauvre hère.
On garottera le reclus,
On le liera pour qu'il ne bouge,
On l'accusera d'être rouge!!!
Le peuple ne chantera plus,
Au nom, etc.[23]

. . . . . .

The existence of the wine tax meant, as Proudhon sardonically observed in *Système des contradictions économiques*, that most French workers could hardly fail to obey the 'prescriptions diététiques de l'Église' seeing that 'grâce à l'impôt, toute l'année est carême pour le travailleur; et son dîner de Pâques ne vaut pas la collation du vendredi-saint de Monseigneur'.[24] Having to choose between a quasi-Lenten abstinence—it is as 'mangeurs de pain noir, buveurs d'eau' that the 'enfants de la terre' are pointedly described in Dupont's song '1852'—and the adulterated concoctions vintners devised to keep costs down, many workers opted for the latter, with the consequences to their health that can be imagined: Garnier-Pagès did not exaggerate when he stated that 'le vin que boivent aujourd'hui les classes pauvres est un poison'.[25] A third alternative —and it was one that thousands of working-class Parisians took every Sunday—was to patronize the innumerable *cabarets* and *guinguettes* that sprang up immediately outside the *mur d'octroi*,

[23] *Le Travail*, 4 (30 Dec. 1849), 'Guerre aux chansons', 4.
[24] Proudhon, *Système*, i. 310.
[25] Antony, *La Politique financière*, 193.

that 'misérable mur de boue et de crachat', as Hugo called it,[26] whose perimeter coincided essentially with that of the present so-called *boulevards extérieurs*, where untaxed liquor was available. The fact that, in order to drink at prices they could afford, lower-class Parisians were forced to go outside the official city limits is the clearest evidence, Alain Faure has written in his fine study of carnival in nineteenth-century Paris, of the 'caractère marginal des plaisirs du peuple dans la société bourgeoise'.[27] To the extent that it normally took place beyond the bounds of the *polis* in the ambiguous in-between world of the *barrières* where crime and prostitution thrived, the drinking of wine by lower-class Parisians already possessed a semi-subversive character both in the eyes of the consumers themselves and, with rather different reactions, in those of the middle classes who anxiously observed their raucous goings and still more riotous returnings every Sunday.

The unavailability of wine to the class that produced it and that most needed the sustenance and comforts it afforded was, in the eyes of a popular *chansonnier* like Altaroche only the most flagrant instance of the unequal distribution of rewards in a society split between a mass of 'actifs' and a tiny handful of 'oisifs' living off their labour:

> Au milieu des rudes travaux,
> Le vin serait d'utile usage:
> Il procure l'oubli des maux;
> Il rend la force et le courage,
>   Force et courage.
> Quand le riche a sa table aura
> Le bordeaux, l'aï, le madère,
> Ta lèvre ne s'humectera
> Que d'aigre piquette ou de bière
> Qui paie autant à la barrière! . . .
> Allons, sème, bon prolétaire,
> C'est l'oisif qui récoltera.
>
> 'Le Prolétaire' (early 1830s)[28]

---

[26] Hugo, *Notre-Dame de Paris*, *Œuvres complètes*, i. 130.

[27] Faure, *Paris carême-prenant*, 17.

[28] Quoted Pierre Brochon, *La Chanson française: Béranger et son temps* (Éditions sociales, 1966), 157–8. *Piquette* was a cheap alcoholic beverage made by running water over the lees of wine. See also Altaroche's 'Le Peuple a faim' and 'L'Impôt du pauvre', ibid. 160–3.

In the circumstances, it is not at all surprising if, for working-class French people of the 1840s and 1850s, the Promised Land should have presented itself to them less as a land of milk and honey than as one of red wine, white bread, and *saucisson* and that working-class singers and their middle-class sympathizers should have evolved an elaborate symbolism derived from the production, distribution, and consumption of wine to express the hopes and longings of a people still largely reduced, in the words of one song, to 'l'eau du ciel pour détremper son pain'.[29] A song such as Dupont's 'Le Vin de la planète' (1846?) is characteristic in that its celebration of present pleasures suggests the promise of still greater joys to come:

> Dieu n'est pas un méchant juge,
> Tout en frappant, il sourit:
> Le lendemain du déluge
> Le cep de Noé fleurit.
> La pluie a noyé les terres,
> Le soleil a cuit les blés,
> Mais la vigne emplit nos verres.
> Buvons à coups redoublés.
>
> C'est une ère qui commence
> L'âge fleuri de l'amour,
> Qu'on cisèle un verre immense
> Où chacun boive â son tour.[30]

Although not itself explicitly political, 'Le Vin de la planète' shows how readily the multiple hazards of viticulture—storms, drought, pests, disease—combined with the processes of wine production itself—the crushing of the grape, fermentation, storage prior to consumption—might lend themselves to the expression of the political hopes and fears of the 1840s and 1850s and even to the symbolization of the revolutionary process itself; 'le peuple bouillonne, la République fermente sourdement', Baudelaire would write in the second number of *Le Salut public* (OC, ii. 1034) and 'Le Vin des chiffonniers' speaks of working-class Paris as a 'labyrinthe fangeux | Où l'humanité grouille en ferments orageux', images which, in the circumstances, take on an unexpected potency and show how readily the discourse of wine and the discourse of revolution could flow one into the other. The whole life-cycle of the vine and the

[29] Altaroche, 'Le Peuple a faim', quoted Brochon, *La Chanson française*, 160.
[30] Pierre Dupont, *Chants et poésies* (Garnier, 1862), 79–81.

months-long process of fermentation, filtering, and bottling followed by perhaps many years of storage before the wine can be drunk mesh in with the perception of politics as a seasonal process of growth, maturation, temporary death or hibernation followed by rebirth and the beginning of another cycle that was so marked in mid-nineteenth-century France. Thus the long winter of the Bourgeois Monarchy was ended by the spring of February–March 1848; its fragile hopes succumbed to the summer heat and drought of June, sank in the winter solstice of the December elections only to be resurrected—all too briefly—in May 1849, pending their entombment in the wintry wastes of December 1851 from which, however, many radicals still had faith that they would rise again. Pierre Dupont's 'Ma vigne' (1846) offers a foretaste, in a form that is pre-political rather than apolitical, of the explicitly political meanings that, in the years to come, poets, singers, and *démoc-soc* pamphleteers would attach to the annual cycle of wine production:

> Au printemps, ma vigne, en sa fleur,
> D'une fillette a la pâleur;
> L'été, c'est une fiancée
> Qui fait craquer son corset vert;
> A l'automne, tout s'est ouvert:
> C'est la vendange et la pressée;
> En hiver, pendant son sommeil,
> Son vin remplace le soleil.[31]

By 1849, when Dupont wrote 'Le Chant des paysans' to promote the *démoc-soc* cause in the May elections, the political message is inescapable. While Napoleon—'non point l'ancien, mais un nouveau'—'laisse les blés sous la neige | Et les loups manger son troupeau', the democratic Republic brings with it the promise of springtime sowing, summer growth, and autumn plenty with bread and wine freely, equally, and fraternally dispensed to all who have worked to produce them:

> La terre va briser ses chaînes;
> La misère a fini son bail;
> Les monts, les vallons et les plaines
> Vont engendrer par le travail.
> Affamés, venez tous en foule

---

[31] Dupont, *Chants et poésies*, 16.

> Comme les mouches sur le thym,
> Les blés sont mûrs, le pressoir coule:
> Voilà du pain, voilà du vin.[32]

The vine's winter 'sleep' pending its springtime reawakening, together with the newly fermented wine's long subterranean confinement before it can be 'resurrected' and drunk (cf. the 'prison de verre' and 'froids caveaux' of 'L'Âme du Vin'), indicate how readily the discourse of wine could be combined with the themes of the Republican Christ and Christ the Republic which, as we have seen, pervaded the entire *quarante-huitard* imagination. The vine, that 'arbre divin', at once 'mère du vin' and 'mère des amours' (Dupont, 'Ma vigne'), reaches out to *l'arbre de la liberté* and, beyond that, in the remarkable culminating image of Eugène Pottier's 'Le Pressoir', to the Cross on which the Republican Christ was crucified in 1851 but from which, by His own efforts, He will, in the harvest-time of Revolution, take Himself down to be born again:

> Quand viendra le beau vendémiaire,
> On verra, des pressoirs sacrés,
> Le vin, l'amour et la lumière
> Couler pour tous les altérés;
> Du gibet quittant les insignes,
> Jésus déclouant ses bras las,
> Au Calvaire planté de vignes
> Mettra sa croix pour échalas.[33]

The discourse of wine is given a strikingly original twist by the Fourierist Alphonse Toussenel with whose work Baudelaire was certainly familiar in the mid-1850s but whom he could also have read by the time he composed the first published version of 'L'Âme du vin'.[34] Toussenel's work *L'Esprit des bêtes: Vénérie française et zoologie passionnelle*, published in 1847, contains a remarkable excursus on the properties of the vine, parts of which had been

---

[32] Quoted Brochon, *La Pamphlet du pauvre: Du socialisme utopique à la Révolution de 1848* (Éditions sociales, 1957), 76–7.

[33] Pottier, *Œuvres complètes*, 108.

[34] See Baudelaire's letter of 21 Jan. 1856 to Toussenel (C, i. 335–7) where he discusses the Fourierist's most recent work *L'Esprit des bêtes: Le Monde des oiseaux. Ornithologie passionnelle* (1853–5), a copy of which, or part of which, he has just received from the author. For the possible influence of this work on Baudelaire, see Hartmut Stenzel, 'Sur quelques souvenirs socialistes dans l'œuvre de Baudelaire', *Bulletin baudelairien*, 12/1 (1976), 3–13.

published earlier in *La Démocratie pacifique* of which we know Baudelaire to have been a reader;[35] other extracts appeared in the Dijonnais newspaper *Le Peuple: Journal de la Révolution sociale* on 5 May 1850, some time after the likely date of Baudelaire's return to Paris, but suggesting that the work had for some time enjoyed both wide diffusion and semi-canonical status in the *démoc-soc* milieu Baudelaire frequented. Whether the Toussenel text is a 'source' for 'L'Âme du vin' cannot, finally, be proved, but the likelihood must be considered high; in any case, even in its most eccentric elaborations, it clearly draws on the same 'vat' of images as that tapped so effectively by the songs of Pottier, Dupont, Mathieu, and others and, it should now be clear, by *Du vin et du haschisch* and the wine poems themselves. 'La vigne aime à jaser,' Toussenel avers, suggesting from the outset a link with the singing wine of 'L'Âme du vin'. It is

une plante dont le jus délie la langue et qui est un emblème cardinal d'amitié. Dans l'ardeur d'expansion qui la brûle, la vigne s'attache avec amour à tout ce qui l'entoure; elle monte familièrement sur l'épaule des pruniers, des oliviers, des aimés; elle tutoie tous les arbres [as wine does the worker in 'L'Âme du vin']. Puisque la vigne module en tonique d'amitié, sa familiarité est légitime.

As in 'L'Âme du vin', there is an osmotic relationship between the vine and human work, though for Toussenel 'le travail de la vigne est en effet le travail attrayant par excellence', generating a sequence of fraternal exchanges between nature and worker, worker and worker, and, beyond them, between producer and consumer, consumer and consumer, consumer and nature, consumer and God: it is not difficult to see why the vine occupies so privileged a place in the Fourierist flora. Not only is its end-product wine, 'la liqueur consolatrice et fortifiante qui récompense le travailleur de toutes ses peines, fait rentrer la souplesse en ses membres fatigués et la gaîté communicative en son cœur', it is also 'le lait des vieillards, le consolateur des affligés, le soutien des faibles, le viatique des forts'. Above all, though, wine is

l'âme des banquets, le mobile d'expansion universel, la pile de Volta, qui met en communication tous les cœurs, qui fait jaillir à la fois de tous les regards l'étincelle, de toutes les poitrines l'enthousiasme, aux grands mots

[35] See Ivanna Bugliani, *Baudelaire: L'Armonia e la discordanza* (Bulzoni, Rome, 1980), 129–31.

de liberté, d'égalité et de fraternité. Égalité, c'est le ton de l'homme à table; avec le vin, plus d'esclave ni de maître; la langue de Bacchus ignore le mot *vous*. Liberté, c'est la première condition du plaisir. Fraternité, c'est l'inspiration naturelle de la liqueur divine. La riante couleur du vin . . . prête son charme à toute la nature, et aime tout le genre humain.[36]

Given the symbolic values that attach to wine in the Republican discourse of the 1840s and 1850s, it becomes possible to see the open-air communal meals of *quarante-huit* as the properly sacramental occasions they were.[37] Gathered around an *arbre de la liberté* bedecked in bunting of red, white, and blue, often (in the early months) with a priest presiding, men, women, and children ate, drank, talked, and sang together in a spirit less carnavalesque than reverential to celebrate the eucharist of the Republican faith: Liberté, Égalité, Fraternité made really present. 'Asseyons-nous à cette table | Et fraternisons tous en chœur', wrote Pierre Dupont in celebration of the Fête du Champ de Mars in 1848.[38] When Republicans of *quarante-huit* sat down at table together, they both bound themselves in spirit to their forebears of 1790 at the first Fête de la Fédération when, said a contemporary, the whole of France sat down simultaneously at the 'grand couvert national'[39] and pointed forward to the huge street parties and open-air beanfeasts with which lower-class French men and women celebrated the *quatorze juillet* in the 1890s and early 1900s.[40] Even today, as anyone who has walked through the table-crammed streets of Paris on the eve of the *Fête Nationale* will know, the old link between food, drink, and the Republic has not been entirely lost.

Two final songs by the great Eugène Pottier, *communard* and composer of the *Internationale*, underline the congruence between the vision of 'L'Âme du vin' and *Du vin et du haschisch* and that of advanced radical Republicanism in mid-nineteenth-century France.

[36] Quotations from Alphonse Toussenel, *L'Esprit des bêtes: Vénérie française et zoologie passionnelle* (Librairie Sociétaire, 1847), 66–7 and *Le Peuple: Journal de la révolution sociale*, 4 (5 May 1850), 2–3.

[37] For a moving description of one such gathering as late as March 1850, see Pauline Roland, 'Chronique des associations ouvrières: Les Cuisiniers', *La République* (31 March 1850), quoted Jacques Rancière, *La Nuit des prolétaires* (Fayard, 1981), 312–13.

[38] Dupont, *Chants et poésies*, 113.

[39] Charles Villette, cited Mona Ozouf, *La Fête révolutionnaire 1789–1799* (Gallimard, 1976), 44.

[40] See Rosamonde Sanson, *Les Quatorze-juillet (1789–1975): Fête et conscience nationale* (Flammarion, 1976), 80–106.

Pottier's 'L'Origine du vin' meshes at every point with the themes and images of 'L'Âme du vin' and, although his radicalism is muted, the antitheistic and revolutionary implications of its conclusion are clear enough:

> Emplis ton verre
> D'un vin vermeil,
> Et bois la terre
> Et le soleil!
>
> .   .   .
>
> Bois, pour tes rêves,
> Monde en haillons,
> Toutes leurs sèves,
> Tous leurs rayons.
>
> Le chaude effluve
> D'un vin nouveau,
> Bouillonne en cuve,
> Flambe au cerveau.
>
> La chair consomme
> Ce sang de feu,
> Le vin fait l'homme
> Fait l'homme dieu! [41]

Still more urgently radical in tone is 'La Bouteille inépuisable':

> Versons! versons enfin
>   La vieille
>   Bouteille,
> Versons! versons enfin
> La bouteille sans fin!
>
> Prise sous les fagots,
>   Bien bouchée
>   Et couchée,
> Prise sous les fagots,
> C'est le vin des égaux.
>
> C'est le prix d'un long bail
>   D'esclavage
>   Et servage,
> C'est le prix d'un long bail,
> C'est le sang du travail!

---

[41] Pottier, *Œuvres complètes*, 77.

Un couple ensorcelé;
   Ignorance,
   Indigence,
Un couple ensorcelé
Tenait ce vin sous clé.

    .   .   .   .

Hôpital et prison,
   Tas d'ordures,
   Et tortures,
Hôpital et prison,
Buvez la guérison.

Fange de la cité,
   Toi, vermine
   Et famine,
Fange de la cité,
Bois-y la dignité.

Bois-y, globe assaini,
   De la vigne
   Enfin digne,
Bois-y, globe assaini,
Le bien-être infini.

Versons! versons enfin
   La vieille
   Bouteille,
Versons! versons enfin
La bouteille sans fin![42]

Nothing could be clearer: from the *Dive Bouteille* of revolution will flow endlessly the deep red wine of *Liberté, Fraternité, Égalité* that 'ce couple ensorcelé', ignorance and poverty and the social and political forces that sustain them, has kept hidden away under lock and key from those whom Pottier, in the one song for which he is now remembered, strikingly called 'les damnés de la terre'. Of course, nothing that Baudelaire says in his wine poems is as explicit as the message of 'La Bouteille inépuisable', but the broad concordances of image and theme suggest a common source in popular political culture and enable us to assign the wine poems to their appropriate place on the political spectrum, a place which, for obvious reasons, cannot be pinpointed with absolute precision but which everything suggests is well to the left of that usually attributed to the poet during his 'republican phase'.

[42] Ibid. 179.

Cabarets *and* goguettes

Many of the songs discussed above would have been performed
'live'—by the composers themselves, by professional singers, or by
ordinary working people—either in neighbourhood *cabarets* or in
the popular singing societies known as *goguettes* that abounded in
mid-nineteenth-century Paris. Baudelaire is known to have frequented working-class *cabarets* in the 1840s—Prarond, for
example, describes how 'nous vagabondions . . . très souvent hors
barrière' and regularly visited 'un bon cabaret bien au-delà du
faubourg Saint-Jacques', 'un endroit méprisé des bourgeois' where
radical songs could well have been sung[43]—and it is clear from the
letter of January 1854 to the actor Jean-Hippolyte Tisserant in
which Baudelaire outlined the plot of his never-to-be-written
'drame populacier' *L'Ivrogne* that, probably (as ever) in the
company of Pierre Dupont, he had visited *goguettes* before and
perhaps after the 1848 Revolution (Baudelaire simply says 'autrefois'), and that he had responded with apparent enthusiasm to the
'échantillons de poésie tout faits' of the songs performed and to 'les
instincts lyriques du peuple, souvent comiques et maladroits' on
display there (OC, i. 631): certainly the links between wine, song,
conviviality, and political radicalism can hardly have failed to
impress themselves upon him. It is even possible that he may have
contributed to some of the songs that appear under Dupont's
name,[44] and that the first version of 'Une gravure fantastique'
(1843–7?) with its singsong rhythm and 'Lariflaflafla' refrain (see
OC, i. 967) may represent an attempt, however improbable, to
reach, via Dupont's singing voice, an audience of *goguettiers*.

  With its limited clientele, often drawn from the same professional
group, the mid-nineteenth-century *cabaret*, whether in town or

[43] BPZ, 174. Asselineau describes how, after meeting at the Salon in 1845, he
and Baudelaire went together 'chez un marchand de vin de la rue du Carousel [sic]
où buvaient des ouvriers et un postillon de la maison du roi en livrée'. Baudelaire
drank 'du vin blanc' and—typically—ordered 'des biscuits et des pipes *neuves*'
to disorientate proprietor and customers: 'commencement de la théorie de
l'*étonnement*', Asselineau comments (BPZ, 205).

[44] The preface to vol. iv of Dupont's *Chants et chansons* (Houssiaux 1851–4)
states that 'on y trouvera aussi des chants dont Pierre Dupont n'a composé que la
musique et dont la poésie est d'autres auteurs avec lesquels il s'est trouvé en relations
de sentiments: Victor Hugo, Gustave Mathieu, Charles Baudelaire, etc.' (OC,
i. 969).

country, was, Maurice Agulhon has written, 'toujours à la limite de l'association volontaire'.[45] It was in the *cabaret* that issues relating to pay, employment, and working conditions were commonly discussed, that newspapers such as *Le Populaire* were read (often out loud to the clients as a group[46]), that many *sociétés de secours mutuel* had their headquarters and that, despite police surveillance, working-class radicals regularly recruited and made contact with each other; in addition, many *cabarets* had adjoining rooms that it was the practice to let out for strike meetings and similar gatherings.[47] The *marchand de vin* was himself often a militant republican-socialist who used his influence and contacts to disseminate radical ideas and to foster radical groupings; ideas, information, and instructions would spread by word of mouth from *cabaret* to *cabaret* in a manner that Renan would later liken to the spreading of the Gospel in early Christian times. The *cabaret* was an all-male society, secular and egalitarian, opposed at every point, as Agulhon says, to traditional forms of sociability such as the *veillée*:

Cabaret, ouverture sur la société globale; veillée, isolement paysan.— Cabaret, ségrégation masculine; veillée, unité de la famille.—Cabaret, culture écrite, française, le journal; veillée, culture orale, dialectale. . . . Cabaret, politique de gauche; veillée, sagesse éternelle, c'est-à-dire ordre moral.[48]

While in Dijon, Baudelaire could have read in *Le Travail* a cogent statement by the prominent *démoc-soc* propagandist Pierre Joigneaux concerning the political role of the *cabaret* in working-class culture: 'C'est là seulement qu'on peut s'asseoir à la même table, trinquer ensemble, dire ce qu'on a sur le cœur, causer de ses blés en herbe, de ses blés en épis, s'instruire les uns les autres, faire de la République et lire le journal de la semaine'.[49] *Faire de la République*: in the human, social, and political values it embodied, the *cabaret* was already a 'République démocratique et sociale' in miniature, and the wine that flowed there was as the nectar of

[45] Maurice Agulhon, 'Le Problème de la culture populaire en France autour de 1848', *Romantisme*, 9 (1975), 51.

[46] Ibid. 55.

[47] See, amongst many possible examples, Martin Nadaud, *Mémoires de Léonard, ancien garçon maçon*, ed. Maurice Agulhon (Hachette, 1976), 226.

[48] Agulhon, 'La Société paysanne et la vie à la campagne', in *Histoire de la France rurale*, iii. 354.

[49] Pierre Joigneaux, 'Les Cabarets dans nos campagnes', *Le Travail*, 40 (26 Dec. 1849), 1.

republican socialist brotherhood. For the Right, of course, the association of radical republicanism and drink added to the sinister implications of each, and, as late as 1872, Zola, no radical but a republican to the bone, found it necessary to defend the Republic against the reactionary taunt that it was a regime of drunkards, sprung from the netherworld of tap-rooms and *estaminets*:

Donc, ils renvoient la République au cabaret; c'est là qu'ils la veulent asseoir, entre les brocs d'étain et les bouteilles vides. Le cabaret est devenu leur suprême injure, leur argument décisif, le gros mot dont ils soufflètent et dont ils condamnent le peuple. Et il semble, à les entendre, que l'esprit révolutionnaire du siècle sorte d'un litre mal bouché, et qu'on ait ramassé dans les rinçures du comptoir les grandes conquêtes legales de 89.

Far from denying or, still less, condemning the links between Republic and *cabaret*, Zola sees in them proof of the new regime's vitality. For him, it seems, not only is the *cabaret* a mini-Republic but the Republic itself is a *cabaret* writ large where Marianne carouses *à la bonne franquette* with her republican brothers and sisters: 'Eh bien! que le peuple aille au cabaret, qu'il y aille boire chopine, bras dessus bras dessous avec la République!'[50] In the wake of June 1848 and December 1851 *cabarets*, as we have seen, were subject to stringent police controls and, in view of the long-standing association between Republicanism and public drinking-places, it is possible that the fifth stanza of 'L'Irréparable' (1855) contains a hidden allusion to the fate of the Republic and its martyred and exiled supporters after the December coup:[51]

> L'Espérance qui brille aux carreaux de l'Auberge
> Est soufflée, est morte à jamais!

[50] 'Causerie du Dimanche', *Le Corsaire* (17 Dec. 1872). Émile Zola, *Œuvres complètes*, ed. Henri Mitterrand (Cercle du Livre Précieux, 1970), xiv. 199–201.

[51] This reading is tentative and takes into account the fact that the image of the 'Auberge' in 'L'Irréparable' is derived from the *féerie* in which Baudelaire saw Marie Daubrun perform in 1847 (see OC, i. 931–2). My (partial) political reading may be supported by the similarities between the images in surrounding stanzas and those in poems undoubtedly stemming from the Second Republic years, e.g. the 'mourant' and 'blessés' of 12–13 of 'L'Irréparable' and the 'blessé' and the 'grand tas de morts' in 'La Cloche fêlée' (1851) in which the image of 'le vieux soldat' also links up with the 'soldat brisé' of the later poem. One might also note the similarity —and still more the contrast—between 'les blessés | Que le sabot du cheval froisse' of 'L'Irréparable' and 'l'ivrogne attardé foulé par les chevaux' of 'Les Litanies de Satan'; while the drunkard of the earlier poem is saved and healed by the (Republican?) Satan, the wounded of 'L'Irréparable' are abandoned to their fate while the (Bonapartist?) Devil extinguishes all hope about them.

Sans lune et sans rayons, trouver où l'on héberge
Les martyrs d'un chemin mauvais!
Le Diable a tout éteint aux carreaux de l'Auberge.

The links between drink, song, and Republicanism were lived
even more intensely in the intimate and highly charged context of
the *goguette*.[52] *Goguettes* originated in the early years of the
Restoration, but it was during the Bourgeois Monarchy that their
numbers proliferated—in 1840 there were said to be over 300 in
Paris alone—and that they came to play a major part in the formation of working-class political consciousness. Sporting agreeably
fantastic names such as *Les Poissons de l'Hippocrène*, *Les Pale-
freniers du Cheval d'Apollon*, *Les Insectes*, or *Les Nourrissons des
Muses*, *goguettes* combined, in proportions that varied from club
to club, drinking, singing, socializing, and what one can only
describe as 'consciousness raising'. Most *goguettes* had between
one and two hundred members, overwhelmingly drawn from
amongst 'le peuple' and, in the case of Paris, normally resident in
the *quartier* where the *goguette* itself was located; meetings were
held weekly and, like *cabarets*, though in a far more structured
manner, *goguettes* constituted micro-democracies with their elected
officials, minutes, subscriptions, insignia, and financial assistance
for members in time of need or bereavement. A meeting took the
form of individual and collective singing, sustained, of course,
by much wine and conviviality; a sympathetic observer such as
L. A. Berthaud, writing in 1840, stresses, however, that 'ce que le
goguettier cherche, ce n'est pas le vin, c'est la compagnie; le vin
qu'il boit est mauvais, les gens qu'il fréquente sont bons'.[53] The
content of the songs—which, as Berthaud suggests, were often
composed as well as performed by the *goguettiers* themselves—was
often anodine, but even in the mid-1820s one observer noted that
'la politique n'a pas épargné les goguettes' and that 'la police veut
être instruite non seulement de ce qui se fait, mais aussi de ce qui se
dit et se chante'.[54] Despite numerous attempts by the police to
prohibit political songs, *goguettiers* continued vehemently to assert

[52] For *goguettes*, see Thomas, *Voix d'en bas*, 41–52 and the three anthologies of
songs edited by Pierre Brochon cited in the bibliography.
[53] L.-A. Berthaud, 'Le Goguettier', in *Les Français peints par eux-mêmes*
(Curmer, 1840), iv. 315–17.
[54] L. Montigny, *Le Provincial à Paris: Esquisses des mœurs parisiennes*
(Ladvocat, 1825), 322–3.

their freedoms—evenings at Le Ménagerie (where all participants bore the names of animals) began with the provocative declaration 'les chansons politiques sont permises, on peut dire merde au roi'[55]—and the intensity with which radical republican songs were performed and received emerges from any number of accounts of the 1830s and 1840s:

Parfois, du milieu des deux cents buveurs d'une Goguette, un homme tout à coup se lève. Cet homme a la figure mâle et énergique, l'œil doux et profond, la bouche calme, le geste sobre, le front sévère. Aussitôt tout bruit cesse, et les mains retombent sans achever de porter aux lèvres le verre qu'elles viennent de remplir. C'est qu'il ne s'agit plus ici de pampres ni de faux dieux, de croyances éteintes, ni de hochets vieillis, ce n'est plus le passé que l'on va chanter, c'est l'avenir.[56]

Having successfully defied the police of the Bourgeois Monarchy, *goguettes* came under still greater pressure after the June uprising and, with the coming of the Second Empire, swiftly succumbed to enforced 'depoliticization'.[57] For *chansonniers*, the 1850s were a time when, as Pottier put it in 1857, 'articulées | Par les grands froids | Les paroles se sont gelées':

> Qui peut entendre
> Si l'on se plaint?
> Il gèle, il gèle à pierre fendre.
> Faut-il attendre?
> D'onglée atteint,
> Le cerveau grelotte et s'éteint . . .[58]

As the cold gathered, republican poets and singers whose lives had revolved around *cabarets* and *goguettes* appear to have retreated for warmth and consolation into private drinking circles where, with woozy nostalgia, they celebrated wine in poems and songs which, lacking the political animus that had sustained them of old, soon became as anodine in content as they were stereotypical in

[55] Brochon, *Le Pamphlet du pauvre*, 95.

[56] Marc Fournier, *Paris chantant* (1845). Cited Brochon, *La Chanson sociale de Béranger à Brassens*, 41.

[57] For a telling discussion of the repression of the *goguettes*, see Jacques Rancière, 'Good Times or Pleasure at the Barricades', in Adrian Rifkin and Roger Thomas (eds.), *Voices of the People: The Social Life of 'La Sociale' at the end of the Second Empire* (Routledge & Kegan Paul, 1988), esp. pp. 45–60. By 1868, according to Rancière (p. 60), 'political songs were rarely censored any more. This was because few political songs were still presented to the censor'.

[58] Pottier, *Œuvres complètes*, 76.

expression. Such a group was that which briefly had as its centre
Jean Raisin, a 'revue joyeuse et vinicole' that appeared twice
monthly between October 1854 and March 1855. Its leading figure
was a republican-socialist poet-singer whose name we have already
encountered, Gustave Mathieu, and who, in the wake of the
December coup, gathered about him other bibulous survivors of
the *bon vieux temps* of Utopian socialism, some of whom were
directly or indirectly known to Baudelaire: Alphonse Toussenel,
Fernand Desnoyers (whose lame *profession de foi*, 'Je crois au vin',
published in the first number of the review is the most telling evidence of the decadence of 'le discours du vin' just three years after
the coup), Antonio Watripon, and, almost inevitably, Pierre
Dupont who, having seriously compromised his Republican purity
after the June uprising and again after the coup, was already
succumbing to the alcoholism which would kill him in 1871.[59] From
Luc Badesco's reconstruction,[60] the poets, singers, and other
writers moving in 'ce milieu republicain, fouriériste et mennaisien'
seem a sad collection of relics from a better time, with only
memories, fantasies, and *le gros rouge* to sustain them in their
despair, and little would be known of them and their review today
had not Baudelaire first published 'Le Vin des chiffonniers' in its
issue of November 1854. It is to this crucial text of Baudelaire's
Second Republic output that we now turn.

[59] For Dupont's later career, see Brochon, *Le Pamphlet du pauvre*, 70–1.
[60] Luc Badesco, 'Baudelaire et la Revue *Jean Raisin*: La Première Publication du
"Vin des Chiffonniers"', *Revue des sciences humaines*, 22/85 (1957), 55–88.

6

Metamorphoses of the Ragpicker: Interpreting 'Le Vin des Chiffonniers'

The Myth of the chiffonnier

'Le Vin des chiffonniers' is without question the most interesting of the wine poems not only because of its amplification of the themes we have been discussing but also through its use of the ragpicker, a figure who is obsessively present in mid-nineteenth-century writings on Paris, both literary and non-literary. Furthermore, no other poem in *Les Fleurs du mal* appears to have been so frequently and so radically reworked by Baudelaire; no fewer than nine separate versions of the poem are known—ten if one includes the prose version in *Du Vin et du haschisch*. According to Prarond, this poem, like 'L'Âme du vin', was composed before 1843, and it is indeed probable that a version existed by that date.[1] The first extant manuscript was sent by Baudelaire to Daumier who had frequently used the ragpicker motif and who may well have been one of the poem's inspirations;[2] the manuscript is signed 'Charles Baudelaire', the signature which, as we have seen, the poet began to use in early 1848. The prose version was published in March 1851 and there are two further manuscripts of the poem, dating from 1851–2, which present substantial differences from the first version, differences not only of expression but also of content; one of these manuscripts was sent—unsuccessfully—to Gautier for publication in the *Revue de Paris* some time between September 1851 and January 1852. As indicated above, the poem (based on the version of 1851–2) was at last published in *Jean Raisin* in November 1854 and, finally, the text of the first edition of *Les*

---

[1] BET, 25.
[2] For a full discussion of the successive versions of the text, see OC, i. 1047–553.

Fleurs du mal shows further major alterations which again substantially change the sense of the poem.

Although briefly mentioned in Mercier's monumental *Tableau de Paris* (1782),[3] the *chiffonnier* is essentially a nineteenth-century phenomenon. His existence is richly documented in the quasi-Linnaean catalogues of Parisian types contained in works such as *Les Français peints par eux-mêmes* (1840), in early investigations into the condition of the urban working classes, notably Frégier's *Des classes dangereuses de la société dans les grandes villes* (1840) and Le Play's massive compilation *Les Ouvriers européens* (1858), and in the work of professional *flâneurs* and observers of urban life such as Alexandre Privat d'Anglemont (*Paris inconnu*, 1861), Victor Fournel (*Ce qu'on voit dans les rues de Paris*, 1858), and Edmond Texier (*Tableau de Paris*, 1853). Poets, painters, and cartoonists were also much drawn to the *chiffonnier*; amongst a mass of possible examples we may single out, in addition to Baudelaire himself, Daumier, Gautier, and the cartoonist Traviès who had collaborated with Baudelaire on *Le Salut public* and whose *chiffonniers* are commended by him in *Quelques caricaturistes français*.[4] It would be idle, therefore, to try to establish a single source for 'Le Vin des chiffonniers' for the simple reason that, as Claude Pichois says in his notes to the poem, 'nous nous trouvons devant un océan' (OC, i. 1048). In writing a poem about the *chiffonnier* Baudelaire was drawing on one of the most hackneyed themes of Parisian literature and art, a theme whose early vitality and capacity to shock had virtually disappeared by the 1840s. Writing in 1858, Victor Fournel sees in the over-use of the *chiffonnier* theme in literature and art evidence not merely of a sentimental *nostalgie de la boue* on the part of writers and painters but also, and more pertinently, of outright commercial exploitation:

Il y a dans leur profession quelque chose de plus original, qui sourit à une imagination vagabonde, quelque chose de plus indépendant, qui semble mieux d'accord avec la dignité d'un homme libre. Aussi le chiffonnier a-t-il eu souvent, trop souvent peut-être, les honneurs du roman et du drame. Des écrivains, entraînés par une sympathie qui n'avait rien au fond de bien

[3] Louis-Sébastien Mercier, *Tableau de Paris* (Amsterdam, 1782), ii. 271–2.
[4] OC, ii. 562. A reproduction of Traviès's 'Le Chiffonnier' in *Les Français peints par eux-mêmes* is to be found in Anne Coffin Hanson, 'Popular Imagery in the Work of Edouard Manet', in Ulrich Finke (ed.), *French Nineteenth-Century Painting and Literature* (Manchester Univ. Press, 1972), 138.

naïf ni de bien désintéressé, mais sentant le besoin de réveiller par de nouveaux aliments, plus piquants et moins délicats, le palais du public, ce gourmet difficile, ont fouillé la place Maubert, frayé avec les clients de l'*Azard de la fourchette*, hanté les guinguettes de la barrière Saint-Jacques, dégusté, au *Bœuf Français*, du bouillon de veau à un sou le litre. Ils se sont faits les Homères de cette existence à part, qui a ses charmes en effet, sinon pour ceux qui la pratiquent, du moins pour ceux qui l'étudient le loin.[5]

The principal elements that go to make up the 'mythological' image of the *chiffonnier* are easily identified and show remarkably little variation from one writer to another. But, as we shall see, this relatively unchanging image evoked a wide variety of reactions ranging from horror and disquiet to romantic glamorization, even sentimental identification, in such a way that a writer's treatment of the *chiffonnier* theme becomes an excellent indicator of his broader social, political, and artistic attitudes.

The root of the myth lies in the *chiffonier*'s apartness, his extreme poverty, his condemnation to a parasitical and largely nocturnal existence in the interstices of urban life. 'Les chiffonniers ont une existence à part dans la société', wrote Barberet in *Le Travail en France* (1882),[6] and his words are echoed, in fearful or admiring tones, by almost every writer on the subject. The *chiffonnier* occupied the lowest rung on the wretched hierarchy of the Parisian *Lumpenproletariat*. He was a creature of the night, contaminated by the filth and detritus from which he eked his living, a taboo figure, *fascinans et tremendus*, utterly alien to the ordered, well-lit world of the Parisian bourgeoisie: 'La forme, le fond, le dessus, le dessous, tout est pourri chez les chiffonniers', wrote Berthaud in *Les Français peints par eux-mêmes*.[7] Each night, *chiffonniers* would pick their way through the deserted streets of the city—particularly on the Montagne Sainte-Geneviève where the *chiffonnier* of *Du vin et du haschisch* plies his miserable trade— shifting through the rubbish left by those who live by day in search of such items as might be kept, sold, or pulped down for further use. Victor Fournel has left a telling image of this parasitical industry:

[5] Victor Fournel, *Ce qu'on voit dans les rues de Paris* (Adolphe Delahaÿs, 1858), 326–7.

[6] Jules Barberet, *Le Travail en France: Monographies professionnelles* (Berger-Levrault, 1886–1890), iv. 91.

[7] L.-A. Berthaud, 'Les Chiffonniers', in *Les Français peints par eux-mêmes*, iii. 333.

Rien ne se perd dans Paris: cette industrie effrayante, gigantesque roue toujours en mouvement pour piler, broyer et renouveler, ne néglige pas le moindre atome de matière, la plus infime parcelle des plus dégoûtants immondices. Les bouts de cigare tombés de la lèvre des fumeurs, les pelures et les trognons de pommes, les fruits pourris jetés au coin des bornes, les os demi-rongés, les croûtes de pain desséchées et moisies, tous ces débris fétides, hideux, repoussants, qui soulèvent le cœur et que les chiens flairent avec dégoût, tout cela se recueille avec soin pour servir de matière première à une industrie occulte et ténébreuse; tout cela va faire peau neuve et se pavaner, dans l'éclat de sa transfiguration, à l'étalage des marchands à prix réduits.[8]

The *chiffonnier* was ostracized not only by respectable middle-class society but also by workers and, indeed, other members of the *Lumpenproletariat*: 'les sentiments généreux qui animent l'ouvrier n'existent pas dans le chiffonnier,' wrote Fregier, 'ce dernier, couvert des lambeaux de la misère, affecte une sorte de cynisme, il s'isole volontiers des masses, peut-être parce que celles-ci s'éloignent elles-mêmes du lui'.[9] *Chiffonniers* often lived on a communal basis in what were, effectively, shanty-towns constructed from whatever they had managed to find on the streets of the capital; in *Paris-anecdote* (1854) Privat d'Anglemont gives a detailed description of one such encampment on the Montagne Sainte-Geneviève, calling it 'une ville dans une ville' inhabited by 'un peuple égaré au milieu d'un autre peuple'.[10] Pockets of *chiffonniers* were to be found in many parts of the city, but the area they most affected was the Faubourg Saint-Marcel, described as follows in Texier's *Tableau de Paris* (1853):

Dans ce quartier, il n'y a pas de rues, mais des ruelles et des impasses; il n'y a pas de maisons, mais des cloaques et des taudis. Il y respire une race hâve, déguenillée, à figure sinistre, vivant des épaves que laisse dans Paris l'insouciance et le mépris de tout le reste; cette race maudite mange les restes dédaignés des chiens errants, se pare des lambeaux rejetés par le pauvre; elle se recrute parmi les criminels qui ont payé leur dette à la justice, parmi les malheureux que l'imprévoyance et l'inconduite mettent entre la mort et la faim. Quand la nuit tombe, on les voit, à demi gris, sortir des trous où ils passent la journée, et suivre la direction des plus riches

[8] Fournel, *Ce qu'on voit dans les rues de Paris*, 329.

[9] H.-A. Frégier, *Des Classes dangereuses de la société dans les grandes villes* (J. B. Baillière, 1840), i. 310.

[10] Cited in Pierre Citron, *La Poésie de Paris dans la littérature française de Rousseau à Baudelaire* (Les Éditions de Minuit, 1961), ii. 317.

quartiers, agitant leur pâle falot, et piquant toute immondice qui les séduit. En vain on a voulu poétiser les chiffonniers: sauf exceptions, ils sont tous tombés à ce degré extrême d'abrutissement qui ne laisse ni sentiments autres que ceux de la brute, ni joies autres que les joies de l'ivresse.[11]

Chiffonniers, indeed, were notorious for their drunkenness and particularly for their addiction to a potent punch-like concoction variously known as *poivre*, *casse-poitrine*, or *camphre*. 'Des huit heures du matin, il s'est défait de sa récolte de la nuit,' wrote Privat d'Anglemont of the typical *chiffonnier*, 'il a donc dix heures devant lui pour se griser, car sa nouvelle journée ne commencera guère qu'à cinq ou six heures du soir. . . . Aussitôt qu'il a vendu sa hottée de chiffons et de débris d'os et de verres cassés, il s'attable dans un coin avec un morceau de pain et de l'eau-de-vie; bientôt il tombe appesanti, ivre-mort, sous la table et s'y endort.'[12] Although comparatively harmless and law-abiding themselves, *chiffonniers* were inevitably surrounded by an aura of vice and criminality; according to Frégier there were 'parmi les chiffonniers beaucoup de repris de justice et, parmi les chiffonnières, un certain nombre de prostituées de bas étage',[13] while criminals were known to disguise themselves as *chiffonniers* in order to escape attention as they prowled through wealthy *quartiers* at night. To cap it all, *chiffonniers* even spoke a language that was unintelligible to the average Parisian whatever his class, those from the Auvergne ('les Auverpins') conversing in *patois* while, said Berthaud, the Paris-born '*entravent bigorne*' and to that extent would be identified with the *argot*-speaking criminal classes.[14]

Everything, then, combined to set *chiffonniers* apart from established society, to make them, as it were, the 'untouchables' of mid-nineteenth-century Paris. The *chiffonnier* was an absolute outsider, detested and feared by bourgeoisie and 'settled' working class alike, and it is hardly surprising that a potent collective myth should have grown up around him, a myth which, like all such group representations, fuses reality and fantasy in a single irresistible compound. The myth's starting-point is invariably the radical otherness of the *chiffonnier*, an otherness that is characteristically expressed in quasi-racial terms. Thus for Privat d'Anglemont, the

[11] Edmond Texier, *Tableau de Paris* (Paulin et Le Chevalier, 1853), ii. 283.
[12] Alexandre Privat d'Anglemont, *Paris inconnu* (Adolphe Delahaÿs, 1861), 51.
[13] Frégier, *Des classes dangereuses*, i. 110.
[14] Berthaud, 'Les Chiffonniers', 22.

'chiffonnier moderne' is the 'sauvage de Paris' and the shanty-town on the Montagne Sainte-Geneviève is 'le camp des barbares de Paris'[15] while, in *Les Dessous de Paris* (1862), Alfred Delvau typically sees the *chiffonniers* of the Place Maubert as the 'Peaux-Rouges du Paris moderne' with whom, intrepid social backwoodsman, he goes to powwow: 'Nous sommes entrés . . . sous leurs *wigwams*, à ces sauvages de Paris! Nous avons fumé avec eux le *calumet de paix*! Nous avons bu l'*eau de feu* avec leurs horribles *squaws*,—et nous sommes sortis tout mélancolisés.'[16] The most common, indeed virtually automatic, assimilations are, however, with the two great 'outside groups' of European society: Jews and gypsies. For Victor Fournel, the *chiffonniers'* haunts are a modern equivalent of the medieval ghetto:

Les chiffonniers sont dédaigneux à l'égard du bourgeois; ils ne frayent qu'entre eux; ils forment une société à part qui a des mœurs à elle, un langage à elle, un quartier à elle, auquel on peut . . . comparer les rues hideuses et méphitiques où était acculée, grouillante et sinistre, la population juive du moyen âge.

Continuing, Fournel compares *chiffonniers* to 'un peuple de Zingaris en campement dans Paris, peuple sombre et déguenillé, ayant l'ivresse bruyante et terrible, le regard fauve sous un sourcil épais, la barbe sale et la voix avinée. Ils inspirent une peur instinctive au digne citadin, qui les regarde comme une famille de réprouvés et de maudits'.[17] Example after example of this kind of social mythopoeisis could be given, but the underlying pattern is clear: for 'respectable' opinion, the *chiffonnier* was, in the first instance, a particularly horrendous specimen of the *classes dangereuses* spawned by the helter-skelter growth of the nineteenth-century city, men wholly *other* in terms of appearance, dress, behaviour, culture, language, even, it seemed, of race.

Yet the very qualities, real or imagined, that struck terror and loathing in the hearts of honest citizens when they viewed the *chiffonnier* appeared, logically enough, in a wholly different light to the political radicals and dissident artists with whom Baudelaire associated in the 1840s and early 1850s. Where the conservative shunned and condemned, the rebel glamorized and identified. As

[15] Privat d'Anglemont, *Paris inconnu*, 49–50.

[16] Alfred Delvau, *Les Dessous de Paris* (Poulet-Malassis, 1862), 75.

[17] Fournel, *Ce qu'on voit dans les rues de Paris*, 327–8.

Walter Benjamin wrote: 'From the *littérateur* to the professional conspirator, everyone who belonged to the *bohème* could recognize a bit of himself in the ragpicker. Each person was in a more or less obscure state of revolt against society and faced a more or less precarious future.'[18] Thus for the socialist he was the epitome of working-class misery and, as such, a ready-made justification for the need for thoroughgoing social and political transformation: such, broadly, is the image of the ragpicker that emerges from the hugely successful play *Le Chiffonnier de Paris* (1847) by the future Communard Félix Pyat, a work which, as Jean Pommier has argued not altogether convincingly, may have had some influence on 'Le Vin des chiffonniers'.[19] Or, as in the elder Vinçard's song 'La Lanterne du chiffonnier' (1849), he is a bringer of light into those recesses of society, its squalid underside, that respectable opinion preferred to remain decently hidden:

> Oui, pour palper les artères
> De notre corps social,
> Et des humaines misères
> Pour éclairer l'arsenal
> Il n'est de lumière externe
> Qui vaille le vieux foyer,
> S'illuminant dans la lanterne,
> La lanterne du chiffonnier.[20]

For the dissident writer, the *chiffonnier* was, needless to say, a symbol not only of his own marginality and parasitical mode of existence but also of his love of freedom and rejection of the society that rejected him: this Bohemian identification with the *chiffonnier* finds its classic statement in *Paris inconnu* (1861) by Alexandre Privat d'Anglemont, one of Baudelaire's closest associates in the late 1840s.[21] For Privat the *chiffonnier* is 'l'enfant du hasard, que la société semble avoir rejeté de son sein'; he ekes out his existence 'au milieu de la grande famille des désherités', and 'sans état civil, il ne connaît jamais son père; la famille, les parents sont pour lui des

---

[18] Walter Benjamin, *Charles Baudelaire: A Lyric Poet in the Era of High Capitalism*, trans. Harry Zohn (New Left Books, 1973), 20.

[19] Jean Pommier, *La Mystique de Baudelaire* (Les Belles Lettres, 1973), 20.

[20] Cited Pierre Brochon, *Le Pamphlet du pauvre: Du socialisme utopique à la Révolution de 1848* (Éditions Sociales, 1957), 45.

[21] For Privat d'Anglemont and Baudelaire, see Jean Ziegler, 'Essai biographique', *Études baudelairiennes*, 8 (1976), 228–32.

mots vides de sens; il connaît sa mère, mais il la dédaigne'. There are, says Privat, different varieties of *chiffonnier*, and the identification with the dissident writer becomes almost complete when he discusses the third category:

La troisième classe est le chiffonnier artiste, le bohème du genre, le philosophe, l'homme qui fut jadis quelque chose, et que des malheurs quelquefois, l'inconduite presque toujours, ont fait rouler de chute en chute jusqu'aux plus bas fonds de la société. Celui-ci parle latin; il s'embarrasse rarement d'une hotte, il a un simple bissac jeté négligemment sur son épaule; il marche raide et fier dans son indépendance et dans sa liberté. La société l'a repoussé, il l'a prise en mépris; il nargue les heureux du monde; il fait chaque matin un repas de roi avec la desserte de leur table, il s'habille de leur défroque et se chauffe des débris de leur feu. Le monde lui a nié sa position sociale: il l'abandonne volontiers, mais, en revanche, ce monde devra lui payer en détail tout ce qu'il lui a pris en un jour.

Oppressed, impoverished, ostracized by society, the *chiffonnier*, as Privat envisages him, enjoys a compensatory freedom and, as 'un homme d'imagination et de savoir' before all else, triumphs inwardly over the wretchedness of his outward condition. 'Une existence déclassée' in which material miseries combine with drink-induced splendours of the imagination: in Privat's *chiffonnier* we find all the essential elements that Baudelaire will incorporate into his poem.[22]

How far *chiffonniers* and their like were involved in political activity during the period that concerns us remains a hotly disputed question. There can be no doubt that on occasions they were capable of taking violent collective action in defence of their material interests as they did, for example, during the cholera epidemic of 1832 when proposals to reform the collection of rubbish from the streets of Paris threatened to deny them access to the 'raw materials' of their 'industry'.[23] From incidents such as these there grew the belief that, in the words of Émile de la Bedollière writing in 1842, 'les chiffonniers ont une vive inclination pour la rixe', an 'amour irrésistible de désordre' inciting them 'au combat toutes les fois que l'émeute se dechaîne' and that they represented a properly revolutionary threat to the structure of existing society:

[22] Privat d'Anglemont, *Paris inconnu*, 52–4.
[23] See Heine's description of this incident in the *Ausbürger Allgemeine Zeitung*, cited in Karlheinrich Biermann, 'Der Rausch des Lumpensammlers und der Alptraum des Bürgers', *Germanisch-Romanische Monatschrift*, 60 (1979), 315.

En entendant leurs cris sauvages, en suivant des yeux dans sa chute cette avalanche de gueux déterminés, le commerçant dit avec terreur: 'Voilà le faubourg Marceau qui descend!' Le plus stable gouvernement tremble sur la base quand, guidée par les Chiffonniers, la hâve population des faubourgs se rue sur les riches quartiers. On appréhende moins le pillage que le bouleversement de la société; on sent combien l'ordre public est faible contre tant de gens qui n'ont rien à perdre; et la protestation armée des misérables fait comprendre à tous la nécessité d'adopter comme règle de conduite ce grand axiome: 'Amélioration du sort de la classe la plus nombreuse et la plus pauvre'.[24]

The belief—amply promoted by Frégier's *Des classes dangereuses*— that it was the most dispossessed, marginalized groups of the sub-proletariat which constituted the major political threat to the Bourgeois Monarchy and the social and economic interests it represented has been decisively disproved by modern historical research.[25] While *chiffonniers* may have rioted on occasions as a group and while some may have formed associations in defence of their interests and even taken part in the June insurrection,[26] there can be no doubt that the real threat to the existing order came from the 'settled' or 'traditional' (i.e. essentially artisanal) working class of Paris, with the *Lumpenproletariat* engaging in, at most, activities of a sectional, 'pre-political' character: ironically, the 'dangerous classes' were, in a political sense, not that dangerous at all. Yet while the *classes dangereuses* as a whole were in principle distinct from the more stable *classes laborieuses* who made up the core of the revolutionary crowd in Paris from 1789 up to and including the *journées de juin*, and while *chiffonniers* in particular were, it

[24] Émile de la Bedollière, *Les Industriels, métiers et professions en France* (Alphonse Pigoreau, 1842), 175.

[25] See George Rudé, 'The Growth of Cities and Popular Revolts 1750–1850', in J. F. Bosher (ed.), *French Government and Society 1500–1850* (Athlone Press, 1973), 184–5 and 189–90, and for a summary of recent research, Mark Traugott, *Armies of the Poor: Determinants of Working-class Participation in the Parisian Insurrection of June 1848* (Princeton Univ. Press, Princeton, NJ, 1985), 171–2.

[26] On *chiffonniers'* associations, see Privat d'Anglemont, *Paris inconnu*, 55, and for the participation of the *chiffonniers* of the Rue Mouffetard in the June uprising, see Georges Duveau, *1848* (Gallimard, 1965), 151. For the possibility that *chiffonniers* had a vested interest in social and political *stability*, see the comment by a ragpicker on the effect of 1848 on his 'business' in Sir Francis Head, *A Faggot of French Sticks, or Paris in 1851* (George P. Putnam, New York, 1852): 'Monsieur, depuis la révolution le monde est plus économique; la consommation est moins grande dans les cuisines; on jette moins d'os et de papier dans les rues. . . . Si la tranquillité vient, nous ferons peut-être quelque chose; mais . . . quand il n'y a pas de luxe, on ne fait rien' (p. 252).

appears, too crushed by immediate necessities to engage in any significant political activity, the conditions of the later years of the Bourgeois Monarchy made it almost inevitable that they would be identified by outsiders with those more political conscious elements of the lower classes who, like the Goths and Visigoths of old, posed a growing threat to the citadel of 'ordered' society:

Les ouvriers sont aussi libres de devoirs envers leurs maîtres que ceux-ci le sont envers eux; ils les considèrent comme des hommes d'une classe différente, opposée et même ennemie. Isolés de la nation, mis en dehors de la communauté sociale et politique, seuls avec leurs besoins et leurs misères, ils s'agitent pour sortir de cette effrayante solitude, et, comme les barbares auxquels on les a comparés, ils méditent peut-être une invasion.[27]

In the bourgeois consciousness of the 1840s, be it conservative or radical, *classes laborieuses* and *classes dangereuses* swirled together as one, and the *chiffonnier*, that emblem of 'le peuple de Paris' at its most dispossessed, became, for the first, an embodiment of all those political fears and traumas by which, from a clearly distinct source, the bourgeois world-view was assailed and, for the latter, a symbol of the forthcoming regeneration by popular revolution of the ossified structures of society. Essentially apolitical himself, the *chiffonnier* had, by the beginning of 1848, been transformed into a political 'myth' of considerable potency for Left and Right alike.

The myth was surprisingly durable, and survived the virtual disappearance of *chiffonniers* as a recognizable sub-class of the *Lumpenproletariat* in the 1860s. Almost thirty years after the first publication of 'Le Vin des chiffonniers', Jules Vallès, in an article entitled 'L'Assommoir des chiffonniers' published in *Gil Blas* in 1882, gave an even more romanticized image of the ragpicker as free-wheeling street-poet whose psychedelic benders are to be applauded not condemned:

Ils flânent heureux dans leurs savates boueuses. Pas de loyer à payer: la plaine immense. Pas de frais de toilette: la guenille abonde. Pas besoin de pain: on repêche les croûtes dans le ruisseau, et même on a le goût du vin, si l'on veut, en rinçant avec de l'eau fraîche un cul de bouteille cassée. Que fait-il de plus? N'est-ce pas assez? ils ont de quoi ne pas mourir, et ils sont libres. Oui, ils sont libres! tandis que l'ouvrier ne l'est pas. Il ne chôme

---

[27] Saint-Marc Girardin in *Le Journal des Débats* (Dec. 1831), quoted Louis Chevalier, *Classes laborieuses et classes dangereuses à Paris pendant la première moitié du XIXe siècle* (Plon, 1958), 453.

jamais, le *Biffin*. Chaque jour amène son épluchure, tandis qu'il y a des grèves la veille des révolutions et que l'on ferme les fabriques le lendemain.[28]

Middle-class bugaboo or peripatetic poet-scavenger of the Bohemians, the *chiffonnier*, it is clear, lent himself only too readily to mythologization: what he may have thought and felt in reality remains almost totally mysterious. Yet the basic significance of Baudelaire's gesture is clear: to write sympathetically of a figure whose mythological meaning was already fixed in conservative and radical writing was, irrespective of the radical-romantic velleities and straight intellectual 'slumming' involved, to align oneself unmistakably with 'les damnés de la terre'. Across the chasm of social divisions, the *déclassé* poet reaches out to the most despised member of the Parisian *Lumpenproletariat* and, through the medium of wine, expresses their joint hostility to the repressive— and sober—world of the bourgeoisie.

'Le Vin des chiffonniers'

In 1957 W. T. Bandy demonstrated the close links between 'Le Vin des chiffonniers' and the portrait of one particular ragpicker in Privat d'Anglemont's *Paris-Anecdote* (1854). Here Privat describes an old *chiffonnier* nicknamed 'le général' who, late at night, drunkenly imagines himself in command of an army in battle. He deploys regiments born of his inebriated fantasy in the backstreets of the Faubourg du Temple, issues orders to imaginary brigadiers and colonels and thereby, says Privat, escapes from the miseries of his real existence into a 'pays des chimères' where he reigns supreme:

Enfin la bataille est engagée sur toute la ligne, canons et caissons roulant font crier leurs essieux, cavalerie, infanterie et artillerie, tous se mêlent, se culbutent, se tuent, le général passe le point du canal; il se remue, marche, court, avance, recule. Puis il pousse un grand cri et s'assied sur une borne.—Encore une victoire, dit-il; oh! la guerre, le sang! . . . Il reprend tranquillement sa hotte et continue sa récolte de chiffonnier comme si rien n'en était. Il se croit sans doute revêtu de son brillant uniforme, distribuant

[28] Jules Vallès, 'L'Assommoir des chiffonniers', *Gil Blas* (30 Mar. 1882), in Vallès, *Le Tableau de Paris*, ed. Marie-Claire Bancquart (Éditeurs Français Réunis, 1971), 79–80.

ses récompenses et ses encouragements à ses troupes rangées sur le champ de bataille conquis par elles.[29]

Privat's text first appeared in *Le Figaro* on 30 July 1854, a few months before the first publication of Baudelaire's poem in *Jean Raisin*. He may, of course, have taken the idea from *Du vin et du haschisch* or from one of the several manuscripts that, as we have seen, were already in circulation. Alternatively, Privat's text may have existed for some time before its publication and Baudelaire— who may, as indicated earlier, be the (part) author of poems published under Privat's name in the mid-1840s—could well have seen it and used it in composing his own poem. The most likely explanation is that advanced by W. T. Bandy. Both Baudelaire and Privat were renowned for their *noctambulisme* and often went together on late-night explorations of the 'labyrinthe fangeux' of Parisian backstreets evoked in the first stanza of the 1857 text of 'Le Vin des chiffonniers'. Together or separately, they both witnessed the ragpicker-general's drunken manœuvres and composed their tributes to him independently, Baudelaire as early as 1841–3, Privat probably somewhat later. Baudelaire's poem, in short, is born of an actual encounter seen and reworked through the prism of, as we have seen, countless literary and visual models. The version-by-version discussion that follows is intended to bring out the progressive transformation of the text from its genesis in 1841–3 to its 'definitive' form of 1857. Only when the major variations have been indicated will an attempt be made to link the text's bewildering metamorphoses to the evolution of Baudelaire's politics during the period spanned by its composition.

Version I: The Godoy Manuscript (1841–3 to 1850–1)

'LE VIN DES CHIFFONNIERS'

Au fond de ces quartiers sombres et tortueux,   1
Où vivent par milliers des ménages frileux,
Parfois, à la clarté sombre des réverbères,
Que le vent de la nuit tourmente dans leurs verres,   4
On voit un chiffonnier qui revient de travers,

---

[29] Quoted W. T. Bandy, 'Le Chiffonnier de Baudelaire', *Revue d'histoire littéraire de la France*, 57/4 (1957), 583.

Se cognant, se heurtant, comme un faiseur de Vers,
Et libre, sans souci des patrouilles funèbres,
Seul épanche son âme au milieu des ténèbres.   8

Un régiment se meut à ses regards trompés,
Et lui, jette aux échos des mots entrecoupés,
Tels que ceux que vaincu par la mort triomphante
L'Empereur exhalait de sa gorge expirante.   12
Oui, ces gens tout voûtés sous le poids des débris
Et des fumiers infects que rejette Paris,
Harassés et chargés de chagrins de ménage,
Moulus par le travail et tourmentés par l'âge,   16
Ont une heure nocturne, où pleins d'illusions,
Et l'esprit éclairé d'étranges visions,
Ils s'en vont, parfumés d'une odeur de futailles,
Commandant une armée et gagnant des batailles,   20
Et jurant qu'ils rendront toujours leur peuple heureux.
Mais nul n'a jamais vu les hauts faits glorieux,
Les triomphes bruyants, les fêtes solemnelles [*sic*],
Qui s'allument alors au fond de leurs cervelles,   24
Plus belles que les Rois n'en rêveront jamais.

C'est ainsi que le vin règne par ses bienfaits,
Et chante ses exploits par le gosier de l'homme.
Grandeurs de la bonté de celui que tout nomme,   28
Qui nous avait déjà donné le doux sommeil,
Et voulut ajouter le vin, fils du soleil,
Pour réchauffer le cœur et calmer la souffrance
De tous les malheureux qui meurent en silence.

(OC, i. 1049–50)

What is presumably the earliest surviving manuscript of 'Le Vin
des chiffonniers', at present in the collection of Armand Godoy,
bears the signature 'Charles Baudelaire' and must therefore date
from the beginning of 1848 at the earliest. Consisting of 32 lines,
divided into three sections of 8, 17, and 7 lines respectively, it
presumably pre-dates the 24-line strophic versions of 1851–4; it was
found among Daumier's papers at his death and is, all editors
assume, close to the version heard by Prarond in or before 1843,
though minor or major revisions could well have occurred any time
between that date and, say, the end of 1850. This first version of
the poem differs in important respects from all those that follow it.
In the first place, it evokes the ragpickers' militaristic fantasies in a
way that leaves no doubt as to their illusoriness. The *chiffonniers*

are 'pleins d'illusions', their collective mind is 'éclairé d'étranges visions', and Baudelaire is only stating the obvious when he observes that 'nul n'a jamais vu les hauts faits glorieux . . . | Qui s'allument alors au fond de leurs cervelles': no subsequent version will present such direct, explicit commentary by the poet, though one should not assume from this that he would later come to view the ragpickers' 'visions' as any less chimerical. Secondly, the reference to Napoleon ('L'Empereur exhalait . . .', l. 12) is made openly and, it would appear, 'innocently', in contrast to the covert and devious way in which, as we shall see, it is insinuated into the later verse texts; it is picked up allusively in 'les triomphes bruyants' and 'les fêtes solennelles' of line 20, these last being said to be 'plus belles que les Rois n'en rêveront jamais'. Claude Pichois reminds us (OC, i. 1049) that Baudelaire had, in the company of Gustave Le Vavasseur, witnessed the return of the Emperor's remains in December 1840, and the link between the *chiffonnier*'s bellowed commands and the barely coherent dying words—reportedly 'à la tête de l'armée'[30]—of Napoleon on Saint-Helena could indeed have been suggested by the stimulus that that most ambiguous of 'fêtes solennelles' had given to the Napoleonic legend. If this were so, the case for regarding the Godoy manuscript as being very close to the early (1841?) draft of the poem heard by Prarond would obviously be strengthened. We shall return in due course to the possible significance of the Napoleonic sub-text that is present, often heavily disguised, but perceptible to those who can recognize the signs, whenever Baudelaire treats the theme of the ragpicker.

The most striking difference between the first extant version of 'Le Vin des chiffonniers' and its successors lies, however, in its conclusion. The world-view contained in its seven lines is, at the very least, theistic; Nature is the creation and image of a loving god who benevolently bestows the gifts of wine and sleep upon 'les malheureux'. To the extent that it echoes the naturalistic theology of such undoubted early poems as 'J'aime le souvenir de ces époques nues . . .' and 'La Géante', this conclusion again points

[30] As reported by General Bertrand in his *Cahiers de Sainte-Hélène* (Éditions Sulliver, 1949), 194. Baudelaire could have heard a version of this report through any number of popular and other sources, for example, Dumas' play *Napoléon Bonaparte ou trente ans de l'histoire de France* (first performed in 1831 with Frédéric Lemaître in the title role), where the Emperor's last words are given as 'Tête armée! Mon Dieu! Mon Dieu!' (cited Jean Tulard, *Le Mythe de Napoléon* (Armand Colin, 1971), 172).

towards the Godoy manuscript's being close to the version Prarond heard before the end of 1843: it conspicuously lacks the antitheistic impulse foregrounded in the somewhat later (1846–7?) 'Révolte' poems and which we have found to be subliminally present in the 1850 'Vin des honnêtes gens'. At the same time, though, the manuscript leaves unanswered the question to which the 1857 text will give a reply that is far more antitheistic—and hence, by implication, far more 'revolutionary'—than any of the earlier versions: why, if both God and Nature (and presumably man) are intrinsically good, should there be any 'malheureux' needing consolation through sleep and wine? It was a question that Baudelaire could discreetly push to one side in the early 1840s. By the end of the decade, and still more by the mid-1850s, such evasions would no longer be possible.

Version II: Du vin et du haschisch *(March 1851)*

Mais voici bien autre chose. Descendons un peu plus bas. Contemplons un de ces êtres mystérieux, vivant pour ainsi dire des déjections des grandes villes; car il y a de singuliers métiers. Le nombre en est immense. J'ai quelquefois pensé avec terreur qu'il y avait des métiers qui ne comportaient aucune joie, des métiers sans plaisir, des fatigues sans soulagement, des douleurs sans compensation. Je me trompais. Voici un homme chargé de ramasser les débris d'une journée de la capitale. Tout ce que la grande cité a rejeté, tout ce qu'elle a perdu, tout ce qu'elle a dédaigné, tout ce qu'elle a brisé, il le catalogue, il le collectionne. Il compulse les archives de la débauche, le capharnaüm des rebuts. Il fait un triage, un choix intelligent; il ramasse, comme un avare un trésor, les ordures qui, remâchées par la divinité de l'Industrie, deviendront des objets d'utilité ou de jouissance. Le voici qui, à la clarté sombre des réverbères tourmentés par le vent de la nuit, remonte une des longues rues tortueuses et peuplées de petits ménages de la montagne Sainte-Geneviève. Il est revêtu de son *châle d'osier avec son numéro sept.* Il arrive hochant la tête et butant sur les pavés, comme les jeunes poètes qui passent toutes leurs journées à errer et à chercher des rimes. Il parle tout seul; il verse son âme dans l'air froid et ténébreux de la nuit. C'est un monologue splendide à faire prendre en pitié les tragédies les plus lyriques. 'En avant! marche! division, tête, armée!' Exactement comme Buonaparte agonisant à Sainte-Helene! Il paraît que le numéro *sept* s'est changé en sceptre de fer, et le *châle d'osier* en manteau impérial. Maintenant il complimente son armée. La bataille est gagnée, mais la journée a été chaude. Il passe à cheval sous des arcs de triomphe. Son cœur est heureux. Il écoute avec délices les acclamations d'un monde enthousiaste. Tout à l'heure il va dicter un code supérieur à tous les codes connus. Il jure solennellement qu'il rendra ses peuples heureux. La misère et le vice ont disparu de l'humanité. Et cependant il a le dos et les reins écorchés par le poids de sa hotte. Il est harcelé de chagrins de ménage. Il est moulu par quarante ans de travail et de courses. L'âge le tourmente. Mais le vin, comme un Pactole nouveau, roule à travers l'humanité languissante un or intellectuel. Comme les bons rois, il règne par ses services et chante ses exploits par le gosier de ses sujets. Il y a sur la boule terrestre une foule innombrable, innomée, dont le sommeil n'endormirait pas suffisamment les souffrances. Le vin compose pour eux des chants et des poèmes. (OC, i. 381–2)

The prose 'doublet' of 'Le Vin des chiffonniers' in *Du vin et du haschisch* is assumed by all editors to post-date the Godoy manuscript, to have been composed specially for the essay of which it forms part and thus to constitute the link between the Ur-text of 1841–3 and the verse manuscripts of 1851–2 on which the *Jean Raisin* text of 1854 is based. The text of *Du vin et du haschisch* is, however, less a recasting in prose of the Godoy manuscript or of the recensions of 1851–2 (on which Baudelaire may already have embarked when he wrote *Du vin et du haschisch*) than an independent composition in parallel to the verse texts considered as an ensemble. Although it preserves the basic pattern of the Godoy manuscript and though it takes over verbatim phrases from this or later verse texts ('à la clarté sombre des réverbères', 'hochant la tête et butant sur les pavés', etc.), the prose text introduces much new material (notably the compelling description of the ragpicker's *modus operandi* ('tout ce que la grande cité a rejeté', etc.)) and also differs significantly from the verse texts in respect of tone, style, and general moral position. Whereas the verse texts are notable for their total absence of first person pronouns,[31] the text of *Du vin et du haschisch* begins with a series of direct and complicitous addresses to the reader ('descendons', 'contemplons') followed by some personal reflections by the author ('J'ai quelquefois pensé', 'je me trompais'); the use of 'voici' three times in the text further intensifies the bond between writer, reader, and the object of their

---

[31] See Biermann, 'Der Rausch', 319 on the 'Abwesenheit eines lyrischen Ich' in the verse texts. This 'disparition élocutoire du poète' is paralleled in other 'Second Republic' texts, notably the two 'Crépuscule' poems. See Ross Chambers, 'Trois paysages urbains: Les Poèmes liminaires des *Tableaux parisiens*', *Modern Philology*, 80/4 (1983), 372–89.

joint attention. At the same time, the overtly moralizing stance of the Godoy manuscript is quietly dropped, in large part because Baudelaire is anxious at all costs to avoid what the paragraph preceding the ragpicker episode calls the 'acharnement' with which 'pseudo-moralistes pharisiens' inveigh against wine and all its works. The illusoriness of the ragpicker's visions is left in no doubt ('et cependant'), but his right to drink and fantasize is vigorously defended. More than in any of the verse texts, the *chiffonnier* of *Du vin et du haschisch* is a poet or, more precisely, the willing medium through which the poetic energies of wine take form and gain release. If the ragpicker's 'monologue splendide' is such as to 'faire prendre en pitié les tragédies les plus lyriques', it is because it is sung by the supreme lyricist, wine, at work within him. Wine is a benevolent despot who, 'comme les bons rois', chooses his favourites amongst the lowest and most unfavoured of his 'subjects' and through them finds a voice: 'Le vin compose pour eux des chants et des poèmes'.

As far as content is concerned, the text of *Du vin et du haschisch* drops the Godoy manuscript's reference to 'patrouilles funèbres' and has no equivalent of the 'mouchards ténébreux' that take their place in the 1851–2 manuscripts. On the other hand, the reference to the dying Napoleon is retained, and the links between ragpicker and Emperor actually strengthened by the transformation of the former's *châle d'osier* 'en manteau impérial' and of his mysterious *numéro sept*—presumably the hooked instrument used by *chiffonniers* to pick through piles of rubbish[32]—'en sceptre de feu'. Given the context of 1851, the reference to Napoleon is no longer as 'innocent' as it was in 1841–3, and the spelling 'Buonaparte', as well as signalling Baudelaire's anti-Bonapartist sentiments to the reader,[33] could also suggest his growing uneasiness with the connection his original text had made between ragpicker and Emperor. In passing from the Godoy manuscript to *Du vin et du haschisch*, the *chiffonnier* has, in keeping with Baudelaire's populist *démoc-soc* politics, become an emblem of the 'le peuple de Paris' at, simul-

---

[32] As illustrated, for example, in Berthaud, 'Les Chiffonniers', 333. See also the description in Head, *A Faggot of French Sticks*, 249. Baudelaire's references are presumably to the imperial regalia at the *sacre* of 1804.

[33] The spelling 'Buonaparte'—here used for, it seems, the only time by Baudelaire —conventionally denoted an anti-Bonapartist stance, as in Chateaubriand's celebrated pamphlet of 1814, *De Buonaparte et des Bourbons* (see Tulard, *Le Mythe de Napoléon*, 47–8).

taneously, its most abject and most 'poetic'; in the circumstances of 1851, his lingering connections with Bonapartism are disconcerting indeed, though, as we shall see, by no means lacking in historical equivalents. The sentences that follow yield further complications. The Godoy manuscript merely had the *chiffonniers* (plural) 'jurant qu'ils rendront toujours leur peuple heureux' with no reference as to how they would do this or indication of what such 'happiness' might involve. If *Du vin et du haschisch* says more about both questions, it does so in a way that mixes Republican-Jacobin, Bonapartist, and even royalist (cf. 'les bons rois') discourses in a most troubling and problematic manner. The ragpicker-Napoleon— one only—passes 'sous des arcs de triomphe' to the tumultuous applause of the crowd and promulgates a code—no need to emphasize *that* word's Napoleonic ring—that will be 'supérieur à tous les codes connus'. But, perplexingly, the language switches next to a register that is more Republican-Jacobin or royalist than Bonapartist (or a bewildering tangle of all three) as the ragpicker 'jure solennellement qu'il rendra ses peuples heureux'. Swears like who? Like Charles X at his coronation in 1824 or Louis-Philippe in 1830? Or the deputies of the Third Estate in 1789? Or Napoleon at his coronation in 1804?[34] Or, dare one say it, like Louis Napoleon at his presidential inauguration on 20 December 1848? To add to the confusion, 'ses peuples' couples a royalist 'ses' to a Jacobin-universalist 'peuples', this last contrasting with 'leur peuple' of the Godoy manuscript but pointing forward uncannily, like the whole development of which it forms part, to the Utopian-socialist treatises of 'Assommons les pauvres!' 'où il est traité de *l'art de rendre les peuples heureux*, sages et riches, en vingt-quartre heures' (OC, i. 357), italics added). The paragraph ends with the dearest dream of *quarante-huit* fulfilled—'la misère et le vice ont disparu de l'humanité'—but fulfilled by means that are at least as much royal and/or imperial as they are republican in character. *Du vin et du haschisch*, in short, does not so much oppose royalist, Bonapartist, and republican discourses as show them continually slipping one into the other. In the 'final' version of 'Le Vin des chiffonniers', this intersecting and merging of competing political discourses will, as we shall see, take on even more disconcerting forms.

[34] At his coronation in 1804, Napoleon swore, amongst other things, to 'gouverner dans la seule vue de l'intérêt du bonheur et de la gloire du peuple français' (Jean Tulard, *Napoléon ou le mythe du sauveur* (Fayard, 1987), 173).

Version III: Jean Raisin *(1854)*

'LE VIN DES CHIFFONNIERS'

Souvent à la clarté sombre des réverbères,
Que le vent de la nuit tourmente dans leurs verres,
Au fond de ces quartiers mornes et tortueux
Où grouillent par milliers les ménages frileux,   4

On voit un chiffonnier qui vient, hochant la tête,
Buttant et se cognant aux murs comme un poète,
Et, sans prendre souci des mouchards ténébreux,
Épanchant tout son cœur dans l'air silencieux.   8

Oui, ces gens harcelés de chagrins de ménage,
Moulus par le travail et tourmentés par l'âge,
Le dos bas et meurtri sous le poids des débris
Et des fumiers infects que rejette Paris,   12

Reviennent parfumés d'une odeur de futailles,
Commandant une armée et gagnant des batailles,
Ils jurent qu'ils rendront toujours leur peuple heureux,
Et suivent à cheval leur [*sic*] destins glorieux.   16

C'est ainsi qu'à travers l'humanité frivole,
Le vin roule de l'or comme un nouveau Pactole.
Par le gosier de l'homme il chante ses exploits,
Et par ses bienfaits règne ainsi que les vrais rois.   20

Pour apaiser le cœur et calmer la souffrance
De tous les innocents qui meurent en silence,
Dieu leur avait déjà donné le doux sommeil:
Il ajouta le vin, fils sacré du soleil.   24

(OC, i. 1050–1)

The first published version of 'Le Vin des chiffonniers' is, in its essentials, identical to the two manuscripts dating from 1851–2 which, for their part, differ significantly both from the Godoy manuscript and from the prose text of *Du vin et du haschisch*. The reference to the dying Napoleon has disappeared, and the Bonapartist resonances of the text have been muffled, surviving only in virtually undetectable form in the 'commandant une armée et gagnant des batailles' of line 14. As in the Godoy manuscript, the word 'oui' (l. 9) marks a progression from one *chiffonnier* in particular to the sub-class as a whole, but the law-making fantasies of the single *chiffonnier* of *Du vin et du haschisch* are now omitted, leaving only the non-specific 'ils jurent qu'ils rendront toujours leur peuple [singular] heureux' that had appeared in slightly different form in the poem's earliest version. As a result of these excisions, the 32 lines of the Godoy manuscript become the 24, divided into four-line stanzas, of the *Jean Raisin* text. The tone of the first published text is neutral and descriptive, lacking both the moralistic perspective of the Godoy manuscript and the personal and compassionate stance of *Du vin et du haschisch*. There are changes of wording which, perhaps of little import in 1854, will have major implications for the radically revised text of 1857. 'Les bons rois' (or 'Rois') of *Du vin et du haschisch* and the 1851–2 manuscripts (cf. 'les Rois' in the Godoy manuscript) became 'les vrais rois' in 1854; 'tous les malheureux' of the last line of the Godoy manuscript give way to 'tous les innocents' in the 1851–2 and 1854 texts; and the *chiffonniers* no longer go away ('s'en vont', l. 19) as they did in the Godoy manuscript but are shown returning in all the subsequent versions of the text ('reviennent', l. 13, cf. 'remonte' in *Du vin et du haschisch*). Finally, God, wholly absent in the prose text, is reinstated in the last stanza of the verse texts that follow, but in, so to speak, a theologically trimmed down form: He simply adds the gift of wine to His earlier gift of sleep, and no reference is made, as it was in the Godoy manuscript, to the abundance of his generosity ('grandeur de la bonté') or to the way in which the whole of His creation bears witness to His existence as creator ('de celui que tout nomme'). All in all, the *Jean Raisin* text is notable for its lack of openly controversial or problematic materials, though the presence of 'mouchards ténébreux' (or 'curieux'[35]) (l. 7) lurking in the interstices of the text and introduced for the first time in the 1851–2 manuscripts functions, perhaps, as a *mise en abysme* of the mechanisms of surveillance and censorship common to the declining Second Republic and Second Empire that have prompted Baudelaire to 'depoliticize' his potentially incendiary text for the purposes of publication.

Version IV: Les Fleurs du mal *(1857)*

> Souvent, à la clarté rouge d'un réverbère
> Dont le vent bat la flamme et tourmente le verre,

[35] 'Curieux' is a deleted reading in the text of 1851–2 entitled 'L'ivresse du chiffonnier' that Baudelaire sent to Achille Ricourt (OC, i. 1050).

Au cœur d'un vieux faubourg, labyrinthe fangeux,
Où l'humanité grouille en ferments orageux,   4

On voit un chiffonnier qui vient, hochant la tête,
Buttant, et se cognant aux murs comme un poète,
Et, sans prendre souci des mouchards, ses sujets,
Épanche tout son cœur en glorieux projects.   8

Il prête des serments, dicte des lois sublimes,
Terrasse les méchants, relève les victimes,
Et sous le firmament comme un dais suspendu
S'enivre des splendeurs de sa propre vertu.   12

Oui, ces gens harcelés de chagrins de ménage,
Moulus par le travail et tourmentés par l'âge,
Le dos martyrisé sous de hideux débris,
Trouble vomissement du fastueux Paris,   16

Reviennent, parfumés d'une odeur de futailles,
Suivis de compagnons blanchis dans les batailles,
Dont la moustache pend comme les vieux drapeaux.
Les banniers, les fleurs et les arcs triomphaux   20

Se dressent devant eux, solennelle magie!
Et dans l'étourdissante et lumineuse orgie
Des clairons, du soleil, des cris et du tambour,
Ils apportent la gloire au peuple ivre d'amour!   24

C'est ainsi qu'à travers l'Humanité frivole
Le vin roule de l'or, éblouissant Pactole;
Par le gosier de l'homme il chante ses exploits
Et règne par ses dons ainsi que les vrais rois.   28

Pour noyer la rancœur et bercer l'indolence
De tous ces vieux maudits qui meurent en silence,
Dieu, saisi de remords, avait fait le sommeil;
L'Homme ajouta le Vin, fils sacré du Soleil![36]   32

It is immediately obvious that the text published as poem 94 in the first edition of *Les Fleurs du mal* represents a fundamental reworking of the *Jean Raisin* version, above all in the final stanza where the substitution of 'l'Homme'—the capital letter is to be noted—for God as the creator of wine inverts the theistic world-view present, in one form or another, in all the previous verse texts of the poem and propels the new version in an antitheistic and implicitly revolutionary direction wholly at variance with what seems to have been the general evolution of Baudelaire's religious,

[36] I have reconstituted the 1857 text on the basis of the notes in OC, i. 1051–2.

ethical, and political thinking since the end of 1852. When this radical rewriting took place cannot be determined, but what evidence we have points to a date closer to 1857 than 1854. Baudelaire sent the manuscript of *Les Fleurs du mal* to Poulet-Malassis at the beginning of February 1857. He received proofs before the end of the month and worked on them right up until *Les Fleurs du mal* went to press in the middle of June, treating them, as Claude Pichois says,[37] less as texts to be checked, corrected, and returned than as 'une simple dactylographie' to which major revisions could legitimately be made. Although the major transformation of the final stanza of 'Le Vin des chiffonniers' had been made before the manuscript was dispatched, the fact that the proof of the poem contained so many changes that Baudelaire had to send a complete fair copy to Poulet-Malassis in Alençon around the middle of May (see C, i. 402) suggests that the rewriting was of recent date, probably the last months of 1856 but conceivably as late as January 1857. To add to the confusion, yet another version of 'Le Vin des chiffonniers' was published in Poulet-Malassis' newspaper, the *Journal d'Alençon*, on 18 June 1857, only a week or so before *Les Fleurs du mal* went on sale in Alençon and Paris. Although *Les Fleurs du mal* had been printed by the time it appeared, the text published in the *Journal d'Alençon* is based on the proof copy minus the changes Baudelaire had made to it in April and May.[38] Still more oddly, the poem was not divided into quatrains (and, to that extent, represents a kind of 'regression' to the Godoy manuscript) and, in two instances, actually reverted to readings from the *Jean Raisin* text which Baudelaire had amended before sending the manuscript to Poulet-Malassis. Instead of 'épanche' in line 8 of the proof, the *Journal d'Alençon* reads 'épanchant', and, more importantly, replaces the proof's line 31 'Dieu saisi de remords avait fait le sommeil' with the reading of *Jean Raisin* and the 1851–2 manuscripts: 'Dieu leur avait déjà donné le doux sommeil'. How this text was constituted, by whom (Baudelaire himself? Poulet-Malassis? Poulet-Malassis' brother-in-law and partner De Broise?) and for what reason remain obscure: its publication only serves to underline further the extraordinary textual instability of 'Le Vin des chiffonniers'. As if this were not enough, the text of the second edition of *Les Fleurs du mal* (1861) brought yet more

[37] BPZ, 338.
[38] See Jacques Crépet and Georges Blin, *Les Fleurs du mal* (Corti, 1950), 209.

revisions, principally at lines 15–16 and 31 where the first edition's 'saisi de remords' was altered to 'touché de remords', a change which makes God even less the loving, generous provider for the weak that He was in the Godoy manuscript and, if anything, pushes the poem still further in the antitheistic direction it had taken in 1857.

Readers alert to the political codes and contexts of mid-nineteenth-century France will not fail to notice how almost all the changes Baudelaire made in 1856–7 to the ostensibly 'dépolitiqué' text published in *Jean Raisin* have contemporary resonances which, taken together, make of this 'definitive' version of 'Le Vin des chiffonniers' one of the richest, most complex and most ambiguous political poems in Baudelaire's entire work. In the very first line, the substitution of 'rouge' for 'sombre' is only the first of a series of politically loaded terms introduced into the 1857 text. The basically neutral and descriptive term 'quartiers' is replaced by 'faubourg' with its potent political associations, the adjective 'vieux' signalling to the reader of 1857—for whom, as 'Haussmannization' proceeded apace, the Paris of even 1848–51 must already have seemed 'le vieux Paris'—that it is out of the very heart ('au cœur' for 'au fond') of the revolutionary city of yore, the Faubourg du Temple, the Faubourg Saint-Marceau, the Faubourg Saint-Antoine, that the ragpicker is staggering drunkenly towards him. The suppression of the two adjectives 'mornes et tortueux' in favour of the appositive noun phrase 'labyrinthe fangeux' transforms the *faubourg* into a single threatening spider's-web of fetid back-streets and alleys in which the individuated households still present in 1854 ('ménages frileux') have collapsed and dissolved into an undifferentiated and faceless 'humanité'. With their 'quartiers mornes [or 'sombres'] et tortueux' and thousands of 'ménages frileux', the 1851–4 texts evoke, appropriately enough, 'les grands froids' (Eugène Pottier) of the post-June and post-December repressions: abruptly, the 'ferments orageux' of 1857 plunge the reader back into the political cauldron of February and June. In the 1857 text everything becomes wildly, drunkenly, alive as city, mind, and poem become images of each other. The ragpicker's brain itself becomes a 'labyrinthe fangeux' sluicing with delirious images and visions, rhythmically the opening stanzas lurch from line to line like the *chiffonnier* staggering from wall to wall, their syntax as complex and disorientating as a knot of streets through which the reader stumbles in confusion before reaching the vantage-point of a subject and main verb ('on voit'), only to be led off forthwith down further syntactical alleyways that draw him deep into the mind and milieu of 'le peuple' at its most dispossessed.[39] The flickering flame of a single *réverbère* is all the (bourgeois) reader has to guide him: this is working-class Paris at its most alien, the very heartland of popular revolution.

Out of that heartland, the ragpicker comes staggering towards us, his head lolling drunkenly from side to side, no longer simply heedless (as he had been in 1854) of the *mouchards* dispatched by the bourgeois state to spy on and report his actions, but actively recruiting them as bit-parts in the power-drunk fantasy unfolding in his brain ('des mouchards, ses sujets'); he is the vagabond king or emperor to whom everyone, not least the hirelings of the rich man's state, is vassal and must pay homage. The further small changes Baudelaire made to the second stanza in 1857 all have the effect of making the *chiffonnier* a more purposive and hence perhaps more threatening figure. The earlier texts had been at pains not only to emphasize the ragpicker's isolation ('seul épanche' (Godoy MS, l. 8), 'il parle tout seul' (*Du vin*)) but to show the outpourings of his 'soul' or 'heart' vanishing like so much breath from his mouth into the frosty silence about him ('au milieu des ténèbres', 'dans l'air froid et ténébreux', 'dans l'air silencieux'): it is the classic Baudelairean image of fruitless self-vaporization, made all the more futile by being frozen, in the *Jean Raisin* text, into an unchanging present by the participle 'épanchant' (l. 8). The *chiffonnier* of 1857 is no less alone than his predecessors nor do his drunken ravings, any more than before, find any response in the void about him, but the fact that he now pours out his soul 'en glorieux projets' marks a significant advance on the content-less *épanchements* of the earlier versions. This *chiffonnier* may be just as drunk as those who staggered their way through the previous texts, but his drunkenness, far more explicitly than theirs, carries with it a longing for change, for power, for glory. Lurching drunkenly towards the reader, his mind afire with Utopian and megalomaniac dreams, the ragpicker embodies in grotesque, debased form the aspirations of 'le peuple' as it streamed from its *faubourgs* in

[39] This section owes much to the excellent comments in T. J. Clark, *The Absolute Bourgeois: Artists and Politics in France 1848–1851* (Thames and Hudson, 1973), 162–3.

February 1848 to establish the Kingdom of republican-socialist Heaven on earth.

The third stanza of the 1857 'Vin des chiffonniers' goes back to the prose text of *Du vin et du haschisch* to reintroduce the theme of the *chiffonnier* as lawgiver which, as we have seen, had been eliminated from the *Jean Raisin* text of the poem. Karlheinz Biermann perceptively links the line 'Terrasse les méchants et relève les victimes' with the 'chiliastic' vision of the Magnificat (cf. especially Luke 1: 52–3: 'Il a renversé les potentats de leurs trônes et élevé les humbles. Il a rassasié de biens les affamés et renvoyé les riches les mains vides' (Jerusalem Bible)), commenting that 'the *chiffonnier* thus assumes the role which Jesus played as revolutionary protagonist in the republican-socialist ideology of 1848, and with him all those who considered themselves his disciples'.[40] It is a suggestive comparison, and one that falls in well with Biermann's broader interpretation of the ragpicker as embodiment of the revolutionary people of 1848 and of the poem as an endorsement by Baudelaire of his—and the people's—revolutionary aspirations. But the Magnificat is not the only text echoed by line 10 of 'Le Vin des chiffonniers'. Equally striking is the parallel with the Virgilian *locus classicus* 'parcere subiectis et debellare superbos' (*Aeneid*, VI. 853) at the climax of Anchises' vision of the future glories of the city and people of Rome:

> Roman, remember by your strength to rule
> Earth's peoples—for your arts are to be these:
> To pacify, to impose the rule of law,
> To spare the conquered, battle down the proud.

Anchises' vision encompasses Rome as kingdom and republic but leaves no doubt that it will be as an Empire, and under one Emperor in particular, that the city will achieve its greatest triumphs:

> Turn your two eyes
> This way and see this people, your own Romans.
> Here is Caesar, and all the line of Iulus,
> All who shall one day pass under the dome
> Of the great sky: this is the man, this one,
> Of whom so often you have heard the promise,
> Caesar Augustus, son of the deified,
> Who shall bring once again an Age of Gold

[40] Biermann, 'Des Rausch', 317 (my translation).

To Latium, to the land where Saturn reigned
In early times . . .[41]

If, therefore, the third stanza of 'Le Vin des chiffonniers' evokes allusively a Republican-socialist Christ, it also contains within it hints of an imperial counter-image that will become more pronounced in the stanzas that follows. Like the parallel prose passage in *Du vin et du haschisch*, lines 9–11 contain a number of terms ('prête des semments', 'dicte des lois sublimes') that belong equally to republican, imperial, and royalist discourses, just as the expression 'sous le firmament comme un dais suspendu' (conceivably an echo of 'caeli . . . sub axcm' of *Aeneid*, VI. 790) seems to evoke the revolutionary feasts of the 1790s and their pale imitations in 1848 but also points forward to the imperial pomp and circumstances evoked in lines 20–1. For the moment, the *chiffonnier* and his language are more republican than imperial, but both contain within them the seeds of a future Bonapartism.

The wholly new line 'S'enivre des splendeurs de sa propre vertu' marks a sharp break with the essentially non-critical stance adopted towards the *chiffonnier* and his laws for instant human happiness in *Du vin et du haschisch* and the texts of 1851–4. The line points forward strikingly to the denunciation of 'l'homme-Dieu' in *Le Poème du hachisch* (first published in *La Revue contemporaine* on 30 September 1858) where, picking up an idea already expressed in *Du vin et du haschisch* ('Nul ne saura jamais à quel degré de vertu et d'intelligence tu es parvenu' (OC, i. 394)), Baudelaire describes how the drug-user becomes 'absorbé dans la contemplation d'une vertu idéale, d'une charité idéale, d'un génie idéal' and gives himself over to a 'triomphante orgie spirituelle' in which, passing 'de la contemplation de ses rêves et de ses projets de vertu' to a belief in his 'aptitude pratique à la vertu', he comes finally to 'décréter son apothéose en ces termes nets et simples, qui contiennent pour lui tout un monde d'abominables jouissances: *"Je suis le plus vertueux de tous les hommes!"*' At this point Baudelaire interrupts his description of *l'homme Dieu*'s mounting *ivresse* to compare him, unexpectedly, to Rousseau:

L'enthousiasme avec lequel il admirait la vertu, l'attendrissement nerveux qui remplissait ses yeux de larmes, à la vue d'une belle action ou à la pensée

---

[41] *The Aeneid*, trans. Robert Fitzgerald (Vintage Books, 1983), 187–90. I am grateful to my former colleague Chris Baxter for pointing out this parallel.

de toutes les belles actions qu'il aurait voulu accomplir, suffisaient pour lui donner une idée superlative de sa valeur morale. *Jean-Jacques s'était enivré sans hachisch.* (OC, 435–6, italics added)

These parallels between the self-righteous intoxication of ragpicker, drug-user, and *philosophe* suggest, first, that, by the time he wrote the 1857 text of 'Le Vin des chiffonniers', Baudelaire had abandoned the distinction—crucial, as we have seen, to the meaning and message of *Du vin et du haschisch*—between wine and drugs as creators of *ivresse*, and, second, that in the *chiffonnier*'s delirious rantings a whole philosophical and political tradition stands condemned. The *chiffonnier* is a tatterdemalion Jean-Jacques, drunk on wine and self where the philosopher was drunk on self alone, bellowing forth a gutter version of the belief, which Baudelaire simplistically associated with the name of Rousseau,[42] that 'nature', in the words of *L'Éloge du maquillage* (1863) constitutes the 'base, source et type de tout bien et de tout beau possibles' (OC, ii. 715), that it is 'society' or 'civilization' that makes man depraved and miserable and that, accordingly, harmony and happiness can be legislated into existence by political fiat. In *Du vin et du haschisch*, Baudelaire had, despite all his misgivings, still been too close to that belief himself to do more than gently mock the ragpicker's Utopian fantasies and, even in 1854, had drawn back from outright condemnation in favour of a stance that is no more than implicitly critical. By 1857, though, such evasions were no longer in order. In the figure of the ragman-Rousseau, there can be no doubt, the utopianism of 1848, and the whole philosophical-political tradition that sustained it, are denounced as so much hubristic verbiage spewed forth by self-drunk, self-deluded ideologues. It is the verdict of 'Assommons les pauvres!' almost ten years before 'Assommons les pauvres!' came to be written. Whether, as in the later text, the Revolution and the Republic themselves are condemned along with the utopianism that accompanied them is a question that we shall have to engage with in due course.

In each of the previous verse texts, the word 'oui' served to mark a shift in perspective from one *chiffonnier* to many, from an individual 'case-study' to a *physionomie* of the sub-class as a whole. In the 1857 text, its function is more complex since, as well

---

[42] See esp. 'Notes nouvelles sur Edgar Poe' (1857) (OC, ii. 325). For Baudelaire and Rousseau, see Melvin Zimmerman, 'Trois études sur Baudelaire et Rousseau', *Études baudelairiennes*, 9 (1981), 31–71.

as marking a change of focus from the particular to the general, it also signals a very marked change in the character of the *chiffonniers* themselves. The ragpicker of the first three stanzas was basically a republican, even though, as we have seen, his republicanism contained a disturbing Bonapartist undercurrent. As they became more numerous, however, the *chiffonniers*—and still more their mysterious battle-hardened 'compagnons' (l. 18) who make their first appearance in the 1857 text of the poem—take on an increasingly Bonapartist air, as the ambivalent language of the first three stanzas is succeeded by terms and images that are explicitly militarist and imperial in their resonance: 'bataille', 'moustache' (the almost iconic attribute of the Napoleonic *grognard*), 'drapeaux', 'bannières', 'arcs triomphaux', 'clairons', 'tambour', 'gloire'. Moreover, in the Godoy manuscript the *chiffonniers* were shown going away ('s'en vont', l. 19) whereas in all the subsequent verse texts, as Karlheinz Biermann has astutely observed,[43] they are depicted in the act of returning ('reviennent'). Biermann glosses this as meaning that the *chiffonniers*—who for him symbolize the defeated insurgents of June 1848—are coming back as 'revenants' to haunt the terrified bourgeois consciousness. It is an intriguing suggestion, and one which could be pushed further if the departing ragpickers of the Godoy manuscript (assuming, for the moment, that it transcribes a post-June version of the poem) were interpreted as representing, in the manner of Daumier's later fugitive *saltimbanques*, those imprisoned, deported, or driven into exile for their participation in the *journées de juin*.[44] Yet the theme of the *Return* is absolutely fundamental to the Napoleonic myth[45] (*le retour de Moscou*, *le retour d'Elba*, *le retour des Cendres*, most recently the return of Louis Napoleon from exile in September 1848), and is evoked on a number of occasions by Baudelaire himself.[46] The

---

[43] Biermann, 'Der Rausch', 320.

[44] See Clark, *The Absolute Bourgeois*, 119–23.

[45] On the widespread belief in France after 1821 that Napoleon was not dead and would shortly return, see Bernard Ménager, *Les Napoléon du peuple* (Aubier, 1988), 19–33.

[46] See e.g. OC, i. 642 and OC, ii. 45 and 124. The second reference (in *L'École païenne* (Jan. 1852)) is particularly complex in that it links the return of Napoleon from Saint-Helena to the return of 'le dieu Pan' from the dead, it having previously been said—though not by Baudelaire—that 'c'est le dieu Pan qui fait la révolution. Il est la révolution'. This could be of relevance to 'Le Vin des chiffonniers' since it was probably at the time that he was drafting *L'École païenne* that Baudelaire made the crucial change from 's'en vont' to 'reviennent'.

salience of this theme in Napoleonic discourse, plus the whole military-imperial resonance of stanzas four to six, must call in question Biermann's interpretation as it stands, though it may be possible to reincorporate parts of it in a more complex and ambiguous reading of the poem. If, then, the returning *chiffonniers* are not—or are not solely, or in any straightforward emblematic way—the insurgents of June 1848, who exactly are they? To answer this, we must examine the whole evolution of Bonapartism in France from the *retour des Cendres* in the aftermath of which Baudelaire first drafted 'Le Vin des chiffonniers', through the crises of 1848–52 (when he wrote *Du vin et du haschisch* and made major changes to the verse text), up to the mid-to-late 1850s when a still more radically altered 'definitive' text of the poem was at last published in *Les Fleurs du mal*.

When, probably in the first half of 1841, Baudelaire first likened the 'mots entrecoupés' bellowed out by the ragpicker-general he had seen on the Paris streets to 'ceux que vaincu par la mort triomphante | L'Empereur exhalait de sa gorge expirante' (Godoy MS., ll. 11–12), the comparison was certainly not politically neutral —no evocation of Napoleon in nineteenth-century France could ever be exactly that—but carried very different meanings from those it would have when he dispatched the manuscript to Daumier some time between the beginning of 1848 and the end of 1850. To allude, even mockingly as Baudelaire does in the Godoy manuscript, to the Bonapartist fervours and fantasies of the Parisian lower classes in the early 1840s was to draw attention to a phenomenon which, particularly in the wake of the labour unrest of the summer and autumn of 1840 and of Louis Napoleon's second bid for power in August that year, the Bourgeois Monarchy was anxious to contain by 'recuperating' the Napoleonic myth for its purposes, notably by taking upon itself the task of returning the Emperor's remains to France. But, far from creating a sense of national unity, the *retour des Cendres* had been greeted with real enthusiasm only by the lower classes, leading the *Gazette de France* to comment on 17 December 1840 that 'aujourd'hui l'image de Napoleon n'apparaît que pour accuser les gouvernants, pour faire ressortir toutes les misères de la situation'.[47] In the context of 1841–3, therefore, Baudelaire's ragman-emperor could well have evoked, for those

---

[47] Quoted A. J. Tudesq, *L'Élection présidentielle de Louis-Napoléon Bonaparte, 10 décembre 1848* (Armand Colin, 1965), 25.

few persons who read or heard the poem, an aura of opposition to the ruling regime, particularly when the rites and ceremonies of royalty are compared so unfavourably to the 'triomphes bruyants' and 'fêtes solemnelles' with which the collective *chiffonnier* mind is drunkenly afire (Godoy MS, 1. 20). One may doubt, however, whether this earliest *chiffonnier* is intended as an explicitly political figure. Like so much else in Baudelaire's writing of the 1840s, the ragpicker of 1841–3 is not so much apolitical as prepolitical, a signifier whose signified has still fully to crystallize in the poet's mind. When, some time between the beginning of 1848 and the end of 1850, Baudelaire went back to his draft of 1841–3, he would have found that, without his needing to make a single important change to the original, his poem's pivotal figure had been transformed by the February revolution itself from the potential revolutionary he had been in the early 1840s into an embodiment of the popular political passions that had swept the Bourgeois Monarchy from power and which were now (or, depending on the exact date of the Godoy manuscript, had recently been) bent on transforming not just the nation's political superstructure but its underlying economic and social structure. It is for this reason, one imagines, that he copied out the poem—hurriedly, in pencil[48]—exactly or almost as it stood, signed it with his new 'republican' signature 'Charles Baudelaire' and dispatched it to his fellow radical Daumier. Without itself undergoing major textual change, the earliest 'Vin des chiffonniers' was thus endowed by the events of 1848 with an explicitly revolutionary meaning that had been only implicit, or barely present at all, in the poem when it was first drafted six or seven years previously.

There was only one problem: the *chiffonnier*'s Bonapartism. If the ragpicker of 1841–3 had been retrospectively 'revolutionized' by the Revolution itself, the significance of Bonapartism also underwent a fundamental transformation as the crisis of the Second Republic unfolded. From the very outbreak of revolution the republican enthusiasms of working-class Paris had possessed a strong Bonapartist undercurrent which, following the crushing of the June insurrection, would come increasingly to the fore, to the consternation of moderate republicans and bourgeois radicals alike; in the provinces, of course, the name of Napoleon had

[48] See OC, i. 1047.

always been a far more powerful mobilizing force than that of the Republic. As early as 1836, Armand Carrel had presciently observed of Louis Napoleon that 'le nom qu'il porte est le seul qui puisse exciter fortement les sympathies populaires'.[49] Those sympathies were soon in evidence in the success of three members of the Bonaparte family in the elections of April 1848, followed by the unexpected triumph of Louis Napoleon himself in four departments (including the Seine) in the complementary elections held on 4 June. It did not escape the attention of observers that, in Paris, it had been the working-class east of the city that had voted most heavily for the ex-prisoner of Ham who, it should be noted, had still to 'return' from exile in England. *La Réforme* astutely linked the rise of popular Bonapartism with mounting working-class disillusion with the Provisional Government, commenting in its number of 12–13 June that 'si le peuple n'avait pas vu ses illusions tomber feuille à feuille comme la fleur; si, comme nos pères, les hommes du jour avaient rempli les devoirs de la politique révolutionnaire, croit-on que le nom du prince Louis agiterait aujourd'hui les rues?' Noting 'le lien mysterieux qui a réuni sur la même liste les noms de Bonaparte, de Lagrange et de Proudhon', *L'Assemblée nationale* drew the conclusion—broadly accepted by modern historians—that it was the same voters who had voted for the far left and for Louis Napoleon.[50] For the moment, though, the Bonapartism of the Parisian working classes remained broadly, if uneasily, compatible with their commitment to the Republic. The cries of 'Vive Barbès! Vive Poléon!' that began to be heard on the boulevards in early June show how readily the language of the ultra-left and the language of Bonapartism flowed into each other as the political and social crisis approached its climax: shortly before the insurrection broke out, the workers of La Villette even demanded that Louis Napoleon be named consul.[51] In the provinces, however, Republicanism and Bonapartism were already at odds with each other. As early as March 1848 cries of 'Vive l'Empereur! A bas la République!' had been reported in places as far apart as Saintes, Chartres, Fécamp, Amiens, and Nîmes.[52] By the time of the June insurrection, the split between the radical Bonapartism of working-class

---

[49] Quoted Tudesq, *L'Élection présidentielle*, 27.
[50] Ibid. 59–63.
[51] Ménager, *Les Napoléon du peuple*, 95.
[52] Ibid. 93.

Paris and the conservative Bonapartism of the provinces was already well established.

Having declined, in the face of parliamentary opposition, to take up the seat he had won in June, Louis Napoleon was none the less re-elected on 17/18 September in the four *départements* that had returned him three months earlier; his majority everywhere increased, and once again working-class voters were held responsible for the bulk of the 110,000 votes that were cast for him in the department of the Seine. On 24 September, Louis Napoleon at last 'returned' to France from exile, prompting the following revealing comment in *L'Événement* on the 25th: 'A l'heure qu'il est le peuple croit vaguement que c'est l'Empereur qui *revient* et non le prince, l'oncle et non le neveu. Depuis 1815 le peuple attend Napoléon. Plongé dans l'ignorance et dans la souffrance, il a besoin d'un idéal, d'une vision, d'un *amour*: cet idéal, cette vision, cet *amour*, c'est l'Empereur'[53] (italics added, cf. l. 24 of the 1847 'Vin des chiffonniers': 'Ils apportent la gloire au peuple ivre d'amour'). Following the prince's return, the Bonapartist propaganda machine, which had begun to function in earnest in May, rapidly gathered momentum in preparation for the presidential elections at the end of the year at which, long before he announced his candidature, it was known that Louis Napoleon would stand. The country was flooded with lithographs, engravings, medallions, beer mugs, and pipes bearing the image of the prince and/or his uncle; abridged versions of *L'Extinction du paupérisme* were distributed free of charge and, of course, the popular song was used systematically to diffuse a composite image of Louis Napoleon as heir of a heroic tradition, disinterested benefactor of the people and, not least, staunch defender of the Republic. The following two songs show how readily Republicanism, Bonapartism and a kind of socialism overlapped and interpenetrated in the autumn and winter of 1848:

> Je suis républicain dans l'âme
> Pourtant j'aime Napoléon
> Peu m'importe à moi qu'on le blâme
> Il fit respecter notre nom.
> Vive la République!
>
> Je suis un franc républicain
> Je vous le donne pour certain

---

[53] Quoted Tudesq, *L'Élection présidentielle*, 93.

> Il faudrait un Napoléon
> Pour soutenir la nation.
> Comment douter de son libéralisme
> Quand pour charmer l'ennui de sa prison
> Il composait son fameux paupérisme
> Du prolétaire il connaît la souffrance
> Lui seul en peut alléger le tourment.[54]

All the evidence suggests that this mixture of Republicanism, Bonapartism, and pseudo-socialism was highly attractive to precisely the people for whom Louis Napoleon's propagandists intended it: the urban working-classes whose disgust with the Provisional Government had not shaken their commitment to the Republic or diminished their desire for fundamental social and economic, as well as political, reform. Of the five and a half million votes for Louis Napoleon in December 1848, fully one quarter are estimated by modern historians to have been cast by voters on the far left,[55] in part, as many commentators observed at the time, in revulsion against the principal republican candidate General Cavaignac—still seen as *le bourreau de juin*—in part, too, because of the long-standing appeal of Bonapartism and the personalized political style it embodied amongst the working classes of Paris, Lyon, Rouen, Limoges, and other large cities.

One can readily see the impact that this upsurge of popular Bonapartism would have on the overall sense of 'Le Vin des chiffonniers'. It is not known, of course, how *chiffonniers* voted—if they voted at all—in December 1848, but, given that so many of them appear, like, presumably, Baudelaire and Privat's ragman-general himself, to have been veterans of Napoleon's armies or, more recently, of the Algerian campaign,[56] it is likely that, if they had any political preferences at all, they would have opted for Louis Napoleon rather than Cavaignac, Ledru-Rollin, Raspail, or the hapless Lamartine, perhaps feeling like the semi-literate voter in the Marne who inscribed his voting-slip as follows: 'Vive Napoléon puisqu'il est bon. En cas de représéntants, je n'en quon n'est pas. Un bon Napoléon les quonnais mieux que moi puisqu'il les choisis lui-même.'[57] The situation became even more problematic in 1849

---

[54] Quoted Ménager, *Les Napoléon du peuple*, 94–5 and 100.
[55] See Tudesq, *L'Élection présidentielle*, 203–5.
[56] See Berthaud, 'Les Chiffonniers', 341.
[57] Quoted Ménager, *Les Napoléon du peuple*, 107.

when, if Marx's memorable account is to be believed, Baudelaire's
Napoleon-obsessed *chiffonnier* would have made a choice recruit
for the notorious *Société du Dix-Décembre* formed for the purpose
of advancing the Bonapartist cause by whatever means might be
necessary:

Under the pretext of founding a benevolent society, the Paris *Lumpenproletariat* had been organized into secret sections, each led by Bonapartist
agents and at the head of the whole a Bonapartist general. Besides ruined
roués of questionable means of subsistence and dubious origins, besides
decayed adventurers, scions of the bourgeoisie, there were tramps, discharged soldiers, discharged convicts, fugitive galley slaves, sharpers,
charlatans, *lazzaroni*, pickpockets, conjurors, gamblers, *maquereaux*,
brothel-keepers, porters, literary drudges, organ-grinders, rag-pickers,
knife-grinders, tinkers, beggars, in short the whole haphazard, dissolute
battered mass which the French call *la bohème*; of these kindred elements
Bonaparte formed the main body of the Society of 10 December.[58]

If Baudelaire's *chiffonnier* of 1841–3 had been transformed overnight into a popular revolutionary by the *journées de février*, events
since then had—again without Baudelaire's necessarily making any
change to his earliest draft of the poem—made of him a much more
complex and, in many ways, sinister figure. The Bonapartist sympathies which, in the early 1840s, had had, if anything, an oppositional or even radical aura about them could, by the end of 1848
and throughout what remained of the Second Republic, be located
at any number of points along the political spectrum that led from
far left to far right. T. J. Clark has made a telling parallel between
Baudelaire's earliest *chiffonnier* and Daumier's Bonapartist hench-
men Ratapoil and Casmajou:[59] one might go further and see him as
a parodic precursor of the parody-prince Louis Napoleon himself.[60]

It may have been unease about his ragpicker's Bonapartism that
deterred Baudelaire from publishing—as presumably he might have
done—'Le Vin des chiffonniers' alongside 'Le Vin des honnêtes
gens' in *Le Magasin des familles* in June 1850. Unease, as we have
seen, is also subliminally present in *Du vin et du haschisch* where
the *chiffonnier*'s Bonapartist enthusiasms assort ill with the aura of

[58] Marx, *The Eighteenth Brumaire of Louis Bonaparte, Surveys from Exile*,
197–8.
[59] Clark, *The Absolute Bourgeois*, 116–17.
[60] Marx himself (*The Eighteenth Brumaire*, 206) described Louis Napoleon as 'a
bohemian, a princely lumpenproletarian'.

proletarian noble savage with which the text invests him; the ironic spelling 'Buonaparte' cannot wholly conceal the tension between the *démoc-soc* inspiration of *Du vin et du haschisch* as a whole and the all too patent attraction of the pivotal figure of one of its central elements towards the totemic hero of the political enemy. Unable to resolve this tension, Baudelaire seems to have chosen simply to suppress it in the revised manuscripts of 1851–2, for, as noted earlier, virtually every trace of the original *chiffonnier*'s Bonapartism has been expunged from the text published in *Jean Raisin*. By 1856, however, Baudelaire had been able to think through the whole question of *quarante-huit* and its consequences in a far more searching—but not for that dispassionate—manner than had been possible in the years immediately following the coup, and his reflections led him to reintroduce into the 1857 text of 'Le Vin des chiffonniers' those Bonapartist resonances he had suppressed or muted after March 1851, but to reintroduce them in a way that gave them a very different meaning from what they had had in *Du vin du haschisch* and the Godoy manuscript, to say nothing of the primitive version of 1841–3.

The result was a poem substantially longer than that published three years previously, and one which, I suggest, is to be interpreted, like 'Le Reniement de saint Pierre', as a coded history of the Second Republic itself, in which the transformation of the *chiffonnier* from the besotted republican-socialist Utopian (with Bonapartist leanings) of stanzas 2 and 3 into the out-and-out Bonapartist of stanzas 4–6 is to be interpreted 'allegorically' as Baudelaire's commentary on the passage, via the débâcle of June 1848, of 'le peuple de Paris' from one form of mystification—the 'illusion lyrique' of February–March with all its 'glorieux projets' —to another—the massive working-class vote for Louis Napoleon in December—and, beyond that, to the subsequent occasions when, by their actions or inaction, the Parisian working classes had deludedly collaborated in the coming tó power of the Bonapartist dictatorship: first in their failure in any way to resist the coup itself, then in their validation of its results in the plebiscite of 21/22 December 1851 and finally in their votes for official government candidates in the legislative elections of February 1852, in the wake of which Baudelaire informed Ancelle in disgust that he had been *'physiquement dépolitiqué'*. The populist sympathies that sustained the *chiffonnier* episode in *Du vin et du haschisch*, and which had already been present, in muted form, in the Godoy manuscript, have now disappeared completely. Whether the *chiffonnier* of stanzas 2 and 3 represents the *peuple* itself or all those—from Louis Blanc, Raspail, or Ledru-Rollin down to the host of 'petits orateurs, aux enflures baroques | Prêchant l'amour' evoked in the projected epilogue to the 1861 *Fleurs* (OC, i. 192)—who presumed to speak in its name or, as is most likely, a combination of both, Baudelaire's verdict on the utopianism of *quarante-huit* is, as we have seen, of quite devastating severity. Viewed from the standpoint of 1857, the *peuple de Paris* and its assorted spokesmen had staggered on to the political stage in February 1848 like so many drunken scavengers, taking oaths they could not keep to, passing grandiloquent resolutions ('lois sublimes') in their clubs and assemblies that they had no power to enforce, taking imaginary vengeance on the rich and powerful ('terrasse les méchants') and raising up the victims of oppression to the status of demi-gods while all the time the real power remained in the hands of the possessing classes and their agents and representatives in parliament and the Provisional Government. Drunk with a sense of their own virtue, the *peuple* and its would-be leaders lurched from one illusion to another in the early months of the Republic until in June, 'harcelés de chagrins de ménage | Moulus pour le travail et tourmentés par l'âge', they—or, more precisely, only the working classes, for their self-elected spokesmen had by now abandoned them—had taken to the barricades from whose 'hideux débris' they emerged 'le dos martyrisé' by the savage repression unleashed upon them by the forces of law and order. Taking a 'realist' text first drafted fifteen years previously and revised, expanded, or abridged on several occasions since, Baudelaire, I am suggesting, finally injected almost all of its originally descriptive elements with an 'allegorical' significance relating to 1848 and, through the image of the drunken *chiffonnier* whose 'glorieux projets' of universal justice and happiness make not a bit of difference, ultimately, to the sordid social and economic conditions under which he labours, recounted, quite simply, and with stunning economy of means, the story of *le peuple de Paris* between February and June 1848.

But the story of February–June is only half the story of 1848, and at the precise median point of the text (l. 17), the crucial word 'reviennent' occurs and so initiates the second of the poem's two 'phases'. If I am right in seeing the verb 'revenir' as a talismanic term in the Bonapartist lexicon, stanzas 5 and 6 of 'Le Vin des chiffonniers' may be opposed after the fashion of a diptych to stanzas 2 and 3, with stanza 4—representing the *journées de juin*— marking the transition from the people's republican fervour of February–June 1848 to the upsurge of popular Bonapartism between July and December. Still reeking with the fumes of their earlier intoxication ('parfumés d'une odeur de futailles'), the *chiffonniers* are shown returning from their ordeal on the streets of Paris, no longer alone but 'suivis de compagnons blanchis dans les batailles | Dont la moustache pend comme les vieux drapeaux'. If the single ragpicker of stanzas 2 and 3 represents, broadly, *le peuple de Paris* in its idealistic republican phase and if, following Karlheinz Biermann, we identify the multiple *chiffonniers* of stanzas 4 and 5 with, in the first instance, the defeated insurgents of June (the passage from one to many perhaps indicating the break-up of working-class unity in the wake of the uprising), who are the mysterious moustachioed 'compagnons' who, introduced for the first time into the 1857 text, follow in the ragpickers' footsteps? Their evident status as army veterans points to a link with the ten to twelve thousand *anciens combattants* who, according to the later testimony of the Bonapartist *agent provocateur* Aristide Ferrère,[61] formed the hard core of Louis Napoleon's support in the months following the June uprising and who, in 1849, would become the backbone of the *Société du Dix-Décembre*: it could even be that Baudelaire took the motifs of the white hair and moustache from Daumier's unforgettable images of Ratapoil and Casmajou. If the 'compagnons' of line 18 are intended to represent Bonapartist agents and propagandists, they gain a swift and easy victory for by lines 20–1 the *chiffonniers* have been wholly taken in by the 'solennelle magie' of the Napoleonic iconography of 'les bannières, les fleurs et les arcs triomphaux'.[62] Converts to the Bonapartist faith, they now become evangelists in their turn:

[61] See Adrien Dansette, *Louis Napoléon à la conquête du pouvoir* (Hachette, 1961), 169.

[62] For confirmation of this interpretation, see Maurice Agulhon's description of Louis Napoleon's triumphalist procession through Marseille in Sept. 1852: 'Louis Napoléon fut reçu avec pompes, salves d'artillerie, volées de cloches, arcs triomphaux, et toute la liesse d'une foule abreuvée de spectacles, de fêtes et de cérémonies. Dans tous les discours, comme au fronton des arcs de triomphe, les allusions à l'Empire, les emblèmes imperiaux ne laissent plus aucun doute sur l'avenir politique' (Agulhon, *1848*, 221).

Et dans l'étourdissante et lumineuse orgie
Des clairons, du soleil, des cris et du tambour,
Ils apportent la gloire au peuple ivre d'amour!

Like the single *chiffonnier* of stanzas 2 and 3, the 'peuple' of line 24 is 'ivre d'amour', but it is not now a love for *Liberté, Égalité, Fraternité* that intoxicates them, but a love for *gloire*, for the person of Louis Napoleon and the heroic tradition he so unheroically embodied and, beyond that, a love of love itself, a need to be cherished and cared for, as Bonapartist propaganda promised, in short, a fear of freedom that leads directly to the sado-masochistic political nightmare of 'Le Voyage' (1859):

Le bourreau qui jouit, le martyr qui sanglote;
La fête qu'assaisonne et parfume le sang;
Le poison du pouvoir énervant le despote,
Et le peuple amoureux du fouet abrutissant . . .

(ll. 93–6)

The people of Paris—and by 'peuple' Baudelaire surely means first and foremost the city's working people—have merely exchanged one form of *ivresse* for another: at the end of the poem they are as intoxicated and mystified as a mass as the *chiffonnier* was as an individual at its outset. But the ragpicker who proclaimed the republican faith in stanzas two and three has evolved, without undergoing any *fundamental* transformation, into the ragpickers who propagate the Bonapartist gospel in stanza six, reminding us that even in the 'republican' *chiffonnier* there was already a concealed Napoleon lurking. Baudelaire's point seems to be that the (cynical) authoritarianism of Bonapartism is already contained *in nuce* in the (idealistic and Utopian) authoritarianism of republican-socialist attempts to legislate for instant human happiness and to shape human beings in accordance with some pre-existing ideological blueprint. Republican-socialist and Bonapartist discourses are not so much opposed to each other as variant forms of the same fundamentally totalitarian world-view, which is why, throughout the *chiffonnier* texts, the two have continually slipped into and intersected with each other and why, finally, the republican ragpicker is metamorphosed so readily into his ideological 'opposite'. A parallel with Flaubert's Sénécal immediately suggests itself.

If the first six stanzas of the 1857 'Vin des chiffonniers' point inescapably to an anti-revolutionary, even frankly reactionary, verdict on the men and ideas of *quarante-huit*, the final two stanzas reintroduce ambiguities that, characteristically, undercut, or seem to undercut, the earlier developments and caution against too hasty a conclusion one way or the other. The principal problem, already indicated, of the final stanzas in the 1857 text may be summarized as follows. In all the previous versions of the poem, wine had been seen as the disinterested gift of an essentially benevolent God to those of His children who, for reasons unspecified, were the victims of unmerited suffering: 'les malheureux' in the Godoy manuscript, 'les innocents' in *Jean Raisin*. In 1857, however, wine suddenly and unexpectedly becomes man-created, created, moreover, as a retort or challenge by man to a seemingly indifferent *deus otiosus*:

> Pour noyer la rancœur et bercer l'indolence
> De tous ces vieux maudits qui meurent en silence,
> Dieu, saisi de remords, avait fait le sommeil;
> L'Homme ajouta le Vin, fils sacré du Soleil!

The development here, in other words, is precisely the reverse of that which we have traced in the case of 'L'Âme du vin'. In the first version of that poem dating from the period of the Second Republic, Baudelaire's vision was humanistic and implicitly antitheistic; in the 1857 text an attempt was apparently made to make the poem more 'pious' by seeing wine which, earlier, had been born solely of the collaboration of man and nature as a 'grain précieux jeté par l'éternel Semeur'. But in the case of 'Le Vin des chiffonniers' it is the earlier, Second Republic, versions that are the more 'pious' and the 1857 text that presents a humanistic vision which teeters on the brink of antitheistic rebellion. The question that all the previous verse texts had significantly 'occulted' is now posed for the first time with the directness its urgency requires. Whence, if both God and Nature—and, by implication, the human race itself—are, as all the earlier texts maintained, essentially good, and if they themselves are innocent, do the unwarranted sufferings of 'les malheureux' derive? Why, amidst all this goodness, should misery requiring consolation by sleep and wine exist in such profusion?

Les yeux des pauvres: there can be no doubt that, throughout his life, Baudelaire was haunted by the 'marks of weakness, marks of woe' that confronted him everywhere on the streets of Paris. His response oscillated between pity and horror, anger and guilt, identi-

fication and sadistic contempt (as in *Assommons les pauvres!*),
before resolving itself, uneasily, into that combination of fascination and repulsion which Baudelaire calls 'curiosité'. During the
years of the Second Republic, however, simple compassion, evident
in the following passage, already quoted, from *Pierre Dupont*, held
sway over the darker, more ambiguous emotions that would
surface in his later work:

Il est impossible, à quelque parti qu'on appartienne, de quelques préjugés
qu'on ait été nourri, de ne pas être touché du spectacle de cette multitude
maladive respirant la poussière des ateliers, avalant du coton, s'imprégnant
de céruse, de mercure et de tous les poisons nécessaires à la création des
chefs-d'œuvre, dormant dans la vermine, au fond des quartiers où les
vertus les plus humbles et les plus grandes nichent à côté des vices les plus
endurcis et des vomissements du bagne. (OC, ii. 31)

Yet, despite the intensity of his emotion, nowhere, it seems, does
Baudelaire at this time directly confront the question of the origin
of these sufferings. Curiously unwilling, even during his 'socialist
phase', to attribute the miseries of the poor unequivocally to an
oppressive social and economic system and unable to invoke the
doctrine of Original Sin since it clashes with the optimistic assump-
tions of his philosophy of the time, Baudelaire cannot escape the
possibility that it is God Himself who wills the innocent to suffer,
either as part of a soteriological design only He understands or—an
explanation as plausible as it is horrifying—because He is no God
of Love but a God of hatred, cruelty, and pain: 'Dieu, c'est le mal'.
In 'Les Litaries de Satan', as we have seen, Baudelaire accepts
Proudhon's proposition as a possibility, even a probability, and
draws the appropriate conclusions—antitheist, humanist, demono-
latrous, 'socialist'—from it, but, even when he shies away from
such extremes, the spectacle of suffering often finds him, as it does
even in a late text such as 'Mademoiselle Bistouri' (1865–6?) poised
on the very brink of impugning God's goodness:

Quelles bizarreries ne trouve-t-on pas dans une grande ville, quand on sait
se promener et regarder? La vie fourmille de monstres innocents.—Seigneur,
mon Dieu! vous, le Créateur, vous le Maître . . . ayez pitié, ayez pitié des
fous et des folles! Ô Créateur! peut-il exister des monstres aux yeux de
Celui-là seul qui sait pourquoi ils existent, comment ils *se sont faits* et
comment ils auraient pu *ne pas se faire*? (OC, i. 355–6)

In a sense, therefore, the 'antitheistic' conclusion of the 1857 version of 'Le Vin des chiffonniers' has a definite metaphysical and moral logic to the extent that it at least implies an origin to miseries that are otherwise unexplained and unexplainable. None the less, the fundamental change of meaning brought about by the substitution of 'l'Homme' (the capital letter, as in 'Le Reniement de saint Pierre', is surely of great significance) for God appears to run completely against the evolution of Baudelaire's thought as we know it from other texts written in the second half of the 1850s. If, in the earlier versions of the poem, God is benevolent and expresses his bountifulness through the gift of wine to 'les malheureux', the source of whose misery is never specified, in the 1857 text He appears as, at best, indifferent to human suffering and, at worst, actively malignant. 'Les innocents' of the 1854 text have become 'tous ces vieux maudits'—cursed by society? cursed by God?— whose 'rancœur' (presumably at the fate that has been arbitrarily forced upon them) God attempts to appease by 'drowning' it in sleep. God acts out of a perfunctory remorse at the sufferings He has inflicted or failed to prevent (and perhaps also to forestall a challenge to His supremacy), but it is Man, Man in collaboration with Nature, who now, as in the first version of 'L'Âme du vin', creates wine as an antidote to suffering and as a source of hope and inspiration. Baudelaire must surely have intended this fundamental transformation of the poem's meaning: why, though, do we get, or appear to get, a revival in 1857 of the antitheistic humanism (with all its potentially revolutionary implications) which the poet would seem from other texts to have thoroughly repudiated by then?

In attempting to explain these shifts and switches of meaning, it will not greatly avail us to fall back on the proverbial waywardness of Baudelaire's convictions, that alleged love of contradiction for contradiction's sake that has so often functioned as an all-purpose stand-by solution to any intractable problem arising from the poet's work. Baudelaire's mind proceeds by contradiction but wayward or whimsical it is not, and if it often seems capable of espousing antithetical positions virtually simultaneously or of oscillating perpetually between affirmation and negation, it is not, as some would have it, through sheer capricious perversity but as part of a tortuous life-long quest for synthesis and totality. Contradiction and its attempted resolution are crucial to the meaning of the wine poems, concerned as they are (amongst other things) with

Baudelaire's relation to revolutionary politics over a period of ten years or more during which his thought, responding to both internal and external pressures, was continually subject to all manner of deviations, forward surges, and abrupt about-turns. Far from denying these repeated changes of direction, Baudelaire draws attention to them, implying on a number of occasions that not only is contradiction an inevitable part of politics but that the full complexity of politics, and of an individual's relation to politics, can only be understood 'synthetically', that is by bringing the maximum number of opposed but complementary viewpoints to bear upon them simultaneously. Baudelaire's adoption, from the mid-1850s onwards, of an increasingly obdurate anti-humanistic anti-democratic position did not, as we have seen, mean that his earlier beliefs had been entirely eradicated, and there is a sense in which the unexpected volte-face of the 1857 text's conclusion could be explained all too easily by invoking that 'vieux fonds d'esprit révolutionnaire' to which Baudelaire confesses in his letter of 1862 to Sainte-Beuve (C. ii, 220). But a 'return of the revolutionary repressed'—a real possibility, at the very least, in the case of a text like 'Assommons les pauvres!'—seems to me unlikely in a work as carefully calculated as the 1857 'Vin des chiffonniers' in which Baudelaire seems to be striving towards some kind of inclusive or objective statement on the whole experience of *quarante-huit* and its aftermath. In the circumstances, it could be that the grafting of a seemingly revolutionary conclusion on to opening stanzas as profoundly non- or anti-revolutionary (or apparently so!) as the first six of 'Le Vin des chiffonniers' is linked in some way to Baudelaire's stated desire (in *Pauvre Belgique!* (OC, ii. 961)) to 'sentir la Revolution des deux manières' or to his observation elsewhere that 'je comprends qu'on déserte une cause pour savoir ce qu'on éprouvera à en servir une autre' (*Mon cœur mis à nu* (OC, i. 676)). In other words, might not the 1857 'Vin des chiffonniers', particularly if read in conjunction with and in opposition to 'L'Âme du vin', be an attempt by Baudelaire to express a 'total' vision of the revolutionary utopianism of 1848 (and of his own relation to it both at the time and later), to grasp the positive and negative aspects of both, and to do so by exploring the contrasting effects of wine and drunkenness? It is this possibility that we must now investigate.

The view of wine expressed in 'L'Âme du vin' is, as we have seen, resoundingly positive; like the 1848 Revolution itself in its earliest stages, it is a source of health, hope, and human love. The verdict of even the earliest version of 'Le Vin des chiffonniers', on the other hand, is considerably more ambiguous, for if wine (temporarily) liberates the ragpickers of 1841–3 from their miseries, it does so only by imprisoning them in a world of fantasy and illusion from which they will emerge only to plunge forthwith into a further bout of drunken hallucination. For political reasons, this negative side of drinking was played down in *Du vin et du haschisch* and the 1851–2 manuscripts, but in the 1857 text the accusation of pride is added to the earlier and less serious charge of delusion, so that the *chiffonnier* now seems drunk less with wine or with his vision of human happiness than with himself: 'S'enivre de splendeurs de sa propre vertu.' Moreover, his republican-socialist *ivresse* is seen to lead directly to the Bonapartist intoxication of stanzas 5 and 6, as though it were Baudelaire's purpose in the 1857 'Vin des chiffonniers' to reveal the underside of the euphoric vision of wine he had elaborated in 'L'Âme du vin'. At the time when he first published that poem as 'Le Vin des honnêtes gens' in 1850, there seems little doubt that it was intended to express, like its slightly later prose 'doublet' in *Du vin et du haschisch*, Baudelaire's enthusiasm for the socialist humanism of the radical republican left; that enthusiasm is also expressed, somewhat more guardedly and equivocally, in the prose text on the *chiffonnier* also published in *Du vin et du haschisch*. Initially, therefore, the two texts in their prose and verse forms were complementary to each other, the *chiffonnier* text furnishing, as it were, a specific illustration of the general (and highly positive) proposition concerning wine expressed in its companion-piece. When, however, Baudelaire, operating now from a very different ideological position than even four or five years previously, came to order his poems into a single 'architectural' whole in the mid-1850s, he decided, I suggest, to set 'Le Vin des chiffonniers' *against* 'Le Vin des honnêtes gens' and to use the former as a means of undercutting the euphoric and potentially hubristic paean to wine contained in the latter. By juxtaposing and contrasting these two poems and by following them with three further sharply differentiated texts on wine ('Le Vin de l'assassin', 'Le Vin du solitaire', and 'Le Vin des amants'), Baudelaire sought to provide a complex, multi-faceted and, so to speak, stereoscopic overview of the whole question of wine and drunkenness in much the same way, for example, that poems VI to IX of *Les Fleurs du mal* attempt a synoptic presentation of the artist's condition by undercutting the 'heroic' vision of his vocation elaborated in 'Les Phares' with the stark and ironic realism of the poems that immediately follow it, 'La Muse malade', 'La Muse vénale', and 'Le Mauvais Moine'.

Put more simply, my argument is that the wine poems as deployed in the 'cardre singulier' of the 1857 *Fleurs du mal* had a very different meaning for Baudelaire from when he first composed them. Originally, it seems clear, Baudelaire basically approved of the process of self-deification they celebrate, just as, at the time when *they* were first written, he had clearly subscribed to the anti-bourgeois Satanism of 'Les Litanies de Satan', 'Abel et Caïn', and 'Le Reniement de saint Pierre'. By the mid-1850s, however, his attitude towards self-deification, whether it be through drink, drugs, sexual perversion, or devil-worship, had undergone a radical change. Satanism he now thoroughly condemned, and his decision to bring together the three poems in question and to set them apart under the distinct rubric 'La Révolte' implies the taking of an 'objective' critical standpoint towards a set of beliefs that, subjectively, he had once approved. Baudelaire may not have provided 'en parfait comédien' the 'pastiche des raisonnements de l'ignorance et de la fureur' that he claimed to have done in the note in the 1857 edition of *Les Fleurs du mal* (OC, i. 1075–6)—he had, we may be sure, originally meant every word he wrote—but it would appear that the final structuring of the 'Révolte' section does indeed respond, as the poet said it did, to a 'douloureux programme' of distancing and (self-) critical simulation that he had imposed upon himself. Similarly, the bringing together of the wine poems as a separate sequence within the wider design of the collection indicates Baudelaire's growing conviction that wine, if not unequivocally evil like Satanism, is none the less ontologically and morally dual, like those other intoxicating entities whose 'composition double' would never cease to haunt him and which he expressly likens to wine in 'Hymne à la Beauté' (1860), woman and art:

> Viens-tu du ciel profond ou sors-tu de l'abîme,
> Ô Beauté? ton regard, infernal et divin,
> Verse confusément le bienfait et le crime.
> Et l'on peut pour cela te comparer au vin.

In all the pre-1857 verse texts of 'Le Vin des chiffonniers' wine had, as it were, come down 'du ciel profond' as a gift of a living and compassionate God to His creatures; in the 1857 text, it is suddenly transformed into a human creation, issuing, like poetry, from the 'abîme' of the collective human soul and rising up to reproach or challenge a cosmic order which, for being divinely instituted, is none the less unjust. At the same time, and in a pointedly contrasting way, the wine that in the original 'Vin des honnêtes gens' was wholly man-created becomes, in the revised 'L'Âme du vin', at least partially or in its origins a gift of God ('Grain précieux jeté par l'éternel Semeur' (l. 22)). Baudelaire could not have revealed his fundamental ambivalence concerning the nature of wine and the moral status of the effect it induces—divine *and* infernal? divine *or* infernal?—more dramatically than by so transposing and inverting the constituent terms of his two poems. Once, therefore, they are assembled as a group, the wine poems add to, comment upon, and qualify one another, suggesting a 'total' view of wine that transcends the view contained in any one poem. And that view is profoundly ambiguous, for if wine inspires the cosmic communalism of 'L'Âme du vin', it also impels the solitary 'I' of 'Le Vin de l'assassin' to put himself entirely outside the human and divine community by killing his wife, just as the wine of revolution inspired equally the carnival of February, the blood-bath of June and the inebriated mystification of December. In stressing, in the 1857 'Vin des chiffonniers' the human origins and character of wine, Baudelaire was reiterating, with a far greater sense of moral urgency, the conclusion he had already reached in *Du vin et du haschisch*: 'Le vin est semblable à l'homme: on ne saura jamais jusqu'à quel point on peut l'estimer ou le mépriser, l'aimer ou le haïr, ni de combien d'actions sublimes ou de forfaits monstrueux il est capable' (OC, i. 380). In 1851, Baudelaire, like all those writers and *chansonniers* on the Left who used wine as a symbol of social(ist) justice and harmony, had had, for obvious reasons, to minimize the 'forfaits monstrueux' of which, as he already knew full well, it was capable. In 1857, no such considerations operated, and Baudelaire, who had moved beyond his radical enthusiasms of 1848–51 without for that reneging totally on his revolutionary past, was able for the first time to express how, like everything else in human affairs, drinking and revolutionary political action involve 'deux postulations simultanées' that tear at the moral being of the *homo duplex* who resorts to them, dragging him down into the realm of Satan and 'animalité' at the very moment that he would obey—indeed that he thinks he *is* obeying—'l'invocation à Dieu, or spiritualité' (*Mon cœur mis à nu* (OC, i. 682–3)). It is in this vision of good and evil, spirituality and animality, God and Satan promiscuously entwined and embattled in the individual and collective human soul that Baudelaire would seem to me to have attained his deepest insight into the reality of revolution.

The Poet as Ragpicker

Despite the major alterations from one version of 'Le Vin des chiffonniers' to the next, one crucial theme remains constant: the assimilation of the ragpicker to the poet. In the first version he is described as 'se cognant, se heurtant, comme un faiseur de Vers' while in his prose avatar in *Du vin et du haschisch* he makes his appearance 'hochant la tête et butant sur les pavés, comme les jeunes poètes qui passent toutes leurs journées à errer et à chercher des rimes' (OC, i. 381); finally, in 1854 the line stabilizes as 'buttant et se cognant aux murs comme un poète'. There are many remarkable parallels between 'Le Vin des chiffonniers' and 'Le Soleil', a poem first published in 1857 but almost certainly dating from the late 1840s or early 1850s,[63] in which the poet is found walking through the streets of a 'vieux faubourg' of Paris with the same halting gait as the *chiffonnier*:

> Le long de vieux faubourg, où pendent aux masures
> Les persiennes, abri des secrètes luxures,
> Quand le soleil cruel frappe à traits redoublés
> Sur la ville et les champs, sur les toits et les blés,
> Je vais m'exercer seul à ma fantasque escrime,
> Flairant dans tous les coins les hasards de la rime,
> Trébuchant sur les mots comme sur les pavés,
> Heurtant parfois des vers depuis longtemps rêvés.

Nor do the parallels with the wine poems stop here, for Baudelaire goes on to trace an extended analogy between the sun (and one recalls, naturally, that wine is the 'fils sacré du Soleil') and the poet which correlates at almost every point with 'L'Âme du vin':

[63] For a searching discussion of the text and dating of 'Le Soleil', see Leakey, *Baudelaire and Nature*, 106–8.

Ce père nourricier, ennemi des chloroses,
Éveille dans les champs les vers comme les roses;
Il fait s'évaporer les soucis vers le ciel,
Et remplit les cerveaux et les ruches de miel.
C'est lui qui rajeunit les porteurs de béquilles
Et les rend gais et doux comme des jeunes filles,
Et commande aux moissons de croître et de mûrir
Dans le cœur immortel qui toujours veut fleurir!
Quand, ainsi qu'un poète, il descend dans les villes,
Il ennoblit le sort des choses les plus viles,
Et s'introduit en roi, sans bruit et sans valets.
Dans tous les hôpitaux et dans tous les palais.

The sun rouses the whole of nature into creativity, awakens 'dans les champs les vers comme les roses' (the later comparison with the poet suggests a deliberate pun here) and, like wine in 'L'Âme du vin', heals and rejuvenates the sick and elderly, entering hospitals 'en roi' just as in 'Le Vin des chiffonniers' wine 'règne par ses dons ainsi que les vrais rois' (1857 text, cf. 'les bons rois (or 'Rois') in the 1851–2 manuscripts). Above all, the sun, in common with wine and poetry, has the power to transfigure, as it were, alchemically the most sordid reality ('Il ennoblit le sort des choses les plus viles'), reminding one, inevitably, of the cry of triumph that the spectacle of Paris wrings from Baudelaire in the projected epilogue to the second edition of *Les Fleurs du mal*: 'Tu m'as donné ta boue, et j'en ai fait de l'or' (OC, i. 192).

The wine poems, it is clear, bear directly upon Baudelaire's image of the poet and upon his conception of the nature and function of poetry. Two issues are involved: the assimilation of the poet to a typical, if especially sordid, member of the Parisian *Lumpenproletariat* and the relationship between the writing of poetry and drunkenness. This second question has been discussed in detail by Victor Brombert in an outstanding analysis of 'La Chevelure', and will accordingly receive less emphasis here.[64] For Baudelaire, writes Brombert, 'true inebriation . . . refers to the poetic sensibility, or more precisely to the poetic function itself'; through the invocation of Hoffmann's *Kreisleriana* at the beginning of *Du Vin et du haschisch*, 'the notion of inebriation is explicitly placed in the service of art', and Baudelaire goes on to describe how

[64] Victor Brombert, 'The Will to Ecstasy: The Example of Baudelaire's "La Chevelure"', *Yale French Studies*, 50 (1974), 55–64.

the 'ivresse' of both wine and drugs produce an 'impersonnalité' or 'objectivisme' which he considers to be 'le développement excessif de l'esprit poétique' (OC, i. 396). Brombert stresses the importance for Baudelaire of the idea of 'artistic self-possession as inebriation', a theme expressed most powerfully in 'Une mort héroïque':

Fancioulle me prouvait, d'une manière péremptoire, irréfutable, que l'*ivresse* de l'art est plus apte que toute autre à voiler les terreurs du gouffre; que le génie peut jouer la comédie au bord de la tombe avec une joie qui l'empêche de voir la tombe, perdu, comme il est, dans un paradis excluant toute idée de tombe et de destruction. (OC, i. 321, italics added)

It is highly significant that both of the questions raised by 'Le Vin des chiffonniers'—the theme of the poet-pariah and the relationship between drunkenness and poetic inspiration—should have been central to the life and work of a writer with whom Baudelaire was becoming steadily more obsessed at exactly the same time that he was working on *Du vin et du haschisch* and revising the early version of 'L'Âme du vin' and 'Le Vin des chiffonniers'. The first article on Poe ('Edgar Allan Poe: Sa vie et ses ouvrages') appeared in the *Revue de Paris* in March and April 1852 and is of direct relevance to the themes we are studying: it contains an exceptionally illuminating discussion of what Baudelaire calls 'l'ivrognerie littéraire' which, perhaps significantly, is not retained in the revised version of the article published in 1856.

On the day that *The Raven* was published, writes Baudelaire, Poe was to be seen staggering drunkenly along Broadway 'en battant les maisons et en trébuchant' (OC, ii. 271), just as the *chiffonnier* picks his inebriated way through the backstreets of Paris 'butant, et se cognant aux murs comme un poète'—the same hampered gait, we might note *en passant*, that characterizes those other emblems of the poet, the albatross, and the swan.[65] Poe is described as 'ivrogne, pauvre, persécuté, paria' (OC, ii. 288)—all terms which, needless to say, could equally well be applied to the *chiffonnier*. Just as Baudelaire sees the ragpicker's drunkenness as a result of social rejection rather than of innate moral degeneracy, so the responsibility for Poe's alcoholism is placed firmly on the shoulders of the society that denied him recognition. In Baudelaire's view poets like Poe are victims of bourgeois indifference or hostility

---

[65] See Richard D. Burton, *The Context of Baudelaire's 'Le Cygne'* (Durham Modern Language Series, Durham, 1980), 78–9.

and, with characteristic hypocrisy, 'la société les frappe d'un anathème spécial, et argue contre eux des vices de caractère que sa persécution leur a donnés' (OC, i. 249). Baudelaire goes on to develop an incisive analysis of the prevalence of drunkenness amongst writers of the nineteenth century:

Aujourd'hui, l'ivrognerie littéraire a pris un caractère sombre et sinistre. Il n'y a plus de classe spécialement lettrée qui se fasse honneur de frayer avec les hommes de lettres. Leurs travaux absorbants et les haines d'école les empêchent de se réunir entre eux. Quant aux femmes, leur éducation informe, leur incompétence politique et littéraire empêchent beaucoup d'auteurs de voir en elles autre chose que des ustensiles de ménage ou des objets de luxe. Le dîner absorbé et l'animal satisfait, le poète entre dans la vaste solitude de sa pensée; quelquefois il est très fatigué par le métier. Que devenir alors? Puis, son esprit s'accoutume à l'idée de sa force invincible, et il ne peut plus résister à l'espérance de retrouver dans la boisson les visions calmes ou effrayantes qui sont déjà ses vieilles connaissances. C'est sans doute à la même transformation de mœurs, qui a fait du monde lettré une classe à part, qu'il faut attribuer l'immense consommation de tabac que fait la nouvelle littérature. (OC, ii. 271–2)

In other words, the writer's recourse to drink is attributed to the fundamental transformation of French society since 1789 in much the same way that the *chiffonnier* is himself a product of the headlong urbanization and attendant social disintegration of the same period. The traditional hierarchical bond of patron (Baudelaire's 'classe spécialement lettrée') and artist was severed by the Revolution, leaving the artist an unprotected individual, rootless, alienated from the wider society. Concomitantly, as Baudelaire had already described in the (strongly Fourierist) section of the *Salon de 1846* entitled *Des écoles et des ouvriers*, the relative unity of style characteristic of pre-revolutionary art had given way to a chaotic individualism in which 'chacun est abandonné à lui-même'. 'La grande tradition' had disintegrated along with the 'organic' society it expressed, leaving a mass of heterogeneous styles and schools all in competition with each other—the artistic equivalent of the competitiveness and centreless individualism of nineteenth-century French society (OC, ii. 490–2). Alienated from each other no less than from the wider society, writers and artists, according to Baudelaire, form 'une classe à part' like the *chiffonniers*, condemned to a pariah-like existence away from the main thoroughfares of society and culture. Like *chiffonniers* they work alone while the rest of society sleeps, surviving on the scraps of detritus left by the wealthy and the fortunate, always subject to harassment by the forces of law and order just as, in the earlier versions of 'Le Vin des chiffonniers', the ragpickers are regularly harried by 'patrouilles funèbres' and 'mouchards ténébreux'. Small wonder, therefore, that for both artist and *chiffonnier* the only solace is that afforded by drink.

But wine is not merely the consolation of the literary sub-class but also a stimulus to creativity. Baudelaire insists that Poe's alcoholism was in no way prejudicial to his genius: 'ni la pureté, ni le fini de son style, ni la netteté de sa pensée, ni son ardeur au travail et à des recherches difficiles ne furent altérés par sa terrible habitude. La confection de la plupart de ses bons morceaux a précédé ou suivi une de ces crises' (OC, ii. 271). In the revised version of the study (1856), Baudelaire stresses that 'les mots *précédé* ou *suivi* impliquent que l'ivresse pouvait servir d'excitant aussi bien que de repos' and goes on to explain at some length what he sees as the catalytic powers of wine, its ability to resurrect the past ('La Chevelure' speaks of 'le vin du souvenir'), to heighten perception ('Le vin rend l'œil plus clair et l'oreille plus fine', we read in 'La Fontaine de sang') and to suggest analogies between disparate phenomena that the sober man would never perceive. He concludes that 'l'ivrogenerie de Poe était un moyen mnémonique, une méthode de travail, méthode énergique et mortelle, mais appropriée à sa nature passionnée. Le poète avait appris à boire, comme un littérateur soigneux s'exerce à faire des cahiers de notes'. Alcoholism, the consequence of society's indifference or hostility to his genius, stimulates him to further creativity; the link between wine, poetry, and social rebellion, suggested by the wine poems themselves, is further strengthened.

Wine consoles and inspires; but it also kills, and the inseparability of creativity, suffering, and death is one of the major themes suggested by the wine poems, *Du vin et du haschisch*, and the essays on Poe. Poe, says Baudelaire,

ne pouvait résister au desir de retrouver les visions merveilleuses ou effrayantes, les conceptions subtiles qu'il avait rencontrées dans une tempête précédente; c'étaient de vieilles connaissances qui l'attiraient impérativement, et, pour renouer avec elles, il prenait le chemin le plus dangereux, mais le plus direct. Une partie de ce qui fait aujourd'hui notre jouissance est ce qui l'a tué. (OC, ii. 315)

The joy of the 'consumer' is directly related to the suffering of the 'producer'. The interdependence of enjoyment and suffering is also suggested by the description of factory workers in *Pierre Dupont* which we have already cited with its stress on 'tous les poisons nécessaires à la création des chefs-d'œuvre' (OC, ii. 31). Similarly, the description of the *chiffonnier* in *Du Vin et du haschisch* offers, as Walter Benjamin says, 'one extended metaphor for the procedure of the poet in Baudelaire's spirit':[66]

Voici un homme chargé de ramasser les débris d'une journée de la capitale. Tout ce que la grande cité a rejeté, tout ce qu'elle a perdu, tout ce qu'elle a dédaigné, tout ce qu'elle a brisé, il le catalogue, il le collectionne. Il compulse les archives de la débauche, le capharnaüm des rebuts. Il fait un triage, un choix intelligent: il ramasse, comme un avare un trésor, les ordures qui, remâchées par la divinité de l'Industrie, deviendront des objets d'utilité ou de jouissance. (OC, i. 381)

The rubbish in the streets is for the *chiffonnier* what external nature as a whole is for the artist: 'un amas incohérent de matériaux que l'artiste est invité à associer et à mettre en ordre' (OC, ii. 752), and the recycling process in which he plays an essential part is akin to the dual character of the creative imagination in Baudelaire's aesthetic:

Mystérieuse faculté que cette reine des facultés! Elle est l'analyse, elle est la synthèse. . . . Elle décompose toute la création, et, avec les matériaux amassés et disposés suivant des règles dont on ne peut trouver l'origine que dans le plus profond de l'âme, elle crée un monde nouveau, elle produit la sensation du neuf. (OC, ii. 620)

Through a kind of imaginative alchemy,[67] the 'ordures' of reality are transformed into 'des objets d'utilité ou de jouissance': 'Tu m'as donné ta boue et j'en ai fait de l'or.'

But, crucially, the *chiffonnier* is only part of the creative or, rather, recreative process. In *Les Industriels* (1842), Émile de la Bedollière described the crucial role of the middleman or *marchand en gros* to whom *chiffonniers* sold their gleanings once they had been 'catalogued' and classified:

Habile alchimiste, le marchand de chiffons transmute en or les objets de

---

[66] Benjamin, *Charles Baudelaire*, 79–80.

[67] The image of alchemy is a commonplace of nineteenth-century writing on the *chiffonnier*, for example, Berthaud ('Les Chiffonniers', 338): 'Avec ces ordures il fera de l'argent, ce pauvre alchimiste . . .'.

rebut qu'on lui rapporte. Avec le produit de la vente du *caron* [old paper] et du *bul* [rags] il achète des rentes sur l'État. Il reçoit les Chiffonniers dans un bouge infect, et ses amis dans un salon élégant. Sa boutique est hideuse à voir; elle est encombrée d'immondices, de guenilles crottées, de bois pourris, d'ossements qui sentent l'amphithéâtre; le tout apporté par des êtres à peine humains, posé dans les balances d'un aspect fantastique, trié par des mégères décrépites . . . Mais si l'on pénètre au delà de cette première pièce, on y remarquera l'attirail ordinaire du luxe bourgeois, la pendule dorée, les scènes gravées de la vie de Napoléon, le cabaret en porcelaine.[68]

In his turn, the *marchand de chiffons* resells what he has bought from 'his' *chiffonniers* to workshops or factories where the pulping and other processes take place, and so on through a host of intermediary stages at the end of which the 'vomissement confus de l'énorme Paris' ('Le Vin des chiffonniers', 1861 text) emerges, unrecognizably, as 'des objets d'utilité ou de jouissance', most commonly, ironically enough, as the pages of a book: the 'vils débris' that the *chiffonnier* picks out of the mud of the Paris streets are, La Bedollière wrote, 'comme de hideuses chrysalides auxquelles la science humaine donnera les formes élégantes et des ailes diaphanes'.[69] Similarly, the poet, after sifting through and giving form to the *disjecta membra* of his personal experience, sells his manuscript to the publisher or editor who, in turn, conveys it to the printers whence it emerges as a finished 'work of art' destined to pass, through the further intermediary of the bookseller, into the hands of the public. Both *chiffonnier* and poet are alienated not only from the final product but also from all but the first stage of the productive process. Through his analogy between poet and ragpicker, Baudelaire appears to be laying emphasis less on the literary work as something fixed, absolute, and atemporal (Mallarmé's 'calme bloc ici-bas chu') but as something tentative, unstable, and provisional, perpetually in the process of becoming. And, as though to underline this, the successive versions of 'Le Vin des chiffonniers' themselves testify to the essentially unfixed, open quality of literary production as the poet-ragpicker—the poet-*bricoleur*—sifts through and tinkers with the rejects of previous versions, trying a piece here, a piece there, as the poem advances haltingly towards a final but by no means definitive state when, as

[68] La Bedollière, *Les Industriels*, 172.
[69] Ibid. 170.

Valéry said, it is abandoned rather than completed. Poet and *chiffonnier*, poet and prostitute, poet and *saltimbanque*: all are creatures of the street, homeless, nomadic beings dependent for their survival on a society which, though it obscurely needs the services they provide, refuses to acknowledge that need and segregates and represses them through fear of contamination. All are *in* the city without being *of* the city, a part of yet apart from its teeming life, living in its interstices rather than, as the common image has it, on its margins.[70] It may be that this image of the poet as urban pariah, at once inside and out, is ultimately more moving and more authentic than that of the metaphysical trailblazer of 'Les Phares' or the aristocratic martyr-figure of 'Bénédiction'.

From L'Ivrogne *to 'Enivrez-vous': Wine in Baudelaire's Later Writing*

Even in its 'definitive' form, 'Le Vin des chiffonniers' draws back at the last from an outright condemnation of wine and drunkenness, and the tension between the poem's first six and last two stanzas may be seen as symptomatic of Baudelaire's own ideological and moral uncertainty concerning wine even as late as 1857. A similar uncertainty is evident in the projected 'drame populacier' *L'Ivrogne*, the plot outline of which Baudelaire sent to the actor Jean-Hippolyte Tisserant in early 1854 in response to Tisserant's suggestion, after hearing Baudelaire recite the poem in question, that he write a two-act play based on 'Le Vin de l'assassin' (OC, i. 629–34). 'Le Vin de l'assassin' is one of the poems Prarond insisted he had heard in or before 1843 and if it was not published, as was long believed, in *L'Écho des marchands de vin* in 1848, the reason is probably, as suggested earlier, that the total absence in the poem of any explicit condemnation of the drunken murderer's action clashed too violently with the eminently moral view of wine and drinking that the Comité Central des Boissons was anxious to promote in its journal. The major difference between *L'Ivrogne* and 'Le Vin de l'assassin' is that while the poem only hints at the drunkard's class, the projected play deliberately endows him with 'une profession lourde, triviale, rude', that of a *scieur de long*, and locates the drama in an unequivocally working-class setting of

---

[70] See Burton, *The Context*, 17–18.

goguettes, *guinguettes*, and *bastringues*, with the murder itself taking place amidst a 'paysage sinistre et mélancolique des environs de Paris': at the very least this suggests that, by early 1854, Baudelaire had got over the romantic populism that, in *Du vin et du haschisch*, had effectively prevented him seeing *any* fault or failing in the working classes and especially in working-class drinking habits. At the same time, *L'Ivrogne* maintains a highly equivocal attitude towards the drunkard and his terrible deed. If the suggested alternative title, 'La Pente du mal' suggests an explicit moral perspective or purpose, the play itself, at least in the fragmentary outline that, needless to say, it was to remain, is notably sympathetic towards the murderer and notably less so towards his victim with her 'puissante religion'. As an 'atrocité sans prétexte', the murder points forward to the violent *actes gratuits* such as those related in 'Le Mauvais Vitrier' and 'Assommons les pauvres!' The murder's 'idée fixe, obsédante', *'Je suis libre, libre, libre'*, is certainly not approved of by Baudelaire, as its equivalent may well have been in the verse text when it was first written, but neither is it subject to outright condemnation. Like the 1854 text of 'Le Vin des chiffonniers', *L'Ivrogne* is located around the mid-point of the political spectrum that leads from the radical republicanism of 1848–51 to the reactionary de Maistrianism of 1855–6 and beyond, closer, perhaps, to the latter, but still retaining much of the former's attachment to individual and collective freedom even if it leads *jenseits des von Gut und Böse* to a revolt against the law of God and man alike.

By the end of the 1850s, however, the ambiguities and equivocations evident even in the 1857 version of 'Le Vin des chiffonniers' had disappeared, and the poet's verdict on wine, in keeping with his now unqualified anti-socialism and anti-humanism, was one of outright condemnation. In *Les Paradis artificiels* (1860) the distinction—fundamental to the whole argument of *Du vin et du haschisch*—between drink- and drug-inspired intoxication has been abandoned; all forms of 'ivresse', except that produced by artistic creation itself, are now condemned as hubristic. It is highly significant that in his blanket condemnation of all forms of excess Baudelaire should reintroduce the *chiffonnier* in an altered but still recognizable form:

C'est dans cette dépravation du sens de l'infini que gît, selon moi, la raison de tous les excès coupables, depuis l'ivresse solitaire et concentrée du littérateur . . . jusqu'à l'ivrognerie la plus répugnante des faubourgs, qui, le cerveau plein de flamme et de gloire, se roule ridiculement dans les ordures de la route. (OC, i. 403)

But it is in 'Le Voyage' that we find the most strident condemnation of 'ivresse' in all its forms. Baudelaire satirizes the utopianism of the men of the Second Republic (including, no doubt, his own) in the line 'Notre âme est un trois-mâts cherchant son Icarie'—a reference, as is well known, to the *Voyage en Icarie* (1840) by the Utopian socialist Étienne Cabet.[71] Almost immediately after this allusion to 1848, there is a further denunciation of drunkenness in which the *chiffonnier* puts in a by now almost obligatory appearance:

> Ô le pauvre amoureux des pays chimériques!
> Faut-il le mettre aux fers, le jeter à la mer,
> Ce matelot ivrogne, inventeur d'Amériques
> Dont le mirage rend le gouffre plus amer?

> Tel le vieux vagabond, piétinant dans la boue,
> Rêve, le nez en l'air, de brillants paradis;
> Son œil ensorcelé découvre une Capoue
> Partout où la chandelle illumine un taudis.

Finally, the whole of humanity stands indicated of drunken vainglory:

> L'Humanité bavarde, ivre de son génie,
> Et folle, maintenant comme elle était jadis,
> Criant à Dieu, dans sa furibonde agonie:
> 'Ô mon semblable, ô mon maître, je te maudis!'

It was symptomatic of this hardening attitude towards wine that, in the revised 1861 edition of *Les Fleurs du mal*, the section *Le Vin* was moved from the position it occupied in 1857 when it came 'comme un apaisement', in Claude Pichois's words, between *Révolte* and *La Mort* and became instead 'une gradation dans la damnation' following *Les Tableaux parisiens* and leading up as a kind of preface in rebellion and excess to *Fleurs du mal* and *Révolte* (OC, i. 1045).

Still more eloquently, when the possibility of a de luxe illustrated edition of *Les Fleurs du mal* was raised by Poulet-Malassis some

[71] For Baudelaire and Cabet, see Peter S. Hambly, 'Baudelaire et l'utopie' and James S. Patty, 'Baudelaire, Cabet et Capé', both in *Bulletin Baudelairien*, 6/1 (1970), 5–7 and 8–10.

time in 1861, Baudelaire suggested 'Eritis sicut Dei' or 'sicut Deus' (Gen. 3: 5) as possible epigraphs for *Le Vin* and proposed the motif of a 'serpent buvant dans une coupe'—to be designed by Bracquemond—as an appropriate *fleuron* for the section concerned: the link between the Fall and the 'divine madness' of wine could hardly be made clearer (C, ii. 179). By 1861, then, Baudelaire's attitude had turned full circle. During the Second Republic, wine represented poetry, revolt against oppression, human genius versus the tyranny of a divinely sanctioned social order; drunkenness was celebrated even—or, rather, especially—when it led man to rise above himself and challenge the power and authority of God. But by 1861 all this has changed. Man is still 'ivre de son génie'—he always was and always will be—but Baudelaire now has nothing but contempt for the heaven-vaulting pretensions of a besotted race. Humanism has given way to a systematic and all-pervasive misanthropy; 'ivresse' connotes vice and vanity that can be held in check only by the divine Cosmocrat who, ten years earlier, had been seen as the major obstacle to the establishment of a wholly human paradise on earth. Yet, as though to underline the message of ambiguity that emerges from the wine poems, Baudelaire's earlier attitude towards wine still survived, buried somewhere deep beneath the incrustations of de Maistrian gloom, and it was to surface briefly but unforgettably once more in 1864 in the greatest of his celebrations of wine, the *Credo*, *Gloria*, and *Sanctus* of every devotee of 'le fils sacré du Soleil', the incomparable prose poem 'Enivrez-vous':

Il faut être toujours ivre. Tout est là: c'est l'unique question. Pour ne pas sentir l'horrible fardeau du Temps qui brise vos épaules et vous penche vers la terre, il faut vous enivrer sans trêve. Mais de quoi? De vin, de poésie ou de vertu, à votre guise. Mais enivrez-vous. Et si quelquefois, sur les marches d'un palais, sur l'herbe verte d'un fossé, dans la solitude morne de votre chambre, vous vous réveillez, l'ivresse déjà diminuée et disparue, demandez au vent, à la vague, à l'étoile, à l'oiseau, à l'horloge, à tout ce qui fuit, à tout ce qui gémit, à tout ce qui roule, à tout ce qui chante, à tout ce qui parle, demandez quelle heure il est; et le vent, la vague, l'étoile, l'oiseau, l'horloge, vous répondront: 'Il est l'heure de s'enivrer! Pour n'être pas les esclaves martyrisés du Temps, enivrez-vous sans cesse—De vin, de poésie ou de vertu, à votre guise'.

'De vin, de poésie ou *de vertu*': perhaps there were times when even the *chiffonnier*, drunk with self-righteousness as much as wine, might have found some grace in the later Baudelaire's eyes.

7

Baudelaire and Proudhon (I): 'Châtiment de l'orgueil' in Context

En ces temps merveilleux où la Théologie
Fleurit avec le plus de sève et d'énergie,
On raconte qu'un jour un docteur des plus grands,
—Après avoir forcé les cœurs indifférents;
Les avoir remués dans leurs profondeurs noires;
Après avoir franchi vers les célestes gloires
Des chemins singuliers à lui-même inconnus,
Où les purs Esprits seuls peut-être étaient venus,—
Comme un homme monté trop haut, pris de panique,
S'écria, transporté d'un orgueil satanique:
'Jésus, petit Jésus! je t'ai poussé bien haut!
Mais, si j'avais voulu t'attaquer au défaut
De l'armure, ta honte égalerait ta gloire,
Et tu ne serais plus qu'un fœtus dérisoire!'

Immédiatement sa raison s'en alla.
L'éclat de ce soleil d'un crêpe se voila;
Tout le chaos roula dans cette intelligence,
Temple autrefois vivant, plein d'ordre et d'opulence,
Sous les plafonds duquel tant de pompe avait lui.
Le silence et la nuit s'installèrent en lui,
Comme dans un caveau dont la clef est perdue.
Dès lors il fut semblable aux bêtes de la rue,
Et, quand il s'en allait sans rien voir, à travers
Les champs, sans distinguer les étés des hivers,
Sale, inutile et laid comme une chose usée,
Il faisait des enfants la joie et la risée.

(Text of 1861 edition)

Few readers of *Les Fleurs du mal*, one imagines, would disagree with F. W. Leakey's verdict that, considered from a purely aesthetic viewpoint, 'Châtiment de l'orgueil' (first published in June 1850 and included as poem XVI in both the 1857 and 1861 editions of

Les Fleurs du mal[1]) 'must be counted amongst the weakest that Baudelaire wrote'.[2] Although 'this edifying but sadly prosaic anecdote' is, as Leakey has shown,[3] typical of the explicitly moralizing poems that Baudelaire was writing in the late 1840s and early 1850s (many of which, but not 'Châtiment de l'orgueil' itself, would be published in the *Limbes* sequence of 1851), it appears to contain little of the intensity of feeling and expression that characterizes other no less directly moralistic texts of the same period such as 'Les Hiboux' and 'Le Tonneau de la Haine': it is likely that the reader who looks to a Baudelaire poem for some manner of 'sorcellerie évocatoire' will find the text almost comically deficient, utterly 'un-Baudelairean' in conception, intention, and style. Not surprisingly, the poem has 'excited' virtually no critical comment, the only point of scholarly interest being the source of the medieval anecdote on which it is based. In 1937 Albert-Marie Schmidt established that the 'docteur des plus grands' of line 3 of the poem is Simon de Tournai, the story of whose theological hubris and subsequent nemesis is recounted by a number of medieval chroniclers, notably the thirteenth-century hagiographer Mathieu Pâris, whence, via an eighteenth-century anthology and commentary, it found its way into Michelet's *Histoire de la France*.[4] The *direct* source of Baudelaire's 'inspiration' was, however, not Michelet but an article by the philosopher Saint-René Taillandier that appeared in the *Revue des Deux Mondes* on 14 October 1848. Entitled 'L'Athéisme allemand et le socialisme français: M. Charles Grün et M. Proudhon', the lengthy forty-page article uses two works: Karl Grün's *Die soziale Bewegung in Frankreich und Belgien* (1845) and Proudhon's *Système des contradictions économiques* (1846)—the celebrated *Philosophie de la misère* which, as we have seen, Baudelaire read in whole or in part some time between 1846 and

---

[1] 'Châtiment de l'orgueil' was also published in *Le Journal d'Alençon* on 17 May 1857. The only significant difference between the text of 1850 and those of 1857 and 1861 is at l. 14 where *Le Magasin des familles* had 'objet dérisoire' instead of 'fœtus dérisoire'.

[2] F. W. Leakey, *Baudelaire and Nature* (Manchester Univ. Press, Manchester, 1969), 100, n. 1.

[3] Id., 'Baudelaire: The Poet as Moralist', in L. J. Austin, Garnet Rees, and Eugène Vinaver (eds.), *Studies in Modern French Literature Presented to P. Mansell Jones* (Manchester Univ. Press, Manchester, 1961), 203.

[4] For a discussion of Schmidt's article, see Peter S. Hambly, 'Notes sur deux poèmes de Baudelaire: "Reversibilité" and "Châtiment de l'orgueil"', *Revue d'histoire littéraire de la France*, 71/3 (1971), 485–8.

1852—as a focus for a sustained attack on the neo-Hegelianism represented by Grün and the 'French socialism' of Proudhon. Towards its conclusion, and at the climax of his denunciation of Proudhon, Taillandier relates the story of Simon de Tournai which, presumably, he had encountered in Michelet:

Il y avait au XIIIe siecle, dans les grandes écoles de la scholastique, un vigoureux dialecticien nommé Simon de Tournay. Un jour qu'il avait admirablement établi la divinité du Christ et ravi l'auditoire, il s'écria: 'Ô petit Jésus! petit Jésus! (*Jesule! Jesule!*) autant j'ai exalté ta loi, autant je pourrais la rabaisser, si je voulais.' Les chroniques rapportent avec un pieux effroi que le sophiste fut incontinent privé de sa raison. Cet homme qui régnait dans les écoles, ce dialecticien enivré de sa logique, ne sut bientôt plus que balbutier au hasard et devint la risée des enfants.[5]

Claude Pichois, who is responsible for pinpointing this source, says no more and makes nothing either of the date of the article— October 1848—nor of the fact that one of the two targets of its invective—Pierre-Joseph Proudhon—was a man and writer for whom, as we have seen, Baudelaire's enthusiasm was at its height at precisely this time. The potentially enormous significance of 'Châtiment de l'orgueil' lies in the fact that, apart from 'Le Vin des honnêtes gens' (the companion-piece of 'Châtiment de l'orgueil' when it was first published in *Le Magasin des familles* in June 1850) and 'Lesbos' (July 1850), it represents the only poem of Baudelaire's to appear in public between November 1847 ('Les Chats') and the *Limbes* sequence of April 1851. But the origins—if not the first published texts—of 'Le Vin des honnêtes gens' and 'Lesbos' (as well as of the bulk of the *Limbes* poems) all lie in the early or mid-1840s. 'Châtiment de l'orgueil', however, could well be the *only* poem Baudelaire actually wrote in its entirety in the confused and painful aftermath of the *journées de juin* and, to that extent at least, merits our very closest attention. The relevant number of the *Revue des Deux Mondes* appeared when, as we have seen, Baudelaire was almost certainly in Châteauroux engaged on his brief stint as *rédacteur en chef* of the local conservative newspaper *Le Représentant de l'Indre*. Baudelaire presumably read Saint-René Taillandier's article, either in Châteauroux or Paris, some time in October–November 1848 and, one may assume, was immediately struck both by its content and by the obscure medieval

5 Quoted from OC, i. 870.

anecdote that serves to clinch the author's attack on the political thinker to whose ideas he was at the time so tightly drawn that to describe him as a disciple seems no exaggeration. When the poem itself was written cannot, of course, be determined with any precision, but, given its evident 'occasional' character, an early rather than a later dating may be in order, at least for the initial drafts: December 1848, perhaps, or January–February 1849, at precisely the time, that is, when, with the election of Louis Napoleon to the Presidency in December 1848, the hopes and dreams of February could be said to have been definitely buried. To understand the possible significance of 'Châtiment de l'orgueil' it is insufficient simply to extract the de Tournai anecdote from Taillandier's article and make of it, as Claude Pichois does, a straightforward textual 'source'. The article needs to be read as a whole and its argument set beside what we know of Baudelaire's political stance(s) in 1848–50 (and particularly beside what we know of his attitude towards Proudhon). If this is done, the poem, for all its dismaying clumsiness (itself, perhaps, of considerable significance), constitutes an important new piece of evidence in the slowly emerging but necessarily fragmentary picture we have of that utterly paradoxical but utterly crucial figure, the Baudelaire of the Second Republic.

Saint-René Taillandier's anti-socialist animus,[6] no less than his post-June relief, is evident from the very outset of his article. With its fatal combination of 'utopies désastreuses' and 'ordonnances dictatoriales', socialism, he says, 'a été maître de la France pendant quelques mois', a chaotic interlude during which 'des voix ont été entendues qui n'avaient rien d'humain, l'air a été souillé de hideuses clameurs' (pp. 280–1).[7] Having made his ideological position

---

[6] René Gaspard Ernest Saint-René-Taillandier (1817–79) was a regular contributor to the *Revue des Deux Mondes* on literary and philosophical questions and was probably the best-informed French intellectual of his day concerning literary and intellectual developments in Germany. His principal writings on philosophy are collected in *Histoire et philosophie religieuse* (1859), and his *Littérature étrangère: Écrivains et poètes modernes* (1861) contains his major studies of German literature.

[7] All quotations from Saint-René-Taillandier, 'L'Athéisme allemand et le socialisme français: M. Charles Grün et M. Proudhon', *Revue des Deux Mondes*, 23 (15 Oct. 1848), 280–322. It may be that Baudelaire recalls this judgement of neo-Hegelianism in *Le Poème du haschisch* when he writes of 'un philosophe français qui, pour railler les doctrines allemandes modernes, disait: "Je suis un dieu qui ai mal dîné"' (OC, i. 437). See Pichois's comments, OC, i. 1381–2.

abundantly clear, Taillandier proceeds to give a lengthy, wide-ranging, and incisive analysis of what he sees as the twofold philosophical foundation of the crisis so recently undergone not only in France but also in Germany and elsewhere: German neo-Hegelianism (as typified by Grün's *Die soziale Bewegung*) and 'French socialism' which, deriving (according to Taillandier) from Holbach, Helvétius, Raynal, and, above all, Rousseau, was elaborated by Fourier, Saint-Simon, Louis Blanc, Leroux, and Cabet and reached its supreme expression in Proudhon's *Philosophie de la misère* of 1846. Taillandier's analysis of the Young Hegelians is of less relevance to the present discussion than his dissection of Proudhon's thought, but, if nothing else, it offers important evidence that Baudelaire was at least indirectly acquainted with the main elements of, in particular, Feuerbach's antitheist humanism and Stirner's anarchistic individualism. Taillandier views neo-Hegelianism essentially as a deification of humanity founded on the conviction that 'il n'y a rien au-dessus de l'humanité', what men call 'God' being no more than 'un reflet de nous-mêmes, une aliénation de nos idées les plus sublimes au profit d'un être imaginaire; *homo homini Deus*' (p. 300). Humanism—by which he means the project of human self-divinization elaborated by Feuerbach and those close to him—is seen as 'la conséquence directe du système de Hegel' (p. 289), the main elements of which he summarizes as follows (p. 303):

'L'infini, s'ignorant d'abord lui-même, se divise pour se déterminer et se connaître; par cette scission, il pose hors de lui son contraire, qui est le fini. Voilà la thèse et l'antithèse; comment se rétablit l'unité? comment reparaît l'harmonie? L'unité, la synthèse harmonieuse de l'infini et du fini, c'est l'esprit absolu qui, sorti d'abord de l'infini et de l'indéterminé, puis longtemps captif dans les formes périssables de l'univers créé, acquiert enfin, après des milliers d'années, la conscience de soi-même, et retrouve, sur les ruines de la nature et de l'homme, sa divinité laborieusement conquise.

The ultimate meaning of neo-Hegelianism is seen by Taillandier to lie in the Stirnerian maxim *Homo sibi Deus* (p. 301). Since 'God' (p. 288) 'n'est autre chose que notre figure reproduite dans un merveilleux mirage; c'est le reflet sublime, l'ombre grandiose du genre humain', it follows that the liberation of humanity lies in its reclaiming its divinity from the alienating image it has produced and which has been turned against it. The relevance of this philosophy of antitheistic humanism to Baudelaire's own writings of the late 1840s—most notably the 'Révolte' poems—should already be obvious.

Although, according to Taillandier, Proudhon does not subscribe to the Young Hegelians' 'croyance anti-chrétienne' (p. 283), he does share with them a belief in the urgent need for human (re)diviniza-tion: Proudhonism, like neo-Hegelianism, is 'une religion dont vous et moi sommes les dieux'. Proudhon's thought, says Taillandier, is drawn inexorably towards what he calls 'la grande et fondamentale antinomie: Dieu d'un côté, l'homme de l'autre. Dieu est infini; l'homme est un être limité; Dieu et l'homme sont deux contraires inconciliables'. 'Puisque Dieu est infini,' he continues summarizing Proudhon's thought, 'sa bonté, sa liberté, sa science, sont exacte-ment le contraire de la bonté, de la liberté et de la science de l'homme'; the whole universe consists, therefore, of 'un antagon-isme immense de principes ennemis', 'une guerre à mort entre l'homme et dieu', at the end of which 'l'homme libre et progressif triomphera de son immense et immobile adversaire: le fini prévoyant triomphera de l'infini hébété, de même, et plus sûrement encore, qu'Ulysse a vaincu le Cyclope' (pp. 309–10). Taillandier goes on to quote the notorious 'Dieu, c'est le mal' passage in *Philosophie de la misère* which, if he did not already know it, we may imagine having a shattering effect on Baudelaire as he read it. Another quotation held to illustrate Proudhon's antitheistic humanism follows ('La profondeur des cieux n'égale pas la profondeur de notre intelligence au sein de laquelle se meuvent de merveilleux systèmes . . . Que dirai-je de plus? C'est la création même prise, pour ainsi dire, sur le fait!' (p. 315)), and it is at this point that Taillandier recounts the story of Simon de Tournai's heaven-vaulting sophistries that would provide the source of Baudelaire's poem. The author concludes by contrasting the Young Hegelians (for whom (p. 315) 'il n'y a pas d'autre Dieu que l'humanité') and Proudhon who is said to recog-nize a God, but a God 'ennemie de l'homme, un Dieu que nous devons combattre et vaincre'. For all his similarities with his German counterparts, Proudhon is held to be opposed to any 'déification de notre espèce' which, allegedly, he believes to represent 'un dernier écho des terreurs religieuses' (p. 318). This refusal (or inability) either to seek to reconcile his antithetical terms of man and god or to resolve their conflict by suppressing or denying the God-term entirely (as the Young Hegelians had done) 'n'a réussi qu'à faire de l'esprit de M. Proudhon un chaos inextricable' (p. 314), a judgement which line 17 of 'Châtiment de l'orgueil' could well echo: 'Tout le chaos roula dans cette intelligence'. All that remains for Proudhon is 'la guerre à outrance de Dieu et de l'homme' (p. 310) which, admitting of neither resolution nor respite, effectively condemns his thought to so many 'sophismes', 'affirmations hautaines', and 'brusques enjambées' which recall all too pertinently the dialectical excesses of the medieval Schoolmen (p. 303). Having demonstrated to his own satisfaction 'l'incurable indigence de tous les systèmes socialistes', Taillandier is able to conclude his article with a series of conventional pieties extolling Christianity, property, and the family: 'Le sentiment du devoir, le sentiment de la liberté, nous ne demandons que cela, et le socialisme est vaincu' (p. 321). Hubris has been punished and Order restored: Baudelaire, we recall, chose to publish *his* version of Pride Chastised under the general rubric of 'Poésies de la famille' in a review called *Le Magasin de la famille*, though the sense of that gesture could, as we have seen, be problematic and provocative in the extreme.

How, reading Taillandier's article towards the end of a year which had swept him, in common with so many of his generation, from the heady enthusiasms of February, via the fury and anguish of June, to the torpor and despondency of October, November, and December, would Baudelaire have reacted to this sustained assault on the philosophical foundations—or what were seen as such—of the whole radical upsurge of *quarante-huit* and, in particular, on the ideas and personality of the socialist thinker—Proudhon—for whom he unquestionably nourished an admiration which, though not wholly uncritical, clearly went beyond anything he felt for any other political theorist of the period? Given this well-documented enthusiasm, Baudelaire may be supposed to have rejected with derision the attack on Proudhon and Proudhonism that is the main thrust of Taillander's invective: it follows that, whatever else it may be, 'Châtiment de l'orgueil' is not, at least not when it was conceived and written (its significance for Baudelaire could, of course, have changed by the time he came to incorporate it into the 1857 edition), an attack on the author of *Philosophie de la misère* and his ideas. Any doubts on this score should be dispelled by an article which appeared in *Le Représentant de l'Indre* just five days after Taillandier's piece was published in the *Revue des Deux Mondes*.

Entitled 'Actuellement' and beyond reasonable doubt the work of Baudelaire,[8] the article in question uses Proudhon, and in particular Proudhon's interpretation of the *journées de juin*, as a yardstick of political correctness: 'Il faut avoir le courage d'avouer les faits tels qu'ils sont. Proudhon l'a dit, le seul et le premier: *L'insurrection est socialiste*. Il ne ment pas celui-là; il est brutal et clair'.[9] Assuming that 'Actuellement' is indeed by Baudelaire and given that, if it is, its composition took place, in all likelihood, either immediately before or immediately after he read the Taillandier article, we can obtain a remarkably clear picture both of the poet's general state of mind in the autumn of 1848 and of his political perspectives in the months that separated the suppression of the June insurrection from the Bonapartist electoral triumph in December; in particular, the article casts valuable light on the possible significance of 'Châtiment de l'orgueil' itself.

'Actuellement' begins by evoking with nostalgia the euphoria of February when 'sauf une très petite quantité d'hésitations et de regrets obstinés, si minime que personne ne la vit, toutes les classes politiques et religieuses, ouvriers prolétaires, ouvriers propriétaires, anciens partisans même de l'opposition légitimiste, républicains traditionnels et de vieille date, se précipitèrent avec enthousiasme dans une fraternelle et mystique union,—union que l'on crut definitive. *Nous nous faisons gloire d'avoir partagé cette sublime illusion*' (italics added). February was a 'moment unique dans l'histoire' when, it seemed, the whole of France was united by an 'immense espérance' in the future, by a collective 'aspiration à la vertu et à la concorde' such as had never before been witnessed. So why, despite 'l'immense bonne volonté de la France' or at least of 'la très grande majorité des citoyens français', was this brief moment of harmony succeeded by weeks and months of discord which, bringing in their train 'le désordre social, la stagnation des affaires, la misère du peuple, les récriminations réciproques, etc.', culminated in 'l'histoire lamentable de l'insurrection de Juin'? Rejecting any notion that a conspiracy, Legitimist, Bonapartist, or foreign, could have precipitated the June crisis, refusing to deny the right of the insurgents to embark upon the desperate course they

[8] See Pichois's comments, OC, ii. 1563–4. For further and, I believe, clinching evidence that 'Actuellement' is by Baudelaire, see conclusion, n. 10, below.
[9] All quotations from 'Actuellement' taken from OC, ii. 1060–3.

took—given the circumstances, says Baudelaire bluntly, 'l'insurrection était légitime, comme l'assassinat'—and, finally, forbearing to blame either the moderate republicans (those whom, borrowing Proudhon's terms, the article calls 'républicains classiques' or 'républicains de tragédie') or the out-and-out reactionaries for what took place, Baudelaire pins the responsibility for the *journées de juin* and the repression that followed squarely on those he calls the 'meneurs vulgaires' who, he says, have led the people to perdition. 'Actuellement' makes it abundantly clear who, in Baudelaire's view, the real culprits are: not the Bonapartists, not the bourgeois republicans, not, above all, the insurgents themselves ('le peuple a raison' is his uncompromising verdict), but all those who, in February and the months that followed, appeared before the people 'les mains pleines de panacées universelles' against every evil and shortcoming imaginable in the belief that 'l'on décrète la vertu, le bonheur, la fraternité et le travail avec de petits carrés de papier, que l'on jette des fenêtres d'un hôtel de ville emporté d'assaut, ou par surprise!' Baudelaire names no names and stigmatizes no specific political tendency, group or party, but there is no mistaking that his deepest contempt, in October 1848 as at the time of 'Assommons les pauvres!' (1865), is reserved for those who imagine themselves in possession of 'l'art de rendre les peuples heureux, sages et riches, en vingt-quatre heures': all those—Fourierists, Blanquists, Icarians, and Saint-Simonians, no doubt, but also dreamers and Utopians of less radical hue—who, in the words of 'Actuellement', cannot or will not see that 'toutes les choses humaines—idées, droits, institutions—ne se génèrent que lentement et que par un progrès successif et analogue à toutes les floraisons, moissons, et récoltes'. If—once again the caution is necessary—'Actuellement' really is by Baudelaire (but who else in Châteauroux at the time could have advanced such an argument in such an assured and striking manner? who else would have quoted Proudhon with approval?), then there is evidence of a remarkable, indeed life-long, continuity in the poet's attitude towards the events, personalities, and programmes of 1848. The celebrated later denunciations of *quarante-huitard* utopianism ('1848 ne fut amusant que parce que chacun y faisait des utopies comme des châteaux en Espagne, 1848 ne fut charmant que par l'excès même du ridicule.' *Mon cœur mis à nu* (OC, i. 679)) are already clearly present in the article of October 1848. What, of course, changes is Baudelaire's emotional stance towards this utopianism, so that that which, writing in the late 1850s or early 1860s, Baudelaire finds (or claims to find) 'charmant' or 'amusant' about 1848 is, in the immediate aftermath of the events themselves, a subject 'pour nous trop triste á développer'. Critical though it is of 'les Attilas de la démagogie' who have undone the people by promising them too much too soon, 'Actuellement' is not for that the work of a reactionary or of an 'uncommitted' spectator; on the contrary, the position that it takes is that of a convinced republican and socialist, in all essentials identical to that taken by Proudhon himself.[10] What is denounced in 'Actuellement' is not socialism or republicanism, but quite simply the hubris of all the Utopians, dreamers, demagogues, and other assorted 'gens à parole dorée' whose rhetorical and other excesses have brought about the current nemesis of reaction and repression. From this point the way back to 'Châtiment de l'orgeuil' should be clear.

When read in the light of the Taillandier article, of 'Actuellement' and of what we know from other sources of Baudelaire's response to 1848, 'Châtiment de l'orgueil' is revealed to be nothing less than a coded commentary by the poet on the turbulent events—tragedy and farce combined—that he, along with the French nation, has so recently lived through. The 'temps merveilleux' with which the poem begins could well evoke the unforgettable collective effervescence of February when 'la Théologie'—quasi-religious doctrines of instant republican-socialist redemption—did indeed flourish 'avec le plus de sève et d'énergie'. The 'docteur des plus grands' stands emblematically, I suggest, for all the Utopian theorists, messianic fantasists, and radical slogan-mongers for whom, even in the springtime of the revolution, Baudelaire had, if the accounts of his contemporaries are to be believed, the most heartfelt contempt. Like the 'gens à parole dorée' denounced in 'Actuellement', the Doctor uses his rhetorical-dialectical skills to 'force' 'les cœurs indifférents' of his listeners, rousing them 'dans leurs profondeurs noires' to heed his heady message of Paradise Now and to hanker for joys beyond his or their imagining. Shedding all anchorage in the real (like the doctrinaire socialists of March and April?), the Doctor 'takes off' 'vers les célestes gloires | Des chemins singuliers à lui-même inconnus | Où les purs Esprits seuls peut-être étaient

---

[10] See van Slyke, 'Dans l'intertexte', 65–8.

venus'. The lines that follow are replete with likely references to the dreams and aspirations of the early months of the Second Republic. When the Doctor calls upon 'Jésus, petit Jésus' to admire his scholastic prowess, the reader familiar with the iconography of 1848 can hardly fail to recall the image of the Republican Christ or Christ the Republic that Baudelaire himself had invoked in *Le Salut public* in March 1848 and of which he would later make such startling use in 'Le Reniement de saint Pierre'. Similarly, as we have seen, the term 'satanique' (l. 10) has a specifically political—and, in republican discourse, normally positive—meaning in the context of the late 1840s, and if the Doctor is 'pris de panique' (l. 9) as he reaches his intellectual empyrean, that, too, may have a political resonance if the reply, recorded by Baudelaire in *L'École païenne* (January 1852), supposedly given by 'un de ces jeunes gens qu'on peut qualifier d'instruits et d'intelligents' to the question 'qu'est-ce que le dieu Pan a de commun avec la révolution?' has any general import:'—Comment donc? répondait-il; mais c'est le dieu Pan qui fait la révolution. Il est la révolution' (OC, ii. 44).

Drawing on the intertextual and other materials assembled so far, and referring also to other texts characteristic of Baudelaire's 'republican interlude', I tentatively suggest the following political reading of a text which, like so many of those Baudelaire wrote between 1846 and 1852, appears devoid of any contemporary reference whatsoever. Just as the sin of Simon de Tournai was to make Jesus' existence (or at least His attributes) dependent on his own reasoning powers (in the same way that, according to Taillandier, the Young Hegelians see 'God' solely as a projection and product of the human mind), so it has been the crime and error of the republican-radical 'doctors' of 1848 to create imaginary Republics out of their own dreams, fantasies, or nostalgias and, in so doing, to reduce the one Republic that actually existed to a 'fœtus dérisoire' (l. 14) of what otherwise it might have become; or, as the representative proletarian of 'Actuellement' retorts to his supposed betters, 'que m'importe la cocarde et l'écriteau républicain que vous portez à votre chapeau, que m'importent les pastiches traditionnels de jacobinisme, de sans-culottisme, si vous perdez la République! Je ne vis pas de poésie historique, mais de pain'. Having trespassed 'comme un homme monté trop haut' (l. 9) beyond the limits of that which is humanly knowable or feasible, the doctor is punished, like the dreamers and demagogues, by the destruction of those rational (or pseudo-rational) powers that constituted his apparent great-ness: 'Immédiatement sa raison s'en alla'. But whereas Simon de Tournai's nemesis was limited to himself, it is 'le peuple' as a whole which, in 1848, is the real victim of its leaders' hubris, and it could be that the unseeing, wholly self-enclosed, barely human creature of the second part of the poem is intended as an image not just of the discomfited 'Attilas de la démagogie' of 1848 but, by extension, of the Republic itself in the sordid aftermath of June, 'sale, inutile et laid comme un chose usée', rejected and despised by those who, in February, had greeted it as their redeemer: 'Il faisait des enfants la joie et la risée' (ll. 25–6).

The word 'ivre' and its cognates is nowhere used in 'Châtiment de l'orgeuil', but the condition evoked in the poem is, self-evidently, one of intoxication: there is an ironic appositeness in the Doctor's ending up imprisoned 'dans un caveau dont la clef est perdue' (contrast the 'froids caveaux' from which wine rises in the accom-panying poem 'Le Vin des honnêtes gens' (l. 12)). Moreover, there are unmistakable parallels between the 'docteur des plus grands' of 'Châtiment de l'orgeuil' and the figure of the *chiffonnier*, particu-larly in his later manifestations. If the ragpicker of the 1857 text 's'enivre des splendeurs de sa propre vertu', the *docteur grandis-simus* had been shown seven years earlier drunk on the no less imaginary splendours of his own *intellect*: it is surely no accident that he ends up as the *chiffonnier* begins, *staggering* blindly 'à travers | Les champs, sans distinguer les étés des hivers', pursued by laughing children rather than by the 'mouchards ténébreux' who dog the ragpicker's steps. Two other texts of the 1840s or early 1850s have a possible bearing on 'Châtiment de l'orgueil'. The Doctor's fate may be seen as a specific illustration of the general thesis, advanced in *L'École païenne*, that 'la spécialisation excessive d'une faculté aboutit au néant', and the punishment that is visited upon him is akin to that suffered by the artist who gives himself over to 'le goût immodéré de la forme': 'Il a banni la raison de son cœur, et, par un juste châtiment, la raison refuse de rentrer en lui' (OC, ii. 48–9). Finally, the explosion of laughter with which the poem concludes suggests a possible connection with *De l'essence du rire*, a text which, as we have seen, Baudelaire had almost certainly drafted in its essentials before 1848 but which must from the outset have contained at least the germs of the moral and metaphysical pessimism commonly attributed to Baudelaire's post-1851 despair

and to his reading of de Maistre. If the Doctor himself is an unmistakably Satanic figure—Satanic, that is, not in the republican
sense of revolutionary Lucifer but in the standard Christian sense
of one who, as Baudelaire says of Melmoth in *De l'essence du rire*,
contains within him 'un côté faible, abject, antidivin et anti-
lumineux'—then the children who laugh after him are themselves
'des Satans en herbe', gratuitously taking pleasure in another's
(albeit merited) discomfiture (OC, ii. 531 and 535). *Qui veut faire
l'ange fait la bête*: by the end of 'Châtiment de l'orgueil' both the
doctor angelicus and his young tormentors have been reduced to
the same sub-human level, all of them just so many 'bêtes de la rue'
(l. 22), an expression which, in the context of the events of 1848–50,
takes on a particularly heavy ironic colouring.

The importance of 'Châtiment de l'orgueil' is that, although it
was written some time between October 1848 and June 1850, it
already contains more than the lineaments of the Augustinian–
Jansenist world-view which, it is often claimed, Baudelaire only
espoused in the wake of, and as a desperate response to, the
Bonapartist coup of December 1851. By publishing 'Châtiment de
l'orgueil' alongside 'Le Vin des honnêtes gens' in *Le Magasin des
familles* in June 1850, Baudelaire may already have been trying to
give an 'objective' or 'stereoscopic' view of revolution by juxtaposing two texts that are thematically related but written from antithetical ideological or ethical standpoints. In 'Le Vin des honnêtes
gens', that supreme poetic expression of Baudelaire republican-
humanist naturalism of 1848, all is sunlight, fecundity, fraternity,
and creative exchange between man and nature. Most strikingly,
too, the poem has, as we have seen, an implicitly hubristic conclusion (nowhere condemned by Baudelaire) as 'la poésie', the child
of the union of man and wine, rises up 'vers Dieu comme un grand
papillon', less in adoration, it would seem, than in revolt against
the creator of 'un monde où l'action n'est pas la sœur du rêve'.
'Châtiment de l'orgueil' is a precise inversion of its companion-
text, confronting it as negative to positive. Hubris now is punished,
the sun is swallowed up by darkness ('L'éclat de ce soleil d'un crêpe
se voila' (l. 16)), harmony and order are succeeded by chaos ('Tout
le chaos roula dans cette intelligence' (l. 17)), speech by silence and
ecstatic fellowship and communion by total self-immured isolation
('Comme dans un caveau dont la clef est perdue' (l. 21)). Everything suggests that the two texts have been coupled together as

contrasting panels of a political and moral diptych. If 'Le Vin des honnêtes gens' is the poem *par excellence* of the Republic's springtime, with all its vainglorious hopes and dreams, then, just as surely, 'Châtiment de l'orgueil' is the poem of its post-June nemesis. The Republic and its supporters have sinned and received due and condign punishment: on the evidence of 'Châtiment de l'orgueil', Baudelaire had reached an essentially de Maistrian verdict on the men of *quarante-huit* some considerable time—conceivably as much as two years—*before* the likely date of his discovery of the author of *Du Pape* and *Les Soirées de Saint-Pétersbourg* some time in 1851.

We may now venture some tentative conclusions. While Baudelaire clearly did not share—at least not when the article first appeared—Saint-René Taillandier's reactionary political perspective (and, in particular, his negative view of Proudhon), reading 'L'Athéïsme allemand et le socialisme français' some time in late 1848 or early 1849 evidently enabled him to clarify his view of the turbulent events of the previous nine to twelve months. In particular, the story of Simon de Tournai offered him a set of 'objective correlatives' whereby he could formulate—indirectly, by way of a fable or homily without obvious political reference—ideas and feelings to which, for a variety of internal and external reasons, he could not yet give satisfactory direct poetical expression. By the end of 1848, Baudelaire could clearly see what the 'sublime illusion' of February–March—an illusion which he had shared in some large measure and which, on the evidence of 'Actuellement', he was not yet ready to abjure—had led to. What, however, he now condemned was not the hopes and dreams of 1848 themselves, but rather the belief, in the later formulation of *Le Poème du haschisch* that Baudelaire took from Barbier (OC, i. 402), that it was possible to 'emporter le paradis d'un seul coup' and, like Simon de Tournai, rise Icarus-like on the wings of rhetoric or dialectic alone 'vers les célestes gloires', bypassing the need for the determined, cumulative work on which all of Baudelaire's writings of the Second Republic insist so strongly. By publishing 'Châtiment de l'orgueil' alongside 'Le Vin des honnêtes gens' in June 1850, Baudelaire provided a critical corrective to the latter text's considerable hubristic potential without, it would seem, necessarily repudiating its optimistic vision as such which, on the evidence of *Du vin et du haschisch* and *Pierre*

Dupont, he would continue to espouse in some form right up to the fall of the Republic itself. But 'Châtiment de l'orgueil' suggests how, in condemning the 'doctors' of the Republic in 1850, Baudelaire was already pointed in the direction of the de Maistrian world-view that he would make his own in the years following the Bonapartist coup; the line that separates denouncing Republicans from denouncing the Republic is a fine one indeed and, if Baudelaire had not crossed it in 1850, the probability is that he had done so— at least in so far as his 'official' ideology was concerned—by the time 'Châtiment de l'orgueil' appeared before a wider public in 1857. Baudelaire's later repudiation of the Revolution of 1848, as well as of the revolutionary 'doctors' he held responsible for its undoing, was not, therefore, the fruit of some 'conversion' undergone after the December coup but a resurfacing, in a heightened and extended form, of an attitude already present in 1848 itself. 'De Maistre et Edgar Poe m'ont appris à raisonner' (OC, i. 669): how to think, not *what* to think. There was nothing Baudelaire found in the author of *Du Pape*, no more than in the author of *The Poetic Principle*, that he had not felt or thought at some level years before his actual encounter with their works,[11] and it is as evidence of Baudelaire's *maistrianisme avant de Maistre* that 'Châtiment de l'orgueil'—arguably the worst poem in *Les Fleurs du mal*—takes on its unexpected significance.

---

[11] See Baudelaire's comments on his first encounter with Poe's work in his letter to Armand Fraisse of 18 Feb. 1860 (C, i. 676).

8

The Revenge of Pluviosus:
Baudelaire and the Agony
of the Second Republic

On 9 April 1851—by design or coincidence his thirtieth birthday
—Baudelaire at last published, under the long-announced title
Les Limbes, a sequence of eleven sonnets in *Le Messager de
l'Assemblée*, the journal in which *Du vin et du haschisch* had
appeared the previous month. The eleven poems in question are, in
the order in which they appeared in *Le Messager*: 'Le Spleen'
(1857: 'Spleen', 'Pluviôse, irrité . . .'), 'Le Mauvais Moine',
'L'Idéal', 'Le Spleen' (1857: 'Le Mort joyeux'), 'Les Chats', 'La
Mort des artistes', 'La Mort des amants', 'Le Tonneau de la Haine',
'La Béatrix' (1857: 'De profundis clamavi'), 'Le Spleen' (1857: 'La
Cloche fêlée'), and 'Les Hiboux'. Some months later, at some
indeterminable date between, according to Claude Pichois (C, i.
803), September 1851 and January 1852, Baudelaire sent Gautier
two 'paquets' containing twelve poems for publication in the
recently founded *Revue de Paris*: 'Les Deux Crépuscules' (1857:
'Le Crépuscule du matin' and 'Le Crépuscule du soir'), 'La Mendiante rousse', 'La Rançon', 'Le Vin des chiffonniers', 'Le Reniement
de saint Pierre', 'La Caravane des Bohémiens' (1857: 'Bohémiens
en voyage'), 'La Mort des pauvres', 'L'Outre de la volupté' (1857:
'Les Métamorphoses du vampire'), 'La Fontaine de sang', 'L'Artiste
inconnu' (1857: 'Le Guignon'), and 'Voyage à Cythère' (1857: 'Un
voyage à Cythère'). Gautier seems to have rejected all these sub-
missions except the most controversial and inflammatory of all, 'Le
Reniement de saint Pierre', which, astoundingly, he published in
the *Revue de Paris* in October 1852, along with 'L'Homme libre et
la mer' (1857: 'L'Homme et la mer'), which Baudelaire presumably
sent to him under separate cover after his other manuscripts had
been turned down. 'Les Deux Crépuscules' were published in *La*

Semaine théâtrale on 1 February 1852, so that if one adds to his publications of 1851–2 those of 1850 ('Châtiment de l'orgueil', 'Le Vin des honnêtes gens', and 'Lesbos'), Baudelaire—who, as Prarond wrote in the preface to his anthology *De quelques écrivains nouveaux* (1852), had long enjoyed 'cette rare fortune, en récitant pour lui seul ou quelques amis de la grande poésie, d'obtenir presque une renommée sans publier un seul vers'[1]—had, by the end of 1852, established a limited reputation for himself as a published poet to set beside the undoubted stature he had acquired—in, admittedly, a restricted circle—as the author of what Prarond called his 'catéchisme de la peinture moderne', the *Salon de 1846*. What Baudelaire had published by the time the Second Republic was officially transformed into the Second Empire (2 December 1852) represented, however, only a tiny selection of the poems he had ready, or almost ready, for publication. It was, as we have seen, some time in the autumn or winter of 1851 that Asselineau was shown the professionally transcribed two-volume manuscript on which the first edition of *Les Fleurs du mal* would be based, thus raising the question of what principles, if any, governed the choice of texts that were published or submitted for publication in 1851 and 1852. Those principles, I shall argue in this chapter, were largely if not exclusively political principles. If Baudelaire published or sought to publish these poems rather than the many others he might have published, it was, I believe, principally because he was anxious to appear as a republican poet, and as a radical republican poet at that. I have already suggested political readings of 'Châtiment de l'orgueil', 'Le Vin des honnêtes gens', 'Le Vin des chiffonniers', 'Le Reniement de saint Pierre', 'La Rançon', and 'Les Hiboux': the task of the present chapter is to investigate the political resonances of the *Limbes* sequence as a whole and the possible political meanings of some, at least, of the poems sent to Gautier (the so-called 'douze poèmes'), most notably 'Les Deux Crépuscules' and 'Voyage à Cythère'.

Such an investigation immediately runs into the inevitable and predictable problem of dating the poems in question. Of the twenty-four poems of 1851–2 (*Les Limbes*, the 'douze poèmes',

---

[1] Quoted BPZ, 302. Prarond—whose 'écrivains nouveaux' included Le Vavasseur and Chennevières as well as established figures like Banville and Mürger—was obviously unaware of the publication of *Les Limbes* in *Le Messager*.

and 'L'Homme libre et la mer'), only three—'La Rançon', 'La Mort des pauvres'[2] and 'Le Reniement de saint Pierre'—can be assigned beyond reasonable doubt exclusively to the Second Republic period. A dozen or more may be confidently said to have been composed or, failing that, drafted in all their essentials, before 1848: 'Les Chats' (cited by Champfleury in November 1847), 'Le Mauvais Moine', 'L'Idéal', 'La Béatrix' ('De profundis clamavi'), 'Le Vin des chiffonniers', 'Voyage à Cythère', 'Le Crépuscule du matin' (all of them recalled, in some form or other, by Prarond[3]), to which may be added, on stylistic, thematic, or other grounds, 'La Mendiante rousse', 'L'Outre de la volupté' ('Les Métamorphoses du vampire'), 'La Mort des artistes', 'La Mort des amants', 'Le Spleen' ('Le Mort joyeux'), and 'La Caravane' ('Bohémiens en voyage'). With the remaining eight poems—'Le Crépuscule du soir', 'L'Artiste inconnu' ('Le Guignon'), 'L'Homme libre et la mer', 'La Fontaine de sang', 'Le Spleen' ('Pluviôse . . .'), 'Le Tonneau de la Haine', 'Le Spleen' ('La Cloche fêlée'), and 'Les Hiboux'—there are three equally plausible alternatives. Each of these poems could have been composed in its entirety before 1848 or exclusively within the Second Republic period; alternatively, Baudelaire could have substantially revised a pre-1848 draft during the Second Republic, giving it, if need be, a political inflexion that it did not originally possess. Even this triple classification does not exhaust the problems of dating—and thus of interpreting—the poems of 1851–2, for, as we have seen in the case of 'Le Vin des chiffonniers', it was perfectly possible for a poem drafted as long ago as 1841–3 to acquire a whole range of new resonances after 1848 without the text itself undergoing any change whatsoever. Such could well be the case with one of the major poems to concern us in this chapter, 'Voyage à Cythère', which Prarond was practically certain he had heard in or before 1846 and whose 'point de départ', for which we have Baudelaire's own testimony (see OC, i. 1069–70), was in the extracts from his future *Voyage en Orient* that Nerval published in *L'Artiste* in June and August 1844. Baudelaire clearly read Nerval's description of the debased modern version,

---

[2] On 'La Mort des pauvres', see OC, i. 1089.

[3] BET, 25–7. It should be stressed that Prarond is not always totally sure about the poems he heard in the 1840s, especially after 1843 when he and Baudelaire were much less close. It seems practically certain, however, that all of the poems mentioned here existed at least in draft form prior to 1848.

Cerigo, of the Cytherea of old when or shortly after it first appeared, and it is reasonable to assume that it made sufficient immediate impact for him to draft a version of the poem forthwith. But even if that version were *essentially the same* as that sent to Gautier in 1851–2, the convulsive changes that he and France as a whole had undergone since 1848 would have injected into it a series of new meanings that it could not have possessed when first drafted in, say, 1844–5. What began as a non-political (or, to use my preferred term, 'pre-political') expression of personal sexual desolation could, by 1851–2, have been transformed by events, but without itself necessarily undergoing any textual change, into a coded political statement of sufferings and revulsions that go far beyond (but still include) the sexual and also, in keeping with the stated programme of *Les Limbes*,[4] reach out beyond Baudelaire himself to embrace the whole of his generation.

'Le Spleen' ('Pluviôse irrité contre la ville entière . . .')[5]

As indicated above, 'Le Spleen' ('Pluviôse . . .')—hereafter referred to by its 1857 title 'Spleen'—is one of the texts of 1851–2 that could have been composed wholly before 1848 or wholly between 1848 and (in this case, early) 1851 or be a post-1848 revision or rewriting of a pre-1848 text. If I treat it here as a product, in its essentials, of the Second Republic period itself, it is principally because it lends itself—I hope without distortion—to the kind of political reading I shall be attempting, but also on the grounds that it seems to me unlikely (though not, of course, unthinkable) that Baudelaire would have begun a poem by invoking the revolutionary month of Pluviôse unless a revolutionary context existed to give point and pertinence to that invocation; in any case, even if Pluviôse were present in a pre-1848 draft, the circumstances of 1848–51 would obviously endow the image with a set of explicit political associations that would have been, for both poet and putative reader alike, barely discernible in the primitive text. In support of a post-

---

[4] A second manuscript of 'Voyage à Cythère', of uncertain date, makes it clear that the poem was intended to form part of *Les Limbes* (OC, i. 1069).

[5] Substantial parts of the discussion that follows first appeared in Richard D. E. Burton, 'Baudelaire and the Agony of the Second Republic: "Spleen" (LXXV) ("Pluviôse, irrité . . .")', *Modern Language Review*, 81/3 (1986), 600–11.

1848 dating, I would also mention, parenthetically and without attaching undue importance to it, the possibility that the image of the 'dame de pique' in the sonnet's final tercet—an image which no editor or exegete has yet fully explained—may have been suggested to Baudelaire by the translation (by Mérimée) of Pushkin's *Queen of Spades* that was published in the *Revue des Deux Mondes* on 15 July 1849.[6] The links between Pushkin's tale and Baudelaire's poem—discussed in the notes below[7]—could not, of themselves, assign 'Spleen' beyond doubt to the Second Republic period; taken with other contextual evidence, however, they do, in my view, make it most likely that the poem as we have it is essentially a post-revolutionary rather than pre-revolutionary work.

LE SPLEEN

Pluviôse irrité contre la ville entière
De son urne à grands flots verse un froid ténébreux
Aux pâles habitants du voisin cimetière
Et la mortalité sur les faubourgs brumeux.

Mon chien sur le carreau cherchant une litière
Agite sans repos son corps maigre et galeux;
L'ombre d'un vieux poète erre dans la gouttière
Avec la triste voix d'un fantôme frileux.

Le bourdon se lamente, et la bûche enfumée
Accompagne en fausset la pendule enrhumée,
Cependant qu'en un jeu plein de sales parfums,

---

[6] ' "La Dame de Pique" de Pouchkine, par Prosper Mérimée', *Revue des Deux Mondes* (15 July 1849), 185–206.

[7] Pushkin's *Queen of Spades*, it will be recalled, concerns a young gambler called Hermann who kills the decrepit Countess Anna Fedotovna as he forces from her the secret of winning at cards that has mysteriously been given her. After a number of wins, Hermann eventually loses when the card he believed to be an ace turns out to be a queen of spades. The crucial passage in Mérimée's translation runs as follows: 'Hermann tressaillit. Au lieu d'un as, il avait devant lui une dame de pique. Il n'en pouvait croire ses yeux, et ne comprenait pas comment il avait pu se méprendre de la sorte. Les yeux attachés sur cette carte funeste, il lui sembla que la dame de pique clignait de l'œil et lui souriait d'un air railleur. Il reconnut avec horreur une ressemblance étrange entre cette dame de pique et la défunte comtesse . . .—Maudite vieille, s'ecria-t-il épouvanté' (p. 206). Although the queen of spades is indeed the 'héritage fatal' of an old woman, the Countess is—'pieds gonflés' (p. 197) apart—anything but 'hydropique', being described variously as 'ce spectre cassé', a 'momie ambulante' and as 'toute jaune, toute ratatinée, les lèvres pendantes' (pp. 195–7). None the less, Baudelaire could have derived the idea of an animated playing-card from Pushkin's story.

Héritage fatal d'une vieille hydropique,
Le beau valet de coeur et la dame de pique
Causent sinistrement de leurs amours défunts.

(Text of 1851[8])

To begin the poem—particularly if it was written, as I am tentatively suggesting, some time between July 1849 and February 1851—by invoking the revolutionary month of Pluviôse (the fifth month of the revolutionary year, coinciding with the period 20 January to 18 February[9]) immediately situates it ironically within a specific historical context and its accompanying political discourse. The replacement, by virtue of the decree of 'octidi, 1ʳᵉ décade de brumaire an II' (otherwise Tuesday, 29 October 1793), of the old Gregorian by the new revolutionary calendar signified, Michelet wrote in Book XIV of his *Histoire de la Révolution Française* (1852), nothing less than a 'changement de religion' or, more accurately, the institution of a secularized man- and nature-centred concept of time in place of one that had its pivot and *raison d'être* in God and religious belief and ritual. Summarizing this revolution in man's being-in-the-world, Michelet argued that, thanks to the new calendar,

la terre, pour la première fois, répondit au ciel dans les révolutions du temps. Et le monde du travail agissant aussi dans les mesures rationnelles que donnait la terre elle-même, l'homme se trouva en rapport complet avec sa grande habitation. Il vit la raison au ciel, et la raison ici-bas. A lui de la mettre en lui-même. Elle absente, le chaos régnait. L'œuvre divine, brouillée par l'ignorance barbare, semblait un caprice, un hasard sans

---

[8] In an otherwise interesting discussion of 'Spleen' (LXXV) ('Baudelaire and the City: 1848 and the Inscription of Hegemony', in Francis Barker *et al.* (eds.), *1848: The Sociology of Literature* (Univ. of Essex, 1978), 225–41), Colin Mercer wrongly maintains that the original (1851) text of the poem had 'vie' rather than 'ville' in the opening line; in fact, 'vie' appears only in the posthumous (1868) edition of *Les Fleurs du mal* and is almost certainly a printer's error (see Pichois's note, OC, i. 974). The 'displacement of meaning from "life" to "town", semantically radically different but phonemically similar' would indeed, as Mercer states (p. 232), be 'crucial' if it had taken place; unfortunately for Mercer's argument, it did not.

[9] Needless to say, 'Pluviôse' does not so much denote the February Revolution as a historical event as connote Revolution as a concept. The February Revolution in fact began on 22 February, in the revolutionary month of Ventôse. It is possible that the image of Pluviôse with his 'urne' was suggested by an actual illustration of a revolutionary calendar known to Baudelaire; all the representations of Pluviôse that I have seen, however, depict a female figure and one that is, one might add, neither 'vieille' nor 'hydropique'.

Dieu. État impie, objection permanente contre toute religion. La science, à la fin des temps, se charge d'y répondre en rétablissant l'harmonie, en détrônant le chaos, en intronisant la Sagesse.[10]

No passage could better bring out the multiple ironies unleashed by Baudelaire's using the revolutionary month Pluviôse to set not merely 'Spleen' but—because it is the first word of the first sonnet of his sequence—the whole of *Les Limbes* in a complex relationship of imitation and opposition to *L'An II* and the heroic traditions of the First Republic. If the institution of the republican calendar in 1793 signified, as Michelet claimed, the creation of a rational man-centred cosmos out of a chaos of unreason and superstition, the return of Pluviôse as the vindictive rain-god Pluviosus in 1849–50 marks a regression to, precisely, the chaos or limbo from which, for a brief time, the *journées de février* seemed to deliver France and its people but eighteen months or two years previously. Far from consecrating the harmony of man and what Michelet called 'sa grande habitation', Pluviosus presides rather over a condition of chronic homelessness in which not even the cemetery's 'pâles habitants' are 'at home' in their graves and in which, as Michael Riffaterre has shown in a justly famous discussion of the poem, the values of inside and outside are inverted and *maison* is systematically transformed into *non-maison*.[11] Furthermore, that Man whom, according to Michelet, the revolutionary calendar had installed at the centre of the universe as the sole measure of Time has now been 'dethroned' like God before him. 'Spleen', as we shall see, is before all else a poem of the dissolution of the subject, of a world which no longer has a centre either in God, King, Republic, or Citizen (nor yet in Emperor), in which all individuated forms are slowly liquefying amidst the remorseless rain and all-encompassing fog.

'Spleen', then, belongs not to the heroic radicalism of 1793 but to the torpid aftermath of the botched and mimetic revolution of 1848. The *faubourgs* that ignited with militant fervour in 1789, 1793, 1830, 1832, and in February and June 1848 are now 'brumeux', shrouded in indifference and despair, their ardour doused by the post-June repression and the right-wing votes that had poured 'à grands flots' from the *urnes de scrutin* of December

[10] Michelet, *Histoire de la Révolution Française* (Robert Laffont, 1979), ii. 623–4.
[11] Michael Riffaterre, *Semiotics of Poetry* (Indiana Univ. Press, Bloomington, Ind., 1978), 67–70.

1848, and the poet himself who had experienced a singular 'ivresse' in communion with the crowds of February and June is once more driven back into the capsule of a privatized and solitary existence. The swirling rain that drenches the whole of Paris is the rain that Baudelaire had already described in *La Fanfarlo*:

Le temps était noir comme la tombe, et le vent qui berçait des monceaux de nuages faisait de leurs cahotements ruisseler une averse de grêle et de pluie. Une grande tempête faisait trembler les mansardes et gémir les clochers; le ruisseau, lit funèbre où s'en vont les billets doux et les orgies de la veille, charriait en bouillonnant ses mille secrets aux égouts; *la mortalité* s'abattait joyeusement sur les hôpitaux . . . (OC, i. 574, italics added)

This text in its turn cannibalizes a poem of 1841 entitled 'Un jour de pluie' of which Baudelaire is surely part-author at the very least:

> Les nuages sont noirs, et le vent qui les berce
> Les heurte, et de leur choc fait ruisseler l'averse.
> Leurs arceaux, se courbant sur les toits ardoisés,
> Ressemblent aux piliers de draps noirs pavoisés,
> Quand, de la nef en deuil qui pleure et qui surplombe,
> Le dôme s'arrondit comme une large tombe.
> Le ruisseau, lit funèbre où s'en vont les dégouts,
> Charrie en bouillonnant les secrets des égouts;
> Il bat chaque maison de son flot délétère,
> Court jaunir de limon la Seine qu'il altère,
> Et présente sa vague aux genoux du passant.
> Chacun, nous coudoyant, sur le trottoir glissant,
> Egoïste et brutal, passe et nous éclabousse,
> Ou, pour courir plus vite, en s'éloignant nous pousse.
> Partout fange, déluge, obscurité du ciel:
> Noir tableau qu'eût rêvé le noir Ezéchiel![12]

As we have seen, Baudelaire's most strongly *démoc-soc* poems of the Second Republic period are essentially celebrations of 'ce père nourricier, ennemi des chloroses', the sun, who 'remplit les cerveaux et les ruches de miel', 'rajeunit les porteurs de béquilles' ('Le Soleil') and, above all, ripens the grapes that will produce the 'fils sacré du Soleil' itself, the rich red wine of revolution which, in February–March 1848, had briefly bound all Parisians together in a communalistic carnival: now, in contrast, the rain of reaction

---

[12] OC, i. 1254. For a discussion of the attribution of these and other *vers retrouvés*, see OC, i. 1249–53.

divides them from each other, sets them once again in individual-
istic competition, enclosing each in the prison of a solitary ego.
Unlike the sunlit earthly paradise celebrated in 'L'Âme du vin', the
in-between world of *Les Limbes* is lit, if at all, by a 'soleil oblique'
('Les Hiboux') or 'un soleil sans chaleur' ('La Béatrix', cf. 'ce soleil
de glace' in the same poem) that 'hovers' for six months over 'un
pays plus nu que la terre polaire' while 'les six autres mois la nuit
couvre la terre'. In the circumstances, it matters little that half or
more of the sonnets in *Les Limbes* had probably been completed
before 1848. In publishing them in the spring of 1851—so different
from the spring of three years before—Baudelaire was indicating as
clearly as he could that the limbo-world they expressed had, after
the brief interlude of February–March 1848, been thoroughly and
inexorably restored. There was only one difference, one that made
the situation of 1849–50 infinitely worse than that, say, of 1845–6:
it was no longer a monarchy but a nominal republic that held sway
over the frozen, sodden, or fog-bound wasteland of France at
mid-century.

With the demise of the revolutionary calendar as a meaningful
system of measuring time—attempts to reintroduce it in 1848 were,
it appears, greeted with derision[13]—Pluviôse has taken on a grotesque, menacing life of his own as a pseudo-classical neo-pagan
godling pouring forth unending torrents of rain from an urn that
could be derived iconographically from an illustrated republican
calendar Baudelaire had seen or, more likely, from the conventional attribute of Aquarius, the eleventh sign of the zodiac which,
by chance or design, covers exactly the same period as the revolutionary month Pluviôse: such a link would yield not merely a nicely
hidden play of words on 'Verseau' / 'verse'[14] but also a further set
of ironies in that Aquarius, according to a modern dictionary of
symbols, traditionally represents 'la solidarité collective, la co-

---

[13] See e.g. the rejection by the *Courrier de Loir-et-Cher* on 6 Mar. 1848 of the
attempt by 'quelques personnes' to 'rétablir les bizarreries de notre révolution': 'Ils
voudraient qu'on reprît le calendrier républicain, qu'on obligeât à se servir des
qualifications républicaines, etc. etc. Nous pensons qu'à cet égard rien ne doit être et
ne sera changé. La forme tue souvent le fond et le ridicule écrase les objets les plus
sains et les plus sérieux' (quoted Maurice Dommanget, 'Velléités de rétablissement
du calendrier révolutionnaire', *Annales historiques de la Révolution Française*, 138
(1955), 67–8).
[14] The link between 'Verseau' and 'verse' is made by Paolo Budini in his article
'Sul "bourdon" polisemico del primo "Spleen"', *Francofonia*, 1 (1981), 110.

opération, la fraternité et le détachement des choses matérielles',[15] the qualities of February 1848 that 1849–50 so conspicuously lacks. The incongruity of a pseudo-Roman rain-god lowering, complete with amphora, above a mid-nineteenth-century metropolis shows Baudelaire parodying to subversive effect the neo-paganism that would be his target in *L'École païenne* written, as we have seen, immediately before or immediately after the Bonapartist coup and published in *La Semaine théâtrale* in January 1852:

Depuis quelque temps, j'ai tout l'Olympe à mes trousses, et j'en souffre beaucoup; je reçois des dieux sur la tête comme on reçoit des cheminées. Il me semble que je fais un mauvais rêve et qu'une foule d'idoles de bois, de fer, d'or et d'argent, tombent avec moi, me poursuivent dans ma chute, me cognent et me brisent la tête et les reins. Impossible de faire un pas, de prononcer un mot, sans buter contre un fait païen.

In *L'École païenne* it is the grotesque inappropriateness of classical mythology, themes, and imagery to the realities of the modern world that is the general object of Baudelaire's invective, but the most striking particular instance of that inappropriateness adduced in the article involves not only the modern city as the celebration of 'l'héroïsme de la vie moderne' in the *Salon de 1846* might lead us to expect but, still more significantly, the modern city during a time of revolutionary turmoil:

La ville est sens dessus dessous. Les boutiques se ferment. Les femmes font à la hâte leurs provisions, les rues se dépavent, tous les cœurs sont serrés par l'angoisse d'un grand événement. Le pavé sera prochainement inondé de sang.—Vous rencontrez un animal plein de béatitude; il a sous le bras des bouquins étranges et hiéroglyphiques.—Et vous, lui dites-vous, quel parti prenez-vous?—Mon cher, répond-il d'une voix douce, je viens de découvrir de nouveaux renseignements très curieux sur le mariage d'Isis et d'Osiris.—Que le diable vous emporte! Qu'Isis et Osiris fassent beaucoup d'enfants et qu'ils nous f—— la paix!

'Combien prête-t-on sur une lyre au Mont-de-Piété?' (OC, ii. 46–7). Such absurd conjunctions and disjunctions of the pseudo-classical and the modern-urban were evidently something of a Baudelairean *idée fixe* around this time. A similar ironic application of pastiche classicism to modern Paris is to be found in a fragment of an undated letter to Gautier which Claude Pichois

---

[15] *Dictionnaire des symboles*, ed. Jean Chevalier (Robert Laffont, 1969), 794.

assigns to the summer of 1852. Once more a recent history of revolutionary upheaval is sardonically alluded to:

Cette année, Paris est rissolé; Phébus-Apollon *verse* tous les jours plusieurs casserolées de plomb fondu sur les malheureux qui se promènent le long des boulevards. Si j'étais au ciel, j'appellerais ceux de l'endroit à faire des barricades contre ce Dieu sans-gêne. (C, i. 206, italics added)

'Urnfuls' of rain in January–February followed by 'saucepans' overflowing with incandescent heat in the dog days of summer: assuredly, the Parisians of the Second Republic and its aftermath were as much victims, climatically, of the vindictive excesses of the demi-gods of rain and sun as they were, politically, of the inadequacies, machinations, and greeds of the pseudo-Girondins and -Jacobins who competed for power in the early months of 1848 until, finally, a bogus Bonaparte appeared like some absurd *Deus ex machina* to put an end to their squabbles. Baudelaire's Pluviôse stands in the same relationship to his prototype of 1793 as Daumier's caricatures in *Histoire ancienne*—discussed with evident approval of their subversiveness in *L'École païenne*—of 'le bouillant Achille, et le prudent Ulysse, et la sage Pénélope, et Télémaque, ce grand dadais' (OC, ii. 46) do to their heroic originals in the pages of the *Iliad* and *Odyssey*. Daumier, Baudelaire wrote elsewhere, was to be commended for having 'spat upon' or 'blasphemed' not against antiquity as such—'car nul ne sent mieux que lui les grandeurs anciennes'—but against 'la fausse antiquité' (OC, ii. 556), that alienating pseudo-classicism which, according to the *Salon de 1846*, prevents modern urban man from perceiving 'une beauté nouvelle et particulière, qui est celle, ni d'Achille, ni d'Agamemnon', but that of himself, his city, and his fellow citizens (OC, ii. 496). By inscribing Pluviôse as a kind of parodic tutelary god at the head of his poetic sequence, Baudelaire contrived to highlight the *décalage* between the neoclassic forms of 'official' art, be it of the political Left or Right, and the contemporary social and political realities it effectively concealed, and thus introduced at the outset of the first of a whole series of dissociations of form and content, signifiers and signifieds, which, as we shall see, constitutes one of the recurring motifs of the whole poem.

In the course of his transplantation from the First Republic to the Second, from the heroic 1790s to the anticlimactic and repressive 1850s, 'Pluviôse' has undergone a fundamental mutation. No longer a conventional designation of a traditionally rainy time of year, nor even a pseudo-classical personification of rain itself, Pluviôse has become a mean and petty-minded demi-god, 'irrité' with the city and its inhabitants rather than 'enragé' or 'furieux', and armed not with the thunderbolts of a Zeus or a Yahweh but with a swirling, remorseless, endlessly corrosive drizzle that saturates and extinguishes the very heart of the city's vital being, exciting not revolt but sullen, impotent submission. Whereas Baudelaire's 'revolutionary' poems of the 1848 period—most notably 'Les Litanies de Satan' and 'Abel et Caïn' but also, as we have seen, most of the 'Vin' sequence in *Les Fleurs du mal*—pit Man and his antitheistic allies, Lucifer and Cain, against the tyrannical order of a bourgeois Cosmocrat, here the demi-god of a spurious revolution has turned in malignant irritation against the very city that brought him into being. It would be difficult to contrive a more telling image of the situation of the Second Republic as it found itself in 1849–50, the likely date of 'Spleen''s composition. Scarcely had the Bourgeois Monarchy been overthrown by the combined forces of 'le peuple' and middle-class republicans than the luminaries of this latter group—the Lamartines, the Marrasts, the Cavaignacs, even the Victor Hugos—had, with the backing of the overwhelming majority of the possessing classes, turned, *in the name of the Revolutionary Republic itself*, against the 'peuple' which alone gave them legitimacy and power. June followed February and December June; in the face of repeated betrayals by the politicians, working-class morale collapsed, so that on the would-be revolutionary *journée* of 13 June 1849 only a handful of middle-class radicals were prepared to defy the increasingly repressive and right-wing Republic in Paris. More and more, Parisian workers withdrew into their *faubourgs* from which not even the Bonapartist *putsch* could bring them to defend the Republic. By the time Baudelaire wrote 'Spleen' some time in 1849–50, the Republic, with its middle- and lower-class support crumbling, and threatened from the Right by organized and aggressive Bonapartism, was indeed at odds with 'la ville entière', even if, in rural areas, support for it had been consolidated by the highly effective *démoc-soc* propaganda campaign launched after the electoral catastrophe of December 1848. As a minor contributor to that campaign, Baudelaire had, in *Du vin et du haschisch*, assumed an optimistic public stance *pour les besoins de la cause* as he would, four months after the publication of *Les Limbes*, in the essay on Dupont. *Les Limbes* as a whole, and the lead-poem 'Spleen' in particular, bears witness to Baudelaire's private despair with a Republic that had so comprehensively betrayed and turned against its revolutionary origins. In common with so many radicals and ex-radicals of his generation, Baudelaire retreated privately into the limbo-world of 'Spleen' even as, in his outward life and public writings, he did what little he could to save a Republic in which, deep down, he no longer believed. It is this collective experience of betrayal, thwarted hope, and fear for the future that provides 'Spleen' with its specific context and makes of it, as Baudelaire always intended that it should, rather more than the purely individual statement that it at first appears to be.

In an interesting discussion of 'Spleen', Victor Brombert has noted that 'faubourgs' 'suggèrent un ensemble qui ne saurait se définir, se délimiter' and that there could be no more appropriate setting for a poem whose central theme is, he claims, the erosion of personality: 'Traumatisant et anesthésiant à la fois, le complexe urbain reste anonyme.'[16] Brombert is only partly correct, for he seems to confuse the traditional and anything but indefinite and anonymous *faubourgs* of 'le vieux Paris'—particularly the Faubourg Saint-Antoine, the Faubourg du Temple and the Faubourg Saint-Denis which collectively constituted the old city's revolutionary heartland—with the comparatively undifferentiated and depersonalized *banlieue* whose existence dates from the 1860s at the earliest. What is undeniable, however, is that, at the time Baudelaire was writing, the old *faubourgs* were, as a result of complex social, political, and structural changes I have discussed elsewhere,[17] progressively losing the highly individuated, self-contained 'urban village' character that had hitherto been theirs: the process would be accentuated and, above all, accelerated by the 'Haussmannization' of Paris in the 1850s and 1860s, but its origins undoubtedly lie in the pre-1850 period. In 1864 Auguste Cochin commented as follows on the destruction of the distinctive personality of the various *arrondissements* brought about by the increasing economic and administrative unification of the city: 'L'arrondissement a perdu son territoire, ses rues, sa milice, ses droits électoraux, son

[16] Victor Brombert, 'Lyrisme et dépersonnalisation: L'Exemple de Baudelaire ("Spleen" LXXV)', *Romantisme*, 6 (1973), 31.
[17] See Burton, *The Context of Baudelaire's 'Le Cygne'* (Durham Modern Language Series, Durham, 1980), 35–47.

numéro, sa vie propre: toute vie est retournée au centre. Ainsi, par des réformes successives, on en est venu à ce point: il y a encore dans Paris des habitants, il n'y a plus de citoyens.'[18] Once the citizen of a clearly defined, personalized locality, the Parisian of the transitional 1840–1860 period came increasingly to inhabit a vast homogeneous urban mass, a faceless sprawl that condemned him to facelessness. As the life of the city retreated to the centre, so the ex-citizen retreated into himself. With the disintegration of the civic framework that bound individuals together as citizens, the Parisian was, in the view of many contemporaries, in the process of becoming a ghost-like, one-dimensional figure, no longer at home in his native city, in many ways scarcely distinguishable from the 'pâles habitants du voisin cimetière'—that cemetery which could well be the dreaded *fosse commune* evoked in 'Spleen' (LXXVI) ('J'ai plus de souvenirs . . .') where, in the decade 1838–48, no less than 79 per cent of Parisians were consigned to definitive anonymity and oblivion:[19]

C'est là que les cercueils des malheureux morts sans ressources sont juxtaposés, c'est jetés, c'est empilés qu'il faudrait dire, sans un pouce de terre entre eux, sans une autre séparation que quelques planches à peine jointes. Là, le vieillard, l'enfant, le débauché, la vierge sont accumulés pêle-mêle, et, chose horrible à dire, à penser plus encore, quand les frêles ais de sapin s'entr'ouvrent, sous la double action de l'humidité et des gaz méphitiques qui les repoussent, les chairs se mêlent et les ossements se confondent.[20]

Death itself is depersonalized, no longer 'la mort' striking at each of the city's inhabitants individually, but as 'Spleen' (LXXV) declares, 'la mortalité' reducing them to no more than a statistic in the Préfecture's files.

The focus of the poem shifts with the second stanza from appalled contemplation of the outside world to a no less agonized 'voyage autour de ma chambre' that moves inexorably towards the centre represented by 'le beau valet de cœur et la dame de pique'. The poem's structure, like that of other poems in the 'Spleen'

---

[18] Auguste Cochin, *Paris, sa population, son industrie* (1864), quoted Louis Chevalier, *La Formation de la population parisienne au XIXe siècle* (Presses Universitaires de France, 1950), 241.

[19] See Peter H. Amann, *Revolution and Mass Democracy: The Paris Club Movement in 1848* (Princeton Univ. Press, Princeton, NJ, 1975), 17.

[20] Félix Mornand, *La Vie de Paris* (Librairie Nouvelle, 1855), 274–5.

sequence,[21] consists of a series of concentric circles pivoted on a beleaguered *moi-centre*, a kind of 'Chinese-box effect' of interlocking containers-within-containers which graphically represents the exacerbated and infinitely multiplied self-consciousness—'une pensée qui se pense et toujours se pense' (Georges Poulet[22])—that characterizes the 'malady' of spleen. The room into which we are introduced is the antitype of the 'chambre paradisiaque' ('La Chambre double'), enclosed but liberating, whose centrality to Baudelaire's 'claustrophiliac' imagination has been so well demonstrated by Victor Brombert.[23] Here, though, the distinction of 'inside' and 'outside' collapses, the 'home' becomes a locus of homelessness, and the insecurities and confusions of 'le dehors' are imported *en bloc* into 'le dedans'. The theme of homelessness within the home is dramatically underscored by the image of the owner's scrawny mange-ridden dog fretfully trying to make itself comfortable on the bare floor-tiles of the cheerless room. By 1857, the dog—never Baudelaire's favourite animal, at least not until he discovered the pariah-dogs of Brussels at the end of his life[24]—would be replaced by a cat, not the sleek, aristocratic creature of 'Le Chat' 'en qui tout est, comme un ange | Aussi subtil qu'harmonieux', but a wretched tom-cat no less agitated and alienated than its master. The spectre of homelessness becomes even more horrifying with the admonitory apparition of the 'vieux poète' to whom not even death has brought repose, a 'limbic' being if ever there was one, marooned, like the poet himself and the 'pâles habitants' of the graveyard nearby, on the marches of life and death, unable fully to die as he had been unable fully to live; just as the dog can find rest neither inside the room nor without in the rain, so the poet's 'fantôme

[21] Most notably that of 'J'ai plus de souvenirs que si j'avais mille ans'.

[22] Georges Poulet and Robert Kopp, *Qui était Baudelaire?* (Albert Skira, Geneva, 1969), 139.

[23] For the whole of this theme, see Victor Brombert, 'Claustration et infini chez Baudelaire', *Actes du Colloque de Nice, Annales de la Faculté des Lettres et Sciences Humaines de Nice* (1968), 49–59.

[24] One of Baudelaire's reasons for breaking with Jeanne in 1852 was—or so he claimed in his letter to his mother of 27 Mar. that year—that she had banished his cat 'qui était ma seule distraction au logis' and introduced in its stead 'des chiens, *parce que* la vue des chiens me fait mal' (C, i. 193). Whether this biographical snippet is of any value in the dating of 'Spleen' is to be doubted: it is, however, worth asking why, in 1851 when his poetic reputation rested almost entirely on 'Les Chats', Baudelaire should have written so unexpectedly of '*mon* chien'.

frileux' is doomed to wander endlessly in the gutter, neither completely inside nor yet completely out. Similar liminal or intermediary beings and states are, appropriately enough, to be found throughout the *Limbes* sequence and in other poems of the final months of the Second Republic. The 'vieux corps sans âme' of 'Le Mort joyeux' craves a state of suspended animation between life and death in which it might 'à loisir étaler [ses] vieux os | Et dormir dans l'oubli comme un requin dans l'onde' while the wounded man in 'La Cloche fêlée' lies trapped beneath 'un tas de morts', interminably engaged 'sans bouger, dans d'immenses efforts' in an apparently vain attempt to die completely. Sleep, no less than death, is denied to the denizens of this in-between world, so that in 'Le Tonneau de la Haine' hatred is said to be 'vouée à ce sort lamentable | De ne pouvoir jamais s'endormir sous la table' while 'La Béatrix' is located in 'un pays plus nu que la terre polaire', neither living nor dead, in which once again the poet is refused 'le sort des plus vils animaux | Qui peuvent plonger dans un sommeil stupide'. Finally, it is worth pointing out that both of Baudelaire's principal 'social realist' poems of this period, 'Le Crépuscule du soir' and 'Le Crépuscule du matin', are situated, precisely, in the twilight-time between day and night and that night no more consoles the sick and suffering in 'Le Crépuscule du soir' than 'l'aurore grelottante' brings genuine rebirth and renewal in 'Le Crépuscule de matin':

> Et le sombre Paris, en se frottant les yeux,
> Empoignait ses outils, vieillard laborieux.

In one way or another, then, the world of 'Les Limbes' and kindred texts is a static or endlessly self-repeating world in which nothing is truly alive or truly dead, wholly asleep or completely awake, a world of phantoms and corpses unable fully to die and of foetal forms like the inchoate art-works of 'Le Mauvais Moine' and 'La Mort des amants'—to say nothing of the sleeping subterranean jewel of 'L'Artiste inconnu'[25]—struggling to be born, a no-man's-land suspended between past and future, life and death: in short, the twilight-world of the dying months of the doomed Republic.

As a further sign of radical displacement and solitude, the

---

[25] For this poem, see Graham Chesters, 'A Political Reading of Baudelaire's "L'Artiste Inconnu" ("Le Guignon")', *Modern Language Review*, 79/1 (1984), 64–76.

'bourdon'[26] begins its melancholy chime, echoing the bells in 'La Cloche fêlée' and pointing forward, above all, to the manic tintinnabulation of 'Spleen' (LXXVIII):

> Des cloches tout à coup sautent avec furie
> Et lancent vers le ciel un affreux hurlement,
> Ainsi que des esprits errants et sans patrie
> Qui se mettent à geindre opiniâtrement.

'The bells, which were once part of holidays, have been dropped from the calendar,' is Walter Benjamin's superb gloss on this stanza, 'they are like the poor souls that wander endlessly, but outside of history'[27]—and, one might add, just as 'Pluviôse' has been 'dropped' from the revolutionary calendar which alone gave it meaning. Unlike 'la cloche au gosier vigoureux' of a past age 'qui, malgré sa vieillesse, alerte et bien portante | Jette fidèlement son cri religieux' ('La Cloche fêlée'), the bells of the modern city no longer denote any precise shared sacred *signifié* but merely connote a largely irrelevant concept of 'sacredness'. In much the same way, 'la pendule enrhumée'—the counterpart indoors of the great bell outside—no longer refers to the time but merely concretizes passing time in the absolute while the Jack of Hearts and the Queen of Spades have also been 'dropped' from the semiological system (the deck of cards as a whole) that endowed them with meaning and having taken on a sinister autonomous existence of their own. Finally, the log gives off smoke but no flame or heat, so that on a whole number of levels 'Spleen' confronts the reader with a set of oppositions between, on the one hand, a former substance and significance and, on the other, a present emptiness and state of non-relatedness. Everywhere the *signifiant* has become separated from the *signifié* and confronts the self with its autonomous presence. 'Spleen' is, in the first instance, the collapse of systems of meaning. Torn from any context of signification, detached from their referents, what were formerly intelligible units of meaning become, quite literally, ob-jects hurled against the beleaguered consciousness that can no longer establish relations between them or between itself and the outside world as a whole. When meaning collapses, all that is left is the irrevocable otherness of reality.

---

[26] On the possible double meaning of 'bourdon' in 'Spleen', see Budini, 'Sul "bourdon" polisemico', 112–16.
[27] Benjamin, *Charles Baudelaire*, 144.

The focus of the poem has moved steadily from the circumferential universe to the centre of the room where, in a final, clinching opposition of past and present, 'le beau valet de cœur et la dame de pique | Causent sinistrement de leurs amours défunts'. But who is the 'vieille hydropique' who has bequeathed or left behind the 'jeu plein de sales parfums' from which the cards are taken? Her bloated form grotesquely parodying that of a pregnant woman, she presides as a kind of anti-mother goddess over this limbo-world of the still-born, the sterile, the stunted, and the still-to-be. If, stranded in the continuum of an unending imperfect tense ('dormaient', 'soufflaient', 'poussaient', 'rentraient', etc.), the 'crepuscular' Paris of 1850–2 is a city in which 'les agonisants dans le fond des hospices' are forever uttering 'leur dernier râle en hoquets inégaux', unable fully to die, so too it is one in which, seemingly incapable of giving birth, 'les femmes en gésine' are doomed to lie in perpetual labour 'parmi le froid et la lésine' ('Le Crépuscule du matin'). Whether she be madam, midwife, or abortionist (or, of course, all three), the 'vieille hydropique'—the thematic aptness of dropsy in this 'poème de la liquidité et de la liquidation' (Victor Brombert) need hardly be stressed[28]—clearly has some unspecified link with the world of prostitution, gambling, and, perhaps, fortune-telling. Gambling and prostitution are explicitly linked in 'Le Crépuscule du soir' ('Les tables d'hôte, dont le jeu fait les délices | S'emplissent de catins et d'escrocs, leurs complices'), but the cards in 'Le Spleen' are probably intended to suggest fortune-telling, in which case the 'vieille hydropique' becomes an aged procuress-cum-cartomancer who has brought together the 'beau valet de cœur' and the 'dame de pique' for her own financial advantage.[29] In a sinister parody of

[28] Brombert, 'Lyrisme et dépersonnalisation', 29. The idea of dropsy may have been suggested to Baudelaire by Goya's engraving 'Dondé vá mamá?' (*Los Caprichos*, 65) which depicts a bloated nude woman of uncertain age being carried by three naked witches and bears the subtitle: 'Mamá esta ydropticá'. This engraving may in its turn have suggested the figure of *la tiá*, the aged procuress-duenna who appears in so many of Goya's works and whom Baudelaire evokes as follows in 'Quelques caricaturistes étrangers': 'toutes ces blanches et sveltes Espagnoles que de vieilles sempiternelles lavent et préparent soit pour le sabbat, soit pour la prostitution, sabbat de la civilisation' (OC, ii. 568). 'Quelques caricaturistes étrangers' was not published until 1857, but its conception dates back to the mid-1840s; Baudelaire undoubtedly knew Goya's work at the time that he wrote 'Le Spleen' (see OC, ii. 1342–5).

[29] Given Baudelaire's fascination with 'hieroglyphic' systems of meaning, it is possible that he knew the significance of certain cards and combinations of cards in cartomancy. For what it is worth, according to a modern cartomancer ('Hadès',

the alchemical marriage, two totally antithetical, indeed literally 'unsuited', terms (the Jack of Hearts and the Queen of Spades) are brought together in a pseudo-relationship thanks to the sordid ministrations of a dropsical *entremetteuse*. Between them only conflict is possible and now, having been 'dropped' from the mercantile or chimerical bond that formerly linked them, they confront each other as irreconcilable antagonists.

Earlier, I described the poem as a series of concentric circles pivoted on a beleaguered *moi-centre*. But where is that pivotal central self? Is this not indeed, as Brombert has written,[30] a poem 'de l'absence, et spécifiquement de l'absence de "sujet"'? The only reference in the poem to a perceiving or organizing subject is to be found in the possessive adjective of 'mon chat': everything, it seems, is centred on a self that has no centre. Created by man but freed now from the fetters of meaning or function, the things assembled in the poem have been transformed into 'strange, parasitic, vampiristic objects, which draw their being from man and drain him of his own in return' (Fredric Jameson[31]). The self is virtually absent, dissolved (Baudelaire would say 'vaporized') in the not-self as in a chaotic *Merzbild* of randomly juxtaposed objects. At the same time, however, the things assembled in the room clearly 'correspond' in some way to a subjectivity of whose inner states they are analogues or exteriorizations in the manner

Cartes et Destins, Arts et Métiers Graphiques (1973), 135 and 144–5), the Jack of Hearts symbolizes 'le jeune amoureux, ardent et irréfléchi, se précipitant sur les êtres comme un jeune chien. Sa folie est des plus sympathiques mais c'est néanmoins une folie. Très jeune, il ne peut proposer à une femme que ses qualités de cœur. . . . Il ne compte pas; en conséquence, tant ses désirs sont multiples et sans frein, la prodigalité n'est jamais loin de lui. . . . C'est le fiancé, l'homme très jeune . . . n'ayant que peu d'expérience de l'amour, porté à idealiser, à rêver, incapable de construire.' For her part, the Queen of Spades denotes 'une femme veuve ou divorcée' who tends 'à apporter des brouilles, des risques de "piques" (ce mot dérive de la couleur) et même des possibilités de vengeance'; the spade suit as a whole is 'redoutable et peut aussi, particulièrement en amour, signifier la fin d'une illusion'. Given all this, the temptation is great to identify the Jack of Hearts with the spendthrift, romantic Baudelaire of the 1840s and the Queen of Spades with Jeanne—though, given the context of widowhood, Madame Aupick might be a no less plausible identification. It is, however, a temptation that we should resist: what is more important, in the context of the poem, is the manner in which the association of gambling, fortune-telling, and prostitution reduces the relations between men and women to a squalid affair of chance and venality.

[30] Brombert, 'Lyrisme et dépersonnalisation', 29.

[31] Fredric Jameson, *Marxisme and Form* (Princeton Univ. Press, Princeton, NJ, 1971), 245.

prescribed in Baudelaire's classic formulation of the late 1850s: 'Qu'est-ce que l'art pur suivant la conception moderne? C'est créer une magie suggestive contenant à la fois l'objet et le sujet, le monde extérieur à l'artiste et l'artiste lui-même' (*L'Art philosophique* (OC, ii. 598)). We are faced, then, with the paradox of objects that are at once totally alien to the self and, just as surely, products and projections of the self. The world of 'Spleen' is, as Brombert says,[32] a *spaeculum* of the self, but the image it discerns therein is irremediably other: the poem expresses essentially the self-alienation of the subject projected on to the world of objects. The self which seemed to be nowhere turns out to be everywhere or, rather, everywhere and nowhere, present and absent, like the God of the medieval Schoolmen: *sphaera cujus centrum est ubique, et circumferentia nusquam*. Without neighbour and without God, the subject becomes a self-alienated god unto itself, a god who cannot but 'prostitute' himself in the world of objects, recreating the universe in his own hideously fragmented image, infecting it with his own inner malady. The world becomes the self, the self becomes the world, and there is no escape from either—perhaps, as the fate of the 'vieux poète' suggests, not even in death.

What, then, is being described in 'Spleen' is, at the very least, a radical crisis of identity, a break-up of relations, a sudden traumatic coming to consciousness of the otherness of things and of the self's dispersal amid that otherness. It is not, of course, a wholly new sensation in Baudelaire's poetry, though we will look in vain amongst the poems that can be assigned unequivocally to the 1840s for a text that displays anything approaching the sense of exile, displacement, and self-estrangement that confronts us here. It would be as absurd to attribute that sense in a univocally deterministic manner to Baudelaire's despair at the collapse of his hopes of February 1848 as it would be to abstract the poem entirely from the probable circumstances of its composition. Nor, of course, was Baudelaire alone in his despair. 'Tout poète véritable doit être une incarnation,' he wrote in *Pierre Dupont*, his fullest Second Republic statement on the poet's role and function. Stationed 'sur un des points de la circonférence de l'humanité,' the authentic poet, says Baudelaire, 'renvoie sur la même ligne en vibrations plus mélodieuses le pensée qui lui fut transmise' (OC, ii. 27). Utterly

---

[32] Brombert, 'Lyrisme et dépersonnalisation', 21.

distinctive in its expression, 'Spleen' may be seen as just such a vibration—harsh and dissonant rather than 'melodious'—from a wider historic tremor.

'Voyage à Cythère'

As we have seen, Baudelaire almost certainly made the first draft of 'Voyage à Cythère' immediately after reading the evocative description of Cytherea ancient and modern that Nerval published in *L'Artiste* in 1844. It is, however, to be expected that he would not have sent a text of 1844–6 to Gautier in 1851–2 without first thoroughly revising it (just as he substantially rewrote 'Le Vin des chiffonniers' before including it in the same batch of manuscripts) and thus making it, in effect, a Second Republic poem; and even if the version sent to Gautier was essentially the same as the version of 1844–6, many of its characteristic images and expressions could, as I have argued, have been invested retrospectively with a political significance, derived from the context of 1848–51, that they did not originally possess. Interestingly, Nerval himself saw fit, in 1849, to insist publicly on the political purpose that lay behind his original description of Cytherea-Cerigo which had since been republished in book form in late 1847 or early 1848. Reviewing the book in *Le Messager des théâtres et des arts* in early May 1849, Champfleury wrote that 'Gérard ne pense ni à la politique ni au socialisme; il débarquerait à Constantinople, et trouverait la ville pleine de barricades, qu'il ne s'en effaroucherait guère. Tout au plus écrirait-il sur son carnet: "J'ai vu tuer aujourd'hui beaucoup de monde. Accident."' Champfleury's claim that Nerval 'se fait mahométan sans trop de remords, ne voit dans l'île de Cythère qu'un pendu' upset its target sufficiently for him to write forthwith to *Le Messager*'s editor to deny that he had ever become a Muslim and to dismiss Champfleury's attack on his alleged apoliticism as 'au fond une parodie de cette phrase célèbre: "J'admirais la sublime horreur de la canonnade"', the reference being to Proudhon's much misunderstood comment on the insurrection of June 1848. Nerval continued as follows:

Il n'est pas moins inexact de prétendre que je n'ai remarqué à Cythère (Cérigo) qu'une potence ornée d'un pendu. Je n'ai fait cette observation que comme critique de la domination anglaise, qui a confisqué les libertés de la république des Sept Îles. Je ne suis donc pas un sceptique ne m'occupant ni de politique ni de socialisme.[33]

Baudelaire was close to both Champfleury and Nerval around this time[34] and it seems unlikely that he would not have heard of the curious dispute between them.[35] Could it be that Baudelaire, having read Nerval's political interpretation of his description of Cytherea-Cerigo, saw how, without making any fundamental change to its overall structure and without discarding its original sexual significance, he could inject his poem with a hidden political meaning, substituting *la République Française* for *la république des Sept Îles* and replacing British imperialism with Bonapartism? Since the only test of this hypothesis is how fully and successfully it can account for all the elements of the text, we may proceed forthwith to an analysis of the manuscript Baudelaire sent Gautier no more than a few weeks before—and conceivably even after—the Bonapartist coup of December 1851.

> Mon cœur comme un oiseau s'envolait tout joyeux,
> Et planait librement à l'entour des cordages.
> Le navire roulait sous un ciel sans nuages,
> Comme un oiseau qu'enivre un soleil radieux.

[33] Champfleury's article and Nerval's reply are reproduced in Champfleury, *Grandes figures d'hier et d'aujourd'hui* (Poulet-Malassis et de Broise, 1861), 171–6. A more detailed reply was published in *Le National* on 1 Nov. 1850.

[34] See his letters to Nerval of 10 and 18 May 1850 (C, i. 164–5). In the second of these letters, Baudelaire asked Nerval to keep for him a copy of the *tirage à part* of the sections of *Voyage en Orient* (*Les Nuits du Ramazan*) that *Le National* had been serializing since March that year. He was obviously, therefore, retaining a keen interest in Nerval's account of his journey, but the evidence points against his having reread the description of Cytherea/Cerigo after 1848.

[35] It is possible that it was to this dispute that Baudelaire was referring when he wrote the following note on one of the manuscripts he sent to Gautier in 1851–2: 'L'*incorrigible* Gérard prétend au contraire que c'est pour avoir abandonné le bon culte que Cythère est réduite en cet état' (C, i. 180). It is a strange comment for if Nerval had certainly shown himself to be 'incorrigible' during his dispute with Champfleury (if that indeed is what Baudelaire is thinking of), he had never, either in his original articles on Cytherea/Cerigo or in his reply to Champfleury, attributed its present state to its having abandoned the cult of the pagan gods. What he had said was that 'la terre est morte, morte sous la main de l'homme, et les dieux se sont envolés', leaving no doubt that, for him, those responsible for the island's present desolation—and not least for the gibbet that disfigured its coast—were the British who had taken it from France in 1814: 'Le premier gibet réel que j'aie vu encore, c'est sur le sol de Cythère, possession anglaise, qu'il m'a été donné de l'apercevoir!' (Gerard de Nerval, *Œuvres complètes*, ed. Jean Guillaume, Claude Pichois, *et al.* (Gallimard, 1984), ii. 234 and 240.) On this whole question, see OC, i. 1073–4.

Quelle est cette île triste et noire? C'est Cythère, 5
Me dit-on. Un pays fameux dans les chansons,
Eldorado banal de tous les vieux garçons.
Regardez, après tout, c'est une pauvre terre.

Île des doux secrets et des fêtes du cœur,
De l'antique Vénus le superbe fantôme 10
Au-dessus de tes mers plane comme un arôme,
Et charge les esprits d'amour et de langueur.

Belle île aux myrtes verts, pleine de fleurs écloses,
Vénérée à jamais par toute nation,
Où les cœurs mortels en adoration 15
Font l'effet de l'encens sur un jardin de roses

Ou du roucoulement éternel d'un ramier.
Cythère n'était plus qu'un terrain des plus maigres,
Un désert rocailleux troublé par des cris aigres.
J'entrevoyais pourtant un objet singulier. 20

Ce n'était pas un temple aux ombres bocagères,
Où la jeune prêtresse errant parmi les fleurs
Allait, le corps brûlé de secrètes chaleurs,
Entre-baîllant sa robe à des brises légères.

Mais voilà qu'en rasant la côte d'assez près 25
Pour troubler les oiseaux avec nos voiles blanches
Nous vîmes que c'était un gibet à trois branches
Du ciel se détachant en noir comme un cyprès.

De féroces oiseaux perchés sur leur pâture
Dévoraient avec rage un pendu déjà mûr, 30
Et chacun jusqu'aux yeux plantait son bec impur
Dans tous les coins saignants de cette pourriture.

Les yeux étaient deux trous, et du ventre effondré
Les intestins pesants lui coulaient sur les cuisses,
L'organe de l'amour avait fait leurs délices, 35
Et ces bourreaux l'avaient cruellement châtré.

Sous les pieds un troupeau de jaloux quadrupèdes
Le museau relevé tournoyait et rôdait;
Une plus grande bête au milieu s'agitait,
Comme un exécuteur entouré de ses aides. 40

Habitant de Cythère, enfant d'un ciel si beau,
Silencieusement tu souffrais ces insultes
En expiation de tes anciens cultes
Et des péchés qui t'ont interdit le tombeau.

Pauvre pendu muet, tes douleurs sont les miennes. 45

Je sentis à l'aspect de tes membres flottants,
Comme un vomissement remonter vers mes dents
Le long fleuve de fiel de mes douleurs anciennes;
Devant toi, pauvre diable au souvenir si cher,
J'ai senti tous les becs et toutes les mâchoires   50
Des corbeaux lancinants et des panthères noires
Qui jadis aimaient tant à triturer ma chair.

Le ciel était charmant, la mer était unie.
Pour moi, tout était noir et sanglant désormais,
Hélas! et j'avais comme en un suaire épais   55
Le cœur enseveli dans cette allégorie.

Dans ton île, ô Venus, je n'ai trouvé debout
Qu'un gibet dégoûtant où pendait mon image.
Oh Seigneur! donnez-moi la force et le courage
De contempler mon cœur et mon corps sans dégoût.[36]   60

(Text of 1851–2)

    There can be no more commonplace motif in nineteenth-century Utopian writing than that of the journey to a fabulous land of love, peace, harmony, and equality, and one need only think of the most celebrated of such allegorical journeys, Étienne Cabet's *Voyage en Icarie* (1840) to see how readily 'Voyage à Cythère' might be injected with a set of supplementary political meanings some years after the poem was first drafted: indeed Baudelaire almost invites us to make the connection between Icaria and Cytherea in the celebrated line in 'Le Voyage', 'Notre âme est un trois-mâts cherchant son Icarie'. Many other words and images in the first stanza of 'Voyage à Cythère' have direct echoes in Baudelaire's republican-socialist writings of 1848–51. Thus 'tout joyeux' (l. 1) is echoed in 'chant plein de joie, de lumière et d'espérance' sung by wine in *Du vin et du haschisch* (OC, i. 380), in the 'joie extrême' with which in *Le Vin des honnêtes gens* wine 'tombe | dans le gosier d'un homme' and in 'cette joie qui respire et domine' in the songs of Pierre Dupont (OC, ii. 34); when 'Voyage à Cythère' was published in the 1857 *Fleurs du mal* 's'envolait' would become 'voltigeait', a word that is already present, along with the crucial bird image, in the prose doublet of 'Le Vin des honnêtes gens' in *Du vin et du haschisch* ('A nous deux nous ferons un Dieu, et nous

---

[36] Quoted (with some corrections) from John W. MacInnes, *The Comic as Textual Practice in 'Les Fleurs du mal'* (Univ. of Florida Press, Gainesville, Fla., 1988), 131–3.

voltigerons vers l'infini, comme les oiseaux . . .' (OC, i. 381)).
'Librement' links up with 'L'Homme libre et la mer' that Gautier
would publish alongside 'Le Reniement de saint Pierre' in October
1852: it may be significant that when the poem reappeared in the
1857 edition, its title had been pared down to the less politically
loaded 'L'Homme et la mer'. Above all, of course, the image of
'un oiseau qu'enivre un soleil radieux' suggests a whole series of
parallels with the celebrations of sunshine and drunkenness that are
the most characteristic expression of Baudelaire's short-lived
republican optimism of 1848. The very interchangeability of the
experience and expression of alcoholic, sexual, and political *ivresse*
indicates once again the ease with which the process of trans-
signification which I am suggesting could have occurred without
substantially altering the language and the imagery of the poem in
question.

The simile 'comme un oiseau' occurs twice in the first stanza and
since, as John W. MacInnes has written in his stimulating discussion of the successive versions of the poem, it was not like
Baudelaire 'to run quickly dry of analogies',[37] we may ask if there
was any political reason—in addition to the rhetorical and other
reasons suggested by MacInnes—why Baudelaire should have
repeated such a rudimentary and hackneyed image in 1851–2 and
yet have eliminated the repetition in the versions he published in
1855 (in the *Revue des Deux Mondes*) and 1857.[38] In the article on
Pierre Dupont, discussing the 'espèce de mysticité amoureuse' in
which his friend's songs and poems are steeped, Baudelaire alludes
to 'une comédie espagnole'—apparently Caldéron's *El mágico
prodigioso*—'où une jeune fille demande en écoutant le tapage
ardent des oiseaux dans les arbres: Quelle est cette voix, et que
chante-t-elle? Et les oiseaux répètent en chœur: l'amour, l'amour!
Feuilles des arbres, vent du ciel, que dites-vous, que commandez
vous? Et le chœur de répondre: l'amour, l'amour!' As well as
linking up with the bird simile of 'Voyage à Cythère', this passage

---

[37] MacInnes, *The Comic*, 13. My reading of 'Voyage à Cythère' is very different
from that elaborated by MacInnes, but it was his study that alerted me to the
complexity of the poem and to its possible links—which MacInnes hints at but does
not fully explore—with the political crisis of 1848–51.
[38] In 1855, Baudelaire altered the first line to 'Mon cœur se balançait comme un
ange joyeux' (thus losing all the ecstatic forward thrust of the original version) and
in 1857 changed the fourth line to 'Comme un ange enivré d'un soleil radieux', the
reading that is retained in the 1861 edition.

offers further evidence, if it were needed, of the inseparability, in Utopian socialist and, more generally, *démoc-soc* discourse, of the language of sexual love and the language of *Liberté, Égalité, Fraternité*: Cytherea and Icaria are sister islands whose common anthem might be the 'refrain sauveur: *Aimons-nous*' of one of Dupont's songs, love being, after all, 'le remède universel' to a society distorted and divided by the *Enrichissez-vous* of Bourgeois Monarchy individualism (OC, ii. 27–32). But if I am right in my suggestion that Baudelaire reworked 'Voyage à Cythère' some time afer reading Nerval's riposte to Champfleury in May 1849, it is possible that the flocks of birds that throng the poem—they have, it should be stressed, no parallel in Nerval's original—possess a political significance to which alert left-wing readers might have responded had the poem been published, as Baudelaire wished, in early 1852. In the first half of 1849, there appeared in *Le Travail affranchi* a series of texts by Alphonse Toussenel that would later, in 1853–5, be incorporated into his extraordinary 'ornithologie passionnelle', *Le Monde des oiseaux*, the possible influence of which on later Baudelairean texts such as 'Le Cygne' (1859) has been raised by a number of scholars and critics.[39] Toussenel's ornithological speculations had also appeared in *La Démocratie pacifique* and *La Presse* before the February revolution, so there is every likelihood—but, as ever, no decisive proof—that Baudelaire would have encountered them before he sent the manuscript of 'Voyage à Cythère' in 1851–2. If he did, he can hardly have failed to be struck by Toussenel's sometimes crude, sometimes highly intricate, political and social allegorizations of different species of birds—the night-owl, for example, symbolizes the priest, the magpie the police informer, the vulture the usurer, the great tit the *petite bourgeoisie*, the turkey the *Parti de l'Ordre*, with, of course, the eagle taking pride of place as an emblem of the Emperor or Prince-President himself. On the evidence of the cartoon, reproduced in Dolf Oehler's *Hollenstürz der Alten Welt*,[40] depicting Louis Napoleon leading an army of turkeys into battle, such ornithological symbolism formed part of current political discourse under the Second Republic, and though it is doubtful whether the

---

[39] See especially Stenzel, 'Quelques souvenirs socialistes', 6–7.

[40] Dolf Oehler, *Ein Hollenstürz der Alten Welt: Der Selbersterforschung der Moderne nach dem Juni 1848* (Suhrkamp, Frankfurt-on-Main, 1988), 201. This whole passage is based on Oehler's discussion of *Le Monde des oiseaux*, pp. 191–206.

birds and beasts of 'Voyage à Cythère' have the kind of precise emblematic significance elaborated by Toussenel (only two actual species, crows and panthers, are mentioned), Baudelaire could well have taken over from *Le Monde des oiseaux* and *L'Esprit des bêtes* the general concept of using birds and animals—especially those belonging to what Toussenel calls the *espèces bourreaux*[41]—as a coded way of representing socio-political groups and conflicts. In the context of 1849–51, therefore, it is not at all fanciful to see the 'troupeau de jaloux quadrupèdes' that prowl, 'le museau relevé', around the foot of the gibbet in 'Voyage à Cythère' as representing the reactionary forces of the Second Republic as a whole, with the 'plus grande bête' who moves around fitfully at their centre 'comme un exécuteur entouré de ses aides' as an image of *le pouvoir exécutif* itself, Louis Napoleon, flanked by his principal collaborators, Odilon Barrot, perhaps, or Fould, Morny, or Persigny.

The political reading of 'Voyage à Cythère'—which, to repeat, I view as supplementary to the more obvious sexual or existential readings, rather than as an alternative to them—is reinforced by the poem's very close thematic links with 'Le Reniement de saint Pierre' which Baudelaire sent to Gautier at the same time. In both texts, the central image is the tormented male body, humiliated and then crucified in 'Le Reniement', hanged, mutilated, and finally castrated in 'Voyage à Cythère'; it is to be noted, too, that the word 'bourreaux' occurs in each poem, and that the same verb 'planter' describes both the driving of the nails into the 'chairs vives' of Christ's martyred body (l. 12) and of the birds' 'bec impur' into 'tous les coins saignants' of the hanged man's dangling corpse (ll. 31–2). As we have seen, the political significance of 'Le Reniement' is in no doubt whatsoever. Baudelaire can hardly have failed to discern the similarity between the two texts, and it is entirely possible that the disembowelled, de-sexed carcass of the pre-1848 version of 'Voyage à Cythère' would come to appear to him, when he returned to the poem some time between 1849 and 1851, as a 'prophetic' image of the fate of the future Second Republic. If this interpretation is admitted, it becomes possible to view 'Voyage à Cythère' and 'Le Reniement' as representing two phases in Baudelaire's changing attitude towards the Republic in its different manifestations: 'Voyage à Cythère' as an expression of impotent

41 Quoted ibid. 199.

disgust and self-disgust at the radical republic's execution and mutilation at the hands of so-called moderate republicans between, say, March 1848 and the botched uprising of June 1849, with 'Le Reniement' as a later—and, just possibly, post-December 1851—repudiation of the Second Republic as such (but not necessarily, or indeed not at all, of *Republicanism*) for its failure physically to resist its arrest, mock trial, and crucifixion at the hands of the assorted Judases, Caiaphases, and Pontius Pilates of the Bonapartist reaction. Between 1849–50 (our putative date for the 'revision' of 'Voyage à Cythère') and 1851 (the likely date of 'Le Reniement''s composition), Baudelaire's attitude has passed from self-disgusted, paralysed identification with the 'pauvre pendu muet' of 'Voyage à Cythère' to angry rejection of Christ's 'corps brisé' in 'Le Reniement'.[42] The reading 'pauvre pendu muet' was retained in the text published in the *Revue des Deux Mondes* in 1855 and in the proofs of the 1857 *Fleurs du mal* until, at the last moment, Baudelaire altered the line in question to '*Ridicule* pendu, tes douleurs sont les miennes'. Purely stylistic considerations may have dictated the change,[43] but how neatly, too, it encapsulates the distance that Baudelaire had travelled politically since 1849–50. In 1857, as in 1861 and throughout the rest of his life, Baudelaire still suffered with and suffered from the ritual killing of the Second Republic, but not only is the murdered Republic itself now 'ridiculous', but his continuing identification with its fate is equally absurd. Enclosed in memories of the Republic 'comme en un suaire épais', his heart remains 'enseveli dans cette allégorie' which like every veteran of *quarante-huit* he decodes over and over again, absurdly, in his brain without ever being able to 'bury' the Republic's corpse (cf. 'des péchés qui t'ont interdit le tombeau' (l. 44)) and so move into the future. It may be, in short, that Baudelaire was emotionally, politically, and poetically castrated by the castration of the Second Republic.[44] Never again—except, as I have argued elsewhere,

---

[42] See MacInnes's comment that the repetition of 'degoûtant' and 'degoût' in the first stanza of the 1851–2 text 'underscores the specular fixity of the speaker's identification: "tes douleurs sont les miennes"; this is my image; it is disgusting and I am disgusting; it is me' (*The Comic*, 13).

[43] See Alison Fairlie's excellent discussion in *Baudelaire: Les Fleurs du mal* (Edward Arnold, 1960), 31–2.

[44] See MacInnes's comment on the final stanza of 'Voyage à Cythère' as 'a prayer to be freed from the power of allegory' and as an expression of 'a wish for deallegorization' (*The Comic*, 41).

almost miraculously and certainly all too briefly in 1859–60[45]—
would he recover that creative fertility as a lyric poet that he had
known, ironically enough, in the other respects sterile limbo-years
of the Bourgeois Monarchy. *Le 2 décembre* may or may not have
left Baudelaire *'physiquement dépolitiqué'* as he claimed; it certainly
seems, however, to have rendered him effectively 'dépoétiqué' for
most of the 1850s until the creative 'explosion' of 1859–60 temporarily restored his lyric fecundity, pending a further relapse into
sterility—at least as far as the writing of verse poetry was concerned
—after the publication of the second *Fleurs du mal* in 1861.

The Poems of 1851–2: An Overview

From the very considerable number of poems he had at his disposal,
it seems clear that Baudelaire selected for publication in 1851–2
texts which—to adopt the thematic opposition of the first section
of *Les Fleurs du mal*—emphatically privileged 'spleen' over 'idéal'.
Even the sonnet 'L'Idéal', published in the *Limbes* sequence,
concerns the poet's frustrated search, amongst the 'produits
avariés' of the age, for 'une fleur qui ressemble à mon *rouge* idéal':
in the context of 1851, Baudelaire's choice of adjective could
hardly be more loaded. The poems are, with no more than three or
four exceptions, dominated by feelings of imprisonment, sterility,
stagnation, impotence, and death as the would-be poet—that 'im-
puissant Orcagna' who, in another age, might have made 'du
spectacle vivant de ma triste misère | Le travail de mes mains et
l'amour de mes yeux'—returns to the 'cloître odieux' ('Le Mauvais
Moine') from which, briefly, the effervescence of February had
released him. It would be a fundamental error, however, to see this
all-encompassing lugubriousness as in some way 'apolitical'; on the
contrary, as our discussion of 'Spleen' ('Pluviôse . . .') tried to
show, Baudelaire's withdrawal into the confines of his own room—
where, as it turns out, there is no more security or comfort than
in the 'faubourgs brumeux' outside—is a politically motivated
response to the gathering political crisis of the Second Republic.
The street, the room: even where a calmer mood prevails, it is the

---

[45] See Burton, *Baudelaire in 1859*, esp. pp. 57–63. The term 'explosion' is
Baudelaire's own, and comes in a letter of 29 Feb. 1859 to Poulet-Malassis (C,
i. 568).

theme of retreat from the public into the private world that is most striking. We have already seen how in 'Paysage'—a very early text which Baudelaire probably returned to immediately after the coup— the poet draws away from the world of political reality represented by 'l'atelier' and 'l'émeute' into the inner sanctum of his room where, like a *fort en thème* crouched in a concentrated ecstasy of creativity at his desk, he deliberately closes eyes and ears to the world without in order to compose poetry of an almost ostentatiously inward- or backward-looking character. Other poems likewise stress the need for self-containment or reclusion, either as a stimulant to creativity ('L'Artiste inconnu') or as a vantage-point from which to contemplate the vain gesticulations of 'l'homme ivre d'une ombre qui passe' ('Les Hiboux'); by the end of the *Limbes* sequence, the drunken activist has been decisively superseded by the 'sage' for whom nothing is more to be dreaded and shunned than 'le tumulte et le mouvement'. Even in a 'populist' poem such as 'Le Crépuscule du soir', the poet's stance is essentially that of a spectator who views with no particular sympathy the underclass of prostitutes, gamblers, and burglars as they creep from their daytime lairs to ply their dubious trades in the nooks and crannies of 'la cité de fange' until, finally turning away from all this pseudo-activity, he withdraws, in a way that points forward to the last stanza of 'Le Cygne', into compassionate but at the same time self-absorbed meditation on the fate of the sick, the lonely and the dying:

> Recueille-toi, mon âme, en ce grave moment,
> Et ferme ton oreille à ce bouillonnement.
> C'est l'heure où les douleurs des malades s'aigrissent;
> La sombre nuit les prend à la gorge, ils finissent
> Leur destinée et vont vers le gouffre commun;
> L'hôpital se remplit de leurs soupirs; plus d'un
> Ne viendra plus chercher la soupe parfumée,
> Au coin du feu, le soir, auprès d'une âme aimée.
> Encore la plupart n'ont-ils jamais connu
> La douceur du foyer et n'ont jamais vecu!
>
> (Text of *La Semaine théâtrale*, February 1852)

It is, finally, the reality of death that provides the thematic link that unites the bulk of the poems of 1851–2. Blood flows through these poems as through no other group of Baudelairean texts. It pours along with sweat from the brow of the crucified Christ in 'Le Reniement de saint Pierre', seeps out of 'tous les coins saignants' of the mutilated corpse in 'Voyage à Cythère'. On one side, we hear the 'grateful dead' of 'Le Spleen' ('Le Mort joyeux') imploring 'les corbeaux | A saigner tous les bouts de ma carcasse immonde', on the other the

> hurlements d'un blessé qu'on oublie
> Auprès d'un lac de sang, sous un grand tas de morts,
> Et qui meurt sans bouger dans d'immenses efforts.

> ('Le Spleen' ('La Cloche fêlée'), text of 1851)

Elsewhere, 'la Vengeance éperdue aux bras rouges et forts' empties endless 'grands seaux pleins du sang et des lames des morts' into the bottomless 'tonneau de la Haine', to no avail, of course, since Hatred will always contrive to 'ranimer ses victimes | Et pour les resaigner galvaniser leurs corps' ('Le Tonneau de la Haine', text of 1851). Most terrifying of all, though, is the unstaunchable haemorrhage in 'La Fontaine de sang':[46]

> Il me semble parfois que mon sang coule à flots,
> Ainsi qu'une fontaine aux tranquilles sanglots.
> Je l'entends bien qui coule avec un long murmure,
> Mais j'ai beau me tâter pour trouver la blessure.

> A travers le marché, comme dans un champ clos,
> Il s'en va, transformant les pavés en îlots,
> Désalterant la soif de chaque créature,
> Et partout colorant en rouge la nature.

In the face of this other red liquid, the wine that flowed so freely in 'L'Âme du vin' and *Du vin et du haschisch* is of no avail whatever:

> J'ai demandé souvent à des vins généreux
> D'endormir pour un jour la terreur qui me mine:
> Mais le vin rend la vue et l'oreille plus fine.

> (Text of *Douze poèmes*)

It is tempting, once again, to follow the invitation of 'Le Reniement de saint Pierre' and interpret in a political sense the 'provision de

---

[46] The present chapter was written before I was able to gain access to Hartmut Stenzel's discussion of 'La Fontaine de sang': 'Frankreich 1850', in Klaus Lindemann (ed.), *europaLyric 1775-heute* (Ferdinand Schöningh, Paderborn, 1982), 181–93.

sang' ('L'Outre de la Volupté') with which the poems of 1851–2 are laden. Although, of course, blood had been present in abundance in such characteristic pre-1848 texts as 'Une martyre', 'Les Bijoux', and 'A Theodore de Banville' ('Poète, notre sang nous fuit par chaque pore'), memories of the blood-letting of June 1848 may have prompted Baudelaire to choose for publication in 1851–2 poems in which blood flowed with such profusion that, as in 'Le Spleen' ('La Cloche fêlée') and 'La Fontaine de sang' it becomes an elemental force of nature capable of inundating whole cities and—like the blood of Christ, as Claude Pichois points out (OC, i. 1064)—of slaking 'la soif de toute créature' ('La Fontaine de sang' (l. 7)). To a reader of 1851–2, lines and images like 'la Vengeance éperdue aux bras rouges et for' ('Le Tonneau de la Haine'), 'un blessé qu'on oublie | Auprès d'un lac de sang, sous un grand tas de morts' ('Le Spleen' ('La Cloche fêlée')) and the blood which, in 'La Fontaine de sang', not only transforms 'les pavés en îlots' but paints the whole of nature incarnadine would surely evoke the carnage on the streets of Paris in June 1848, even if, as is always possible, the poems themselves had been written before the revolution. More than that one cannot say: it would be particularly interesting to know whether the unexpected 'marché' of the 1851–2 text of 'La Fontaine de sang' (l. 5) refers obliquely to any particularly bloody confrontation of June 1848.

We may appropriately conclude this survey of the poems of 1851–2 with a discussion of 'La Mort des pauvres', a poem which was almost certainly written during the Second Republic and which recapitulates by way of a farewell many of the most characteristic images and themes of Baudelaire's poetry of the period:

> C'est la mort qui console et la Mort qui fait vivre,
> C'est le but de la vie et c'est le seul espoir
> Qui comme un élixir nous monte et nous enivre,
> Et nous donne le cœur de marcher jusqu'au soir;
>
> A travers la tempête, et la neige et le givre,
> C'est la lampe brillante à notre horizon noir;
> C'est l'auberge fameuse inscrite sur le livre,
> Où l'on pourra manger et dormir et s'asseoir;
>
> C'est un Ange qui tient dans ses doigts magnétiques
> Le sommeil et le don des rêves extatiques
> Et qui refait le lit des gens pauvres et nus;

C'est la gloire des Dieux, c'est le grenier mythique,
C'est la bourse du pauvre et sa patrie antique;
C'est le portique ouvert sur les Cieux inconnus!

(Text of *Douze poèmes*, slightly modified)[47]

Previously it was wine that poured out 'l'espoir, la jeunesse et la vie' ('Le Vin du solitaire'), that was 'l'espoir des dimanches' (*Du vin et du haschisch*) and which opened the way 'pour un ciel féerique et divin' ('Le Vin des amants'): now the only intoxicant left to the poor is the hope that death will open up to them the 'grenier mythique' where they can enjoy treasure in heaven in default of the 'granges pleines de moissons' ('La Rançon') that their labour has filled but to which they are forever denied access. By 1851–2 the 'auberge' is no longer somewhere to drink, make merry, and, in Pierre Joigneaux's phrase, *faire de la République* but simply a place to 'manger et dormir et s'asseoir'. Amidst the rain and the snow and the ice of reaction, the one hope is that death will at last grant the poor man his 'bourse' and restore him to his lost 'patrie'. In the early 1860s, discussing a possible *fleuron* for the 'Mort' sequence in a projected de luxe edition of *Les Fleurs du mal*, Baudelaire proposed the striking image of 'une tête de mort avec les attributs de la Liberté, coiffée du bonnet phrygien' (C, ii. 179): Death, not Revolution, is now the only true Liberator of care- and strife-worn mankind. It is a conclusion Baudelaire had already reached in 'La Mort des pauvres', a poem which, more than 'Le Cygne' itself, more even than 'Le Reniement de saint Pierre', is truly the poet's swan-song to the intoxicating hopes of February 1848.

---

[47] The *Douze poèmes* manuscript of this poem bears the title 'La Mort', but the title 'La Mort des pauvres' is included on a list of titles that accompanied the manuscripts (OC, i. 1089). I have corrected the 'à Travers' of l. 5 of the manuscript to 'A travers'.

9

Baudelaire and Proudhon (II): A Reading of 'Assommons Les Pauvres!'

Pendant quinze jours je m'étais confiné dans ma chambre, et je m'étais entouré des livres à la mode dans ce temps-là (il y a seize ou dix-sept ans); je veux parler des livres où il est traité de l'art de rendre les peuples heureux, sages et riches, en vingt-quatre heures. J'avais donc digéré,—avalé, veux-je dire,—toutes les élucubrations de tous ces entrepreneurs de bonheur public,—de ceux qui conseillent à tous les pauvres de se faire esclaves, et de ceux qui leur persuadent qu'ils sont tous des rois détrônés.—On ne trouvera pas surprenant que je fusse alors dans un état d'esprit avoisinant le vertige ou la stupidité.

Il m'avait semblé seulement que je sentais, confiné au fond de mon intellect, le germe obscur d'une idée supérieure à toutes les formules de bonne femme dont j'avais récemment parcouru le dictionnaire. Mais ce n'était que l'idée d'une idée, quelque chose d'infiniment vague.

Et je sortis avec une grande soif. Car le goût passionné des mauvaises lectures engendre un besoin proportionnel du grand air et des rafraîchissants.

Comme j'allais entrer dans un cabaret, un mendiant me tendit son chapeau, avec un de ces regards inoubliables qui culbuteraient les trônes, si l'esprit remuait la matière, et si l'oeil d'un magnétiseur faisait mûrir les raisins.

En même temps, j'entendis une voix qui chuchotait à mon oreille, une voix que je reconnus bien; c'était celle d'un bon Ange, ou d'un bon Démon, qui m'accompagne partout. Puisque Socrate avait son bon Démon, pourquoi n'aurais-je pas l'honneur, comme Socrate, d'obtenir mon brevet de folie, signe du subtil Lélut et du bien-avisé Baillarger?

Il existe cette différence entre le Démon de Socrate et le mien, que celui de Socrate ne se manifestait à lui que pour défendre, avertir, empêcher, et que le mien daigne conseiller, suggérer, persuader. Ce pauvre Socrate n'avait qu'un Démon prohibiteur; le mien est un grand affirmateur, le mien est un Démon d'action, un Démon de combat.

Or, sa voix me chuchotait ceci: 'Celui-là seul est l'égal d'un autre, qui le prouve, et celui-là seul est digne de la liberté, qui sait la conquérir.'

Immédiatement, je sautai sur mon mendiant. D'un seul coup de poing, je lui bouchai un œil, qui devint, en une seconde, gros comme une balle. Je cassai un de mes ongles à lui briser deux dents, et comme je ne me sentais pas assez fort, étant né délicat et m'étant peu exercé à la boxe, pour assommer rapidement ce vieillard, je le saisis d'une main par le collet de son habit, de l'autre, je l'empoignai à la gorge, et je me mis à lui secouer vigoureusement la tête contre un mur. Je dois avouer que j'avais préalablement inspecté les environs d'un coup d'œil, et que j'avais vérifié que dans cette banlieue déserte je me trouvais, pour un assez long temps, hors de la portée de tout agent de police.

Ayant ensuite, par un coup de pied lancé dans le dos, assez énergique pour briser les omoplates, terrassé ce sexagénaire affaibli, je me saisis d'une grosse branche d'arbre qui traînait à terre, et je le battis avec l'énergie obstinée des cuisiniers qui veulent attendrir un beefsteak.

Tout à coup,—ô miracle! ô jouissance du philosophe qui vérifie l'excellence de sa théorie!—je vis cette antique carcasse se retourner, se redresser avec une énergie que je n'aurais jamais soupçonnée dans une machine si singulièrement détraquée, et, avec un regard de haine qui me parut de *bon augure*, le malandrin décrépit se jeta sur moi, me pocha les deux yeux, me cassa quatre dents, et avec la même branche d'arbre me battit dru comme plâtre.—Par mon énergique médication, je lui avais donc rendu l'orgueil et la vie.

Alors, je lui fis force signes pour lui faire comprendre que je considérais la discussion comme finie, et me relevant avec la satisfaction d'un sophiste du Portique, je lui dis: 'Monsieur, *vous êtes mon égal!* veuillez me faire l'honneur de partager avec moi ma bourse; et souvenez-vous, si vous êtes réellement philanthrope, qu'il faut appliquer à tous vos confrères, quand ils vous demanderont l'aumône, la théorie que j'ai eu la *douleur* d'essayer sur votre dos.

Il m'a bien juré qu'il avait compris ma théorie et qu'il obéirait à mes conseils.

The text reproduced above is the first published text of 'Assommons les pauvres!', that of the first edition of the *Petits poèmes en prose* which appeared in 1869, two years after Baudelaire's death; it is this text, the forty-ninth of fifty prose poems, that figures in all the standard modern editions of Baudelaire's works. It is first referred to by name in a list of prose poems drawn up in February 1865 (OC, ii. 1306), though it is possible that Baudelaire continued to work on it right up to the time when, on a flying visit from Brussels to Paris in July 1865, he submitted it and a number of other prose poems for inclusion in the *Revue nationale et étrangère* whose editor, Gervais Charpentier, promptly rejected it as unpublishable, along with three other scarcely less provocative texts: 'Mademoiselle Bistouri', 'Le Galant Tireur', and 'La Soupe et les nuages'. The manuscript submitted to the *Revue nationale* has survived and shows only one major departure—but that utterly crucial—from the first published text. Instead of ending at 'Il m'a bien juré qu'il avait compris ma théorie, et qu'il obéirait à mes conseils', the manuscript continues with, on a new line and indented to form a separate paragraph, the following words: 'Qu'en dis-tu, (Pro) [*crossed out*], Citoyen Proudhon?' It remains unclear whether the suppression of this parting *boutade* in the first published text was of Baudelaire's doing or of that of his posthumous editors, Asselineau and Banville, acting on their own initiative.

Readings of 'Assommons les pauvres!' can be divided into two broad categories:[1] those which take into account the reference to Proudhon and those which confine themselves to the first published text, and it is hardly surprising if the interpretations that result, without necessarily being totally discrepant, show very marked differences of emphasis and focus. Readings that, for whatever reason, give little or no attention to the deleted conclusion, tend to take Nietzsche or Freud, or a combination of both, as their frame of reference. In 1947, Benjamin Fondane wrote that 'avant Nietzsche, précurseur de Nietzsche, Baudelaire dénonce la pitié, l'orgueil et l'impuissance de la pitié; ce n'est pas dans l'obéissance qu'il voit la vertu, mais dans la fierté, dans l'audace'.[2] In *Le Dernier Baudelaire* (1966), Charles Mauron, while noting the reference to Proudhon *en passant*, also dwells on the poem's Nietzschean resonances—'Ainsi parlera Zarathustra,' he says nicely of the narrator's 'Celui-là seul est l'égal d'un autre qui le prouve, et celui-là seul est digne de la liberté, qui sait la conquérir' (words that are in fact an obvious reworking of a famous passage in the second *Faust*[3])—before going on to interpret the confrontation of narrator

---

[1] The present chapter was written before I discovered the excellent article by Jonathan Monroe, 'Baudelaire's Poor: The *Petits poèmes en prose* and the social reinscription of the lyric', *Stanford French Review*, 9/2 (1985), 169–88. Monroe's interpretation intersects at many points with my own: the most illuminating parallels and divergences are indicated in the notes.

[2] Benjamin Fondane, *Baudelaire et l'expérience du gouffre* (Seghers, 1947), 156.

[3] See Melvin Zimmerman, 'Quelques allusions dans "Assommons les pauvres!" ou du nouveau sur Baudelaire et Nerval', *Bulletin baudelairien*, 14 (supplément) (1979), 1–2. The lines in question are *Faust* II. 574–5: 'Nur der verdienst sich Freiheit wie das Leben | Der täglich sie erhoben muss', which Nerval translates as 'Celui-là seul est digne de la liberté comme de la vie, qui tous les jours se dévoue à les conquérir'.

and beggar as an unresolved and essentially masochistic conflict between Baudelaire's *moi social* (represented by the narrator) and his *moi créateur* (represented by the beggar), a dyadic opposition of *bourreau* and *victime* which he finds replicated throughout the *Petits poèmes en prose*, most notably in 'Le Mauvais Vitrier' and 'Une mort héroïque'.[4] With somewhat different emphases and with, perhaps, a keener sense than Mauron of the way in which, in Baudelaire's work, the categories *bourreau* and *victime* slide continually in and out of each other, Jeffrey Mehlman[5] and Leo Bersani[6] have developed this psychoanalytical interpretation of 'Assommons les pauvres!' in the light, in particular, of Freud's 'A Child is Being Beaten' and, in Mehlman's case, of Deleuze's reading of Nietzsche. Neither Mehlman nor Bersani so much as mentions the reference to Proudhon and, perhaps in consequence, neither gives the social and political dimension of the *corps à corps* of narrator and beggar the weight it surely deserves.

Those readers of 'Assommons les pauvres!' who do take the Proudhonian allusion into account and who are alert to the poem's social and political resonances themselves fall into two distinct camps. On the one hand, there are those—one might call them representatives of the mainstream of Baudelaire criticism—who see what they invariably take as a sarcastic denunciation of Proudhon as Baudelaire's final and most extreme repudiation of his radicalism of 1848–9 (clearly referred to in the 'il y a seize ou dix-sept ans' of the poem's opening paragraph) when, as they do not fail to point out, Baudelaire was sufficiently close to Proudhon in political terms to be counted amongst his followers in the bitter months after the June uprising. In this reading of 'Assommons les pauvres!', the by now comprehensively de Maistrianized Baudelaire is seen to denounce not only *all* forms of socialism—Utopian or whatever—but also liberalism, humanism, rationalism, democracy, republicanism, and their ilk for their collective failure to account for the ineradicable, in-born perversity of fallen humanity. Proudhon becomes merely one of a host—no better, no worse—of self-appointed 'entrepreneurs de bonheur public' whose 'formules de bonne femme' must sooner or later collapse before the unregenerate

[4] Charles Mauron, *Le Dernier Baudelaire* (José Corti, 1966), 113–14.

[5] Jeffrey Mehlman, 'Baudelaire with Freud: Theory and Pain', *Diacritics* (Spring 1974), 7–13.

[6] Leo Bersani, *Baudelaire and Freud* (Univ. of California Press, Berkeley, Calif., 1977), 139–50.

savagery that lurks in the depths of all human beings. Read in this light, 'Assommons les pauvres!' is a supremely provocative illustration of the general thesis expounded in that masterpiece of Baudelaire's exacerbated Augustinianism, 'Éloge du maquillage': 'C'est la philosophie (je parle de la bonne), c'est la religion qui nous ordonne de nourrir des parents pauvres et infirmes. La nature (qui n'est pas autre chose que la voix de notre intérêt) nous commande de les assommer' (*Le Peintre de la vie moderne* (1863) (OC, ii. 715)).

In contrast to this reading of 'Assommons les pauvres!' as an allegory of ultra-conservatism, there is the view, vigorously espoused by Dolf Oehler[7] and, rather more circumspectly, by T. J. Clark,[8] that the poem shows rather Baudelaire's continuing allegiance to his supposedly ultra-leftist political stance of February–June 1848 and beyond. According to this interpretation, 'Assommons les pauvres!' denounces not only the official discourse of Second Empire philanthropy—that, in particular, of Napoleon III's own *Extinction du paupérisme* (1844)—but also the counter-discourse of its *apparent* rival (but *de facto* ally), Proudhonian mutualism, which, in its (alleged) denial of class conflict, is held to be deflecting its numerous working-class adherents in France and Belgium in the mid-1860s from the out-and-out revolutionary struggle against their class enemies which they should be waging. In this perspective, the narrator of 'Assommons les pauvres!' functions as a Satanic liberator of the oppressed who, by inflicting gratuitous violence on one of their number, incites in him the counter-violence and hatred which alone can deliver him and his *confrères* from their bondage. Proudhon is repudiated not in the name of de Maistre but of someone of whose work as theoretician and activist Baudelaire was unaware but to whose conclusions regarding the necessity of violent inter-class conflict he had independently arrived. There are no prizes for guessing that that someone is Marx.

It is no part of my purpose here either to attempt to reconcile these highly divergent interpretations of 'Assommons les pauvres!' or to propose a single univocal interpretation of my own to take their place. Rather I want to emphasize what seems to me to be the irreducible ambiguity of the text and, by exploring a number of

---

[7] Dolf Oehler, ' "Assommons les pauvres!": Dialektik der Befreiung bei Baudelaire', *Germanisch-Romanisch Monatschrift*, 56 (1975), 454–62.

[8] T. J. Clark, *The Absolute Bourgeois: Artists and Politics in France 1848–1851* (Thames and Hudson, 1973), 176–7.

manifest or concealed allusions within it, to situate it in the context of a triple ambiguity: the ambiguity of Proudhon's thinking on class conflict, social and economic organization and the role of politics and the State, the ambiguity of the situation confronting working-class radicals in France and Belgium in the mid-1860s, and, finally, in the context of the ambiguity of Baudelaire's own politics, particularly as that ambiguity expresses itself in response to Proudhon as human being, political radical, and theoretician of mutualism. The gist of my argument is that 'Assommons les pauvres!' is shot through from beginning to end with concepts drawn from Proudhonian discourse, that the text is at one and the same time a celebration, parody, and subversion of that discourse and that, correspondingly, the final 'Qu'en dis-tu, Citoyen Proudhon?' is by no means the straightforward *denunciation* of Proudhon that both the 'de Maistrian' and the 'Marxist' readings of the text take it to be, but something far more equivocal: an amalgam of tribute, provocation, and loathing rendered still more problematic by being addressed *outre-tombe*, for Proudhon had died on 19 January 1865 and it could well have been the news of his death, reported in *L'Indépendance belge* the following day, that prompted Baudelaire to use an incident in which he had been involved some months earlier, in August 1864, to confront head-on the complexity of his reactions to the man and his doctrine and, in so doing, to compose a text in which political and psychological ambivalences are fused with an intensity unique in his work.

After having, as we have seen, exercised a perhaps determining influence on Baudelaire's political thinking and actions between July 1848 (or even 1846–7) and early 1852, Proudhon had, by the middle of the latter year, been supplanted as Baudelaire's *maître à penser* by Poe and de Maistre, and there is only one further reference to him in Baudelaire's correspondence—and none at all in his published writings—until his arrival in Belgium in 1864. The reference in question—in a letter of 14 June 1858 to Sainte-Beuve (C, i. 505)—concerns Proudhon's recently published *De la justice dans la Révolution et dans l'Église* and is notable only for what it fails to say. Neither book nor author is mentioned by name (Baudelaire refers obliquely to 'l'œuvre du stoïcien'—which he has not read—and only the context makes possible the identification with Proudhon) and—remarkably, in view of Baudelaire's own condemnation in 1857 and of the suppression of the *Revue de Paris* in January 1858 that so enraged him—nothing whatsoever is said of the fact that, less than a fortnight before, on 2 June 1858, Proudhon had been condemned to three years' imprisonment and fined 4,000 francs for 'outrage à la morale publique et religieuse' in having published *De la justice*, hundreds of copies of which had been seized by the police when it appeared in April 1858.[9] On 20 January 1858, on learning of the suppression of the *Revue de Paris*, Baudelaire had written to his mother of his fear that 'une nouvelle période *encore plus dénuée de liberté* que celle qui vient de s'écouler' was about to begin (C, i. 447); his apparent indifference, less than six months later, to Proudhon's fate is an indication, surely, of how far he had moved politically since December 1851.

Proudhon escaped imprisonment by fleeing, in the time-honoured manner of French dissidents, to Belgium where he remained from September 1858 to September 1862 when he was compelled to return to France on the absurd grounds that his *La Fédération et l'unité en Italie* (1862) contained an incitement to Napoleon III to invade and annex Belgium.[10] Baudelaire himself arrived in Brussels in April 1864 and in July twice referred to the 'dégoûtante émeute' which, he says, obliged Proudhon to flee the country, allegedly '*à coups de pierre*', 'pour s'être permis quelques plaisanteries très innocentes dans un journal' (C, ii. 388 and 391). If Proudhon's treatment at the hands of 'les Belges' prompted Baudelaire into the kind of identification with a fellow-victim or -exile to which he was perhaps all too susceptible, he says nothing further of him until news of his death reached him in January 1865. It seems, however, that, although rumours were circulating that he was an 'affilié de la police française' (see C, ii. 370, 375, 387, 437, etc.), Baudelaire soon made contact—probably through Poulet-Malassis, who had himself fled to Belgium in September 1863—with the substantial number of supporters, both French and Belgian, that Proudhon had left behind him in Brussels, a point of some importance for my argument since it gave him private access to letters and *inédits* of Proudhon's which are pertinent to an understanding of 'Assommons les pauvres!'.[11] In August 1864 there occurred an incident, reported in a letter to Nadar (C, ii. 401), which, it has been speculated,

[9] See Pierre Haubtmann, *Pierre-Joseph Proudhon: Sa vie et sa pensée (1849–1865)* (Desclée de Brouwer, Bruges, 1988), 95–100.

[10] Ibid. 201.

[11] See Gretchen Van Slyke, 'Dans l'intertexte de Baudelaire et de Proudhon: Pourquoi faut-il assommer les pauvres?', *Romantisme*, 45 (1984), 57–77.

provides the biographical basis for the confrontation of narrator and beggar that takes place in 'Assommons les pauvres!':

Croirais-tu que *moi*, j'aie pu *battre* un Belge? C'est incroyable, n'est-ce pas? Que je puisse battre quelqu'un, c'est absurde. Et ce qu'il y avait de plus monstrueux encore, c'est que j'étais complètement dans mon tort. Aussi, l'esprit de justice reprenant le dessus, j'ai couru après l'homme pour lui faire des excuses. Mais je n'ai pas pu le retrouver.

Nothing, of course, indicates that the luckless Bruxellois was a beggar, and it is to be noted that Baudelaire's reaction could hardly be further removed from that of the narrator in the poem. In itself insignificant, the incident could none the less have provided Baudelaire's imagination with the—to use his own terms—*pabulum* or *incitamentum* it always needed, a set of circumstances which he could reinvest with, in this instance, profound political, social, and psychological meanings not necessarily involved at all in the original incident.

Moving now a little closer to the central themes of 'Assommons les pauvres!', a reading of Baudelaire's correspondence in 1864–5 and of the early entries in *Pauvre Belgique!* offers ample evidence that his reaction to poverty and the poor in Belgium differed significantly from that expressed in most of the prose poems completed before his departure from France. In poems such as 'Le Vieux Saltimbanque' and 'Les Veuves' (first published November 1861) and, above all, in 'Les Yeux des pauvres' (first extant text 1862), the spectacle of lower-class poverty had remained just that: a spectacle capable of exciting a complex of emotions—that enigmatic combination of pity, revulsion, guilt, and fear which Baudelaire sometimes calls 'curiosité' but one from which person-to-person contact, above all speech contact, is significantly absent and in which, with the very notable exception of 'Le Mauvais Vitrier' (August 1862), feelings of aggression are directed against the self rather than at the object of the self's 'curiosité'. In Belgium, however, the elements of pity and interest, already ambiguous in themselves, seem to have disappeared completely, leaving only repulsion and aggression (now explicitly directed outwards), the two exacerbated by the poor's passive acceptance of their degradation. Typical of this new attitude towards the poor is an early entry in *Pauvre Belgique!* entitled 'Laideur et misère':

La misère, qui dans tous les pays, attendrit si facilement le cœur de philosophe, ne peut ici que lui inspirer le plus irrésistible dégoût, tant la face du pauvre est originellement marquée de vice et de bassesse incurable! (OC, ii. 869–70)

It is entirely possible that, taking the August incident as his narrative basis, and drawing on his reading, both recent and remote, of Proudhon's works (including letters and *inédits* to which his contacts gave him access), Baudelaire had begun writing, or even completed, 'Assommons les pauvres!' before news of Proudhon's death reached him in late January 1865; equally, it could have been the news itself that detonated the imaginative process that, with great rapidity (possibly as early as 3 February, and almost certainly by the 15th of the month), produced a complete or near-complete text which Baudelaire may have continued to tinker with—'triturer' is the word he uses (C, ii. 443)—right up to the time that he took his manuscripts to Paris in July. Either way, the comments, reminiscences, and judgements concerning Proudhon that abound in his correspondence of February 1865 and which continue at intervals throughout the year and into early 1866 offer valuable clues to the meaning of 'Assommons les pauvres!' and need to be given close attention here before we move on to a study of the text itself.

Some time in late 1864 or early 1865, Baudelaire had got hold of a letter which Proudhon had written to a Belgian supporter, Félix Delhasse, on 9 October 1864. The content of the letter, to which I shall return, had obviously made an impact on Baudelaire and, somewhat improbably, he had sent a copy or summary of it to Ancelle for his comments. The worthy lawyer was not impressed and plainly thought the letter to be the work of a madman, prompting the following response from Baudelaire on 8 February 1865:

La lettre de Proudhon ne vous a pas assez frappé, et vous le traitez de fou beaucoup trop légèrement. Je vous ai envoyé cette lettre pour vous prouvez que Proudhon, quoi qu'on ait dit, *n'avait jamais varié*. A la fin de sa vie, comme à ses debuts, les questions de production et de finance étaient celles qui l'obsédaient particulièrement. S'il était question d'art, oui, vous auriez raison de dire de Proudhon: Il est fou.—Mais en matière d'économie, il me paraît singulièrement respectable. (C, ii. 453)

On 12 February, Baudelaire wrote again to Ancelle and, amongst other matters, mentioned a visit he had received 'il y a quelque temps' (before or after Proudhon's death is not clear) from the republican art critic Théophile Thoré, also in exile in Belgium, whom, he says, he had not seen 'depuis vingt ans, ou peu s'en faut'. Obviously the two men had talked about what, with the comment 'Que c'est vieux, déjà!', the same letter refers to as 'les enthousiasmes et les drôleries de Février' and, inevitably, the conversation had turned to Proudhon. The whole passage is worth quoting, not only for the clues it gives to the ambivalence of Baudelaire's attitude towards Proudhon but also for its incidental opening comment on the tension between dandyism and radical republicanism, the importance of which to the understanding of 'Assommons les pauvres!' will become clear as we proceed:

Thoré, quoique républicain, a toujours eu des mœurs élégantes. Il me racontait qu'il avait fait une fois un voyage avec Proudhon, mais qu'il avait été obligé d'abandonner celui-ci, à cause du dégoût que lui inspirait, à lui Thoré, l'affectation rustique de Proudhon, affectation de grossièreté, en toutes choses, impertinence de paysan.—Ainsi, on peut être à la fois un *bel esprit* et un *rustre*,—comme on peut en même temps posséder un *génie spécial* et être un *sot*. Victor Hugo nous l'a bien prouvé.

The mention of Hugo prompts Baudelaire to tell an amusing story of Proudhon reading and annotating *Les Misérables*—'le déshonneur de Hugo', Baudelaire calls it, in total contrast to the terms of pious admiration he had used in his review of the book in April 1862. Baudelaire's comment—'Ce devait être une merveille de drôlerie; la logique corrigeant l'absence de logique!' (all quotations: C, ii. 459–60)—is again important, not only for the further evidence it offers of Baudelaire's respect for Proudhon's intellect, but because it suggests the possibility that, to anticipate a question to which I shall return in due course, Proudhon was, in Baudelaire's mind, not at all one of those 'entrepreneurs de bonheur public' so scathingly dismissed in the first paragraph of 'Assommons les pauvres!' but, precisely, an *anti-Utopian* for whom the vacuous if well-meaning philanthropism of *Les Misérables* was simply *quarante-huitard* utopianism in another souped-up guise. Proudhon versus Hugo, logic versus illogic, realism versus utopianism: in May 1865 Baudelaire had the dubious pleasure of being invited to dinner by Madame Hugo and her sons and spent the evening— 'moi, républicain avant eux', he says significantly—being regaled with 'un plan majestueux *d'éducation internationale*'. 'Je crois', he comments, 'que c'est une nouvelle toquade de ce grand parti qui a accepté l'entreprise du bonheur du genre humain' (letter to mother, 24 May 1865, C, ii. 501): the echo of 'Assommons les pauvres!' could not be clearer.

Baudelaire was not, of course, the only veteran of 1848 to dwell on memories of Proudhon in the weeks following his death. On 25 February, that 'vieux faubourien' Poulet-Malassis (Baudelaire's description, see C, i. 557) had published an article entitled 'Proudhon en Belgique' in *La Petite Revue* which included the following anecdote:

Un citoyen le [Proudhon] contemplait dans les bureaux du *Peuple*, précipitant les morceaux de son déjeûner énorme et frugal: 'Vous vous étonnez de me voir tant manger, citoyen, lui dit-il joyeusement; mon appétit est en raison des grandes choses que j'ai à faire. (C, ii. 902)

The 'citoyen' was, of course, Baudelaire and the occasion his meeting, referred to earlier,[12] with Proudhon in 1848 (or 1849, according to some scholarly opinion). Poulet-Malassis had, however, got the story slightly wrong and some time around the beginning of March, Baudelaire wrote him an open letter, published in *La Petite Revue* on 11 March, to set the record straight:

Mon cher ami, je viens de lire vos curieuses notes sur Proudhon, et je trouve, à la page II du soixante-huitième numéro de *La Petite Revue*, une anecdote que je vous ai contée, il y a longtemps, et qui s'est transformée dans votre mémoire.

Un citoyen le contemplait dans les bureaux du *Peuple*, etc. . . .

Ce citoyen, mon ami, c'était moi. J'étais allé, un soir, chercher le citoyen Jules Viard dans les bureaux du *Représentant du peuple*.

Proudhon y était, entouré de ses collaborateurs, et leur distribuait des instructions et des conseils pour le numéro du lendemain.

Peu à peu, chacun le quitta, et je restai seul avec lui; il me dit que Viard était parti depuis longtemps, et nous nous mîmes à causer. Comme je lui appris, dans la conversation, que nous avions quelques amis communs, entre autres Ricourt, il me dit: 'Citoyen, voilà l'heure du dîner; voulez-vous que nous dînions ensemble?'

Nous allâmes chez un petit traiteur récemment installé rue Neuve-Vivienne; Proudhon jasa beaucoup, violemment, amplement, m'initiant, moi, inconnu pour lui, à ses plans et à ses projets, et lâchant involontairement, pour ainsi dire, une foule de bons mots.

[12] Monroe ('Baudelaire's Poor', 184) has valuable comments on 'Assommons les pauvres!' as 'a displacement and prose-poetic reworking' of this encounter in 1848.

J'observai que ce polémiste mangeait énormément et qu'il ne buvait presque pas, tandis que ma sobriété et ma soif contrastaient avec son appétit. 'Pour un homme de lettres, lui dis-je, vous mangez étonnamment.'

'C'est que j'ai de grandes choses à faire', me répondit-il; avec une telle simplicité que je ne pus deviner s'il parlait sérieusement ou s'il voulait bouffonner.

Je dois ajouter,—puisque vous attachez aux plus petits détails une importance souvent légitime,—que, le repas fini, quand je sonnai le garçon pour payer notre dépense commune, Proudhon s'opposa si vivement à mon intention que je le laissai tirer sa bourse, mais qu'il m'étonna un peu en ne payant que strictement son dîner.—Peut-être en inférerez-vous un goût décidé de l'égalité et un amour exagéré du droit?

Tout à vous. (C, ii. 469–70)[13]

The letter calls for a number of comments, most obviously on the extraordinary vividness of Baudelaire's memory, sixteen or seventeen years after the event, of the one occasion—or, possibly, one of only two occasions—when he and Proudhon had met. Read closely, however, the letter reveals many of the ambiguities in Baudelaire's attitude towards Proudhon, not least his uncertainty concerning the character of his writings and his stature as a writer. In the opening paragraph, Baudelaire had first described Proudhon as 'ce singulier écrivain' before deleting these words and substituting 'ce véritable écrivain'; a further hesitation led to the suppression of any reference to Proudhon as *écrivain* and his relegation, later in the letter, to the level of *polémiste*; similarly, when it came to restoring their dialogue of 1848, Baudelaire again hesitated between calling Proudhon an 'homme de travail' and an 'homme de lettres' (see C, ii. 902–3). One notes, too, the contrast between the dandy's restraint of appetite and language and the gluttony and garrulousness of the radical who speaks as he eats, 'violemment, amplement', almost 'involontairement': if the narrator of 'Assommons les pauvres!' chooses to 'digér[er],—aval[er], veux-je dire,—toutes les élucubrations de tous ces entrepreneurs de bonheur public', Baudelaire is forced to swallow all the 'plans' and 'projets' that Proudhon

---

[13] On the contrast between Proudhon's *vouvoiement* of Baudelaire in 1848 and Baudelaire's *tutoiement* of him in 1865, see Monroe, 'Baudelaire's poor', 184. Baudelaire's use of *tutoiement* with 'Citoyen' conforms with strict republican usage. On 10 brumaire an II, the Convention passed a motion decreeing that 'tous les républicains français . . . seront tenus de tutoyer ceux ou celles à qui ils parleront, à peine d'être déclarés suspects . . . car ils se prêteraient en ne le faisant pas au soutien de la morgue qui sert de prétexte á l'inégalite entre nous'. (See Michel Péronnet, *Les 50 mots clefs de la révolution française* (Privat, 1988), 63.)

spouts forth though, unlike the narrator, he appears to be able to slake the 'grande soif' induced by this ideological forced feeding. Then there is the way in which Baudelaire's one encounter with Proudhon raises *en petit*, but in a manner that plainly troubled Baudelaire, all the massive questions to which his life and work were devoted, questions which are, moreover, in heavily ironic form, the salient concerns of 'Assommons les pauvres!' itself: reciprocity, distribution, giving and receiving, justice, equality. And, finally, Proudhon's response to Baudelaire's comment raises precisely the same questions as 'Assommons les pauvres!': are his words intended 'sérieusement' or does he merely want to 'bouffonner' and disorientate his interlocutor? Like *Pauvre Belgique!* ('un livre . . . à la fois bouffon et sérieux' (C, ii. 409)) and the *Petits poèmes en prose* themselves with their characteristic association of 'l'effrayant avec le bouffon' (C, ii. 473), Proudhon's conversation confronts the receiver with almost insuperable problems of *interpretation*.

Two final letters will complete this survey of Baudelaire's attitudes towards Proudhon. On 2 January 1866, Baudelaire wrote to Sainte-Beuve[14] (who between October and December had published in *La Revue contemporaine* a series of articles—which Baudelaire duly read—on Proudhon's early life) and made explicit the opposition between dandy and radical which had been implicit in many of his earlier recollections and judgements:

Je l'ai [Proudhon] beaucoup lu, et un peu connu. La plume à la main, c'etait un *bon bougre*; mais il n'a pas été et n'eût jamais été, même sur le papier, *un Dandy!* C'est ce que je ne lui pardonnerai jamais. (C, ii. 563)

On 5 January Sainte-Beuve wrote back[15] with some general comments on the relationship between literature, socialism, and humanitarianism with which Baudelaire appears to have been in agreement since he transcribed them (minus some derogatory comments on Hugo the 'prédicateur' and 'patriarche' whose 'humanitarisme se retrouve jusque dans ses goguettes') in a letter he sent to Madame Hugo a week later:

[14] On the links between Baudelaire, Proudhon, and Sainte-Beuve, and the presence of Sainte-Beuve in the subtext of 'Assommons les pauvres!', see Monroe, 'Baudelaire's Poor', 183–4.

[15] Sainte-Beuve's letter is reproduced in full in *Lettres à Charles Baudelaire*, ed. Claude Pichois and Vincenette Pichois (*Études baudelairiennes*, 4–5 (1973)), 346–7.

Proudhon, duquel vous me parlez, devait être l'homme qui vous était le plus antipathique. Tous ces philosophes et socialistes ne veulent de la littérature que comme d'une institution ou d'un instrument de moralisation pour le peuple. (C, ii. 568)

There is, then, a basic tension in Baudelaire's attitude towards Proudhon. If he admires most things about the thinker (his logical rigour, his intellectual and political consistency, his economic theory, everything, in fact, except—crucially—his view of art), he loathes almost everything about the man (his gross habits of eating and speaking, his (pseudo-) peasantish mannerisms, his lack of dandyesque refinement as man and writer): whether Proudhon was, in Baudelaire's eyes, himself a Utopian or anti-Utopian (or a mysterious mixture of both) is still to be resolved. At this point, we may briefly leave Baudelaire to one side and consider another set of questions vital to the understanding of 'Assommons les pauvres!': the condition of working-class politics in France in the mid-1860s and Proudhon's attitude towards developments that were taking place.

'Le socialisme,' Louis Reybaud wrote in 1854, 'est mort, parler de lui, c'est faire son oraison funèbre'.[16] In the early 1860s, however, government policy towards the working classes shifted from its earlier combination of repression, state-sponsored work schemes, direct charitable hand-outs, and the propagation, by every means at its disposal, of Napoleon III and the imperial family as the disinterested saviours and benefactors of 'le peuple' to a more subtle and supple policy that, within duly prescribed limits, gave greater freedom to workers to organize amongst themselves and to pursue their own interests and objectives under the general aegis of state supervision; it was in the spirit of this new policy, for instance, that, in 1862, Napoleon III himself had encouraged workers to come together and elect delegates to attend the Industrial Exhibition held in London that year.[17] The object of government policy was, of course, to defuse and recuperate growing working-class discontent and militancy by diverting them into politically acceptable

[16] Quoted Jean Bruhat, 'Le socialisme français de 1848 à 1871', in Jacques Droz (ed.), *Histoire générale du socialisme* (Presses Universitaires de France, 1972), i. 511.
[17] See David T. Kulstein, *Napoleon III and the Working Class: A Study of Government Propaganda under the Second Empire* (California State Colleges Publications, 1969), 120–30.

channels and, to the extent that some working-class leaders—particularly the so-called Palais Royal group patronized by the Emperor's 'left-wing' cousin Prince Jérôme—were prepared, in effect, to collaborate with the government, the policy enjoyed a certain limited success. Other working-class leaders, however, sought to constitute themselves as a political, and specifically parliamentary, force distinct from both the state-sponsored working-class organizations and from the middle-class republican opposition for whose candidates most workers, at least in Paris, had hitherto cast their votes. To this end, in February 1864, a group of sixty working-class militants from the department of the Seine published a document—immediately dubbed the 'Manifeste des Soixante'—that for the first time proposed that working-class candidates stand *as workers* in the *élections complémentaires* to be held in Paris the following month. Their case was that, though they agreed entirely with the political objectives of the bourgeois republican opposition, that opposition was incapable of representing the social objectives of workers who voted for it: 'Le suffrage universel nous a rendus majeurs politiquement, mais il nous rest encore à nous émanciper socialement'.[18] What is of particular significance as far as 'Assommons les pauvres!' is concerned is the manifesto's vigorous rejection of all forms of public and private charity as a remedy to working-class social and economic misery: 'Nous ne voulons pas être des clients ou des assistés; nous voulons devenir des égaux; nous repoussons l'aumône; nous voulons la justice.'

The radicalism of the Manifeste des Soixante should not be exaggerated,[19] for though it recognized the existence of classes, it stopped well short of asserting the existence of—let alone the necessity for—class conflict; the signatories' principal aim was to create a group of working-class deputies who would speak for working-class interests in parliament but would in other respects collaborate with the bourgeois parliamentary opposition. The Manifesto confronted Proudhon's working-class supporters with an immediate dilemma for, true to Proudhon's unwavering rejection of parliamentary politics as a means of achieving social change, they had until now abstained from voting in parliamentary

---

[18] The Manifeste des Soixante is reproduced in Proudhon, *De la capacité politique des classes ouvrières* (Marcel Rivière, 1924), 409–17. The present quotations are on pp. 410 and 412–13.

[19] See Bruhat, 'Le socialisme français', 521.

elections and plebiscites alike. Following the publication of the Manifesto a group of workers from Rouen wrote to Proudhon seeking his opinion and advice, and on 8 March 1864 Proudhon replied with a lengthy 'Lettre aux ouvriers' whose arguments were widely diffused and with which, it is reasonable to assume, Baudelaire must have come into contact some time during the months following his arrival in Belgium in April 1864.

The Manifesto presented Proudhon with a dilemma no less acute than that of his supporters for though he endorsed all of the signatories' social and economic objectives, he disagreed entirely with the political means they proposed for achieving them. The 'Lettre aux ouvriers' goes much further than the Manifesto in asserting the existence not only of classes but of class conflict. For Proudhon what defines existing society is its division

en deux catégories de citoyens, vulgairement nommés *bourgeoisie et plèbe, capitalisme et salariat*. . . . Toute notre politique, notre Économie politique, notre organisation industrielle, notre histoire, notre littérature, notre société reposent sur cette distinction que la mauvaise foi et une sotte hypocrisie paraissent seules nier.[20]

Given this division, it is unthinkable for Proudhon that the working classes should participate *in any way* in the political process of the enemy camp. For him, the bourgeois parliamentary opposition cannot possibly be an ally of the working classes for what defines bourgeois republicanism is not so much its opposition to the Empire but its opposition to socialism; on social issues (which for Proudhon are, of course, the only issues of importance), 'les membres de l'opposition prétendue démocratique sont d'accord avec le gouvernement; il sont plus anti-socialistes que le gouvernement lui-même'.[21] The bourgeois opposition, like the government, has, in Proudhon's view, separated itself from the working classes; it would be self-defeating folly for French workers to look to the institutions and representatives of their class enemies for the advancement of their cause. 'C'est pourquoi je vous le dis de toute l'énergie et de toute la tristesse de mon âme,' Proudhon concludes, 'Séparez-vous de ce qui s'est le premier séparé, séparez-vous, comme autrefois le peuple romain se séparait de ses aristocrates.

[20] 'Lettre aux ouvriers', in Proudhon, *Contradictions politiques* (Marcel Rivière, 1952), 134.
[21] Ibid. 321.

Separamini popule meus. C'est par la séparation que vous vaincrez; point de représentants, point de candidats!'[22] 'La séparation que je recommande est la condition même de la vie,' Proudhon wrote shortly afterwards in *De la capacité politique des classes ouvrières*, 'Se distinguer, se définir, c'est être; de même que se confondre et s'absorber, c'est se perdre'.[23] By the time he came to write 'Assommons les pauvres!', Baudelaire would probably not have read these words; they represent, though, Proudhon's final thinking on the options open to the working classes, and I cite them here for the light they may throw on the confrontation of middle-class aggressor and lower-class victim in the text that concerns us.

I mentioned earlier a letter addressed by Proudhon in October to a Belgian supporter, Félix Delhasse;[24] Baudelaire gained private access to it and, since it links up directly with the themes of 'Assommons les pauvres!' I will discuss it in some detail here. The letter is apocalyptic in tone, written half in dread, half in eager expectation, and concerns the increasing interconnectedness of the European—indeed the global—economy, the escalating indebtedness not only of individuals, private companies, and banks but also of governments and nation-states and the way in which if one major economic concern were to default on its debts, first a national, then a continental, and finally a global economic catastrophe would ensue. 'Le commerce, par toute l'Europe, est solidaire,' says Proudhon,

la banque est solidaire, les capitaux sont solidaires; toutes les entreprises, toutes les fortunes, de même que tous les États sont solidaires. Eh bien, au premier accroc que va-t-il arriver? Supposez que la débâcle commence sur ce point, au Comptoir d'escompte, par exemple, au Crédit mobilier, ou ailleurs; toute l'industrie, tout le commerce, la banque et l'agriculture suivront comme un feu de file; le gouvernement suivra; à la suite de la France, la Belgique, l'Italie, l'Angleterre, l'Allemagne, la Hollande, l'Autriche, etc.

Proudhon's reaction to the prospect of 'la banqueroute universelle, européenne, politique et économique, morale, sociale' is characteristically ambivalent. On the one hand, he admits that 'la terreur sera immense; il y aura, par milliers, des gens qui meurent de peur,

---

[22] Proudhon, *Contradictions politiques*, 325.
[23] Proudhon, *De la capacité politique*, 237.
[24] See id., *Correspondance* (A. Lacroix, Brussels, 1875), xiv. 62–8.

frappés d'apoplexie ou désespérés de leur ruine'; on the other, the collapse of the creaking superstructure of accumulated indebtedness would bring about what he calls a 'rafraîchissement universel' of the world's economies and social structures. For, as he asks, 'au fond, qu'y aurait-il de perdu?'

Rien, pas un grain de blé, pas un morceau de betterave, pas un fragment de fer ou de houille, pas un fil de soie, coton, laine ou chanvre. Nos livres seront brûlés: voilà tout. Les grandes propriétés pourront bien éclater en morceaux; en ce qui touche les petites propriétés, il n'y aura pas un patrimoine d'usurpé, ni de confondu.

With the existing economic order collapsing like a house of cards, a new world would emerge which, delivered from the shackles of credit, would be based on what, in his *Idée générale de la révolution* (1851), Proudhon had called 'la communication directe des producteurs et des consommateurs'.[25] 'Propriété', in the specifically Proudhonian sense of the unearned income which, in the existing order, accrues from ownership, would be supplanted by 'possession' (the simple fact of ownership[26]), goods would be exchanged directly between producers and, with the collapse of 'la grande propriété' and its agent, the State, society would henceforth consist of a multitude of autonomous producers, possessing their own means of production, and linked one to the other by bonds of reciprocal need rather than of hierarchy and oppression. It is the old mutualist-anarchist dream of *Qu'est-ce que la propriété?* and the Banque du Peuple, borne apocalyptically out of the 'explosion générale' to which the present economic order is careering.

It was precisely the consistency between what Proudhon stood for in the 1840s and what he stood for at the end of his life that, as we have seen, prompted Baudelaire's admiration and led him, in his letter to Ancelle of 8 February 1865 to describe Proudhon the economist as 'singulièrement respectable'. The letter continues as follows:

Je ne vois qu'une seule manière de mettre à néant les utopies, les idées, les paradoxes et les prophéties de Proudhon sur la rente et sur la propriété, c'est de prouver péremptoirement (l'a-t-on fait? je ne suis pas érudit en

---

[25] Quoted Pierre Ansart, *Proudhon* (Librarie Générale Française, 1984), 288.

[26] On this crucial distinction, see Charles Gide, 'Proudhon and the Socialism of 1848', in Charles Gide and Charles Rihs, *A History of Economic Doctrines from the Time of the Physiocrats to the Present Day* (trans. R. Richards, Harrap, 1948), 301.

ces choses) *que les peuples s'enrichissent en s'endettant.* Vous êtes plus financier que moi; vous devez savoir si cette thèse a été soutenue. (C, ii. 453)

This, it should be noted, is the only occasion on which Baudelaire uses the term 'utopie' in relation to Proudhon, and in a way that is immediately undercut by the implication that the future evoked in the letter to Delhasse may not be 'Utopian' at all. Still more significantly, when a few days earlier he had sent a copy of Proudhon's letter to Ancelle, he had spoken of its author's 'idée fixe de la banqueroute comme *salut*, et de l'abolition de la rente' (C, ii. 452). *Bankruptcy as salvation*: the parallels between Proudhon's chiliastic economic vision and the root and branch transformation of society implicit in 'Assommons les pauvres!' will emerge as we proceed. The Delhasse letter may not be the 'source' of 'Assommons les pauvres!', but the fact that Baudelaire was almost certainly familiar with it when he wrote the poem gives precision to the final reference to Proudhon and makes of it something other—or, at least, something more—than the generalized denunciation of so-called Utopian socialism for which it is almost always taken.

Assommons les pauvres! The verb 'assommer', taken by most modern readers to mean simply 'to beat up', had particular connotations in the 1830s and 1840s which need to be taken into account if all the ironies of the title—itself thudding down like an *assommoir* on the unprepared reader's sensibilities—and the text it introduces are to be understood. Early in *L'Éducation sentimentale*, when Frédéric and Hussonnet witness the beating up of Dussardier by a group of *sergents de ville*, students and onlookers shout in protest 'A bas les assommeurs!', and Flaubert, referring to widespread anti-tax riots in the provinces in 1838, gives the following clarification for his readers of 1869: 'C'était une injurer usuelle depuis les troubles du mois de septembre'.[27] In *Quelques caricaturistes français* (first published 1857), Baudelaire too uses a cognate of 'assommer' to refer specifically to police violence in evoking Daumier's depiction of the turbulent years 1830–4 with their litany

[27] Gustave Flaubert, *L'Éducation sentimentale*, ed. Édouard Maynial (Garnier, 1964), 29–30. Flaubert's *carnets* refer to a work entitled *Les Assommeurs du Châtelet*, an open letter to the Prefect of Police Gabriel Delessert by one Bienvenu G. M. Daernvaelt, author of 'Je casse les vitres'. (See Flaubert, *Carnets de travail*, ed. Pierre-Marc de Biasi (Balland, 1988), 449).

of 'massacres, emprisonnements, arrestations, perquisitions, procès, assommades de la police' (OC, ii. 550), and an entry in *Pauvre Belgique!* similarly refers, in connection with a recent 'unofficial' act of censorship in Ghent, to 'des officiers qui se mettent à cinq pour assommer un journaliste dans son bureau' (OC, ii. 46). It seems likely, then, that, for writers of Baudelaire's generation, the verb 'assommer' had something of the ring of 'tabasser' in modern French argot: though it could (as in the extract from *Le Peintre de la vie moderne* cited earlier) mean any kind of beating-up, it almost automatically evoked beatings-up administered by the police or their paramilitary associates in the name of public order and the public good. It is interesting, therefore, that, before putting his own conception of *le bien public* into action, the narrator of 'Assommons les pauvres!' makes sure that he will remain 'pour un assez long temps hors de la portée de toute police'; free from any threat of *assommades*, the narrator can take the place of the absent *sergent de ville* or *agent de police* and *assommer* at will until mind, heart, and body are fully satisfied. In other words, the narrator—whose similarity to the bored sadistic dandy-prince of *Une mort héroïque* is evident—usurps the function of power to test a 'theory' of human happiness which, to say the least, calls in question the whole power structure of existing society. Narrator and dictator are disturbingly alike: like Napoleon III, the narrator has his vision of how *l'extinction du paupérisme* can be brought about, and he is prepared to go even further than the Emperor—and far, far further than the cautious and conspicuously non-violent Proudhon—to make that 'Utopian' vision real. 'En politique,' reads a chilling entry in *Fusées* dated May 1856, 'le vrai saint est celui qui fouette et tue le peuple pour le bien du peuple' (OC, i. 655).

Bored stupid—*assommé*[28]—by 'toutes les élucubrations de tous ces entrepreneurs de bonheur public'—the narrator at last breaks out of the room in which he has been 'confiné' for the last fortnight and, 'une grande soif' raging within him, heads out on to the streets of Brussels or Paris in search of 'grand air' and 'rafraîchissants'. As he is about to enter a *cabaret* (that focus of working-class radicalism 'il y a seize ou dix-sept ans', now no more than an

---

[28] On the multiple meanings of the verb 'assommer', see Marie Maclean, *Narrative as Performance: The Baudelairean Experiment* (Routledge, 1988), 165–71.

assommoir where the lower classes go to drown their sorrows and frustrations and perhaps, like the workers in Zola's novel, bibulously to relive their Utopian delusions of *quarante-huit*), he encounters a beggar who holds out his hat, hoping, one assumes, for a few coppers that will enable him to *s'assommer à son tour*. In the manuscript, the beggar is first described simply as a 'vieillard', then more precisely as a 'sexagénaire affaibli' as though Baudelaire sought to situate him in relation to the historical events of his own shattered life: 60-odd in 1864–5, say 40 to 45 'il y a seize ou dix-sept ans', 25 in 1830, now a broken-down beggar, a republican exile, perhaps, reduced to penury on the streets of Brussels, but in those far-off *journées* of July, February, and June perhaps one of those *cordonniers*, *bijoutiers*, or *bronziers* whose 'regards inoubliables' did indeed '(culbuter) les trônes' and who might have created *la République démocratique et sociale* 'si l'esprit remuait la matière, et si l'œil d'un magnétiseur faisait mûrir les raisins', for which read: if only Utopian theory could have ripened the grapes and brought forth the rich red wine of a full socialist revolution.

As the beggar stretches out his hat to the bourgeois, one may recall the famous song of February 1848, 'La Casquette', to which Flaubert makes sardonic reference in *L'Éducation sentimentale*:

> Chapeau bas devant ma casquette,
> A genoux devant l'ouvrier![29]

But the narrator, as the reader knows and as the beggar must learn, is no 'ordinary' bourgeois, and it is thus all the more interesting that his first reaction—not to respond to the beggar's mute request for alms—is, or appears to be, identical to that condemned with a force remarkable even for Baudelaire in a text published in 1853 and still shot through with his radical republicanism of the recent past, *Morale du joujou*. Parents who refuse their children toys, says Baudelaire, are

les mêmes gens qui donneraient volontiers un franc à un pauvre, à condition qu'il s'étouffât avec du pain, et lui refuseront toujours deux sous pour se désaltérer au cabaret. Quand je pense à une certaine classe de personnes ultra-raisonnables et anti-poétiques par qui j'ai tant souffert, je sens toujours la haine pincer et agiter mes nerfs. (OC, i. 586)

[29] Flaubert, *L'Éducation sentimentale*, 304.

Once again, therefore, the narrator takes over the discourse of the powerful—*moralisons les pauvres!*—only to turn it comprehensively on its head in the sequence that follows. What prompts the narrator to act as he does is not an abstract conception that precedes the act in the manner of a Utopian blueprint for the ideal society, but one which is formed even as he acts, a theory which begins as a 'germe obscur . . . confiné au fond de mon intellect' (cf. 'confiné dans ma chambre' of the opening sentence) but which only comes to fruition in and through praxis.[30] The narrator's Daemon, whispering to him from the depths of his Unconscious, is, unlike that of Socrates, 'un grand affirmateur . . . un Démon d'action, un Démon de combat' whose nature it is to 'conseiller, suggérer, persuader'.[31] Not for the first time one notes the meticulous plotting of the text in the way in which 'conseiller' and 'persuader' repeat verbs used of the Utopians in the opening paragraph and in which 'suggérer' both echoes and deforms 'digérer' as though, having 'digéré' the theories of others, the narrator will now exercise his right to 'suggérer' on his own account.

What follows is an extraordinary process of exchange, a veritable pugilistic potlatch, which I propose to interpret here as at once a celebration, parody, and subversion of the Proudhonian theory and practice of mutualism. I will begin by noting the way in which, in the very first paragraph, Baudelaire insidiously introduces the themes of numerical increase and incremental growth that will be taken up later in the text: 'quinze jours' leads to 'seize ou dix-sept ans' which leads in its turn to 'vingt-quatre heures'. '*Tout* est nombre,' runs a celebrated entry in *Fusées*, 'le nombre est dans *tout*' (OC, i. 649): $15 + 16 + 17 = 48$, 2×24, and 'Assommons les pauvres!' is poem 49 in the *Petits poèmes en prose*, a location which Richard Terdiman, to whom I owe this last insight, sees as 'an oblique numerological warning of an inevitable movement to follow 1848'.[32] In his excellent discussion of the poem, Terdiman

30 See the excellent comments in Maclean, *Narrative*, 165–6.

31 Monroe ('Baudelaire's Poor', 183–4) draws attention to the similarity between the 'Démon d'action' celebrated in 'Assommons les pauvres!' and Baudelaire's admiration, in 1851, for 'le génie de l'action' as expressed in Dupont's songs. The Dupont article also notes the existence of 'quelque secrète affinité' between Proudhon and the Lyon *chansonnier* (OC, ii. 34).

32 Richard Terdiman, *Discourse/Counter-Discourse: The Theory and Practice of Symbolic Resistance in Nineteenth-Century France* (Cornell Univ. Press, Ithaca, NY, 1985), 315–16.

describes the narrator's 'impulsive and hilarious mock-utopian experiment' as 'a burlesque Hegelian remake of the master–slave dialectic. He tries to induce self-consciousness through the beating he administers to the decrepit beggar. In the second moment the social force potential in the class opponent rebounds, and the punishment is returned double upon its bourgeois instigator.' As a description of what happens between narrator and beggar this could scarcely be bettered, but I am inclined to disagree with Terdiman when he argues that the suppression of the reference to Proudhon marks a retreat *on Baudelaire's part* (rather than, as seems far more plausible, on that of his posthumous editors) from the unpalatable political implications of his text: 'Baudelaire's prose poems can thematize the conflict of classes,' is Terdiman's conclusion, but not, he adds, '*that* openly'. My feeling is rather that Baudelaire not only endorses the thesis of inevitable and necessary class conflict which we have seen Proudhon defending in his 'Lettre aux ouvriers' of 1864 but actually pushes it further than Proudhon would ever do, since 'Assommons les pauvres!' explicitly raises the issue which Proudhon himself always seems to side-step, gloss over, or simply suppress in his writings as in his actions, namely the place of politics, and specifically of political violence, in the achievement of his social and economic objectives. I shall return to this question in my conclusion when I have considered some of the ways in which, to use Terdiman's expression, 'Assommons les pauvres!' 'burlesques'—while paying ambiguous homage to—both the Proudhonian concept of mutualism and the idea of 'la banqueroute comme *salut*' which Baudelaire correctly inferred from the letter to Félix Delhasse.

As its name suggests, mutualism is founded on, in Proudhon's words, the 'idée de mutualité, réciprocité, échange, JUSTICE, sub-stituée à celles d'autorité, communauté ou charité' and, through a transformation of the system of distribution rather than of relations of production, aims to 'construire un système de rapports qui ne tend à rien de moins qu'à changer de fond en comble l'ordre social'.[33] In an ideal society, he says, goods and services would be exchanged directly between producers and consumers at their real value rather than, as they are at present, at prices distorted and inflated by the vast number of intermediate institutions and charges —principally credit institutions and charges—that stand between

---

[33] Proudhon, *De la capacité politique*, 124.

producer and consumer. The goal of mutualism is to restore or to institute for the first time conditions of complete reciprocity and equality between producer and consumer and, to this end, Proudhon proposed, in 1848–9, the creation of a Banque du Peuple which, financed by its members' subscriptions and, initially, a state subvention, would issue paper money equivalent to the combined output of its members, paper money that would be negotiable only amongst members and convertible only into goods and services, not into cash. Such arrangements would, Proudhon argued, create conditions of interest-free credit and would logically draw customers away from banks that continued to lend at interest; as the numbers of subscribers to the Banque du Peuple increased, so would the amount of paper money in circulation, progressively driving existing banks out of business and, as a kind of side-effect, causing their political expression and agent, the State, to 'wither away'. What would remain would be, in Proudhon's words, a condition of 'anarchie positive',[34] a self-regulating society and economy delivered of all political superstructures and consisting of voluntary associations of autonomous but interdependent citizen-producers interacting with each other according to principles of mutualism foreign to both the untrammelled individualism of laissez-faire capitalism and to the 'concentration liberticide, absorbante'[35] of the state, society, and economy envisaged by those Proudhon called 'communists', namely proponents of state-directed socialism such as Louis Blanc and Étienne Cabet. In creating the Banque du Peuple, Proudhon sought, as he put it, to 'opérer la Révolution *par en bas*'[36] by encouraging producers to associate freely, equally, and fraternally with each other and create counter-systems of production and distribution which would supplant those in existence by virtue of their economic and social superiority, thus bypassing the need for political revolution from above. 'Procéder à la réforme sociale par l'extermination du pouvoir et de la politique' was the means; the goal 'point d'autorité, point de gouvernement, même populaire: la Révolution est là.'[37]

[34] Id., *Solution du problème social* (1848), cited Pierre Ansart, *Sociologie de Proudhon* (Presses Universitaires de France, 1967), 52.

[35] Proudhon, *Idée générale de la révolution* (1851), cited Ansart, *Sociologie de Proudhon*, 116.

[36] Id., *Les Confessions d'un révolutionnaire pour servir à l'histoire de la Révolution de Février* (Marcel Rivière, 1929), 80.

[37] Id., *Système des contradictions économiques* (1846) and *Idée générale*, cited Ansart, *Sociologie de Proudhon*, 124–5.

In *De la capacité politique des classes ouvrières*, Proudhon defines the 'principe mutuelliste' as meaning 'service pour service
... produit pour produit, prêt pour prêt, assurance pour assurance, crédit pour crédit, caution pour caution, garantie pour garantie, etc.' and comments: 'C'est l'antique talion, *œil pour œil, dent pour dent, vie pour vie*, en quelque sorte retourné, transporté du droit criminel et des atroces pratiques de la *vendetta* dans le droit économique, les œuvres du travail et les bons offices de la libre fraternité.'[38] It is at this point that one can begin to discern the ironic congruence between Baudelaire's text and the theory of mutualism, for what 'Assommons les pauvres!' does is bring together a producer (the narrator) and a consumer (the beggar) in the unmediated person-to-person relationship advocated by Proudhon and then cause them to engage in a series of exchanges, not of goods, services, or even cash, but of blows, which represent a regression to the conditions of *l'antique talion* which, according to Proudhon, mutualist theory had 'turned on its head'. If it were only a *retournement du retournement* operated by Proudhon, 'Assommons les pauvres!' could indeed legitimately be read, as it commonly has been, as a sarcastic but ideologically straightforward refutation, in the name of what Baudelaire elsewhere calls 'la grande vérité oubliée, la perversité primordiale de l'homme' (*Notes nouvelles sur Edgar Poe* (1857) (OC, ii. 323)) of all the Utopian illusions of 1848 of which Proudhonian mutualism is held to be entirely typical.

But the relationship between text and intertext is considerably more complex than this, for while 'Assommons les pauvres!' sends up the Proudhonian ideal of unmediated reciprocal exchange by precipitating an exchange of evils rather than of good(s), the net result of the narrator's theory and practice of 'negative mutuality' is, or appears to be, identical to the goals of 'positive mutuality' as propounded by Proudhon, namely the creation of a relationship of liberty, equality, and fraternity between the two parties to the exchange which is no less real for having been sealed by reciprocal violence: out of the exchange of evils, an apparently positive good has been born. Moreover, the exchange has, in its negative-ironic way, been notably productive, not simply a case, as in *l'antique talion*, of *œil pour œil* and *dent pour dent* but of *deux yeux pour un œil* and *quatre dents pour deux dents*, suggesting, perhaps, a

[38] Proudhon, *De la capacité politique*, 125.

parody of the way in which, in Proudhon's theory of the Banque du Peuple, the combined wealth of subscribers would increase exponentially as they conducted their credit-free exchanges with each other. More cynically, one might observe that it is the party that possesses more at the outset, the narrator, who, at the end, possesses twice as much 'capital'—two black eyes and four broken teeth—than the beggar who is now supposedly his equal. The two parties may divide the narrator's purse equally between them, but the narrator still possesses resources far in excess of the beggar's. All mutualists may be equal but some, it seems, are more equal than others.

'Assommons les pauvres!', then, presents a series of bizarre convergences with and divergences from Proudhonian theory. From Proudhon's economic theory it takes the idea of equal and reciprocal exchange, turns it on its head but then shows apparently positive results accruing from this *retournement*. From the letter to Félix Delhasse it takes over the idea that a single 'raccroc' in a complex system of interlocking interdependencies has potentially limitless consequences of a catastrophic but liberating kind. The narrator's defaulting on the obligation to give charity corresponds, in Proudhon's apocalyptic vision, to the failure of a single company, bank, or government to honour its obligations, thereby unleashing the concatenation of defaults that leads to the 'rafraîchissement universel' of global bankruptcy. Having taken half of the narrator's purse, the beggar agrees to repeat his benefactor's 'experiment' on the person of every *confrère* who approaches him for charity, each of whom will, after the ritualized exchange of *assommades*, presumably make a similar commitment, leading logically to further divisions, sub-divisions, and sub-sub-divisions of the combined 'capital' of the beggar population until finally the mutualist Utopia —a confraternity of completely free and completely equal citizens— will have been realized amongst them. By following the narrator's example and obeying his instructions—the equivalent, in the circumstances, of Proudhon's urging his working-class followers to 'se distinguer' and 'se séparer' to achieve self-identity—the beggars will have separated themselves completely from bourgeois society and, through their exchanges with each other, have created a parodic version of that self-subsistent, self-sustaining federation of mutualist associations that Proudhonian theory urged workers to create within the interstices of capitalist society, pending the collapse—for reasons that, crucially, are never fully spelt out—of the capitalist system itself.

It is at this point that the ambiguities in the narrator's position—not to mention in Baudelaire's—become too numerous and too complex to be grasped in a single formulation. There can be no doubt that 'Assommons les pauvres!' brings out a fatal flaw—perhaps *the* fatal flaw—in Proudhon's whole conception of mutualism, namely the uncertainty surrounding the part to be played by politics and, above all, by political revolution in the creation of a socialist society. Proudhonian theory held that if workers—not necessarily all workers but, presumably, a sizeable majority amongst them—formed their own mutualist associations and their own mutualist exchange system within and alongside the structures of existing capitalist society, those structures would sooner or later cease to be viable and would disintegrate of their own accord, thus obviating the need for the kind of political revolution 'from above' advocated by Proudhon's great rivals, the neo-Jacobins and their leftist descendants, the Blanquists. The great paradox of Proudhon's thought is that, despite spending a lifetime denouncing 'la bancocratie' and 'l'État-ulcère', he none the less failed to grasp that neither the capitalist system nor the capitalist state was likely simply to allow itself to 'wither away' in the manner mutualist theory predicted, and that if either were to be *seriously* threatened 'from below' by autonomous workers' institutions, as would happen six years after Proudhon's death, and four years after Baudelaire's, in 1871, they would retaliate with quite massive political force to maintain their position. 'Assommons les pauvres!' could, therefore, be read, as Dolf Oehler does, as a warning, delivered from a standpoint that is *marxiste sans le savoir*, against the illusion of mutualist anti-politicism to which, it should be stressed, thousands of French and other workers subscribed in the mid-1860s. In this perspective, the narrator becomes, in Oehler's expression, a 'Satanic liberator' of the oppressed, heightening the misery of one docile member of 'le peuple' to make him fight back against his tormentor and so force him and his *confrères* to realize that only violence—violence directed against the bourgeoisie—can remove their misery by destroying its source and that to look to charity, either in its 'philanthropic' bourgeois form or in the supposedly radical disguise of Proudhonian mutualism, is not to challenge the existing system but to reinforce and perpetuate it.

This is a seductive thesis, but one which, I think, is contradicted once one examines closely the actual results and likely implications of the narrator's 'experiment'.

In the first place, the beggar is urged by the narrator not to *assommer les bourgeois* but to apply his 'theory' 'à tous (ses) confrères qui (lui) demanderont l'aumône'. As a result of their 'exchanges' with each other, the beggars may well create a confraternity of equals amongst themselves, but, like Proudhon's mutualist associations, this need have no necessary effect on the profoundly unequal and anti-mutualist structures of existing society which could hardly be weakened, and could well be confirmed, by the application of the narrator's 'theory'. Secondly, the idea that the narrator's experiment has 'liberated' the beggar from his subservience and has transformed him into an 'equal' is decisively negated by the final sentence of the first published version: 'Il m'a bien juré qu'il avait compris ma théorie, et qu'il obéirait à mes conseils.' The reader can hardly fail to make the connection between the narrator's 'conseils' and the 'ceux qui conseillent à tous les pauvres de se faire esclaves' of the opening paragraph. The narrator's 'conseils' may be different in content from those of the 'entrepreneurs de bonheur public' he detests, but his status as 'counsellor' is much the same. The hierarchical relationship between narrator and beggar is ultimately unchanged by their supposedly equalizing exchange of blows. The narrator theorizes, experiments, instructs, and confers 'equality': the beggar swears that he will obey, promptly exchanging one form of 'esclavage' for another.

Finally, it seems to me that, far from being a liberator—'Satanic' or otherwise—of 'le peuple', the narrator of 'Assommons les pauvres!' is a brother-in-perversity of the narrator of 'Le Mauvais Vitrier' or of the central figure of 'La Fausse Monnaie', the close relationship of which to 'Assommons les pauvres!' is indicated by its probable original title: 'Le Paradoxe de l'aumône' (OC, ii. 607). In this poem, it will be recalled, a friend of the narrator gives a beggar a counterfeit coin of apparently considerable value in order at once to delight and delude the recipient and, like the narrator of 'Assommons les pauvres!', to introduce a 'raccroc' into a series of commercial exchanges with unforeseeable, and possibly disastrous, consequences for one or more of the parties concerned. The narrator condemns his friend not simply because 'il avait voulu faire à la fois la charité et une bonne affaire' and so 'emporter le paradis économiquement', but more because of the *inconscience* with which he acted: 'On n'est jamais excusable d'être méchant, mais il y a quelque mérite à savoir qu'on l'est; et le plus irréparable des vices est de faire le mal par bêtise' (OC, i. 324). In contrast, there is no better commentary on the state of mind of the narrator of 'Assommons les pauvres!' as he decides, consciously and deliberately, to obey his 'daemon' than the remarkable concluding entry of *Pauvre Belgique!* (OC, ii. 961):

MOI, quand je consens à être républicain, *je fais le mal, le sachant.* Oui! *Vive la Révolution!* Toujours! quand même! Mais moi je ne suis pas dupe, je n'ai jamais été dupe! je dis *Vive la Révolution!* comme je dirais: *Vive la Destruction! Vive l'Expiation! Vive le Châtiment! Vive la Mort!* Non seulement je serais heureux d'être victime, mais je ne haïrais pas d'être bourreau, pour sentir la Révolution des deux manières! Nous avons tous l'esprit républicain dans les veines, comme la vérole dans les os, nous sommes démocratisés et syphilisés.

Yet from first to last the narrator of 'Assommons les pauvres!' is *bourreau* not *victime*, and never more *bourreau*, ironically, than when he is reeling under the beggar's blows, just as the beggar is most the victim at the moment of his specious triumph. Far from being a parable of revolutionary liberation, 'Assommons les pauvres!' seems to me to be a sinister, nihilistic *blague*, a perverse illustration of the rhetorical question posed in *Mon cœur mis à nu*: 'Vous figurez-vous un Dandy parlant au peuple, excepté pour le bafouer?' (OC, i. 684).[39] 'Assommons les pauvres!' was first published in June 1869, a little more than a year before the fall of the Second Empire, and eighteen months or so before the proclamation of the Commune. It may be a *blague* but, as Baudelaire pointed out in a letter to Sainte-Beuve of 30 March 1865 (C, ii. 491), there is nothing more significant or prophetic than a certain kind of joke: 'Quand les gens s'amusent d'une certaine façon, c'est un bon diagnostic de révolution.'

---

[39] Stenzel, (*Der historische Ort Baudelaires: Untersuchungen zur Entwicklung des französischen Literatur um die Mitte des 19. Jahrhunderts* (Wilhelm Fink, Munich, 1980), 211) sees 'Assommons les pauvres!' as an expression of 'eine Politik der Katastrophe' linked to 'eines gesellschaftlichen Zustanden, in dem alles auf Negativität hinauslauft'.

Conclusion: Ni Droite ni Gauche?
Baudelaire and the Politics of
Nineteenth-Century France

On the basis of the basis of the evidence discussed in the previous
chapters, I would like to conclude with a number of comments on
the general trajectory of Baudelaire's political thinking, and on its
relationship to the broader political development of nineteenth-
century France, that range from the confident to the tentative to
the unabashedly speculative. Where I feel most confident is on the
central subject of this book, the period February 1848 to December
1851, during which, it seems to me, Baudelaire displays every sign
in what he did and in what he wrote of being a committed and
consistent radical republican, close initially to the Blanquist camp
and then, after the June insurrection, and under the determining
influence of Proudhon, to the *démoc-socs* with whom the evidence
suggests Baudelaire consciously aligned himself, publishing a
number of texts, notably *Du vin et du haschisch* and the first essay
on Pierre Dupont, that can be described without exaggeration as
démoc-soc propaganda. The widely held view that Baudelaire
participated in the street-fighting of 1848 as a *bourgeois révolté*
rather than as a *révolutionnaire* is plausible in the case of February
but, I would argue, wholly false in the case of June: to fight, as
Baudelaire undoubtedly did, on the June barricades required real
revolutionary commitment if one was middle class, and implies, in
Baudelaire's case, an intensification of his radicalism between
February and June rather than, as is commonly asserted, a diminution or dilution.

The evidence also suggests that, in the aftermath of June, Baudelaire in no way lost interest in radical politics and still less that he
in some way moved from 'left' to 'right'. What happened rather
was that the character of his radicalism shifted, as did that of
thousands of radical republicans (often influenced, as Baudelaire
was, by Proudhon's post-June speeches and writings), from the
old-style confrontational model of the Blanquists to the new

démoc-soc strategy of eschewing head-on clashes with the forces of
reaction that could only lead to further defeats, and concentrating
instead on building up a nation-wide (rather than merely Parisian)
republican party that would oppose the right first through the
ballot-box and then, if necessary, by force. After June, conscious
now if he had not been before that 'toutes les choses humaines—
idées, droits, institutions—ne se génèrent que lentement et que par
un progrès successif et analogue à toutes les floraisons, moissons et
récoltes' ('Actuellement' (OC, ii. 1063)), Baudelaire, in common
with the emerging *démoc-soc* party, stressed the need for purposive
collective action in pursuit of the possible. When this pragmatic but
still radical progressivism proved incapable of containing the
advance of the right, Baudelaire, like many middle-class republicans in Paris, took to the streets in a last-ditch attempt to save the
Republic, distraught that the working-class *faubourgs* themselves
showed no similar will to defend the Republic against its enemies by
force. Several shaken by *le 2 décembre* and still more by the ensuing
plebiscite that effectively legitimized the Bonapartiste putsch,
Baudelaire's radical populist faith collapsed in the face of the elections of 29 February 1852 in which a predominantly lower-class
electorate overwhelmingly endorsed Bonapartist candidates: it was
this, rather than the coup itself, that 'depoliticized' Baudelaire in
the restricted Proudhonian sense of destroying forever his faith in
electoral politics. Shakily sustained in the immediate aftermath of
the coup by Proudhon's dubious arguments in *La Révolution
sociale démontrée par le coup d'état de deux décembre*, what was
left of Baudelaire's radicalism disintegrated in the course of 1852
and, with Poe and de Maistre replacing Proudhon as his *maîtres à
penser*, may be said to have disappeared by the time the Second
Empire was proclaimed a year after the coup. By the beginning of
1853 the way was clearly open for the virulent anti-humanism and
anti-naturalism—to say nothing of the anti-feminism that explodes
in 'A une femme trop gaie' (December 1852)—of the 'mature'
Baudelaire of the late 1850s and 1860s.

Conclusions as to the pre-1848 and post-1852 periods must be
much more tentative, particularly where the earlier period is
concerned. The view, strenuously advanced by Dolf Oehler, that
the *Salon de 1846* articulates a coherent, if deviously expressed,
radical republican (or, at the very least, 'anti-bourgeois') position
does not seem to me to have been proven and, given the nature of

that text, may indeed be neither provable or disprovable. On the other hand, the *Salon de 1846*—written, as I have tried to show, at a time when nothing seemed more unlikely than that, less than two years later, the Bourgeois Monarchy would disappear virtually overnight in a puff of smoke—does contain the lineaments or nucleus of a radical republican position. If it does not lead directly to the barricades of February and June, neither does it lead away from them, which is why I have preferred to call it a 'pre-political' text rather than an 'apolitical' or 'anti-political' one. For reasons I have tried to explain, something more was required to make a revolutionary out of Baudelaire than simple opposition (in de Certeau's sense) to the orthodoxies of Bourgeois Monarchy thought and art, but, given the absence of published texts between January 1847 and January 1848, that extra ingredient is unlikely ever to be pin-pointed. If we knew more of what Baudelaire did, wrote, and, above all, read in 1847—and particularly if we could prove that he read *Philosophie de la misère* some time before the outbreak of revolution—the road from the *Salon de 1846* to the February barricades and beyond, while hardly smooth and level, would probably not contain the qualitative leap from one world-view to another that, as things stand, it seems necessarily to involve.

But if the *Salon de 1846* contains *in nuce* the radical republicanism of 1848–51, it also carried within it the rudiments, as we have seen, of an élitist, anti-democratic world-view centred on the moral superiority of the authentic artist which, following the essentially populist theory of poetry and the poet elaborated in *Pierre Dupont (I)*, would resurface with a vengeance after the December coup. If, in addition, we accept Claude Pichois' view that *De l'essence du rire*, complete with its insistent sense of the reality of original sin, is, in its essentials, a pre-1848 composition, then it is clear that, at the very least, the rudiments of Baudelaire's post-1851 thought were present, along with its opposite, in his pre-revolutionary writings. While reading Poe and de Maistre in 1851–2 may, as Baudelaire said, have taught him to 'raisonner' (OC, i. 669), that is all they did. In other words, they did not give him any new ideas, but taught him how to articulate and express thoughts and feelings which, in varying degrees of consciousness, were present within him before 1848: the superstructure of Baudelaire's post-1851 thought may be de Maistrian, but its infrastructure is authentically and, so to speak, aboriginally Baudelairean. Baudelaire's mind was, in Philip Larkin's striking phase, a mind 'double-yolked with meaning and meaning's rebuttal', capable of sustaining antithetical propositions and even conflicting world-views more or less simultaneously, and it required only some seismic event—such as the December coup—to bring to the surface elements which, for one reason or another, had been repressed and denied during the years immediately preceding. If there is an underlying continuity between the *Salon de 1846* and the radical republicanism of 1848–51, there is also no fundamental discontinuity between it and Baudelaire's post-1851 world-view. The only enduring characteristic of the Baudelairean *homo duplex* is the consistency of his contradictions, the constancy of his dubieties and divisions. Small wonder that, some time around mid-century, Baudelaire should have noted the following *pensée* in an album belonging to Philoxène Boyer: 'Parmi les droits dont on a parlé dans ces derniers temps, il y a un qu'on oublie, à la démonstration duquel *tout le monde* est intéressé,—le droit de se contredire' (OC, i. 709).

After 1851 (or, more precisely, after 1852), Baudelaire reverted to the kind of oppositional tactics he had adopted in the mid-1840s but which the possibility of a strategy of resistance opened up by the events of 1847–8 had temporarily made redundant.[1] While Baudelaire, it seems to me, never made his peace with either Empire or Emperor (though he was strongly drawn despite himself to the person of the latter), it is important to distinguish his opposition to the Bourgeois Monarchy with its left-revolutionary potential from the very different political implications of the stance he adopted towards the wealth- and pleasure-seeking mentality of the Second Empire. Baudelaire was no less 'anti-bourgeois' after 1852 than he had been before 1848 nor was his disaffection from the dominant ethos any less great, but since there is a bourgeoisophobia of the right as well as of the left, a bourgeoisophobia which, in its extreme forms, points more in the direction of fascism than of socialism in any left-wing sense, it is vital to examine the values and beliefs that underpinned his opposition to the regime installed by the December coup. Those values and beliefs are, it is immediately clear, antithetical to those that Baudelaire 'officially' espoused between 1848 and 1851 but at the same time embody and bring to the surface a set

[1] For a full discussion of Baudelaire's oppositional textual practice after 1851, see Ross Chambers, *Mélancolie et opposition: Les Débuts du modernisme en France* (Corti, 1987), esp. chap. 5, 'Un despotisme oriental', 131–66.

of conscious or unconscious urges that, subliminally present but for the most part held in check before and during the Second Republic, exploded with quite prodigious force in the wake of the Republic's collapse: 'Ma tête devient littéralement un volcan malade', as Baudelaire wrote to Ancelle in the crucial letter of March 1852 (C, i. 188), 'De grands orages et de grandes aurores'. What the political eruption of late 1851 and 1852 brought to the surface was a lava-flow of fears and hates that Baudelaire's progressive, optimistic, humanistic republican ideology of the preceding years had, with some difficulty, been able to contain: hatred and fear of nature, hatred and fear of women, hatred and fear of 'le peuple', hatred and fear of self, all flowing one into the other, and needing only an intellectual mould or matrix such as that furnished by *Du Pape* and *Les Soirées de Saint-Pétersbourg* to harden into an ideological crust of an explicitly, though not—being Baudelaire—an unambiguously reactionary kind.

On the surface, Baudelaire's political trajectory between the February revolution and the mid-1850s has much in common with that of Flaubert, Leconte de Lisle, the Goncourt brothers, and other writers who, having supported, usually without much enthusiasm, the Republic in its earliest days, subsequently—in most cases by December 1848 at the latest—turned against it and took refuge in a stance that combined an 'apolitical' aestheticism in literary practice with cynicism and indifference in everyday life.[2] What makes Baudelaire different is first that, having espoused the revolutionary cause much more passionately and, above all, for much longer than such contemporaries, his volte-face was that much more extreme and violent than theirs and, second, that it was not into a set of postures and attitudes that he retreated after 1851 but into a systematic, all-embracing *ideology*—the authoritarian hyper-Augustinianism of de Maistre—that enabled him to theorize his antagonism not only to the Republic and the Empire that displaced it but also to all possible socio-political systems that might appear in the future. Thanks to his reading of de Maistre, Baudelaire was able to posit himself as an absolute outsider, beyond people and bourgeoisie, revolution and reaction, left and right, as an extra-social, almost extra-terrestrial observer of 'le spectacle ennuyeux de l'immortel péché' ('Le Voyage') for whom the whole

---

[2] See Paul Lidsky, *Les Écrivains contre la Commune* (Maspéro, 1970), 12–39.

of human history is a predictable sado-masochistic horror-story: 'Le canon tonne . . . les membres volent . . . des gémissements de victimes et des hurlements de sacrificateurs se font entendre . . . C'est l'Humanité qui cherche le bonheur' (OC, i. 371).

In the course of the 1850s and 1860s, the de Maistrian crust hardened, thickened, deepened until it held almost the totality of Baudelaire's thought-processes in its grip and threatened his very survival as a lyric poet. If from time to time (most notably, as I have argued elsewhere, in 1859[3]), a more spontaneous, creative, and fecund self was able to manifest and express itself, it did so in the teeth of an 'official' ideology whose principal components— anti-humanism, anti-democracy, anti-populism, anti-feminism combined with a leavening of anti-semitism that, in 1865, enabled Baudelaire casually to describe his publisher Michel Lévy as 'appartenant à une race qui a crucifié Notre-Seigneur' (C, ii. 490)[4] —seem, judged by the criteria of the late twentieth century, to belong unambiguously to the political right. If 'Assommons les pauvres!' marks Baudelaire's final, if highly ambivalent, repudiation of the radicalism of 1848, a reading of the contemporaneous *Pauvre Belgique!* leaves little doubt concerning his still greater disdain for the new generation of French socialists of the 1860s. Some time in late 1865, Baudelaire extracted for contemptuous quotation a number of statements, reported in *La Rive gauche*,[5] made by French socialist students at a recent joint meeting with their counterparts in Belgium. Characteristically, many of the statements Baudelaire singled out for derision are shot through with precisely the kind of radical antitheism that he himself had passionately endorsed during his 'socialist interlude' fifteen or twenty years earlier:

Le citoyen Tridon, étudiant français: *La lutte est en ce moment entre l'Homme et Dieu, l'avenir et le passé.* Le citoyen Sibrac, étudiant français: *C'est Eve qui a jeté le premier cri de révolte contre Dieu.*[6] Le citoyen Lafargue, étudiant français: Les hommes sont solidaires, ils

---

[3] See Burton, *Baudelaire in 1859: A Study in the Sources of Poetic Creativity* (Cambridge Univ. Press, 1988), esp. pp. 83–6 where the tension between de Maistrianism and lyricism is discussed.

[4] See also the entry in *Mon cœur mis à nu*, possibly the theme of a never-written short story: 'Belle conspiration à organiser pour l'extermination de la Race Juive' (OC, i. 706).

[5] Reproduced in *Pauvre Belgique!* OC, ii. 908–12.

[6] Cf. another entry in *Pauvre Belgique!*: 'Toast à Eve. Toast à Caïn' (OC, ii. 918).

doivent s'unir dans le grand principe de la mutualité et repousser toute idée extra-humaine qui n'a de fondement nulle part. *Guerre à Dieu! le progrès est là.*

Baudelaire's sarcastic use of 'citoyen' to designate the student radicals plainly links up with his parallel denunciation of 'Citoyen Proudhon' in 'Assommons les pauvres!' It is of some interest to note that his 'citoyen Lafargue' is none other than Paul Lafargue (1842–1911), Marx's son-in-law and, with Jules Guesde, the pioneer of Marxist theory and practice in France in the 1870s and 1880s.[7]

But Baudelaire's evident contempt for socialism in the late 1850s and 1860s did not mean that he had ceased to be a republican, an implacable enemy of the bourgeoisie and, in the broadest sense of the word, a revolutionary. As to the first, what evidence there is suggests that, notwithstanding his 'depoliticization' of 1851–2, Baudelaire remained a republican until the end of his creative life, at least in the minimum sense of rejecting both royalism (in either its legitimist or Orleanist form)[8] and Bonapartism. He clearly thought of himself as a republican, describing himself as such in a letter of May 1865, already quoted, concerning a recent meeting with Madame Hugo and her sons,[9] and insisting, in a letter to Victor de Laprade of December 1861, that 'malgré l'obligation apparente pour tout républicain d'être athée', he himself had always remained 'un fervent catholique' (C, ii. 198): the implication is plainly that he for his part is that mid-nineteenth-century anomaly, both a republican and a (Catholic) Christian. Secondly, any notion that Baudelaire in some way made his peace with the bourgeois hegemony after 1851 should be quashed by the following invective in the *Salon de 1859*:

Dans la Thebaïde que mon cerveau s'est faite . . . je dispute parfois avec des monstres grotesques du plein des spectres de la rue, du salon, de l'omnibus. En face de moi, je vois l'Âme de la Bourgeoisie, et croyez bien que si je ne craignais pas de maculer à jamais la tenture de ma cellule, je lui

[7] See OC, ii. 1497. It is likely that the Tridon referred to is Gustave Tridon, the future Communard and subsequent author of *Du molochisme juif* (1884).

[8] In the letter to Victor de Laprade referred to in the next sentence of the text, Baudelaire describes himself as being 'à l'antipode' of Laprade's real or alleged royalism (C, ii. 198).

[9] Baudelaire claims in this letter to have been a republican well before Hugo and his 'clan' and implying that he has never ceased to be one.

jetterais volontiers, et avec une vigueur qu'elle ne soupçonne pas, mon écritoire à la face. (OC, ii. 654)

Finally, in a letter to Nadar of May 1859 (C, i. 579), Baudelaire revealingly criticized his photographer friend for not being 'Jésuite et Révolutionnaire, comme tout vrai politique doit l'être, ou l'est fatalement'. The implication is once again that, politically speaking, he himself is, or likes to think of himself as, precisely that disquieting and paradoxical combination of ultra-Catholic authoritarian and revolutionary, and it is indeed a radical ultra-Catholicism that gives ideological coherence to the diatribes and denunciations of *Pauvre Belgique!*, that 'livre anti-libre penseur, fortement tourne au bouffon' (C, ii. 443) whose purpose, Baudelaire told Ancelle in February 1866 (C, ii. 611), was to combine 'la raillerie de tout ce qu'on appelle *progrès*, ce que j'appelle, moi: *le paganisme des imbéciles*' with nothing less than 'la démonstration du gouvernement de Dieu'. For Baudelaire, writing just a month before the fall in the Église Saint-Loup at Namur that put an end to his creative life, his politico-religious position was plainly clarity itself. To many modern readers, however, it will seem a tangle of contradictions, a congeries of 'right-' and 'left-wing' impulses. By situating these seemingly contradictory impulses within the broader contexts of French political thought in the second half of the nineteenth century, I hope, in conclusion, to be able to locate an underlying coherence in Baudelaire's political thinking as it had defined itself by the end of his life, to indicate the ideological direction in which it was pointing and so to link it with emerging currents of thought whose underlying meaning would not be fully revealed until the century that followed.

A republican contemptuous, as we have seen, of elections and constitutions ('Les constitutions sont du *papier*. Les mœurs sont *tout*.' (*Pauvre Belgique!* (OC, ii. 914)));[10] a hater of democracy convinced that 'il n'y a de gouvernement raisonnable et assuré que l'aristocratique' (*Mon cœur mis à nu* (OC, i. 684)); a de Maistrian theocrat whose 'sympathie visible pour les Jésuites' (C, ii. 388)

[10] Cf. the statement in 'Actuellement' (*Le Représentant de l'Indre*, 20 Oct. 1848) to the effect that 'on ne décrète pas la vertu, pas plus que la renonciation; il faut que ces choses soient d'abord dans les mœurs. Ce qui n'est pas dans les mœurs n'est que chiffons de paper' (OC, ii. 1063). The exact parallel between this and the entry in *Pauvre Belgique!* makes it virtually certain, in my view, that 'Actuellement' is by Baudelaire.

made him many enemies in Belgium but whose faith in a divine principle of power and order, let alone of love, was at best vacillating and abstract;[11] at once a strident anti-socialist and an anti-capitalist for whom 'le commerce est, par son essence, *satanique*' (*Mon cœur mis à nu* (OC, i. 703)); misogynist,[12] paedophobe,[13] probable anti-Semite and hater of 'Peuple' and 'Bourgeoisie' alike: it is immediately evident that such a creature of contradiction cannot readily be assigned a precise location on the conventional political continuum of 'left' and 'right'. Accordingly, I propose to use—though in a broader and looser sense than he[14]—Zeev Sternhell's category of *ni droite ni gauche* as the best available designation of Baudelaire's political position during the last six or seven years of his creative life when his thinking had stabilized—some might say rigidified—around certain fundamental convictions, prejudices, and hatreds after the confusions and uncertainties of the early and middle 1850s.

Ni droite ni gauche is how Sternhell characterizes in the first instance that current of French political thought and practice, originally exemplified by Edouard Vaillant, Benoît Malon, and Henri Rochefort, which, with its political roots (as were Baudelaire's) in Fourierism, Blanquism, and Proudhonism, vigorously espoused the Communard cause in 1871 but which, veering to the right in the late 1870s and 1880s, elaborated an authoritarian, anti-bourgeois, anti-capitalist, anti-semitic but still 'socialist' model of society, backed Boulanger in 1888–9 and so provided the link between the socialism of 1848 and 1871 and the anarcho-syndicalism of the 1890s and 1900s which, in its turn, would debouch in the proto-fascism of Georges Sorel, Georges Valois and the Cercle Proudhon just before the outbreak of the First World War. More

---

[11] See the letter to his mother of 6 May 1861 (C, ii. 151) on his longing to believe that 'un être extérieur et invisible s'intéresse à ma destinée; mais comment faire pour le croire?'

[12] In Belgium Baudelaire even came to hate old women who elsewhere, he said, have the 'grand mérite . . . d'attendrir l'esprit sans émouvoir les sens' (*Pauvre Belgique!*, OC, ii. 870).

[13] See the prose poem 'Le Gâteau' (1862) and the view, expressed in *L'Œuvre et la vie de Delacroix* (1863), that the child is 'en général, relativement à l'homme, en général, beaucoup plus rapproché du péché originel' (OC, ii. 767). Needless to say, Belgian children are the worst of all: 'L'enfance, jolie presque partout, est ici hideuse, teigneuse, galeuse, crasseuse, merdeuse' (OC, ii. 870).

[14] See Zeev Sternhell, *La Droite révolutionnaire 1885–1914: Les Origines françaises du fascisme* (Seuil, 1978) and *Ni droite ni gauche: L'idéologie fasciste en France* (Seuil, 1983).

generally, the term is used to designate all those political ideologies, programmes, and organizations of the Third Republic—most notably Action Française, the Ligue des Patriotes and the explicitly fascist formations of the 1920s and 1930s—that were at once reactionary (in that they sought to overthrow the 'bourgeois' republic and establish a monolithic authoritarian regime), revolutionary (in that they advocated violence in furtherance of their aims and had nothing but contempt for the 'bourgeois' values of humanism, liberalism, and scientific rationalism) and, in the sense that they opposed capitalism and sought the support of working-class radicals, socialist. Such ideologies and formations did not emerge until the 1890s but were preceded and, to some considerable degree, prepared, by the formidable assault unleashed against the Third Republic and its secular liberal-humanist values by the ultra-Catholic intelligentsia of the 1870s and 1880s.[15] What we know of Baudelaire's political thinking of the 1860s suggests that, had he lived on through and beyond the Paris Commune, he would have been powerfully attracted to the ultra-Catholic reaction of which his mentor de Maistre and close friend Barbey d'Aurevilly were leading forebears and inspirations. With the Catholic reactionaries of the early Third Republic the Baudelaire of the 1860s shared a detestation of humanism, liberalism, rationalism, and progressivism combined with an obsessive sense of 'la perversité primordiale de l'homme' (OC, ii. 323). Lacking their faith in the redemptive power of the God-Man Christ, he none the less believed, like them, in the virtue of suffering ('Je crois qu'il est bon que les innocents souffrent,' he told Madame Paul Meurice in 1865 (C, ii. 500)) and, as his remarkable speculations on capital punishment reveal, in the redemptive value of *self*-sacrifice;[16] it might be said, in short, that he anticipated all of a Léon Bloy's phobias and morbidity but none of his positive faith in God's love for the weak and suffering. Similarly, while Baudelaire's loathings of the late 1850s and 1860s point forward unmistakably to the hatreds of Maurrasians, Barrèsians, anarcho-syndicalists, and the like, neither letters, notes, nor published works give any evidence that he would have endorsed the monarchism of the first, the nationalism of the second, or the militant atheism of the last, though the tactic of the *grève générale*

---

[15] See Richard Griffiths, *The Reactionary Revolution: The Catholic Revival in French Literature 1870–1914* (Constable, 1966), esp. ch. 8, 'Vicarious suffering'.
[16] See esp. OC, i. 683.

is curiously anticipated in the social and economic chaos implicit in 'Assommons les pauvres!''s 'theory' of proletarian liberation. Thus, while there are no grounds for seeing 'late Baudelaire' as a pre- or proto-fascist in any 'positive' sense, negatively, in terms of what he despised and detested, he had much in common with the revolutionary ultra-Right of the 1890s and 1900s and, by the same token, much in common with the revolutionary ultra-Left whose detestation of bourgeois democracy and its associated values had, as Sternhell and others have shown, caused their ideas and interests to converge with those of men and movements which, by conventional criteria of 'left' and 'right', should have been their bitterest enemies.

It is perhaps as an anticipation of this *fin de siècle* meeting of the categories of 'left' and 'right' and their eventual amalgamation in something close to fascism that the historical significance of 'Assommons les pauvres!' may be said to lie. The very fact that the text can be plausibly interpreted either as an incitement to revolutionary violence (in a left-wing, proto-Marxist sense) or as a nihilistic *reductio ad absurdum* of all forms of leftism already locates it at or close to the point—so fateful for the twentieth century— where the opposition between left and right ceases to be operable. 'Assommons les pauvres!' does not, as I have tried to show, attack (Proudhonian) socialism from a clear-cut right-wing or reactionary standpoint but uses the very terms of Proudhonism to turn it against itself and in so doing deconstruct the opposition of 'left' and 'right' on which conventional political perceptions and judgements largely depend. In this light, the narrator appears not so much as a 'Satanic liberator', as one critical view would have it, of the beggar but as one who satanically parodies socialism and twists it into its opposite, leaving the beggar deludedly grateful for the pseudo-freedom (in fact a still greater bondage) that has been conferred upon him. In Baudelaire's nihilistic narrator with his satanic (in)version of the revolutionary trinity of *Liberté, Égalité, Fraternité* is prefigured the twentieth century hater of capitalism, democracy, and socialism alike who would use society's rejects and victims to set in motion his own perverted 'entreprise du bonheur public'. Beyond 'Assommons les pauvres!''s duo of *bourreau* and *victime*, demagogue and Lumpenproletarian, a still more fateful sado-masochistic pairing—*Führer* and *Volk*—comes dimly into view.

If, then, the literary practice of 'late Baudelaire' points beyond romanticism, realism, and classicism toward modernism, his politics, it seems to me, point beyond 'left' and 'right', 'revolution' and 'reaction', to something resembling fascism, the whole of his post-1851 development posing the question, fifty or more years in advance of Pound, Eliot, T. E. Hulme, Yeats, and Wyndham Lewis, of the relationship—still fully to be charted and explained[17] —between modernism, prejudice (both racial and sexual), and political authoritarianism. Baudelaire was no less a 'revolutionary' (and certainly no less 'anti-bourgeois') when he wrote 'Assommons les pauvres!' and *Pauvre Belgique!* than when he fought on the barricades in 1848, but if he continued to cry '*Vive la Révolution!*', it was, as he admitted in the conclusion of *Pauvre Belgique!*, eerily anticipating as he did so the *¡Viva la Muerte!* of Spanish fascism, 'comme je dirais: *Vive la Destruction! Vive l'Expiation! Vive le Châtiment! Vive la Mort!*' (OC, ii. 961). By the time Baudelaire wrote these words, the slight hopes he may once have had of re-making his life in Belgium had collapsed, and if *Pauvre Belgique!* has about it something of the demented fury of *Bagatelles pour un massacre*, it is because Baudelaire's omnipresent, identical *Belges* are, like Céline's Jews, creatures born of his self-loathing and despair, paranoid projections of that all-encompassing horror of life to which he repeatedly gives voice in his letters of the 1860s. In Belgium Baudelaire experienced 'le regard et le visage de l'ennemi, partout, partout' (OC, ii. 868), encountering at every step in the 'stupidité menaçante des visages' an expression of 'cette bêtise universelle inquiète comme un danger indéfini et permanent' (OC, ii. 826). It was the familiar 'tyrannie de la face humaine, plus dure qu'ailleurs' (OC, ii. 868)—more threatening because the ever-identical Belgian face was a 'chaos' without consciousness, something 'informe, difforme, rêche, lourd, dur, non fini', a 'visage obscur sans regard, comme celui d'un cyclope, d'un cyclope, non pas borgne, mais aveugle', prompting Baudelaire revealingly to comment: 'Absence de regard, chose terrible' (OC, ii. 829). *Pauvre Belgique!* evokes a world without or beneath thought, in which the

---

[17] See, though, John R. Harrison, *The Reactionaries* (Gollancz, 1966); Fredric Jameson, *Fables of Aggression: Wyndham Lewis, the Modernist as Fascist* (California Univ. Press, Berkeley, Calif., 1979), and, most recently, Christopher Ricks, *T. S. Eliot and Prejudice* (Oxford Univ. Press, 1989).

processes of eating, drinking, and excretion[18] have swallowed up mind, leaving only a gross materiality, existence without essence, that moulds itself unthinkingly according to whatever models are offered it: 'Il est *singe*,' Baudelaire wrote of his identikit *Belge*, 'mais il est *mollusque*' (OC, ii. 844).

Brussels, then, confronted Baudelaire with a heightened version of the inauthentic, reified, mimetic urban space he had already come to dread in Haussmann's Paris. It was, in the worst sense of the word, a democratic city, dominated by 'la tyrannie des faibles' and 'la fatuité des infiniment petits' (OC, ii. 914), a city from which every trace of the 'aristocratic chrétienne' he so admired in the work of Barbey d'Aurevilly had been resolutely banished (letter of July 1860 (C, ii. 61)). It embodied the 'fadeur universelle' of a massified, despiritualized, anti-aesthetic society, a society in which even 'le piment devient concombre' (OC, ii. 824) and in which the peripatetic pleasures of the dandy-aesthete, not least 'la flânerie devant les boutiques, cette jouissance, cette instruction' have become a 'chose impossible' (OC, ii. 827). It was a society equally far removed from the socialist republic he had fought for in 1848 and the hierarchical (but still, it seems, republican) theocracy to which his later reading of de Maistre had converted him. In 1848, sustained by a belief in the fundamental goodness of man and nature, Baudelaire had fought for the People in the name of *Liberté, Égalité, Fraternité*. By the mid-1860s, both man and nature were irredeemably corrupt, and the intoxicating revolutionary fervour he had celebrated during the Second Republic had been supplanted by the '*effroyable* ivrognerie du peuple' in Brussels (OC, ii. 836) with all its attendant barbarities: 'Caractère particulièrement sauvage et bestial de l'ivresse belge. Un père est ivre. Il châtre son fils. Observez dans ce crime non seulement la férocité, mais le mode du crime' (OC, ii. 843). In 1851, Baudelaire had called in desperation on 'un Attila dévastateur et égalitaire' (OC, i. 1076) to save the Republic from its enemies. In 1865, exiled now in a city that was both a grotesque parody of the already parodic city he had left and, politically, morally, and in every other way, the epitome of everything he had come to loathe, he invoked once more the barbarian king, and in the savage glee with which he calls down

---

[18] Excretion is one of the obsessions of *Pauvre Belgique!*, particularly the 'pisseries et chieries des dames belges' performed, Baudelaire alleges, in common and in public (OC, ii. 839). See also OC, ii. 836.

destruction and disease upon *les Belges*, as much as his antitype of civilization as Céline's Jews, one glimpses with a shudder the holocaust of the century to come:

Aujourd'hui lundi, 28 août 1865, par une soirée chaude et humide, j'ai erré à travers les méandres d'une Kermesse de rues, et dans les rues du *Coin du Diable*, du *Rempart des Moines*, de *Notre-Dame du Sommeil*, des *Six Jetons*, et de plusieurs autres, j'ai surpris suspendus en l'air, avec une joie vive, de frequents symptômes de choléra. L'ai-je assez invoqué, ce monstre adoré? Ai-je étudié assez attentivement les signes précurseurs de sa venue? Comme il se fait attendre, l'horrible bien-aimé! Cet Attila impartial, ce fléau divin qui ne choisit pas ses victimes! Ai-je assez supplié le Seigneur Mon Dieu de l'attirer au plus vite sur les bords puants de la *Senne?* Et comme je jouirai enfin en contemplant la grimace de l'agonie de ce hideux peuple embrassé par les replis de son Styx-contrefaçon, de [son] *ruisseau-Briarée* qui charrie encore plus d'excréments que l'atmosphère au-dessus se nourrit de mouches!—Je jouirai, dis-je, des terreurs et des tortures de la race aux cheveux jaunes, nankin et au teint lilas! (OC, ii. 956)

Bibliography

This bibliography includes only the more important items referred to in the text or notes; the editions referred to are those actually used. Unless otherwise stated, all items in English are published in London, those in French in Paris.

EDITIONS, CRITICAL APPARATUS, AND WORKS OF REFERENCE

Complete Works

PICHOIS, CLAUDE (ed.), Œuvres complètes de Baudelaire, 2 vols. (Gallimard, Bibliothèque de la Pléiade, 1975–6).

Correspondence

PICHOIS, CLAUDE (ed.), Correspondance de Baudelaire, 2 vols. (Gallimard, Bibliothèque de la Pléiade, 1973).

Miscellaneous

BANDY, W. T., and PICHOIS, CLAUDE (eds.), Baudelaire devant ses contemporains (Éditions du Rocher, Monaco, n.d.).

MAITRON, JEAN, Dictionnaire biographique du mouvement ouvrier français, Première partie, 1789–1864, 3 vols. (Les Éditions ouvrières, 1964–6).

PICHOIS, CLAUDE, Album Baudelaire (Gallimard, Bibliothèque de la Pléiade, 1974).

—— (with PICHOIS, VINCENETTE), Lettres à Charles Baudelaire, Études baudelairiennes, 4–5 (La Baconnière, Neuchâtel, 1973).

OTHER WORKS BY NINETEENTH-CENTURY WRITERS

BERTHAUD, L.-A., 'Le Goguettier', in Les Français peints par eux-mêmes (Curmer, 1840), iv. 313–21.

—— 'Les Chiffonniers', in Les Français peints par eux-mêmes (Curmer, 1840), iii. 333–44.

DELACROIX, EUGÈNE, Journal, ed. André Joubin (Plon, 1960).

DUPONT, PIERRE, Chants et poésies (Garnier, 1862).

FERRARI, GIUSEPPE, 'Des idées et de l'école de Fourier depuis 1830', Revue des Deux Mondes, 11 (1845), 389–434.

FLAUBERT, GUSTAVE, *L'Éducation sentimentale*, ed. Edouard Maynial (Garnier, 1964).

FOURNEL, VICTOR, *Ce qu'on voit dans les rues de Paris* (Adolphe Delahaÿs, 1858).

HUGO, VICTOR, *Choses vues*, i (Éditions Rencontre, Lausanne, 1968).

—— *Choses vues, 1847–1848* (Gallimard, Folio, 1972).

LA BEDOLLIÈRE, ÉMILE DE, *Les Industriels, métiers et professions en France* (Alphonse Pigoreau, 1842).

LEFRANÇOIS, GUSTAVE, *Souvenirs d'un révolutionnaire* (Bibliothèque des Temps Nouveaux, Brussels [1902]).

MARX, KARL, *Surveys from Exile* (Penguin, Harmondsworth, 1973).

POTTIER, EUGÈNE, *Œuvres complètes*, ed. Pierre Brochon (Maspéro, 1966).

PRIVAT D'ANGLEMONT, ALEXANDRE, *Paris inconnu* (Adolphe Delahaÿs, 1861).

PROUDHON, PIERRE-JOSEPH, *Correspondance* (A. Lacroix, Brussels, 1875).

—— *De la capacité politique des classes ouvrières* (Marcel Rivière, 1924).

—— *Les Confessions d'un révolutionnaire pour servir à l'histoire de la Révolution de Février* (Marcel Rivière, 1929).

—— *La Révolution sociale démontrée par le coup d'état du deux décembre* (Marcel Rivière, 1936).

—— *Contradictions politiques* (Marcel Rivière, 1952).

SAINTE-BEUVE, CHARLES-AUGUSTIN, 'Quelques vérités sur la situation en littérature', *Revue des Deux Mondes*, 3 (1843), 5–20.

SAINT-RENÉ-TAILLANDIER, RENÉ GASPARD ERNEST, 'L'Athéïsme allemand et le socialisme français: M. Charles Grün et M. Proudhon', *Revue des Deux Mondes*, 23 (1848), 280–322.

STERN, DANIEL, *Histoire de la Révolution de 1848* (Charpentier, 1862).

TOCQUEVILLE, ALEXIS DE, *Œuvres complètes*, xii., *Souvenirs*, ed. Luc Monnier (Gallimard, 1964).

BOOKS AND ARTICLES ON BAUDELAIRE

ASSELINEAU, CHARLES, *Baudelaire et Asselineau*, ed. Jacques Crépet and Claude Pichois (Nizet, 1953).

BADESCO, LUC, 'Baudelaire et la *Revue Jean Raisin*: La Première Publication du "Vin des chiffonniers"', *Revue des sciences humaines*, 22/85 (1957), 55–88.

BANDY, W. T., 'Le Chiffonnier de Baudelaire', *Revue d'histoire littéraire de la France*, 57/4 (1957), 580–4.

BECQ, ANNIE, 'Baudelaire et "l'Amour de l'Art": La Dédicace "aux bourgeois" du *Salon de 1846*', *Romantisme*, 17–18 (1977), 71–8.

—— 'Energie, nostalgie et création artistique selon Baudelaire: A propos du *Salon de 1846*', in *Approches des Lumières: Mélanges offerts à Jean Fabre* (Klincksieck, 1974), 31–7.

BENJAMIN, WALTER, *Charles Baudelaire: A Lyric Poet in the Era of High Capitalism*, trans. Harry Zohn (New Left Books, 1973).

BIERMANN, KARLHEINRICH, 'Der Rausch des Lumpensammlers und der Alptraum des Bürgers', *Germanisch-Romanische Monatschrift*, 60 (1979), 311–21.

BROMBERT, VICTOR, 'Lyrisme et dépersonnalisation: L'Exemple de Baudelaire' ("Spleen" LXXV)', *Romantisme*, 6 (1973), 29–37.

BUDINI, PAOLO, 'Sul "bourdon" polisemico del primo "Spleen"', *Francofonia*, 1 (1981), 105–18.

BUGLIANI, IVANNA, *Baudelaire: L'Armonia e la discordanza* (Bulzoni, Rome, 1980).

BURTON, RICHARD D. E., *The Context of Baudelaire's 'Le Cygne'* (Durham Modern Language Series, Durham, 1980).

—— *Baudelaire in 1859: A Study in the Sources of Poetic Creativity* (Cambridge Univ. Press, 1988).

—— 'Baudelaire and Lyon: A Reading of "Paysage"', *Nottingham French Studies*, 28/1 (1989), 26–38.

BUTOR, MICHEL, *Histoire extraordinaire* (Gallimard, 1961).

CHAMBERS, ROSS, 'Le Fade et le pimenté: Modes de séduction dans *La Fanfarlo*', in Ronald W. Tobin (ed.), *Littérature et gastronomie*, *Biblio*, 17 (1985), 175–201.

CHESTERS, GRAHAM, 'A Political Reading of Baudelaire's "L'Artiste inconnu" ("Le Guignon")', *Modern Language Review*, 79/1 (1984), 64–76.

EMMANUEL, PIERRE, *Baudelaire, la femme et Dieu* (Seuil, 1982).

HAMBLY, PETER S., 'Idéologie et poésie: Notes sur Baudelaire et ses contemporains', *Australian Journal of French Studies*, 16/2 (1979), 198–213.

HIDDLESTON, J. A., 'Baudelaire et le rire', *Études baudelairiennes*, 12 (1987), 85–98.

HOWELLS, BERNARD, 'Baudelaire: Portrait of the Artist in 1846', *French Studies*, 37 (1983), 426–39.

HYSLOP, LOIS B., 'Baudelaire, Proudhon, and "Le Reniement de saint Pierre"', *French Studies*, 30/3, (1976), 273–86.

JASENAS, ELIANE, 'Stendhal et Baudelaire: La Dédicace "Aux bourgeois", la problématique d'un texte', *Nineteenth-century French Studies*, 9/3–4 (1981), 192–203.

JOUVE, NICOLE WARD, *Baudelaire: A Fire to Conquer Darkness* (Macmillan, 1980).

LEAKEY, F. W., 'Baudelaire: The Poet as Moralist', in L. J. Austin, Garnet Rees, and Eugène Vinaver (eds.), *Studies in Modern French Literature*

Presented to P. Mansell Jones (Manchester Univ. Press, Manchester, 1961), 196–219.

LEAKEY, F. W., 'Les Esthétiques de Baudelaire: Le "Système" des années 1844–1847', *Revue des sciences humaines*, 32/127 (1967), 481–96.

—— *Baudelaire and Nature* (Manchester Univ. Press, Manchester, 1969).

—— 'Baudelaire's *Les Limbes* (1848–52): "The Agitations and Melancholies of Modern Youth"', *French Studies Bulletin*, 26 (1988), 4–8.

MACINNES, JOHN W., *The Comic as Textual Practice in 'Les Fleurs du mal'* (Univ. of Florida Press, Gainesville, Fla., 1988).

MACLEAN, MARIE, *Narrative as Performance: The Baudelairean Experiment* (Routledge, 1988).

MAURON, CHARLES, *Le Dernier Baudelaire* (Jose Corti, 1966).

MONROE, JONATHAN, 'Baudelaire's Poor: The *Petits poèmes en prose* and the Social Reinscription of the Lyric', *Stanford French Review*, 9/2 (1985), 169–88.

MOUQUET, JULES, and BANDY, W. T., *Baudelaire en 1848* (Éditions Émile-Paul Frères, 1946).

OEHLER, DOLF, ' "Assommons les pauvres!"': Dialektik der Befreiung bei Baudelaire', *Germanisch-Romanische Monatschrift*, 56 (1975), 454–62.

—— 'Le Caractère double de l'héroïsme et du beau modernes: A propos de deux faits divers cités par Baudelaire en 1846', *Études baudelairiennes*, 8 (1976), 187–216.

—— *Pariser Bilder*, i *(1830–1848): Antibourgeoise Ästhetik bei Baudelaire, Daumier und Heine* (Suhrkamp, Frankfurt-on-Main, 1979).

PACHET, PIERRE, *Le Premier Venu: Essai sur la politique baudelairienne* (Denoël, 1976).

PICHOIS, CLAUDE, *Baudelaire à Paris* (Hachette, 1967).

—— *Baudelaire: Études et témoignages* (La Baconnière, Neuchâtel, 1967).

—— 'Baudelaire devant la socio-critique ouest-allemande', *Études baudelairiennes*, 9 (1981), 226–33.

—— and ZIEGLER, JEAN, *Baudelaire* (Julliard, 1987).

RUFF, MARCEL, 'La Pensée politique et sociale de Baudelaire', in *Littérature et société: Recueil d'études en l'honneur de Bernard Guyon* (Desclée de Brouwer, Bruges, 1973), 65–75.

SARTRE, JEAN-PAUL, *Baudelaire* (Gallimard, 1966).

STARKIE, ENID, *Baudelaire* (Penguin, Harmondsworth, 1971).

STENZEL, HARTMUT, 'Sur quelques souvenirs socialistes dans l'œuvre de Baudelaire', *Bulletin baudelairien*, 12/1 (1976), 3–13.

—— 'Les Écrivains et l'évolution idéologique de la petite bourgeoisie dans les années 1840: Le Cas de Baudelaire', *Romantisme*, 17–18 (1977), 79–91.

—— *Der historische Ort Baudelaires: Untersuchungen zur Entwicklung des französischen Literatur um die Mitte des 19. Jahrhunderts* (Wilhelm Fink, Munich, 1980).

—— 'Frankreich 1850', in Klaus Lindemann (ed.), *europaLyric 1775-heute* (Ferdinand Schöningh, Paderborn, 1982), 181–93.

VAN SLYKE, GRETCHEN, 'Dans l'intertexte de Baudelaire et de Proudhon: Pourquoi faut-il assommer les pauvres?', *Romantisme*, 45 (1984), 57–77.

—— 'Riot and Revolution in the *Salon de 1846*', *French Forum*, 10/3 (1985), 295–306.

WING, NATHANIEL, 'The Poetics of Irony in Baudelaire's *La Fanfarlo*', *Neophilologus*, 59/2 (1985), 165–89.

WRIGHT, BARBARA, and SCOTT, DAVID H. T., *'La Fanfarlo' and 'Le Spleen de Paris'* (Grant and Cutler, 1984).

ZIEGLER, JEAN, '"Le Vin de l'assassin": 1848?', in *Du romantisme au surnaturalisme: Hommage à Claude Pichois* (La Baconnière, Neuchâtel, 1985), 189–97.

BOOKS AND ARTICLES ON OTHER SUBJECTS

AGULHON, MAURICE, *1848 ou l'apprentissage de la république 1848–1852* (Seuil, 1973).

—— *Les Quarante-huitards* (Gallimard/Julliard, 1975).

—— 'Le Problème de la culture populaire en France autour de 1848', *Romantisme*, 9 (1975), 50–64.

—— 'Attitudes politiques' and 'La Société paysanne et la vie à la campagne', in Étienne Juillard (ed.), *Histoire de la France rurale*, iii, *Apogée et crise de la civilisation paysanne 1789–1914* (Seuil, 1976), 143–75 and 307–55.

AMANN, PETER H., *Revolution and Mass Democracy: The Paris Club Movement in 1848* (Princeton Univ. Press, Princeton, NJ, 1975).

ANSART, PIERRE, *Sociologie de Proudhon* (Presses Universitaires de France, 1967).

—— *Proudhon* (Librairie Générale Française, 1984).

ARNAND, FÉLIX, *Les Fouriéristes et les luttes révolutionnaires de 1848 à 1851* (PUF, 1948).

BERENSON, EDWARD, *Populist Religion and Left-wing Politics in France 1830–1852* (Princeton Univ. Press, Princeton, NJ, 1984).

BOWNESS, ALAN, 'Courbet and Baudelaire', *Gazette des Beaux-Arts*, 90 (Dec. 1977), 189–99.

BROCHON, PIERRE, *Le Pamphlet du pauvre: Du socialisme utopique à la Révolution de 1848* (Éditions sociales, 1957).

—— *La Chanson sociale de Béranger à Brassens* (Éditions sociales, 1961).

—— *La Chanson française: Béranger et son temps* (Éditions sociales, 1966).

BURTON, RICHARD D. E., 'The Unseen Seer, or Proteus in the City:

Aspects of a Nineteenth-Century Parisian Myth', *French Studies*, 42/1 (1988), 50–68.

CHAMBERS, ROSS, *Mélancolie et opposition: Les débuts du modernisme en France* (Corti, 1987).

CITRON, PIERRE, *La Poésie de Paris dans la littérature française de Rousseau à Baudelaire* (Les Éditions de Minuit, 1961).

CLARK, T. J., *The Absolute Bourgeois: Artists and Politics in France 1848–1851* (Thames and Hudson, 1973).

—— *Image of the People: Gustave Courbet and the 1848 Revolution* (Thames and Hudson, 1973).

CUVILLIER, ARMAND, *Hommes et idéologies de 1840* (Marcel Rivière, 1956).

DE CERTEAU, MICHEL, 'On the Oppositional Practices of Everyday Life', *Social Text*, 3 (1980), 3–43.

DOLLÉANS, ÉDOUARD, and PUECH, J.-L., *Proudhon et la Révolution de 1848* (Presses Universitaires de France, 1948).

DOMMANGET, MAURICE, *Auguste Blanqui et la Révolution de 1848* (Mouton, 1972).

DUVEAU, GEORGES, *1848* (Gallimard, 1965).

FAURE, ALAIN, *Paris Carême-prenant: Du carnaval à Paris au XIXe siècle, 1800–1914* (Hachette, 1978).

FORSTENZER, THOMAS R., *French Provincial Police and the Fall of the Second Republic: Social Fear and Counterrevolution* (Princeton Univ. Press, Princeton, NJ, 1981).

GALLAHER, JOHN G., *The Students of Paris and the Revolution of 1848* (Southern Illinois Univ. Press, Carbondale and Edwardsville, 1980).

GRAS, PIERRE (ed.), *Histoire de Dijon* (Privat, Toulouse, 1981).

HAUBTMANN, PIERRE, *Pierre-Joseph Proudhon: Sa vie et sa pensée (1809–1849)* (Beauchesne, 1982).

—— *Pierre-Joseph Proudhon: Sa vie et sa pensée (1849–1865)* (Desclée de Brouwer, Bruges, 1988).

HALÉVY, DANIEL, *Le Mariage de Proudhon* (Stock, 1955).

JARDIN, A., and TUDESQ, A. J., *La France des notables*, i. *L'Évolution générale 1815–1848* (Seuil, 1973).

KELLEY, DAVID, 'L'Art: L'Harmonie du beau et de l'utile', *Romantisme*, 5 (1973), 18–36.

LAURENT, ROBERT, *Les Vignerons de la Côte-d'Or au XIXe siècle* (Les Belles Lettres, 1958).

LÉVÊQUE, PIERRE, *La Bourgogne de la Monarchie de Juillet au Second Empire*, 5 vols. (Université de Lille III, 1980).

LIDSKY, PAUL, *Les Écrivains contre la Commune* (Maspéro, 1982).

MAGRAW, ROGER, *France 1815–1914: The Bourgeois Century* (Fontana, 1983).

MARRINAN, MICHAEL, *Painting Politics for Louis-Philippe: Art and*

Ideology in Orleanist France 1830–1848 (Yale Univ. Press, New Haven, Conn., and London, 1988).

MÉNAGER, BERNARD, *Les Napoléon du peuple* (Aubier, 1988).

MERRIMAN, JOHN M., *The Agony of the Republic: The Repression of the Left in Revolutionary France 1848–1851* (Yale Univ. Press, New Haven, Conn., and London, 1978).

MILNER, MAX, *Le Romantisme 1820–1843* (Arthaud, 1973).

MURAY, PHILIPPE, *Le 19ᵉ siècle à travers les âges* (Denoël, 1984).

OEHLER, DOLF, *Ein Hollenstürz der Alten Welt: Der Selbsterforschung der Moderne nach dem Juni 1848* (Suhrkamp, Frankfurt-on-Main, 1988).

PAYNE, HOWARD C., *The Police State of Louis Napoleon Bonaparte 1851–1860* (Univ. of Washington Press, Seattle, 1966).

PINKNEY, DAVID H., *Decisive Years in France 1840–1847* (Princeton Univ. Press, Princeton, NJ, 1986).

PRICE, ROGER (ed.), *Revolution and Reaction: 1848 and the Second French Republic* (Croom Helm, 1975).

STERNHELL, ZEEV, *La Droite révolutionnaire 1885–1914: Les Origines françaises du fascisme* (Seuil, 1978).

—— *Ni droite ni gauche: L'Idéologie fasciste en France* (Seuil, 1983).

TERDIMAN, RICHARD, *Discourse/Counter-Discourse: The Theory and Practice of Symbolic Resistance in Nineteenth-Century France* (Cornell Univ. Press, Ithaca, NY, 1985).

THOMAS, EDMOND, *Voix d'en bas: La poésie ouvrière du XIXᵉ siècle* (Maspéro, 1979).

TRAUGOTT, MARK, *Armies of the Poor: Determinants of Working-Class Participation in the Parisian Insurrection of June 1848* (Princeton Univ. Press, Princeton, NJ, 1985).

TUDESQ, A. J., *L'Élection présidentielle de Louis-Napoléon Bonaparte, 10 décembre 1848* (Armand Colin, 1965).

VIGIER, PHILIPPE, *La Seconde République* (PUF, 1967).

VINCENT, K. STEVEN, *Pierre-Joseph Proudhon and the Rise of French Republican Socialism* (Oxford Univ. Press, 1984).

WEBER, EUGEN, *Satan Franc-maçon* (Julliard, 1964).

Index of Works by Baudelaire

'Abel et Caïn' 197, 199, 263, 302
'A celle qui est trop gaie' ('A une femme trop gaie') 128, 182–4, 354
'Actuellement' 136, 283–5, 286, 354, 360 n.
'L'Albatros' 76
'L'Ame du vin' ('Le Vin des honnêtes gens') 30, 128, 132, 153, 185, 191–6, 203, 204, 209, 210, 211, 212, 220, 234, 258, 260, 261, 262, 264, 266, 278, 287, 288–9, 299, 314, 321
'Assommons les pauvres!' vii, viii, xii, 44, 112, 124, 164, 172, 181, 182, 237, 246, 259, 261, 273, 284, 324–52, 358, 359, 363
'A une dame créole' ('A une Créole') 57
'A une mendiante rousse' 41

'Bénédiction' 17, 191, 272

'La Chambre double' 305
'Une charogne' 51, 52, 183, 194
'Le Chat' 305
'Châtiment de l'orgueil' 128, 136, 153, 192, 276–90
'La Chevelure' 269
Choix de maximes consolantes sur l'amour 57
'La Cloche fêlée' 216 n., 293, 306, 307, 321, 322
Conseils aux jeunes littérateurs 39
'Les *Contes* de Champfleury' 88, 90–1, 97
'Le Crépuscule du matin' 157, 293, 306, 308
'Le Crépuscule du soir' 157, 293, 306, 308, 320
'Le Cygne' 76, 316, 320, 323

De l'essence du rire 49–52, 70–1, 287–8, 355

'De profundis clamavi' ('La Béatrix') 209, 306
'Les Derniers Buveurs' 154, 204
'Don Juan aux Enfers' ('L'Impénitent') 39, 58, 154
Les Drames et les romans honnêtes 156, 159, 160–2
Du vin et du haschisch 131, 156, 159, 167, 168, 169, 186–91, 194–6, 204, 210, 211, 220, 234–7, 246, 262, 302, 314, 353

L'École païenne 157, 196, 247 n., 286, 287, 300–1
Edgar Allan Poe, sa vie et ses ouvrages 173, 267
'Enivrez-vous' 275
Exposition universelle de 1855 51

La Fanfarlo 9, 10, 11, 12, 23–4, 44, 58–9, 65, 71–82, 89, 144, 298
'La Fausse Monnaie' 351–2
'Femmes damnées (Delphine et Hippolyte)' 49
La Fin de Don Juan 39
'La Fontaine de sang' 269, 293, 321, 322
'Les Foules' 102

'Le Gâteau' 44, 361 n.
'Une gravure fantastique' 214
'Le Guignon' ('L'Artiste inconnu') 306, 320

'Les Hiboux' 174–5, 277, 292, 293, 299, 320
'L'Homme et la mer' (L'Homme libre et la mer') 291, 293, 315
'Hymne à la Beauté' 263

'L'Idéal' 323
'L'Irréparable' 216–17
L'Ivrogne 128, 186, 214, 272–3

Les Lesbiennes 48, 58
'Lesbos' 49, 153, 191
Les Limbes 15, 39, 60, 70, 137–8, 140, 145, 154, 156–7, 158, 192, 204, 291–311, 319–23
'Les Litanies de Satan' 29, 197, 199, 216 n., 259, 263, 302

'Mademoiselle Bistouri' 44, 128, 259, 326
'Le Mauvais Moine' 263, 293, 306, 319
'Le Mauvais Vitrier' 44, 273, 326, 331, 351
Morale du joujou 176, 190–1, 344
'La Mort des pauvres' 322–3
'Une mort héroïque' 72, 127–8, 267, 327, 343, 351
'Le Mort joyeux' 306, 321
Le Musée classique du Bazar Bonne-Nouvelle 9, 33, 42–6
'La Muse vénale' 43, 263

'Notes diverses sur *L'Art philosophique*' 196

Les Paradis artificiels 186, 245, 273
Pauvre Belgique! 360, 364–6
'Paysage' 175–6, 320
'Les Phares' 17, 263, 272
Pierre Dupont (1851) 131, 156, 159, 167, 169, 170, 186–91, 203, 259, 270, 290, 303, 310, 314, 315, 353, 355
'Le Poison' 190
Puisque réalisme il y a 92

Quelques caricaturistes étrangers 115

'La Rançon' 132–3, 150, 187, 293, 323
'Le Reniement de saint Pierre' 30, 128, 132, 157, 176–82, 197, 198, 254, 258, 260, 263, 286, 291, 293, 317–18, 321, 323
'La Révolte' (section of *Les Fleurs du mal*) 40, 41, 49, 197–9, 234, 263, 274, 281

Salon de 1845 14, 33–5, 37, 58, 91
Salon de 1846 4, 5, 6, 7, 8, 9, 10, 12, 14, 15, 16–17, 19, 20, 21, 23, 26–7, 30, 31, 32, 40, 41, 42, 45, 50, 51, 60, 67, 68, 74, 91, 98, 189, 268, 300, 301, 354–5
'Le Soleil' 76, 265–6, 298
'Spleen' ('J'ai plus de souvenirs . . .') 304, 305 n.
'Spleen' ('Pluviôse, irrité . . .') 129, 293, 294–311, 319

'Le Thyrse' 76
'Le Tonneau de la Haine' 189, 277, 293, 306, 321, 322

'Les Veuves' 331
'Le Vieux Saltimbanque' 44, 331
'Le Vin' (section of *Les Fleurs du mal*) 49, 263–5, 274, 275, 302
'Le Vin de l'assassin' 41, 138, 186, 189, 192, 197, 262, 264, 272
'Le Vin des amants' 197, 262, 323
'Le Vin des chiffonniers' 30, 76, 128, 157, 176, 185, 192, 196, 207, 219, 220–75, 287, 293
'Le Vin du solitaire' 190, 196, 262, 323
'Le Voyage' 18, 164, 257, 274, 314, 357
'Un voyage à Cythère' 52, 183, 293–4, 311–19, 321

'Les Yeux des pauvres' 331

General Index

L'Aimable Faubourien 113, 158, 193 n.
Altaroche 206, 207
L'Ami du Peuple 27, 102, 104
Ancelle, Narcisse 80, 161
  Baudelaire's letter of March 1852 to 96, 109, 167, 171, 182, 254, 319, 357
arbres de la liberté 96, 155, 179, 180, 209, 211
Asselineau, Charles 12, 36 n., 63, 65, 154, 156, 157, 214 n., 326
  on Baudelaire and 1848 100
L'Atelier 2, 18
Aupick, Caroline 55–6, 62, 86, 114, 140
  on Baudelaire in 1851 170
Aupick, Jacques 2, 29, 38, 55, 56, 57, 62, 80–1, 101, 104, 114, 118, 140
  'il faut aller fusiller le général Aupick' v, 40, 100

Balzac, Honoré de 67
  see also under Baudelaire
banquets 84–5, 157–8, 211
Banville, Théodore de 65, 191, 326
Barbey d'Aurevilly, Jules 362, 365
barrières 201, 205–6
Barthet, Armand 99
Baudelaire, Charles:
  as 'anti-bourgeois' viii, 32–40, 182, 356, 359–60, 364
  on Balzac 91
  and Blanquism 29, 105–8, 116, 353, 361
  at Châteauroux 133–6, 278
  and *conseil judiciaire* 11, 12, 55–6, 64
  and dandyism 59–60, 63, 64–71, 73
  'depoliticization' of vi, viii, 96, 109, 140, 142, 165, 167–76, 182, 254, 319, 354, 357, 359
  and *le 2 décembre* 13, 46, 162–7, 354
  at Dijon 145–53, 204–5, 215
  and drugs 169, 187, 245–6, 263, 273–4

  and figure of Cain 40, 49, 198–9, 302, 358 n.
  and figure of Christ 96, 103, 130–1, 132, 177–9, 180–2, 198, 209, 244, 245, 286
  and figure of Don Juan 39–40, 49, 58
  and figure of Satan 40, 41, 47, 49, 197–9, 286, 288, 302
  and Fourierism 14–19, 30, 31, 36, 74, 93, 132, 361
  and *Le Hibou philosophe* 173, 174
  and *Jean Raisin* 128, 219
  and *journées de février* 94–6, 98–105, 176, 283, 333
  and *journées de juin* 46, 116–19, 283, 353
  and Louis Napoleon 163, 165–6, 172, 356
  and Marat 9, 104, 134, 150
  and 'nature' 88–9, 189, 194–5, 197, 233–4, 246, 266–7, 365
  and 'opposition' 10–11, 13, 33, 356
  and original sin 50–2, 259, 355, 362
  and 'le peuple' 40–6, 62, 69, 101–2, 103, 163–4, 187, 188, 195, 255, 257, 331–2
  physical appearance 64–71, 102, 134–5, 154
  pseudonyms 54–60, 97
  and *Le Représentant de l'Indre* 111
  and republicanism in 1840s 19–23
  and Robespierre 134–5
  and Rousseau 245–6
  and *Le Salut public* 102–5
  and socialism in 1840s 23–32
  and *Société Républicaine Centrale* 105–7
  and theme of *ivresse* 102, 104, 190, 191, 245–6, 266–7, 273–5, 287, 315, 365
  and theme of work 131, 150, 167, 187–8, 194–5, 289

Baudelaire, Charles (*cont.*):
  and theme of youth 39–40
  and *La Tribune nationale* 110–14
  and wine 69, 129, 175, 185–96, 260;
    see also wine in nineteenth-century
    French society *and* individual works
    on theme of wine
  see also Courbet; Hugo; Maistre;
    Poe; Proudhon
Baudelaire, Claude-Alphonse 57, 160
Baudelaire, Félicité (née Ducessois) 57
Baudelaire, François 55, 56, 101
Blanc, Louis 2, 18, 27, 85, 109, 113,
  117, 121, 136, 255, 280
Blanqui, Auguste 20, 29, 105–8, 109,
  116, 119
blouse, significance of 96, 102, 103,
  154–5
Bonapartism 237, 238, 245, 247, 248–57,
  262
  see also Louis Napoleon
Bourgeois Monarchy:
  decline of 82–5, 94
  'depoliticization' of 1, 4, 5, 6, 8, 9
  as 'limbo-age' 60, 63, 68, 70, 72–4,
    86, 90, 93, 299
Bouzeran, Joseph 168
Buisson, Jules vi, 100

cabarets see *marchands de vin*
Cabet, Étienne 2, 18, 27, 32, 109, 274,
  280, 314
Cain, figure of in nineteenth-century
  French politics 40, 49, 198–9, 302,
  358 n.
casquette, significance of 96, 103, 344
Champfleury (Jules Husson, dit) 12,
  54, 88, 89, 90, 91, 98, 102, 145,
  173, 311
  on Baudelaire in 1840s 69
chiffonniers 42, 220–30
  poet as *chiffonnier* 265–72
  see also 'Le Vin des chiffonniers'
Christ, figure of in nineteenth-century
  French politics 96, 103, 130–1,
  132, 177–9, 180–2, 198, 209, 244,
  245, 286
classes dangereuses 41–2, 62, 225, 228–9
Considerant, Victor 15, 18, 19
Constant, Abbé 10, 14, 26, 48, 49, 105
Courbet, Gustave 13, 30, 92, 98, 103,
  144
  Baudelaire and 89–92

L'Enterrement à Ornans 91
  portrait of Baudelaire 66–7

Daumier, Honoré 62–3, 178, 220, 221,
  232, 247, 248, 249, 253, 256, 301
Delacroix, Eugène 4, 35, 37, 60 n., 70
  Baudelaire's visit to in early 1849 142
La Démocratie pacifique 14, 15, 16, 18,
  22, 79, 89, 210
démoc-socs 136, 146, 148, 149–53, 163,
  186, 187, 189, 192–3, 194, 202, 204,
  208, 210, 215–16, 236, 254, 302,
  316, 353, 354
Deroy, Émile, portrait of Baudelaire
  65–6
Dupont, Pierre 13, 22–3, 27–9, 31, 88,
  105, 116, 117, 132, 137, 139, 159,
  203, 210, 211, 214, 219, 316, 345 n.
  'La Chanson du banquet' 87
  'Le Chant des Ouvriers' 27–9, 40, 88,
    200
  'Le Chant des paysans' 208–9
  'Ma vigne' 137, 208, 209
  '1852' 205
  'Le Vin de la planète' 207
  see also Pierre Dupont (1851)
Durand, Claude, 'Le Chant des
  vignerons' 202
Duval, Jeanne 114, 131, 134, 136–7,
  140, 145

L'Écho des marchands de vin 15, 128,
  137–8, 203–4
Esquiros, Alphonse 10, 14, 25, 26, 48,
  105, 107, 108–9, 116, 117

Ferrari, Giuseppe 17, 18, 19
La Feuille de village 24, 147
Flaubert, Gustave 9, 47, 95, 141, 357
  L'Éducation sentimentale 22, 85, 100,
    155, 178, 257, 342, 344
Flotte, Paul de 105, 107–8, 116, 166
Fourier, Charles 13, 14–19, 20–1, 26,
  27, 30, 31, 47, 50, 51
Fournel, Victor 221, 222–3, 225

Gautier, Théophile 63, 65, 66
Girardin, Émile de 1, 98, 111, 112
goguettes 88, 214–19
Grün, Karl 277–8, 280–1

Le Hibou philosophe 173, 174
honnêtes gens, meaning of 192–3

Houssaye, Arsène 108
Hugo, Victor 3, 6, 7, 45–6, 47, 82, 84, 95, 164–5, 166
   Baudelaire and 333–4

Joigneaux, Pierre 147, 215, 323

Lamartine, Alphonse de 47, 85, 87, 113, 114
Lamennais, Félicité de 7, 48, 127, 178
Laverdant, Désiré 14, 15, 16
Leconte de Lisle, Charles 19, 105, 357
Ledru-Rollin, Alexandre-Auguste 117, 136, 137, 203–4, 255
Lefrançais, Gustave 4, 94, 108, 139, 146 n., 153
Lemer, Julien 153, 191, 192
Leroux, Pierre 26, 47, 48, 113, 117, 166, 280
Le Vavasseur, Gustave 3, 233
   on Baudelaire during *journées de juin* 107, 108, 116
Louis Napoleon 3, 39, 139–40, 142–3, 163, 165–6, 172, 202, 208, 247, 250, 252, 256 n., 257, 316–17, 337, 356
   L'Extinction du paupérisme 251, 328, 343
   see also Bonapartism

Madier de Montjau, Noël 151–2, 166
Le Magasin des familles 128, 191–2
Maistre, Joseph de, Baudelaire and 50–1, 110, 119, 132, 169, 172, 173, 176, 183, 288, 289, 290, 329, 354, 355, 357, 358, 360, 362
'Manifeste des Soixante' 338–9
marchands de vin 88, 149, 155, 167, 203, 205, 214–19, 323, 343
Marx, Karl 201, 253, 328
Mathieu, Gustave 210, 219
   'La Chanson de Jean Raisin' 204–5
Ménard, Louis 48, 54, 106, 107, 117, 166
Michelet, Jules 47, 48 n., 85, 88, 97, 296–7
Montégut, Émile 159

Nadar (Félix Tournachon, dit) 139
   Baudelaire's letter of 1859 to 54, 64, 65, 171
Napoleon I 3, 201, 233, 236, 238, 247, 251
Napoleon III *see* Louis Napoleon

Le National 21, 22, 23, 112
Nerval, Gérard de 54, 311–12
Nisard, Désiré 23, 80–1

Le Peuple 123, 129, 147
La Phalange 14, 15, 16, 22
Poe, Edgar Allan, Baudelaire and 47, 50, 89, 91, 110, 168, 173, 267–8, 269, 290, 329, 354, 355
Pottier, Eugène 96, 210
   'La Bouteille inépuisable' 212–13
   'Le Fumier' 87
   'L'Origine du vin' 212
   'Les Paroles gelées' 218, 242
   'Le Pressoir' 209
   'La République honnête' 192–3
Poulet-Malassis, Auguste 113, 117, 123, 124, 158, 330, 334
Poulmann, Pierre-Joseph 41–2
Prarond, Ernest 62, 64, 65, 185, 186, 191, 214, 220, 232, 292
Privat d'Anglemont, Alexandre 14, 62–3, 221, 223, 224–5, 226–7, 230–1
Proudhon, Pierre-Joseph:
   and 1848 95, 98, 117, 119–26, 283, 311
   and Banque du Peuple 111–12, 122, 341, 347, 349
   Baudelaire and 13, 29–31, 93, 110, 112, 119, 121, 123–6, 131–2, 138–9, 142, 150, 159, 163, 173, 194, 278, 282–5, 327, 329–30, 332–7, 353, 361, 363
   De la capacité politique des classes ouvrières 340, 346, 348
   De la justice dans la Révolution et dans l'Eglise 329–30
   and hostility to 'politics' 25, 109, 119–20, 171, 338–40, 347, 350
   Idée générale de la révolution 341
   and letter to Félix Delhasse 340–2, 346, 349
   Lettre aux ouvriers 339–40, 346
   and Louis Napoleon 142–4, 165, 172
   Manifeste du peuple 129–31, 136
   Qu'est-ce que la propriété? 2, 29, 341
   Système des contradictions économiques (Philosophie de la misère) 25, 30, 31, 32, 92–3, 199, 205, 259, 280, 281–2, 347, 355

Quinet, Edgar 1, 26, 47, 48, 166

Raspail, François 27, 102, 104, 139, 155, 255
red, significance of 68–9, 155, 167, 174 n., 211, 213, 242, 319
Le Représentant de l'Indre 111, 133–6
Le Représentant du Peuple 30, 112, 120, 121, 122, 123, 124, 125
Rethel, Alfred 144, 145
Rousseau, Jean-Jacques 50, 51, 245–6, 280

Sainte-Beuve, Charles-Augustin 6, 105, 336
 Baudelaire's letter of 1862 to vi, 171, 261
Saint-René Taillandier, René 277, 278, 279–82, 286, 289
Le Salut public 48 n., 88, 102–5
Sand, George 47, 48 n., 113
Satan, figure of in nineteenth-century French politics 40, 41, 47, 49, 197–9, 286, 288, 302
Scheffer, Ary 34, 35, 37
Schmeltz, Jules 111, 112
Société du Dix-Décembre 253, 256

Thoré, Théophile 105, 106, 117, 333
Tocqueville, Alexis de 83, 84, 85, 95
Toubin, Charles 30, 68–9, 102
 on Baudelaire in 1848 98–9, 104
Toussenel, Alphonse 15, 209–11, 219, 316–17
Le Travail 145–6, 149–50, 193
La Tribune nationale 110–14

Vallès, Jules 229–30
Vernet, Horace 34, 35, 37, 38, 39, 80
Viard, Jules 30, 124, 146, 150
Vinçard *aîné* 226

Wagner, Richard 105, 144, 145
Wallon, Jean 15, 105, 168
 on *Les Limbes* 138–9
wine in nineteenth-century French society 96, 137, 147–8, 149, 153, 158, 167, 186, 189, 194, 200–19, 264
 see also marchands de vin
Wronski, Hoëné 169

Zola, Émile 216

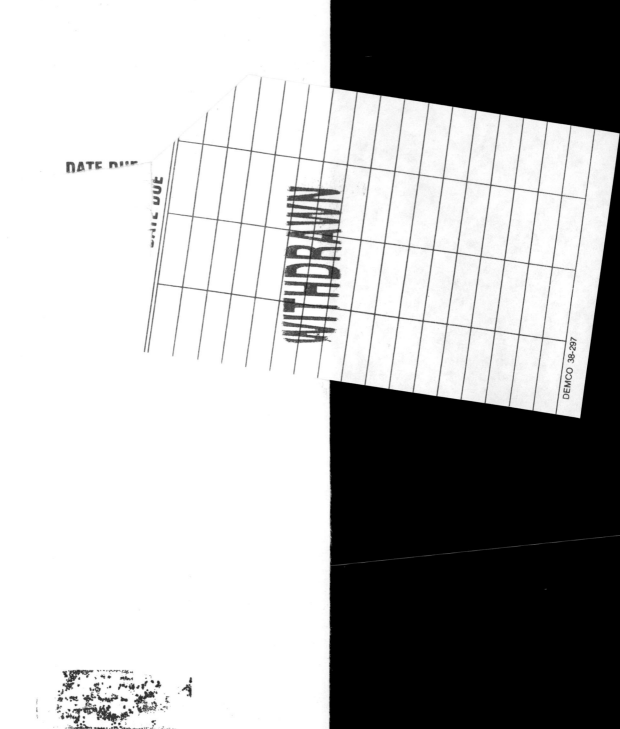